Theory now and then

Theory now and then

J. Hillis Miller
University of California at Irvine

Duke University Press
Durham 1991

Published in 1991 in the United States
by Duke University Press

First published 1991 by
Harvester Wheatsheaf
66 Wood Lane End, Hemel Hempstead,
Hertfordshire, HP2 4RG
A division of
Simon & Schuster International Group

© J. Hillis Miller 1991

All rights reserved. No part of this publication may be reproduced, stored in a retrieval system, or transmitted, in any form or by any means, electronic, mechanical, photocopying, recording or otherwise, without prior permission, in writing, from the publisher.

Printed and bound in Great Britain

Library of Congress Cataloging-in-Publication Data
Miller, J. Hillis (Joseph Hillis), 1928–
Theory now and then / J. Hillis Miller.
p. cm.
Includes bibliographical references and index.
ISBN 0–8223–1112–7 (cloth)
1. Criticism. I. Title.
PN81.M528 1991
801'.95–dc20   90–44884
                                          CIP

Contents

Preface	*vii*
Acknowledgements	*xiii*
1. The antitheses of criticism: reflections on the Yale Colloquium	*1*
2. The Geneva school: the criticism of Marcel Raymond, Albert Béguin, Georges Poulet, Jean Rousset, Jean-Pierre Richard, and Jean Starobinski	*13*
3. Geneva or Paris: Georges Poulet's "Criticism of identification"	*31*
4. Literature and religion	*63*
5. Tradition and difference	*79*
6. Deconstructing the deconstructers	*95*
7. The year's books: literary criticism	*111*
8. Stevens' Rock and criticism as cure, II	*117*
9. Beginning with a text	*133*
10. The critic as host	*143*
11. On edge: the crossways of contemporary criticism	*171*
12. The function of rhetorical study at the present time	*201*
13. English romanticism, American romanticism: what's the difference?	*217*
14. Composition and decomposition: deconstruction and the teaching of writing	*227*
15. Constructions in criticism	*245*
16. The search for grounds in literary study	*263*
17. *Gleichnis* in Nietzsche's *Also Sprach Zarathustra*	*277*
18. How deconstruction works	*293*
19. President's column	*295*
i. Responsibility and the joy of reading	*295*
ii. Responsibility and the joy(?) of teaching	*297*
iii. The obligation to write	*299*

iv. The future for the study of languages and literatures	302
20. The imperative to teach	305
21. Presidential Address 1986: The triumph of theory, the resistance to reading, and the question of the material base	309
22. The ethics of reading	329
23. "Reading" part of a paragraph in *Allegories of Reading*	341
24. Paul de Man's wartime writings	359
25. An open letter to Professor Jon Wiener	369
26. The function of literary theory at the present time	385
Index	395

Preface

Theory Now and Then collects my more overtly theoretical essays published between 1966 and 1989. Even more evidently than the studies gathered in *Victorian Subjects* and *Tropes, Parables, Performatives*, the essays here are marked by their occasions. Each is a punctuation in time, something that occurred now and then over the years, intermittently. Each essay was a response to a specific historical moment in the institutionalizing of theory in the United States. By being spoken or printed, each entered that history in a certain way, at a certain time and place, to effect such changes as may have occurred when it was heard or read.

Theory, paradoxically, is more time-bound than reading. A good reading of a poem, novel, or play always exceeds its historical occasion. To some extent it disqualifies the theoretical presuppositions that apparently enabled it. However much a reading is made possible by the specific historical, institutional, gender, or class situation of the reader, a reading, once it is written down, joins the work in a trans-temporal region where it may be repeated at any time, like the work itself. This renewed act of reading gives access again to the work or to that to which the work itself gives access.

Another way to express this is to say that theory, much more than reading, has an explicitly performative, as opposed to cognitive, function. This is so in spite of the fact that the word "theory" comes, etymologically, from Greek *thea*, "a viewing," as in a "theater." But the function of theory is to enable readings, in the broadest sense of that term, readings of cultural signs generally, not just works of literature. Theory therefore works as performative praxis. It does not in itself give knowledge. We need theory now and then, to help us get on with the serious business of reading. If each performative speech act is unique, for just this time, place, and occasion only, so a work of theory, insofar as it is performative, is oriented toward its own time and place. It is what is needed now and then, not for all time, to make reading possible. Reading then takes place for present purposes that are always political as well as personal, though the results, as I have said, are certain to be asymmetrical with the theoretical intent.

Each essay here marks a distinct moment in the evolution of literary theory over the last thirty-five years, but I identify three episodes of special salience. To call them "crises" or turning points would be to create a historical fiction. Nevertheless they may be identified as nodes in a complex and overdetermined continuum of change, as "theory" has become more and more important to literary study in the United States.

The first essay here is a response to a Symposium on Literary Criticism held at Yale in the spring of 1965. The Yale Symposium was even prior to the more celebrated Symposium at Johns Hopkins in 1966 that brought Jacques Derrida and Jacques Lacan to the United States for the first time. The Yale Symposium, with its papers on Lukács, Auerbach, Curtius, and others, along with the Hopkins Symposium, may be taken as public events that signaled the gradual displacement in the United States of the indigenous New Criticism by "continental criticism" generally. For me this meant initially adopting the theoretical presuppositions of "criticism of consciousness" in place of the Burkean or Empsonian New Criticism I had appropriated in graduate school. The second and third chapters here define the theoretical presuppositions of the so-called "Geneva School" through discussion of Marcel Raymond, Albert Béguin, Jean Rousset, Jean-Pierre Richard, Jean Starobinksi, and, especially important for my own early work, Georges Poulet. These critics practiced perhaps the most important form of "phenomenological criticism." This criticism challenged the New Criticism by shifting the focus away from the attempt to identify the organic unity of individual works. In place of that Poulet and his colleagues defined the project of criticism as description through citation and thematic paraphrase of a single author's "interior space." I thought then, and still think, that wonderful results, for example in those admirable essays by Poulet, can be obtained in this way. But even then, as chapter three shows, I saw that Poulet's actual work of reading, like that of any great critic, goes beyond its stated presuppositions. Poulet came to recognize, almost in spite of himself, the constitutive role of language in shaping consciousness if not actually in making it. In my own work, then, I tended to see consciousness as constitutive and originary. I would by no means now say that there is no such thing as consciousness, or that we have gone "beyond the subject," but I no longer see the subject as original and originating. A subjectivity is rather a constantly displaced function in an immensely complex web of signs. Those signs call the subject into being as a knowing and responsible center of consciousness, for example in the act of reading. But to ascribe consciousness and selfhood to the work of an author, the words on the page, is a species of prosopopoeia, the assigning of a face, a name, a voice, to the absent, the inanimate, or the dead. And to suppose that the work speaks to us or answers back when we speak to it is to yield to the "telepathy effect" that makes literature a massive extension of anthropomorphism, as when Milton says books "contain a potency of life in them to be as active as that soul whose progeny they are."[1]

The second extended moment represented in these essays is the reception, assimilation, and transformation in America of so-called "deconstruction." The reading of what was to become Derrida's *Of Grammatology*, as parts came out in periodical form, was an epoch in my intellectual life, as were my attendance at seminars Derrida gave at Johns Hopkins in the late 1960s and my early encounters with Paul de Man, first at that Yale Symposium of 1965, then at Johns Hopkins, where he presented "The Rhetoric of Temporality" as two seminars, then in Zürich a little later at another conference on criticism sponsored by The Hopkins.

Chapters seven and eight here contributed, somewhat later on, to the creation of the myth of the "Yale School." This preface is not the place to try to say what "deconstruction in America" is, but three points should be stressed:

1. The diversity of "deconstruction" is so great that it would be better to speak of "*deconstructionisms* in America." Those five "Yale critics" gathered within the covers of one book in *Deconstruction and Criticism* ("The Critic as Host" here was part of that book) are about as different from one another as friendly colleagues at one university can be. The subsequent dissemination of deconstructionisms to theology, philosophy, anthropology, architecture, law, and even to the creative arts has led to even more diversity and downright heterogeneity. Sentences that take the form of "Deconstruction *is* so and so" are bound to be aberrant.
2. The great attraction of deconstructionisms, for me at least, has not been their theoretical formulations but exactly the same feature that drew me originally to the work of Poulet: the penetrating and original readings of specific works: works by Plato, Mallarmé, Hegel, and a host of others for Derrida; by Rousseau, Nietzsche, Wordsworth, Kant, Kleist, and many others for de Man; by Shelley, Brontë, or Kleist for Carol Jacobs; by Hölderlin and Hegel for Andrzej Warminski; by Wordsworth, Freud, or Kleist for Cynthia Chase; by Kierkegaard, Nerval, or Proust for Kevin Newmark: the list could be extended indefinitely to a large group of brilliant younger critics.
3. Throughout all their diversity deconstructionisms have performed their liberating critique of "logocentrism" not just to dismantle and undo, but as an affirmative solicitation gesturing toward new institutional and cultural forms. These prospective affirmations are speech acts. They invoke as yet unimagined disciplinary studies, new forms of democracy, new forms of obligation and creative responsibility.

The third moment registered in these essays is the negotiation between deconstructionisms and the almost universal turn in the 1980s to forms of literary study oriented toward society, toward history, toward ethical questions and questions of institutional organization, toward questions of race, class, and gender, toward the reformation of the canon. Though some of these cultural and historical critics have been unwilling to recognize the fact, their work would have been impossible without "deconstructionisms," as Alan Liu has recently demonstrated for the "New Historicism."[2] These recent forms of "cultural critique" are more the continuation of deconstruction than its cancellation. Recent rereadings of Derrida and de Man recognize that they have always been vitally concerned with history. About the wartime writings of de Man I have had my say in two essays collected here, but those writings certainly show that de Man never underestimated the role of literature and even the role of the study of literature in the making of history. The work he was engaged on at the end of his life focused on a critique of the baneful historical effects of what he called "aesthetic ideology," one of the features of which is a spurious sequestering of literature from history, or, what amounts to the same thing, a spurious aestheticizing of history.

As I write this preface in the early weeks of 1990 I am persuaded that we are on the threshold of an enormous transformation both in cultural practices and in their understanding through theory and reading. Such understanding will also help bring about the transformation. Rapid technological changes are moving us all out of the Gutenberg era into an era of multimedia, hypertext or hypermedia, a mixing of alphabetic, iconic, and auditory signs. These new technologies are already transforming both the cultures we study and our ways of studying them, including even our ways of studying the literature of the past. An example is our recognition that "literature," especially the novel, is the product of what Nicholas Royle, following Derrida, calls a "telepathy effect."[3] This telepathy effect has been objectified in telephones, computers, television, xerox, electronic mail, modems, networking, increasing availability of enormous data bases, machine possibilities of multiple authorship, as more than one person keys into the same file, fax machines, VCRs, laser videos, CD-ROMS, satellites, and all the rest of the new communications technology. This technology embodies a species of universal telepathy in physical artifacts that we may manipulate or that may manipulate us, in a relation that is beyond any opposition between active and passive, as it is beyond any opposition between chance and destiny, and beyond even the opposition between life and death, or between mind and machine, natural and artificial intelligence. These machines, exhilarating and at the same time terrifying in their power, interpellate us into being what we are today. We are subject to these new technologies but also their users, able to make them instruments of freedom as of domination, as earlier readers were subject to the novels they read, made subjects by them, but also used them to become what they were. The novel as a genre is a critique of the ideology that it also represents and reinforces.

Those new and as yet not fully shaped forms of democracy I have mentioned are not some utopian hope. They are appearing at the moment I write this all over the world, for example in the extraordinary events of the past few months in Eastern Europe, or in the democracy movement in the People's Republic of China, surely destined ultimately to triumph, though no doubt in unforeseen ways, or even in South Africa, where "sweeping changes" have just been announced including the recent release of Nelson Mandela after so many years of imprisonment. These events have been facilitated if not necessitated by the new communications technology, the transistor radios, for example, that are available to Chinese peasants, or the videos that have played such a role in the recent revolutions in Eastern Europe. Far from being necessarily the instruments of thought control, as Orwell in *1984* foresaw, the new "technological regime of telecommunications"[4] seems to be inherently democratic. It has helped bring down dictator after dictator in the past few months.

In this new and as yet almost unimaginable global economy we are entering, made one world by these new technologies, the isolated study of single national literatures will soon seem as outmoded as old-fashioned nationalisms themselves. Such study must be replaced by multi-lingual and multi-ethnic disciplines of collective research and teaching. These new disciplines are themselves as yet hardly imagined, like the new world we are entering. They will borrow from anthropology and studies of popular culture as much as those disciplines have borrowed from literary theory. That new transnational democracy, whatever it will be like, must be based on the recognition and enhancement of cultural and individual differences. Here so-called "deconstructionisms" in their many forms will play an indispensable role. A constant focus of Derrida's work, for example, has been on heterogeneity in cultural forms, on the idiomatic in signature or text, and on what he calls the "invention of the other." "Invention" here means both creation and discovery, both making up and fortuitous coming upon, as if by chance, as when a book just happens to fall under a reader's eye and makes that reader different through the encounter with difference. The new technologies make such encounters universal. They also give us new ways to preserve and enhance difference, if we will take advantage of them.

I have said that theory is nothing without praxis and that reading is the praxis that theory makes possible, though theory and reading are asymmetrical. Only readings can respect the idiosyncratic in texts, what there is in them that resists the generalizations of theory. Though the essays gathered here are overtly "theoretical" or even polemical, theory in them nevertheless is constantly substantiated and made more complicated by readings. This includes readings of other theorists. Works of theory, if they are worth reading at all, must be read as scrupulously as literary works themselves. In these essays, in addition, the theoretical affirmations are "illustrated" (in all the ambiguity of that term) by many readings of literary works along the way – readings of works by Milton, Shelley, Wordsworth, Emerson, George Eliot, Nietzsche, Stevens, and Williams. Now as then, I find those acts of reading the place where the most happens in these essays and where the most may still again happen when they are read. Each of these essays belongs to the 'then' of its occasion. I have made no attempt to bring bibliographical or biographical facts fully up to date, much less to make the essays conform to what I would say now.

J. Hillis Miller
Irvine, California
3 February 1990

Notes

1. As I have argued in *Versions of Pygmalion* (Cambridge, Mass., 1990). See also references below to Derrida's "Télépathie" and Nicholas Royle's *Telepathy and Literature*.
2. See Alan Liu, "The Power of Formalism: The New Historicism," *ELH*, LVI, 4 (Winter 1989), 721–71.
3. See Nicholas Royle, "Telepathy: From Jane Austen and Henry James," *Oxford Literary Review*, X, 1–2 (1988), 43–60, and his *Telepathy and Literature*, forthcoming from Blackwell.
4. The phrase is Jacques Derrida's: *régime technologique des télécommunications*, in *La carte postale* (Paris, 1980), p. 212; in English in *The Post Card*, tr. Alan Bass (Chicago & London, 1987), p. 197.

Acknowledgements

I am grateful to the publishers and editors for permission to reprint the following essays:

"The Antitheses of Criticism: Reflections on the Yale Colloquium," *Modern Language Notes*, LXXXI, 5 (1966). Reprinted in *Velocities of Change: Critical Essays from MLN*, Richard Macksey, ed. (Baltimore and London: The Johns Hopkins University Press, 1974).

"The Geneva School: The Criticism of Marcel Raymond, Albert Béguin, Georges Poulet, Jean Rousset, Jean-Pierre Richard, and Jean Starobinski," *The Critical Quarterly*, VIII, 4 (Winter, 1966). Reprinted in *The Virginia Quarterly Review*, XLIII, 3 (Summer 1967) and in *Modern French Criticism*, J. K. Simon, ed. © 1972 by the University of Chicago.

"Georges Poulet's 'Criticism of Identification,'" *The Quest for Imagination*, O. B. Hardison, Jr., ed. (Cleveland, Ohio: The Press of Case Western Reserve University, 1971). The first half of this essay was first published as "The Literary Criticism of Georges Poulet," *Modern Language Notes*, LXXVIII (December 1963). The second half was published as "Geneva or Paris: The Recent Work of Georges Poulet," *University of Toronto Quarterly*, 39 (1970).

"Literature and Religion," *Relations of Literary Study: Essays on Interdisciplinary Contributions*, James Thorpe, ed. (New York: MLA, 1967).

"Tradition and Difference," *diacritics*, II, 4 (Winter 1972).

"Deconstructing the Deconstructers," *diacritics* (Summer 1975).

"The Year's Books: Literary Criticism," *The New Republic*, (29 November 1975).

"Stevens' Rock and Criticism as Cure, II," *The Georgia Review*, XXX, 2 (Summer 1976).

"Beginning with a Text," review article on E. W. Said's *Beginnings*, *diacritics*, VI, 3 (Fall 1976).

"The Critic as Host," *Deconstruction and Criticism* (New York: The Seabury Press, 1979). The opening part of this essay appeared in preliminary form in *The Critical Inquiry*, III, 3 (Spring 1977).

"On Edge: The Crossways of Contemporary Criticism," *Bulletin of the*

American Academy of Arts and Sciences, XXXII, 4 (January 1979). Reprinted, with a "Postscript 1984," in *Romanticism and Contemporary Criticism*, Morris Eaves and Michael Fischer, eds. Copyright © 1986 by Cornell University. Used by permission of the publisher, Cornell University Press. The postscript has been added here to the original essay.

"The Function of Rhetorical Study at the Present Time," *The State of the Discipline: 1970s–1980s, ADE Bulletin*, 62 (September–November 1979). Reprinted with slight changes in *Teaching Literature, What is Needed Now*, James Engell and David Perkins, eds, © 1988 by the President and Fellows of Harvard College. I have reprinted the later version here.

"Composition and Decomposition: Deconstruction and the Teaching of Writing," *Composition and Literature*, Winifred B. Horner, ed. © 1983 by the University of Chicago.

"Constructions in Criticism," *Boundary 2*, XII, 3/XIII, 1 (Spring/Fall 1984).

"The Search for Grounds in Literary Study." From *Rhetoric and Form: Deconstruction at Yale*, with an introduction by Robert Con Davis and Ronald Schleifer, eds. Copyright © 1985 by the University of Oklahoma Press.

"Gleichnis in Nietzsche's *Also Sprach Zarathustra*," *International Studies in Philosophy*, XVII, 2 (1985).

"How Deconstruction Works," *The New York Times Magazine*, (9 February, 1986), p. 25.

"President's Column," *MLA Newsletter*.
   Responsibility and the Joy of Reading (Spring 1986).
   Responsibility and the Joy(?) of Teaching (Summer 1986).
   The Obligation to Write (Fall 1986).
   The Future for the Study of Languages and Literatures (Winter 1986).

"The Imperative to Teach," *Qui Parle*, I, 2 (Spring 1987).

"Presidential Address 1986. The Triumph of Theory, the Resistance to Reading, and the Question of the Material Base," *PMLA* (May 1987).

"The Ethics of Reading," *Style*, XXI, 2 (Summer 1987).

"Paul de Man's Wartime Writings," *The Times Literary Supplement* (June 17–23, 1988).

"'Reading' Part of a Paragraph in *Allegories of Reading*." Copyright ©

1989 by the University of Minnesota. Reprinted from *Reading de Man Reading*, Lindsay Waters and Wlad Godzich, eds, by permission of the University of Minnesota Press.

"An Open Letter to Professor Jon Wiener." Reprinted from *Responses on Paul de Man's Wartime Journalism*, Werner Hamacher, Neil Hertz and Thomas Keenan, eds, by permission of University of Nebraska Press. Copyright © 1989 by the University of Nebraska Press.

"The Function of Literary Theory at the Present Time." First published in *The Future of Literary Theory*, Ralph Cohen, ed. (New York & London: Routledge, 1989). Copyright © Routledge, Chapman and Hall, Inc. Reprinted here by permission of Routledge.

1

The antitheses of criticism: reflections on the Yale Colloquium

I

This Colloquium testifies to an important shift of focus in American literary criticism. The temper of the conference can be accounted for partly by the topics chosen for papers and partly by the fact that so many of the participants are European-trained or teach in departments of romance language or of comparative literature. Even so, the new orientations of the Colloquium have significance for American criticism generally. A few years ago one would have expected an American colloquium on literary criticism to be a dialogue between our native formalism and other approaches. Quite recently, for example, Professor Murray Krieger described present-day literary criticism in America in terms of a conflict between a fading "new criticism" and the archetypal approach. The latter is, for Krieger, the most viable alternative. At the Yale Colloquium, however, neither the new criticism nor archetypal criticism figured centrally, in spite of the fact that there was a paper on the work of Northrop Frye. There was hostility to neither, but a sense that their lessons can be taken for granted. For most of the participants part of the impetus for the next advances in literary study will come from one form or another of European criticism. Assimilating the best recent continental criticism, American scholars may come to develop new forms of criticism growing out of American culture as well as out of the encounter with European thought. The Yale Colloquium suggests that this is in fact already taking place.

Tensions between antithetical approaches are fundamental to the critical enterprise. The Colloquium brought a number of the most important of these into the open where their variety and complexity could be seen. Sometimes these tensions were present in the mind of a

---

This article was written to comment on papers given at the Yale Colloquium on Criticism and was published in *MLN* 81 (December 1966).

single participant. Sometimes they emerged in the clash of the discussions, or from the juxtaposition of two papers. In any case, they governed our thinking.

Among the antitheses were the following: the nominalization of literature versus its periodization; reification versus totalization; the notion that an authentic image in poetry is unique versus investigation of literature in terms of *topoi*, archetypes, or other fixed forms transcending the particular; novelty versus tradition; relativity or historicism versus some form of absolutism; the end of history (or history transformed into an "eternal Platonic state") versus endless history; temporal form versus spatial form; hermeneutic, polyrhythmic, dialectical, or discontinuous time versus linear, organic, "natural," or continuous time; structure versus form; the notion that literature is autonomous versus the notion that it should be studied in terms of some context, biographical, social, metaphysical, or religious; microscopism versus the panoramic view; poetry as an end versus poetry as a means; yielding to the work as an experience or meaning which is its own justification versus the attempt to do something with the work for oneself, to assimilate it into the critic's own patterns of meaning; subjectivity versus reality; metaphysics versus science; poetry versus the novel; angelism versus original sin; alienation versus authenticity; disengagement, objectivity, or detachment versus engagement, commitment, or involvement; ontology versus intersubjectivity; dualism versus monism (a conviction that observer and observed are two or a conviction that they are one); criticism as interpretation versus criticism as the means of developing a theory of literature; criticism as a form of literature versus criticism as the science of interpretation or as the practice of a certain methodology.

It will be seen that some groups of these pairs interpenetrate and overlap bewilderingly, while some pairs seem to stand by themselves or to be related only distantly to the others. The opposition between the notion that literature and ontology may be one and the notion that literature deals with the relation between several minds is related, for example, to the opposition between poetry and the novel. The critic interested in the way literature may express truths about ultimate being will find more to his taste in Stevens or Keats than in Thackeray or even in Proust. On the other hand, the acceptance or denial of original sin seems to have little to do with the opposition between time and space, though there may in fact be secret connections between the two antinomies. In any case, the presence of these oppositions is visible everywhere in the papers of the Colloquium. In fact they cover the whole field of critical theory, if not in themselves, certainly in their implications, as contour lines do not touch every square foot of a mountain, but taken together outline its complex surface. The work of a particular critic tends to be defined by where he stands on the mountain, by his perspective, explicit or implicit, on the issues raised by the oppositions I have listed. This placing is often so taken for granted that it is never recognized for what it is – the foundation of a critical method.

Though the antitheses of criticism overlap, they do not form a neat continuum. There are breaks and contradictions between any one opposition and some of the others. They cut the field of criticism in different and often incompatible ways. To borrow a word from Gerard Manley Hopkins, the oppositions might better be thought of as so many topographical "cleaves" of the landscape of criticism, rather than as logically connected pairs. Nor are the antitheses dialectical. It is not possible to proceed from their opposition to some grand synthesis transcending the problems of criticism in a comprehensive system – with all the critics clasping hands and singing a final chorus. Ours is a fallen world, and literary critics, like everyone else, must endure the *malconfort* of a pull between opposing tendencies of the spirit. In the case of literary criticism, it is the peculiarity of these tensions that to ignore the attraction in one direction and yield without reservation to the lure of the other is to court disaster.

I shall now try to follow several of the lines suggested by the antitheses I have named. To do this will show how the oppositions melt into one another, how it is possible to move from one to another within the space of criticism, and how various methods of criticism can be placed according to coordinates within that space.

II

A constant source of quarrels among critics is disagreement about the context in which a work of literature should be studied. The oppositions within an important set of the antitheses of criticism are implicit in these quarrels.

Perhaps the poem should be studied by itself. Each poem has a unique meaning, and this meaning is generated solely by the words of the poem. Poetic language is self-contained or self-referential. Whatever meanings it has are there on the page, shining forth from the words themselves, and not to be found in other works by the author or in books read by the author. Perhaps the location of uniqueness in literature is the image, and the critic should, like Gaston Bachelard, detach each authentic image from its surrounding words. These blur the freshness and generative integrity of the image. The image is poetry at its source, and therefore each should be studied in isolation. Only in this way can its psychic dynamism, its intrinsic originating power, be identified.[1]

Such microscopism is opposed by all those theories of literature which argue that a word or image in a poem is of little meaning in itself. It gets its meaning from its context. Words after all, have a complicated cultural history. The notion of intrinsic meaning is not incompatible with the idea that each image draws into itself all those connections it has with its various contexts. The critic must identify those connections, not for their own sake, but in order to show what is really there in the words of the work. He must show how a certain text draws its life from similar passages in other works by the author, or from books read by the author, or from the social and historical milieu in which it came into existence, or from the tradition to which it belongs. A work of literature is defined by what is around it. Literary criticism must therefore take a wide view and see both the work and all its environments. But the work may then disappear into its context. If, on the other hand, the critic cuts it off from its contexts, it may appear so unique that there is nothing to say about it.[2]

If the critic avoids this penchant of literary study and returns to the poem itself, another danger awaits him. The more completely he cuts the poem off from its mesh of defining circumstances, the less he can allow himself to say about it. The poem means only itself, and any commentary falsifies it by turning it into something other than itself. Fearing the heresies of paraphrase and explanation, he is reduced to silence, or to repeating the poem itself as its only adequate commentary.[2]

Literary criticism disappears at either extreme, and any valid criticism must stand somewhere between. The choice of a place to stand plays a large role in determining the procedure of any critic. Bachelard sees a dichotomy between the image and its contexts, and can say *Entre le concept et l'image, pas de synthèse*.[3] Many other critics feel that the context of an image, far from being a conceptual abstraction, is its latent meaning and inheres in its being. For Georges Poulet or Jean-Pierre Richard, Albert Béguin or Marcel Raymond, the essential context of any passage is everything else its author wrote. The meaning of a text can be defined only in terms of the system of relations which ties it to the patterns of an *oeuvre*. Psychological criticism does not have that respect for the manifest meaning of a text which Poulet, for example, shares with Bachelard. Nevertheless, it is like the criticism of the *école de Genève* in assuming that the proper context for literary interpretation is the coherence of one man's life. For the Freudian, Sartrean, or Lacanian critic, however, the meaning of a passage is latent. A given paragraph can only be deciphered when it is understood to be the disguised expression of the author's governing complex or project, or of the occult chain of meanings which rules his life.[4]

Other critics assume that the proper context for criticism is social or cultural. Sociological, Marxist, structuralist, or anthropological criticism received much attention at the Yale Colloquium, as did the idea of "structure". This word is often used today to describe a notion of context in which the element to be studied participates in its environment rather than being surrounded by it or being determined by it from the outside. "Structure" may be used in opposition to the idea of "form" to suggest a many-layered system of meanings made up of dynamic interchanges rather than being fixed in a static pattern. (Many formalists would reply that if structure means this, they have been structuralists all along.) Or "structure" may suggest the notion of a system in which any element is meaningless except in its relation to the others. A word in a sentence, an image in a poem, a gesture, action, or speech performed by a person, a Sioux among the Sioux or a Parisian in Paris – each of these is a center of exchange for meanings, but is without meaning in isolation. The notion of structure is similar in all these contexts (as is suggested by the influence of structural linguistics on anthropological structuralism), but it makes a great difference for literary criticism which context is taken as most important.

The critics who choose the context of society as the essential one for literature would deny that the *oeuvre* of a writer is any more self-sufficient than a single poem by that writer. Both are parts of a social or cultural system and are irradiated with social meanings. If critics who choose smaller contexts are often most interested in poetry, sociological critics often choose fiction. The novel, they argue, is the genre developed to explore the relation of the individual and society. The social system in which a man lives determines the form of his subjective life, and even poetry, which often seems exclusively concerned with epistemological or ontological problems, will reflect the class-structure or the economic structure of its author's society. For a critic like Georg Lukács or Lucien Goldmann a man is so pervaded by the structures of the society surrounding him that these seize him and force him to express them, wittingly or unwittingly. There is no simple notion of determinism here. A man is free to respond slavishly, rebelliously, or creatively to his society, but however he responds his work will be testimony to the nature of his society. The great realists are those who mirror their societies without distortion. This often means that their work as dramatic expression is truer to the facts than their conscious beliefs or than the meanings they thought they were putting into their work.

Most of the kinds of criticism I have discussed so far, with the notable exception of the *école de Genève*, are in one way or another "scientific" or "objective," conceiving the language of literature as being "out there," and as forming objective systems of meaning which inhere in other larger objective systems. These structures can be studied in a way which will make literary study part of the collective body of research to which we give the name of science. Structural linguistics, Russian formalism, the American new criticism, Lacan, Lukács, Lévi-Strauss – all in one way or another consider language and literature in this way. Another important group of critics agree that the study of literature should be objective and scholarly, but disagree with most forms of criticism so far mentioned in their conception of the nature of literature. For them literature tends to be thought of as a self-enclosed spiritual sphere. This sphere is inhabited by all the good writers and forms a sealed tradition with an evolution of its own which can be studied in isolation. Such critics often cut literature off from the structures which seem all-important to a Lukács or a Lévi-Strauss, but on the other hand they see Western literature as forming a system of its own in which the meaning of a writer's work is determined by its relation to the whole. An individual image is authentic not because it represents the absolute novelty Bachelard finds in it, but because it repeats or embodies some *topos*, archetype, or other fixed form of the culture to which it belongs. This culture is imaged as a spatial panorama in which each new valid image finds a place determined by its relations to the other images already there. In such critics the same idea of structure may be found as is present in structural linguistics or in the thought of Lévi-Strauss, but the reality seen as so structured is very different. T. S. Eliot, in *After Strange Gods*, shows the intolerance to which such a position can lead. He rejects Hardy, Yeats and Lawrence because they do not fit the tradition as he defines it.[5]

If Eliot's book expresses the extreme consequences of a certain notion of tradition, this notion nevertheless has great strength among critics. It is represented in different versions by three of the critics discussed in the Colloquium: Frye, Auerbach, and Curtius. The papers at the Colloquium showed the complex forms this kind of criticism takes in the work of these men: the eternal archetypes of Frye in their spatialized fixity mirrored in the cyclic evolutions of literature; the nostalgia for a unified European culture in Curtius' admirable gathering of *topoi* in *Europäische Literatur und lateinisches Mittelalter*; the tension in Auerbach's thought between an idealism seeing history as an eternal Platonic state and a historicism seeing literature as responding to social forces almost as much as it does for Lukács.

From the microscopism of Bachelard, with its call for an exclusive focus on a single image, to the varied forms of panoramic criticism in Lukács, Curtius, or Auerbach the antithesis between no context and an ever-widening context may be followed as one of those topographical guide-lines crossing the landscape of criticism. My own position is near the middle. In my reading of literature the single poem or novel is never enough. It can never be made fully transparent or fully comprehensible if it is kept in isolation. On the other hand, I become uneasy when the work is placed in the context of a whole period or culture. The qualities and themes which Matthew Arnold or Wallace Stevens share with their ages seem often the least important aspects of their work, and I fear the dissolution of their uniqueness in the gray dusk of historical or parahistorical generalizations. When I read an author I have the conviction that my experience is most like that of encountering another human being, a mediated encounter it is true, and unsatisfactory for that reason, and yet in another way giving deeper and more intimate knowledge than I have even of those persons I am closest to in the "real world." Though the people I know are fully present in each gesture or phrase, nevertheless this presence of the whole in the part can never be understood without knowledge of the whole, without prolonged acquaintance with the person in various situations, so that what is most personal and characteristic of him may be detected as the constant presence in the variety of his behavior. In the same way, a single novel or poem can be understood only if it is read in the context of the other work by that author. Only then will what Proust called the "novel and unique beauty" of the author become visible.

III

My discussion of the problem of context has touched on many of the other antitheses of criticism. One of these is of great importance at the moment: the opposition between monism and dualism. The assumption that existence is divided into subject and object, mind and things, is deeply a part of our culture. It is present in many forms: in the philosophical traditions stemming from Descartes and Locke; in romanticism in poetry, with its preoccupation with epistemological themes; in the habitual technique of fiction, with its dependence on "point of view" as a generative structural principle; in the methodology of science, with its setting of the knowing mind against knowable things.

Much modern criticism inherits this dualism. This is to be expected, since modern criticism is the child of its culture, and in particular the child of romanticism, though often the ungrateful and rebellious child. The presence of dualistic assumptions is especially evident in the quarrels between those who want to make criticism a science, or who want to judge literature by its correct "mirroring" of reality, and their opponents, whom they accuse of "subjectivizing" literature. On the one hand, Curtius and Eliot tend to think of European culture as a self-contained spiritual whole, and a critic like Georges Poulet describes criticism as consciousness of consciousness. Poulet's dependence on the dualism descending from Descartes is apparent in the way he seeks in each writer for the *Cogito*, a unique version of the act of coming to self-consciousness in which what persists through all the experiences of the self is revealed. From this *point de départ* all the spiritual adventure of the writer is generated. If this adventure participates in anything outside itself, it shares in the collective consciousness of the age. This again is something subjective, and can be described in the same terms as individual consciousnesses. Poulet attempts to do this in the chapters on the Renaissance, baroque, the eighteenth century, and romanticism in *Les métamorphoses du cercle*.

On the other hand, a critic like Lukács also assumes a dualism of subject and object, though he uses it in an opposing way. Nineteenth- and twentieth-century "bourgeois" thought, in his view, is undermined by subjectivism, which he defines as a withdrawal into an unreal never-never-land of the mind. This detachment from reality is a symptom of the decadence of the bourgeois intellectual. Opposed to subjectivistic writers like Kafka, Beckett, or Joyce are the true realists like Thomas Mann, Conrad, or Shaw. The latter mirror modern social and economic reality accurately rather than inhabiting a non-existent domain of the mind. Lukács' dependence on a rather simple version of dualism is especially apparent in this metaphor of the mirror. The figure is of course traditional, and goes back in particular to nineteenth-century theories of realism in fiction. Just as Stendhal defines the novel as *un miroir promené par les grands chemins*, and just as George Eliot, in a famous chapter in *Adam Bede*, says that her aim is "to give a faithful account of men and things as they have mirrored themselves in my mind,"[6] so Lukács praises Mann for being "an extreme type of the writer whose greatness lies in being a 'mirror of the world.'"[7]

Georges Blin has shown how paradoxical is the concept of realism in fiction.[8] His analysis is based on one version of that monism which is as characteristic of twentieth-century thought as the persistence of dualism. This unification of existence is not, in its most persuasive forms, attained by the dialectical transcendence of dualism. If the latter is accepted as a starting point it is impossible to think or feel one's way out of it. At best one can experience, as some English romantic poets do, a momentary coalescence of subject and object, followed by a fall back into the normal bifurcation of existence. Many important twentieth-century writers and artists have avoided this situation by assuming that a union of subject and object is the primordial situation, the "given." Dualism is a derived state, perhaps cultural in origin, perhaps an almost irresistible illusion.

There is a tradition for this monism, too, though it is usually of an idealist cast. Blake, like Smart and Macpherson, expresses in his poetry a visionary or apocalyptic unity of subject and object, and Shelley holds that mind and world are one realm which has been artificially divided in our experience of them. T. S. Eliot in his dissertation picks out as central in F. H. Bradley's thought the notion that dualism is an inevitable illusion following upon the breaking apart of the original unity of "immediate experience." Since that unity is what "really is," any system of thought which begins with the assumption that either subject or object is primary will be led into contradiction.⁹

The most appealing twentieth-century versions of monism, however, are neither idealist nor materialist. This opposition, a contemporary monist would say, is itself a product of dualist thought. In spite of the continued strength of dualistic thinking, and in spite of the resistance of thinkers like A. O. Lovejoy,¹⁰ the new monism has strengthened and has appeared more or less spontaneously in widely different areas. Its most elaborated philosophical form is in the phenomenology of Husserl, Heidegger, and Merleau-Ponty, but it is present too in the linguistic philosophy of Wittgenstein's *Philosophical Investigations*, or in the insistence that a work of art means itself, rather than "representing" anything, made by the American abstract expressionists, or in the transcendence of dualism in the later work of Wallace Stevens, or in the affirmation that "anywhere is everywhere" of William Carlos Williams.

The new way of thinking has important implications for literary criticism. An understanding of dualistic thought is essential to the interpretation of those works which embody it, and even a monist would see a derived truth in dualistic experience. Nevertheless, it is possible to distort novels and poems in the direction of a dualism which they do not in fact express. The form of nineteenth-century English fiction, for example, is determined by dualistic thinking. Even so, George Eliot, Trollope, Meredith, or Hardy often present with admirable concreteness the inherence of a person's mind in his/or her body and in physical and social surroundings. Fiction was taking for its province an exploration of the nuances of intersubjectivity long before this category became important for twentieth-century philosophy. To the degree that the insights of twentieth-century monism are compelling they can usefully determine the procedures of criticism – the questions it asks and the range of its assumptions. This has in fact already happened, as in the influence of phenomenology, in various ways, on the criticism of Sartre, Poulet, or the later Bachelard, or in the monism implicit in the various forms of structuralism.

IV

One of the areas where the opposition between dualism and monism has especial force in contemporary criticism is that named by another antithesis of criticism, the one between temporal form and spatial form. This opposition is nearly the same as that between linear, organic, natural, or continuous time and hermeneutic, polyrhythmic, dialectical, or discontinuous time. Linear time is spatialized time, whereas for Heidegger space is a modification of existential time. One of the accomplishments of the Yale Colloquium was to bring this opposition to the surface, most explicitly in the admirable paper of Paul de Man, but less overtly at other times in the papers and discussions.

There is some evidence that a tendency to think either in spatial, visual terms or in dynamic, temporal terms may be innate in individuals. Each of us may be born either a little Platonist, with a penchant for thinking in terms of visual figures, optical space, and geometrical diagrams, or a little Aristotelean, with a penchant for thinking in terms of interacting energies in movement. Nevertheless, many qualities of our culture, and in particular those associated with dualistic assumptions, work to make spatialized thinking easy for us. The domination of eyesight over the other senses follows naturally from an assumption that man is subjective mind opposed to a physical world spread out before him. The passivity, detachment, and abstraction of a book culture may reinforce this, as does our habit of assuming that man's proper business is the reduction of the world to abstractions, numbers, patterns, maps, charts, and diagrams. Time, according to this way of thinking, becomes a fourth dimension of space, something open to linear representation. The charts of dates in history books, for example, suggest that time is a line stretching backward through the French Revolution to the Norman Conquest, then to the birth of Christ, with other events at measured intervals between, and in many forms of applied mathematics there is a coordinate showing time as a line.

Much modern literary criticism is permeated by spatial thinking. This may be seen in the diagrammatic patterns of Northrop Frye's *Anatomy of Criticism*,[11] or in some of the habitual metaphors of the "new criticism," or in discussions of fiction in terms of the "curve of the plot," or in the insistence, in Joseph Frank's celebrated essay, that modern literature has a "spatial form," or in the spatialized model of literary history in T. S. Eliot's "Tradition and the Individual Talent." There is a tension in Georges Poulet's criticism, to give another example, between an interest in time and a habit of dialectical thought, on the one hand, and the attraction to spatial form evident in the key image of *Les métamorphoses du cercle* and in *L'espace proustien*. Even the concept of structure, which is often explicitly opposed to that of form in a dichotomy between dynamic movement and fixed design, has a tendency to become geometrical pattern after all. Lévi-Strauss offers his spatial diagrams of exogamy and other forms of social relationship, and in the work of Jacques Lacan there is an interesting conflict between the use of diagrams and the employment of non-spatial mathematical models to express chains or transformations of meaning.

The tradition in modern thought and art which rebels against dualism would also claim that spatial thinking is an abstraction from the concrete richness of experience. Human existence is fundamentally temporal, and even our experience of space is falsified if it is described in terms of geometrical abstraction. Among those forms which are falsified by spatialization, such thinkers would say, is literature. Literature is a temporal, not a spatial art, and should be described as such, in vocabulary proper to its temporality.

Bergson of course is an important innovator in this twentieth-century reaction against spatialization, but Paul de Man properly pointed to Bachelard's *La dialectique de la durée* and to Heidegger's *Sein und Zeit* as important parts of this tradition. In the latter there are provocative comments on the way spatial metaphors are native to our language and natural to our thinking, and Heidegger provides a classic analysis of time as the basic dimension of human existence. Once again, however, there are parallels between modern philosophy and modern literature, parallels which are not a matter of influence but of simultaneous manifestations of similar tendencies of thought. Much modern poetry, for example, is poetry of the moment. It often describes the moment as an evanescent flowing, each instant appearing out of nowhere and reaching toward a goal which transcends it, so that it vanishes in the reaching. An example of such poetry is the late work of Wallace Stevens, as in the fluid improvisations of "An Ordinary Evening in New Haven" or of "A Primitive Like an Orb." William Carlos Williams, to give another example, expresses his denial of dualism by an avoidance of abstract visual images and by an emphasis on the more intimate senses, hearing, tasting, touching, and that kinesthetic mimesis whereby we internalize the world with our muscles and nerves. The verbal forms appropriate to these senses cooperate, in poems like "To All Gentleness," Book Five of *Paterson*, or "Asphodel, That Greeny Flower," to take the reader into a region of immanence, where space is the expansive movement of the instant in its flowing.

The affirmation of the unity of subject and object and a replacement of space by time as the basic dimension of existence are two salient characteristics of twentieth-century thought. Literary criticism has developed modes of interpretation which match the new attitudes, but in many areas this development is not complete. No one yet, for example, has done full justice to the complexity of temporal structure in fiction or to the subtle variation in grasp of interpersonal relations from one novelist to another. These are not a matter of the curve of the action, or of the design of the whole, or of the patterns of imagery, but are concretely present from paragraph to paragraph in the language of the novel as it opens temporal perspectives and relates minds to one another in ever-changing ways. It is extremely difficult to honor in criticism the flow of our experience as we read the words of *Middlemarch* or *To the Lighthouse*. In the interpretation of fiction, more perhaps than with any other literary form, it is hard for the critic to remain in touch with the immediate quality of the work. It is easier to create a structure of one's own than to identify the living structures of the novel in question. The Yale Colloquium in its discussion of the masters of recent criticism recognized our necessary dependence on their work, but the papers and especially the discussions were also oriented toward the criticism that has not yet been written. The antitheses of criticism will remain, but perhaps in the years to come some of the most important criticism will be done on the basis of the swing to monism and temporality in twentieth-century thought. It is by their fruits that you will know them. No critical method, no presuppositions about man and the world, will guarantee the writing of good critical studies. New perspectives may sometimes, however, reveal aspects of works of literature which have so far remained hidden.

Notes

1. See especially the introductory chapter of Bachelard's *La poétique de la rêverie* (Paris, 1960).
2. Jean Starobinski has eloquently described this paradox of criticism in *L'oeil vivant* (Paris, 1961), pp. 24–7.
3. *La poétique de la rêverie*, p. 45.
4. A recent example of such criticism, in this case influenced by the work of Jacques Lacan, is Jean Laplanche, *Hölderlin et la question du père* (Paris, 1961).
5. See p. 69 of the present book for further discussion of this.
6. The passage is in Chapter xvii.
7. *Essays on Thomas Mann*, tr. Stanley Mitchell (London, 1964), p. 16.
8. See "Liminaire," *Stendhal et les problèmes du roman* (Paris, 1960), pp. 5–16.
9. See *Knowledge and Experience in the philosophy of F. H. Bradley* (London, 1964).
10. See *The Revolt against Dualism* (New York, 1930).
11. Another good example of Frye's use of spatial metaphors is his essay, "Myth, Fiction, and Displacement." "We are," says Frye of our reading of a novel, "continually, if often unconsciously, attempting to construct a larger pattern of simultaneous significance out of what we have so far read. . . . We expect a certain point near the end at which linear suspense is resolved and the unifying shape of the whole design becomes conceptually visible" (*Fables of Identity* [New York, 1963], p. 25).

2

The Geneva school:

the criticism of Marcel Raymond,
Albert Béguin, Georges Poulet, Jean Rousset,
Jean-Pierre Richard, and Jean Starobinski

I

Consciousness of consciousness, literature about literature – all six of the critics to be discussed here would accept in one way or another these definitions of literary criticism. The similar assumptions of these critics about the nature of criticism may justify speaking of them as a "school," in spite of the important differences among them. Moreover, all but two (Georges Poulet and Jean-Pierre Richard) have been formally associated with the University of Geneva, and close ties of friendship and reciprocal influence have linked all six.

The members of the Geneva school share common sources in earlier criticism. Their work stems directly from that of the critics of the Nouvelle Revue Française, especially Jacques Rivière and Charles du Bos, and the filiation may be extended behind them through Proust to mid-nineteenth-century writers like Pater and Ruskin, and so back to romantic criticism. Moreover, the older members of the Geneva school, especially Marcel Raymond and Georges Poulet, were strongly influenced in their development by the work of two German critics who continued the romantic and historicist traditions: Wilhelm Dilthey and Friedrich Gundolf. The presuppositions of the criticism of the Geneva school may therefore be defined as a unique version of attitudes toward literature and criticism which are our heritage from romanticism.

Literature about literature – such a definition of criticism sharply differentiates the work of the Geneva critics from that of those scholars – French structuralists, Russian formalists, or American new critics – who tend to think of criticism as a mode of objective knowledge. For such critics criticism is one of the "human sciences," and therefore, like anthropology, history, or sociology, part of the university based enterprise of analysis and description which works toward a definitive conceptualization of the world. The Geneva critics, on the other hand, consider literary criticism to be itself a form of literature. It is a form which takes as its theme not that experience of natural objects, other people, or supernatural realities about which the poet and novelist write, but those entities after they have been assimilated into the work of some author. Literary criticism is literature at a second degree. It reaches the subject matter of literature by way of the intercession of poems, novels, plays, journals, and letters which others have written. In order to attain this subject matter literary criticism must not describe from the outside, as a scientist describes a flower or an atom. It must extend, complete, and constitute in a new form the themes which are already present in literature. It therefore makes the same use of language as literature does, and it expresses the same kinds of reality.

This means, among other things, that the literary critic, like the novelist or poet, is pursuing, however covertly or indirectly, his own spiritual adventure. He pursues it not by way of his own experience, but by the mediation of the experience of others. His work is far from disinterested or detached. "The most valuable criticism," says Albert Béguin,

> is . . . that criticism . . . in which the writer continues his own private adventure in his writing, in which through the very finding of the words he enacts one of the stages of his own personal spiritual adventure. Subjective criticism seems to me entirely justifiable and defensible.

It is therefore proper that Georges Poulet should have written a number of his most important recent essays on the work of other members of his own group: Raymond, Béguin, and Starobinski. This is not some final rarefying of criticism, the mirror mirroring the mirror. It is significant evidence that for the Geneva critics criticism is a form of literature and may itself be criticized in turn. If the work of these critics is literature about literature, it might be best to define it not in terms of its relation to other kinds of literary criticism, but as a special form of that literature of meditation, reverie, or spiritual quest which is historically associated with Switzerland and most often with Geneva. One thinks of Rousseau, of Sénancour, of Constant, of Amiel, of Ramuz. The Geneva critics continue in a new way this native tradition.

If criticism is literature about literature, what then is literature? The definition will determine not only the nature of the subject matter of criticism, but also the nature of criticism itself. For the Geneva critics literature is a form of consciousness. This conception of literature once more separates these critics from many current kinds of criticism. For Poulet or Raymond literature is neither an objective structure of meanings residing in the words of a poem or novel, nor the tissue of self-references of a "message" turned in on itself, nor the unwitting expression of the hidden complexes of a writer's unconscious, nor a revelation of the latent structures of exchange or symbolization which integrate a society. Literature, for them, is the embodiment of a state of mind. In the language of a text from Rousseau's "Rêveries," a poem by Hugo, or a novel by Balzac a certain mode of consciousness has been brought into the open in a union of mind and words. This union incarnates the consciousness and makes it available to others.

Criticism must therefore begin in an act of renunciation in which the critic empties his mind of its personal qualities so that it may coincide completely with the consciousness expressed in the words of the author. His essay will be the record of this coincidence. The "intimacy" necessary for criticism, says Georges Poulet, "is not possible unless the thought of the critic *becomes* the thought of the author criticized, unless it succeeds in re-feeling, in re-thinking, in re-imagining the author's thought from the inside. Nothing could be less objective than such a movement of the mind . . . for what has to be reached is a *subject*, that is to say a spiritual activity which cannot be understood unless the critic puts himself in its place and makes it play again within him its subjective rôle."

For the Geneva critics, then, criticism is primordially consciousness of the consciousness of another, the transposition of the mental universe of an author into the interior space of the critic's mind. Therefore these critics are relatively without interest in the external form of individual works of literature. Often the subject of one of their essays is the total work of an author, including his notes, his diaries, his unfinished works, his fragmentary drafts. Such incomplete writings may allow better access to the intimate tone or quality of a mind than a perfected masterpiece. "Subjectively," says Poulet, "there is nothing formal about literature. It is the reality of a thought which is always particular, always anterior and posterior to every object. . . ." A living mind is a protean energy which can never express itself fully in any objective form. "It is characteristic of a work," says Poulet,

> at once to create its structures and to transcend them, I should even say to destroy them. So the work of an author is certainly the collection of texts which he has written, but in the sense that as they follow one another, each replaces the last and reveals thereby a movement toward a liberation from structures.

Even Jean Rousset, the critic among the group most concerned with the form of individual works, defines structures in literature as "formal constants" or "relationships" whose function is precisely to reveal a "mental universe." A mental universe, however, has a structure of its own, and the critics of the Geneva school do not altogether reject structures in literature. Rather, they replace a concern for the objective structure of individual works with a concern for the subjective structure of the mind revealed by the whole body of an author's writings.

Though the Geneva critics would agree that literature is a form of consciousness, they would disagree in their assumptions about what consciousness is. The differences here are more than nuances within a single tradition of criticism. The varying intuitions of the nature of consciousness in the Geneva critics manifest fundamental oppositions within current thought and art, oppositions which suggest that we are living at the point of intersection of several incompatible conceptions of the nature of man. If the aim of literary criticism is to reach a coincidence of the critic's mind and the mind of the author, the nature of this experience will be determined by the nature of consciousness itself. What does one reach when one reaches the mind of another person and relives from the inside, by way of his writing, his thoughts and emotions? To identify the differing answers to this question among the critics of the Geneva school will be to specify the particular quality of the work of each.

II

Born in 1897, Marcel Raymond has recently retired after many years as a professor at the University of Geneva. He may be considered the founder and senior member of the Geneva school. No criticism could fulfill better than his the requirement that criticism should be consciousness of consciousness. Criticism begins for him with "a sort of ascesis." The critic must "enter into a state of profound receptivity in which his being becomes extremely sensitized." This preliminary state must "yield bit by bit to a penetrating sympathy." Only such a *sympathie pénétrante* will allow the critic to accomplish his primary task, which is to "relive from the inside," by a sort of "knowledge from within," the experience of the author as it is embodied in his words. The critic's job is to "transform states of existence into states of consciousness." He must "re-create" the work of art "within himself, but in conformity to itself." The work must be born anew within him, rising up again in his mind by means of an act which is fundamentally to be defined as "creative participation."

Raymond distinguishes two kinds of knowledge. There is intellectual, scientific, or objective knowledge, knowledge which holds everything at arm's length, separating the mind from its objects and all objects from one another, and there is that inward, affective knowledge in which the mind and its objects become one, or rather, in the case of criticism, in which the critic's mind and the mind expressed in the work become one. This experience is not so much intersubjective as introspective, for the mind of the author must be as much interior to the critic as his own sense of himself. Raymond's genius as a critic has depended on an extreme inner plasticity which has allowed him to duplicate within himself the affective quality of the mind of each of his authors, that profound note of selfhood which persists as the same throughout the work of each. Repeating it within himself, he is able to reproduce it with marvelous economy in a brief quotation or in an image of his own.

This admirable dispatch, which gets to the heart of an author in an instant, is essential to the atmosphere of Raymond's criticism and makes it very different from that of his immediate predecessors, Jacques Rivière and Charles du Bos. In Raymond's work there is neither Rivière's hesitating approach to the mind of an author (which Georges Poulet has called "asymptotic"), nor du Bos' tendency to be led to digressive expansion by way of his coincidence with the mind of the writer. For a great many authors, especially those of the baroque period and those of the period which begins with Rousseau and extends to surrealism, Raymond has performed the basic critical act of reproducing in the words of his essay the unique affective quality of the mind of the writer. Raymond's masterpiece, *From Baudelaire to Surrealism*, inaugurated in 1933 a new epoch in French criticism. Its greatness lies as much in its succinct presentations of a multitude of individual poets as in its grasp of the inner unity of modern French poetry. With unrivaled sympathy and tact he identifies distinguishing characteristics in the work of Baudelaire, Rimbaud, and Mallarmé, and then traces the development from these fathers of modern French poetry in brief essays on Valéry, Apollinaire, Breton, Eluard, and many other twentieth-century poets.

Raymond's insight into the unity of what he calls "the modern myth of poetry" is, however, no less important than his ability to identify what is unique in each poet he discusses. What qualities does Raymond most often find in the authors he admires? A text in *From Baudelaire to Surrealism* will give the answer:

> While the classical writer, anxious to know himself, relied on introspection and transposed the result of his observations to the plans of discursive reasoning, the romantic poet, renouncing any form of knowledge which was not at the same time a feeling and an enjoyment of himself – and a feeling of the universe, experienced as a presence – charged his imagination with the task of composing a metaphoric or symbolic portrait of himself in his metamorphoses.

The two elements which Raymond finds essential in authentic poetry are here neatly juxtaposed: "feeling of the self" and "feeling of the universe, experienced as a presence."

The self-consciousness of others with which Raymond seeks to identify himself is neither that lucid awareness of the self in its isolation and distinctness dear to Descartes and the intellectualist tradition, nor is it a mind filled to brimming with the various objects and thoughts which occupy it. It is rather a primitive sense of existence, prior to the identification of any distinct objects, a state of mind more emotive than rational, scarcely differentiated as that of one particular self. Expressions for this quality of mind run all through Raymond's work. It is "the feeling of existence in what it can have of most elementary and least differentiated," or "the feeling of our profound life," or "the elementary and quasi-mystical feeling of existence," or "a general sense of existence," or "an apprehension or a presentiment of the opaque, irrational nebula – or of existence as such – which subsists beyond knowledge by means of the intellect."

Only this *nébuleuse, opaque, irrationnelle* state breaks down the barriers which rational consciousness sets up between the mind and the world and gives the critic, by way of the words of the poet, an experience of the universe as a communion of all objects and persons in an intimate overlapping. Such an interpenetration of all things will be pervaded throughout by a fugitive spiritual reality, "a mysterious presence . . . seductive and overwhelming, like a miracle." The ultimate goal of all true poetry is to reach this state. Raymond's criticism seeks in its turn to capture in poetry this mysticism of immanence, a "confused and delicious feeling of existence" in which "the sense of the self and the sense of the whole can no longer be distinguished." "Dream of a magical universe," says Raymond, "in which man would not feel himself to be distinct from things."

Since 1950 the instinctive mysticism of this earth in Raymond, closer perhaps to primitive or pre-logical forms of participation than to Platonic or Christian mysticism, has been modified by the sudden appearance of a more traditional form of religious experience. This has to some degree cut Raymond off from his earlier attitudes and has opened the way for him to the confrontation of a transcendent personal divinity. The extremely beautiful and moving account of this experience in *La Maladie et la guérison*, however, reaffirms Raymond's conviction that the deepest joy, whether in this world or in another, consists in a free communion of all objects and persons by way of a supreme Being or spiritual power. Poetry, for Raymond, is still in its essence a testimony to the possibility of this fusion.

Albert Béguin was born in 1901 and died in 1957. In his youth he taught for several years in Germany and was then appointed to a chair at Basel. In 1950 he succeeded Emmanuel Mounier as editor of the distinguished Catholic magazine, *Esprit*. He remained with *Esprit* until his death. He was the friend and, in early years, the disciple of Marcel Raymond, and his greatest book, *L'Âme romantique et le rêve* (1937) was presented as a dissertation at the University of Geneva.

Like Raymond, Béguin affirms that authentic literary criticism is only possible "if the commentator situates himself in the interior of the universe created by the author." The critic must "coincide with the spiritual adventure of the poet." But in place of the self-effacement and reticence characteristic of Raymond, Béguin is willing to say that the critic should be overtly "interested, engaged in an adventure, pursuing, under the guardianship of his familiar poets, a continuous research." The poets and novelists about whom he has written – Pascal, the German and French romantics, Nerval, Balzac, Claudel, Péguy, Bloy, Bernanos, Ramuz, Supervielle – are in his criticism openly encountered as intercessors. They are mediators who make it possible for him to reach, through their works, a physical and spiritual reality which might otherwise be unattainable. *L'Âme romantique et le rêve* was not undertaken as a work of objective scholarship, though it is in fact a landmark in the interpretation of romanticism. Béguin's encounter with the work of Hamann, Saint-Martin, Novalis, Tieck, Hoffmann, and the rest, and the intimate re-creations of the spiritual adventures of each in his book were crucial stages in his own religious quest. He does not show the same sympathy for writers who do not help him in this quest, and has, for example, great distaste for the idealism, the icy subjectivism, of a writer like Mallarmé. Béguin's identification with the consciousness of a poet has value for him only if that consciousness is one which participates in a transcendent reality of a certain kind.

"To restore in their integrity a contemplation characterized by *wonder* and the primary *presence of things*" – this phrase expresses concisely Béguin's definition of true poetry. The poet is a man who by way of dream, or reminiscence, or a heightened sensitivity to physical objects can break through the veil of familiarity which hides reality from us and return to the naïveté of infancy. The theme of childhood recurs throughout Béguin's criticism – childhood of the individual, but also childhood of the race, time of the beginning of things and of myth. His interest in this theme determines not only his approach to the romantic writers, but also his admiration for a twentieth-century author like Bernanos. His study of Bernanos in the *Par lui-même* series, one of the most important of his later books, is organized around the analogous themes of childhood innocence, the vocation of the priesthood, and the vocation of the writer. For Béguin, as for Bernanos or Dostoevsky, each human being contains hidden somewhere within himself, amid the distractions and corruptions of adulthood, a portion of the immaculate purity of a child. This secret purity is his true self. If he is granted grace to recover even for a moment the innocence of the buried self he will recover at the same time the golden age of our first parents, and with it a perfect openness to the natural world and to other people.

Such openness is the special virtue of childhood for Béguin. It is characterized by a sudden recognition of the concrete existence of physical objects. "On returning from the world of dreams," says Béguin in the admirable recapitulation of the adventure of romanticism at the end of *L'Âme romantique et le rêve*,

> human vision is capable of that amazement which one experiences when suddenly things take on for an instant their primal novelty. I am born to things; they are born to me. The exchange is re-established as in the first minutes of existence; this astonishment endows the world again with its marvelous appearance of fairyland.

This text will allow a further distinction to be made between Béguin's criticism and Raymond's. The concrete presence of substantial objects so cherished by Béguin in the work of the writers he admires is different from the *nébuleuse, opaque, irrationnelle* state of Raymond. Raymond prizes a vague indistinction, a state in which all things and persons seem to melt into one another. Béguin, on the other hand, most values a state of lucid astonishment in which each thing is distinctly present to the contemplating mind in all its exact weight and texture, and can be incarnated in the words of the poet. He praises the work of Claudel, for example, for its "strong taste of life": "The robust language of the poet is completely charged with the savor of terrestrial things. Things which are delectable and solid, loved in their solidity, things which keep, in their verbal evocation, their entire force of presence, their full weight."

This *force de présence* which the child and the poet can see in things is, however, by no means limited to their physical pressure on the senses. In the presence of objects the poet also encounters the presence of the Creator who has everywhere incarnated himself in his creation. The word *présence* is the key word in Béguin's criticism. It names both the physical tangibility of objects and the habitation of God within that tangibility. The notion of Incarnation is at the center of his concept of poetry, and for him all true poetry has as its goal a revelation of "the presence of the spiritual in the terrestrial." Poetry must, as he puts it in a succinct formulation, "touch in the concrete the presence of the Invisible."

Béguin finds in all the poets he admires something like the analogical symbolism of the middle ages or Renaissance which allows an object to express some specific quality of the divine life without ceasing to be itself. The paradise poetry glimpses is characterized by resonance at a distance. All three realms – divine, natural, and human – vibrate musically together in the diapason of creation. Of the work of all the poets Béguin most loves he could say what he says of the "profound realism" of Péguy:

> At every moment, in every object named, it evokes, demonstrates, installs the unique Presence; and before this, on its side, like every believer at the hour of prayer, it performs an *act of presence*. Presence of God to the world and to man; presence of the soul to God; presence of man to his universe.

To this "triple witness" must be added two more forms of presence. These will complete the system of musical accords Béguin finds in poetry. The first is language itself, the instrument of poetic revelation and the indispensable means of its "act of presence." The words of the poet stand in the middle, facing in turn toward the poet's consciousness, toward God, and toward the objects of the creation. Poetic language incarnates the affinities and harmonies of the other three realms, for the poet is the man who knows how to "call things by their true names, by their secret names," and his words bring into the open the hidden presence of God in things.

There is, finally, the presence of all the men and women of history to one another and to the world. The writers Béguin came especially to admire – Bernanos, Bloy, Claudel, Péguy – are those Catholic writers who recognize most clearly the communion of mankind in suffering which is a perpetual re-enactment of the Incarnation and Crucifixion. "All the saints – and all the faithful, and all the sinners –," says Béguin, "form through the ages a continuous chain." To this brotherhood of pain poetry presents evidence of the possibility of redemption, evidence of a sacred freshness still present beneath the surface of things and uncorrupted by the long centuries since the Fall. Béguin's criticism, in the end, is an apologetic addressed to all men in their solidarity in suffering. It brings them the precious witness poetry offers of God's presence in the creation.

Georges Poulet was born in Belgium in 1902 and was educated at the University of Liège. From 1927 to 1952 he taught at the University of Edinburgh; in 1952 he became Professor of French at The Johns Hopkins University; in 1958 he became Professor of French Literature at the University of Zürich. [He completed his teaching career at the University of Nice – JHM 1990.]

Like the other members of his group, Poulet thinks of criticism as beginning and ending in a coincidence of the mind of the critic and the mind of the author. There must be what he calls an "absolute transparency with the soul of the other." Poulet differs from the rest, however, in his unwillingness to use this transparency as a means to reach some further end. His "criticism of pure identification" is an end in itself. This means that Poulet is somewhat broader in his sympathies than either Raymond or Béguin. Seeking nothing beyond consciousness in consciousness, he has been able to concern himself with a wide variety of authors, from the Church Fathers through the writers of the middle ages, the poets, dramatists, and religious thinkers of the seventeenth century, the sensationalists of the eighteenth century, and a multitude of nineteenth- and twentieth-century writers. He can take the same interest, for example, in Casanova as in Pascal or Mallarmé. As long as some specific quality of inner experience is successfully expressed in the work of a writer, Poulet will find it worthwhile to relive that quality from within. The aim of each of his critical essays is to re-create as precisely as possible the exact tone which persists in a given writer throughout all the variety of his work.

For this reason he puts great value on defining the *Cogito* of each writer. The *Cogito* is the primary moment of the revelation of the self to itself in "an act of self-consciousness" separating the mind from everything which may enter it from the outside. All those exterior things are for Poulet somewhat accidental and unimportant. The affective quality of a consciousness is the source of everything else in a writer. It is an invariant element, present as a necessary coefficient of all the things the consciousness is conscious of. A moment of self-consciousness is therefore the "invariable starting point of every human existence perceived from within." The aim of criticism must be to disengage the mind of the writer from everything extraneous to it, to catch it "in the surging forth and genetic action of its power," when it exists "in a nearly virginal state, not yet invaded and as it were masked by the thick mass of its objective contents." One of Poulet's most admirable books, a study of a group of twentieth-century writers, is called *Le point de départ*. In each essay in this book, as in the rest of his criticism, he attempts to "go back in the work of the author all the way to that act from which each imaginary universe opens out. . . ."

This concern for the intimate texture of each writer's mind explains Poulet's special admiration for a writer like Amiel, whose journal lets one hear in its purity the murmur of "the original and final activity of the human consciousness, which consists in thinking itself, and again, and always, in thinking itself." Or it explains his fondness for Joubert, whose *Pensées* bring clearly into the open something different from any specific thought they may express, that is, the "interior distance" of the mind, that transparent space of "pure vacancy and latency" whose luminous expanses offer themselves to everything the mind may come to think.

Poulet's commitment to the idea that consciousness is the living source of literature distinguishes his work from all that criticism which presupposes a Husserlian conception of consciousness. For Husserl, for Martin Heidegger, for Maurice Merleau-Ponty, for Gaston Bachelard, for Jean-

Pierre Richard, and for many other contemporary thinkers and artists, consciousness is always consciousness *of* something or other. For such men there is never an act of self-consciousness in which the mind is aware of nothing but its own native affective tone. However far back one goes, however seemingly far away from the world, no state of mind can be encountered which is not already an inextricable interpenetration of subject and object, mind and things. This categorical rejection of any complete division of consciousness and the world, so fecund in recent developments in philosophy and art, is fundamentally anti-Cartesian. It rejects the idea of a *Cogito* in which the mind knows nothing but itself. Poulet, on the other hand, maintains the traditional dualism and affirms the priority of consciousness as the genetic energy in literature. This commitment appears clearly in an important letter of 1961. Distinguishing the presuppositions of his criticism from those of his friend and follower Jean-Pierre Richard, Poulet here rejects all that modern tradition of thought which may be called phenomenological and states his allegiance to the tradition of Descartes:

> I should readily consider that the most important form of subjectivity is not that of the mind overwhelmed, filled, and so to speak stuffed with its objects, but that there is another [kind of consciousness] which sometimes reveals itself on this side of, at a distance from, and protected from, any object, a subjectivity which exists in itself, withdrawn from any power which might determine it from the outside, and possessing itself by a direct intuition, infinitely different from the self-knowledge which is the indirect result of our relations with the world. In other words, I should say that subjectivity is the consciousness of the critic coinciding with the consciousness of the thinking or feeling person, located in the heart of the text (of every literary text), in such a way that this double consciousness appears less in its multiplicity of sensuous relation with things, than prior to and separate from any object, as self-consciousness or pure consciousness. . . . As you have seen, in this I remain faithful to the Cartesian tradition.

Poulet's criticism, then, may more exclusively be defined as "consciousness of consciousness" than either the religiously oriented criticism of Raymond and Béguin or the thematic criticism of Bachelard and Richard. For Poulet neither the dense substance of physical objects nor any extra-human presence within them is as important as the consciousness of the writer who describes them. If anything other than consciousness enters for him as an essential element into literature, it is something located not beyond or outside the mind, but precisely at its deepest center, for "the profundity of the interior [of consciousness] is such that one can never see the edge or the end of it, and, as in the case of Pascal, there is a transcendence of the center." This transcendence is reached not by going outside the minds of the writers criticized, but by "prolonging in its very interiority the spirituality of all the authors." In doing this "one comes to glimpse something which transcends them, to establish a convergence."

The notion that the minds of all authentic authors converge toward a transcendent point which is the hidden center of every human consciousness is in part the rationale of the essays in *Les métamorphoses du cercle* in which Poulet re-creates not the mind of a single author, but the mind of an age. For him, all human minds form a living whole, and the history of literature may therefore be defined as "a history of the human consciousness."

The idea of a transcendence at the center also explains Poulet's interest in authors like Pascal, Maurice de Guérin, or Nerval, for whom writing is the quest for a goal which can never be reached in this world. A transcendent presence is one which always remains beyond and unattainable. "I am above all attracted," says Poulet,

> by those for whom literature is – by definition – a spiritual activity which must be gone beyond in its own depths, or which, in failing to be gone beyond, in being condemned to the awareness of a non-transcendence, affirms itself as the experience and verification of a fundamental defeat.

The dialectical development of each critical essay by Poulet follows a writer in his attempts to reach the depths of his mind. His encounters with things other than that mind are often important in these attempts. Poulet tries to clarify these encounters as much as possible, to put them in order according to their interconnections. Order and transparence are two fundamental aspects of his criticism. Transparence is attained by seeing through an author, by bringing to light the intimate reason for each quality of the consciousness expressed in his works. Though Poulet likes a consciousness which is semi-opaque, a half-darkness penetrated with difficulty, this may be because such a mind is a challenge to his powers of clarification. Even when he talks about darkness or irrationality, he transforms muddle into clarity by demonstrating its plausibility. To show its plausibility means to show its connection to all the other salient motifs in the author's work. Order is attained in criticism through a demonstration of the mutual implication of all the characteristics of the consciousness being criticized. All the contents of the bubble of consciousness must be shown to be acting and reacting on one another, in reciprocal interchange.

Though Poulet concerns himself with the ways his authors have assimilated parts of the world into their writings, nevertheless his essential aim is to detach each mind from its contents. In relation to the characteristic texture or grain of a writer's interior space, the objects which happen to traverse it seem, to Poulet, more or less "a matter of indifference." Marcel Raymond may have been the first to use the concept of the *Cogito* in literary criticism, but Poulet's most important accomplishment is his extensive and deliberate investigation of the variations from writer to writer and from century to century in the ways men have come to self-consciousness. From the mobile self-awareness of Montaigne, to the intellectualist *Cogito* of Descartes, the sensationalist *Cogito* of Rousseau, or the voluntarist *Cogito* of Balzac, down to contemporary forms of self-consciousness in Proust, Claudel, Eluard, Char, and many others, Poulet has distinguished the manifold ways in which the human mind has become aware of its own "indescribable intimacy."

Jean Rousset was born in Geneva in 1910. After studies at Geneva he was a lecturer in various German universities, and then returned to the University of Geneva, where he became Professor of Literature. Disciple and colleague of Marcel Raymond, also close friend of Georges Poulet, his work differs somewhat from theirs in its concern for structure in works of literature, and in the fact that he often devotes an essay to a single work – to a play by Corneille, or to a novel by Flaubert or Proust. Raymond too affirms that "it is impossible to escape from forms," but he tries to go as much as possible beyond them in order to reach the obscure sense of existence which is at the heart of each author's work. Rousset, on the other hand, is, in his interest in individual works, much closer to American new criticism, to Russian formalism, or to a French critic like Gaëton Picon. For Rousset each work has its own unique form. This form brings into existence meanings which could become articulated in no other way. *Madame Bovary*, for example, "constitutes an independent organism, an absolute which is entirely self-sufficient, a whole which can be understood and clarified in itself."

Unlike Picon, however, or the Anglo-American formalists, Rousset affirms that the new presence which an authentic work brings into the world is not something impersonal, but is precisely the identity of its creator. If form for Poulet is something external which masks the consciousness which created it, Rousset sees in form the indispensable means by which a mind emerges from indistinction and becomes aware of itself in its individuality. The true structure of a work is nothing like a superficial framework or shape, for "in art there is no form which is not experienced and worked out from the inside." Only such an interior form can be one in which the artist discovers himself in the process of making his work. "The writer," says Rousset, "does not write in order to say *something*, he writes in order to *say himself*, as the painter paints in order to express himself in paint." "It is not before or after, it is by way of his creation that [the artist] becomes the person he is," and therefore the writing of *Madame Bovary* "reveals to Flaubert what he could know only through it: Flaubert himself."

Rousset's most important theoretical statement, the introduction to *Forme et signification*, makes explicit the presupposition of his critical studies, the notion that a work of literature is "the simultaneous development of a structure and of a way of thinking, the amalgamation of a form and of an experience which are interdependent in their genesis and growth." The critic must reverse this process, and "seize the dream by way of the form." For this reason Rousset is most interested in those structural themes or motifs in a work which seem to converge toward what Claudel calls its "dynamic source," "the foyer from which all the structures and meanings radiate." Examples of such themes in Rousset's criticism are the motifs of windows and views from above in *Madame Bovary*, or the motif of the separating screen in the plays of Claudel. This desire to reach through structural motifs to the spiritual quality at the origin of form may also explain Rousset's interest in moving, unstable forms, forms behind which one can see the shaping experience at work. In *La littérature de l'âge baroque en France* he has described with delicate sensitivity and great refinement of taste the development of a multitude of such forms in baroque art.

Jean-Pierre Richard was born in 1922. Though he has been strongly influenced by the older members of the Geneva school, particularly by Poulet, he stands a little apart from the others. He was educated at the École normale supérieure and at the Sorbonne, and he also followed Georges Poulet's courses at the University of Edinburgh. He has taught at the French Institutes in London and, more recently, in Madrid. His work derives as much from the criticism of Gaston Bachelard as it does from the Geneva critics. He has applied to the work of individual writers the insights into poetic language which Bachelard has expressed for that universal poetry diffused in the work of all the poets.

Like Bachelard, like Merleau-Ponty, Richard believes that there is no originating moment when consciousness is empty of any content but the presence of the self to itself. Like Bachelard, Richard affirms that the origin of poetry is material images, phrases or passages which express one or another of the thousands of ways in which subject and object can be joined by way of a bodily sensation. "It is in sensation that everything begins," says Richard: "flesh, objects, moods, compose for the self a primal space, an horizon of density or dizzying emptiness." Since everything, literature included, starts with sensation, Richard has in his criticism attempted, "by way of obsessive landscapes or visibly pre-occupying reveries, a direct study of sensation" in literature. His aim is to remain as close as possible to the primary physical level, from which forms and ideas in literature are born. This aim implies Richard's conviction that ideas and forms are in fact less fundamental than sensations, material images, or obscure reveries in which the soul marries itself by way of the body to some objective quality. "I have tried," says Richard,

> to seize [the *fundamental project* of the author] at its most elementary level, that at which it affirms itself with the greatest humility, but also most openly: level of pure sensation, of crude emotion, or of the image in the process of being born.

This is Richard's intention in criticism, but the intention does not prepare one for the great richness and weight of his critical language, his astonishing ability to re-create in the words of his essay the most evasive bodily or vegetative forms of life, the patient way in which he takes the reader through the network of recurrent physical images which organizes the work of Nerval or Flaubert, Baudelaire or Rimbaud, Mallarmé or Char. In each of Richard's essays certain fundamental images are shown to embody, in carnal concreteness, one writer's search for a "happy relation" to the world, his attempt to find an "experienced joy" in which "the most contradictory needs come to be satisfied together." *L'univers imaginaire de Mallarmé* is Richard's most challenging work. It brings to light an entirely new Mallarmé, not the cold symbolist seeking to capture "nothingness" in words, but a poet enamored of the substances of this earth and seeking his happiness there.

Littérature et sensation, the title of Richard's first book, gives a name to one orientation of his criticism. *Poésie et profondeur*, the title of his next book, names another. Poetry for him must have depth as well as sensations. The writers he most admires seek to reach through sensations something secretly present in sensations, something glimpsed in an emptiness or limitless depth which opens beneath them, something which is the ground of them all, the "being" which is present in each sensation because it so substantially *is*. "Figures of a being at once radiant and withdrawn," says Richard.

> Separation here becomes the very proximity of the distant. The void opens to reveal that there is something there, or rather to reveal the ground, the *foundation of things* which allows all things to be, to be in the distance which divides them from their depths.

This fugitive being which is the ground of things is not to be identified with the divine presence which Béguin and Raymond find. Richard's "being" is more closely tied to the physical substance of things. It is something present in them and absent from them at the same time. His interest in this theme in poetry connects his work, in this way at least and in spite of great differences in tone and atmosphere, to the criticism of Maurice Blanchot or to the philosophical thought of Heidegger. Unlike Blanchot or Heidegger, however, Richard always seeks to glimpse being by way of the concrete and intensely specific images in poetry which reveal it, as, for example, in one of his later books, *Onze études sur la poésie moderne*, a series of essays on contemporary French poets, Reverdy, Perse, Ponge, Du Bouchet, Jaccottet, and others.

Jean Starobinski, the last critic to be discussed here, was born in Geneva in 1920 and educated at the University of Geneva. He completed medical as well as literary studies. From 1954 to 1956 he taught at The Johns Hopkins University. Since 1958 he has been at the University of Geneva, where he now holds a professorship.

Starobinski sides with Husserl and Merleau-Ponty in his conception of consciousness. "Consciousness exists," he says, "because it appears to itself. But it cannot appear to itself without bringing into existence a world to which it is indissolubly connected." The locus of this connection is the body and its behavior. "We perceive, we express ourselves," says Starobinski,

> by our body, by our gestures, by our words. . . . Our consciousness is from the beginning engaged in a body and in an experienced situation. . . . Merleau-Ponty refuted the presuppositions . . . of intellectualism, which endows with special privileges a consciousness entirely separated from the world and from the body. . . .

Though Starobinski agrees with the phenomenologists that the mind is always inextricably intermingled with a body and with a world which it knows by way of the body, nevertheless he has been haunted since his earliest writing by the dream of a perfect intellectualization of the body and of the world's density. In this transformation the mind becomes a limpid transparency open to a world also made transparent. This is "the illusion of a sovereign look, which would encounter no obstacle and for which the universe would be a palace of crystal." This state is most nearly made real in literature, for Starobinski, in those ecstatic reveries in which Jean-Jacques Rousseau "enjoys his own transparency by way of the presence of a universe which makes everything transparent." Such an ecstasy fulfills man's desire to "destroy the obstacle of material passivity," to "escape from his carnal condition and make himself an angel." Starobinski's book on Rousseau is a brilliantly detailed analysis of the alternation in Rousseau's work between expressions of a paradisiacal openness to the world and descriptions of the various barriers which may isolate a man from the world and from other people.

Back and forth, in Starobinski's interpretations of literature, human existence swings between a state of dense incarnation and a state of angelic intellectualization in which everything becomes so pellucid that it can be pierced by a single look. Among the obstacles which may resist this look are other persons. More than any other of the critics discussed here Starobinski is interested in the theme of intersubjective relations in literature. This interest associates his work not only with that of Jean-Paul Sartre, but also with the work of Georges Blin, who has, especially in his books on Stendhal, investigated interpersonal relations in literature. Starobinski himself, in long sections of *Jean-Jacques Rousseau: la transparence et l'obstacle* and in the various essays in *L'oeil vivant*, has made admirably concrete analyses of the interplay between consciousness and consciousness as it is expressed in literature by means of motifs like the mask, the look, the secret witness, or the village festival.

For Starobinski literary criticism is also a form of inter subjectivity, and, as he explains in the important theoretical chapter prefixed to *L'oeil vivant*, criticism too must live in a movement between proximity and distance, opacity and transparency, "a total complicity with the creative subjectivity" and a "panoramic look from above." Understanding the work of literature alternately from the inside and from the outside, the critic may come to attain what is otherwise unavailable to him, a full understanding of himself. Starobinski, in affirming this, is consistent with his description of himself as a man for whom "there will be no access to himself except by way of the world."

III

For all the critics of the Geneva school criticism is fundamentally the expression of a "reciprocal transparency" of two minds, that of the critic and that of the author, but they differ in their conceptions of the nature of consciousness. From the religious ideas of human existence in Raymond and Béguin, to the notion in Poulet's criticism that what counts most is "the proof, the living proof, of the experience of inner spirituality as a positive reality," Rousset's belief that the artist's self-consciousness only comes into existence in the intimate structure of his work, the unquestioning acceptance of an overlapping of consciousness and the physical world in Richard's criticism, and the fluctuation between incarnation and detachment in the work of Starobinski, these six critics base their interpretations of literature on a whole spectrum of dissimilar convictions about the human mind.

3

Geneva or Paris: Georges Poulet's "criticism of identification"[1]

I

Prior to criticism, and the origin of it, is the act of reading. The special virtue of reading, for Georges Poulet, is that it gives a man unique access to another mind: "without leaving oneself, without abandoning one's own interiority, the person who, as they say, 'plunges' into reading, by this fact alone sinks within the depths of a second interiority, with which his spirit coincides."[2] To plunge into a book does not mean entering an impersonal realm created by words. It means entering another consciousness, for "the consciousness of the reader, and, *a fortiori*, the consciousness of that special type of reader who is the critic, have as their characteristic trait the habit of identifying themselves with a thought other than their own."[3]

A central theme of much literature, especially of fiction, is the interplay of consciousness with consciousness. One writer may be distinguished from others according to his assumptions about the way one person exists for another. For example, the relative opacity of person for person in Jane Austen's novels may be set against the relative transparency of Trollope's people to each other. The theme of intersubjectivity is rarely treated directly in Poulet's criticism. To read one of his essays is usually to be transported into a consciousness which exists almost as if there were no other minds in the world. Nevertheless, his criticism comes into being only through an act of reading which is the complete entry of the critic into the mind of the author criticized.

For Poulet the relation of two subjectivities in reading is rarely an interchange or dialogue, neither the marriage of true minds, in which each self enhances and supports the other, nor the implacable battle of mind with mind described by Sartre. The plunge into a book is achieved only in the perfect *coincidence* of the reader's mind with the "indescribable intimacy"[4] of the author's mind. Criticism derives from an act of rigorous self-dispossession. "To read or criticize," says Poulet, "is to

31

make a sacrifice of all [our] habits, desires, beliefs."[5] Having abandoned all particular commitments, the reader becomes a neutral power of comprehension. This neutrality is not a lazy yielding to external forces. Literary criticism, in Poulet's view, "is possible only insofar as the critical thought *becomes* the thought which is criticized, insofar as it succeeds in re-feeling, rethinking, re-imagining the latter from within."[6]

In his essay on Marcel Raymond, Poulet compares the critic's act of self-sacrifice to those Christian virtues of self-effacement which, in the epochs of faith, made it possible for a man to empty himself of himself and become a vessel fit for the presence of God.[7] This receptivity is characteristic of all that group of critics of the so-called Geneva School. One quality, however, especially distinguishes Poulet: his *disinterestedness*. Like those seventeenth-century quietists whom he especially admires, Poulet does not ask anything for himself. Though he likes certain authors (the young Goethe, Byron, Chateaubriand, an aesthete like Pater) for whom the act of writing is a means of salvation, his own criticism has no Promethean or egotistical motive. The re-creation of the mind of the author in the mind of the critic is not performed for the sake of any good it may do the critic, but for the sake of the author criticized. If Poulet's criticism, like Raymond's, is the twentieth-century equivalent of a seventeenth-century book of devotion, it has not that last vestige of egotism present in the quietist's awareness that his effacement of himself before God is a way, perhaps the only way, to win a place in heaven. For Poulet the "absolute transparence with the soul of the other"[8] is an end in itself, not a means to some further end.

This gratuitousness may be seen in another characteristic which distinguishes Poulet's criticism. He never tries to reach, through his identification with the mind of an author, anything beyond or outside that mind. Almost all the other critics of his school, however self-effacing they are, secretly or openly try to attain through literature to something beyond literature. Albert Béguin seeks through poetry to possess "the full garden of things."[9] Having attained objects in the created world, he tries to reach, beyond them, their Creator. The criticism of Gaston Bachelard and Jean-Pierre Richard also goes through poetry to the material world, and experiences, from within, all the nuances of texture and substance which words borrow from things. Maurice Blanchot seeks through a patient and systematic destruction of words to reach a dark and devouring absence which those words reveal and hide. The fatal glance of Orpheus at Eurydice, model for all literature, is a look beyond literature and beyond the consciousnesses expressed in literature. Jean Starobinski, it seems, seeks through literature indirect access to himself, "that visage of ourselves which we cannot bear to look at except on the strict condition that we see it reflected in a play of mirrors."[10] Even Marcel Raymond, closest of all these critics to Poulet, reaches through literature to a silence beyond literature. He goes through consciousness toward a confused and obscure "subconsciousness" in which "things are no longer things, and objects, objects in such a way that consciousness and things, melted together, constitute a universal non-duality, within which the immanence of the divine everywhere shines."[11] Physical objects, a transcendent or immanent deity, the hidden self of the critic, the being at the base of all beings – these critics seek, through identification with the mind of an author, to attain something otherwise unattainable, something which transcends that mind and differs from it in substance. For these critics literature is in one way or another a form of mediation.

Not so for Poulet. He wants to reach, through his "criticism of pure identification,"[12] the mind of the author and nothing beyond that. Material objects, other people, God in his various modes, all are present in Poulet's criticism, but only as they have been turned into words, that is, into a form of consciousness. Everything that exists must exist as contained in the globular bubble of the mind of the author, and that bubble is never allowed to burst. For Poulet criticism "must define itself primordially as a taking into consciousness [*prise de conscience*] of consciousness."[13] What criticism is in the beginning it remains to the end: consciousness of consciousness and nothing more.

II

Having identified himself with another mind, what does the reader do then? Though reading is in one sense a purely verbal activity, since it consists in the assimilation by the reader of the meanings of words, in another sense it is mute. Reading reaches, beyond words, an ineffable presence of one consciousness within another. When the reading is over, this presence vanishes, leaving the mind of the reader once more empty, ready to be invaded and possessed by another book, another mind. Moreover, the presence of one mind to another in reading is vivid, but blurred, disordered. It is the result of the piling up of all the furniture of that other mind, like a storeroom full of a great mass of bric-a-brac, chairs, tables, sofas, lamps, all in pell-mell confusion. Reading, in short, is not yet criticism.

Criticism, for Poulet, is the putting in order and clarification of the identification attained through reading. Order and transparence are two fundamental needs of his mind. Transparence is attained only by *seeing through* the author, bringing to light the intimate reason for each quality of the consciousness expressed in his works. Though Poulet likes a consciousness which is semi-opaque, a half-darkness penetrated with difficulty, this may be because such a mind is a challenge to his powers of clarification. Even when he talks about darkness or irrationality, he transforms muddle into clarity by demonstrating its plausibility. To show its plausibility means to show its connection to all the other salient motifs in the author's work. Transparence is attained only through a demonstration of the mutual implication of all the characteristics of the consciousness being criticized. If obscurity pains Poulet, so equally does any discontinuity, any description of an author which limits itself to a listing, without connection, of motifs. All the contents of the bubble of consciousness must be shown to be acting and reacting on one another, in reciprocal interchange. The works of an author make up a complex, three-dimensional structure, a palace of crystal filling the mind and integrated organically in its interplay of part with part, aspect with aspect.

Two fundamental assumptions of Poulet's criticism can be seen in this: the notion that all the works of an author form an indissoluble unity and the notion that the mode of interconnection of the parts of this unity is dialectical. Criticism, like all literature, is temporal, hence sequential. Dialectic is one way of defeating the mutual exclusion of words and moments. All the stages of a dialectical progression are present at once in any stage, and the development does no more than unfold the implications of some moment chosen as the beginning. These implications are not the necessary and determined ones of a logical progression. They are free and unpredictable, in the sense that any one stage might have been followed by other stages than the ones which actually occur, and yet the sequence seems, in retrospect, inevitable. Dialectic is a way of presenting the complexities of the palace of crystal from all its aspects, as though a consciousness were slowly revolved, still continuing its own intrinsic movement, until, finally, through time, time is transcended and an atemporal unity is revealed.

The special quality of Poulet's dialectic can be seen in the fact that he has written more than one essay on the work of several writers. There are two essays on Pascal, two on Rousseau, two on Balzac, two on Baudelaire – and each of these is a full study of the ensemble of the author's work. Even though each consciousness is one space, not a house of many mansions, and even though the contents of this space may be finite, nevertheless there are many ways of proceeding from one place to another in a critical essay. Poulet's two essays on Rousseau (or Balzac, or Baudelaire) are the same and yet different. The same intuition of the unity of the author's work governs each essay, but the itinerary through that work is different. Sometimes the same quotations are used in both essays, but, approached from a new direction, they reveal a new aspect of their inherence in all the other motifs, as, in *A la recherche du temps perdu*, the towers of Martinville remain the same and yet seem different when approached by a novel route. If limpidity is a characteristic of Poulet's criticism, this transparency is achieved through an agility in making existential associations rather than through the solemn march of logical inference. This means that an indefinite number of valid critical essays could be written on the same writer.

The fluid structure of dialectic is sharply opposed to the objective structure which some critics find essential in literature. For Poulet, the structure of a single work is something supplementary and superficial, since "subjectively literature has nothing formal about it."[14] No objective form can hold or express so protean a force as a living mind.

> It is a characteristic of the work at once to invent its structures and to go beyond them. I should even say to destroy them. Thus the work of an author is certainly the collection of the individual works he has written, but in the degree to which, following one after the other, they replace one another and reveal in that very fact a movement of liberation from structures.[15]

If the school of criticism to which Poulet belongs defines criticism as "a sort of prolongation and deepening of poetic thought,"[16] the means of this extension is the language of the critic. Language is used in three interconnected ways in Poulet's criticism. It is first "the indispensable medium by means of which the 'critical' identification takes place."[17] The poet's words are the initial means of this identification, but the critic's own words complete it. The critic's language is a grappling of one mind with another which ultimately attains complete assimilation. The sign of this assimilation is the coincidence of the language of the critic and the language of the author. If Poulet's criticism makes much use of direct quotation, the status of quotation is defined by the fact that the critic's language is as much as possible in the style and vocabulary of the author. Poulet's criticism is first of all mimesis, and the duplication of an author's mind in a critic's mind is accomplished when the critic can, as it were, speak for the author, alternately in the author's language and in the critic's language, for the two languages have become the same. In this coincidence comes to the surface the connection of Poulet's criticism with the romantic strategy of role-playing. Like Keats, Browning, or Dilthey, Poulet wants to relive the inner lives of other people, as if they were his own life.

Nevertheless, a critical essay by Poulet is not a curious kind of ventriloquism. Such a criticism would be "a crude sort of mimicry,"[18] an impoverished reduplication of the poet's voice. If criticism is to be "literature about literature,"[19] if it is to prolong and deepen literature, it must add something to it. This addition is never, in Poulet, that distant and detached "view from above" which Starobinski sometimes recommends. Such detachment would separate critic from author and make intimate comprehension impossible: "A critic who does not wish or who is unable to attain the properly subjective comprehension of which I speak, is condemned by this fact to see and to express beings and things only from the outside."[20] Poulet is completely unwilling to detach himself from the author in hand, to judge from a distance according to criteria other than those of the author himself, to put in question the validity, sanity, authenticity, or plausibility of anything he finds in the author's work. The critic must never withdraw from the mind of his author, but his own language may deepen the poet's language, that is, define it more precisely, and it may prolong that language, prolong it by establishing connections and implications which the poet may never have stated explicitly. Deepening and prolonging are in fact the exact equivalents of that clarification and putting in order which are the habitual needs of Poulet's mind in its relation to other minds.

Clarification is attained by intense concentration on one or another aspect of the author's work. As long as Poulet remains within one area of an author's thought it is as if nothing could be more important than the exact definition of the quality of that area. This definition is performed by a series of ever finer distinctions which gradually closes in on the specific nuance of the motif in question and pins it down with the sharpest possible precision. This relentless approach toward ever finer and finer clarification is like getting a microscope into focus, as more powerful lenses are substituted one for another. In the end, an area heretofore blurred or invisible fills the entire field of vision with all its delicate details laid bare. Habitual in the language of Poulet's criticism is a sequence of distinctions; when one is rejected as too coarse, it is replaced by another sharper one, until finally the requisite precision is attained: "Then occurs the strange apparition, in the depths of the self, of the thought, is that enough to say? no, of the life, more still, of the *being* of another."[21]

Along with clarification goes putting in order. If Poulet has a great power to concentrate on a single passage in an author's work, in order to establish its exact flavor of meaning, an essay of his is concentrated in yet another way. Unlike Jean-Pierre Richard, Poulet rarely attains density in his criticism by minute attention to the texture and substance of material images. The material world may enter into poetry, but by the time that world has become poetry it is disembodied. Density in an essay by Poulet results chiefly from an extreme compression of the author's thought or feeling. Such an essay seeks to put within the limits of a brief study the essential structure of an oeuvre which may include dozens of volumes. The energy of Poulet's intelligence appears as much in an extreme firmness of dialectical structure as in his power to distinguish subtle nuances of feeling or thought. Firmness of structure is attained by a great power of reduction. Passages from different books by an author, written at different times of his life, are set side by side, so that their similarity can be seen. All the apparent heterogeneity of a multiform author like Balzac or Baudelaire is reduced to a manageable number of motifs. These motifs are put in a sequence showing how each leads to the next and how all are connected. The critic may confirm his coincidence with the mind of his author when he discovers, in a work before unread, the explicit expression of a connection which he had seen to be present latently. If Poulet dislikes the sequence of mere addition, no words are more important in his criticism than words of dialectical connection: "but", "then," "or," "therefore," "nevertheless," "however," "in other terms," "that is to say," "moreover," "not only . . . but also."

III

Clarification and ordering, deepening and prolonging – these are the ways in which Poulet's criticism goes beyond mimetic doubling. A problem arises at this point. If the work of an author is like a transparent crystal, and if all can be shown to follow naturally from a beginning, where, exactly, is the proper place to begin? Perhaps there is no proper beginning, so that the sequence of an essay is arbitrary. Starting anywhere, the critic will ultimately be led everywhere, for all the aspects of an author's mind exist simultaneously, and each implies the rest. Poulet would be dissatisfied with this uncertainty. One of the strongest penchants of his mind leads him to search for the true beginning of his author's spiritual adventure.

The *Cogito* is that true beginning. It is for this reason that the theme of the *Cogito* has such importance in Poulet's work. No concept occurs more constantly than that of the *Cogito*, and almost all his essays begin with an attempt to establish the unique version of the *Cogito* which is the starting point for the author in question. Poulet names Marcel Raymond as the first critic "who has applied the principle of the *Cogito* to the critical knowledge of literary thoughts and works, and who has made that criticism begin in a *moment* of the same nature as the moment of the *Cogito*, since the being discovers himself there in the activity of his present thought."[22] If Raymond was the first to use the *Cogito* as an instrument of criticism, Poulet is surely the critic who has most systematically studied all its varieties.

It is easy to see why the *Cogito* should be important for Poulet. A criticism directed exclusively toward the consciousness of others will want to identify the quality of the other mind in its purest form, not as it is modified by one content or another, but as it exists in itself. If consciousness is a kind of "interior depth"[23] which may be occupied by all the contents of consciousness, that inner space is not a hollow shell, neutral, unqualified; it is "an ambient milieu, a unifying field."²⁴ Each consciousness has its own precise texture or tone. This texture or tone is the invariant which persists through all the diverse experiences of the self. It is an irreducible X, necessary coefficient of all the things that consciousness is conscious of. Since the invariant note distinguishing one man from all others is hidden or distorted when consciousness is engaged with some object, the critic will want to surprise it at a moment when nothing exists but a naked presence of consciousness to itself. This is the moment of the *Cogito*.

For Poulet this moment is radically original and originating. A criticism oriented entirely toward consciousness cannot allow consciousness to have any cause or source outside itself. Consciousness appears from nowhere. It is a beginning before which it is impossible to go. In assuming this Poulet shows himself to be the heir of a certain mode of idealism. If nothing is prior to consciousness, if nothing causes it or explains it or supports it in being, then consciousness is, from the point of view of human existence, the origin of everything else, and "an act of selfconsciousness" is the "invariable point of departure for every human existence perceived from within."²⁵ The moment of the revelation of the self to itself, before the assimilation of any of its objects, is the true beginning not only because nothing exists before it, but also because the moment of the *Cogito* is the ground or foundation of everything else. Everything follows from it, as a tiny cube of paper unfolded may be a map of the world, or as a colorless button grows, in a glass of water, into a magic Japanese garden full of flowers, trees, and shrubs. If the *Cogito* has this marvelous power of expansion, the critic will want to catch it "in the surging forth and genetic exercise of this power," in the moment before it explodes into form, when it exists "in a nearly virginal state, not yet invaded and, as it were, masked by the thick heap of its objective contents."²⁶

The proper beginning for the critic's reliving and reconstruction of the inner experience of an author must always be the *Cogito*, but the *Cogito* exists not only in its Cartesian or rationalist form, the putting in doubt of all the contents of the mind in order to reach a clear and distinct thought which proves that the self exists. The *Cogito* exists in a multitude of versions, a different one for each age or author, and Poulet has in his criticism identified a great variety of these: the Christian *Cogito* in all its modes, the intellectualist one, the romantic or sensationalist *Cogito*, the *Cogito* of Mallarmé, and so on, down to the last page of *Les métamorphoses du cercle*, which ends with a definition of the *Cogito* of Jorge Guillén.

The supreme importance of the moment of self-awareness makes Poulet especially delighted by passages where an author describes his awaking from sleep. If the moment of waking is like a repetition of the creation of the world, so that the waker is seized with an astonishment before things comparable to that of Adam or Miranda, waking is also a daily repetition of the *Cogito* and is a fresh enactment of the discovery of the self. From the waking of Montaigne, of the statue of Condillac, or of Rousseau, to the waking of Poe, Proust, or Béguin, Poulet follows the theme of "the moment of awakening," and in each case waking is the way in which the *Cogito* is intimately known. The *Cogito*, for Poulet, is no theoretical abstraction, but is always the most immediate and inward of experiences.

IV

The universality of the *Cogito* solves the problem of the starting point for both Poulet and Raymond, but Poulet differs radically from Raymond in his use of this instrument of criticism. Raymond's criticism goes against the stream, as it were. It works backward from the mass of motifs and details which fill a consciousness toward the virginal moment when consciousness is as yet empty of all but itself. To attain identification with this moment is Raymond's ultimate aim, for in that moment only, a moment on the frontier between consciousness and unconsciousness, the critic has a chance to reach a sense of the confused co-presence of all things and people in the universe. Poulet, on the other hand, goes out from the moment of the *Cogito* to follow the adventures of a mind at grips with its objects. The crystalline bubble of consciousness is made up of the engagement of a mind with things, and the critic must go with his author as he assimilates the world. Poulet wants to see just how far a particular author will take him and follows without questioning to the farthest distance he can reach while still remaining inside the sphere of a single mind.

Consciousness may engage itself with physical objects, with time and space, with other consciousnesses, with God. In his criticism Poulet explores each of these modes of relation, but all tend to be transformed into one or another of the endless possible interchanges of subject and object within the inner space which Poulet calls "the interior distance." In this allegiance to the primacy of the subject–object relation Poulet shows himself once again the inheritor of romanticism and idealism. From Montaigne, Descartes, and Rousseau, to Coleridge, Fichte, or Amiel, on down to Yeats, Claudel, or Proust, the continuity of literature and philosophy since the Renaissance is marked by the dualism of subject and object, self and world. Taken as a whole, Poulet's criticism may be said to approach a recapitulation of all the varieties of experience possible within the limits of this dualism.

Only if it is true that this tradition is coming to an end in our day is it possible to give assent to a curious passage about *Les métamorphoses du cercle* in a review of 1963 by Maurice Blanchot: "I asked myself, having closed this book, why there closed with it the very history of criticism and of culture and why it seemed with a melancholy serenity to dismiss us and at the same time to authorize us to enter into a new space."[27] Without sharing Blanchot's desire to destroy all the forms of subjectivity which Poulet so cherishes, it is possible to say that certain contemporary authors, like Jorge Guillén or William Carlos Williams, have gone beyond the division of subject and object, as they have gone beyond the tradition of a transcendent power dwelling beyond the world. Such writers hardly represent the end of culture, but they contradict some of the habitual assumptions of Poulet's criticism. Poulet is not unaware of this:

> Guillén's poetry separates itself sharply from the rest of European poetry. It does not begin from the interior, but from the exterior. It situates that which is, not in the central hollow of a consciousness, but in the peripheral manifestation of a tangible reality. . . . A singular relation, which seems to reverse the habitual direction of thought. What? everything then no longer springs forth from the interior? What? it is no longer *beginning from the center* that life is born and propagates itself?[28]

The "What?" here might be defined as the moment of encounter with a new tradition, reversing earlier habits of thought. Since the essay on Guillén forms the conclusion of *Les métamorphoses du cercle*, that book does not so much celebrate the funeral of literature and criticism, as move toward the confrontation of a new age, an age in which consciousness will no longer be defined as "that interior vacancy within which the world redisposes itself."[29]

So habitual is this image of an interior milieu to Poulet that his thought may be defined as fundamentally spatial. Though his earliest book is entitled *Etudes sur le temps humain,* time is there often treated in terms of a relation of the mind to objects which are presented to it across a kind of subjective distance. The notion of interior distance provides the title for his next book, *La distance intérieure,* and in his more recent work he has yielded overtly to the spatializing tendency of his criticism. In *Les métamorphoses du cercle* writers from Parmenides to T. S. Eliot are presented in terms of relations, within the spheric bubble of the mind, between center and periphery. The center is the *Cogito*, source of all, and at various places within consciousness all the objects of consciousness are located in a moving totality which sometimes expands to infinity and sometimes contracts to a point, but always remains enclosed in itself. Through the whole history of Western thought Poulet explores the varieties of spatial relation: distance, closeness, or union; continuity or discontinuity; condensation or dilation; thickening or rarefaction – all the categories by which center and circle may be separated, identified, or brought into some form of association.

Throughout all this development two states of consciousness are most important for Poulet. As long as there is distance there is a failure of consciousness to coincide unequivocally with itself. One way to avoid this has been discussed: the *Cogito*, reduction of all to a central point. The other possibility is an expansive diffusion of that point until it includes everything, as, according to an image which Poulet especially likes to find in his authors, a stone dropped in water will start a series of concentric circles radiating outward to infinity. Poulet could say of many of his authors what he says of Amiel: "Particular activities are here only a middle term between the unextended depth of a life seized in the eternity of its principle and, on the other hand, the expansion of an existence dilating by means of thought to coincide with the full dimensions of the universe."[30] In his latest books as in his earlier ones Poulet pursues the dream of a *totum simul*, the enclosure by consciousness of all existence, in an infinite moment of expansion transcending time and space. If Jean Starobinski in his early critical essays yields to "the sin of angelism,"[31] a central motif in Poulet's criticism is the desire to be not like an angel, but like a God. In his essay on Gérard de Nerval, Poulet observes that "all thought which draws its life only from itself is unable to suffice to itself," and that "human thought cannot endure being substituted either for the totality of the real or for its simplicity."[32] Nevertheless, Poulet is fascinated by writers who approach as close as is humanly possible to a divine self-sufficiency. For this reason, perhaps, Rousseau holds a place of special importance in his work, for Rousseau was the first man to achieve a state of expansive revery in which the self, dwelling in a realm where only the solitary mind and its objects exist, possesses all, and therefore "suffices to itself, like God."[33] With each of his authors Poulet goes as far as he can toward the attainment of this *totum simul*, human equivalent of divine simultaneity and ubiquity. His essays often end at the stage closest to this ultimate victory, or in the recognition of a failure to win it or hold it.

Failure is in fact more important than temporary success. For Poulet, human consciousness, both in its widest expansion and in its contraction to the purity of the *Cogito*, is marked by a sense of "existential insufficiency, the feeling of contingency and incapacity."[34] Hence the importance in his criticism of the theme of continuous creation. Unless some power sustains the self it will be powerless to bring into existence its own future. Each man is "called by an immense demand, [but] discovers within himself an immense weakness."[35]

V

When the critic has gone as far as he can with an author, the essay is over. The silence after the ending marks the evaporation of that union of critic's mind and author's mind which has made the essay possible. After coincidence, separation. Having investigated to its limit the effect of being occupied by the consciousness of another person, the critic's mind returns to attentive vacancy. He must turn now to another author, and, once more forgetting all other writers, begin again the process which will culminate in a critical essay.

It is not true, however, to say that all other authors are forgotten. There is in Poulet's criticism a constant comparison between one author and another. He rarely uses it to show how two authors are alike, but almost always to identify more precisely the uniqueness of the author at hand. The notion of the singularity of each consciousness is central in Poulet's criticism, and this is often shown by the juxtaposition of ideas or motifs from two authors, as a color can be more clearly perceived if it is set against a different hue. Just as a comparison with another author, within the body of an essay, will make possible more precise definition of a certain motif, so the setting side by side, within the covers of a single book, of essays on a number of authors is a way of demonstrating that no two consciousnesses are alike. Poulet has an intense dislike for any blurring or smudging of the integrity of a writer's thought. If he concerns himself with the history of ideas, it is chiefly with "that still neglected part of the history of ideas which we could call the history of consciousness,"[36] and it seems that a study of the history of consciousness must be based on the Leibnizian assumption that each mind is unique and isolated from all the others.

In spite of the importance of this assumption, however, there is a counter assumption of equal importance. This new assumption provides an escape from an apparent dilemma. If each consciousness excludes all the others, how can the critic include a number of essays together in a book, and by implication possess a group of minds at once? "It is impossible to escape from this difficulty," says Poulet, "except by imagining for each epoch a consciousness common to all the contemporary minds. It is within this general consciousness that the individual thoughts and feelings are bathed."[37] At any one time each consciousness, however particular, participates in the general consciousness. Its particularity consists in the unique version or organization it makes of ideas common to the age, not in its power to think ideas unheard-of in that time and place. This notion is, in Poulet's earlier books, present overtly only in the prefatory chapter to *Etudes sur le temps humain*, but *Les métamorphoses du cercle* contains a number of chapters of a kind new in

Poulet's criticism: essays on ancient and medieval thought, on the Renaissance, on "the baroque epoch," on the eighteenth century, and on romanticism. The presupposition of these essays is that the consciousness of an age forms a closed unity, a crystalline sphere much like that of a single mind. Such a collective mind can be seized by the same consciousness of consciousness which grasps the mind of a single author, and it can be followed through its structure by the same kind of dialectical route.

Enclosing the consciousness of an age is the genius of a language or of a culture. It may be that Poulet is motivated in his reading and criticism by a desire to follow through all its changes the flowering of the French language as an expression of the varieties of human existence. Outside the French language there is Western culture as a whole. Like T. S. Eliot, Poulet has a strong sense of the oneness of Western civilization and thinks of it as an immense consciousness which contains in moving simultaneity the thought of all the members of that culture from the early Church Fathers to the latest authentic poet who adds his work to the whole and thereby changes that whole in every part. From the single writer to the mind of an age, to all the writings in one language, to all of Western culture – each of these larger wholes encloses the next smaller and forms its milieu. Taken together, they are so many concentric circles of consciousness, each inside the next larger, like a Chinese carving.

Why should Western culture form the largest bubble of all? Can it not be said that Poulet's criticism implies the notion of the unity of the consciousness of all mankind in its historical development? The history of literature can therefore be defined as "a history of human consciousness."[38] The model of history suggested by *Les métamorphoses du cercle* is that of a progressive diversification, from the relatively homogeneous thought of antiquity, the Middle Ages, the Renaissance, and the eighteenth century to the explosion into individuality in the nineteenth and twentieth centuries, when every important writer deserves a full essay to himself. Significantly, the chapter on romanticism twice ceases to be a rendering of the consciousness of an age and for a time concentrates on an individual mind, that of Coleridge and that of Goethe. But though the recent history of consciousness is more diversified it still remains continuous. All individual consciousnesses still dwell together within an embracing general mind, and Balzac and Baudelaire belong as much to the same age as Montaigne and Pascal belong to theirs.

Poulet's sense of the continuity of history does not lead him to be tempted by Dilthey's notion of an exhaustive reliving of all possible human points of view, so that man might go through history beyond history. No, for Poulet the human spirit is inexhaustible in its potential variety, and its development is always incomplete, still moving toward the realization of its infinite possibilities. If this is the case, then the literary critic can never hope to reach an equivalent of the *totum simul* of God. The best he can do is to make a concentration, re-creation, and coordination of all mankind's thought so far. Through this strategy he can move with that ever-developing consciousness as it approaches toward a completion it can never attain. The critic can perhaps exhaust the mind of a single writer, for each individual mind may be finite, but criticism can never come to the end of the human mind in its totality. That mind will always be open-ended, unfinished.

Recognition of the essential historicity of Poulet's criticism will lead to a final definition of it. History, for Poulet as for the romantics, is not a linear development, but a spherical expansion. A criticism which re-creates history will also be spherical, not, like the thought of Jacques Rivière and Robert Browning, asymptotic, but not less an approach toward infinity. As a curve sweeps toward its asymptote, Rivière moves always closer to that coincidence with the mind of another person which he never quite attains, and Browning sees all human history as a gradual movement toward the plenitude of God. Poulet's criticism remains faithful to its exclusive commitment to human consciousness, and, for this, an image of three-dimensional enclosure is more appropriate. Like a sphere dilating toward the infinity it will never reach, his criticism follows the mind of mankind as it uncovers the limitless riches of interior space.

VI

The preceding parts of this essay were written in 1963. It may stand as an introduction to the scope of Georges Poulet's criticism and as an outline of its theoretical presuppositions. In what follows I shall take notice of the many books and essays Poulet has published since 1963,[39] and I shall try to proceed further in an interpretation of the significance of his work.

Poulet's recent publications have filled out the contours of his lifework in several ways. New programmatic statements have confirmed his commitment to a "criticism of consciousness": "I wish to save at any price the subjectivity of literature," he says,[40] and he defines his kind of criticism firmly as "above all, a criticism of participation, better still, of identification. There is no true criticism without the coincidence of two consciousnesses."[41] The literary text is a means by which the critic can achieve an identification with "a consciousness which is in the work,"[42] and his criticism is an expression of the results of this identification.

The publication of *Le point de départ* and *Mesure de l'instant*, the third and fourth volumes of the *Etudes sur le temps humain*, has made clearer than before the monumental and inclusive nature of Poulet's work, its unity as an attempt to relive from within and to express in criticism more or less the whole range of French literature from the Renaissance to the present, placing it in the context of a less complete treatment of ancient and medieval literature, and of major modern writers in other European languages: Goethe, the English romantics, Poe, Whitman, Henry James, Guillén, and so on. In fact *Les métamorphoses du cercle* is only somewhat arbitrarily excluded from the *Etudes sur le temps humain* (on the grounds, presumably, that its leitmotif is a spatial rather than a temporal form). The five volumes together, *Etudes sur le temps humain, I, La distance intérieure, Les métamorphoses du cercle, Le point de départ,* and *Mesure de l'instant,* form a single comprehensive work consisting of seventy essays on various writers, groups of writers, or literary periods. Most of the essays are on single authors, and each follows a dialectical itinerary through the interior space of the author in question, drawing quotations from the whole range of his writing to trace out a spiritual adventure leading the author from some beginning in an awakening to consciousness toward an end of triumph or defeat. The seventy essays may be thought of as juxtaposed side by side in a spatial panorama, somewhat as, in Poulet's interpretation of Proust in *L'Espace proustien,* the various times of Marcel's life are set side by side in *A la recherche du temps perdu* like the paintings of different events from a saint's life in a triptych. To borrow another Proustian metaphor, the five major volumes of Poulet's criticism are like five bays within the voluminous interior of a cathedral, the smaller books on Proust, Constant, etc., forming adjacent chapels. The introduction to each major volume identifies the special commitment of that collection within the all-inclusive themes of literary time and space: the range of literary experiences of human temporality in the first volume of *Etudes,* the exploration of the distance within literature between consciousness and what it is conscious of in *La distance intérieure,* the inexhaustibly renewed movement of the mind's spherical expansion and contraction in *Les métamorphoses du cercle,* the special commitment of twentieth-century poets to the genetic energy of the moment in *Le point de départ,* and in *Mesure de l'instant* the power of the instant, as it has been "measured" by various writers, to move between nullity and totality. Each volume is organized within itself chronologically. Each moves through an historical trajectory, sometimes from the Renaissance to the present, as in the eighteen essays going from Montaigne to Proust by way of Descartes, Pascal, Molière, Corneille, Racine, Madame de La Fayette, Fontenelle, Abbé Prévost, Rousseau, Diderot, Benjamin Constant, Alfred de Vigny, Théophile Gautier, Flaubert, Baudelaire, and Paul Valéry in the first volume of *Etudes,* or as in the twenty essays of *Les métamorphoses du cercle* going from "La renaissance" to Rilke, Eliot, and Guillén, by way of "L'epoque baroque," Pascal, "Le dix-huitième siècle," Rousseau, "Le romantisme," Lamartine, Balzac, Vigny, Nerval,

Poe, Amiel, Flaubert, Baudelaire, "La 'prose' de Mallarmé," Henry James, and Claudel, or as in the fourteen essays of *Mesure de l'instant* going from Maurice Scève through Saint-Cyran, Racine, Fénelon, Casanova, Joubert, "Les romantiques anglais," Madame de Staël, Lamartine, Stendhal, Michelet, Amiel, and Proust to Julien Green. Sometimes the trajectory is less inclusive, as in the movement from Marivaux to Mallarmé by way of Vauvenargues, Chamfort, Laclos, Joubert, Balzac, Hugo, Musset, and Maurice de Guérin in *La distance intérieure*, or in the concentration on nine recent writers in *Le point de départ*: Whitman, Bernanos, Char, Supervielle, Eluard, Saint-John Perse, Reverdy, Ungaretti, and Sartre.

This recapitulated historical movement in each of the volumes, going over and over the same periods of literary history from the Renaissance to the present, has brought more clearly into the open the historical schema assumed in Poulet's criticial enterprise. For him European literature took a new turn in the Renaissance when consciousness became conscious of itself with a new acuteness in writers like Montaigne and Descartes. In the seventeenth century Poulet is especially interested in those religious writers (Pascal, Saint-Cyran, Racine, and Fénelon) who experienced with most intensity the contingency of the human spirit in relation to a divine transcendence. This distant deity must intervene continuously, creating the soul anew from moment to moment and preventing it from falling into nothingness. Poulet sees the eighteenth century as the time when belief in the sustaining power of God fades. Man finds himself alone, in the moment, forced to create a duration and a self through expansive revery, through feeling, or through affective memory. The romantic writers, from Rousseau on, seek to create, in rare moments of secular ecstasy, a human equivalent of the divine *totum simul*. In the twentieth century this historical movement is continued by a tendency to "break with every a priori conception of time," to reject all but the living moment of experience. Twentieth-century authors use this moment as a point of origin on the basis of which the writer must "invent or rediscover [a] duration."[43]

When this historical pattern gradually emerges as a structuring constant, it becomes clear that Poulet considers each writer limited to some degree by the time in which he is born as to the possible spiritual experiences open to him. At the same time there is a contrary recognition of the complexity and multiplicity of each writer. This is implied in the increasing number of examples of Poulet's power to return to a writer treated in an earlier essay and to find something new to say about him. In *Mesure de l'instant*, for example, there are new essays on Racine, Joubert, Amiel, and Proust, all of whom had been treated at least once before. Works published since 1963 make even more evident the fact that for

Poulet a great writer is inexhaustible. The voluminous imaginative space of a writer like Proust may always be entered again from a different point and traversed anew by a different route.

Poulet's recent work, finally, has more clearly exposed the deeper commitments of his enterprise, the assumptions which lie beneath those he overtly affirms in his statements about the nature of criticism. It is not wholly true to say that Poulet is to be distinguished from other critics in his group (Albert Béguin, say, or Marcel Raymond) by his disinterestedness, by the fact that he is unwilling to use the transparency of one mind to another attained in criticism "as a means to reach some further end."[44] Though Poulet differs from his colleagues in the breadth and catholicity of his sympathy, in his openness to a wider variety of writers, nevertheless his criticism is motivated, one begins to suspect, by a covert personal quest, a quest of whose guiding assumptions he may not be entirely conscious. As Paul de Man has recently asserted, it may be that each writer or critic has a blind spot which is the pivot around which his whole work turns, its hidden energizing source. In Poulet's case, this central concern may govern more or less covertly the search he has conducted by way of other writers for answers to questions which are his own. This aspect of his work is one factor which justifies defining it as authentically a work of literature in its own right, perhaps one of the most important of our time. In these areas, moreover, Poulet's work is most problematical and raises in its own way those questions which are most crucial in twentieth-century literature, philosophy, and criticism. What, in Poulet's case, is the genetic concern? And what, in his case, is the unspoken system of assumptions establishing the rules according to which the exploration of literature is conducted?

VII

Poulet inherited from Bergson, a philosopher who much influenced his earliest work,[45] the distinction between inauthentic spatialized time and authentic duration. In his own writing, however, this theme takes the form of a concern for the opposition between a human time of transient flowing and the all-embracing fixed time of the divine eternity. The search for an escape from the human time of evanescence to a time of plenitude governs Poulet's exploration of literature. He finds some version of this search in most of the various writers he studies. His criticism is therefore not so much a series of studies of human time as it has been experienced by major authors since the Renaissance as it is a study of the various attempts made by these authors to escape from the fluidity and instability of everyday time – escape through the discovery of a transcendent power outside time by the Christian writers, or through the discovery of a sensationalist equivalent of the *totum simul* of

God by a writer like Rousseau, or through a dismissal of all other times but the present instant in certain modern writers. In some cases Poulet finds an expansion of the self to include all the universe, in others a reduction of the self to a self-sufficient point. In all these variations the constant is an escape by one form or another of spatialization from the transience of time.

This search for an escape from temporal flowing may also be defined as the search for some authentic point of departure, some solid beginning from which all else will follow. To escape from fluidity one must find some motionless rock in the flux. Poulet's criticism makes the a priori assumption that this beginning before, behind, or below which one cannot go is to be found in consciousness, in the authentic *moi*, in the self as it is to itself when it is deprived of all its contents. In each of his essays he attempts to "go back in the work of the author all the way to that act from which each imaginary universe opens out."[46] This act is a moment of self-consciousness. Such a moment, says Poulet, is the true point of departure for every human existence.[47] An important letter of 1961 defines in detail the quality of this act of self-awareness and specifies the tradition to which it belongs:

> I should readily consider that the most important form of subjectivity is not that of the mind overwhelmed, filled, and so to speak stuffed with its objects, but that there is another [kind of consciousness] which sometimes reveals itself on this side of, at a distance from, and protected from, any object, a subjectivity which exists in itself, withdrawn from any power which might determine it from the outside, and possessing itself by a direct intuition, infinitely different from the self-knowledge which is the indirect result of our relations with the world. In other words, I should say that subjectivity [in criticism] is the consciousness of the critic coinciding with the consciousness of the thinking or feeling person located in the heart of the text (of every literary text), in such a way that this double consciousness appears less in its multiplicity of sensuous relations with things, than prior to and separate from any object, as self-consciousness or pure consciousness. . . . As you have seen, in this I remain faithful to the Cartesian tradition.[48]

Here is that *Cogito* which Poulet seeks to identify initially in each of his essays as the source of everything of importance in the author in question. He tries to identify it in a moment of "double consciousness," the pure intuitive grasp of the unique affective tone of the mind of the author by himself, doubled in the intuitive insight into that self-reflecting mind by the receptive mind of the critic. Both in this pure subjectivity without content and in all the transformations it goes through when it opens out to the world "in the multiple effects of its fecundating power,"[49] one quality is assumed by Poulet to be fundamental: the quality of *presence*. This condition is the basic test of authenticity which Poulet applies to the various experiences he finds recorded in literature. It persists as a constant among the motifs which recur in proliferating variety throughout his criticism – as the presence of the mind to itself in the "indescribable intimacy" of the genetic moment of self-consciousness; as the presence of one consciousness to another in the coincidence of two minds which takes place in the reading which precedes criticism; as the priority accorded to the instant, to the present, to immediate experience within the presence of the present; as the presence of objects to the mind in the instant of sensation or perception; as the presence of past moments of sensation to the now of consciousness in that recovered present of affective memory which Poulet finds in so many of his authors; as the presence of the whole world to the mind in the immediacy of the *totum simul* which imitates in the finite and fleeting consciousness of man the infinite and eternal consciousness of God. If Rousseau's importance lies in the fact that in his writing "for the first time there appears in literature a text which claims to retrace, not as a didactic development nor as a mystic vision, but as an experience personally lived, the *totum simul* of the Alexandrians and the scholastics,"[50] the English romantic poets, in the essay on them in *Mesure de l'instant*, are described as all seeking in one way or another a human version of the divine *totum simul*, "a personal, subjective eternity; an eternity for their own use";[51] of Paul Claudel Poulet says in *Le point de départ* that no one "has more amply depicted the *totum simul* of that eternity at once cosmic and human."[52] From the presence to itself of consciousness in the contentless point at the origin of the mind's adventures to the most expansive revery in which the mind contains all existence in panoramic simultaneity, the priority and supreme value of the present and of presence are everywhere assumed in Poulet's criticism.

This means the implicit acceptance, in spite of the prolonged meditation which Poulet has applied to the theme of time in literature, of a spatial model of temporality, a model determined by the Christian–Platonic inheritance of the Western tradition of metaphysics. Poulet finds this spatialized time in multiplied variations in the writers he discusses from the Presocratics to Proust. It is no accident that in spite of his commitment to an exploration of human time spatial images become increasingly dominant in his criticism, as in the notion of interior distance, or in the title image of *Les métamorphoses du cercle*, or in the concept of juxtaposition in *L'Espace proustien*. Poulet is correct in claiming that this spatial image of time is a fundamental constant in our tradition, occurring in countless variations among philosophers and writers. A spatial model of time is, for example, present in Plato's *Timaeus*, in Aristotle's *Physics*, in Book Eleven of St Augustine's

Confessions, and on down even to Edmund Husserl's *Vorlesungen zur Phänomenologie des inneren Zeitbewusstseins* in our own century.[53] The continuity of this image of time is suggested by the fact that Husserl praises St Augustine's Book Eleven at the beginning of his own discussion of time.[54]

The spatiality of this Christian–Platonic image of time, accepted for the most part without question by Poulet when he encounters it in his writers, is systematically associated with the acceptance of presence as an original category from which other categories are derived. Plato, Aristotle, Augustine, and Husserl all build their image of time on the priority of the present, viewing past and future as presents which once happened or which will one day happen. In such a view, temporality, however complex its structure, is still a pattern of interrelated presents or "now-points," as in Husserl's diagrammatic representation of the "running-off phenomena" of time in the *Vorlesungen*.[55] This view of time is traditionally associated with the contrast, so frequently referred to by Poulet, between the *nunc fluens* of human time, to which only one present moment can be present at a time, and the *nunc stans* of God's eternity, to which all moments are perpetually present in an all-inclusive spatialized now, guaranteeing the substantial presentness of those moments which, to a given human experience, are not at present present. For Poulet, as for the tradition generally, each man wishes intuitively to obtain an experience of all times as immediately present. He wants to achieve in one way or another something like the *nunc stans* of God.

This priority of presence in Poulet's criticism is associated, finally, with a tendency to take language for granted in literature. For the most part he does not put the language of his authors in question, hold it at arm's length and analyze it, interrogate it suspiciously for distinctions between what it apparently says and what it really says. He does not scrutinize the language of his texts for the covert assumptions of its metaphors, its tense structures, its silences. Part of Poulet's generosity toward his authors is a taking for granted not only of the authenticity of their experiences, but also of the authenticity of the words in which they have expressed these experiences. It is scarcely an exaggeration to say that for Poulet the language of the works he discusses is seen as a perfectly transparent medium through which the mind of the author passes into the mind of the critic. If Poulet apparently accepts without question the Western tradition of presence he also accepts the Western tradition of representation or mimesis. His relatively infrequent stylistic analyses tend to assume that the language of literature is the undistorting mirror of a state of mind which precedes it and can exist in full authenticity without it. Consciousness, it seems, is the genetic source of literary language, and words like "express," "reflect," or "imitate" are usually present when Poulet calls attention to some characteristic of an author's style. I shall cite two from the abundant examples of this which could be given. Speaking of the habit of ejaculatory syntax in Gide's writing, Poulet says: "Better than any other syntactical form, the exclamation expresses the moment, responds to it in instantaneous echo, marks it, in its springing forth, with an exclusively present life."[56] Writing of Proust, he says:

> *Au-devant, devant!* [Beyond, before!] Few adverbial expressions appear more frequently in the work of Proust and express more precisely at once the forward élan of the spirit and the perpetual impossibility for that spirit to attain its goal.[57]

Here one can better identify the role of citation, so important a feature of Poulet's procedure in criticism. If the critic must use as much as possible either the writer's own terminology or a neutral vocabulary which will not impose an alien screen between the reader and the mind of the author in question, this is because it is assumed that in the citation the minds of author, critic, and reader of the criticism coincide in a perfect presence of three consciousnesses to one another. To put in question the power of language to make possible this merger of minds would be to put in question the quality of presence, as a category of space, time, and consciousness, which is the true point of departure in Poulet's criticism.

VIII

The right of this quality of presence, however, to be called the basis which has priority over all forms of absence or distance has been challenged by much recent philosophy, literature, linguistics, and criticism. Under the aegis of such nineteenth-century predecessors as Marx, Freud, and Nietzsche recent writers of many different orientations have addressed themselves to what is sometimes called the "deconstruction of metaphysics." In one way or another all the forms in which the priority of the present and of presence appears in Poulet's work have come under attack.

The Freudian concept of the unconscious, for example, puts in question the notion that consciousness is a beginning or basis which cannot be gone beneath. Freud's unconscious is a region of the mind which never was present to consciousness and which can never be brought wholly out of obscurity into the bright realm of the mind's presence to itself. The concept or word "consciousness," or even consciousness itself, it is often suggested today, is generated as one element in a systematic interplay of linguistic elements which is the ground of the mind, rather than the other way around. The "I" or "me" which seems to prove its own existence in the *Cogito* may be no more than a grammatical term of a peculiar sort, as Emile Benveniste has suggested recently and as Nietzsche in a somewhat different way had already proposed in 1885: "It is within and by language that man constitutes himself as a *subject [comme sujet]*," says Benveniste, "because language alone in reality founds, in *its* reality which is that of being [*de l'être*], the concept of the 'ego.'"⁵⁸ "We used to believe in the 'soul,'" states Nietzsche,

> as we believed in grammar and the grammatical subject; we used to say that "I" was the condition, "think" the predicate that conditioned, and thinking an activity for which a subject *had to be* thought of as its cause. But then we tried, with admirable persistence and guile, to see whether the reverse might not perhaps be true. "Think" was now the condition, "I" the thing conditioned, hence "I" only a synthesis which was *created* by thinking [*"ich" also erst eine Synthese, welche durch das Denken selbst gemacht wird*].⁵⁹

Many recent linguists and literary critics, to take another such topic, inherit the tradition of Saussure, who denies that meaning pre-exists language or that a word can be a sign pointing toward some idea or thing which was present before the word was invented. Language, according to such thinkers, creates meaning in the differential relation of sounds or signifiers to one another. This means that language is never a matter of immediate presence, nor a matter of mimetic representation. Meaning arises from the reference of one signifier or phoneme to another, in the interplay of their differences. Meaning in language is always deferred, always in movement away from the present toward the no longer or the not yet. If language constitutes consciousness rather than the reverse, then such critics are right to argue that the structural, syntactical, and metaphorical details of languages are the proper subjects of literary criticism, not the state of mind which they generate rather than reflect. The concept of representation or of imitation has in fact been subjected to a searching criticism by such recent writers as Roland Barthes, Jacques Derrida, and Gilles Deleuze.⁶⁰

To take another of Poulet's motifs, the search for a point of departure in literature or in life has recently been questioned by such thinkers as Michel Foucault. Here Nietzsche is again a forerunner, the Nietzsche who in *Jenseits von Gut und Böse* describes the radical thinker who believes that behind every beginning there is another beginning more original still: "He will suspect behind each cave a deeper cave, a more extensive, more exotic, richer world beyond the surface, a bottomless abyss beyond every 'bottom,' beneath every 'foundation' [*ein Abgrund hinter jedem Grunde, unter jeder 'Begründung'*]."⁶¹ Foucault, speaking of the nineteenth-century revolution in interpretation initiated in part by Nietzsche, has spoken recently of a *refus du commencement*, a refusal to believe that it is in any way possible in an act of interpretation to go back to a beginning before which one cannot go.[62]

As for Poulet's founding of criticism on an act of reading which attains an identification or overlapping of two minds, Emmanuel Levinas has based his recent work on a belief in the radical otherness of the other person. Another mind is so alien, so impenetrable, that it is never possible by any means to lift the veil which hides the other from me. This means that I can never confront the other person as an immediate presence, only encounter indirect signs and traces of his passage.[63]

A critic like Paul de Man, to turn to another structuring motif of Poulet's criticism, would put in question the concept of literary history on which Poulet's interpretations of literature appear to be based. For de Man and other present-day critics, literary history is not a sequence of self-enclosed "periods," each with its own unique set of assumptions determining the themes of literature written during that time. The human condition remains the same throughout history, de Man would argue, and the great writers of every epoch rise above the superficial configurations of thought in their age to express in authentic language the human predicament, in particular the abysses in man's experience of temporality.[64]

Martin Heidegger, finally, in the most celebrated twentieth-century analysis of time, *Sein und Zeit*, has subjected the spatialized model of time coming down from the Greeks and the Church Fathers to a penetrating criticism. For Heidegger authentic human time is never an experience of unmediated presence, but is a complex structure of "ecstasies" in which time arises from the not yet present future. Each dimension of time reaches out toward the others and forms an incomplete system moving toward a finite totality it never attains while a man is alive. "Temporality," says Heidegger, "temporalizes itself as a future which makes present in the process of having been [*Zeitlichkeit zeitigt sich als gewesende-gegenwärtigende Zukunft*]."[65] On the basis of this conception of time Heidegger argues that the Platonic or Christian idea of time as a succession of nows which is grounded in the static and infinite eternity of a God to whom all times are co-present arises as a false projection from the inauthentic everyday conception of time as an infinite succession of equivalent nows stretching before and after in a spatial row. So Heidegger affirms in a footnote in *Sein und Zeit* that

> the traditional conception of "eternity" as signifying the "standing 'now'" [*nunc stans*], has been drawn from the ordinary way of understanding time [*aus dem vulgären Zeitverständnis geschöpft*] and has been defined with an orientation toward the idea of "constant" presence-at-hand [*der "ständigen" Vorhandenheit*]. . . . If God's eternity can be "construed" philosophically,

then it may be understood only as a more primordial temporality which is "infinite."[66]

Time as presence, the other as presence, the presence of consciousness to itself, language as the pure reflection of the presence of consciousness, literary history as a history of consciousness, the possibility of reaching an original presence from which all the others derive – each of these forms of presence has been rejected by a central tradition of modern thought. Perhaps the most radical and comprehensive of these attempts to dismantle metaphysics from within is that being mounted by Jacques Derrida.[67] All the apparent assumptions of Poulet's criticism are interrogated by Derrida and found wanting (though without specific reference to Poulet), for example in the more or less comprehensive taking of position in his recent essay, "La 'différance.'"[68] The privilege accorded to the "living present," says Derrida,

> is the ether of metaphysics, the element of our thought insofar as it is caught in the language of metaphysics. It is impossible to escape from the limitations of such an enclosure except by interrogating today that value of presence which Heidegger has shown to be the ontotheological determination of being; and therefore by interrogating that value of presence, by a putting in question the status of which must be altogether singular, we interrogate the absolute privilege of that form or of that epoch of presence in general which is consciousness as the will to meaning [*comme vouloir-dire*] within its presence to itself.[69]

IX

It would seem that the tradition represented by Derrida and that represented by Poulet must be set against one another as an irreconcilable either/or. A critic must choose either the tradition of presence or the tradition of "differance," for their assumptions about language, about literature, about history, and about the mind cannot be made compatible. The more deeply and carefully one reads Poulet's criticism, however, the more clearly it emerges that it challenges its own fundamental assumptions and that as his work gradually develops it encounters in its own way the same problematical issues which are central for a critic like Derrida. It encounters them through the pursuit of its own avowed goals, that is, the reliving from within of the spiritual adventures of major Western writers in an attempt to see whether any of them has been able to find an escape from the flowing of time and in an attempt in each case to discover the point of departure within consciousness from which all aspects of the work in question have derived. As Derrida has repeatedly affirmed, the "deconstruction of metaphysics" takes place within metaphysics and remains within metaphysics, since we have no language but one version or another of the Western metaphysical tradition. However different in tone and attitude a critic like Derrida is from Poulet, their procedures are, in one way at least, the same. Derrida, like Poulet, calls for a reliving of the fundamental texts of our tradition, in his case a following through of the basic metaphorical strands which make up the texture of these texts. Far from going "beyond metaphysics" now, says Derrida,

> it is necessary . . . to remain within the difficulty of this passage [back through the metaphysical tradition], to repeat it by way of the rigorous reading of metaphysics wherever it normalizes Western discourse and not only in the texts of "the history of philosophy."[70]

Poulet's criticism may be described as one form of such a rigorous reading, and in making a concentrated image of the literary tradition since the Renaissance, Poulet, however indirectly, puts that tradition to the test.

Moreover, if Poulet's "rigorous reading" is motivated covertly by a desire to discover an escape from the flowing of time in a stable point of departure, the result of this search is failure. In no writer, for more than an illusory moment, does he find what he seeks. Again and again in his criticism he experiences by way of his re-experience of the experience of others the inability of consciousness ever to reach back to its *point de départ*. He discovers the existence within the mind of a fathomless abyss, a deeper bottom beneath every bottom. Poulet's exploration of the *Cogito* of each of his writers leads to the recognition that the *Cogito* is the experience of a lack of a beginning, of an irremediable instability of the mind. The search for a beginning leads to a discovery of the impossibility of ever reaching an origin. This coincides with a revelation that the present moment of consciousness, from which all else follows, is undermined by absence and is a movement which can never be stopped in its reaching toward an ungraspable totality. Unlike Derrida, Poulet has no desire to "deconstruct" metaphysics. Quite the reverse. He wants to prolong it and to maintain it. But in reliving it from within he has participated in that deconstruction by encountering the instability of the foundation on which the tradition is based: consciousness and the present. "I believe," says Poulet in perhaps the most revealing statement he has made about the outcome of his study of literature,

> that in prolonging in its very interiority the spirituality of all the authors, one comes to glimpse something which exceeds them, to establish a convergence. . . . [T]he profundity of the interior [of the mind] is such that one can never see the edge or the end of it, and, as in the case of Pascal, there is a transcendence of the center.[71]

This transcendence of the center is the absence of any attainable origin. However far back or far below one goes, the center still eludes the searcher. Beneath the deepest deep a deeper deep still opens, and the authenticity of literature is constituted by this experience of failure to reach the bottom. "I am above all attracted," continues Poulet,

> by those for whom literature is – by definition – a spiritual activity which must be gone beyond in its own depths or which, in being unable to succeed in this, in being condemned to the consciousness of a failure to go beyond itself [*un non-dépassement*], affirms itself as the experience and verification of a fundamental defeat.[72]

This insight into the fact that the central movement of literature is an experience of failure explains the crucial importance for Poulet of writers like Pascal, Rousseau, Baudelaire, and Proust, those problematical authors in whom especially appears in one way or another the insufficiency of consciousness to sustain itself or in whom, as in the case of Rousseau, the attempt to make it sustain itself has been most heroic. Marcel Proust is above all other writers important here as an indication of the inner drama of Poulet's criticism. He has returned many times to Proust, in the climactic essay of *Etudes sur le temps humain, I*, in a book-length essay, *L'Espace proustien*, in the admirable recent essay included in *Mesure de l'instant*. There are crucial pages on Proust at the end of the introduction to *Le point de départ*, and in the preliminary essay in *Les chemins actuels de la critique* Poulet salutes Proust as the founder of "thematic criticism," that criticism which, having "plunged into the apparent disorder which almost always constitutes the collection of works by the same author, discovers there . . . the *themes* common to all these works."[73] To follow the sequence of these essays on Proust is to trace by way of a series of salient points the development of Poulet's work, and it is to discover that if Poulet in his own way questions the value of presence and the definition of consciousness which seem to be postulates of his work, he also, in spite of appearance, does not view as trivial the fact that literature is made of words. His distaste for the objective study of literary language springs from a desire to protect what is most unsettling about literature from those who would turn it into a fixed spatial structure which can be held at arm's length and safely studied as an external object. To turn a work of literature into an object in this way is to be unable to experience it from the inside and thereby to be unable to discover the record it contains of the failure of the mind ever to coincide with its point of origin. The relation of consciousness to language, when this failure is recognized, comes to be seen as no longer that of a passive mirroring of a preexistent state of mind in words. Language is rather the instrument by which the mind explores its own depths, discovers there is no attainable point of origin within it, and ultimately recognizes that language itself must be used as the means by which the mind attempts to constitute its own continuity and duration over the unfathomable gulf within itself.

Poulet's first essay on Proust explores the way in which in *A la recherche du temps perdu* a fragile and wavering present self founds itself on a recovery of the apparently solid ground of its own past. *L'Espace proustien* looks upon the vast expanse of *A la recherche* as a spatial panorama of events recorded in language and juxtaposed in the present within the covers of a book. The essay in *Mesure de l'instant* reveals a new Proust, a Proust oriented toward the future, toward a prospectivity which will be created from instant to instant in the act of writing, that is, through language. *A la recherche*, says Poulet, leads to a decision

> to draw from past existence a future work, in such a way that the final decision of the hero becomes the initial point of a new novel, the point of departure of a new future. . . . The Proustian novel does not lead up to a simple grasp of the past as past. It creates its own future; it reestablishes . . . the primacy of the prospective élan in the expression of a duration.[74]

This insight into the indispensable, and yet precarious, function of language as the true "point of departure" of literature, this recognition that language is an instrument of revelation and creation rather than merely of reflection or mimesis, had already been affirmed in *Le point de départ*, where Poulet speaks of the special discovery in twentieth-century literature of the naked present as that on the basis of which it is necessary for literature "to invent or recover that [lost] duration."[75] This invention or recovery, continues Poulet, is "a work not impossible, but difficult, and in which the defeats are more frequent than the victories. There are numerous examples in the literature of the twentieth century of durations, sketched out, aborted, exploded, in short of non-durable durations."[76]

Of those writers who have best demonstrated the difficulty of creating a duration through words none stands, for Poulet, above Proust, but Poulet's criticism is itself such a construction. Far from being a mere representation of the work of others, it is the creation of a duration out of all the detached moments of experience founded on words and strewn here and there in all the books. This creation, like Proust's creation of *A la recherche du temps perdu*, moves forward with language toward a never-completed future in the act of recapitulating and organizing the past:

> One cannot . . . understand the literary work except by placing oneself in the *nisus formativus* by which, as it gradually unveils itself to the eyes of the reader, it reveals to him at the same time how it moves from

instantaneousness, that is to say, from the detached sequence of the sensible events which constitute it, to a structural temporalism, that is to say, toward the gradual cohesion which takes hold of the different parts, puts them in positive or dialectical relation to one another and brings into the open with the same stroke the ideological and stylistic constants and the formal sequences. . . . Contrary to what one supposes, time does not go from the past to the future, nor from the future to the past, in traversing the present. Its true direction is that which goes from the isolated instant to temporal continuity. Duration is not, as Bergson believed, an immediate given of consciousness. It is not time which is given us; it is the instant. With that given instant, it is up to us to make time.[77]

All Poulet's investigation of literature approaches toward this affirmation of the reciprocal dependence of consciousness and language in the progressive unfolding of the creative act. Mind and words balance and sustain each other in a wavering at the point of origin which can never be stilled. In saying this Poulet moves beyond any spatialized conception of time to confront the fact that the true beginning of both subjectivity and language, if the concept of origin may still be preserved, is the insecurity of human temporality, the fissures and dislocations which open up for man within time.

Notes

1. The first five sections of this essay are a somewhat shortened and revised version of an essay originally printed as "The Literary Criticism of Georges Poulet" in *Modern Language Notes*, LXXVIII, 5 (Dec., 1963), pp. 471–88, here reproduced with the kind permission of the Johns Hopkins Press. At that time Poulet had published three books: *Etudes sur le temps humain* (Edinburgh, 1949; Paris, 1950); *La distance intérieure* (Paris, 1952); *Les métamorphoses du cercle* (Paris, 1961). These three books have been translated into English and published by the Johns Hopkins Press. In 1963 Poulet had also published three of the essays on French (or in these cases Swiss) critics of his group which are ultimately to form part of the "Essai sur la pensée critique de notre temps" which he is preparing: "La pensée critique d'Albert Béguin," *Cahiers du Sud*, 360 (1961), pp. 177–98; "La pensée critique de Marcel Raymond," *Saggi e ricerche di letteratura francese* (Milan, 1963), pp. 203–29; "La pensée critique de Jean Starobinski," *Critique*, XIX, 192 (Mai, 1963), pp. 387–410.

    Sections six through nine of this essay attempt to extend what I originally wrote in the light of work Poulet has published since 1963. Since then five books and a number of essays have appeared: *L'Espace proustien* (Paris, 1963); *Le point de départ* (Paris, 1964); *Trois essais de mythologie romantique* (Paris, 1966); *Mesure de l'instant* (Paris, 1968), and *Benjamin Constant par lui-même* (Paris, 1968). Though the book on contemporary criticism has not yet appeared, several additional essays likely to form part of that study have been published in the interim: "Bachelard et la conscience de soi," *Revue de métaphysique et de morale*, LXX, 1 (Jan.–Mars, 1965), pp. 1–26; "Bachelard et la critique contemporaine," *Currents of Thought in French Literature: Essays in Memory of G. T. Clapton*, J. C. Ireson, ed. (New York, 1966), pp. 353–57; "La pensée critique de Charles du Bos," *Critique*, XXI, 217 (Juin, 1965), pp. 491–516: "Maurice Blanchot, critique et romancier," *Critique*, XXII, 229 (Juin, 1966), pp. 485–97. In addition Poulet has directed an important conference at Cerisy-la-Salle on criticism, the transactions of which have been published as *Les Chemins actuels de la critique* (Paris, 1967), with an introductory essay by Poulet on his immediate predecessors in criticism – Thibaudet, Jacques Rivière, Charles du Bos, Ramon Fernandez, and Marcel Proust. A new book on Baudelaire, *Le visage de Baudelaire* (Geneva, 1969), has recently appeared.

Further discussion of Georges Poulet's work has also been published since 1963. A good study in English of his criticism is included in Sarah Lawall's *Critics of Consciousness: The Existential Structures of Literature* (Cambridge, Mass., 1968), pp. 74–135. There is a criticism of Poulet in Geoffrey Hartman's "Beyond Formalism," *Modern Language Notes*, LXXXI, 5 (December, 1966), pp. 550–5. I have discussed Poulet's work again briefly in "The Geneva School," *The Virginia Quarterly Review*, XLIII, 3 (Summer, 1967), pp. 477–82 (also available in *The Critical Quarterly*, VIII, 4 [Winter, 1966], pp. 313–16). An admirably full and perceptive essay on Poulet by Paul de Man, entitled "Vérité et méthode dans l'oeuvre de Georges Poulet," has appeared in *Critique*, XXV, 266 (July, 1969), pp. 608–23. [This note dates from 1971 – JHM 1990.]
2. Poulet, "La pensée critique d'Albert Béguin," p. 178. I am responsible for the translations of citations from Poulet's criticism which appear in this essay.
3. Poulet, "La pensée critique de Marcel Raymond," p. 203.
4. *Ibid.*, p. 209.
5. *Ibid.*, p. 203.
6. Poulet, Réponse," *Les lettres nouvelles* (24 Juin, 1959), p. 10.
7. Poulet, "La pensée critique de Marcel Raymond," p. 204.
8. Poulet, "La pensée critique de Jean Starobinski," p. 408.
9. Poulet, "La pensée critique de Albert Béguin." p. 178.
10. Poulet, "La pensée de Jean Starobinski," p. 409.
11. Poulet, "La pensée critique de Marcel Raymond," p. 228.
12. Poulet, "La pensée critique de Jean Starobinski," p. 408.
13. Poulet, "La pensée de Marcel Raymond," p. 208.
14. Poulet, *La distance intérieure*, p. ii.
15. Poulet, *Les lettres nouvelles* (24 Juin, 1959), p. 12.
16. Poulet, "La pensée critique de Marcel Raymond," p. 225.
17. *Ibid.*, p. 224.
18. Poulet, "La pensée critique de Jean Starobinski," p. 408.
19. Preface by Georges Poulet to Jean-Pierre Richard's *Littérature et sensation* (Paris, 1954), p. 9.
20. Poulet, *Les lettres nouvelles* (24 Juin, 1959), p. 11.
21. Poulet, "La pensée critique de Marcel Raymond," p. 205.
22. *Ibid.*, p. 210.
23. Poulet, *La distance intérieure*, p. i.
24. *Ibid.*
25. Poulet, "La pensée critique de Marcel Raymond," p. 209.
26. *Ibid.*, p. 208.

27. Blanchot, "Ars Nova," *La Nouvelle Revue Française*, 125 (Mai, 1963), pp. 886–7.
28. Poulet, *Les métamorphoses du cercle*, pp. 515–16.
29. Poulet, *La distance intérieure*, p. ii.
30. Poulet, *Les métamorphoses du cercle*, p. 339.
31. Poulet, "La pensée critique de Jean Starobinski," p. 397.
32. Poulet, *Les métamorphoses du cercle*, p. 263.
33. Poulet, *Etudes sur le temps humain*, I. 176.
34. From a letter of 1963.
35. Poulet, *La distance intérieure*, p. 251.
36. Poulet, "La pensée critique de Marcel Raymond," pp. 212–13.
37. Poulet, *Les lettres nouvelles* (24 Juin, 1959), p. 12.
38. *Ibid.*
39. See note 1 above for a list of these. [Sections six through nine of this essay were published in 1970 – JHM 1990.]
40. Poulet, *Les chemins actuels de la critique*, p. 251.
41. *Ibid.*, p. 9.
42. *Ibid.*, p. 55.
43. Poulet, *Le point de départ*, p. 37.
44. See my essay, "The Geneva School," p. 477.
45. As Paul de Man has shown in his discussion in the article cited above in note 1 of Poulet's pseudonymous novel, *La poule aux oeufs d'or* (Paris, 1927), and of his uncollected periodical essays of the early 1920s.
46. Poulet, *Trois essais de mythologie romantique*, p. 11.
47. See the discussion of the *Cogito* in section III above.
48. From a letter to this author.
49. Poulet, "La pensée critique de Marcel Raymond," p. 208.
50. Poulet, *Etudes sur les temps humain*, I, 174.
51. Poulet, *Mesure de l'instant*, p. 164.
52. Poulet, *Le point de départ*, p. 34.
53. For recent discussions of the complexities of Husserl's position on this point see Gérard Granel, *Le Sens du temps et de la perception chez E. Husserl* (Paris, 1968), and also Jacques Derrida, *De la grammatologie* (Paris, 1967), pp. 97–8, and his *La voix et le phénomène* (Paris, 1967), especially pp. 93–6.
54. For the English translation see Edmund Husserl, *The Phenomenology of Internal Time-Consciousness*, tr. James S. Churchill (Bloomington, 1964), p. 21: "For no one in this knowledge-proud modern generation," says Husserl of Augustine, "has made more masterful or significant progress in these matters than this great thinker who struggled so earnestly with the problem."
55. *Ibid.*, p. 49.
56. Poulet, *Le point de départ*, p. 9.
57. Poulet, *Mesure de l'instant*, 315.
58. Benveniste. *Problèmes de linguistique générale* (Paris, 1966), p. 259.
59. Nietzsche, *Jenseits von Gut und Böse*, Section 54, *Werke*, ed. Karl Schlechta, II (Munich, 1954), p. 616; English tr. Marianne Cowan, *Beyond Good and Evil* (Chicago, 1955), pp. 62–3.
60. See, for example, Roland Barthes, "L'effet de réel," *Communications*, 11 (1968), pp. 84–9; Jacques Derrida, "La théâtre de la cruauté et la clôture de la représentation," *L'écriture et la différence* (Paris, 1967), pp. 341–68; Gilles Deleuze, "Simulacre et philosophie antique," *Logique du sens* (Paris, 1969), pp. 292–324.

61. Nietzsche, *Jenseits von Gut und Böse*, Paragraph 289, p. 751; tr. Cowan, p. 232.
62. Foucault, "Nietzsche, Freud, Marx," *Nietzsche* (Paris, 1967), pp. 187–92.
63. See, for example, "Le Temps et l'autre," *Le choix, le monde, l'existence* (Grenoble, 1949), and *Totalité et infini, essai sur l'extériorité* (The Hague, 1961): "If one could possess, seize, and know the other, he would not be the other."
64. See de Man's essay on "The Rhetoric of Temporality," in *Interpretation: Theory and Practice* (Baltimore, 1969), and see also his comments on the historical assumptions of Poulet's work in the essay on Poulet in *Critique*, cited above. De Man argues that the historical schema of Poulet's criticism is apparent rather than real. [The essay on Poulet was later included in *Blindness and Insight* – JHM 1990.]
65. Heidegger, *Sein und Zeit*, tenth ed. (Tübingen, 1963), p. 350; English tr. John Macquarrie and Edward Robinson, *Being and Time* (New York, 1962), p. 401.
66. *Ibid.*, p. 427; p. 499.
67. In addition to the three books mentioned above Derrida has published "La pharmacie de Platon," *Tel Quel*, 32, 33 (1968), pp. 3–48, 18–59; "La 'différance,'" *Bulletin de la Société Française de Philosophie*, 62ᵉ année, 3 (Juillet–Septembre, 1968), pp. 73–120; "ΟΥΣΙΑ et ΓΡΑΜΜΗ," *L'Endurance de la pensée* (Paris, 1968), pp. 219–66; "La Dissémination," *Critique*, 262, 263 (Mars, Avril, 1969), pp. 99–139, 215–49.
68. See above.
69. Derrida, "La 'différance,'" pp. 89–90.
70. *Ibid.*, p. 96.
71. From a letter of 1963.
72. *Ibid.*
73. Poulet, *Les chemins actuels de la critique*, p. 23.
74. Poulet, *Mesure de l'instant*, p. 335.
75. It is worth noting, however, that a fundamental question is begged in the either/or here. Invent or recover, which is it?
76. Poulet, *Le point de départ*, p. 37.
77. *Ibid.*, p. 40.

4

Literature and religion

The relations of religion and literature involve methodological problems which may be specified easily enough. To specify them, however, is not to solve them. They constitute one version of that tension between extremes which characterizes all interpretation of literature. One set of these problems has to do with the relation between the critic and the work criticized. Another has to do with the relation between the work and the personal, cultural, or spiritual reality it expresses. I shall discuss the problems in that order.

I

Most students of literature today would agree that the aim of their discipline is elucidation of the intrinsic meanings of poems, plays and novels. They want to know exactly what a sonnet by Shakespeare, an ode by Keats, or a novel by Trollope *means*. Poetic language, they tend to assume, is self-contained or self-referential. Whatever meanings a poem has are there on the page, shining forth from the words and their relations.

But though the words of a poem may contain its meaning, they do not do this in the way a cigarette package contains its cigarettes, or even in the way a tree contains its sap, a flower its aroma. A poem is not just black marks on the page or sonorous vibrations in the air. It comes into existence as a poem only in the mind and feelings of its reader or auditor. Though its meanings are intrinsic, they are intrinsic to an experience which includes the reader as well as the black marks, the listener as well as the sounds. A poem, unlike a scientific formula or a mathematical proof, cannot even be understood if the reader is too detached from it and regards it with too critical an eye. It exists partly as the emotions inhering in it, and these come into being only when it is read with sympathy. The reader or listener, however, is not a neutral machine for

---

"Literature and Religion." Reprinted by permission of the Modern Language Association of America from *The Relations of Literary Study: Essays on Interdisciplinary Contributions*, James Thorpe, ed. (New York: Modern Language Association, 1967; copyright 1967 by the Modern Language Association of America).

bringing verbal meanings into existence. He has a personality and a history of his own. The inherence of the reader in the poem leads to one of the difficulties involved in the relation of religion and literature.

It is natural for the reader of literature to have religious convictions, however vague or contradictory these may be. Even indifference to religious questions or rejection of them is of course a religious position. On the other hand, many works of literature have religious themes, whether overtly, as in the case of *The Divine Comedy*, the poems of St John of the Cross, or *Murder in the Cathedral*, or more indirectly, as in the case of the poems of Hölderlin, Keats or Arnold. The problem arises when a critic, with his own religious convictions, confronts the religious subject matter of a work of literature. Critics have usually chosen one of three characteristic ways of dealing with this problem. Each may lead to its own form of distortion. The critic may tend to assimilate writers to his own religious belief. He may be led to reject writers because they do not agree with his religious views. He may tend to trivialize literature by taking an objective or neutral view towards its religious themes.

Certainly a critic should be granted the right to his religious opinions. The mature person is the committed person, and where is it more important to be committed than in the area of religion? But even though religious faith is not incompatible with the view that God's house has many mansions, nevertheless in practice there is often conflict between the strength of a religious commitment and the historical relativism which the study of literature seems to demand and confirm. An evident fact about literature is the diversity of beliefs which have characterized poets of various times and places, and the knowledge of the way "world views" have varied throughout history is as much a part of present-day assumptions about literature as are the notions of intrinsic meaning and organic form. At one time and place people saw the world in one way and at another time and place in another way, and these endlessly changing views of things are incompatible. Homer, Dante, Shakespeare, Blake, and Wallace Stevens have different ideas about the nature of things. Since this is the case, the first responsibility of the critic, it appears, is to abnegate his own views so that he may re-create with objective sympathy the way things seemed to Homer, Shakespeare, or Stevens. Literary study must be pluralist or relativist because its object is so. The literary critic must be a shape-shifter, a twentieth-century descendant of Keats' poet of negative capability. Having no nature of his own, he must be able to take on the nature of whatever poet he studies, wearing for a time the mask of Shelley, Marlowe, or Chaucer.

And yet to ask the man who holds religious views of his own to give these up when he studies literature is to ask him to become a divided man, keeping two important areas of his life separate. It is not easy, however, to open the frontiers between these areas.

If the critic tries to reconcile his religious belief and his love of literature he may be led to say that the works he reads agree with the insights of his faith, though when viewed with different eyes they do not appear to do so. After all, such a critic says, the world is really as my faith tells me it is, and even those writers who do not know this will testify unwittingly to the truth. Greek and pagan myths, it was once thought, are really distorted versions of Christian revelation. This view, or some modification of it, is still occasionally held. Medieval and Renaissance commentators were able to make Virgil into something like a great Christian poet. In our own day critics both Catholic and Protestant have sometimes argued that the works of a writer like Kafka or Camus are centrally Christian in meaning or at least may be assimilated into a Christian view of things. Another version of this is the anachronism of reading a writer like Coleridge or Shakespeare as a great "existentialist" poet. Such readings may import the categories of the modern religious or quasi-religious philosophy into works of literature to which they are alien. Jean-Paul Sartre, in his book on Baudelaire and in other studies, and Martin Heidegger, in his essays on Hölderlin, have found support for their views in interpretations of earlier works of art or literature, though their studies have been criticized for representing that form of distortion I am discussing.[1] But if Sartre and Heidegger are right about human existence there seems no reason why their insights should not be confirmed by anticipation in earlier poems or paintings. To hold this, however, is implicitly to contradict the notion that there is an intrinsic particularity in the world view of each age or individual, a particularity which may not with impunity be blurred by trans-historical schemes of interpretation.

Even the best of the overtly Christian critics, Jacques Maritain, Allen Tate, or Thomas Gilby among the Catholics, Amos Wilder, Nathan Scott, or W. H. Auden among the Protestants,[2] though they may respect the individuality of non-Christian works, tend to make criticism a dialogue between their own religious views and the world views of the writers they discuss. They ask in effect: "Of what use is Camus, or Kafka, or Melville to a man who believes as I do?" and their studies often have compound titles which suggest this confrontation: *Modern Literature and the Religious Frontier, The Christian and the World of Unbelief, Christianity and Existentialism, The Tragic Vision and the Christian Faith*.[3]

It is easy to see why it is that the relations of religion and literature are now of special concern. In a time when the power of organized religion has weakened, people have turned, as Matthew Arnold said they would, to poetry as a stay and prop, even as a means of salvation. Many people who are authentically religious in the sense that they seek a supernatural meaning for their lives have made for themselves a religion compounded of a bit of their own inherited faith, a bit of existentialism, a bit of Maritain, a bit of Kafka, a bit of Zen Buddhism, a bit of Rilke, a bit of Ananda K. Coomaraswamy, and so on.

Arnold, however, was wrong, and T. S. Eliot was right. Literature is not a means of salvation. It is the Virgil which can take the pilgrim only so far. Beyond that point only Beatrice can lead the pilgrim farther.[4] Nevertheless, to take a man even so far is in a way a religious service. It may seem unpredictable but scarcely absurd that Paul Claudel should have been converted to Catholicism in part at least by his reading of Rimbaud.[5] Kafka's writings, for example, do have religious themes, as do Rimbaud's, and a critic needs much theological acumen to understand them. It is natural that scholars trained in theology should concern themselves with Kafka's work, or with Shakespeare's, or even with Camus'. Yet such scholars, if they wish to remain literary critics and not become something else, must resist the temptation to grind their own axes.

Nor are critics without explicit religious commitment exempt from this danger. Even a great critic like R. P. Blackmur could, because of his distaste for what seemed to him the weirdly heterodox metaphysics of Yeats' poems, sometimes argue that since the poems are so beautiful the bad metaphysics cannot be an intrinsic part of their meaning,[6] and some of the early criticism of Gerard Manley Hopkins' work is marred by the assumption that Hopkins' Catholicism must be more or less irrelevant to his poems.[7]

Another case in point is the work of the brilliant French critic Maurice Blanchot. Blanchot is fascinated by a certain conception of the relation between literary creation and a devouring darkness which, for him, underlies language and the human mind. He has written dozens of essays on widely different authors, many of them most impressive in the depth of their penetration. Nevertheless a curious process of assimilation operates in these essays. Whatever Mr B. reads turns into Mr B. Though he may begin with objective discussion, his own obsessive ideas are an engulfing whirlpool which sweeps Kafka, Beckett, Joubert, Musil, Rilke, and the rest into an irresistible swirling of language, dissipates their individual contours, and absorbs them into itself, so that each essay can end with another statement of those notions which are, in Blanchot's criticism, repeated again and again in almost the same form. The essays are in their movement a perfect imitation of the conception of literature which they presuppose, but the reader is left wondering whether he should call Blanchot's work literary criticism or give it some other name.[8] Only the wisest and best of critics can avoid distorting the writers they study in the direction of their own beliefs, and this tendency is all the more powerful the more firmly they hold those beliefs.

Suppose, then, we imagine a critic who recognizes this danger and who wishes nevertheless to remain a whole person. She or he will take a work of literature seriously enough to put in question the truth of its picture of things, and will have the courage to reject those works which seem morally or religiously mistaken. What use can a poem have, however beautiful it may be, if it pictures the world falsely? If such a critic finds Wagner salacious, Milton the holder of an inhuman theology, or Yeats' metaphysics absurd, he or she will not think these elements extrinsic to their art.[9]

T. S. Eliot was a man of such courage. He expounds in "Tradition and the Individual Talent" a view of history which sees the literature of Europe from Homer to the present as forming a harmonious whole. If this is the case, then the addition of an authentic new work will alter the meanings of all the works back to *The Iliad*, and the meaning of the new work will lie in its relation to the others, its conformity to them.[10] But what of the work which does not conform? In a sense such a work will not exist at all, as, in Christian theology, evil has only a negative existence. The consequences for analysis and judgment of this view of literature are expressed in *After Strange Gods*, Eliot's most intransigent polemic.[11] Hardy, Lawrence, and Yeats receive the harshest criticism. Because they thought for themselves, or dared, as Yeats said of himself, to make a new religion "of poetic tradition, of a fardel of stories,"[12] they are heretics all. They dwell outside the closed community of European letters and must be condemned for whoring after strange gods. This condemnation follows logically enough from Eliot's religious commitment, and yet his paragraphs on Yeats, Hardy, and Lawrence (as F. R. Leavis has argued for the latter[13]) are hardly satisfactory as criticism, hardly give the reader much sense of the richness and complexity of the work of these writers. Eliot here comes close to substituting censorship for criticism.

The work of Albert Béguin offers another striking example of this. His early book, *L'âme romantique et le rêve*, is one of the masterpieces of twentieth-century criticism. With great learning, subtlety, and penetration, and above all with an unparalleled power of sympathetic understanding, Béguin re-creates the spiritual itineraries of the major German and French romantic writers. As the years passed, however, his capacity for sympathetic identification gradually narrowed. In the end his full sympathy and approval could go out only to a small group of writers, those representing a certain kind of modern Catholic spirituality: Dostoevsky, Georges Bernanos, Léon Bloy, Charles Péguy. Even Pascal, who might be expected to fit Béguin's definition of authentic writing, did not escape his growing tendency to exclusions. Certain pages in one of Béguin's last books, the "Par lui-même" volume on Pascal, describe Pascal as alien to the deepest spiritual experience of today. A remorseless logic seems to have led this great critic to narrow more and more the circle of admissible writers.[14]

Suppose then that the critic decides to keep his own views out of his work. Literary study is objective and public, the establishment of the facts about literary history, part of that vast collective body of research which makes up the teamwork of modern scholarship. A man's religious views are his private business and need have nothing to do with his public life as a scholar. Even if literary analysis is to be thought of as the reliving from within of the world view of an author and its creation anew in the words of the critic, still this need have nothing to do with the critic's religious life. He must efface himself before the experience of literature, seek nothing for himself, give his mind and feelings to understanding the work at hand and to helping others to understand it through his analysis.

The problem of the relation between the religiously committed critic and the work of criticism seems to have been solved at one stroke. If this solution is followed rigorously, however, it may turn literary criticism into a trivial pastime. The secret possibility of this triviality undermines the attitude of historicism, as it is present in Nietzsche's thought or in Ortega y Gasset's, or is developed in the criticism of Wilhelm Dilthey, Bernhard Groethuysen, and others, or is present in another form in the work of A. O. Lovejoy and other students of the so-called history of ideas.[15]

Historical relativism has close connections, as Nietzsche's work shows, with that modern form of nihilism which sees all cultural attitudes, all the masquerades that time resumes, as hollow because based on nothing outside man himself. Nietzsche tells man to experiment tirelessly with new life-forms, new world views. This experimentation is a way man can affirm his freedom from any supernatural law and assert his sovereign will to power over the world. What Nietzsche called the "death of God" is the presupposition of his historicism. Dilthey's aim of an exhaustive re-creation of all the types of life-forms leads to admirable works of criticism, but these may leave the reader in the end asking, "Wherefore? If all these forms of life are relative, what value do they have, and why should I bother to relive them?" Dilthey was not unaware of this implication of his work. The conflict between historical relativism and man's need for a universally valid knowledge seemed to him the essential problem raised by historicism.[16] This problem, he felt, could be solved only by pushing the historical sense to its limit. Man can go beyond history only through history. But where would a man be if he were beyond history? To have exhausted all cultural forms, in W. B. Yeats' view at least, is to be face to face with what he calls in "Meru" the "desolation of reality." The vision of all personages of history as relative to their times and places is likely to lead to the world-weariness of Paul Valéry in "La crise de l'esprit," or to the rage for destruction of Yeats in "Nineteen Hundred and Nineteen."

The negative energy present in a rigorous historicism is especially apparent in the work of A. O. Lovejoy. Lovejoy had immense learning and an indefatigable power to understand the logic of ideas, including religious ones, in their development through history. He also had a great distaste for ambiguities and confusions of thought, and yet he felt that most writers are ambiguous or confused, often expressing conflicting ideas or incongruous feelings on a single page of their writing. Lovejoy's attitude toward Western history was a bit like that of a positivistic anthropologist collecting the strange myths and beliefs of the aborigines. This detachment is apparent in his habit of separating the statement of a "unit-idea" from its living context in the thought of a writer and presenting it in cold isolation where it can be subjected to his merciless power of logical analysis. This analysis puts in question both the idea that there is a unity in the culture of a period and the idea that there is a unity in the thought of an individual man. Examples of this are Lovejoy's fragmentation of romanticism and his discrimination of sixty-six different senses in which the idea of nature was, in antiquity, connected with "norms."[17]

Neither objective description of historical facts nor sympathetic re-creation of the life-forms of the past can be a self-sufficient end in itself. A twentieth-century inheritor of historicism, Wallace Stevens, recognizes this when, in "The Noble Rider and the Sound of Words," he rejects Plato's image of the charioteer of the soul and Verrocchio's splendid equestrian statue of Bartolomeo Colleoni.[18] They are of little interest to us now, he says, if they are no more than outmoded forms of the past, a stage set which has been taken down and carted away. The study of the supreme fictions of history has value only if it is related to our search for the supreme fictions of today. Dilthey himself, at the end of *Die Einbildungskraft des Dichters*, an essay of 1887, affirms that though there is something universal about the work of the greatest poets, nevertheless even they are creatures of history. This means that the poets of the past can never move us as they did their contemporaries. The poets of most value to us are the poets of today, those who can speak to us of our own experience.[19] The study of literature cannot be justified in the same way as scientific research can. Each new scientific fact builds up man's picture of the universe and may have practical applications in the great technological civilization he is creating. The student of literature, quite properly, wants to know what's in it for him, and a pure historical relativism, to the degree that it answers that there's nothing in it for him, reduces the study of literature to triviality. Homer's work, or Dante's, or Hardy's must be more than just one way of looking at things among innumerable others, and yet the consequences of assuming this involve the difficulties I discussed earlier.

No doubt in practice a good critic can reconcile his religious convictions with catholicity of taste and wide-ranging sympathy for many authors, but still he must be on guard against the dangers of unwittingly making works of literature over in his own image, or of unjustly condemning them, or of failing to take them seriously enough to put in question the authenticity of their religious themes. The tension between dispassionate objectivity and engagement is in the nature of literary study and must be lived by each critic as best he or she can.

II

Even if critics interested in the religious aspects of literature make their peace with this tension, a new set of problems faces them when they consider the external context of a poem or novel. I said at the beginning that a poem embodies its meaning. This is true, but words are not, after all, like notes in music, meaningless except in their relation to one another. They have a complicated cultural history. The notion of intrinsic meaning is not incompatible with the idea that each poem draws into itself all those connections it has with its various contexts. It is often useful to have those connections identified, not only for their own sake, but for the light they may shed on meanings which are there in the words of the work. Such investigations may show how a certain text draws its life from similar passages in other works by the author, or from books read by the author, or from the social and historical milieu in which it came into existence, or from the tradition to which it belongs.

But where does the context of a poem stop? Its relations to its surroundings radiate outward like concentric circles from a stone dropped in water, and it may be extremely difficult to give a satisfactory inventory of them. Moreover, this investigation tends to disperse the poem into the multiplicity of its associations until it may become little more than a point of focus for the impersonal ideas, images, and motifs which enter into it. Instead of being a self-sufficient entity, it is only a symptom of ideas or images current in the culture which generated it.

If the critic rejects this implication of contextual study and returns to the poem itself, another danger awaits him. The more completely he cuts the poem off from its mesh of defining circumstances, the less, it may be, he can allow himself to say about it. The poem means only itself, and any commentary falsifies it by turning it into something other than itself.

Fearing the heresies of paraphrase and explanation, he may be reduced to silence, or to repeating the poem itself as its only adequate commentary.[20]

No doubt there is validity in both these views of literature. Each authentic poem is something altogether individual, and even other poems by the same writer are more or less irrelevant to its self-enclosed integrity. On the other hand, the insights gained by study of a poem's context may help the critic in many ways in his attempt to understand this particularity.

The problem of the proper focus to choose for the interpretation of a given work or author has, however, special difficulties in relation to the study of religious themes in literature. How is the critic to treat these? Is he to hold that each religious poem has a meaning which is peculiar to that poem alone? If this is the case then there is, for example, one religious view of things for Gerard Manley Hopkins' "The Windhover," another for "God's Grandeur," another for "Spelt from Sibyl's Leaves," another for "The Wreck of the Deutschland," and so on. In each case the religious meanings must be developed solely from the words of the particular poem, and this means that each religious poem will have a unique religious meaning. A strict "new critical" approach to Hopkins' work would follow this path, and in fact many of the essays on "The Windhover" assume that it can be understood more or less in isolation from the rest of Hopkins' work.

Obviously, however, there are echoes, resemblances, fraternal similarities between one poem by Hopkins and the others. Nor are his letters, notebooks, essays, and devotional writings without relevance to an understanding of his poems. Each poem lives in a context which includes everything Hopkins ever wrote. Should the critic therefore attempt to show how that circumambient milieu is a complex harmony of related themes?[21] But then, once more, the individual poem is in danger of losing its integrity and becoming a node in a web of connections or a moment in a spiritual history which transcends it.

On the other hand, why should the critic stop with Hopkins' own writings? The poet was a nineteenth-century Jesuit and a graduate of Oxford. His reading in Scotus, Ignatius, and Suárez, his knowledge of the Bible and of Catholic liturgy, the influence of his tutor at Oxford, Walter Pater, his readings in Greek philosophy as an undergraduate, his place in the Oxford movement or in the general history of Victorian religious experience – none of these associations is irrelevant, and yet their investigation tends, as it proliferates, to dissolve Hopkins into what influenced him, to make his work no more than a "product" of its time.

Certainly all three focuses of criticism are valid, the study of the individual work, the study of all the works of one author, the study of the ideas or sensibility of an age, but each tends to imply a different notion of the way religious themes are present in literature.

The contextual problems in the interpretation of religious literature are especially apparent in the scholarship on medieval and Renaissance poetry. A complex body of learning – traditional topoi, subtle methods of allegory, many-layered symbols – may be hidden in an apparently simple lyric of these periods. For an educated person of the Middle Ages or Renaissance, it is argued, all literature, philosophy, and theological writing from Greek times to the present form a single tradition which should determine the shape and content of any authentic poem. This tradition was taken for granted by a contemporary reader of Chaucer, Spenser, or Milton, and guided the understanding of their poems. The twentieth-century reader must labor to recover the context permitting a just interpretation of such writers, just as a reader of the twenty-fifth century will no doubt have to labor to recover what must be known in order to read Faulkner, Camus, or Beckett, not to speak of Eliot or Joyce. To understand Dante, Chaucer, or Donne, or at least to understand them in relation to the traditions in which their work participates, the scholar must be steeped in these traditions, know Greek and Latin literature, classical philosophy, medieval encyclopedias, Biblical commentaries, and so on. Admirable work has been done in this way by scholars as different in their methods and commitments as E. R. Curtius, Erich Auerbach, D. C. Allen, C. S. Singleton, Morton Bloomfield, and D. W. Robertson, Jr.[22]

Critics still differ, however, about the proper way of interpreting medieval and Renaissance literature. Their recent disagreements have often had to do with the question of the way religious meanings inhere in secular literature. C. S. Singleton and R. H. Green, to cite one example, have argued about whether *The Divine Comedy* is to be considered allegory of the poets or allegory of the theologians.[23] The question at issue is whether or not it is proper to read Dante's poem strictly on the model of the four-level allegorical interpretation which was applied in the Middle Ages to the Bible. The answer to this question will determine what is meant when *The Divine Comedy* is called a religious poem.

Quarrels about context arise as much or more from disagreement about which is the important context for a given poem as from disagreement about whether or not a given poem can be understood in isolation. Even though all scholars would probably now agree that *Beowulf* is a Christian poem, still the poem changes magically if it is moved from the milieu of the Bible and Latin literature of the Middle Ages to the milieu of Germanic heroic poetry. On the other hand, a secular lyric of the Middle Ages or Renaissance may appear innocent of religious meaning when it is looked at in isolation, but when it is set against texts from the Bible, St Augustine, St Gregory, Rhabanus Maurus, and so on, images which seemed realism or decoration take on another meaning and reveal themselves to be symbols of transcendent truths. Who is to say that this symbolism is in the text itself and has not been installed there by the legerdemain of the learned critic? Only the tact born of long immersion in the literature of the period can tell, but the long immersion produces different results in different cases. A consensus among critics in these areas is an ideal to be worked toward rather than a goal yet attained.

III

The problem of context is associated with another problem, the last of the issues involved in the relation of religion and literature which I shall discuss. Exactly what does it mean to say that religious meanings are present in a poem or a play? It may mean the following: The poet belonged to a certain culture. Among the elements of that culture were religious beliefs. These were part of the world view of his age, and naturally they enter into his poems, since all men are subject to the spirit of their times. To take this view is to accept that historicism which, as I argued earlier, tends to turn religious themes in literature into something other than themselves. Of what religious interest are such themes in Dante's poems, or George Herbert's, or T. S. Eliot's if they are accidents of a certain time and place, determined horizontally, as it were, by the influence of other men and their books? Religious themes in literature are without religious significance unless they spring from a direct relationship between the poet and God, however much they may take a form dictated by the age. If human history is made by men alone, then religious elements in culture have only a human meaning. For Ludwig Feuerbach and other such humanists religious ideas are symptoms of the way men lived together at a certain time. Religion for Feuerbach or for George Eliot is the cement of culture, a collective belief which holds people together.[24]

A similar transmutation of the religious import of literature is implicit in an exclusive commitment to either of the other focuses of criticism I have identified. If, as the structural linguists and some "new critics" tend to assume, the meanings of a work of literature are entirely intrinsic, generated by the interaction among its words, then the symbolizing process predominates over what is symbolized, and literature is in danger of becoming a play of words mirroring one another vacantly. In such a case, religious themes will not be different in kind from any other themes in literature, since poetry on any subject does no more than demonstrate the power of language to develop complex symbolic structures. To such a view of literature someone interested in religious themes in poetry could make the same approach Paul Ricœur directs against the anthropological structuralism of Claude Lévi-Strauss. Ricœur sees in Lévi-Strauss' work "an extreme form of modern agnosticism." "For you," he said to Lévi-Strauss in a public discussion of June 1963,

> there is no "message," not in the cybernetic sense, but in the "kerygmatic" sense; you give up meaning in despair; but you save yourself by the notion that if human beings have nothing to say, at least they say it so well that one can subject their discourse to a structural analysis. You save meaning, but it is the meaning of meaninglessness, the admirable syntactic arrangement of a discourse which says nothing. I see you at that point of conjunction of agnosticism and an acute understanding of syntaxes."[25]

The same kind of restriction may limit that form of criticism which takes as its goal the comprehension of the mind of an author as revealed in the ensemble of his works. If each writer's mind is autonomous, the sole originator of the meanings which are expressed in his works, then any seemingly religious themes in those works will have a human rather than a divine meaning. They will be nothing but a part of the pageant of human history.

Any method of criticism which presupposes that meaning in literature is exclusively derived from the interrelations of words, or from the experiences of a self-enclosed mind, or from the living together of a people will be unable to confront religious themes in literature as such. Only if some supernatural reality can be present in a poem, in a mind, or in the cultural expressions of a community can there be an authentic religious dimension in literature. Only if there is such a thing as the spiritual history of a culture or of a person, a history determined in part at least by God himself as well as by man in his attitude toward God, can religious motifs in literature have a properly religious meaning. The scholar's position on this issue will follow from his or her religious convictions, which returns me to the assertion that the religious commitment of the critic, or lack of it, cannot be considered irrelevant to his work.

In the relation of the critic to the work criticized and in the relation of the work to its context there are methodological problems which take especially difficult forms when the connections of religion and literature are in question. Though there is no easy way to solve these, no golden mean which will allow a happy steering between extremes, there is an attitude toward literary study which will escape some of its dangers. The scholar-critic must be as learned as possible, not only in literature itself, but in history, philosophy, theology, the other arts, and so on. Only in this way can she or he avoid egregious errors caused by ignorance. Nevertheless, the end of literary study is still elucidation of the intrinsic meanings of poems, plays, and novels. In the effort toward such elucidation the proper model for the relation of critics to the work they study is not that of scientist to physical objects but that of one person to another in charity. I may love another person and know him as only love can know without in the least abnegating my own beliefs. Love wants the other person to be as he is, in all his recalcitrant particularity. As St Augustine puts it, the lover says to the loved one, "Volo ut sis!" – "I wish you to be." If we approach the poem with this kind of reverence for its integrity, it will respond to our questioning and take its part in that dialogue between reader and work which is the life of literary study.

The metaphor of lover and beloved will also indicate what tone the critic should take with the reader. I may tell you what the man or woman I love is like, but this is no substitute for your direct confrontation with that person. Criticism too is only a preliminary to the reader's own dialogue with the work. In the end criticism must efface itself before the texts, stand back, having done the work of interpretation, to let the works show themselves forth as they are. Only in this way will those religious meanings which are in the work and not in the beholder's eye be made visible.

Notes

1. See Jean-Paul Sartre, *Baudelaire* (Paris, 1947), and Martin Heidegger, *Erläuterungen zu Hölderlins Dichtung* (Frankfurt am Main, 1951).
2. See Jacques Maritain, *Art and Scholasticism*, tr. J. F. Scanlan (London, 1930); *Frontières de la poésie et autres essais* (Paris, 1935); with Raïssa Maritain, *Situation de la poésie* (Paris, 1938); *Creative Intuition in Art and Poetry* (New York, 1953); Allen Tate, *Reason in Madness* (New York, 1941); *On the Limits of Poetry* (New York, 1948); *The Man of Letters in the Modern World* (New York, 1955); *Collected Essays* (Denver, Colo., 1959); Thomas Gilby, *Poetic Experience: An Introduction to Thomist Aesthetic* (London, 1934); Amos Wilder, *The Spiritual Aspects of the New Poetry* (New York, London, 1940); *Modern Poetry and the Christian Spirit* (New York, 1952); *Theology and Modern Literature* (Cambridge, Mass., 1958); W. H. Auden, *The Enchafèd Flood* (New York, 1950); *The Dyer's Hand and Other Essays* (New York, 1962); Nathan A. Scott, Jr., *Rehearsals of Discomposure: Alienation and Reconciliation in Modern Literature* (New York, 1952); *Modern Literature and the Religious Frontier* (New York, 1958); *The Broken Center: Studies in the Theological Horizons of Modern Literature* (New Haven, London, 1966).
3. For *Modern Literature and the Religious Frontier* see n. 2; *The Christian and the World of Unbelief* (New York, 1957) is by Libuse Lukas Miller; *Christianity and the Existentialists* is a collection of essays edited by C. Michalson; *The Tragic Vision and the Christian Faith* (New York, 1957) is a collection of essays edited by Nathan A. Scott.
4. See T. S. Eliot, *On Poetry and Poets* (New York, 1957), p. 94.
5. See Arthur Rimbaud, *Oeuvres*, préface de Paul Claudel (Paris, 1912).
6. A single sentence cannot do justice to the subtlety of Blackmur's essays on Yeats and to the energy with which he grapples with the problem of belief in

Yeats. See, however, p. 97 in "The Later Poetry of W. B. Yeats," *Language as Gesture* (New York, 1952), where he proposes the following "remedy" for our inability to accept Yeats' "magical mode of thinking": "to accept Yeats's magic literally as a machinery of meaning, to search out the prose parallels and reconstruct the symbols he uses on their own terms in order to come on the emotional reality, if it is there, actually in the poems – when the machinery may be dispensed with."

7. See, for one example of this, Vivian de Sola Pinto, *Crisis in English Poetry, 1880–1940* (London, 1952), p. 72.
8. See Maurice Blanchot, *La part du feu* (Paris, 1949); *Lautréamont et Sade* (Paris, 1949); *L'espace littéraire* (Paris, 1955); *Le livre à venir* (Paris, 1959).
9. See William Empson, *Milton's God* (London, 1961), and Yvor Winters, *The Poetry of W. B. Yeats* (Denver, Colo., 1960). The books of Basil Willey and H. N. Fairchild attempt to combine historical objectivity with judgment based on religious commitment, but in the work of these scholars, particularly in Fairchild's, the religious conviction sometimes enters into the historical description and makes what began as unbiased research turn into polemical judgment. Fairchild's last three volumes, for example, are often an argument against the evil effects of romanticism and science on English poetry. See Basil Willey, *The Seventeenth Century Background* (London, 1934); *The Eighteenth Century Background* (London, 1940); *Nineteenth Century Studies* (London, 1949); *More Nineteenth Century Studies* (London, 1956); Hoxie Neale Fairchild, *Religious Trends in English Poetry*, Vol. I: 1700–1740, *Protestantism and the Cult of Sentiment* (1939); Vol. II: 1740–1780, *Religious Sentimentalism in the Age of Johnson* (1942); Vol. III: 1780–1830, *Romantic Faith* (1949); Vol. IV: 1830–1880, *Christianity and Romanticism in the Victorian Era* (1957); Vol. V: 1880–1920, *Gods of a Changing Poetry* (1962) (all published in New York).
10. See T. S. Eliot, *Selected Essays: 1917–1932* (New York, 1947), pp. 4–11.
11. New York, 1934.
12. *The Autobiography of William Butler Yeats* (New York, 1953), p. 70.
13. See *D. H. Lawrence, Novelist* (London, 1955).
14. See *L'âme romantique et le rêve*, 2 vols. (Marseille, 1937), nouvelle édition (Paris, 1939); *La prière de Péguy* (Neuchâtel, 1944); *Léon Bloy: Mystique de la douleur* (Paris, 1948); *Poésie de la présence* (Paris, 1957); *Bernanos par lui-même* (Paris, 1954); *Pascal par lui-même* (Paris, 1952). For Béguin's reservations about Pascal, see "Pascal sans histoire," in *Pascal par lui-même*, pp. 59–111.
15. See W. Dilthey, *Gesammelte Schriften*, 12 vols. (Leipzig and Berlin, 1923–36); Bernhard Groethuysen, *Die Entstehung der bürgerlichen Welt- und Lebensanschauung in Frankreich*, 2 vols. (Halle/Saale, 1927, 1930); *Philosophische Anthropologie* (München & Berlin, 1934), French version: *Anthropologie philosophique* (Paris, 1952); *Mythes et portraits* (Paris, 1947); A. O. Lovejoy, *Essays in the History of Ideas* (Baltimore, 1948); *The Great Chain of Being* (Cambridge, Mass., 1933); *The Reason, the Understanding and Time* (Baltimore, 1961); *Reflections on Human Nature* (Baltimore, 1961); *The Thirteen Pragmatisms and Other Essays* (Baltimore, 1963). For an interesting book on Dilthey's work, see Kurt Müller-Volmer, *Towards a Phenomenological Theory of Literature: A Study of Wilhelm Dilthey's "Poetik"* (The Hague, 1963), and for a recent discussion of Lovejoy's methodology, see Maurice Mandelbaum, "The History of Ideas, Intellectual History, and the History of Philosophy,"

The Historiography of the History of Philosophy, Beiheft 5 of History and Theory (The Hague, 1965), pp. 33–42.
16. See, e.g., the end of his speech on the occasion of his seventieth birthday, in Die Geistige Welt, Part 1, Gesammelte Schriften, V, 9.
17. See "On the Discrimination of Romanticisms," Essays in the History of Ideas, pp. 228–53, and the Appendix to A. O. Lovejoy and G. Boas, A Documentary History of Primitivism and Related Ideas (Baltimore, 1935).
18. See The Necessary Angel: Essays on Reality and the Imagination (New York, 1951), pp. 7, 9.
19. Die Geistige Welt, Part 2, Gesammelte Schriften, VI, 241.
20. Jean Starobinski has eloquently described this paradox of criticism in L'oeil-vivant (Paris, 1961), pp. 24–7.
21. As, e.g., I have tried to do in my chapter on Hopkins in The Disappearance of God: Five Nineteenth-Century Writers (Cambridge, Mass., 1963).
22. See E. R. Curtius, Europäische Literatur and lateinisches Mittelalter (Bern, 1948), English tr. Willard R. Trask, (New York, 1953); Erich Auerbach, Mimesis (Bern, 1946), 2nd ed. (Bern, 1959), English tr. Willard R. Trask (Princeton, N. J., 1953); Literatursprache und Publikum in der lateinischen Spätantike und im Mittelalter (Bern, 1958), English tr. Ralph Manheim (New York, 1965); "Figura," Archivum Romanicum, XXII (1938), pp. 436–89; "Typological Symbolism in Mediaeval Literature," Yale French Studies, No. 9 (1952), pp. 5–8; D. C. Allen, The Harmonious Vision: Studies in Milton's Poetry (Baltimore, 1954); Image and Meaning: Metaphoric Traditions in Renaissance Poetry (Baltimore, 1960); C. S. Singleton, An Essay on the Vita Nuova (Cambridge, Mass., 1949); Dante Studies (Cambridge, Mass., 1954–); Morton Bloomfield, The Seven Deadly Sins (East Lansing, 1952); Piers Plowman as a Fourteenth-Century Apocalypse (New Brunswick, N.J., 1962); D. W. Robertson, Jr., and B. F. Huppé, Piers Plowman and Scriptural Tradition (Princeton, N.J., 1951); D. W. Robertson, Jr., A Preface to Chaucer: Studies in Medieval Perspectives (Princeton, N.J. 1963).
23. See C. S. Singleton, "Dante's Allegory," Speculum, XXV (1950), pp. 78–83; "The Other Journey," Kenyon Review, XIV (1952), pp. 189–206; "The Irreducible Dove," Comparative Literature, IX (1957), pp. 129–35, and Richard Hamilton Green, "Dante's 'Allegory of Poets' and the Mediaeval Theory of Poetic Fiction," Comparative Literature, IX (1957), pp. 118–28.
24. See Ludwig Feuerbach, Das Wesen des Christenthums, Bd. 7 of his Sämmtliche Werke (Leipzig, 1849), English translation by George Eliot (London, 1854), also available in Harper Torchbook series.
25. Esprit, 31ᵉ année, No. 322 (Novembre 1963), pp. 652, 653: "Je penserais plutôt que cette philosophie implicite entre dans le champ de votre travail, où je vois une forme extrême de l'agnosticisme moderne; pour vous il n'y a pas de 'message': non au sens de la cybernétique, mais au sens kérygmatique; vous êtes dans le désespoir du sens; mais vous vous sauvez par la pensée que, si les gens n'ont rien à dire, du moins ils le disent si bien qu'on peut soumettre leur discours au structuralisme. Vous sauvez le sens, mais c'est le sens du non-sens, l'admirable arrangement syntactique d'un discours qui ne dit rien. Je vous vois à cette conjonction de l'agnosticisme et d'une hyperintelligence des syntaxes." See also, in the same number of Esprit, the essay by Paul Ricœur entitled "Structure et herméneutique" (pp. 596–627). Ricœur's essay is an excellent discussion of the relation between the

objectivity proper to structuralism and that form of interpretation from within which he calls, after Dilthey and others, "la compréhension herméneutique." The latter he sees as most appropriate for reaching, by way of sympathetic participation in a tradition, religious meanings in literature and in other cultural forms.

5

Tradition and difference

> There is, hidden within *language*, a philosophical mythology which appears and reappears at every moment, however careful one is.
> Nietzsche, *Human, All Too Human*, II, 2, 11

"Natural supernaturalism"; "tradition and revolution": the oxymorons in Abrams' title and subtitle (the first taken of course from Carlyle) express, like all such contradictions, the force of a desire. They express exactly the equivocal wish lying behind this admirable book. On the one hand, Abrams wants to affirm the continuity between Romantic literature and its Christian and classical antecedents. At the same time he wants to argue that Blake, Hölderlin, Wordsworth, and the rest have "translated" the supernaturalism of the Platonic and Christian tradition into a humanism. As Wallace Stevens puts it: "Aquinas spoke,/kept speaking of God, I changed the word to man." However, as Stevens also says in the same poem, "Theology after breakfast sticks in the eye." This means, among other things, that metaphysics is adhesive. It gets between the eye and a plain seeing of the object. As I shall try to argue, Abrams' clinging metaphysical presuppositions obscure a clear vision of what is most problematical in the historical sequence he describes.

This is a book, however, that one does not challenge lightly. *Natural Supernaturalism* is in the grand tradition of modern humanistic scholarship, the tradition of Curtius, Auerbach, Lovejoy, C. S. Lewis. Learned, elegantly and lucidly composed, equable and sane throughout, generously humane in its appreciation of the great works of the past and in its desire to perpetuate their values through our dark time, Abrams' book is a worthy successor to its line. Like its predecessors, Curtius' *European Literature and the Latin Middle Ages* or Lovejoy's *The Great Chain of Being*, *Natural Supernaturalism* assumes the unity of Western culture through all its modifications. Like *The Great Chain of Being* it attempts to construct a vision of the whole by way of the perspective afforded by one aspect of that whole. In Abrams' case the perspective is the Platonic paradigm of a primal unity then fragmented and finally to be brought back to unity again. This sequence is a "circuitous journey" from creation and fall to the final apocalypse. The eight sections of *Natural Supernaturalism* discuss different versions of this paradigm: the persistence of the motif of apocalypse from the Bible, along with the metaphor of marriage as an expression of the return to unity, from the same source; the narrative pattern of "crisis-autobiography" in its various ways of telling the story of the Prodigal Son's journey away from home through alienation and back home again; the image of the circle or of the spiral which returns on itself at a higher level; the various ways in which Romantic and post-Romantic writers "translate" traditional religious patterns into humanistic terms, promising a secular apocalypse through political revolution (the role of the French Revolution in the writings of the Romantics is discussed at length), through the exercise of the poetic imagination, or through philosophical cognition. By an admirable synecdoche, Wordsworth's Prospectus for *The Recluse* is taken as the starting place and the end of Abrams' own circuitous journey of interpretation. All the motifs Abrams wants to explore are contained in one way or another in this brief passage and in that proof text for any theory of Romanticism, *The Prelude*. The multiplicity of authors, citations, and themes discussed by Abrams is in a sense only a set of footnotes, an elaborate commentary on the Prospectus with which he begins and which he reintegrates at the end in an appendix printing the three extant versions.

In the course of his spiraling journey Abrams discusses with magisterial authority a wide variety of texts. This variety falls into six main groups: the Bible, especially *Revelation* and the prophetic books of the Old Testament; early Christian writers, of whom St Augustine is, properly, the most important for Abrams' purposes; classical authors in the Platonic tradition, Plotinus at most length; the esoteric tradition in the Renaissance: Boehme, Paracelsus, Gerrard Winstanley; the English Romantic poets: Wordsworth, Coleridge, Blake, Keats, Shelley, and their English predecessors, especially Milton; the German Romantic philosophers and poets: Hamann, Schiller, Hölderlin, Novalis, Hegel, Fichte, Schelling; post-Romantic authors from Carlyle through Marx, Nietzsche, Eliot, Lawrence, Stevens, and even down to Allen Ginsberg. All of these authors and all of these motifs have been discussed before, as have, in specialized or in general studies, all the filiations Abrams proposes. The connections between Romantic poetry and the esoteric tradition going back through Hamann to Boehme and Paracelsus, for example, are studied in a masterwork of modern criticism nowhere mentioned by Abrams: Albert Béguin's *L'âme romantique et le rêve*. In fact some of the novelty of Abrams' discussion of the major German Romantic poets and philosophers vanishes if one happens to know Béguin's book. To a considerable extent *Natural Supernaturalism* repeats in a different mode of criticism some of the ground already admirably covered by Béguin. (From the point of view of purely objective "scholarship," one might observe in passing, a weakness of Abrams' book is the relatively small role played in the drama he constructs by primary and secondary sources in French, as compared to the deep familiarity he has with corresponding works in German and English. There is no reason, for example, why he should not have discussed Amiel, Nerval, or even Balzac with the same attention he devotes to Novalis or Hölderlin, and his treatment of Rousseau, Baudelaire, or Rimbaud, for example, is relatively perfunctory.)

Even so, there are important novelties of emphasis and perspective in Abrams' book. Béguin, for example, pays relatively little attention to the English Romantic writers, though there are a few pages on them assimilating them into his general picture of Romanticism in unpublished lectures given as a course at Mills College in California shortly before Béguin's death and now preserved in the Béguin archives at the University of Zürich. No one before Abrams, however, has so comprehensively read the English Romantic poets in the light of their German contemporaries, both poets and philosophers. No one has so persuasively shown the consonance, not in "concept," but in organizing ground plan, between Wordsworth's *The Prelude*, for instance, and Hegel's *Phenomenology* or Hölderlin's *Hyperion*. To assimilate German Romantic philosophy into the pattern of the *Bildungsreise*, the educative journey of the Prodigal Son, and therefore to show its similarity to *The Prelude* or to *Prometheus Unbound*, will remain one of the accomplishments of Abrams' book. Second, no one has in such persuasive detail demonstrated the congruence of the basic myths, metaphors, and concepts of Romantic poetry to patterns not invented by them but inherited from the Biblical, Christian, and Neo-Platonic tradition. No one has so cogently defined Romanticism as no more than a "scene" in the twenty-five-hundred-year "drama of European literature," to borrow a phrase from Erich Auerbach. Third, perhaps no one has so patiently and so wisely discussed what the secularization of theological tradition by the Romantic poets and philosophers might mean. Finally, no one has demonstrated so clearly the persistence of these patterns into modern literature. For Abrams, the best of Victorian and twentieth-century literature is essentially a continuation of the Romantic tradition. We are still, for him, within Romanticism. This is by now a familiar notion. The difference in Abrams' version of it is his insistence that to be within the Romantic tradition means to be still under the domination of metaphors and concepts inherited from Christianity and Neo-Platonism. We are still within the shadow, or illumined by the light, of Western metaphysics. As Abrams puts it, in sentences which might serve as a summary of the position taken in his book: "We in our time are thus the heirs of a very old and expanding tradition – pagan and Christian, mythical and metaphysical, religious and secular – that it is the lot of man to be fragmented and cut off, but haunted in his exile and solitariness by the presentiment of a lost condition of wholeness and community. [. . .] The old images and structural patterns survive, as well as the concepts" (313).

To this list of the virtues of *Natural Supernaturalism* must be added the attractive enthusiasm Abrams expresses for his authors, a warmth that conveys itself in his reconstruction of the knotty polemics of German idealism as well as in his discussion of *The Prelude* or *Jerusalem*. *Natural Supernaturalism* is a defense of the rightness and relevance of Romanticism, a defense in which Abrams' warmth sometimes rises to polemical heat against what he calls, following Lionel Trilling, our "adversary culture." Near the conclusion, for example, he asserts:

> The Romantic writers neither sought to demolish their life in this world in a desperate search for something new nor lashed out in despair against the inherited culture. The burden of what they had to say was that contemporary man can redeem himself and his world, and that his only way to this end is to reclaim and to bring to realization the great positives of the Western past. (430)

These great positives are then listed as "life, love, liberty, hope, and joy" (431), virtues no sane man would lash out against.

In the presence of so much good-humored learning and such faith in humane values, it seems niggling to pick holes in the admirable fabric Abrams has woven. Nevertheless, *Natural Supernaturalism* is questionable, it seems to me, both in its fundamental assumptions and in the more or less unspoken methodology it employs. My putting in question will be divided into several topics, but these overlap or branch into one another. They are different projections of the same landscape rather than distinct topographies.

One topic covers the concepts of tradition, of period, of innovation, of "source," and of filiation. What is involved in the repetition of a motif or narrative pattern from one writer to another? This is the question of family resemblance. What does it mean to have literary or philosophical "ancestors" or to have as "progeny" innumerable books following the same pattern as one's own book, as St Augustine is said to have had in the descendants of the *Confessions*?

Second, there is the question of what is involved in the humanization of theological patterns. If I redefine the Christian and Neo-Platonic tradition as a human creation and take possession of it as such, it would seem that I have destroyed it in the sense that I might be able to create something entirely different. Why is it that Wordworth, Blake, Novalis, and the rest, in Abrams' interpretation of them, created the same patterns all over again?

There is, third, the question of the status of the means by which these patterns have been expressed through the centuries. *Natural Supernaturalism* pays notably little attention throughout to the question of signs or of language. Little space is given either to the theories of language in the authors discussed or to the status of the linguistic terms habitually used throughout Abrams' analysis: "myth," "concept," and "metaphor," to name the most important. One way to put this would be to say that the missing term in Abrams' book is precisely language. By limiting himself for the most part to the other three nodes in the usual dynamics of such analysis (subject, object, and God), he has, to say the least, oversimplified the problem.

Finally, one may question the implicit assumptions Abrams makes about what is involved in the interpretation of a literary or philosophical text.

Abrams' presuppositions, in these four aspects of his book, are themselves a version of Western metaphysics, even a version which might be defined as Romantic. *Natural Supernaturalism* therefore presents the familiar spectacle of a book about Romanticism which is permeated through and through with Romantic assumptions. Though the challenging of these assumptions has always been part of the Western tradition from the beginning, as in the self-subversion of Plato in *The Sophist*, certain recent writers have brought these issues once more to the forefront of attention. One knows the familiar litany of the names of these doubters, underminers of the Occidental tradition in its economic and political theory, in its ethical and ontological notions, in its concept of human psychology, and in its theory of language: Marx, Nietzsche, Freud, Saussure. These writers, it might be argued, are the true "adversary culture," rather than the scurvy crew of Abrams' description who have sought to demolish their life in this world in a desperate search for something new. Marx, Nietzsche, Freud, and Saussure might be called the initiators of several modern revolutions, except that the opposition between "tradition" and "revolution" in Abrams' subtitle is itself a part of that metaphysical tradition which they challenged. Moreover, it is easy to show that all four of these writers belong to the tradition of metaphysics, even in what is apparently most "novel" in their thought. Rather than the notion of revolution one needs the more enigmatic concept of repetition (repetition as displacement or decentering) to describe the effect of these writers on the culture to which, like all of us, they belong. By resurrection, rearrangement, re-emphasis, or reversal of old materials they have made a difference.

Abrams pays scanty attention to these writers, and when he does, as in his brief discussions of Marx and Nietzsche, it is for the most part to affirm the presence in their works of the old millennial paradigm. The plausibility of his account of Nietzsche, supported as it is by abundant citations, mostly from *The Birth of Tragedy*, does not make it the less wrong. Or rather, since the concept of "rightness" in interpretation was one of the ideas Nietzsche most wanted to challenge, one might put this in Nietzschean terms by saying that Abrams' discussion of Nietzsche is evidence of his will to power over the texts he reads, his desire to assimilate them to the pattern he has brought to them. In any case, one of the most fully articulated explorations of alternatives to the assumptions of Abrams' book is to be found in the writings of Nietzsche and in a remarkable series of recent books which have reinterpreted Nietzsche or which have been written directly or indirectly under his aegis. I am thinking of books by Gilles Deleuze, Jacques Derrida, Paul de Man, Bernard Pautrat, Jean-Michel Rey, and Sarah Kofman.[1]

Abrams tends to assume a direct, one to one relation between a work and its "source," so that the meaning of the derived work will be "analogous," "cognate," or "in consonance" with its source. Nietzsche, Deleuze, and the rest would hold instead that all imitation is subversive. It transforms or destroys what it copies. The authentic "progeny" of a literary work are all bad sons who kill their father, or try to, prodigal sons who never return home. An especially important case of this is the use by a "secular" writer like Proust or Wordsworth of structural patterns and terminology drawn from the theological tradition. Abrams, after what, in view of much of the recent work on Proust, by Gérard Genette, Roland Barthes, and others, may seem an oversimplified description of *A la recherche du temps perdu*, observes of the structural similarities between *The Prelude* and Proust's novel:

> such similarities are the less surprising when we realize that these works are cognate, and that their ultimate source (as the densely religious vocabulary of both writers indicates) is not secular, but theological. This source is the fifteen-hundred-year-old tradition of religious confessional writings, and within the tradition the first and greatest example, and one of the most influential of all books, in Catholic as in Protestant Europe, was the *Confessions* of St Augustine. (83)

This is true enough. It is, however, misleading. In spite of Abrams' attention to the differences between St Augustine's *Confessions* and a work "based on it" like Proust's *A la recherche*, the implication is that there is an essential continuity, a preservation of value and meaning, between the work and its "source." In fact both Proust and Wordsworth, in different ways, turn that source upside down, repeat it in parody, hollow it out, manipulate it as a fictive pattern. Just as Abrams' conception of metaphor tends to see it as a representational tool, only another way to express conceptual thought (of which more later), so his terminology for the relation between works in the religious tradition and their secular counterparts betrays his assumption that there can be a "translation" without loss from "source" to "copy." For example, he says of *Prometheus Unbound* that "Demogorgon's summation repeatedly echoes the book Shelley knew almost by heart [the Bible], *translated* to a human center of reference 'in the wise heart'" (460, my italics), or on the next page he says that Wordsworth, in the Prospectus to *The Recluse*, "represented" his meditations "on Man, on Nature, and on Human Life" "as a *translation* to his age of the values embodied in Milton's religious epic" (461, my italics).

Another way to put this is to say that Abrams' humanistic position does not lead him to take the Christian and Platonic tradition seriously enough, or not as seriously as did, say, St Augustine. For Abrams, apparently, it is a grand fiction, the best of human creations, the support of the best human values, love, liberty, hope, and the rest. For St Augustine it was "the truth," founded on an eternal being. For example, Abrams says of St Augustine that in interpreting his own life according to the pattern of Biblical history "he imposed on the flux of experience, the randomness of events, and the fugitive phenomena of memory the enduring plot-form and the standard concepts and imagery of that unique and characteristic genre of Christian Europe, the spiritual autobiography" (83–4). St Augustine, one may be permitted to believe, would have been scandalized by this description of his procedure. He thought the pattern was really there, put there by God in his Providential manipulation of Augustine's life down to the last detail. The other side of this blurring of distinctions is Abrams' minimizing of the differences between a writer like Augustine who believed in the divine origins of the structural patterns of his narrative and a writer like Proust who knows they are fictions and manipulates them as such. To manipulate them in this way means to demystify them, as Proust systematically demonstrates the fictive nature of the patterning analogies which apparently organize his life.

This leads to a second opposition between Abrams' assumptions and those of Nietzsche. Against Abrams' view that the Romantic writers effected a benign secularization of the Western theological tradition, Nietzsche and the others would put a more complex double notion. On the one hand, when one has changed the word from God to man, one is still entirely within the metaphysical tradition. The concept of subjectivity is as much a part of metaphysics as the notion of God, or "the One," or "Being." Nietzsche devoted as much care in the notes now collected as *The Will to Power* to the attempt to deconstruct the idea of the unity of the "thinking I" as he did to undermining the reification of "being." The humanizing of metaphysics is still metaphysical. On the other hand, Nietzsche saw the attempt within "humanism" to maintain theological values after abandoning belief in God as essentially a precarious and momentary prolonging, the attempt to preserve a flower cut off from its roots. The idea of man is inextricably entangled with the idea of God and cannot be maintained without it. Nietzsche gave the name "nihilism" to the moment of the discovery that all man's values, even the idea of man itself, are a baseless fabrication, created and supported only by frail weavings of words. In *Twilight of the Idols* he speaks sardonically of those like George Eliot who do not see that the whole structure of Christian morality collapses with loss of belief in God:

> They are rid of the Christian God and now believe all the more firmly that they must cling to Christian morality. That is an English consistency; we do not wish to hold it against little moralistic females à la Eliot. In England one must rehabilitate oneself after every little emancipation from theology by showing in a veritably awe-inspiring manner what a moral fanatic one is. That is the penance they pay there.
>
> We others hold otherwise. When one gives up the Christian faith, one pulls the right to Christian morality out from under one's feet. This morality is by no means self-evident: this point has to be exhibited again and again, despite the English flatheads. Christianity is a system, a *whole* view of things thought out together [*ein System, eine zusammengedachte und ganze Ansicht der Dinge*]. By breaking one main concept out of it, the faith in God, one breaks the whole: nothing necessary remains in one's hands. (IX, 5; tr. Walter Kaufmann)

Insofar as *Natural Supernaturalism* is a conclusive demonstration that the Romantic writers, while abandoning belief in God, did in fact preserve Christian morality along with its basic concepts, metaphors, and narrative patterns, it poses an unanswered question. This question might be phrased by asking, "Why was it that Blake, when he, or his spokesman, Los, the archetypal artist, determined that he must 'Create a System, or be enslav'd by another Man's,' succeeded only, as Abrams shows, in creating another version of the twenty-five-hundred-year-old myth of an original unity, followed by fragmentation, to be followed at last by spousal reunification?" The demonstration of the relation of the Romantic texts to their Christian and classical prototypes, the revelation of the homogeneity, or even the monotony, of the tradition through the centuries, in its alchemical, theological, hermetical, Kabbalistic, Romantic, and "modern" incarnations, raises a question: "Why?" Why has it been so difficult to awaken from this particular nightmare? Why did this scheme have such power to repeat itself through the centuries? This question imposes itself with great force as soon as one comes to view the scheme as a human construction. Why, if it was a fiction all along, did this fiction dominate and no other? Where did it get the strength to be reborn in so many diverse forms, even in those thinkers and poets who set themselves deliberately to win liberation from it? Why were there not several or innumerable alternatives, divergent, incompatible myths? Would it be possible, by any conceivable regimen, exercise, study, or violence, to free oneself from the scheme? What would it be like to be liberated? What tools might be used to win freedom?

There are several possible answers to these questions. One answer is that the pattern Abrams finds in all his writers is in fact "the truth," God's writing inscribed in the creation, not an illusion or fiction at all. This is what Christian and Neo-Platonic tradition has held and what Wordsworth, for example, apparently still believed when he claimed, in a letter of 1815 (cited by Abrams, 527) that he had "transfused" into *The Excursion* "the innumerable analogies and types of infinity [. . .] from the Bible of the Universe as it speaks to the ear of the intelligent, as it lies open to the eyes of the humble minded." Another answer is that man is a kind of sheep, recalcitrant to change, willing to have his predecessors do his thinking for him, able to impose only minor modifications on the cage of language within which he finds himself when he is born. Western man, it may be, is so stolid, so lacking in invention, that he has been willing to let a few myth-makers, fabricators of supreme fictions, Plato and Aristotle, those fatherly old scarecrows, do most of the creating for once and for all. A third possible answer recognizes that creative energy has been distributed more or less evenly over the centuries. Man is not congenitally obtuse or wholly recalcitrant to change. The third possibility is that the scheme Abrams so lucidly identifies – concepts, metaphors, myths, narrative patterns, the "whole shebang," as Stevens calls it in "The Comedian as the Letter C" – is, as one might say, "programmed into" our Western family of languages. If this is the case, then the continuity of the tradition is not determined by coercive "sources" which have imposed themselves century after century, but is a matter of concepts, metaphors, and myths, each generating the others, which are latently there in the lexicon, the grammar, and the syntax of our languages. To say this would not deny the influence of the paternal sources, Plato, Plotinus, the author of *Revelation*, St Augustine, and the rest, but it would indicate why they have had such power to replicate themselves. It would also explain the ability of the scheme to reproduce itself even when there are no plausible explanations by way of source or influence. It would explain why the scheme is so contagious. As soon as there are people at all, people and their power of speaking, then the whole scheme is already latently there. Such an explanation might also provide a clue to a means of liberation, for those who might wish to "create a

System": by a patient living through of the whole tradition, a reinterpretation which is also a deconstruction, as in the case of Nietzsche's *The Genealogy of Morals*, and by the attempt, also present in Nietzsche, to construct an alternative scheme, to put together the same materials in a different way. As Jacques Derrida has argued, however, the alternative schemes have a way of turning out to be another version of metaphysics.[2] There are no tools or materials for their construction but language, and our languages contain no terms, no concepts, and no metaphors which are not inextricably implicated in the patterns of metaphysical thinking.

This brings me to the third area in which Abrams' assumptions may be put in question: the area of language and its role in human life. I have suggested that this is the missing term in Abrams' analysis. Another way to put this is to say that his own theory of language is implicitly mimetic. Language is taken for granted as the straightforward mirror of an interchange between mind and nature, or between mind, nature, and God. But what, exactly, is a metaphor? What is a concept? What is the relation of metaphors to concepts? What is a "myth"? Is it anything more than the making of a linear narrative out of a metaphor? Is a concept anything more than the abstraction or reifying of a metaphor? "Metaphor," "myth," "concept": the fabric of Abrams' analysis is woven out of assumptions about the interrelation of these three, but their nature as such and the nature of their interrelation is never sufficiently interrogated. An example is a passage on pp. 171–2. "Certain major poets of the Romantic Age, as we shall see," says Abrams, "incorporated into their writings myths and imagery which are recognizably esoteric in origin. They used such elements, however, as symbolic conveniences, 'metaphors for poetry.' The older view of the world helped them to define the malaise of their own time." There is, however, no such thing as an innocent image or myth, in spite of the conventional appeal here to a problematic phrase taken out of context from Yeats to justify the idea that there is. No metaphor or myth is a mere "symbolic convenience," separable from the thought it embodies. It is the body of that thought, the secret generator of the concepts it incarnates. In spite of the careful attention throughout *Natural Supernaturalism* to the fundamental metaphors and narrative patterns of the tradition Abrams describes, the tendency of his book is to imply that these figurative elements are no more than "symbolic conveniences," vivid or lively ways of representing concepts or moral abstractions ("love," "liberty," "hope," and the rest). Or they are ways of expressing states of mind which exist prior to them and are not essentially dependent on them.

In place of this taking for granted of languages and of figures of speech, Nietzsche and others would see language as a constitutive factor in human life. They would see language as basically metaphorical,

metaphorical in its origin. Rather than figures of speech being derived or "translated" from proper uses of language, all language is figurative at the beginning. The notion of a literal or referential use of language is only an illusion born of the forgetting of the metaphorical "roots" of language. Language is from the start fictive, illusory, displaced from any direct reference to things as they are. The human condition is to be caught in a web of words which weaves and reweaves for man through the centuries the same tapestry of myths, concepts, and metaphorical analogies, in short, the whole system of Occidental metaphysics. Nietzsche in "Truth and Lie in an Extra-Moral Sense," from *The Book of the Philosopher*, puts it this way:

> Truths are illusions whose illusory nature we have forgotten, metaphors (*Metaphern*) which have deteriorated through usage and have lost their material force, pieces of money which have lost their effigies and which are then to be taken as metal and no longer as pieces of money.

The difficulty, for Nietzsche, is that we cannot free ourselves from this bondage to signs and to the fictions they have such power to perpetuate. As he says in *The Will to Power*, "We cease to think when we refuse to do so under the constraint of language; we barely reach the doubt that sees this limitation as a limitation./Rational thought is interpretation according to a scheme that we cannot throw off."[3] There would appear to be no escape from the prison of language except by way of a radical theory of fictions and of the interpretation of fictions, a theory which would recognize that "there are no 'facts-in-themselves,' for a sense must always be projected into them before there can be 'facts'" (*WP*, 301).

This brings me to the fourth area in which Abrams' procedure in *Natural Supernaturalism* may be challenged: his notions of the way texts have meaning and the way that meaning may be explicated and identified. Though Abrams recognizes that the texts he discusses are complex, his discussion suggests that he regards this complexity as superficial rather than fundamental. In each case a basic "ground-plan" can be described, which turns out to be another example of the metaphysical scheme which is the subject of his book. Evidence for this is his most common mode of citation, which is to illustrate some straightforward point with a quotation which is not "interpreted," in the sense of being teased for multiple meanings or implications, but which is taken as the confirmation of the "point" which has just been made. A text like *The Prelude* or *Jerusalem* or even *The Phenomenology of Mind*, though it is no doubt "complicated," nevertheless is organized around a relatively simple structural scheme which may be described accurately, summarized in a few lucid pages supported by appropriate citations. The assumption is that a text has a single meaning which is more or less independent of the play of relations, repetitions, and differentiations within the work itself.

The same directness characterizes Abrams' view of the relation of one text to another, for example in his interpretation of the striking "consonance" he finds among the texts of the Romantic period, in spite of apparent diversities and distinctions: "[O]ur present point of vantage," he says, "enables us to discern in *The Prelude* a coherent understructure of ideas and a sustained evolution of images which mark its consonance with the thought and design of a number of other, and very diverse, Romantic works of literature and philosophy" (281). The "diversity" is by implication contingent rather than constitutive. The "understructure" contains the essence. The same sort of "consonance" is seen in the relation of the works of one period to their antecedents in earlier periods, in spite of Abrams' presentation of Romanticism as the "translation" of the supernaturalism of the Bible and the Platonic tradition into a humanism appropriate for our enlightened age. A literary or philosophical text, for Abrams, has a single unequivocal meaning "corresponding" to the various entities it "represents" in a more or less straightforward mirroring: the subjectivity of the author, his "thought," the general conditions of the age (such as the French Revolution or the industrial revolution), the patterns of earlier texts in the tradition to which it is "analogous" (St Augustine's *Confessions*, the Bible, the *Enneads*, or whatever), or the ideal paradigm distilled by Abrams himself from the multitude of books he discusses.

In all these modes of interpretation Abrams perhaps takes his writers a little too much at face value, summarizes them a little too flatly, fails to search them for ambiguities or contradictions in their thought, does not "explicate" in the sense of unfold, unravel, or unweave. One example of this is his straightforward and perspicuous summary of Hegel's argument, in the Preface and Introduction to the *Phenomenology*, that the end of a dialectical train of reasoning must be there in its beginning, must have already been obtained before it starts:

> the road [*Weg*] to *Wissenschaft* is itself already *Wissenschaft*; by the nature of its content, it is the *Wissenschaft* of the experience of consciousness. [. . .] It is a circle that returns into itself, that presupposes its beginning, and reaches its beginning only in its end. (cited from Hegel by Abrams, 235)

Against Abrams' reading of this aspect of Hegel might be set Jacques Derrida's interpretation of the same Hegelian theme in the preface on prefaces ("Hors livre") in *La dissémination* (15–43). Derrida finds much more enigmatic than does Abrams the paradox whereby the impossibility of a preface or introduction outside the magic circle of knowledge is expressed in a preface which both affirms the circle and, by existing outside it, at the same time anuls or breaks it. In place of the theory of interpretation presupposed in *Natural Supernaturalism*, Derrida, Nietzsche, and the others would put the notion that a text never has a single meaning, but is the crossroads of multiple ambiguous meanings. A poem or a philosophical work is a "suspens vibratoire" of meanings, in Mallarmé's phrase. For Nietzsche there is no "objective" interpretation. The reading of a work involves an active intervention on the part of the reader. Each reader takes possession of the work for one reason or another and imposes on it a certain pattern of meaning. "The fundamental presupposition on which you base yourself," wrote Nietzsche in a letter of 26 August 1885, to K. Fuchs,

> that is, that there is in general a correct interpretation, seems to me psychologically and by experience, false. One can in fact determine, in innumerable cases, what is incorrect, what is correct, never [. . .] in short, the old philologist, strengthened by his philological experience, says there is no sacred single interpretation.

In another place Nietzsche argued that, "The same text authorizes innumerable interpretations (*Auslegungen*): there is no 'correct' interpretation" (*Nietzsches Gesammelte Werke, Musarionausgabe*, XVI, 64). There is a cascade of statements in the third book of *The Will to Power* relating the existence of innumerable interpretations of a given text to the fact that reading is never the objective identifying of a sense but the importation of meaning into a text which has no meaning "in itself." A text becomes meaningful only when it is read: "Our values are interpreted into [*hineininterpretiert*] things"; "'Interpretation' [*Auslegung*], the introduction of meaning – not 'explanation' (in most cases a new interpretation over an old interpretation that has become incomprehensible, that is now itself only a sign)"; "Ultimately, man finds in things nothing but what he himself has imported into them"; "In fact interpretation is itself a means of becoming master of something" (*WP*, 323, 327, 342).

The relation between one text and its "sources," like the relation among the elements in a single text, is an ambiguous interplay of sameness and difference, "repetition" in the Nietzschean sense of that term as it has, for example, been identified by Deleuze in *Différence et répétition* or in *Logique du sens*. Moreover, the "sources" (Plato, St Augustine, or whoever) are no more simple than their progeny. Like the "derived" texts, the primary texts contain their own contradictory elements and have ambiguous relations to their own sources. They can therefore never serve as unequivocal principles of explanation for the meaning of the later texts they have engendered. In all these relations, within the text and between the text and what is outside it, the interaction is never between signs and something safely outside their enigmatic play, but always a relation between one sign and another, between one text and another, the relation Paul de Man has termed "allegorical" (see "The Rhetoric of Temporality").

From the point of view of such a theory of interpretation all of Abrams' readings can be put in question, for example his reading of the opening of *The Prelude*, a passage important for his purposes ("to the open fields I told/A prophecy: poetic numbers came/Spontaneously," I, 59–63). Abrams' interpretation of this or other passages is to be challenged not in the sense that one can show that it means something other than what he says it means, though this could be done, but in the sense that his conception of the way texts have meanings is awry. Every one of his passages means in a different way from the way he assumes it does. Its meaning is multiple, vibrating, ambiguous. It cannot be reduced to a single, univocal statement but is "equivocal" or "multivocal."

In all these ways the methodology of *Natural Supernaturalism* is open to challenge. Abrams has identified exactly a basic paradigm of Occidental metaphysics – the picture of an original unity, lost in our present sad dispersal, to be regained at some point in the millennial future, or, in Lewis Carroll's cruel infantile parody: jam yesterday, jam tomorrow, but never jam today. Nietzsche and the others I have cited do not so much reject this scheme (it cannot be rejected, for our languages repeat it to us interminably), as deconstruct it by turning it inside out, by reinterpreting it. They affirm that the situation of dispersal, separation, and unappeasable desire is the "original" and perpetual human predicament. The dream of primal and final unity, always deferred, never present here and now, is generated by the original and originating differentiation. The beginning was diacritical.

Such an alternative pattern to the one Abrams traces would deny that the One comes first. It would deny the existence of "opposites" which are fragmented parts of an original whole. It would deny that history has a goal of reunification. In place of the notion that the origin is unity, Nietzsche, Deleuze, or Derrida would put the idea of a primal difference or differentiation, as Deleuze does in *Différence et répétition* and as Derrida does, for example, in the position-taking essay, "La différance." In place of the notion of opposites ("Without contraries is no progression," said Blake), Nietzsche would put the idea of degrees of difference, differentiated forces which are not opposites, but points on the same scale, distinctions of the same energy, as reason is nature deferred or separated from itself.[4] "There are no opposites:" wrote Nietzsche, "only from those of logic do we derive the concept of opposites – and falsely transfer it to things" (*WP*, 298). In place of the notion of the unity of the thinking subjectivity so essential to the project of the humanization of metaphysics, Nietzsche would put the idea of a multiplicity of forces struggling for dominion within the "self": "The assumption of one single subject is perhaps unnecessary; perhaps it is just as permissible to assume a multiplicity of subjects, whose interaction and struggle is the basis of our thought and our consciousness in general? A kind of aristocracy of equals, used to ruling jointly and understanding how to command?/*My hypothesis*: The subject as multiplicity" (*WP*, 270).

The image of circle and center has played a key role in the tradition, as Abrams shows, as a model for various relations – between God and the creation, between the soul and its forms, between the idea or source of a literary work and the "organic unity" of its parts which copies or imitates its model – or as the image for the single soul or the race in its journey of exile and eventual return to its starting place. In place of this image Nietzsche, Derrida, or Deleuze would put the notion of decentering or displacement, and the concept of a centerless repetition in which no element in the series is the commanding exemplar of which the others are copies. In such a chain of repeating elements similarity arises from difference rather than difference from similarity.[5] In place of the notion that history proceeds in stages from a beginning toward some preordained goal, Nietzsche puts the idea of an eternally repeated situation, without origin or end. If history has no origin and no goal, then it is not going anywhere, getting neither better nor worse, or sometimes better and sometimes worse, according to arbitrary principles of evaluation, and according to no externally operating power but by the momentary successes of ordering energy in one person or group or another. "It is only late," writes Nietzsche in an ironic note of 1887, "that one musters the courage for what one really knows. [. . .] When one moves toward a goal it seems impossible that 'goal-lessness as such' [*die Ziellosigkeit an sich*] is the principle of our faith" (*WP*, 18).

This alternative scheme, with its various aspects or motifs, has always been present as a shadow or reversed mirror image within the Western tradition, even in the texts Abrams discusses, for example, in the Platonic dialogues or in *The Prelude*.[6] His failure to recognize its pervasive presence in texts both traditional and modern is perhaps the chief limitation of *Natural Supernaturalism*.

Notes

1. Gilles Deleuze, *Différence et répétition* (PUF, 1968), *Logique du sens* (Paris, 1969), and most recently, with Félix Guattari, *L'anti-Oedipe* (Paris, 1972); Jacques Derrida, *L'écriture et la différence* (Paris, 1967), *De la grammatologie* (Paris, 1967), *La dissémination* (Paris, 1972), "La différence," in *Théorie d'ensemble* (Paris, 1968), and, for a translation into English of one essay, "Structure, Sign, and Play in the Discourse of the Human Sciences," in *The*

Languages of Criticism and the Sciences of Man, R. Macksey and E. Donato, eds (Baltimore, 1970); P. de Man, *Blindness and Insight* (New York, Oxford, 1971), and "The Rhetoric of Temporality," in *Interpretation: Theory and Practice*, C. S. Singleton, ed. (Baltimore, 1969); Bernard Pautrat, *Versions du soleil: Figures et système de Nietzsche* (Paris, 1971); Jean-Michel Rey, *L'Enjeu des signes: Lecture de Nietzsche* (Paris, 1971); Sarah Kofman, *Nietzsche et la métaphore* (Paris, 1972). Place of publication is Paris unless otherwise noted.

2. See his discussion of this at the beginning of "Structure, Sign, and Play in the Discourse of the Human Sciences."
3. Walter Kaufmann (New York, 1968), p. 283. Further citations from *The Will Power* will be from this translation and will be identified as *WP*, with page numbers in parentheses after the citations. Other translations are my own, unless otherwise noted.
4. In fact Blake's conception of contraries may be closer to Nietzsche's idea of degrees of difference than to the traditional notion of opposites which Abrams reads into it.
5. See Derrida, "La différance," and Deleuze, "Platon et le simulacre," in *Logique du sens*, pp. 292–307, as well as *Différence et répétition*.
6. See Derrida, "La pharmacie de Platon," in *La Dissémination*, pp. 71–197, and my "The Stone and the Shell," a reading of the dream of the Arab at the opening of Book V of *The Prelude*, forthcoming in the *Festschrift* for Georges Poulet.

6
Deconstructing the deconstructers

> *the* most bloody inarticulate animal that every gargled
> Pound on Williams
>
> Since these concepts are not elements or atoms and since they are taken from a syntax and a system, every particular borrowing drags along with it the whole of metaphysics. This is what allows these destroyers to destroy each other reciprocally.
> Derrida, "Structure, Sign and Play"

There can be no doubt that Joseph Riddel's task in *The Inverted Bell* is of great importance for literary criticism now. Perhaps it is even a main task for American criticism in the immediate future. Riddel's job, at least implicitly, is to take possession of the most advanced developments in continental philosophy and criticism and then to ask the question, "What difference does this make to the interpretation of English and American literature?" Though there are of course already many workers in this vineyard, Riddel's book is an early example of a large-scale attempt to answer this question. His book may therefore afford an opportunity to reflect on the enterprise itself, since we are certain to have a good many more books of this sort, or of related sorts, translations, for example, or expositions of the European critics.

Inclusive generalizations about poetics and literary history are made by Riddel. He makes use of a wide range of writers in the tradition he is assimilating – Nietzsche, Valéry, Bataille, Barthes, Foucault, Jakobson, de Man, etc., as well as Heidegger and Derrida. A large number of "Modernist" and "Post-Modernist" writers are discussed – Eliot, Pound, Stevens, H. D., Zukofsky, Olson, etc. Nevertheless, Riddel's book works, as any book of this sort would be likely to do, by a method of synecdoche. The focus is primarily on one example of "Post-Modernist" poetry, William Carlos Williams. Within Williams, primary attention is paid to his critical prose and to *Paterson*. Among the continental writers, Heidegger and Derrida are chosen as the most important for the work at hand. *The Inverted Bell*, then, is essentially a reading of Williams' *Paterson* in five chapters each roughly corresponding to a book of the poem. There is a constant triangulation from Heidegger and Derrida. Detours are made into other work by Williams, into other modern poets, and into other continental writers. The thematic focus can be even more narrowly defined. Riddel's chief topic, whatever his ostensible subject at a given moment may be, is the problematic of origins and beginnings of poetry.

Such an enterprise is difficult. It raises immediately a host of questions. First there is the question of Riddel's reading of Heidegger and Derrida. Has he got them right? What would it mean to "get them right?" If all interpretation is misinterpretation, this would be as true of Riddel's reading of Heidegger as of Wordsworth's reading of Milton. Does the necessity of misreading mean the same thing in each case? Then there is the question of Riddel's reading of Williams. Has he got Williams right? Even if the law of misreading applies here also, there are obviously strong and weak critical misreadings, more or less vital ones.

For Hugh Kenner in *A Homemade World* (New York, 1975), Williams is primarily a poet of brief lyric poems, poems in which "meaning" is minimal and structure everything: "a poem as a structure of little blocks," as Wallace Stevens paraphrased this theory. Kenner's Williams is a poet of the "rebirth" of things into the "Imagination," which means into the realm of literature, words on the page. For Williams, in Kenner's reading of him, poems are handmade objects fashioned of words placed cunningly here and there on the typed page, like the dangling figures of a mobile. An example is "The Red Wheelbarrow."

> Not only is what the sentence says banal, if you heard someone say it you'd wince. But hammered on the typewriter into a *thing* made, and this without displacing a single word except typographically, the sixteen words exist in a different zone altogether, a zone remote from the world of sayers and sayings [. . .]. This ability to move close to quite simple words, both hearing them spoken – not quite the same thing as hearing their sounds – and seeing them interact on a typewritten page, gave Williams the sense of constant discovery that saved him from feeling constantly responsible for weighty problems. He liked a poem he could spin round on one corner, and it freed him not to be encumbered with pronouncements. He typed and retyped sequences of a few dozen words, changing a word or two, or shifting the point in a phrase at which the eye must turn back round a line's end. (*A Homemade World*, 60, 86–7)

For Riddel, on the other hand, Williams is a much more portentous and solemn poet. Riddel's Williams *is* responsible for weighty problems, the weightiest, and he does constantly make pronouncements. Riddel's Williams is the poet of *Paterson* rather than of the fragile lyrics.

He is a "metaphysical" poet concerned with ultimate questions of "Being," language, "primordial origins," "bringing into the light," and so on. Which reading of Williams is the "right" one? Could both be right? Which Williams should we admire, Kenner's "New Jersey physician who had been abroad a few times but seemed to write like an impassioned though grammatical hick" (*A Homemade World*, xiv), or Riddel's Williams, worthy to stand with Hölderlin, Rilke, and George in Heidegger's pantheon of "authentic" poets? In what sense could the discourse of the critic, set side by side with his citations from the poet, "say the same thing" as the poetic texts say? Is there a difference between paraphrase, explication, commentary, citation, and "interpretation"? Even though one may agree that both citation and commentary do violence to the original, it may be that there are different forms of that violence. Would this account for the difference between Riddel and Kenner? Or does Williams offer himself to at least two radically different "correct" readings? Is Riddel's own critical language coherent? Does he say the same thing from one end of his book to the other? Riddel tends to assume that Heidegger, Derrida, Williams, and he himself are each more or less self-consistent, and that all four are saying roughly "the same thing." This means that one can follow Heidegger and Derrida at once. Is this in fact the case?

Then there are problems raised by the assumptions about literary history in *The Inverted Bell*. These assumptions are coming to be a critical commonplace these days, For Riddel, there was a movement called "Modernism," perhaps best represented by Eliot. More recent poets, with Williams their father-figure, have gone beyond Modernism to something called "Post-modernism." Post-Modernism has radically different assumptions about poetry and about its powers. This notion of a progress of poetry seems hardly consistent, by the way, with Williams' claim, abundantly demonstrated by Riddel, that he was returning to the origins of poetry, recovering a constant of authenticity present in Western poetry since Homer. Is there in fact such a thing as Post-Modernism? What validity, in any case, does periodization any longer have in the study of literature?

Finally there is the question of Riddel's source texts for his understanding of Heidegger and Derrida. This general question deserves a comprehensive essay in itself. Though Riddel makes some use of works by Derrida not yet translated into English, his chief reference is to two essays which had been translated at the time his book was written, "La Structure, le signe et le jeu dans le discours des sciences humaines" and "La différance." In the case of Heidegger the primary reference is again to English translations, *An Introduction to Metaphysics* and the essays on poetry and language translated in *On the Way to Language* and *Poetry,*

Language, Thought. The assimilation of new work in one language by readers of other languages tends to be delayed by the time it takes for the work to become well enough established to make the labor of translation seem desirable and economically feasible. Kojève's book on Hegel, for example, was a good many years ago assimilated into the development of twentieth-century French thought. It has just now been published in English and will have a new life in the context of the current American revival of interest in Hegel. Moreover, the wrong works or at any rate works inviting misleading reductions tend to be translated first, or to receive the most attention. An example is the early availability, in French, of Heidegger's polemical and somewhat strident "Letter on Humanism," scarcely the best text with which to begin to understand Heidegger. In America the first translations from Heidegger were of the essays on Hölderlin. The two books by Heidegger in English most used by Riddel continue this tradition of making available the later, more oracular Heidegger. *Sein und Zeit,* the essential beginning for any understanding of Heidegger, has been available for a good while now in a careful English translation. Though *Being and Time* is mentioned by Riddel, his central Heideggerian texts are those late ones on poetry and language, just as Derrida, for him, is essentially represented by the two essays which happened to be first translated into English.

It is easy to see that distortions are likely to result when one's knowledge of a difficult writer is more or less limited to a fragment of his work, and that fragment not in the original language. Exactly what kinds of distortion result in a given case may not be so easy to establish. Why should a fragment of Derrida not be an adequate sample or synecdoche of the whole? Does one have to read all of a writer to understand him? If not, how much? One would like to know when to be free to stop. What about translations? Surely it must be possible to put Heidegger or Derrida into English so that they "say the same thing" in English as in French or German? Is there any way, some coming and going between languages, for us, monolingual Americans, to recover what is lost of Heidegger if his German is left behind? The problem is not made any simpler by the fact that so many of Heidegger's most important essays are interpretations of Greek terms. Must we learn Greek too? Williams defines *Paterson* as "a reply to Greek and Latin with the bare hands" (*Paterson,* 10). "Bare hands" here is the vitality of the native American lingo, sprung from our local ground. As Riddel abundantly demonstrates, however, the pervasive metaphors and concepts of *Paterson* or of Williams' critical prose are heavy with a long history going back precisely to that hated Greek and Latin, back to those terms which Heidegger and Derrida are concerned to interpret.

The problem in this case is made even more complicated by the fact that Heidegger and Derrida are not isolated mountain peaks, indifferent, aloof, on which Riddel may stand to get a bead on Williams. A long dialogue with Heidegger, even a somewhat subterranean battle with Heidegger, is one of the threads winding its way through Derrida's essays. An understanding of Derrida, even of the two essays Riddel uses, both of which mention Heidegger at decisive points, cannot be separated from the question of Derrida's reading of Heidegger. "Sometimes [I] have the feeling" says Derrida, "that the Heidegger problematic is the 'deepest' and most 'powerful' defense of what I am attempting to call into question under the heading of *thought of presence*" (*Positions*, 75).[1] Is Derrida's understanding of Heidegger correct? This is once more a question of translation, of the difficulty of "saying the same" in a different form of discourse, in another language or in one text and its adjacent commentary. Derrida, as a matter of fact, in an important footnote to "Ousia et grammè," puts his whole reading of Heidegger under the aegis of this problem of translation:

> The pages which follow can be read as timid prolegomena to a problem of translation. But who has taught us better than Heidegger to think what is involved in such a problem? Here the question would be the following one: how to transfer, or rather what has happened when we transfer into the single Latin word *presence* this whole differentiated system of Greek and German words, already the whole *system of translation*, in which the Heideggerian language develops (ousia, parousia, Gegenwartigkeit, Anwesen, Anwesenheit, Vorhandenheit, etc.)? And along with this, taking into account the translations laden with history (essence, substance, etc.) that the two Greek words, and those associated with them, already have in French. Especially, how does one transfer into the single word *presence*, at once too rich and too poor, the *history* of the Heideggerian text which associates or disjoins these concepts, in a subtle and controlled fashion, throughout an itinerary covering more than forty years? *Marges* (Paris, 1972), 35–6

"A problem of translation." This is Riddel's problem too, in all the areas where, as I have tried to suggest, his book raises questions. Or, more precisely, Riddel's problem is the problem of the possible sameness of the different, in which Riddel's critical language and Williams' American idiom add themselves to Derrida's French, Heidegger's German, and the Greek of Anaximander or Parmenides. The question of the relation of sameness and difference is a traditional metaphysical problem, perhaps even *the* metaphysical problem, as Heidegger argues in *Identität und Differenz*, and as Aristotle asserted in affirming that the law of non-contradiction ("A is A": "A cannot at the same time be A and not A") is the most certain of all principles and the ground of all logical discourse. The problem may be said to begin, for the Western tradition, with Parmenides' enigmatic, "thought and being are the same," or "the same thing exists for thinking and for being."[2] Obviously much of importance is at stake here – for philosophy, for literature, and for criticism. I cannot hope to do more than to raise a few questions and to follow one or two a little further.

One implication of the questions I have been raising is obvious enough. Though this implication is in principle taken for granted in Riddel's book as in most such books, its full import is extremely difficult to see clearly and to respect fully in doing criticism. This is the fact that in an effort of "triangulation" such as Riddel undertakes, in which one writer is interpreted by juxtaposing him to one or two other writers, the other writers can never be taken for granted as solid standing ground on the basis of which to assess the primary writer. The "other writers" must themselves be fully worked through, what is most problematic about them fully confronted. The difficulty is that in the case of Heidegger, of Derrida, or of other writers of similar importance, this might take a lifetime. The apparently solid basis for interpretation becomes a labyrinth of endless wanderings, including wanderings back to the precursors of the precursors, the labyrinths behind, within, or beneath each labyrinth. How can one understand Heidegger without confronting the Pre-Socratics directly, as "primary" texts?

Let me try some paraphrase myself. I shall attempt to produce something which will say the same thing as Riddel's reading of Williams, of Heidegger, of Derrida, though with the awareness that all paraphrase is periphrasis, parody. Basic to Riddel's argument is a more or less strict equivalence between "Modernism" and what Derrida, in "Structure, Sign, and Play" calls the "nostalgia for origin" ["la nostalgie de l'origine"] of Rousseau or of Lévi-Strauss. On the other hand, Riddel makes an equivalence between "Post-Modernism" and what Derrida describes as "the Nietzschean *affirmation* – the joyous affirmation of the freeplay of the world and without truth, without origin, offered to an active interpretation" (*l'affirmation* nietzschéene, l'affirmation joyeuse du jeu du monde et de l'innocence du devenir, l'affirmation d'un monde de signes sans faute, sans vérité, sans origine, offert à une interprétation active": note, by the way, the "difference" here, the absence from the English of any equivalent for "l'innocence du devenir" or "l'affirmation d'un monde de signes sans faute," in spite of the fact that the French for this particular passage is given as a footnote in the English translation in *The Languages of Criticism and the Sciences of Man: The Structuralist Controversy*, ed. R. Macksey and E. Donato [Baltimore, 1970], 264; is this omission of the translator, elision of the editors, error of the printer?). An example of what Riddel means by Modernism is T. S.

Eliot, the Eliot of *Four Quartets*, with their longing for a revelation of the absent center – beginning, end, and ground of human history. Williams is a Post-Modern writer because he puts all origin in question and gives to language a generative power, even a power to generate that nostalgia for the absent origin. "Writing," says Riddel roundly in the concluding sentences of his book, "can only comment on itself [. . .]. Knowledge [. . .] is the ultimate recognition of freeplay, that there is no Truth and that that truth has made us free: 'to dance to a measure/contrapuntally' (*Paterson*, 239)" (Riddel, 301). This sounds indeed like an approximation of Derrida's notion of *la différance*.

Matters are not quite so straightforward with Riddel's interpretative language, however. In every case where something like the clear distinction between Modernism and Post-Modernism is affirmed, Williams put with the Post-Moderns in his commitment to "freeplay," Riddel immediately (or even simultaneously) contradicts himself. He says something which affirms that Williams shares the nostalgia for origins of the Moderns. There are a great many examples of this ambiguity in Riddel's commentary. It forms in fact the basic substance of his interpretative language. An example is the full text of the concluding passage I quoted above. The omitted sentences are pure "metaphysics," with their Heideggerian (and Williamsian) metaphors of hidden light revealed, of "measure" as *logos*, ratio, or "knowledge," and of a "fall" or "transgression" from some primordial state into "language," that is, into differentiation. Such metaphors express that version of Occidental metaphysics which Heidegger has made familiar in his interpretations of art as "aletheia," for example in "Der Ursprung des Kunstwerkes." According to the formula from Derrida which I have quoted as an epigraph, these metaphors are not innocent. They may not be twisted to express the "deconstruction" of metaphysics which is Riddel's ostensible reading of Williams. They drag the metaphysical system of which they are a part in with themselves. This makes Riddel's text not say what it "means to say," or say what it means to say and something else. (But how does one tell what a text "means to say"?) In any case, Riddel's criticism is heterogeneous, dialogical rather than monological. His commentary wavers or oscillates. It can be read in two incompatible ways. Riddel keeps saying there is no origin and then immediately talks about the "mysterious origin." Here is the full text of his ending, with its self-undermining elements restored: "Writing can only comment on itself. This is the 'luminous background' (Williams, *Imaginations*, 315) that shines through the 'interstices' of the poem's measured dance, the difference of the converging lines. The poem reveals to us the first measure, and thus reveals to us that 'to measure is all we know' (*Paterson*, 239). Knowledge, that is, is our knowledge of transgression and of the ambiguous 'light' that lies within the language into which we fell. It is the ultimate recognition of freeplay, that there is no Truth and that that truth has made us free: 'to dance to a measure/contrapuntally' (*Paterson*, 239)" (Riddel, 301).

I have said that such heterogeneity constitutes the basic texture of Riddel's language. Here is another example. At one moment Riddel sounds something like Derrida: "When art asserts its fictiveness, its apartness from nature, its non-representational totality, it asserts itself as the Word, but a Word already demystified. Reflecting itself, the post-Modern poem brings itself into question." The next moment, on the same page, he falls back into Heidegger: "Each poem recalls its departure from the origin and its involvement in the transgression of 'inaugural naming'" (261). Here is another example, in two sequential sentences, the first sounding like Derrida, the second back to Heidegger again: "Williams' 'thing itself' [. . .] is his word for the poem as dance or as city, as the space of a gathering which has no origin outside itself and no fixed center within. The poem speaks the 'myth/that holds up the rock' (*Paterson*, 39), and thus speaks of what can never be unconcealed, the 'secret' of the origin" (75).

The pervasive self-contradiction in *The Inverted Bell* might be defined as the assumption, in spite of Riddel's early recognition of Derrida's "difference from Heidegger" (37), that the metaphysical patterns of Heidegger's late essays and the deconstruction of centered structure in Derrida's "Structure, Sign, and Play" are saying the same thing. They are not. In the case of Derrida there is an attempt to reject all origins and to replace the notion of origin with the difficult notion of *dissémination*, *jeu*, *différance*, or *trace*. In the case of Heidegger, at least when he is reduced to this group of metaphors, the "origin" is seen as an initial splitting of Being, a "fall into language." This has put the poet in the situation of trying to return by way of language to that which even the most authentic poetic language hides as much as reveals. Whether either Derrida or Heidegger can be encompassed in such formulations is not the question here. Of course they cannot. The point is that the two formulations cannot by any means be reconciled. Riddel appears to assume that they can, and so his interpretative language wavers continually back and forth between them.

Heidegger, on the whole, wins the day. There is a continual, somewhat incantatory, repetition, with slight variation, throughout Riddel's book of the same Heideggerian and Williamsian metaphors: "site," "measure," "whored virgin," "mystery at the origin," "original violence," "bringing to light," "regathering," "house of language," "e-mergence," "presence of a presence," "original cleaving," "primordial dance," and so on. The implication is that these figures are privileged in the way they are affirmed to be by Heidegger. They are magical formulas which open the way back to the ground of language and poetry. Riddel's basic paradigm, in fact, and perhaps that of Williams as well, is not that of Derrida's "freeplay." It is the paradigm of a "mysterious" source which violently broke apart or was broken apart into opposites – sexual opposites, opposites of nature and culture, reason and feeling, light and dark, form and power, and so on. The business of poetry is to reveal the radiant gist hidden behind the multiplicity. The notion of primordial opposites locked in some polemical or sexual combat is entirely compatible, however, with metaphysics, with what Riddel defines as "Modernism." It is by no means to be identified with Derrida's *différance*.

Here is a sequence of such formulations from *The Inverted Bell*, to give some idea of the pervasive weave of Riddel's critical language: "But the mysterious unknown, the ground within the ground, remains, and thus the problem of man's measure remains. [. . .] The presence of 'light' is encased in the darkness of the earth, like a primal energy, and revealed or discovered only as the alien of the dark, like the radium within the pitchblende in the Curies' laboratory" (30); "The measure which Williams' poems repeatedly seek is the measure which takes place on this original site, where the pre-tragic steps into the tragic, where the primordial dance of form and power, or word and thing, broke off" (35); "a desire to know the original point where water and rock were one, where time and place were married. [. . .] These are figures of a primordial time of emergence" (53); "The poem, like thought, is the trace of a lost origin, an image of original cleavage" (75); "This origin is only remembered, like a trace that ambiguously signifies a lost power. [. . .] The language of history speaks the silence of a primordial mystery, the enigmatic 'grin' that is a sign of the unconcealed, not a symbol for it" (83); "this history 'grins' its enigmatic secret, but conceals the Word. [. . .] It is also, then, a labyrinth, concealing the mystery of origins. [. . .] It is the mystery of origins that gives history its true presence" (161); "It is [. . .] an effort to restore himself at the violent origins of history, where he can once more be held in the presence of a presence, of a mother and a first wife without whom there is no time" (162–3); "the center of death from which all utterance issues and to which all names of presence return. The old names reveal themselves as simply substitutions for all the other names of presence. For we must name the 'Beautiful Thing' and in naming it violate it, like whoring a virgin, by bringing it to light, to time and place" (170); "That which shows itself comes to light; to come to light is to leave the origin behind. To know the source, then, one must reconstitute it as a fiction" (192); "The deconstructive art of these poems functions linguistically, thematically, stylistically, structurally, to embody as well as exemplify the violence of *aletheia*:

springing, unconcealing, flowering, bursting out, e-merging, and this is the simultaneous breaking down of some previous unity, idea, concept, 'World'" (218); "It is a dance of beginnings, a Dionysian rout, a breaking up of the sacred unity into an original difference, a first measure. And just as it celebrates the original breaking out, the original difference, it celebrates the original regathering, the pleonasm of primordial language" (294).

The constant barrage of such formulations, in slightly modified repetition throughout *The Inverted Bell*, tends to obscure those places where Riddel plausibly argues for finding in Williams the denial that there is any extralinguistic origin which precedes the words of a poem. In such passages Williams is said to hold something like Derrida's notion that all concepts or metaphors of origin are generated as a phantasm by the play of differences within language. Such a notion is carefully formulated in the two essays by Derrida to which Riddel makes most reference. Its differences from the Heideggerian formulas which dominate Riddel's language are exactly set down. One of the clearest of such statements comes, significantly, in a passage in *La différance* where Derrida, by way of a reading of Heidegger's "Der Spruch des Anaximander" (1946), scrupulously identifies the presence within Heidegger's language of something different from the paradigm Riddel has abstracted. This is the notion of "the primordial trace" [*die frühe Spur*] which precedes the metaphysical system and encloses it. The passage is as transparent as any single statement of Derrida's fundamental theme:

> The trace not being a presence but the simulacrum of a presence which is dislocated, deferred [*se renvoie*], which does not in a proper sense take place, effacing belongs to its structure [. . .] In the language of metaphysics, the paradox of such a structure is that inversion of the metaphysical concept which produces the following effect: the present becomes the sign of the sign, the trace of the trace; it is no longer that to which every reference ultimately refers. It becomes a function in a structure of generalized reference. It is a trace and a trace of the effacing of the trace. (*Marges*, 25)

One would need to read sentence by sentence all the pages on Heidegger in *La différance* in order to assess what he is saying. Having found, or claimed to have found, the idea of "archi-trace" in Heidegger, Derrida goes on to distinguish himself from Heidegger on a point which is relevant to Riddel's use of the magical Heideggerian figures. For Derrida there is no single word, no master word, certainly not the term *différance* ("there will never be a single word, a master-name") (*Marges*, 28), whereas Heidegger, in "Der Spruch des Anaximander," retains this much of metaphysics at least, that he still hopes to find some single word, the unique word ["ein einziges, das einzige Wort"]. The Heidegger text, like Riddel's, like Williams', and like that of Derrida himself, is heterogeneous, though this is true in a different way in each case.

What conclusions can be drawn from this incomplete attempt to indicate an incoherence in the critical language of Riddel's book? Is he confused in a way which might have been clarified, or is there some necessity in the deconstructive enterprise which means that it is always open in its turn to deconstruction? I began by saying that Riddel's project is of great importance and that *The Inverted Bell* could be exemplary for many similar studies. There are genuine insights into Williams in his book, insights which put him closer to what is at stake in Williams' work than the far more adroit, witty, and economical reading by Kenner in *A Homemade World*. Nevertheless, Riddel's book may be as valuable for the questions it raises about the procedures of such criticism as for its undeniable accomplishments. There is no doubt that Riddel has been hampered by remnants in his thinking of forms of criticism he intends to abandon, for example, the periodization of literary history or the assumption that the work of a good writer ought somehow to make a self-consistent whole. He perhaps accepts a bit too much at face value the Heideggerian formulas about "*aletheia*: springing, unconcealing, flowering, bursting out, e-merging." His book would have been clarified if he had remained more faithful to his intermittent insight into the difference between Heidegger and Derrida. Though he uses at one point with insight the Jakobsonian distinction between metaphor and metonymy, he would have been aided by a more elaborate rhetorical theory and by a more discriminating attention to the play of figures in his authors.

Another way to put this is to say that in spite of much talk about language in his book Riddel does not enter into the linguistic moment, that is, the moment of criticism which hovers in a prolonged interrogation of language as such. Such a "moment" recognizes that literature accomplishes whatever it can accomplish by means of language. If it is true, as Vico says, that we can know only what we have made, the means of this making is language, or, more precisely, the play of figure in language. Riddel's theory of language, like that of Heidegger, with his belief in "ein einziges, das einzige Wort," is in fact literal or mimetic. He tends to take the Heideggerian figures literally, as referring to extralinguistic reality. For him, there really was some "primordial violence," a "cleavage at the origin" recurrently literalized in the pathos of sexual terms, as the "whoring of a virgin." The violence of literature is, however, in fact all in the words. It leaves things just as they were, with everything changed and yet nothing changed by a single word.

Though Riddel sees that "site," "cleavage," "dance," "light," "measure," and so on are figures, they are, as in the Heideggerian theory of language, figures for a literal happening, an original opening out which the poet re-enacts by means of language. For Derrida, on the other hand, language is "originally" figurative, or rather, since in the absence of literal or "unique" naming the distinction between literal and figurative breaks down, each word is seen as a link in an endless chain of substitutions and displacements, with nowhere a fixed extralinguistic beginning or ending: "there is no *name* for that, not even the name of essence or being, not even that of '*différance*' which is not a name, which is not a pure nominal unit and which ceaselessly dislocates itself in a chain of deferring [*différantes*] substitutions" (*Marges*, 28). This view of language would imply a different theory of the rhetoric of "figure" from that of Heidegger as Riddel presents it. Without denying the necessary referentiality of any text, such a rhetoric would be equipped to identify the way that referentiality always depends on a misreading of figure, for example on a reversal of polarity in an inside/outside figure (metonymy or synecdoche taken as metaphor) or in an early/late figure reversed (metalepsis). The development (or recovery from the past) of such an analytical rhetoric, flexible enough to be used with a wide range of literary and philosophical texts, with prose fiction, for example, as well as lyric poetry, is a major task for literary studies in the immediate future.

Perhaps the most difficulty is caused in Riddel's book, however, by his failure to recognize consistently the necessary heterogeneity of any text. Williams' poetry opens itself to Kenner's reading as well as to Riddel's. Riddel's own critical language is inconsistent. Neither Heidegger nor even Derrida say the same thing, monologically. Nor can the four be reconciled with one another. They can only be juxtaposed in their manifold differences. Riddel's book may in fact have its greatest value in its apparently unintentional demonstration of the irreducible heterogeneity of the languages of poetry, of philosophy, and of criticism. A corollary of this would be the fact that deconstructive discourse can never reach a clarity which is not vulnerable to being deconstructed in its turn. However clarified, refined, or sophisticated Riddel were to become it would still be possible to show that his work is incoherent. In the same way, Heidegger can be shown by Derrida to be "unreadable," "dialogical." Derrida, in his turn, can be dismantled by Paul de Man in "The Rhetoric of Blindness: Jacques Derrida's Reading of Rousseau" (*Blindness and Insight*, 102–41). There are, however, distinctions between more or less self-aware forms of this impasse of deconstruction. I shall conclude by attempting to define the reasons for this impasse, taking *The Inverted Bell* as my example.

Deconstructive discourse, in criticism, in philosophy, or in poetry itself, undermines the referential status of the language being deconstructed. In Riddel's case this is the notion of an extralinguistic origin, the "radiant gist" from which Williams' poetry "flowers." The deconstruction of such referential statements by Riddel or by Williams himself necessarily takes the form of a statement which is itself capable of being taken referentially. It may be read as referring to some extralinguistic situation or event. In Riddel's case this is the idea that the origin was a moment of violent cleavage into sexual opposites. The beginning is defined as difference.

Opposition or difference understood in this sense, however, implies the acceptance of the law of non-contradiction. It can easily be assimilated into a dialectic of contraries and so returned back to some monological reading. The heterogeneity of a text (and so its vulnerability to deconstruction) lies rather in the fact that it says two entirely incompatible things at the same time. Or rather, it says something which is capable of being interpreted in two irreconcilable ways. It is "undecidable." One way is referential (there is an origin), and the other the deconstruction of this referentiality (there is no origin, only the freeplay of linguistic substitution). The deconstruction, however, is necessarily formulated in such a way that it can be taken as referential in its turn, or else it would not be able to perform its act of deconstruction. But the deconstruction has been undertaken in order to deny the referentiality of the language in question. Aporia, impasse, *malconfort*, in which one can neither sit nor stand.[3]

Rather than rejecting the idea of a center, such formulations as Riddel provides merely redefine the center. They are therefore open to a further deconstruction, that in its turn being vulnerable to a further untwisting. This chain is not, however, an infinite regress or a vicious circle. Each such deconstruction is a version of the basic act of reading. It may be performed on any literary, philosophical, or critical text. Each such reading moves through the figurative complexities of a given text and reaches, in the particular way the given text allows it, the "same" moment of an aporia. The act of reading undermines its own status as "act," since it is unable to efface wholly the referentiality of the text in question and also unable to return in peace to a naive mimetic interpretation. The repetition with different texts of this act or non-act of deconstruction leads to a gradual clarification, as the reading comes back again and again, with different texts, to the "same" impasse.

The clearer deconstructions are those which are most sensitive to the complexities of figure, to that range of different figures which current rhetoric is recovering as a tool of literary analysis: metonymy, synecdoche, metalepsis, catachresis, and so on. Attention to the play of figure in a literary or philosophical text is necessary not because figurative language provides an easy transition from the reference of "literal language" to the "freeplay of fiction." Figure is the essential means of mimesis, for example in the assertions of substantial identity or analogy by way of metaphor. Attention to the play of figure is necessary rather because the heterogeneity of any text expresses itself in the fluctuations of figure. Figure is the battleground between reference and the deconstruction of reference. An example is a figure which functions simultaneously as a metaphor, therefore as mimesis, and as metonymy, therefore as the assertion of a discontinuity or contingency which destroys mimesis. Wallace Stevens' last lyrics can be shown to function in this way throughout and therefore to be self-destructive, open to two simultaneous incompatible readings. This is also true, however, of such a Romantic poem as Wordsworth's "Resolution and Independence," with the blank ambiguity of its formulations: "And the whole body of the Man did seem/Like one whom I had met with in a dream;/Or like a man from some far region sent" (ll. 109–11). What is the exact force of "seem" and "like" here? In fact the life of any text is made up of such irresolvable oscillations of meaning.

My account of deconstruction has been misleading, however, if it has suggested that the dismantling is performed from the outside by the critic on a piece of language which remains innocently mystified about its own status. This is by no means the case. The "unreadability" (if there is such a word) of a text is more than an experience of unease in the reader, the result of his failure to be able to reduce the text to a homogeneous reading. It is also always thematized in the text itself in the form of metalinguistic statements. These may take many different forms. The text performs on itself the act of deconstruction without any help from the critic. The text expresses its own aporia, as in the mélange of three incompatible theories of poetry in the prose parts of *Spring and All*,[4] or in the incoherent clues in the text of *Paterson* indicating how the poem should be read. Riddel for the most part does not face explicitly the heterogeneity of Williams or of the other authors he discusses. The result is that he contradicts himself, rather than recognizing fully the contradictions in the texts he discusses. An example is his argument that "Asphodel that Greeny Flower" represents a backsliding to the nostalgia for origins which Riddel finds characteristic of Modernism, while Book Five of *Paterson* is presented as the fullest example of deconstructive Post-Modernism. The fact is that with both poems it is not a matter of either/or but of both/and. Both "Asphodel" and *Paterson Five* are Modernist and Post-Modernist at once, and can be shown to be so.

A recognition of the necessary heterogeneity of any text will allow one to untangle another knot in Riddel's argument, the assertion that there were two distinct literary periods, Modernism and Post-Modernism. If every text is "dialogical," no text will fit any univocal period definition. The idea of homogeneous literary periods must be discarded. Each period is itself equivocal. Periods differ from one another because there are different forms of heterogeneity, not because each period held a single coherent "view of the world." There is literary history because texts are "undecidable," rather than the other way around, since one side of the aporia of deconstruction is always referential statements, that is, statements which point to time and to history. The question of the kind of literary history which would result from the application of a deconstructive rhetoric to the study of literature has hardly yet begun to be answered, though Harold Bloom and Geoffrey Hartman, in their different ways, have begun to write a revisionist literary history. Such a history will no doubt differ radically from the familiar description of periods in sequence with some implicit "progress" from one to the next. One place, however, where Riddel's acceptance of a period theory conflicts with his insight into the complexity of the texts he discusses may be given. Riddel presents T. S. Eliot initially as a prime example of Modernism. By the time he has finished discussing him, however, he is saying the same things about Eliot that he has been saying about Williams: "But such signs in Eliot repeatedly become comments on themselves, and point to the silence of their own center. [. . .] The enigmatic thing about Eliot's poetics [. . .] is the urgency with which it detached art from life into its own self-contained system, thus affirming the artifice of the center as the fiction of presence" (266). If this is true, then *Paterson* is not something wholly different from *Four Quartets* but a permutation of the same irreconcilable elements. This is true, but it is not what Riddel apparently started out to say, and it undermines the period theory on which his book is in part based.

Another way to put this is to say that great works of literature are likely to be ahead of their critics. They are there already. They have anticipated explicitly any deconstruction the critic can achieve. A critic may hope with great effort, and with the indispensable help of the writers themselves, to raise himself to the level of linguistic sophistication where Chaucer, Spenser, Shakespeare, Milton, Wordsworth, George Eliot, Stevens, or even Williams are already. They are there already, however, necessarily in such a way that their works are open to mystified readings. The critic, then, still has his uses, though this use may be no more than to identify an act of deconstruction which has always already, in each case differently, been performed by the text on itself.

Notes

1. Unless otherwise identified, the translations are the editor's. Page numbers refer to the original.

2. τὸ γὰρ αὐτὸ νοεῖν ἐστίν τε χαὶ εἶναι.
3. See Paul de Man's "Rhetoric of Persuasion (Nietzsche)," *Allegories of Reading* (New Haven and London, 1979), pp. 119–31.
4. I have attempted a preliminary description of these in "Williams' *Spring and All* and the Progress of Poetry," *Daedalus*, (Spring 1970), pp. 405–34.

7

The year's books:
Literary criticism

A distinctive feature of English and American literary criticism in 1975 has been its naturalization of recent continental criticism. This is an obvious enough fact, but its full implications are perhaps not so easy to pin down. Another way to put this is to say that literary criticism at this moment is an international enterprise. Even if one is working on an entirely English or American topic, to ignore criticism in other countries is to risk being provincial. It is to risk repeating methodological developments already performed in France, in Germany or in Russia. The opposite is also of course the case, and it is refreshing to see the important French periodical, *Poétique*, giving occasional space to English and American criticism. Literary criticism in the West has always been a multilingual effort, for example in Coleridge's dependence on Kant and Schelling, or in William Empson's early use of Freud, or in Kenneth Burke's brilliant appropriation of Marx and Freud. In the high days of the New Criticism, however, or, more recently, when Northrop Frye commanded much of the scene in Anglo-American criticism, it was easier than it is now to think that one could ignore the blue fumes of Gauloises or the tinkling of Swiss cowbells.

An exploration of this turn in criticism would leave out a number of important books published in 1975. These continue indigenous approaches and are often implicitly hostile to continental criticism or indifferent to it. Helen Vendler in *The Poetry of George Herbert* (Harvard) shows herself to be the most distinguished contemporary practitioner of the New Critical tradition of "close reading." The same tradition is continued in James Kincaid's *Tennyson's Major Poems* (Yale), with its somewhat unexpected use of the terms "irony" and "comedy" to account for Tennyson. Hugh Kenner's *A Homemade World* (Knopf) is *sui generis* like all Kenner's criticism. It is a lively extended footnote or cadenza for *The Pound Era* (1971). *A Homemade World* is a description of the tradition which is antithetical to Pound's and Eliot's: the home-made, American tradition of Williams, Marianne Moore, Hemingway, Fitzgerald and Stevens, though Kenner hardly does justice to Stevens.

Sacvan Bercovitch's *The Puritan Origins of the American Self* (Yale) stays within the continuity of history-of-ideas based American studies, the discipline which has Perry Miller and A. O. Lovejoy as father figures. Robert Penn Warren's Jefferson Lecture, *Democracy and Poetry* (Harvard) is a moving meditation on the fate of the self in American culture and in American letters. Robert Alter's *Partial Magic: The Novel as a Self-Conscious Genre* (California) traces, with elegance and perception, the tradition of the novel which reflects on itself. With the exception of a few references to Roland Barthes, Marthe Robert and Jean-Jacques Mayoux, Alter ignores for the most part the abundant French, German, Russian and Italian secondary literature on this topic. And, as some would say, who cares? Literary biographies, finally, like R. W. B. Lewis' distinguished *Edith Wharton* (Harper and Row) or C. P. Snow's *Trollope* (Scribners) while containing valuable insights into the works of these writers, assume on the whole that the work is a more or less straightforward reflection of the life or commentary on it.

Such work remains mostly innocent, whether innocently or not, of any continental tinge. It is still the case, however, that much of the most significant Anglo–American literary criticism of 1975 would have been impossible without the continental "influence". I use the word here etymologically, following Harold Bloom. Influence is an occult invasion, a flowing in, almost a disease, like influenza. What is meant here by "continental criticism," and how has it been "accommodated," "translated," "appropriated" (all the terms for this are figurative and ambiguous) into English and American? It is an oversimplification to say that the only influence has been French structuralism. There is still a vital borrowing from phenomenology or the "criticism of consciousness," as in Jay Fellows' admirable *The Failing Distance: The Autobiographical Impulse in John Ruskin* (Johns Hopkins). This book is intelligently informed by the critical procedures of Georges Poulet and Gaston Bachelard. Modern Russian criticism continues to exert an influence, as is indicated by the publication this year of *Twentieth-Century Russian Literary Criticism*, a collection of representative Russian essays in translation edited by Victor Erlich (Yale). The strength and applicability of Mikhail Bakhtin's criticism is beginning to be felt. (The translation by R. W. Rotsel of his *Problems of Dostoevsky's Poetics* [Ardis] was published in 1973.) The work of the group centered at the new German university of Konstanz is becoming more widely known, with the translation of work by Hans Robert Jauss in the journal *New Literary History* and in the volume of essays from that journal, *New Directions in Literary History*, edited by Ralph Cohen (Johns Hopkins). Johns Hopkins also published in 1974 *The Implied Reader*, by Wolfgang Iser, another member of the Konstanz group. So-called structuralism, moreover, turns out when inspected closely to be riven into sects and schools and warring individualities, as is always the case with such movements. It divides into Marxists, Lacanians, Derridians, Lévi-Straussians, Foucaultians, Barthesians, Jakobsonians and so on. These can by no means be reconciled to one another as a single homogeneous critical method. One important feature of "structuralism" is its reappropriation, reinterpretation or even "deconstruction" of the seminal masters of modern thought: Hegel, Marx, Nietzsche, Freud, Heidegger, Saussure. It makes a difference, obviously, whether one's father-text is Marx or Nietzsche or Freud.

Continental criticism, then, is sufficiently complex to be irreducible to a single paradigm. Moreover, it intervenes in many different ways in current English and American criticism. One way is by direct translation, as in the translations (the most important being of Derrida's essay on Lacan) in the valuable issue of *Yale French Studies*, no. 52, *Graphesis: Perspectives in Literature and Philosophy*, edited by Marie-Rose Logan. This issue is mostly a repertoire of essays in the current mode, essays by Jean-Francois Lyotard, Shoshana Felman, Michel Serres, Paul de Man, and others, as well as the one by Derrida. Several new or newly oriented literary journals are in fact one conduit whereby continental criticism flows into America: *New Literary History, diacritics, Critical Inquiry, MLN* and *The Georgia Review* under its new editor, John Irwin: it is significant that these contain the most lively literary criticism in any American periodicals today. Translations of books by Roland Barthes have been recently published, and we are promised translations from Genette's three volumes of *Figures* (Johns Hopkins), as well as of Derrida's *De la grammatologie*, with an excellent long introduction by Gayatri Spivak (Johns Hopkins). These will be major events for those who do not read French, as Walter Kaufmann's translations of Nietzsche have been essential to the current revival of interest in that writer in America. Many Americans, alas, if not many Englishmen, are still monolingual and so dependent on the accidents of translation.

Another way European criticism becomes present in the English-speaking world is by direct exposition, as in Jonathan Culler's well-informed and argumentative *Structuralist Poetics* (Cornell). Another way is by overt application, for example in Joseph Riddel's Derrida and Heidegger-inspired book on Williams, *The Inverted Bell* (Louisiana; 1974), or in Herbert Schneidau's admirable forthcoming book on Biblical culture, *Sacred Discontent* (Louisiana, 1976), or in Culler's own essay in application, *Flaubert: The Uses of Uncertainty* (Cornell), or in Jeffrey Mehlman's Lacanian *The Structural Study of Autobiography: Proust, Leiris, Sartre, Lévi-Strauss* (Cornell, 1974), or in Edward Said's brilliant meditation on *Beginnings* (Basic Books). The latter is one of the most successful overt appropriations in English of the new continental tradition.

In other books the presence of such criticial methodologies is more covert. Gilles Deleuze's concept of repetition intervenes briefly in Avrom Fleishman's *Virginia Woolf* (Johns Hopkins). John Hollander makes use of structural linguistics in his elegant, learned, and sensitive *Vision and Resonance: Two Senses of Poetic Form* (Oxford), a book that could only have been written by someone himself a distinguished poet. There is a somewhat hidden use of Foucault in Ronald Paulson's splendid account of the development of "sign systems" in English art from Hogarth to Gainsborough *Emblem and Expression* (Harvard; Thames and Hudson). Paulson's book is informed throughout by a literary sensitivity and by literary parallels, and so may be included here. An encounter with contemporary French criticism emerges somewhat unexpectedly as the most interesting part of Frank Kermode's *The Classic* (Viking), though Kermode wishes to maintain, as against Barthes or Derrida, the notion of a persistence in each literary text, of "a substance that prevails." James M. Redfield makes unostentatious use of structural anthropology in *Nature and Culture in the Iliad: The Tragedy of Hector* (Chicago). John Irwin's decision to juxtapose Nietzsche and Freud with Faulkner in his lively and challenging *Doubling and Incest, Repetition and Revenge: A Speculative Reading of Faulkner* (Johns Hopkins) shows that he too has caught the continental flu. Irwin's account in his introduction of how his book came to be written is a good example of how these influences occur. They seem more likely to happen these days in certain universities than in others: Johns Hopkins, Buffalo, Cornell, Iowa, Yale.

Finally, and most important in the criticism of 1975, are those critics who are themselves central forces in the new criticism, or who are developing a strongly individual criticism partly in deliberate antithesis to it. These would include Jacques Derrida, whose *Glas* (Galilée, 1974) has already established itself as a masterwork in the "deconstructive" mode. A new book of essays by Derrida and several of his French associates, *Mimesis* (Flammarion), has just been published. Paul de Man, one of the most rigorous and pervasively influential of present American critics has published two important essays during the year, one on Nietzsche in the issue of *Yale French Studies* mentioned above, the other, on Rousseau, in the fall issue of *The Georgia Review*. Geoffrey Hartman's brilliant *The Fate of Reading* (Chicago) is at crucial moments a dialogue with what he calls "the School of Derrida." Hartman has dealt at length with *Glas* in the most important English essay on Derrida since de Man's "The Rhetoric of Blindness" (which appeared in *Blindness and Insight* [Oxford, 1971]). Hartman's essay is "Monsieur Texte: On Jacques Derrida, his *Glas*," *The Georgia Review* (Winter). From his first book, *The Unmediated Vision*, to his current work, Hartman has been one of those writing in English who has been most aware of the international scope of the enterprise of criticism, and one of those able to enact most subtly in his writing the drama of reading, criticism being, as has been said, an "allegory" or putting otherwise of the act of reading.

Harold Bloom has published three books in this year, each adding to the evidence that he is perhaps the most dazzlingly creative and provocative of critics writing in English today: *A Map of Misreading* (Oxford), *Kabbalah and Criticism* (Seabury), and *Poetry and Repression* (Yale). In these books de Man and Derrida, "the School of Deconstruction," are the dark shadows Bloom would exorcise, but they are also the antithetical doubles he needs for his own formulations, temptations of the abyss he would fill or show to have a bottom. All three of these books, like their precursor, *The Anxiety of Influence* (Oxford, paper, 1973), and like Geoffrey Hartman's *The Fate of Reading*, have great, if controversial, importance in the *mise en scène* of contemporary criticism. They must be understood, however, in order to be persuasively controverted. Bloom's *Poetry and Repression* will have the advantage, from this point of view, of being a full-scale "practical" application of the theories worked out in the earlier books to readings of the range of modern poets from Blake, Wordsworth, and Shelley through Browning and Tennyson on down to Yeats and Stevens. Bloom is attempting in these books to appropriate the renewed understanding of the rhetorical, that is, figurative, basis of literature. This means, for Bloom, going back through the rhetorical insights of the Kabbalah to those of classical rhetoric. At the same time Bloom wants to preserve the priority of the psyche over language, the priority of the living voice over writing. This is a neat trick if you can do it, and more power to him, since it is a question of power, of the energy which creates and sustains fictions, including even the "bedrock" fiction of the self. That fiction, in Bloom's view, forms and reforms itself as a solid-seeming base, even when it is most put in question.

The exuberant word play of Geoffrey Hartman, on the other hand, is no play, but serious game. It is part of Hartman's developing interrogation of the word. The continuity of this questioning may be followed, for example, by setting Hartman's newest essay on Valéry in *The Fate of Reading* against the essay on Valéry in *The Unmediated Vision* or the crucial use of Valéry in the essay on Virginia Woolf in *Beyond Formalism*. Hartman's work has always been concerned not only with the fate of reading but also with the fate of poetry, which is to some degree the same thing. This has meant a concern with literary history. The somewhat covert center of Hartman's recent work has been a vision of the development of post-enlightenment poetry which wants to keep open the way to the ground of this poetry (the word!), while conducting a somewhat circumspect testing of that ground.

Hartman, Bloom and de Man are members, in fact, of a new group of critics centered at Yale. These critics are by no means unified in their methodological commitments. They share questions rather than answers, but draw strength, often by opposition, from one another's example. To this group may be added Jacques Derrida, who now presents a seminar at Yale in the early fall of each year. The fundamental issue at stake among the members of this group is the question whether the "cure of the ground" which Stevens demands of poetry and of discourse about poetry is to be a "grounding," a making solid of the foundation, as one "cures" a fiberglass hull, or whether the ground is to be cured by being effaced, made to vanish, as medicine cures a man of disease by taking it away. As Stevens says, the rock is air, "nothingness," "the dominant blank, the unapproachable." Is a "cure of the ground" the clearing away of the ground, leaving nothing to stand on, or is it a securing of the ground, making it firm, so one can build on it? Space limitations forbid exploring this difference now. It must suffice here to say that the difference generates the inner drama or *polemos* of contemporary criticism, for example that among the members of the Yale group.

8
Stevens' Rock and criticism as cure, II

> O Socrates, make music and work at it.
> *Phaedo*, 60e

As readers drown under the ever-accumulating flood of criticism, they are justified in asking, why is there criticism rather than silent admiration? If every literary text performs already its own self-interpretation, which means its own self-dismantling, why is there any need for criticism? A poem, for example Stevens' "The Rock," is entirely self-sufficient. It does not need to have one word added to it. Why does it nevertheless call forth so many supplementary words? The publication, in any given year, of an apparently ungovernable multiplicity of critical texts raises the question of the validity of the whole enterprise. Why must there be literary criticism at all, or at any rate more literary criticism? Don't we have enough already? What ineluctable necessity in literature makes it generate unending oceans of commentary, wave after wave covering the primary textual rocks, hiding them, washing them, uncovering them again, but leaving them, after all, just as they were?

The answer to these questions, insofar as there is an answer, is provided by the formulation of the questions themselves, as well as by what can be seen in such a poem as "The Rock." If that poem is a continuous *mise en abyme*, forming and re-forming itself around words or images – "icon," "rock," "cure," and so on – which both name the "alogical" and cover it over, criticism is a continuation of that activity of the poem. If the poem is a cure of the ground which never succeeds, criticism is a yielding to the temptation to try once more for the "cure beyond forgetfulness," and then once more, and once beyond that, in an ever-renewed, ever-unsuccessful attempt to "get it right," to name things by their right names. As Stevens says, "They will get it straight one day at the Sorbonne," and when "I call you by name, my green, my fluent mundo,/You will have stopped revolving except in crystal" ("Notes Toward a Supreme Fiction"). They never get it right, however, neither in poetry nor in the criticism of poetry, neither at the Sorbonne nor in generations of ordinary evenings in New Haven. The work continues, and the world keeps fluently turning, never called by name, never fixed in a definitive formulation. The critic cannot by any means get outside the text, escape from the blind alleys of language he finds in the work. He can only rephrase them in other, allotropic terms. The critical text prolongs, extends, reveals, covers, in short, cures, the literary text in the same way that the literary text attempts to cure the ground. If poetry is the impossible possible cure of the ground, criticism is the impossible possible cure of literature.

A recognition of the incorporation of the work of criticism into the unending activity of poetry itself seems especially to characterize criticism today. Literature, however, has always performed its own *mise en abyme*, though it has usually been misunderstood as doing the opposite. It has often been interpreted as establishing a ground in consciousness, in the poem as self-contained object, in nature, or in some metaphysical base. Literature therefore needs to be prolonged in criticism. The activity of deconstruction already performed and then hidden in the work must be performed again in criticism. It can be performed, however, only in such a way as to be misunderstood in its turn, like the work itself, so that it has to be done over, and then again. If a work of literature must be read in order to come into existence as a work of literature, and if, as Charles Sanders Peirce said, the only interpretation of one sign is another sign, then criticism is the allegory or putting otherwise of the act of reading. This response of new sign generated by old sign continues interminably as long as the work is read.

What, then, can be said to be special in the present moment in criticism? Each such moment tends to feel itself to be a turning point, an instant of crisis, a crossroads, a time when important new developments are taking place or are about to take place. A recent announcement of a new institute of criticism and theory speaks of our time as "a period of crisis for the humanistic disciplines and of concurrent excitement (and attendant confusion) in the area of critical theory." No doubt this is true, though the odds are strongly against 1976 being as important in literary criticism as, say, 1798. Moreover, it can always be demonstrated that the apparent novelty of any new development in criticism is the renewal of an insight which has been found and lost and found again repeatedly through all the centuries of literary study since the first Homeric and Biblical commentaries. The novelty of any "new criticism" is not in its intrinsic insights or techniques but rather in the "accidents" of its expression, though how can "accident" here be distinguished from "substance"? The novelty of an innovative criticism, nevertheless, is in large part in its institutionalization, in the mode of its insertion into the teaching or reading of literature at a given historical moment, rather than in any absolute originality of terminology or insight.

A distinctive feature of English and American literary criticism today is its progressive naturalization, appropriation, or accommodation of recent continental criticism. Much, though by no means all, of our current criticism in English would be impossible without the continental "influence," meaning primarily, at the moment, so-called structuralism. Structuralism, however, can in no way be described in a single coherent paradigm. It divides and subdivides into warring sects, Saussurians, Barthesians, Marxists, Foucaultians, Lacanians, Lévi-Straussians, Derridians, and so on. No critic would accept a lumping of his work with that of the others. Nevertheless, some paths in this labyrinth may be mapped.

The "new turn" in criticism, which is a return of the old, is characterized by a focus on language as the central problematic of literary study. This focus determines a breaking down of barriers and a putting in question of grounds, even of the apparently solid basis of new linguistic theory. This rediscovery of an often hidden center of gravity in literature might be called the linguistic moment. This moment may have such moment or momentum that it prolongs and expands itself to attract into orbit around its mass all the other themes and features of a given work. These become planets around its solar focus, the other focus being that nameless *abyme* with which language can never coincide. This breaking of barriers and questioning of grounds involves a return to the explicit study of rhetoric. Rhetoric means in this case the investigation of figures of speech rather than the study of the art of persuasion, though the notion of persuasion is still present in a more ambiguous displaced form, as the idea of production, or of function, or of performance. The new turn in criticism involves an interrogation of the notion of the self-enclosed literary work and of the idea that any work has a fixed identifiable meaning. The literary work is seen in various ways as open and unpredictably productive. The reading of a poem is part of the poem. This reading is productive in its turn. It produces multiple interpretations, further language about the poem's language, in an interminable activity without necessary closure.

The boundaries between literature and criticism are broken down in this activity, not because the critic arrogates to himself some vague right to be "poetical" in his writing, but because he recognizes it as his doom not to be able to be anything else. The critic is not able by any "method" or strategy of analysis to "reduce" the language of the work to clear and distinct ideas. He is forced at best to repeat the work's contradictions in a different form. The work is seen as heterogeneous, dialogical rather than monological. It has at least two apparent grounds, centers, foci, or *logoi*, and is therefore incapable of being encompassed in any single coherent or homogeneous interpretation. Any reading can be shown to be a misreading on evidence drawn from the text itself. Moreover, any literary text, with more or less explicitness or clarity, already reads or misreads itself. The "deconstruction" which the text performs on itself and which the critic repeats is not of the superstructure of the work but of the ground on which it stands, whether that ground is history, or the social world, or the solid, extra-linguistic world of "objects," or the givenness of the generative self of the writer, his "consciousness."

If the literary work is within itself open, heterogeneous, a dialogue of conflicting voices, it is also seen as open to other texts, permeable to them, permeated by them. A literary text is not a thing in itself, "organically unified," but a relation to other texts which are relations in their turn. The study of literature is therefore a study of intertextuality, as in the recent work of Harold Bloom, or, in a different way, in that of Geoffrey Hartman. The relation between text and precursor text is devious, problematic, never a matter of direct cause and effect. For this, as for other reasons, such criticism puts in question the traditional notions of literary history as a sequence of self-enclosed "periods," each with its intrinsic characteristics: motifs, genres, ideologies, and so on. It also brings into question the traditional study of "sources."

The boundaries, finally, between literary texts and other kinds of texts are also perforated or dismantled. If insights or methods developed in psychology, anthropology, philosophy, and linguistics are appropriated by literary criticism, linguistics, on the other hand, broadens out imperialistically to redefine all of those disciplines. The founding or fathering texts of these disciplines are reinterpreted according to new notions about language, as Freud is reread in the light of modern linguistics by the school of Jacques Lacan. Lacanian psychoanalysis becomes in its turn the basis of a kind of literary criticism. From the point of view of literary criticism, this blurring of traditional boundaries means that a "philosophical" or "psychological" text, a work by Hegel, say, or one by Freud, is to be read in the same way as a "literary" text. This is done, for example, by Jacques Derrida in his reading of Plato in "La pharmacie de Platon" or in his reading of Hegel in *Glas*. It is done in Edward Said's interpretation, in *Beginnings*, of Freud's *Die Traumdeutung* as a narrative text like a novel.

These assumptions about literature are sufficiently different from the traditional assumptions of much literary study in England and America as to take some time to be assimilated. In time they will be naturalized, tested, challenged, refuted, and perhaps ultimately in some form institutionalized in courses, curricula, and the programs of "departments" in our colleges and universities. This give and take will no doubt characterize literary study, in the United States at least, during the coming years, though with how much giving and how much taking remains to be seen.

Already a clear distinction can be drawn, among critics influenced by these new developments, between what might be called, to conflate two terminologies, Socratic, theoretical, or canny critics, on the one hand, and Apollonian/Dionysian, tragic, or uncanny critics, on the other. Socratic critics are those who are lulled by the promise of a rational ordering of literary study on the basis of solid advances in scientific knowledge about language. They are likely to speak of themselves as "scientists" and to group their collective enterprise under some term like "the human sciences." The human sciences – it has a reassuringly logical, progressive, quantifiable sound, "canny" in the sense of shrewd or practical. Such an enterprise is represented by the discipline called "semiotics," or by new work in the exploration and exploitation of rhetorical terms. Included would be aspects of the work of Gérard Genette, Roland Barthes, and Roman Jakobson, as well as that of scholars like A. J. Greimas, Tzvetan Todorov, Cesare Brandi, and Jean-Claude Coquet. Jonathan Culler's *Structuralist Poetics* is a canny and wholesomely sceptical introduction to the work of such critics.

For the most part these critics share the Socratic penchant, what Nietzsche defined as "the unshakable faith that thought, using the thread of logic (*an den Leitfaden der Kausalität*), can penetrate the deepest abysses of being, and that thought is capable not only of knowing but even of correcting (*corrigiren*) it" (*The Birth of Tragedy*, 15). Here is another meaning for "cure." Socratic or scientific criticism, criticism by what Nietzsche calls *theoretischen Menschen*, criticism as cure, would be not only a penetration of the ground but also its correction, its straightening out. The inheritors today of the Socratic faith would believe in the possibility of a structuralist-inspired criticism as a rational and rationalizable activity, with agreed-upon rules of procedure, given facts, and measurable results. This would be a discipline bringing literature out into the sunlight in a "happy positivism." Such an appropriation of the recent turn in criticism would have the attractive quality of easily leading to institutionalizing in textbooks, courses, curricula, all the paraphernalia of an established academic discipline.

Opposed to these are the critics who might be called "uncanny." Though they have been inspired by the same climate of thought as the Socratic critics and though their work would also be impossible without modern linguistics, the "feel" or atmosphere of their writing is quite different from that of a critic like Culler, with his brisk common sense and his reassuring notions of "literary competence" and the acquisition of "conventions," his hope that all right-thinking people might agree on the meaning of a lyric or a novel, or at any rate share a "universe of discourse" in which they could talk about it. "Uncanny" critics would include, each in his own way, a new group of critics gathered at Yale: Harold Bloom, Paul de Man, and Geoffrey Hartman. Jacques Derrida teaches a seminar early each fall at Yale and so may be included among the Yale group. These critics may be taken by a convenient synecdoche as "examples" of criticism as the uncanny, but there are of course others, for example Derrida's associates in France, Sarah Kofman, Philippe Lacoue-Labarthe, Jean-Luc Nancy, Bernard Pautrat (essays by all of whom are gathered in their new book, *Mimesis*.) The American critic Edward Said admirably explores an uncanny topic in *Beginnings*.

These critics are not tragic or Dionysian in the sense that their work is wildly orgiastic or irrational. No critic could be more rigorously sane and rational, Apollonian, in his procedure, for example, than Paul de Man. One feature of Derrida's criticism is a patient and minutely philological "explication de texte." Nevertheless, the thread of logic leads in both cases into regions which are alogical, absurd. This might find a fit emblem not only in the *polemos* of Apollo and Dionysus but also in the marriage of Dionysus to Ariadne. The work of these critics is in one way or another a labyrinthine attempt to escape from the labyrinth of words, an attempt guided not only by the Apollonian thread of logic but by Ariadne's thread as she might be imagined to have rescued it from the too rational and betraying Theseus, or to have incarnated it in herself as the clue to an escape from the abyss by a cure of the ground. As Ruskin says, in *Fors Clavigera*, "The question seems not at all to have been about getting in; but getting *out* again. The clue, at all events, could be helpful only after you had carried it in; and if the spider, or other monster in midweb, ate you, the help in your clue, for return, would be insignificant. So that this thread of Ariadne's implied that even victory over the monster would be vain, unless you could disentangle yourself from his web also."

Ariadne's thread, then, is another *mise en abyme*, both a mapping of the abyss and an attempted escape from it, criticism as cure. This escape can never succeed, since the thread is itself the interminable production of more labyrinth. What would be outside the labyrinth? More labyrinth, the labyrinth, for example, of the story of Ariadne, which is by no means over with the triumphant escape of Theseus from the maze. According to Ruskin, the traditional labyrinth is "composed of a single path or track, coiled, and recoiled, on itself," and "the word 'Labyrinth' properly means 'rope-walk,' or 'coil-of-rope-walk,' its first syllable being probably also the same as our English name 'Laura,' 'the path.'" This is, apparently, a false, but suggestively false, etymology. At the center, "midweb," of Ruskin's image is no male minotaur, but a female spider. The labyrinth is spun from the spider's belly, and Arachne is here conflated with Ariadne. Far from providing a benign escape from the maze, Ariadne's thread makes the labyrinth, is the labyrinth. The interpretation or solving of the puzzles of the textual web only adds more filaments to the web. One can never escape from the labyrinth because the activity of escaping makes more labyrinth, the thread of a linear narrative or story. Criticism is the production of more thread to embroider the texture or textile already there. This thread is like the filament of ink which flows from the pen of the writer, keeping him in the web but suspending him also over the chasm, the blank page that thin line hides. In one version of Ariadne's story she is said to have hanged herself with her thread in despair after being abandoned by Theseus.

In a different way in each case, the work of the uncanny critics, however reasonable or sane their apparent procedure, reaches a point where it resists the intelligence almost successfully. At this point it no longer quite makes rational sense, and the reader has the uncomfortable feeling that she cannot quite hold what is being said in her mind or make it all fit. Sooner or later there is the encounter with an "aporia" or impasse. The bottom drops out, or there is an "abyssing," an insight one can almost grasp or recognize as part of the familiar landscape of the mind, but not quite, as though the mental eye could not quite bring the material into lucid focus. This "abyssmal" discomfort is no doubt the reason why the work of these critics sometimes encounters such hostility from Socratic reviewers and readers. In fact the moment when logic fails in their work is the moment of their deepest penetration into the actual nature of literary language, or of language as such. It is also the place where Socratic procedures will ultimately lead, if they are carried far enough. The center of the work of the uncanny critics is in one way or another a formulation of this experience which momentarily and not wholly successfully rationalizes it, puts it in an image, a figure, a narrative, or a myth. Here, however, the distinction between story, concept, and image breaks down, at the vanishing point where each turns into something other than itself, concept into the alogical, figure into catachresis, narrative into ironical allegory.

In Paul de Man's essays, for example (example in what sense?), there is a sober and painstaking movement through a given text or set of citations. This leads rather suddenly, usually at the end of the essay, to an aporia, a formulation which is itself, necessarily, paradoxical or self-contradictory. The Apollonian here reaches its limits and becomes uncanny, without ceasing for all that to be coolly rational in its tone, keeping its balance over the abyss. De Man might be called "the master of the aporia," though this would be an oxymoron, since the aporia, like the chasm it opens, cannot, in fact, be mastered. "This complication," to give one example of this, in de Man's analysis of Nietzsche's deconstruction of the principle of identity,

> is characteristic for all deconstructive discourse: the deconstruction states the fallacy of reference in a necessarily referential mode. . . . The differentiation between performative and constative language (which Nietzsche anticipates) is undecidable; the deconstruction leading from one model to the other is irreversible, but it always remains suspended, regardless of how often it is repeated. . . . The aporia between performative and constative language is merely a version of the aporia between trope and persuasion that both generates and paralyzes rhetoric and thus gives it the appearance of a history.

In Harold Bloom's case, for example in *Kabbalah and Criticism*, there is the lucid, learned, patient presentation of a systematic terminology, or rather a terminology drawn simultaneously from three or four different language systems, that of somewhat esoteric Greek philosophy (*clinamen, tessera,* etc.), that of Freudian psychology (anxiety, repression, etc.), that of Kabbalah (*tikkun, Zimzum,* etc.), and that of classical rhetoric (synecdoche, hyperbole, metalepsis, etc.). The presentation is so reasonable, so genuinely learned, and so sane in tone, that it is with something of a start that the reader wakes up to realize what outrageous demands are being made on him. Can he adopt such a wildly eclectic vocabulary? *Tikkun? Zimzum? Clinamen?* Transumption? *Nachträglichkeit? Sefirot?* Can he really be expected to make practical use of such terms? Moreover, if the central insight of Bloom's new work is into the rhetorical and figurative relations of intertextuality, into the way each sign or text is a misreading or verbal swerving from a previous sign or text and calls forth new signs or texts which are misinterpretations in their turn, this insight is with difficulty reconciled with his repeatedly affirmed Emersonian desire to maintain the "bedrock" priority of the strong self as the motivating momentum in this dynamic play of sign with sign, text with text. The conflicting demands of sign and self in his criticism form a blind alley, a bifurcated root in his thinking. This double source cannot be synthesized into a logical or dialectical totality. Bloom's self-contradiction is generative rather than paralyzing, however, as is proven by the admirable essays on the major poets of the Romantic tradition in *Poetry and Repression: Revisionism from Blake to Stevens*. The cogs and levers in Bloom's "machine for criticism" proliferate inexhaustibly, six terms becoming twenty-four, the six original ratios becoming in his most recent work doubled again in twelve *topoi* or crossings. The machine, nevertheless, works. It keeps working perhaps through its own constant autodestruction and triumphant hyperbolic replication. It works to produce splendid essays of interpretation (or misinterpretation, misprision, since all strong reading, for Bloom, must be misreading). After Bloom's work we shall never be able to read Shelley or Browning, Tennyson or Stevens, in the same way again. They are changed by being shown to have made their poetry out of changes, anamorphoses, of their precursors.

In Geoffrey Hartman's case there is an increasing tendency to puns and to wordplayfulness. As he says in his essay on Derrida's *Glas*, "I must pun as I must sneeze." This wordplay is carried on, in all Hartman's books from *The Unmediated Vision* to *The Fate of Reading*, for the sake of an interrogation of the *logos*, the ground or *Grund* at the base of all wordplay. The question, for him, is not so much of the fate of reading as of the fate of poetry. It is a question of the vitality of words, their rootedness, the question whether poetry can survive in a post-enlightenment culture. The danger, for Hartman, as he puts it in "False Themes and Gentle Minds," one of the key essays in *Beyond Formalism*, is an uprooting of poetry such as that of "eighteenth century topographical fancies with their personification mania": "Romance loses its shadow, its genuine darkness: nothing remains of the drama of liberation whereby ingenium is born from genius, psyche from persona, and the spirit of poetry from the grave clothes of Romance." True poetry must be like Milton's *L'Allegro* and *Il Penseroso*, which "show a mind moving from one position to another and projecting an image of its freedom against a darker, demonic ground. Poetry, like religion, purifies that ground: it cannot leave it." On the other hand, the danger is that this return from differentiation, which leads from one word to another in endless punning permutation, will reach not a vital source, the ground of puns, but an undifferentiated blur, a meaningless Blouaugh!, like the roar of William Carlos Williams' sea-elephant. Hartman's essay on Gerard Manley Hopkins in *Beyond Formalism* argues that Hopkins' ways with words "evoke the tendency of semantic distinctions to fall back into a phonemic ground of identity. There is, in other words, a linguistic indifference against which language contends, and contends successfully, by diacritical or differential means." Hartman is caught in the aporia of these two irreconcilable models, whose incompatibility both motivates his criticism and prevents it from becoming clear, wholly enlightened. Hovering between a need for the clarifying distinctions of wordplay and a need for the "rich, dark nothing" of the chthonic ground, a ground which may or may not (such uncertainty is the curse of enlightenment) be a vital source, a source in any case both desired and feared, stretched in this double bind, Hartman's criticism conducts its testing of the ground and its covering of the ground, its mode of criticism as cure.

If Paul de Man is the master of the unmasterable aporia, Jacques Derrida is, as Geoffrey Hartman calls him, a "boa-deconstructor." His prodigious effort in the disarticulation of the major texts of Western metaphysics, philosophical and literary, might, however, be more aptly figured in the sinuous emblem of some slenderer and more insinuating serpent than a snake that crushes. Deconstruction as a mode of interpretation works by a careful and circumspect entering of each textual labyrinth. The critic feels his way from figure to figure, from concept to concept, from mythical motif to mythical motif, in a repetition which is in no sense a parody. It employs, nevertheless, the subversive power present in even the most exact and unironical doubling. The deconstructive critic seeks to find, by this process of retracing, the element in the system studied which is alogical, the thread in the text in question which will unravel it all, or the loose stone which will pull down the whole building. The deconstruction, rather, annihilates the ground on which the building stands by showing that the text has already annihilated that ground, knowingly and unknowingly. Deconstruction is not a dismantling of the structure of a text but a demonstration that it has already dismantled itself. Its apparently solid ground is no rock but thin air.

The uncanny moment in Derrida's criticism, the vacant place at the non-center around which all his work is organized, is the formulation and reformulation of this non-existence of the ground out of which the whole textual structure seems to rise like the pleasure dome of Kubla Khan. Derrida has shown marvelous fecundity in finding or inventing new terms to express this generative non-source, absence, forking, or scattering beneath all appearances of presence: *le supplément, le pharmakon, la différance, l'hymen, la dissémination, la marge, le cadre, la signature*, and so on. Each of these both is and is not concept, figure, and infolded narrative. No one of them may be made the ground of its own textual structure, for example, of a discipline of critical studies. Each is eccentric, like all genuine terms, for example those bizarre terms used by Bloom. Of all these critical terms in Derrida's work one could say what he says of *la dissémination* in "La double séance," his essay on Mallarmé:

> In spite of appearances, the endless work of condensation and displacement does not lead us finally back to dissemination as its ultimate signification, or to its initial truth. . . . According to a scheme which we have experienced with the word "between" (*entre*), the quasi "meaning" of dissemination is the impossible return to the rejoined, reattached unity of a meaning, the closed-off way to such a *reflection* [in the sense of veering back]. Is dissemination nevertheless the *loss* of such a truth, the *negative* interdict against reaching such a signification? Far from allowing in this way the supposition that a virgin substance preceded or surveys it from above, dispersing or obstructing itself in a secondary negativity, dissemination *affirms* the always already divided generation of meaning. . . .

No more than castration can dissemination, which entails, "inscribes," reprojects it, become an original, central, or ultimate signification, the proper place of the truth. It represents on the contrary the affirmation of that non-origin, the empty and remarkable place of a hundred blanks to which one cannot give meaning, multiplying to infinity supplementary marks and games of substitution.

In *Positions*, Derrida provides a commentary on "hundred blanks" (*cent blancs*) by making it one link in a chain generating a complicated multiple pun. It is a phrase, like the word "cure" in Stevens' poem, which is a node or knot of irreconcilable or undecidable meanings: *sens blanc, sang blanc, sans blanc, cent blancs, semblant*. Such words, says Derrida, "are not *atoms*, but points of economic condensation, necessary stations along the way for a large number of marks, for somewhat more effervescent crucibles. Then their effects not only turn back on themselves through a sort of closed self-excitation, they spread themselves in a chain over the theoretical and practical whole of a text, each time in a different way." These proliferating supplements and substitutions are the other possible words, none equivalents of one another, which may express the chasm of the alogical, each time in a different way. Each term has its own systematic play of concepts and figures folded into it, incompatible with the self-excitation of any other word.

De Man, Bloom, Hartman, and Derrida, then, come together in the way their criticism is an interrogation of the ground of literature, not just of its intrinsic structure. They come together also in the way the criticism of each, in a different manner each time, is uncanny, cannot be encompassed in a rational or logical formulation, and resists the intelligence of its readers. They differ greatly, however, in their modes of uncanniness and in their attitudes toward their own insights. Even so, their criticism seems at the opposite pole from that of the canny critics, the semioticians or structuralists, diagram- and system-makers, seekers for a sound scientific base for literary study.

The most uncanny moment of all, however, in this developing polarity among critics today, is the moment when the apparent opposites reverse themselves, the Socratic becoming uncanny, the uncanny, canny, sometimes all too shrewdly rational. Recognition of this movement of reversal or exchange is the second climax of *The Birth of Tragedy*, the first being the insight into the interchangeability of the Apollonian and the Dionysian in tragic art, according to the formulation that, in tragedy, "Dionysus speaks the language of Apollo; and Apollo, finally, the language of Dionysus" (*Dionysus redet die Sprache des Apollo, Apollo aber schliesslich die Sprache Dionysus*). If tragedy is this fraternal union (*Bruderbund*), a union which is also a constant brother-murder, Socratic or scientific thought seems at first the escape from all such paradoxes into the clear light of logical insight. Insight, however, becomes blindness when it reaches its limits, and science turns back into tragic art, the art of the abyss, the alogical. "This sublime metaphysical illusion," says Nietzsche, the illusion, that is, that science can penetrate and correct or "cure" the deepest abysses of being, "accompanies science as an instinct, and leads science again and again to its limits (*zu ihren Grenzen*), at which it must turn into art – *which is really the aim of this mechanism*" *(auf welche es eigentlich, bei diesem Mechanismus, abgesehen ist)*.

Such a reversal is occurring or has already occurred in a number of ways within the Socratic penchant of contemporary criticism. It has occurred most strikingly, perhaps, in the way the rational and reassuringly "scientific" study of tropes by present-day rhetoricians – though it depends fundamentally on an initially clear distinction between literal and figurative uses of language, and on clear distinctions among the tropes – ends by putting these distinctions in question and so undermines its own ground. This movement is clear in the best of such critics, for example in Gérard Genette's three volumes of *Figures*. His admirable "Métonymie chez Proust," in *Figures III*, aims to build itself on Roman Jakobson's firm distinction between metonymy and metaphor and even to show them working harmoniously to make *A la recherche du temps perdu* possible: "For it is metaphor which recovers lost time, but it is metonymy which reanimates it, and puts it in motion again: which returns it to itself and to its true 'essence,' which is its proper fleeting away and its proper Research. Here then, here alone – by metaphor, but *in* metonymy – here begins Narrative." But, as Genette's essay has shown, almost in spite of itself, if metaphor is so dependent on the accidental contiguities of metonymy, then the apparent continuity both of the text of *A la recherche* and of Marcel's life fragment irreparably and become mere juxtapositions of broken shards. The "true" insight of Genette's essay, skirted, avoided, circled around with averted eyes, but unmistakably brought to the surface nevertheless, is the exact opposite of its happy claim that metonymy can be a form of cohesion and therefore a support of metaphor, as Paul de Man has obliquely demonstrated, in "Proust et l'allégorie de la lecture," in *Mouvements premiers*. In fact the same contamination of the substantial similarities of metaphor by the external contingencies of metonymy had already undone the clear distinction between metaphor and metonymy in the precursor texts for Genette's essay, Roman Jakobson's brilliant and influential "Two Aspects of Language and Two Types of Aphasic Disturbances," in *Fundamentals of Language*, and "Linguistics and Poetics," in *Style in Language*. A flash of self-subverting genius in the later essay, aided by an aphorism from Goethe, *Alles Vergängliche ist nur ein Gleichnis* ("Anything transient is but a likeness"), breaks down the polarity between the two figures on which the genuinely productive insights (for example into the role of metonymy in realistic fiction) were based: "In poetry where similarity is superinduced upon contiguity, any metonymy is slightly metaphorical and any metaphor has a metonymical tint." The word "slightly" here has the same force as in the phrase "slightly pregnant." It echoes backward to unravel the whole theoretical basis of the essay on aphasia.

If the uncanny turn of current criticism is partly the moment when "the human sciences" reach their limits and become absurd, the fact that this moment recurs is also uncanny. Criticism repeats or reformulates again and again "the same" blind alley, like Freud in "Das Unheimliche" finding himself repeatedly coming back to the bordello section of that Italian town, however hard he tried to escape it. Any "Socratic" method in criticism, if carried far enough (not very far, actually), reaches its limits and subverts itself. The emblem for this might be that recurrent dream Socrates describes in the *Phaedo*. The dream brought an injunction which implictly challenged Socrates' lifelong commitment to reason and logical thought. "'O Socrates,' it said, 'make music and work at it'" (*O Sokrates, ephe, mouskien poiei kai ergathon*).

Examples of this reversal abound in modern criticism. The New Criticism discovered irony and the irresolvable ambiguities of figure. These discoveries subverted, at least implicitly, its presupposition that a poem is a self-contained "object," an organic unity. The criticism of Georges Poulet, basing itself on the assumption of the irreducible priority and "givenness" of the self, of the presence of consciousness to itself, ends by recognizing in consciousness a fathomless chasm. It ends also in recognizing that any stability or coherence in the self is an effect of language. The self is a linguistic construction rather than being the given, the rock, a solid *point de départ*. A similar self-subversion occurs from the other direction in structuralism. In this case, however, it is not the symmetrically opposite discovery that consciousness is the base of language, but rather the discovery that language is not a base. This is the moment of the self-deconstruction of rhetoric. The study of tropes looks at first like a safely scientific, rational, or logical discipline, but it still leads to the abyss, as it did for the old rhetoricians in the endless baroque, though entirely justifiable, proliferation of names for different figures of speech. More fundamentally, the study of rhetoric leads to the abyss by destroying, through its own theoretical procedures, its own basic axiom. Broadening itself imperialistically to take in other disciplines (philosophy, anthropology, literary criticism, psychology), rhetoric ultimately encounters, within itself, the problems it was meant to solve. Nietzsche expressed this aporia of Socratism or scientism in a brilliant passage in the fifteenth section of *The Birth of Tragedy*. The passage matches the double structure of the "cure of the ground" in Stevens' "The Rock":

> But science [*Wissenschaft*], spurred by its powerful illusion, speeds irresistibly towards its limits [*bis zu ihren Grenzen*], where its optimism, concealed in the essence of logic, suffers shipwreck [*scheitert*]. For the periphery of the circle of science [*des Kreises der Wissenschaft*] has an infinite number of points; and while there is no telling how this circle could ever be surveyed completely, noble and gifted men nevertheless reach, e'er half their time [*noch vor der Mitte seines Daseins*] and inevitably, such boundary points [*Grenzpunkte*] on the periphery from which one gazes at what defies illumination. When they see to their horror how logic coils up at these boundaries and finally bites its own tail – suddenly the new form of insight breaks through, *tragic insight*, which, merely to be endured, needs art as a protection and remedy [*als Schutz und Heilmittel*].

If the canny becomes the uncanny and deconstructs itself, the uncanny is also in perpetual danger of becoming Apollonian in a bad sense. Nietzsche also anticipated this moment of reversal. *The Birth of Tragedy* is often erroneously read as granting superior authenticity to the Dionysian, to music, to the irrational, to the formless, which are supposed to be closer to the eternal stream of the underlying universal will. There are passages which seem unequivocally to support such a reading. In fact, however, this error is at crucial moments deconstructed by the text itself. If science is the illusion that seeks to "correct" the abyss, straighten it out, make it solid or rigid, or if science attempts to heal the wound of the abyss, with the suggestion of a sexual absence that must be repaired or filled by some prosthesis, the Apollonian art which intervenes when science fails and recoils in horror from its glimpse of an unfillable, incurable, incorrigible abyss, is no less an illusion than science itself. No less an illusion too is that image of a formless will flowing beneath the forms of both science and of Apollonian beauty. In one extraordinary passage of *The Birth of Tragedy*, the book expresses its own aporia. The terminology of the underlying chaos, of the universal will, "the eternal life beyond all phenomena," on which the book as a whole has been based, the source of the validation of "unconscious Dionysiac wisdom," is rejected as being as much an illusion as the "lies from the features of nature" which are the basis of Apollonian healing and "triumph over the suffering inherent in life." Socratic logic, Apollonian plastic form, and Dionysian music – all three are illusions, and Nietzsche's book becomes itself a *mise en abyme*, the self-subversion of the distinctions on which it seems to be solidly founded. If all three of these "panaceas" are illusions, what then is the will, the "insatiable will" which the passage posits in order to define all veils of the will as illusions? Is it not an illusion too, the third or Buddhistic illusion that the stream flows on beneath all phenomena? The passage, one can see, destroys its own terminology:

It is an eternal phenomenon: the insatiable will always finds a way [*ein Mittel*] to detain its creatures in life and compel them to live on, by means of an illusion spread over things. One is chained by the Socratic love of knowledge and the delusion of being able thereby to heal the eternal wound of existence [*die ewige Wunde des Daseins heilen zu können*]; another is ensnared by art's seductive veil of beauty fluttering before his eyes; still another by the metaphysical comfort that beneath the whirl of phenomena eternal life flows on indestructibly – to say nothing of the more vulgar and almost more powerful illusions which the will always has at hand. These three stages of illusion are actually designed only for the more nobly formed natures, who actually feel profoundly the weight and burden of existence, and must be deluded by exquisite stimulants [*ausgesuchte Reizmittel*] into forgetfulness of their displeasure [*Unlust*]. All that we call culture is made up of these stimulants: and, according to the proportion of the ingredients, we have either a dominantly *Socratic* or *artistic* or *tragic* culture; or, if historical exemplifications are permitted, there is either an Alexandrian or a Hellenic or a Buddhistic culture.

The *mise en abyme* of uncanny criticism, for example in the passage by Nietzsche just cited or in those present-day critics of the uncanny I have discussed, is not the abyss itself in the sense of some direct representation of the truth of things, as Dionysian music may seem to be in *The Birth of Tragedy*. There is no "truth of things," as such, to be represented. The *mise en abyme* of uncanny criticism is rather the ordering of the abyss, the blank, *cent blancs*, its formulation in one or another terminology or figure. Any such formulation, whether it is called "the Dionysian," "the uncanny," "allegory," "*la dissémination*," "the aporia," "*la différance*," "decentering," "deconstruction," "double bind," "cure," "*mise en abyme*," "transumption," "the voice of the shuttle," "signature," or whatever, can quickly become, like any other critical word, a dead terminology able to be coldly manipulated by epigones, mere leaves covering the ground rather than a means of insight into it. The critics of the uncanny must be exceedingly nimble, as de Man, Hartman, Derrida, and Bloom in their different ways conspicuously are, in order to keep their insights from becoming pseudo-scientific machines for the unfolding (explication), or dismantling (deconstruction), of literary texts. This uncanny and yet wholly inevitable reversal of the Apollonian into the Dionysian and of the tragic into the Socratic, the Socratic into the tragic again, like a Möbius strip which has two sides but only one side, is the inner drama or warfare of current literary criticism. The task of criticism in the immediate future should be the further exploration, as much by practical essays of interpretation as by theoretical speculation, of this coming and going in quest and in questioning of the ground.

9
Beginning with a text

The joy in shaping and reshaping – a primeval joy! We can comprehend only a world that we ourselves have made. (*Die Lust am Gestalten und Umgestalten – eine Urlust! Wir können nur eine Welt begreifen, die wir selber gemacht haben.*) Nietzsche, *The Will to Power*, Sec. 495

How should I begin to write about Edward Said's *Beginnings*? Both the author and the book are going to be a little hard to place, both for me and for readers generally. They do not quite fit any of our fixed categories. They represent therefore to some degree the scandal of the unclassifiable, the *sui generis*. Edward Said is a Palestinian from a family long Christian, whose native language is Arabic, but whose early schooling was, as the striking interview essay in this issue of *Diacritics* indicates, in English-speaking British schools in Egypt and Palestine. Said's family has lived for many years in Lebanon, that country whose present disaster, so difficult, if not impossible, for a Westerner to understand, might be taken by synecdoche (whole for part) as an emblem of the violent complexity of a Near-Eastern heritage.

On the other hand, Said's higher education was at Princeton and Harvard (primarily in English literature). He teaches literary theory and modern literature now at Columbia. This puts him within a reassuringly familiar rubric. It would explain the general focus of *Beginnings* on "modernism" in literature, on contemporary continental criticism, and on its antecedents, for example, Vico. This material, however, is put to slightly unexpected uses. *Beginnings* is in various ways unlike any other book on its topics. It resists pigeonholing, like its author. Nor would it have been easy or indeed possible, for me at least, to predict on the basis of *Beginnings* that Said's next book would be the impressively learned and yet polemical study of one aspect of modern Western intellectual and political history, *Orientalism*, which he is just now completing. In the same way, it would have been impossible, for me at least, to have predicted *Beginnings* on the basis of the excellent but still relatively conventional study of *Joseph Conrad and the Fiction of Autobiography* (Cambridge, 1966), which was Said's doctoral dissertation and first book.

There is, in both Said and in his work, that discontinuity which is one of the central themes of *Beginnings*: the difficult concept of a production or assemblage which is not disorder or heterogeneity, and yet not assimilable to the familiar models of order – organic unity, dialectical progression, or genealogical series – in which origin fathers forth a sequence leading without break to some foreordained end. In place of these models Said puts – in himself, in his work, and in what *Beginnings* says about "textual" or "discursive" order – the notion of an assemblage broken by gaps, lacunae, and incompatibilities, a "sort of multileveled coherence of dispersion" (373), which is nevertheless rigorously held together by what Said calls a "beginning intention" and by "method." What such an alternative form of order might be is the subject of *Beginnings*.

I have said that *Beginnings*, like Said's more recent work, resists categorizing. It is, for example, political, even Marxist, in the sense that its ultimate intention is to change the social, political, and intellectual worlds, not merely to describe them. Nevertheless, Said's Marxism is not quite the same as that more usual sort of academic Marxism familiar in America and in Europe as one mode among others of literary analysis, nor is it incompatible with a deep cultural conservatism which immensely respects, for example, the work of such scholars as Auerbach, Curtius, and Spitzer, and which wants to preserve and extend in its own way their example of philological breadth. Said is as much Vichian or Auerbachian as he is Marxist, and in spite of his deep and acknowledged debt to Foucault, it would be reductive to call *Beginnings* simply Foucaultian.

The genre of *Beginnings* is also difficult to define. It is not exactly a work of literary criticism, though it contains brilliant readings of works by Dostoevsky, George Eliot, Conrad, Hardy, T. E. Lawrence, Mann, Hopkins, and others. Texts by "non-literary" writers like Nietzsche, Freud, and Renan are, however, "read" in the same way as the more traditionally "literary" ones, and one of the effects of *Beginnings* is to break down the traditional divisions between literary criticism, on the one hand, and the discussion of philosophical or psychological texts, on the other. One of the most impressive sections of purely "literary" analysis in *Beginnings* is the discussion of Freud's *The Interpretation of Dreams* as a narrative text analogous in form to certain "modern" novels.

On the other hand, if *Beginnings* is not a work of literary criticism in the ordinary sense, it is not a descriptive study of modern literary theory either, in the sense that the works on structuralism by Robert Scholes or by Jonathan Culler are comprehensive handbooks meant to introduce English readers to current continental linguistics and literary criticism through authoritative description and discussion of the salient works in the field. The range of reference and analysis in *Beginnings* is extremely wide. It may appear at first even miscellaneous, but it is in fact highly selective, focused by Said's intentions for his book. The range of authors interpreted extends from Vico through Milton and Swift to Flaubert, Renan, Marx, Hopkins, Hardy, Conrad, Mallarmé, Valéry, Freud, Wittgenstein, Foucault, Barthes, Derrida, and so on – the list could be expanded. One of Said's most attractive traits, in fact, or, rather, one of the most attractive traits of *Beginnings* as a text (since a separation of each work from any paternal authoring or authorizing "origin" is one of "Said's" themes), is a kind of courageous generosity, a willingness to take on and take in an extremely broad spectrum of books, authors, and ideas, both "fashionable" and "unfashionable" (Merleau-Ponty, for example, as well as Foucault; Mann as well as Borges). *Beginnings* both accepts all these scarcely reconcilable "sources" open-mindedly as they are, or as they seem to Said to be, through citation and exegesis, and at the same time it uses them, judges them, appropriates them, reshapes them for its own purpose. This purpose is to make a beginning of its own, and, extending that beginning, to produce a new book, a "text" which will cut out a place for itself and displace the others, at least in the sense that it will take up its own room and keep any other book from occupying the same room on the shelf, or, as the Foucaultians say, in the "archives." *Beginnings*, then, far from being a miscellaneous or encyclopedic survey, a description of books Said happens to have read, is a radiantly productive work of its own. It "intends" "methodologically" to continue until it has made a text, the fat, square book, a material object, the reader holds in his hands when he has obtained a copy.

A further difficulty in placing *Beginnings*, along with the ones involving its politics, its intellectual allegiances, its genre, its form, and its attitude toward other texts, is the way it is in fact about its own mode of production, its own mode of existence, its own function, while seeming to describe, in an "objective" or "scholarly" way, a historical change, "about the last quarter of the nineteenth century in Europe generally and in Britain and France especially" when "the idea of a poetic or authorial vocation as a common cultural myth underwent severe change" (227). The fourth chapter, "Beginning with a Text" (with its description of the "modern" text which copies no archetype and obeys no fathering origin, but goes on constantly beginning again as it produces itself and makes room for itself), is a self-portrait of *Beginnings*, with its internal contradictions and discontinuities, its constant returnings, circling back in slightly different ways to the same themes, its constant self-revision, its beginning anew in each chapter with a new way of moving through the same topics or "places" rather than marching from chapter to chapter through a logical, genealogical, or dialectical argument oriented toward some triumphant QED. The detailed interpretations of this previous text or that, Conrad's *Nostromo*, or Freud's *The Interpretation of Dreams*, or Vico's *The New Science*, are not there for their own sakes or even as "examples" (the notion of exemplification is in any case extremely problematic), but as material essential, like language itself, to the production of the new text Said is making. This new text in the process of making itself makes over those old texts, like all strong interpretation, does violence to them, and thereby constantly and deliberately makes itself open to the challenges of alternative readings. *Beginnings* is an admirable "exemplification" of the aphorism from Nietzsche I have cited as an epigraph, an example of the primeval joy of shaping and reshaping all those prior texts in order to make a new one, a new text which will be known by its producer because it will be a verbal world Said himself has made.

"Said himself has made?" Does not this formulation falsify the detachment of text from authorial origin which is one of *Beginnings*' chief points? Even the circumspect Nietzsche, "for example," in Section 477 of *The Will to Power*, cannot deconstruct the notion of the subject and its power of acting or thinking ("both the deed and the doer are fictions" [*sowohl das Tun, als der Täter sind fingiert*]), without positing at the beginning of the section exactly those fictions of the ego and its actions which he is going to deconstruct and which are nevertheless the essential tools of the deconstruction. Section 477 begins: "I maintain [*Ich halte*] the phenomenality of the inner world too." In the same way, *Beginnings* must constantly reaffirm that concept of the authoring, willing, intentional, appetitive, productive self which its analysis of the "modern" revolution in the notion of the text denies. If one can ask Nietzsche, "Who is this *Ich* who says there is no *Ich*," one can in the same way ask Said, "Who is the 'I' who speaks, for example, on p. 227 of *Beginnings* of 'what I have been saying so far about the writer,' or on p. 226 speaks of 'my notion' that for 'certain writers' 'producing a text is an achievement fraught with problems'?" Like Nietzsche, Said is caught in one important version of the universal impasse of every deconstructive discourse. In order to free the text from the "classical" notion of an authoring origin, he must use as an instrument of disarticulation the concept he intends to deny, thus depriving himself of that instrument in the act of performing the disarticulation, which nevertheless gets performed (or does it?), in an oscillating torsion of thought which twists or bends the mind, when the mind happens to become aware of it.

The reader of a text, according to Said, and according to the theoretician of the text he most often cites, Michel Foucault, should look for what cannot be said as well as for what can be said within the limits of a given "discursivity," and he should look for the creative or enabling contradictions which make the text possible. In the case of *Beginnings* these generative contradictions have precisely to do with the central affirmations and denials of the book, with the constant affirmation and denial of the notion of the willing, productive, generative self, with the constant affirmation and denial of the uniqueness of the "modern" period of literary and intellectual history, and with the constant recognition and denial of the fact that if the notion of "beginning" is to be genuinely different from the notion of "origin," then it must be a beginning which can never begin except over the gulf of its own impossibility, that is, fictitiously, phantasmagorically. Said quotes a striking passage from Freud's *The Interpretation of Dreams* about the creative nub of a dream, out of which the whole tangle of dream-thoughts grows. This nub cannot be reached or named by any mode of analysis:

> there is often a passage in even the most thoroughly interpreted dream which has to be left obscure; this is because we become aware during the work of interpretation that at that point there is a tangle of dream-thoughts which cannot be unravelled and which moreover adds nothing to our knowledge of the content of the dream. This is the dream's navel, the spot where it reaches down into the unknown. The dream-thoughts to which we are led by interpretation cannot, from the nature of things, have any definite endings; they are bound to branch out in every direction into the intricate network of our world of thought. It is at some point where this network is particularly close that the dream-wish grows up, like a mushroom out of its mycelium. (168)

What "cannot be said" in *Beginnings*, without making the production of the book impossible, is just those latent aporias about the self and its intentions, about history, and about beginnings, out of which the book constantly goes on producing itself, like a mushroom out of its mycelium. *Beginnings* constantly recognizes these contradictions, without quite recognizing them, in passages which are like slips of the tongue or of the pen, or like scarcely visible geological faults in the strata of thought making up the book, traces almost but not quite covered over, evidences that something has been repressed which is nevertheless explicitly revealed, in the text, according to that formulation which Said cites, once more from Freud, as an example of the "reconstructions of the examining critic" which "answer" the "violence in texts" with a reciprocal violence of interpretation. "Thus almost everywhere," says Freud in *Moses and Monotheism*, "noticeable gaps, disturbing repetitions and obvious contradictions have come about – indications which reveal things to us which it was not intended to communicate. In its implications the distortions of a text resemble a murder: the difficulty is not in perpetrating the deed, but in getting rid of the traces" (59).

An example of the traces left behind by the murdering effacement of the aporias in Said's thought, aporias which cannot be clearly said or fully followed out without inhibiting the forward movement of that thought, appears on p. 233:

> Another necessary qualification is that whereas I am primarily discussing a period of about fifty years in European (particularly British and French) literary history – years that give rise to a radical rethinking of what it means to create a text – there are examples from other periods for which some of the modern examples are relevant. All writers have faced the problems of the conflict between coherent development, let us say, and the mere dispersion of energy. All writers, certainly from the Renaissance on, have meditated in language upon the peculiarities of language. So while we can and do cite examples from many periods in history, these fifty years provide us with a sustained examination of the issues at other times. Such writers as Wilde, Hopkins, Proust, James, Conrad, and T. E. Lawrence in their works and lives completely transform the text from an object to be gained into an unceasing struggle to be a writer, into what Lawrence called "the everlasting effort to write."

The passage is not wholly coherent. It is a tangle of thoughts which cannot be logically unravelled and which indicates that the reader is here near the "navel" of the book, that which it cannot allow itself to say clearly. The passage says simultaneously three incompatible things: (1) that the modern period (i.e. from about 1875 to 1925) witnessed a radical transformation in the older notion of a text; (2) that this opposition between two notions of a text (as an object to be gained and as a production, is in fact a universal and appears in one form or another in any period of history; (3) that, no, it is not a universal, and not something that appeared more or less suddenly in 1875, but something that appeared apparently with the Renaissance. Similar passages in *Beginnings* reveal momentarily the contradictions in its other enabling assumptions, that about the self, that about the distinction between beginning and origin. The keeping more or less secret of these fissures of thought is the blank spot leading down to the unknown which generates the admirable generosity and forward-moving hopefulness, the superb confidence that beginnings will get somewhere, of *Beginnings*. The motto for this hopefulness might be that phrase from *The Prelude* which Said quotes (47): "a cheerful confidence in things to come."

Let me examine a little more closely the three closely intertwined, reciprocally necessary, affirmations *Beginnings* makes over the hidden abysses of its blind alleys of thought. These abysses lead down into the unknown not in the sense of some extra-linguistic unnamable substance transcending the text (whatever may be the case with dreams in Freud's interpretation of them). There is nothing transcending the text, since with texts all is on the surface. Their mystery is in the open. The unknown is rather that which this particular text cannot say, what is implicit in its words but must not be made explicit, the unsayable whose unexpressed status facilitates the text, makes it possible for it to go on producing itself. The unsaid is in a peculiar sense the characteristic signature of the text. It is what is everywhere and nowhere said by it, like that name hidden (exposed) in large letters across the map in Poe's (or rather Dupin's) illustrative figure for that which is kept secret by being left in the open, said unsaid or unsaid said, in "The Purloined Letter." In any case, all three of Said's basic affirmations are involved in a summary passage not far from the beginning of *Beginnings*. The passage will allow Said to speak for himself. It may be taken as a synecdochic emblem (part for whole this time) of the fundamental positings generating the book:

> The net result [Said has been discussing Freud as an example of the new "method"] is to understand language as an intentional structure signifying a series of displacements. Words are the beginning sign of a method that replaces another method. The series being replaced is the set of relationships linked together by familial analogy: father and son, the image, the process of genesis, a story. In their place stands: the brother, discontinuous concepts, paragenesis, construction. The first of these series is dynastic, bound to sources and origins, mimetic. The relationships holding in the second series are complementarity and adjacency; instead of a source we have the intentional beginning, instead of a story a construction. I take this shift to be of great importance in twentieth-century writing. Indeed, a principal argument of this book is that a strong rationalist tradition in modern writing has for too long been hidden behind a facade of gloomy, irrational nihilism linked to a dynastic ideology. The progressive advance of knowledge, to which this shift belongs, displaces the burden of responsibility from origin to beginning. (66)

The reader will see how all three of Said's positings are interconnected and necessary to one another. He will see also why it is necessary to repress or efface what Said calls, speaking of Jacques Derrida, "awareness of the debilitating paradoxes that hobble knowledge" (341). The primary intention of *Beginnings* is to affirm the possibility of a form of writing which will free man from the oppressions of past cultural, political, and psychological forms, habits of mind, or institutions. Such writing would enter culture to change it. Said wants to believe that writing, even "critical" writing, can make something happen in the "real world," and so he praises "philosophers like Foucault, novelists and critics like Butor, Garcia Marquez, Borges, and Beckett [who] today research, and chart, the possibilities of a new inventive order." (343)

In order to posit a belief that writing can change society, that it is "not the solitary act of an individual, nor the imprisonment of sense in graphological inscription, but rather an act that constitutes participation in various cultural processes" (205), Said must free writing from what he calls the dynastic, genealogical, paternalistic tradition, the tradition of origin. In the tradition of origin, "like father, like son" is the rule. What comes after can only copy, continue, or weakly supplement what comes before. Since the notion of the self as authoring source is an integral part of the dynastic tradition, the self must be denied along with the other elements of that tradition. A beginning, on the other hand, is an act of paragenesis. It starts from scratch.

In order to posit this fraternal form of initiation, however, that "immediate practical application of the mutuality between men which ensues when a repressive central authority is removed" (174), Said must obliquely affirm just that notion of self which he must so vehemently deny when he is cutting off beginnings from dynastic authorities, joining his brothers in killing off the father, so to speak. The self returns in the form of will, a notion essential to beginnings and to *Beginnings*. A beginning is impossible without a willed intention to continue, to create meaning. This intention must be constantly sustained and reworked as the text continues to be produced. The technical term in phenomenological discourse, "intention" (which defines the fact that consciousness is always "intentional," always consciousness of something or other), is here returned to its everyday use, as in "I intend to do so and so." With this return returns also the idea of an authoring self, in however disguised or fraternal a form.

In the same way, the concept of beginning, as Said here and there recognizes, for example in his discussions of Husserl and Valéry, cannot be protected from one form or another of paralysis, or fictionalizing, or infinite regress unless it returns in fact to another form of origination. I will so and so, have an intention to begin in a certain direction, and that intention is the origin of the text which follows from it, however much that willed intention to begin may have successfully cut itself off from prior paternal authority. The brothers become fathers in their turn, as Marx authorized the form of writing we call "Marxist." The responsibility of initiation is shifted from the prior origin of the father to the present power to begin and continue of the posited will. It must be so shifted, if Said is to confirm his positing of the possibility of new texts which will change the world, and if he is to avoid the "debilitating paradox" of beginning, in the sense of paragenesis without origin. This paradox is expressed, for example, by "A," the "either" of Kierkegaard's *Either/Or*, whom Said might have appropriately cited on this topic:

But for those who follow me [says "A"], although I do not make any progress, I shall now unfold the eternal truth, by virtue of which this philosophy remains within itself, and admits of no higher philosophy. For if I proceeded from my principle, I should find it impossible to stop; for if I stopped, I should regret it, and if I did not stop, I should also regret that, and so forth. But since I never start, so I can never stop; my eternal departure is identical with my eternal cessation. Experience has shown that it is by no means difficult for philosophy to begin. Far from it. It begins with nothing, and consequently can always begin. But the difficulty, both with philosophy and for philosophers, is to stop. This difficulty is obviated in my philosophy; for if any one believes that when I stop now, I really stop, he proves himself lacking in the speculative insight. For I do not stop now, I stopped at the time when I began. (Anchor ed., 1, 38)

The irony of this passage is bracing and irresistibly funny, but it is not wholly attractive as a basis for praxis. In fact it is not a basis for praxis at all. One may be grateful to Said for so insistently and so openly raising the question, both in *Beginnings* and in the interview in this issue of *diacritics*, of the possible function or productive effect (or lack of it) of criticism and humanistic scholarship. One may be grateful to him also for affirming a way in which it may begin to have such an effect, even if that requires leaping beyond paradoxes that might block his thought and action, rather than resolving them (which would in any case be impossible).

The third essential element in Said's project in *Beginnings*, the positing of a decisive historical shift in the fifty years following 1875, has already been shown to be built on aporia similar to the other two. It is easy to see why Said's notion of literary history is a necessary presupposition of the project of the productive text which *Beginnings* affirms and exemplifies. It should be said, moreover, that the new reading of major authors of the period called "modernism" as affirmative, rational, and productive, not gloomy nihilists at all but only appearing to be so when measured by inappropriate "dynastic" standards, is one of the most impressive accomplishments of Said's admirable book. His assumptions about literary history are nevertheless problematic, on his own terms. Unless Said can believe in a literary history which is a series of discrete "periods" essentially different from one another, he cannot posit the existence of a period called "modernism" during which a radically new idea of the productive, non-genealogical text was introduced, the idea of beginning "begun." If he admits too openly the implications of the passage about literary history I quoted above, that is, that the elements with which his book deals – the model of paternal origin, the model of fraternal beginning – are permanent aspects of Western culture, present in one form or another, in one proportion or another, and in one intricate relationship or another to one another, in any "period," then the drama of sudden discontinuous change, for example, from the "classical," genealogical novel to the modern novel of beginnings becomes a piece of story-telling or narration by the critic, a fictive projection along a diachronic scale of what is always present as a synchronic tension in any moment of literary history.

If this recognition is allowed, however, it becomes much more difficult to believe that this text being begun and continued now, *Beginnings*, might produce change, and one is back in that scepticism about "going beyond" "logocentrism" or "Occidental metaphysics" by merely willing to do so, which Said associates, correctly, with Derrida. On the other hand, as Said well knows, it is difficult to detach the notion of a literary history which moves from period to period by "the progressive advance of knowledge" from the dynastic assumptions which fathered that view of history in the first place, and so Said must both affirm and deny the uniqueness of "modernism," just as he must affirm and deny the authority of the self, and affirm and deny the distinction between beginning and origin.

Said's choice of Foucault over Derrida, reaffirmed in the interview here, is a necessity of the productivity of his project. Derrida is discussed intelligently but somewhat negatively on pp. 339–43 of *Beginnings*, nor is this surprising, since Derrida might be defined as the overt insistence on the "undecidability" of those contradictions whose partial repression makes *Beginnings* possible. Derrida's work, accordingly, is defined as possessing "nihilistic radicality" (343), but Said finds him "incorrect" in concluding that it is "not a real current possibility" to "choose" for Nietzsche's "affirmative, joyous, forward-looking" attitude as against Rousseau's "negative, guilty, nostalgic" regret for the loss of the Logos at the center. As Nietzsche says in Section 493 of *The Will to Power*, "The value for *life* is ultimately decisive" (*Der Wert für das Leben entscheidet zuletzt.*), and Said chooses resolutely for life.

Beginnings is throughout the enactment or performance of this choice, for example, in its endorsement of Foucault's "attitude . . . in its affirmativeness, its progressivism, and its energetic discoveries" (342). In the courage, intelligence, and generosity of its performance of this "beginning intention," as well as in its comprehensive consideration of the issues involved, even of the inhibiting or, to use his word, "molesting" ones, Said's *Beginnings* is a major work of creative humanistic scholarship, a splendid demonstration of the way it might be possible, after all, to go "beyond deconstruction," though without wholly forgetting its insights.

10
The critic as host

"Je meurs où je m'attache," Mr. Holt said with a polite grin. "The ivy says so in the picture, and clings to the oak like a fond parasite as it is." "Parricide, sir!" cried Mrs. Tusher.

Henry Esmond, Bk. I, ch. 3

I

At one point in "Rationality and Imagination in Cultural History" M. H. Abrams cites Wayne Booth's assertion that the "deconstructionist" reading of a given work "is plainly and simply parasitical" on "the obvious or univocal reading."[1] The latter is Abrams' phrase, the former Booth's. My citation of a citation is an example of a kind of chain which it will be part of my intention here to interrogate. What happens when a critical essay extracts a "passage" and "cites" it? Is this different from a citation, echo, or allusion within a poem? Is a citation an alien parasite within the body of the main text, or is the interpretive text the parasite which surrounds and strangles the citation which is its host? The host feeds the parasite and makes its life possible, but at the same time is killed by it, as criticism is often said to kill literature. Or can host and parasite live happily together, in the domicile of the same text, feeding each other or sharing the food?

Abrams, in any case, goes on to add "a more radical reply." If "deconstructionist principles" are taken seriously, he says, "any history which relies on written texts becomes an impossibility" (458). So be it. That's not much of an argument. A certain notion of history or of literary history, like a certain notion of determinable reading, might indeed be an impossibility, and if so, it might be better to know that. That something in the realm of interpretation is a demonstrable impossibility does not, however, prevent it from being "done," as the abundance of histories, literary histories, and readings demonstrates. On the other hand, I should agree that the impossibility of reading should not be taken too lightly. It has consequences, for life and death, since it is incorporated in the bodies of individual human beings and in the body politic of our cultural life and death together.

"Parasitical" – the word suggests the image of "the obvious or univocal reading" as the mighty oak, rooted in the solid ground, endangered by the insidious twining around it of deconstructive ivy. That ivy is somehow feminine, secondary, defective, or dependent. It is a clinging vine, able to live in no other way but by drawing the life sap of its host, cutting off its light and air. I think of Hardy's *The Ivy-Wife* or of the end of Thackeray's *Vanity Fair*: "God bless you, honest William! – Farewell, dear Amelia – Grow green again, tender little parasite, round the rugged old oak to which you cling!"

Such sad love stories of a domestic affection which introduces the parasitical into the closed economy of the home no doubt describe well enough the way some people feel about the relation of a "deconstructive" interpretation to "the obvious or univocal reading." The parasite is destroying the host. The alien has invaded the house, perhaps to kill the father of the family in an act which does not look like parricide, but is. Is the "obvious" reading, though, so "obvious" or even so "univocal"? May it not itself be the uncanny alien which is so close that it cannot be seen as strange, host in the sense of enemy rather than host in the sense of open-handed dispenser of hospitality? Is not the obvious reading perhaps equivocal rather than univocal, most equivocal in its intimate familiarity and in its ability to have got itself taken for granted as "obvious" and single-voiced?

"Parasite" is one of those words which calls up its apparent opposite. It has no meaning without that counterpart. There is no parasite without its host. At the same time both word and counterword subdivide. Each reveals itself to be fissured already within itself, to be, like the word *Unheimlich*, itself *unheimlich*. Words in "para," like words in "ana," have this as an intrinsic property. "Para" as a prefix in English (sometimes "par") indicates alongside, near or beside, beyond, incorrectly, resembling or similar to, subsidiary to, isomeric or polymeric to. In borrowed Greek compounds "para" indicates beside, to the side of, alongside, beyond, wrongfully, harmfully, unfavorably, and among. Words in "para" form one branch of the tangled labyrinth of words using some form of the Indo-European root *per*. This root is the "base of prepositions and preverbs with the basic meaning of 'forward,' 'through,' and a wide range of extended senses such as 'in front of,' 'before,' 'early,' 'first,' 'chief,' 'toward,' 'against,' 'near,' 'at,' 'around.'"[2]

If words in "para" are one branch of the labyrinth of words in "per," the branch is itself a miniature labyrinth. "Para" is a double antithetical prefix signifying at once proximity and distance, similarity and difference, interiority and exteriority, something inside a domestic economy and at the same time outside it, something simultaneously this side of a boundary line, threshold, or margin, and also beyond it, equivalent in status and also secondary or subsidiary, submissive, as of guest to host, slave to master. A thing in "para," moreover, is not only simultaneously on both sides of the boundary line between inside and out. It is also the boundary itself, the screen which is a permeable membrane connecting inside and outside. It confuses them with one another, allowing the outside in, making the inside out, dividing them and joining them. It also forms an ambiguous transition between one and the other. Though a given word in "para" may seem to choose univocally one of these possibilities, the other meanings are always there as a shimmering in the word which makes it refuse to stay still in a sentence. The word is like a slightly alien guest within the syntactical closure where all the words are family friends together. Words in "para" include: parachute, paradigm, parasol, the French *paravent* (windscreen), and *parapluie* (umbrella), paragon, paradox, parapet, parataxis, parapraxis, parabasis, paraphrase, paragraph, paraph, paralysis, paranoia, paraphernalia, parallel, parallax, parameter, parable, paresthesia, paramnesia, paramorph, paramecium, Paraclete, paramedical, paralegal – and parasite.

"Parasite" comes from the Greek *parasitos*, "beside the grain," *para*, beside (in this case) plus *sitos*, grain, food. "Sitology" is the science of foods, nutrition, and diet. A parasite was originally something positive, a fellow guest, someone sharing the food with you, there with you beside the grain. Later on, "parasite" came to mean a professional dinner guest, someone expert at cadging invitations without ever giving dinners in return. From this developed the two main modern meanings in English, the biological and the social. A parasite is "Any organism that grows, feeds, and is sheltered on or in a different organism while contributing nothing to the survival of its host"; or "A person who habitually takes advantage of the generosity of others without making any useful return." To call a kind of criticism "parasitical" is, in either case, strong language.

A curious system of thought, or of language, or of social organization (in fact all three at once) is implicit in the word parasite. There is no parasite without a host. The host and the somewhat sinister or subversive parasite are fellow guests beside the food, sharing it. On the other hand, the host is himself the food, his substance consumed without recompense, as when one says, "He is eating me out of house and home." The host may then become host in another sense, not etymologically connected. The word "host" is of course the name for the consecrated bread or wafer of the Eucharist, from Middle English *oste*, from Latin *hostia*, sacrifice, victim.

If the host is both eater and eaten, he also contains in himself the double antithetical relation of host and guest, guest in the bifold sense of friendly presence and alien invader. The words "host" and "guest" go back in fact to the same etymological root: *ghos-ti*, stranger, guest, host, properly "someone with whom one has reciprocal duties of hospitality." The modern English word "host" in this alternative sense comes from the Middle English *(h)oste*, from Old French, host, guest, from Latin *hospes* (stem *hospit-*), guest, host, stranger. The "pes" or "pit" in the Latin words and in such modern English words as "hospital" and "hospitality" is from another root, *pot*, meaning "master." The compound or bifurcated root *ghos-pot* meant "master of guests," "one who symbolizes the relationship of reciprocal hospitality," as in the Slavic *gospodi*, Lord, sir, master. "Guest," on the other hand, is from Middle English *gest*, from Old Norse *gestr*, from *ghos-ti*, the same root as for "host." A host is a guest, and a guest is a host. A host is a host. The relation of household master offering hospitality to a guest and the guest receiving it, of host and parasite in the original sense of "fellow guest," is inclosed within the word "host" itself.

A host in the sense of a guest, moreover, is both a friendly visitor in the house and at the same time an alien presence who turns the home into a hotel, a neutral territory. Perhaps he is the first emissary of a host of enemies (from Latin *hostis* [stranger, enemy]), the first foot in the door, followed by a swarm of hostile strangers, to be met only by our own host, as the Christian deity is the Lord God of Hosts. The uncanny antithetical relation exists not only between pairs of words in this system, host and parasite, host and guest, but within each word in itself. It reforms itself in each polar opposite when that opposite is separated out. This subverts or nullifies the apparently unequivocal relation of polarity which seems the conceptual scheme appropriate for thinking through the system. Each word in itself becomes divided by the strange logic of the "para," membrane which divides inside from outside and yet joins them in a hymeneal bond, or which allows an osmotic mixing, making the stranger friend, the distant near, the *Unheimlich heimlich*, the homely homey, without, for all its closeness and similarity, ceasing to be strange, distant, and dissimilar.

One of the most frightening versions of the parasite as invading host is the virus. In this case, the parasite is an alien who has not simply the ability to invade a domestic enclosure, consume the food of the family, and kill the host, but the strange capacity, in doing all that, to turn the host into multitudinous proliferating replications of itself. The virus is at the uneasy border between life and death. It challenges that opposition, since, for example, it does not "eat," but only reproduces. It is as much a crystal or a component in a crystal as it is an organism. The genetic pattern of the virus is so coded that it can enter a host cell and violently reprogram all the generic material in that cell, turning the cell into a little factory for manufacturing copies of itself, so destroying it. This is *The Ivy-Wife* with a vengeance.

Is this an allegory, and if so, of what? The use by modern geneticists of an "analogy" (but what is the ontological status of this analogy?) between genetic reproduction and the social interchanges carried by language or other sign systems may justify a transfer back in the other direction. Is "deconstructive criticism" like a virus which invades the host of an innocently metaphysical text, a text with an "obvious or univocal meaning," carried by a single referential grammar? Does such criticism ferociously reprogram the *gramme* of the host text to make it utter its own message, the "uncanny," the "aporia," "la différance," or what have you? Some people have said so. Could it, on the other hand, be the other way around? Could it be that metaphysics, the obvious or univocal meaning, is the parasitical virus which has for millennia been passed from generation to generation in Western culture in its languages and in the privileged texts of those languages? Does metaphysics enter the language-learning apparatus of each new baby born into that culture and shape the apparatus after its own patterns? The difference might be that this apparatus, unlike the host cell for a virus, does not have its own pre-existing inbuilt genetic code.

Is that so certain, however? Is the system of metaphysics "natural" to man, as it is natural for a cuckoo to sing "cuckoo" or for a bee to build its comb in hexagonal cells? If so, the parasitical virus would be a friendly presence carrying the same message already genetically programmed within its host. The message would predispose all European babies or perhaps all earth babies to read Plato and become Platonists, so that anything else would require some unimaginable mutation of the species man. Is the prison house of language an exterior constraint or is it part of the blood, bones, nerves, and brain of the prisoner? Could that incessant murmuring voice that speaks always within me or constantly weaves the web of language there, even in my dreams, be an uncanny guest, a parasitical virus, and not a member of the family? How could one even ask that question, since it must be asked in words provided by the murmuring voice? Is it not that voice speaking here and now? Perhaps, after all, the analogy with viruses is "only an analogy," a "figure of speech," and need not be taken seriously.

What does this have to do with poems and with the reading of poems? It is meant as an "example" of the deconstructive strategy of interpretation. The procedure is applied, in this case, not to the text of a poem but to the cited fragment of a critical essay containing within itself a citation from another essay, like a parasite within its host. The "example" is a fragment like those minuscule bits of some substance which are put into a tiny test tube and explored by certain techniques of analytical chemistry. To get so far or so much out of a little piece of language, context after context widening out from these few phrases to include as their necessary milieux all the family of Indo–European languages, all the literature and conceptual thought within those languages, and all the permutations of our social structures of household economy, gift-giving and gift-receiving – this is an argument for the value of recognizing the equivocal richness of apparently obvious or univocal language, even of the language of criticism. Criticism is in this respect, if in no other, continuous with the language of literature. This equivocal richness, my discussion of "parasite" implies, resides in part in the fact that there is no conceptual expression without figure, and no intertwining of concept and figure without an implied narrative, in this case the story of the alien guest in the home. Deconstruction is an investigation of what is implied by this inherence in one another of figure, concept, and narrative.

My example presents a model for the relation of critic to critic, for the incoherence within a single critic's language, for the asymmetrical relation of critical text to poem, for the incoherence within any single literary text, and for the skewed relation of a poem to its predecessors. To speak of the "deconstructive" reading of a poem as "parasitical" on the "obvious or univocal reading" is to enter willynilly into the strange logic of the parasite, to make the univocal equivocal in spite of oneself, according to the law that language is not an instrument or tool in human hands, a submissive means of thinking. Language rather thinks human beings and their "world," including poems, if they will allow it to do so.

The system of figurative thought (but what thought is not figurative?) inscribed within the word parasite and its associates, host and guest, invites us to recognize that the "obvious or univocal reading" of a poem is not identical to the poem itself. Both readings, the "univocal" one and the "deconstructive" one, are fellow guests "beside the grain," host and guest, host and host, host and parasite, parasite and parasite. The relation is a triangle, not a polar opposition. There is always a third to whom the two are related, something before them or between them, which they divide, consume, or exchange, across which they meet. The relation in question is always in fact a chain. It is a strange sort of chain without beginning or end, a chain in which no commanding element (origin, goal, or underlying principle) may be identified. In such a chain there is always something earlier or something later to which any link on which one focuses refers and which keeps the series open. The relation between any two contiguous elements in this chain is a strange opposition which is of intimate kinship and at the same time of enmity. It cannot be encompassed by the ordinary logic of polar opposition. It is not open to dialectical synthesis. Each "single element," moreover, far from being unequivocally what it is, subdivides within itself to recapitulate the relation of parasite and host of which, on the larger scale, it appears to be one or the other pole. On the one hand, the "obvious or univocal reading" always contains the "deconstructive reading" as a parasite encrypted within itself as part of itself. On the other hand, the "deconstructive" reading can by no means free itself from the metaphysical reading it means to contest. The poem in itself, then, is neither the host nor the parasite but the food they both need, host in another sense, the third element in this particular triangle. Both readings are at the same table together, bound by a strange relation of reciprocal obligation, of gift or food-giving and gift or food-receiving.

The poem, in my figure, is that ambiguous gift, food, host in the sense of victim, sacrifice. It is broken, divided, passed around, consumed by the critics canny and uncanny who are in that odd relation to one another of host and parasite. Any poem, however, is parasitical in its turn on earlier poems, or it contains earlier poems within itself as enclosed parasites, in another version of the perpetual reversal of parasite and host. If the poem is food and poison for the critics, it must in its turn have eaten. It must have been a cannibal consumer of earlier poems.

Take, for example, Shelley's *The Triumph of Life*. It is inhabited, as its critics have shown, by a long chain of parasitical presences – echoes, allusions, guests, ghosts of previous texts. These are present within the domicile of the poem in that curious phantasmal way, affirmed, negated, sublimated, twisted, straightened out, travestied, which Harold Bloom has begun to study and which it is one major task of literary interpretation today to investigate further and to define. The previous text is both the ground of the new one and something the new poem must annihilate by incorporating it, turning it into ghostly insubstantiality, so that the new poem may perform its possible–impossible task of becoming its own ground. The new poem both needs the old texts and must destroy them. It is both parasitical on them, feeding ungraciously on their substance, and at the same time it is the sinister host which unmans them by inviting them into its home, as the Green Knight invites Gawain. Each previous link in the chain, in its turn, played the same role, as host and parasite, in relation to its predecessors. From the Old to the New Testaments, from Ezekiel to Revelation, to Dante, to Ariosto, to Spenser, to Milton, to Rousseau, to Wordsworth and Coleridge, the chain leads ultimately to *The Triumph of Life*. That poem, in its turn, or Shelley's work generally, is present within the work of Hardy or Yeats or Stevens and forms part of a sequence in the major texts of Romantic "nihilism" including Nietzsche, Freud, Heidegger, and Blanchot. This perpetual re-expression of the relation of host and parasite forms itself again today in current criticism. It is present, for example, in the relation between "univocal" and "deconstructionist" readings of *The Triumph of Life*, between the reading of Meyer Abrams and that of Harold Bloom, or between Abrams' reading of Shelley and the one I am proposing here, or within the work of each one of these critics taken separately. The inexorable law which makes the "alogical" relation of host and parasite re-form itself within each separate entity which had seemed, on the larger scale, to be one or the other, applies as much to critical essays as to the texts they treat. *The Triumph of Life* contains within itself, jostling irreconcilably with one another, both logocentric metaphysics and nihilism. It is no accident that critics have disagreed about it. The meaning of *The Triumph of Life* can never be reduced to any "univocal" reading, neither the "obvious" one nor a single-minded deconstructionist one, if there could be such a thing, which there cannot. The poem, like all texts, is "unreadable," if by "readable" one means a single, definitive interpretation. In fact, neither the "obvious" reading nor the "deconstructionist" reading is "univocal." Each contains, necessarily, its enemy within itself, is itself both host and parasite. The deconstructionist reading contains the obvious one and vice versa. Nihilism is an inalienable alien presence with Occidental metaphysics, both in poems and in the criticism of poems.

II

Nihilism – that word has inevitably come up as a label for "deconstruction," secretly or overtly present as the name for what is feared from the new mode of criticism and from its ability to devalue all values, making traditional modes of interpretation "impossible." What is nihilism? Here the analysis may be helped by a chain which goes from Friedrich Nietzsche to Ernst Jünger to Martin Heidegger.

The first book of Nietzsche's *The Will to Power*, in the ordering by his sister, Elizabeth Förster-Nietzsche, of the *Nachlass*, is entitled "European Nihilism." The beginning of the first section of this book is as follows: "Nihilism stands at the door: whence comes this uncanniest of all guests?" (*"Der Nihilismus steht vor der Tür: woher kommt uns dieser unheimlichste aller Gäste?"*)[3]

Heidegger's comment on this comes near the beginning of his essay on Ernst Jünger's *Uber die Linie*. The title of Heidegger's essay was later changed to *Zur Seinsfrage, The Question of Being*. Heidegger's essay takes the form of a letter to Jünger:

> It is called the "uncanniest" [*der "unheimlichste"*] because as the unconditional will to will, it wants homelessness as such [*die Heimatlosigkeit als solche*]. Therefore, it does not help to show it the door because it has long since and invisibly been moving around in the house. The important thing is to get a glimpse of the guest and to see through it. You [Jünger] write:

"A good definition of nihilism would be comparable to making the cancer bacillus visible. It would not signify a cure but perhaps the presupposition of it, insofar as men contribute anything toward it." . . . Nihilism itself, as little as the cancer bacillus, is something diseased. In regard to the *essence* of nihilism there is no prospect and no meaningful claim to a cure. . . . The essence of nihilism is neither healable nor unhealable. It is the heal-less [*das Heil-lose*], but as such a unique relegation into health [*eine einzigartige Verweisung ins Heile*].[4]

For these three writers, link after link in a chain, the confrontation of nihilism cannot be detached from the system of terms I have been exploring. To put this another way, the system of terms involves inevitably a confrontation with the uncanniest of guests, nihilism. Nihilism is somehow inherent in the relation of parasite and host. Inherent also is the imagery of sickness and health. Health for the parasite, food and the right environment, may be illness, even mortal illness, for the host. On the other hand, there are innumerable cases, in the proliferation of life forms, where the presence of a parasite is absolutely necessary to the health of its host. Moreover, if nihilism is the "heal-less" as such, a wound which may not be closed, an attempt to understand that fact might be a condition of health. The attempt to pretend that this uncanniest of guests is not present in the house might be the worst of all illnesses, the nagging, surly, covert, unidentified kind, there as a general malaise which undermines all activities, depriving them of joy.

The uncanniest guest is nihilism, "*hôte fantôme*," in Jacques Derrida's phrase, "*hôte qui hante plutôt qu'il n'habite*, guest *et* ghost *d'une inquiétante étrangeté.*" Nihilism has already made itself at home within Occidental metaphysics. Nihilism is the latent ghost encrypted within any expression of a logocentric system, for example in Shelley's *The Triumph of Life*, or in any interpretation of such a text, for example in Meyer Abrams' reading of *The Triumph of Life* or in reversed form in Harold Bloom's reading. The two, logocentrism and nihilism, are related to one another in a way which is not antithesis and which may not be synthesized in any dialectical *Aufhebung*. Each defines and is hospitable to the other, host to it as parasite. Yet each is the mortal enemy of the other, invisible to the other, as its phantom unconscious, that is, as something of which it cannot by definition be aware.

If nihilism is the parasitical stranger within the house of metaphysics, "nihilism," as the name for the devaluation or reduction to nothingness of all values, is not the name nihilism has "in itself." It is the name given to it by metaphysics, as the term "unconscious" is given by consciousness to that part of itself which it cannot face directly. In attempting to expel that other than itself contained within itself, logocentric metaphysics deconstitutes itself, according to a regular law which can be demonstrated in the self-subversion of all the great texts of Western metaphysics from Plato onward. Metaphysics contains its parasite within itself, as the "unhealable" which it tries, unsuccessfully, to cure. It attempts to cover over the unhealable by annihilating the nothingness hidden within itself.

Is there any way to break this law, to turn the system around? Would it be possible to approach metaphysics from the standpoint of "nihilism"? Could one make nihilism the host of which metaphysics is the alien guest, so giving new names to both? Nihilism would then not be nihilism but something else, something without a melodramatic aura, perhaps something so innocent-sounding as "rhetoric," or "philology," or "the study of tropes," or even "the trivium." Metaphysics might then be redefined, from the point of view of this trivium, as an inevitable rhetorical or tropological effect. It would not be a cause but a phantom generated within the house of language by the play of language. "Deconstruction" is one current name for this reversal.

The present-day procedure of "deconstruction," of which Nietzsche is one of the patrons, is not, however, new in our own day. It has been repeated regularly in one form or another in all the centuries since the Greek Sophists and rhetoricians, since in fact Plato himself, who in *The Sophist* has enclosed his own self-deconstruction within the canon of his own writing. If deconstruction could liberate us from the prisonhouse of language, it would seem that it should have long since done so, and yet it has not. There must be something wrong with the machinery of demolition, or some inexpertness in its operator, or perhaps the definition of it as liberating is incorrect. The *fröhliche Wissenschaft* of Nietzsche, his attempt to move beyond metaphysics to an affirmative, life-enhancing, performative act of language, is posited on a dismantling of metaphysics which shows it as leading to nihilism by an inevitable process whereby "the highest values devaluate themselves." The values are not devaluated by something subversive outside themselves. Nihilism is not a social or psychological or even world historical phenomenon. It is not a new or perhaps cyclically reappearing phenomenon in the history of "spirit" or of "Being." The highest values devalue themselves. Nihilism is a parasite always already at home within its host, Western metaphysics. This is stated as a "point of departure" (*Ausgangspunkt*) at the beginning of *Zum Plan* ("Towards an Outline"), at the opening of Book I of *The Will to Power*, just after the sentence defining nihilism as "this uncanniest of all guests":

> . . . It is an error to consider "social distress" or "psychological degeneration" or, worse, corruption as the *cause* of nihilism. . . . Distress, whether of the soul, body, or intellect, cannot of itself give birth to nihilism (i.e. the radical repudiation of value, meaning, and desirability).

Such distress always permits a variety of interpretations. Rather: it is in one particular interpretation, the Christian-moral one, that nihilism is rooted.[5]

Would it be possible, then, to escape from the endless generation out of itself by metaphysics of nihilism, and the endless resubmission of nihilism to the metaphysics which defines it and is the condition of its existence? Is "deconstruction" this new way, a new threefold way out of the labyrinth of human history, which is the history of error, into the sunlit forum of truth and clarity, all ways made straight at last? Can semiotics, rhetoric, and tropology substitute for the old grammar, rhetoric, and logic? Would it be possible to be freed at last from the nightmare of an endless brother battle, Shem replacing Shaun, and Shaun Shem?

I do not think so. "Deconstruction" is neither nihilism nor metaphysics but simply interpretation as such, the untangling of the inherence of metaphysics in nihilism and of nihilism in metaphysics by way of the close reading of texts. This procedure, however, can in no way escape, in its own discourse, from the language of the passages it cites. This language is the expression of the inherence of nihilism in metaphysics and of metaphysics in nihilism. We have no other language. The language of criticism is subject to exactly the same limitations and blind alleys as the language of the works it reads. The most heroic effort to escape from the prisonhouse of language only builds the walls higher.

The deconstructive procedure, however, by reversing the relation of ghost and host, by playing on the play within language, may go beyond the repetitive generation of nihilism by metaphysics and of metaphysics by nihilism. It may reach something like that *fröhliche Wissenschaft* for which Nietzsche called. This would be interpretation as joyful wisdom, the greatest joy in the midst of the greatest suffering, an inhabitation of that gaiety of language which is our seigneur.

Deconstruction does not provide an escape from nihilism, nor from metaphysics, nor from their uncanny inherence in one another. There is no escape. It does, however, move back and forth within this inherence. It makes the inherence oscillate in such a way that one enters a strange borderland, a frontier region which seems to give the widest glimpse into the other land ("beyond metaphysics"), though this land may not by any means be entered and does not in fact exist for Western man. By this form of interpretation, however, the border zone itself may be made sensible, as quattrocento painting makes the Tuscan air visible in its invisibility. The zone may be appropriated in the torsion of the mind's expropriation, its experience of an inability to comprehend logically. This procedure is an attempt to reach clarity in a region where clarity is not possible. In the failure of that attempt, however, something moves, a limit is encountered. This encounter may be compared to the uncanny experience of reaching a frontier where there is no visible barrier, as when Wordsworth found he had crossed the Alps without knowing he was doing so. It is as if the "prisonhouse of language" were like that universe finite but unbounded which some modern cosmologies posit. One may move everywhere freely within this enclosure without ever encountering a wall, and yet it is limited. It is a prison, a milieu without origin or edge. Such a place is therefore all frontier zone without either peaceful homeland, in one direction, land of hosts and domesticity, or, in the other direction, any alien land of hostile strangers, "beyond the line."

The place we inhabit, wherever we are, is always this in-between zone, place of host and parasite, neither inside nor outside. It is a region of the *Unheimlich*, beyond any formalism, which reforms itself wherever we are, if we know where we are. This "place" is where we are, in whatever text, in the most inclusive sense of that word, we happen to be living. This may be made to appear, however, only by an extreme interpretation of that text, going as far as one can with the terms the work provides. To this form of interpretation, which is interpretation as such, one name given at the moment is "deconstruction."

III

As an "example" of the word "parasite" functioning parasitically within the "body" of work by one author, I turn now to an analysis of the word in Shelley.

The word "parasite" does not appear in *The Triumph of Life*. That poem, however, is structured throughout around the parasitical relationship. *The Triumph of Life* may be defined as an exploration of various forms of the parasitical relation. The poem is governed by the imagery of light and shadow or of light differentiated within itself. The poem is a series of personifications and scenes each of which gives a figurative "shape" (Shelley's word) to a light which remains the "same" in all its personifications. The figurative shape makes the light a shadow. Any reading of the poem must thread its way through repeated configurations of the polarity of light and shadow. It must also identify the relation of one scene to the next which replaces it as sunlight puts out the morning star, and the star again the sun. That star is Lucifer, Venus, Vesper, all at once. The polarity constantly reforming itself within a light which turns into shadow in the presence of a novel light is the vehicle which carries, or is carried by, the structure of dream vision within dream vision and of person confronting or replacing precursor person. This structure is repeated throughout the poem. These repetitions make the poem a *mise en abyme* of reflections within reflections or a nest of Chinese boxes. This relation exists within the poem, for example, in the juxtaposition of the poet's vision and the prior vision which is narrated by Rousseau within the poet's vision. Rousseau's vision comes later in the linear sequence of the poem but earlier in "chronological" time. It puts early late, metaleptically, as late's explanatory predecessor. The relation in question also exists in the encapsulation in the poem of echoes and references to a long chain of previous texts in which the emblematic chariot or other figures of the poem have appeared: Ezekiel, Revelation, Virgil, Dante, Spenser, Milton, Rousseau, Wordsworth. Shelley's poem in its turn is echoed by Hardy, by Yeats, and by many others.

This relation inside the poem between one part of it and another, or the relation of the poem to previous and later texts, is a version of the relation of parasite to host. It exemplifies the undecidable oscillation of that relation. It is impossible to decide which element is parasite, which host, which commands or encloses the other. It is impossible to decide whether the series should be thought of as a sequence of elements each external to the next or according to some model of enclosure like that of the Chinese boxes. When the latter model is applied it is impossible to decide which element of any pair is outside, which is inside. In short, the distinction between inside and outside cannot be held to across that strange membrane, wall at once and copulating hymen, which stands between host and parasite. Each element is both exterior to the adjacent one and at the same time encloses and is enclosed by it.

One of the most striking "episodes" of *The Triumph of Life* is the scene of self-destructive erotic love. This scene matches a series of scenes elsewhere in Shelley's poetry in which the word "parasite" is present. The scene shows sexual attraction as one of the most deadly forms of the triumph of life. The triumph of life is in fact the triumph of language. For Shelley this takes the form of the subjection of each man or woman to illusory figures projected by his or her desire. Each of these figures is made of another substitutive shape of light which fades as it is grasped. It fades because it exists only as a transitory metaphor of light. It is a momentary lightbearer. Venus, star of evening, as the poem says, is only another disguise of Lucifer, fallen star of the morning. Vesper becomes Hesper by a change of initial consonant, masculine H for feminine V.

When the infatuated lovers of *The Triumph of Life* rush together, they annihilate one another, like particle and antiparticle, or, in the metaphors Shelley uses, like two thunderclouds colliding in a narrow valley, or like a great wave crashing on the shore. This annihilation, nevertheless, is not complete, since the violent collision leaves always a trace, a remnant, foam on the shore. This is Aphrodite's foam, egg or sperm which starts the cycle all over again in Shelley's drama of endless repetition. The darkest feature of the triumph of life, for Shelley, is that it may not even be ended by death. Life, for him, though it is a living death, may not die. It regenerates itself interminably in ever-new figures of light:

> . . . in their dance round her who dims the Sun
>
> Maidens & youths fling their wild arms in air
>   As their feet twinkle; they recede, and now
> Bending within each other's atmosphere
>
>   Kindle invisibly; and as they glow
> Like moths by light attracted & repelled,
>   Oft to new bright destruction come & go.
>
> Till like two clouds into one vale impelled
>   That shake the mountains when their lightnings mingle
> And die in rain, – the fiery band which held
>
>   Their natures, snaps . . . ere the shock cease to tingle
> One falls and then another in the path
>   Senseless, nor is the desolation single,
>
> Yet ere I can say *where* the chariot hath
>   Past over them; nor other trace I find
> But as of foam after the Ocean's wrath
>
>   Is spent upon the desert shore.
>
>   (ll. 148–64)[6]

This magnificent passage is the culmination of a series of passages writing and rewriting the same materials in a chain of repetitions beginning with *Queen Mab*. In the earlier versions the word "parasite" characteristically appears, like a discreet identifying mark woven into the texture of the verbal fabric. The word appears in *Queen Mab* and in the version of one episode of *Queen Mab* called *The Daemon of the World*. It appears then in *Alastor*, in *Laon and Cythna*, in *The Revolt of Islam*, in *Epipsychidion*, and in *The Sensitive Plant*, always with the same surrounding context of motifs and themes. These include narcissism and incest, the conflict of generations, struggles for political power, the motifs of the sun and the moon, the fountain, the brook, the caverned enclosure, ruined tower, or woodland dell, the dilapidation of man's constructions by nature, and the failure of the poetic quest.

That part of *Queen Mab* which Shelley reworked under the title *The Daemon of the World* contains the earliest version of the complex of elements (including the chariot from Ezekiel) which receives its final expression in *The Triumph of Life*. There Ianthe's "golden tresses shade/ The bosom's stainless pride,/Twining like tendrils of the parasite/ Around a marble column" (ll. 44–7).

In *Alastor* the doomed poet, like Narcissus searching for his lost twin sister, seeks the "veiled maid" (l. 151) who has come to him in dreams. He seeks her in a woodland glen with a "well/Dark, gleaming and of most translucent wave" (ll. 457–8), but he finds only his own eyes reflected there. These eyes, however, are doubled by "two eyes,/Two starry eyes" (ll. 489–90), which meet his eyes when his look rises. They are perhaps actual stars, perhaps the eyes of his evasive beloved. This play of eyes and looks had been prepared a few lines earlier in a description of "parasites,/Starred with ten thousand blossoms" (ll. 439–40), which twine around the trees of the dense forest hiding this well.

In Canto VI of *Laon and Cythna*, then again in the revised version, *The Revolt of Islam* (which veils the theme of incestuous love), Cythna rescues Laon from defeat in battle and takes him for a wild ride on a Tartar's courser to a ruined palace on a mountain top. There they make love, in another scene involving eyes, looks, stars, and Narcissus' well: "her dark and deepening eyes,/Which, as twin phantoms of one star that lies/O'er a dim well, move, though the Star reposes,/Swam in our mute and liquid ecstasies" (ll. 2624–8). This lovemaking takes place in a "natural couch of leaves" in a recess of the ruin. The recess is shaded in spring by "flowering parasites" which shed their "stars" on the dead leaves when the wandering wind blows (ll. 2578–4).

In *Epipsychidion*, the poet plans to take the lady Emily to an island with a ruined tower where, as he says, "We shall become the same, we shall be one/Spirit within two frames" (ll. 573–4). This ruin too is shaded by "parasite flowers" (l. 502), just as, in *The Sensitive Plant*, the garden which the lady personifies contains "parasite bowers" (l. 47) which die when winter comes.

A special version of the undecidable structure contained within the word "parasite" operates in all these passages. One could say either that the word contains the passages in miniature within itself or that the passages themselves are a dramatization of the word. The passages limit the word's meaning and expand it at the same time, tracing out one special design within the complex system of thought and figuration contained within the word.

These passages might be defined as an attempt to get a complicated group of themes to come out right. Their aim is magical or Promethean. They attempt to describe an act of Narcissistic self-begetting and self-possession which is at the same time an incestuous lovemaking between brother and sister. This lovemaking shortcircuits the differences of the sexes and the heterogeneity of families in an unlawful sexual coupling. At the same time this act is a breakdown of the barrier between person and nature. It is also a political act putting an end to a tyranny which is imaged as the familial domination of a bad father over his children and over his progeny in all succeeding generations. It is, finally, an act of poetry which will destroy the barriers between sign and signified. Such poetry will produce an apocalypse of immediacy in which no more poetry will be needed because no more figures will be needed, no metaphors, no substitutions or "standings for," no veils. We will then stand in the presence of a universal present which will be all light. It will no longer require Luciferic shapes, persons, figures, or images from nature to bear that light and in the bearing hide it.

All these projects fail at once. They fail in a way which *The Triumph of Life* makes clearest in showing that the conjunction of lovers, clouds, wave and shore, or words both destroys what it conjoins and always leaves a reminder. This genetic trace starts the cycle of lovemaking, attempts by the self to possess itself, self-destructive political tyranny, and poetry-writing all over again. Shelley's poetry is the record of a perpetually renewed failure. It is a failure ever to get the right formula and so end the separate incomplete self, end lovemaking, end politics, and end poetry, all at once, in a performative apocalypse in which words will become the fire they have ignited and so vanish as words, in a universal light. The words, however, always remain, there on the page, as the unconsumed traces of each unsuccessful attempt to use words to end words. The attempt must therefore be repeated. The same scene, with the same elements in a slightly different arrangement, is written by Shelley over and over again from *Queen Mab* to *The Triumph of Life*, in a repetition ended only with his death. This repetition mimes the poet's failure ever to get it right and so end the necessity of trying once more with what remains.

The word "parasite," for Shelley, names the bridge, wall, or connecting membrane which at once makes this apocalyptic union possible, abolishing difference, and at the same time always remains as a barrier forbidding it. Like the thin line of Aphrodite's foam on the shore, this remnant starts the process all over again after the vanishing of the previous couple in their violent attempt to end the interminable chain. The parasite is, on the one hand, the barrier and marriage hymen between the horizontal elements which make some binary opposition. This opposition generates forms and generates also a narrative of their interaction. At the same time the parasite is the barrier and connecting screen between elements on different planes vertically, Earth and Heaven, this world and a spiritual one above it. The world above is the white radiance of eternity. This world's opposing pairs, male, for example, against female, both figure forth and hide that white fire.

Parasites for Shelley are always parasite *flowers*. They are vines which twine themselves around the trees of a forest to climb to light and air, or they grow on a ruined palace to cover its stone and make fragrant bowers there. Parasitical flowering vines feed on air and on what they can take from their hosts. Those hosts they join with their stems. Shelley's parasites flower abundantly, making a screen between sky and earth. This screen remains even in winter as a lattice of dried vines.

A final ambiguity of Shelley's version of the system of parasite and host is the impossibility of deciding whether the sister-beloved in these poems is on the same plane as the desiring poet or a transcendent spirit infinitely above him. She is both at once. She is a sister to whom the protagonist might make love, incestuously. At the same time she is an unattainable muse or mother who governs all, as the spirit eyes Alastor pursues are those of no earthly sister, or as the poet's love for Emily in *Epipsychidion* is also an attempt, like that of Prometheus, to steal heavenly fire, or as the scene of erotic love in *The Triumph of Life* is presided over by the devouring female goddess, riding in her triumph, Life, or as, in the first version of this pattern, the earthly Ianthe beloved by Henri is doubled by the female Daemon of the World who presides over their relation and who is present at the end of the poem as the star repeating the heroine's eyes. These star-like eyes are a constant symbol in Shelley of the unattainable transcendent power in its relation to the earthly signs of it, but at the same time they are no more than the beloved's eyes, and also, at the same time, the protagonist's own eyes reflected back to him.

IV

The motif of a relation between the generations in which one generation is related parasitically to another, with the full ambiguity of that relation, appears in *Epipsychidion* in its most complete form. This version makes clearest the relation of this theme to the system of parasite and host, to the theme in Shelley of a repetition generated always by what is left over after an earlier cataclysmic self-destruction, to the political theme which is always present in these passages, to the relation of man's works to nature, and to the dramatization of the power of poetry which is always one of Shelley's themes.

The ruined tower in the Sporades to which the poet will take his Emily in *Epipsychidion* is said, in one of the drafts of the preface, somewhat prosaically, to be "a Saracenic castle which accident had preserved in some repair." In the poem itself this tower is a strange structure which has grown naturally, almost like a flower or stone, saxifrage and saxiform. At the same time it is almost supernatural. It is a house for a god and a goddess, or at any rate for a semi-divine Ocean-King and his sister-spouse. The building brackets the human level. It is above and below that level at once:

> But the chief marvel of the wilderness
> Is a lone dwelling, built by whom or how

> None of the rustic island-people know:
> 'Tis not a tower of strength, though with its height
> It overtops the woods; but, for delight,
> Some wise and tender Ocean-King, ere crime
> Had been invented, in the world's young prime,
> Reared it, a wonder of that simple time,
> An envy of the isles, a pleasure-house
> Made sacred to his sister and his spouse.
> It scarce seems now a wreck of human art,
> But, as it were Titanic; in the heart
> Of Earth having assumed its form, then grown
> Out of the mountains, from the living stone,
> Lifting itself in caverns light and high:
> For all the antique and learned imagery
> Has been erased, and in the place of it
> The ivy and the wild-vine interknit
> The volumes of their many-twining stems;
> Parasite flowers illume with dewy gems
> The lampless halls, and when they fade, the sky
> Peeps through their winter-woof of tracery
> With moonlight patches, or star atoms keen,
> Or fragments of the day's intense serene; –
> Working mosaic on their Parian floors.
>   (ll. 483–507)

An "Ocean-King" is, possibly, a human king of this ocean isle and at the same time, possibly, a King of the Ocean, an Olympian or a Titan. In any case, this dwelling was built "in the world's young prime." It was built near the time of origin, when the opposites were confounded or nearly confounded and when incest was not a crime, as it was not for those Egyptian pharaohs who always mated with their sisters, only fit spouses for their earthly divinity. In the same way, in that young time, nature and culture were not opposed. The palace seems at once "Titanic," the work of a superhuman strength, and at the same time human, since it is, after all, "a wreck of human art," though it scarcely seems so. At the same time it is natural, as though it had grown from the rock, not been built by human art at all. Though the building was once adorned with elaborate carved inscriptions and images, those have been effaced by time. Its towers and facades now seem once more natural rock, grown out of the mountains, living stone. The natural, the supernatural, and the human were reconciled in a union whose symbol was brother–sister incest, the same mating with the same, so short-circuiting normal human love with its production of new genetic lines. The prohibition against incest, as Lévi-Strauss has argued, is both human and natural at once. It therefore breaks down the barrier between the two. This breaking was doubly broken by the Ocean-King and his sister. Their copulation kept crime from being invented. It held nature, the supernatural, and the human together – mimicking and maintaining that vision of unity which can be seen from the palace. This seascape–landscape, two in one, makes the particulars of nature seem the ideal dream of a fulfilled sexuality between two great gods, Earth and Ocean:

> And, day and night, aloof, from the high towers
> And terraces, the Earth and Ocean seem
> To sleep in one another's arms, and dream
> Of waves, flowers, clouds, woods, rocks, and all that we
> Read in their smiles, and call reality.
>
> (ll. 508–12)

To this place the poet plans to bring his Emily, promising a renewal of that ideal sexual union of the prime time. This renewal will magically renew the time itself. It will take them back to a time prior to the invention of crime and reconcile once more, in a performative embrace, nature, supernature, and man.

This performance, however, can never be performed. It remains at the end of *Epipsychidion* a proleptic hope which is forbidden by the words which express it. It can never be performed because in fact this union never existed in the past. It is only a projection backward from the present. It is a "seeming" created by reading the signs of remnants still present in the present. The Ocean-King, wise and tender though he may have been, was human after all. The prohibition against incest precedes the committing of incest. It precedes the division between natural and human while at the same time creating that division. The lovemaking of the Ocean-King and his spouse was itself the act which "invented crime." Though it was a mating of the same with the same, it did not put a stop to the difference of sexes, families, and generations, as the peopling of the earth, the presence of political and paternal tyranny, the existence of the poet with his unassuaged desire for Emily all demonstrate.

Moreover, the building only seemed to be natural, divine, and human at once. Though its stone is natural enough, its shape was in fact a product of human art, as is demonstrated by the presence on it once of "antique and learnèd imagery." This imagery was learned because it pointed back still further to a human tradition already immemorial. The "volumes" of the ivy and the wild vine, that screen of parasite flowers, the former making a hieroglyphic pattern on the stone, the latter casting mosaic patterns in tracery on the marble floors, are substitutes for that effaced writing. The purely natural vines and parasites here paradoxically become a kind of writing. They stand for the erased pattern of learned imagery carved in the stone by the Ocean-King's builders. They stand also by implication for writing in general, the writing for example of the poem itself which the reader is at that moment retracing. Yet the pattern of parasite vines is no legible language. It remains "in place of" the erased human language. In this "in place of" all the imaginary unity of "the world's young prime" breaks down. It is dispersed back into irreconcilable compartments separated by the dividing textured membrane which tries to bring them together. Male and female; divine, human; supernatural, natural – all become separate. They are realms separated by language itself and by the dependence of language on figure, on the "in place of" of metaphor or allegorical subsitution. Any attempt to cross the barrier and unify what have from all time been separated by the language which brings them together (that antique and learned imagery which was already there even for the wise and tender Ocean-King and his sister spouse), leads only to an exacerbation of the distance. It becomes a transgression which creates the barrier it attempts to efface or ignore. Incest cannot exist without kinship names and is "invented" as a crime not so much in sexual acts between brother and sister as in any imagery for them. This imagery, however, is always there, of immemorial antiquity. It joins nature and culture in what divides them, as the living stone is covered with carved images making it humanly significant, and as the parasite vines or rather the filigrees of their shadows are taken as signs.

In the same way the poet's attempt to repeat with Emily the pleasure of the Ocean-King and his sister only repeats the crime of illicit sexual relations, always at least implicitly incest for Shelley. "Would we two had been twins of the same mother!" (l. 45) says the protagonist to his Emily. The speaker's love only prolongs the divisions. His union with Emily remains always in the future, as is Henri's love in *The Daemon of the World*, or as is the hero's love in *Alastor*, and as the union of Laon and Cythna is paid for when they are burned at the stake. The lovemaking of Laon and Cythna does not in any case produce the political liberation of Islam. In the same way, the poet's attempt in *Epipsychidion* to express in words this union becomes itself the barrier forbidding it. It forbids also the poet's Promethean attempt to scale heaven and seize its fire through language and through erotic love. The passage is one of Shelley's grandest symphonic climaxes, but what it expresses is the failure of poetry and the failure of love. It expresses the destruction of the poet-lover in his attempt to escape his boundaries, the chains at once of selfhood and of language. This failure is Shelley's version of the parasite structure.

Who, however, is "Shelley"? To what does this word refer if any work signed with this name has no identifiable borders, and no interior walls either? It has no edges because it has been invaded from all sides as well as from within by other "names," other powers of writing – Rousseau, Dante, Ezekiel, and the whole host of others, phantom strangers who have crossed the thresholds of the poems, erasing their margins. Though the word "Shelley" may be printed on the cover of a book entitled *Poetical Works*, it must name something without identifiable bounds, since the book incorporates so much outside within its inside. The parasite structure obliterates the frontiers of the texts it enters. For "Shelley," then, the parasite is a communicating screen of figurative language which permanently divides what it would unify in a perpetual "in place of" forbidding union. This screen creates the shadow of that union as an effect of figure, a phantasmal "once was" and "might yet be," never "now" and "here":

> Our breath shall intermix, our bosoms bound,
> And our veins beat together; and our lips
> With other eloquence than words, eclipse
> The soul that burns between them, and the wells
> Which boil under our being's inmost cells,
> The fountains of our deepest life, shall be
> Confused in Passion's golden purity,
> As mountain-springs under the morning sun.
> We shall become the same, we shall be one
> Spirit within two frames, oh! wherefore two?
> One passion in twin-hearts, which grows and grew,
> Till like two meteors of expanding flame,
> Those spheres instinct with it become the same,
> Touch, mingle, are transfigured; ever still
> Burning, yet ever inconsumable:
> In one another's substance finding food,
> Like flames too pure and light and unimbued
> To nourish their bright lives with baser prey,
> Which point to Heaven and cannot pass away:
> One hope within two wills, one will beneath
> Two overshadowing minds, one life, one death,
> One Heaven, one Hell, one immortality,
> And one annihilation. Woe is me!
> The wingèd words on which my soul would pierce
> Into the height of Love's rare Universe,
> Are chains of lead around its flight of fire –
> I pant, I sink, I tremble, I expire!
> (ll. 565–91)

No reader of these extraordinary lines can fail to feel that the poet here protests too much. Every repetition of the word "one" only adds another layer to the barrier forbidding oneness. The poet protests too much not only in the attempt in words to produce a union which these words themselves keep from happening, but even in the concluding outcry of woe. Not only does the poet not achieve union through words with his Emily and so climb to Love's fiery heights. He does not even "expire" through the failure of these magic performatives. Words do not make anything happen, nor does their failure to make anything happen either. Though the "Advertisement" to *Epipsychidion* tells the reader the poet died in Florence without ever reaching that isle, "one of the wildest of the Sporades," the reader knows that words did not kill him, for "I pant, I sink, I tremble, I expire!" is followed by the relatively calm post-climax dedicatory lines beginning: "Weak Verses, go, kneel at your Sovereign's feet" (l. 591).

The grand climactic passage itself is made of variations on the paradoxical parasite structure. The verbal signs for union necessarily rebuild the barrier they would obliterate. The more the poet says they will be one the more he makes them two by reaffirming the ways they are separated. The lips that speak with an eloquence other than words are doors which are also a liminal barrier between person and person. Those lips may eclipse the soul that burns between them, but they remain as a communicating medium which also is a barrier to union. The lips are the parasite structure once more. Moreover, the voice that speaks of an eloquence beyond words uses eloquent words to speak of this transverbal speech. By naming such speech it keeps the soul from being eclipsed. In the same way, the image of the deep wells reaffirms the notion of cellular enclosure, just as the clash of fire and water in the figure of the mountain-springs being "confused" under the morning sun tells the reader that only by evaporating as entities can lovers become one. The images of two frames with one spirit, the double meteors becoming one floating sphere, the pair each both eater and eaten ("in one another's substance finding food"), are the parasitical relation again. All play variations on "Shelley's" version of the parasite structure, the notion of a unity which yet remains double but in the figurative expression of that unity reveals the impossibility of two becoming one across a parasitic wall and yet remaining two.

This impossibility is mimed in the final *mise en abyme*. This is a cascade of expressions describing a twoness resting on the ground of a oneness which then subdivides once more to rest on a still deeper ground which ultimately reveals itself to be, if it exists at all, the abyss of "annihilation." The vertical wall between cell and cell, lover and beloved, is doubled by a horizontal veil between levels of being. Each veil when removed only reveals another veil, ad infinitum, unless the last veil exposes an emptiness. This would be the emptiness of that oneness which is implored into existence in the reiteration of "one," "one,", "one," "one": "One hope within two wills, one will beneath/Two overshadowing minds, one life, one death/One Heaven, one Hell, one immortality,/And one annihilation. Woe is me!" The language which tries to efface itself as language to give way to an unmediated union beyond language is itself the barrier which always remains as the woe of an ineffaceable trace. Words are always there as remnant, "chains of lead" which forbid the flight to fiery union they invoke.

This does not mean that lovemaking and poetrymaking are the "same thing" or subject to the same impasses determining their failure as performatives magically transforming the world. In a sense they are antagonists, since lovemaking attempts to do wordlessly what poetry attempts to do with words. No one can doubt that Shelley believed sexual experience "occurs" or that he "describes" it in his poetry, for example in *Laon and Cythna* and in the great passage on erotic love in *The Triumph of Life*. Lovemaking and poetrymaking are not, however, stark opposites in Shelley either. Each is, so to speak, the dramatization of the other or the figure of it. This is an elliptical relation in which whichever of the two the reader focuses on reveals itself to be the metaphorical substitution for the other. The other, however, when the reader moves to it, is not the "original" but a figure of what at first seemed a figure for it. Lovemaking, as *The Triumph of Life* shows, is a way to "experience," as incarnate suffering, the self-destructive effects of signmaking, sign-projecting and sign-interpretation. The wordlessness of lovemaking is only another way of dwelling within signs after all, as is shown in *The Triumph of Life* by the affirmed identity between Venus, evening star of love, and Lucifer, star of morning, "light-bearer," personification of personification and of all the other tropes, all the forms of the "in place of."

Poetrymaking, on the other hand, is for Shelley always a figure of, as well as figured by, the various forms of life – political, religious, familial, and erotic. It does not have priority as an origin but can exist only embodied in one or another of the forms of life it figures. There is, for Shelley, no "sign" without its material carrier, and so the play of substitutions in language can never be a purely ideal interchange. This interchange is always contaminated by its necessary incarnation, the most dramatic form of which is the bodies of lovers. On the other hand, lovemaking is never a purely wordless communion or intercourse. It is in its turn contaminated by language. Lovemaking is a way of living, in the flesh, the aporias of figure. It is also a way of experiencing the way language functions to forbid the perfect union of lovers. Language always remains, after they have exhausted or even annihilated themselves in an attempt to get it right, as the genetic trace starting the cycle all over again.

V

Five times, or seven times if one counts *The Daemon of the World* and *The Revolt of Islam* as separate texts, seven times, or even more than seven if one includes other passages with the same elements where the word "parasite" does not appear – more than seven times, then, throughout his work, Shelley casts himself against the lips of the parasitical gate. Each time he falls back, having failed to make two into one without annihilating both. He falls back as himself the remainder, the power of language able to say "Woe is me!" and forced to try again to break the barrier only to fail once more, in repetitions which are terminated only by his death.

The critic, in his turn, like those poets, Browning, Hardy, Yeats, or Stevens who have been decisively "influenced" by Shelley, is a follower who repeats the pattern once again and once again fails to "get it right," just as Shelley repeats himself and repeats his precursors, and just as the poet and Emily follow the Ocean-King and his sister spouse.

The critic's version of the pattern proliferated in this chain of repetitions is as follows. The critic's attempt to untwist the elements in the texts he interprets only twists them up again in another place and leaves always a remnant of opacity, or an added opacity, as yet unraveled. The critic is caught in his own version of the interminable repetitions which determine the poet's career. The critic experiences this as his failure to get his poet right in a final decisive formulation which will allow him to have done with that poet, once and for all. Though each poet is different, each contains his own form of undecidability. This might be defined by saying that the critic can never show decisively whether or not the work of the writer is "decidable," whether or not it is capable of being definitively interpreted. The critic cannot unscramble the tangle of lines of meaning, comb its threads out so they shine clearly side by side. He can only retrace the text, set its elements in motion once more, in that experience of the failure of determinable reading which is decisive here.

The blank wall beyond which rational analysis cannot go arises from the copresence in any text in Western literature, inextricably intertwined, as host and parasite, of some version of logocentric metaphysics and its subversive counterpart. In Shelley's case these are, on the one hand, the "idealism" always present as one possible reading of his poems, even of *The Triumph of Life*, and on the other hand, the putting in question of this in Shelley's "scepticism" by a recognition of the role of projections in human life. This is that law of shadowing which deconstructs idealism. It is most explicitly formulated in *The Triumph of Life*:

> Figures ever new
> Rise on the bubble [of the phenomenal and historical world],
> paint them how you may;
> We have but thrown, as those before us threw,
>
> Our shadows on it as it past away.
>
> (ll. 248–51)

The "deconstruction" of metaphysics by an appeal to the figurative nature of language always, however, contains its own impasse, whether this dismantling is performed within the writing of the author himself or in the following of that in repetitive retracing by the critic who comes after, as in my discussion here. This impasse is itself double. On the one hand, the poet and his shadow, the critic, can "deconstruct" metaphysics only with some tool of analysis which is capable of becoming another form of metaphysics in its turn. To put this another way, the differentiation between metaphysics and scepticism reforms itself as a new form of doubleness within "scepticism." Scepticism is not a firm and unequivocal machine of deconstruction. It carries within itself another form of the parasite structure, mirror image with the valences reversed of that within metaphysics itself.

The appeal to language from idealism is an admirable example of this. As is abundantly apparent in criticism at the present time, rhetorical analysis, "semiotics," "structuralism," "narratology," or the interpretation of tropes can freeze into a quasi-scientific discipline promising exhaustive rational certainty in the identification of meaning in a text and in the identification of the way that meaning is produced. The appeal to etymologies can become another archeology. It can become another way to be beguiled by the apparent explanatory power of seeming "origins" and the accompanying explanatory power of the apparently causally determined chains which emerge from a starting point in some "Indo–European root." Insofar as this move in contemporary criticism is motivated by an appeal to Freud's linguistic insights, such critics should perhaps remember Freud's demonstration, in *The Psychopathology of Everyday Life* and in *Jokes and the Unconscious*, of the way wordplay in all its forms is superficial. Wordplay is the repression of something more dangerous. This something, however, interweaves itself with that wordplay and forbids it to be merely verbal or merely play. Rhetorical analysis, the analysis of figure, and even an investigation of etymologies are necessary to put in question a heavily idealist reading of Shelley, but these must be dismantled in their turn in an interminable movement of interrogation which is the life of criticism. Criticism is a human activity which depends for its validity on never being at ease within a fixed "method." It must constantly put its own grounds in question. The critical text and the literary text are each parasite and host for the other, each feeding on the other and feeding it, destroying and being destroyed by it.

The dismantling of the linguistic assumptions necessary to dismantle Shelley's idealism must occur, however, not by a return to idealism, and not by the appeal to some "metalanguage" which will encompass both, but by a movement through rhetorical analysis, the analysis of tropes, and the appeal to etymologies, to something "beyond" language which can yet only be reached by recognition of the linguistic moment in its counter-momentum against idealism or against logocentric metaphysics. By "linguistic moment" I mean the moment in a work of literature when its own medium is put in question. This moment allows the critic to take what remains from the clashing of scepticism and idealism as a new starting place, for example by the recognition of a performative function of language which has entered into my discussion of Shelley. This again, in its reinstating of a new form of referentiality and in its formation of a new clashing, this time between rhetoric as tropes and rhetoric as performative words, must be interrogated in its turn, in a ceaseless movement of interpretation which Shelley himself has mimed in the sequence of episodes in *The Triumph of Life*.

This movement is not subject to dialectical synthesis, nor to any other closure. The undecidable, nevertheless, always has an impetus back into some covert form of dialectical movement, as in my terminology here of the "chain" and the "going beyond." This is constantly countered, however, by the experience of movement in place. The momentary always tends to generate a narrative, even if it is the narrative of the impossibility of narrative, the impossibility of getting from here to there by means of language. The tension between dialectic and undecidability is another way in which this form of criticism remains open, in the ceaseless movement of an "in place of" without resting place.

The word "deconstruction" is in one way a good one to name this movement. The word, like other words in "de," "decrepitude," for example, or "denotation," describes a paradoxical action which is negative and positive at once. In this it is like all words with a double antithetical prefix, words in "ana," like "analysis," or words in "para," like "parasite." These words tend to come in pairs which are not opposites, positive against negative. They are related in a systematic differentiation which requires a different analysis or untying in each case, but which in each case leads, in a different way each time, to the tying up of a double bind. This tying up is at the same time a loosening. It is a paralysis of thought in the face of what cannot be thought rationally:

analysis, paralysis; solution, dissolution; composition, decomposition; construction, deconstruction; mantling, dismantling; canny, uncanny; competence, incompetence; apocalyptic, anacalyptic; constituting, deconstituting. Deconstructive criticism moves back and forth between the poles of these pairs, proving in its own activity, for example, that there is no deconstruction which is not at the same time constructive, affirmative. The word says this in juxtaposing "de" and "con."

At the same time, the word "deconstruction" has misleading overtones or implications. It suggests something a bit too external, a bit too masterful and muscular. It suggests the demolition of the helpless text with tools which are other than and stronger than what is demolished. The word "deconstruction" suggests that such criticism is an activity turning something unified back to detached fragments or parts. It suggests the image of a child taking apart his father's watch, reducing it back to useless parts, beyond any reconstitution. A deconstructionist is not a parasite but a parricide. He is a bad son demolishing beyond hope of repair the machine of Western metaphysics.

In fact, insofar as "deconstruction" names the use of rhetorical, etymological, or figurative analysis to demystify the mystifications of literary and philosophical language, this form of criticism is not outside but within. It is of the same nature as what it works against. Far from reducing the text back to detached fragments, it inevitably constructs again in a different form what it deconstructs. It does again as it undoes. It recrosses in one place what it uncrosses in another. Rather than surveying the text with sovereign command from outside, it remains caught within the activity in the text it retraces.

To the action of deconstruction with its implication of an irresistible power of the critic over the text must always be added, as a description of what happens in interpretation, the experience of the impossibility of exercising that power. The dismantler dismantles himself. Far from being a chain which moves deeper and deeper into the text, closer and closer to a definitive interpretation of it, the mode of criticism sometimes now called "deconstruction," which is analytic criticism as such, encounters always, if it is carried far enough, some mode of oscillation. In this oscillation two genuine insights into literature in general and into a given text in particular inhibit, subvert, and undercut one another. This inhibition makes it impossible for either insight to function as a firm resting place, the end point of analysis. My example here has been the co-presence in the parasite structure in Shelley of idealism and scepticism, of referentiality which only proleptically refers, in figure, therefore does not refer at all, and of performatives which do not perform. Analysis becomes paralysis, according to the strange necessity which makes these words, or the "experience," or the "procedure," they describe, turn into one another. Each crosses over into its apparent negation or opposite. If the word "deconstruction" names the procedure of criticism, and "oscillation" the impasse reached through that procedure, "undecidability" names the experience of a ceaseless dissatisfied movement in the relation of the critic to the text.

The ultimate justification for this mode of criticism, as of any conceivable mode, is that it works. It reveals hitherto unidentified meanings and ways of having meaning in major literary texts. The hypothesis of a possible heterogeneity in literary texts is more flexible, more open to a given work, than the assumption that a good work of literature is necessarily going to be "organically unified." The latter presupposition is one of the major factors inhibiting recognition of the possibly self-subversive complexity of meanings in a given work. Moreover, "deconstruction" finds in the text it interprets the double antithetical patterns it identifies, for example the relation of parasite and host. It does not claim them as universal explanatory structures, neither for the text in question nor for literature in general. Deconstruction attempts to resist the totalizing and totalitarian tendencies of criticism. It attempts to resist its own tendencies to come to rest in some sense of mastery over the work. It resists these in the name of an uneasy joy of interpretation, beyond nihilism, always in movement, a going beyond which remains in place, as the parasite is outside the door but also always already within, uncanniest of guests.

Notes

1. *Critical Inquiry*, II, 3 (Spring 1976), pp. 457–8. The first phrase is quoted from Wayne Booth, "M. H. Abrams: Historian as Critic, Critic as Pluralist," *Critical Inquiry*, II, 3 (Spring 1976), p. 441. The opening pages of the present essay appeared in a preliminary form in *Critical Inquiry*, III, 3 (Spring 1977), pp. 439–47, by permission of The University of Chicago Press.
2. All definitions and etymologies in this essay are taken from *The American Heritage Dictionary of the English Language*, William Morris, ed. (Boston, 1969).
3. Walter Kaufmann and R. J. Hollingdale, tr., *The Will to Power* (New York, 1968), p. 7; Friedrich Nietzsche, *Werke in Drei Bänden*, ed. Karl Schlechta, III (Munich, 1966), p. 881.
4. Jean T. Wilde and William Kluback, tr., *The Question of Being* [a bilingual text] (New Haven, Conn., 1958), pp. 36–9.
5. Kaufmann and Hollingdale, p. 7; Schlechta, III, p. 881.
6. *The Triumph of Life* is cited from the text established by Donald H. Reiman in *Shelley's "The Triumph of Life": A Critical Study* (Urbana, Ill., 1965). All other citations from Shelley are taken from *Poetical Works*, ed. Thomas Hutchinson, corrected by G. M. Matthews (London, Oxford, New York, 1973).

11

On edge: the crossways of contemporary criticism

The word "crossways" in my title is meant to suggest borders as well as crossroads. This double image is implicit in the poem by Wordsworth I shall discuss. It is also appropriate to the present state of criticism. Literary study often develops through genetic crossings; it brings together different disciplines or different modes of literary study. I shall attempt now to describe the present moment in literary study. The description will by no means pretend to be a sovereign overview. Any such description is necessarily from within, at the crossroads. This is the case not so much because every view is interested, a biased perspective, as because on principle there is no conceivable metalanguage outside one or another of the languages of criticism.

The institutionalized study of vernacular literature is of course a fairly recent development in the West. Matthew Arnold was in 1857 the first Professor of Poetry at Oxford to give his lectures in English. Although departments of English seem now a necessary part of any college or university – a natural feature of the academic landscape, part of nature, so to speak – until not too many decades ago they did not exist at all. They could of course again easily cease to exist or become marginal, as have, alas, departments of Greek and Latin. Some experts believe that this is in fact happening. A new discipline of rhetoric and the teaching of composition, they say, is developing across the nation. This new discipline will displace the departments of English or relegate them to the status departments of classics presently hold. This would in fact be a return to the situation in late nineteenth-century America, when all colleges and universities had substantial staffs in composition and in rhetoric. The discipline of the study of vernacular literature was just establishing itself. Thus the presence in American universities of large and strong departments of literary history and literary criticism may be a relatively shortlived phenomenon, lasting less than a century. The alternative would be for them to make changes which would allow them to survive in a new cultural situation.

Changes in literary study, however, as in other disciplines, usually take place with glacial slowness. Such study is strongly institutionalized in secondary school curricula; in college and university departments of English, French, German, comparative literature, and so on; in textbooks and editions; in curricula inscribed in catalogues as though fixed for the ages; and in graduate programs turning out new Ph.D.s, far too many of them for the available positions. These new Ph.D.s tend to be trained to teach only literature and to teach it only in certain ways; their training in the teaching of composition is often minimal. The greatest institutionalized resistance to change is in the more or less fixed presuppositions, prejudices, and feelings of those who teach literature and write about it.

This institutional continuity in the study of literature of course has great advantages. It would be impossible for all teachers to make up the whole discipline anew each time they confronted a text or a class. Even the most innovative scholar, teacher, or critic depends on the presence of a relatively stable and conservative academic organization in order to get on with his or her own work. Much time these days is in fact wasted in the humanities on the endless concoction of new courses and new curricula. There are problems, however, if the institution no longer responds fully to the demands made on it by society, in one direction, nor fits the actual state of the discipline involved, in the other, which, I believe, is to a considerable degree the case at present. Nevertheless, in spite of the inertia of its institutional embodiments, the study of literature in America is at this moment changing with unusual rapidity.

One change is being imposed from outside the discipline, from the direction of society. By society here I mean the context within which literary study in America dwells, which it serves and is served by: parents, school boards, trustees, regents, legislatures, the "media." We teachers of literature have fewer students already and will apparently have still fewer as the years go by, both in individual courses and as majors in the various departments of literature. Those fewer are steadily less well prepared, both in literature itself and in what are called "basic language skills." They cannot write well. They cannot read well either. The reading of works of literature appears to be playing every day a less and less important role in our culture generally. The complex social function performed in Elizabethan and Jacobean England by going to the theater and in Victorian England by the reading of novels is performed these days by other activities, mostly, so it seems, by watching television. The reading of a novel, poem, or play, or even the watching of a play, is likely to become an increasingly artificial, marginal, or archaic activity. It is beginning to seem more and more odd, to some people, to be asked to take seriously the literature of a small island on the edge of Europe, a small island, moreover, which has ceased to be a major world power. It might be more important to learn Russian or Chinese or Arabic. At the same time, American society has begun to recognize that we are to a considerable degree a multilingual people, not only because many of us have Spanish or some other tongue as a first language, but because we speak and write many different forms of English besides the idiolect and grapholect of standard English. For better or worse, much "standard English as a second language" must be taught, even to college students.

As College Board scores go down from year to year, our society is demanding in a louder and louder chorus that schools and colleges do something soon about the fact that our young people cannot read and cannot write. This demand, at the college and university level, is being made on professors who have been trained to teach the details of literary history and the intricacies of meaning in works by Shakespeare or Milton, Keats or Woolf. Even before they found themselves asked to teach more and more composition, many departments of English had been demoralized by declining enrollments and had begun to set their Shakespeareans and medievalists to teach classes in modern fiction, in film, or in continental novels in translation, just as the department of classics in one large state university justifies its existence at the undergraduate level by a lecture course on "mythology." A large proportion of the courses offered by the department of English in one good liberal arts college I visited recently included at least one work by J. L. Borges. This department is for all practical purposes a department of continental literature in translation, and the departments of Spanish, French, and German at the same college are small and ineffective.

In the area of expository writing a large industry is being mobilized to create a new discipline. This mobilization includes distinguished literary theorists and historians like E. D. Hirsch, Wayne Booth, and Stanley Fish, who began as literary critics, not as experts on the teaching of composition. At the same time, more and more bright young people are already making careers in composition, seeking training in rhetoric, in linguistics, and in educational psychology rather than narrowly in traditional literary history and criticism. This is all to the good, but it will obviously weaken further the traditional activities of the study of literature as such.

At the same time, from the other direction, there have been unusually rapid changes within the discipline of literary study proper. Thirty years ago the field of literary study in America was more or less completely dominated by the method of intrinsic reading called the "New Criticism" and by a positivistic literary history committed to gathering facts and establishing texts. The latter mode was associated with the method of scientific research. It descended from such nineteenth-century metaphorical assimilations of literary study to scientific method as that of Hippolyte Taine, as well as from the long European tradition of philology and textual criticism originally coming from the study of Greek and Latin literature and from Biblical hermeneutics. The archetypal criticism of Northrop Frye was in 1948 just appearing as the first strong alternative to the New Criticism. There was a somewhat marginal presence of the great German philological tradition in the form of refugee scholars like Erich Auerbach and Leo Spitzer. Some news of continental formalism – Russian, Czech, and Polish – was seeping through in the influential book by René Wellek and Austin Warren called *The Theory of Literature*. In spite of the latter book, however, literary study in America was still insular. It was a more or less self-enclosed Anglo-American tradition confident that it could go on going it alone.

Today the situation is greatly changed. No serious student of literature can fail to think of it as an international enterprise. It is just as important for students of Chaucer, of Shakespeare, or of Dickens to know about continental criticism and to read such an international journal as *PTL*, which is edited at the Institute for Poetics and Semiotics in Tel Aviv, as it is for them to know the tradition of secondary works on these authors in English or to read *The Publications of the Modern Language Association*.

Moreover, the range of viable alternatives in literary methodology has become bafflingly large. These alternatives can, so it seems, hardly be reconciled in some grand synthesis. *Il faut choisir*. Along with the still powerful New Criticism, archetypal criticism, and positivistic literary history, there is a more or less fully elaborated phenomenological or hermeneutic criticism, a "criticism of consciousness" as it is sometimes called. A new semiotic formalism inspired by linguistics has been developed. There is a structuralist criticism deriving from structural linguistics and structural anthropology. A powerful new form of psychoanalytic criticism, mostly imported from France, has become influential. A revived Marxist and sociological criticism is beginning to take strong hold in America. Another new kind of criticism focuses on reader response and on what is called in Germany *Rezeptiongeschichte*. There is, finally, a form of literary study which concentrates on the rhetoric of literary texts, taking rhetoric in the sense of the investigation of the role of figurative language in literature. This method is sometimes called "deconstruction," which as a name at least has the advantage of distinguishing it firmly from any form of "structuralism." It is associated with the name of Jacques Derrida in France and with certain critics at my own university, Yale, as well as, increasingly, with younger critics at other universities in the United States. It has distinguished native grandsires or at least great-uncles in Kenneth Burke and William Empson. All these new forms are international in scope. The master works in each are as likely to have been written in Russian, German, French, or Italian as in English. This means that the delays and inadequacies of translation have made particular difficulties for literary study recently in America. Few students and young teachers here can read even one foreign language fluently, much less the whole necessary panoply.

This is not the place to attempt a description of each of these modes. It takes a whole semester of an elaborately team-taught course at my university to provide even a relatively superficial introduction to them for undergraduates. My aim here is to suggest that literary study in America now is in an unusually fluid or unstable condition. It is likely to change much more rapidly than usual, as much from forces within itself as from the pressures from without sketched earlier. This makes it somewhat unpredictable; only a remarkably insensitive or secluded person would be complacently at ease. It is in fact an exciting field to work in at the moment, though it is also no wonder so many members of my profession feel on edge, edgy.

In spite of the bewildering array of possibilities in literary methodology, the methods available may, for the purposes to which I want to turn now, be reduced to two distinctly different sorts. One kind includes all those methods whose presuppositions are in one way or another what I would call "metaphysical." The other kind includes those methods which hypothesize that in literature, for reasons which are intrinsic to language itself, metaphysical presuppositions are, necessarily, both affirmed and subverted. By "metaphysical" I mean the system of assumptions coming down from Plato and Aristotle which has unified our culture. This system includes the notions of beginning, continuity, and end, of causality, of dialectical process, of organic unity, and of ground, in short of *logos* in all its many senses. A metaphysical method of literary study assumes that literature is in one way or another referential, in one way or another grounded in something outside language. This something may be physical objects, or "society," or the economic realities of labor, valuation, and exchange. It may be consciousness, the *cogito*, or the unconscious, or absolute spirit, or God. An antimetaphysical or "deconstructive" form of literary study attempts to show that in a given work of literature, in a different way in each case, metaphysical assumptions are both present and at the same time undermined by the text itself. They are undermined by some figurative play within the text which forbids it to be read as an "organic unity" organized around some version of the *logos*. The play of tropes leaves an inassimilable residue or remnant of meaning, an unearned increment, so to speak, making a movement of sense beyond any unifying boundaries. The following out of the implications of the play of tropes leads to a suspension of fully rationalizable meaning in the experience of an aporia or boggling of the mind. This boggling sets up an oscillation in meaning. Dialectical opposites capable of synthesis may break down into the contradictory elements which are differences among the same.

This distinction between two kinds of criticism must not be understood, as it sometimes is, to be a historical one, or rather, it challenges a certain historical patterning. What I have been saying must be understood as putting in question the familiar historical scheme which presupposes that there was once an age of faith or of metaphysics which was followed by the skepticism, disintegration, or fragmentation of modern times. The argument, rather, is that the literary and philosophical texts of any period of Western culture contain, in a different way each time, both what I am calling metaphysics and the putting in question of metaphysics. The test of this hypothesis is the interpretation of the texts themselves. It is here that the battle should be fought. What does this given poem or passage *mean*? In principle, and in fact, a Greek tragedy, an episode in Ovid, in Dante, or in *The Faerie Queene* would be as good a testing ground for this as any Romantic or post-Romantic poem, though I have chosen a well-known text from English Romanticism as my example.

The relation of metaphysics and the deconstruction of metaphysics finds a parable in the strange relation of kinship among apparent opposites in Wordsworth's "A Slumber Did My Spirit Seal." Here is the poem:

> A slumber did my spirit seal:
> I had no human fears:
> She seemed a thing that could not feel
> The touch of earthly years.
>
> No motion has she now, no force;
> She neither hears nor sees;
> Rolled round in earth's diurnal course,
> With rocks, and stones, and trees.

This beautiful, moving, and apparently simple poem was written at Goslar in Germany in the late fall or early winter of 1798–9, during Wordsworth's miserable sojourn there with his sister Dorothy. It seems at first to be organized around a systematically interrelated set of binary oppositions. These seem to be genuinely exclusive oppositions, with a distinct uncrossable boundary line between them. Such a systematic set of oppositions, as always, invites interpretation of the dialectical sort. In such an interpretation, the oppositions are related in some scheme of hierarchical subordination. This makes possible a synthesis grounded in an explanatory third term constituting the *logos* of the poem. This *logos* is the poem's source and end, its ground and meaning, its "word" or "message." This particular text, I am arguing, forbids the successful completion of such a procedure. The method does not work. Something is always left over, a plus value beyond the boundaries of each such interpretation.

A surprising number of oppositions are present in the poem. These include slumber as against waking; male as against female; sealed up as against open; seeming as against being; ignorance as against knowledge; past as against present; inside as against outside; light as against darkness in the "diurnal" course of the earth; subject or consciousness, "spirit," as against object, the natural world of stones and trees; feeling as "touch" as against feeling as emotion, "fears"; "human fears" as against – what? – perhaps inhuman fears; "thing" in its meaning of "girl," young virgin, as against "thing" in the sense of physical object; years as against days; hearing as against seeing; motion as against force; self-propulsion as against exterior compulsion; mother as against daughter or sister, or perhaps any female family member as against some woman from outside the family, that is, mother, sister, or daughter as against mistress or wife, in short, incestuous desires against legitimate sexual feelings; life as against death.

The invitation to interpret the poem in terms of oppositions is sustained in part by its syntactical and formal structure. Syntactically it is structured around words or phrases in apposition or opposition. The second line, for instance, repeats the first, and then lines three and four say it over again:

> A slumber did my spirit seal;
> I had no human fears:
> She seemed a thing that could not feel
> The touch of earthly years.

To have no human fears is the same thing as to have a sealed spirit. Both of these are defined by the speaker's false assumption that Lucy will not grow old or die. Formally the poem is organized by the opposition between the first stanza and the second. Each stanza sets one line against the next, the first two against the last two; each also sets line one against line three and line two against line four, by way of the interlaced pattern of rhymes – abab, cdcd. The bar or barrier or blank on the page between the two stanzas constitutes the major formal structuring principle of the poem. In the shift from past to present tense this bar opposes then to now, ignorance to knowledge, life to death. The speaker has moved across the line from innocence to knowledge through the experience of Lucy's death. The poem expresses both eloquently restrained grief for that death and the calm of mature knowledge. Before, he was innocent.

His spirit was sealed from knowledge as though he were asleep, closed in on himself. His innocence took the form of an ignorance of the fact of death. Lucy seemed so much alive, such an invulnerable vital young thing, that she could not possibly be touched by time, reach old age, and die. Her seeming immortality reassured the speaker of his own, and so he did not anticipate with fear his own death. He had no human fears. To be human is to be mortal, and the most specifically human fear, it may be, is the fear of death.

Wordsworth, in fact, as we know from other texts both in poetry and in prose, had as a child, and even as a young man, a strong conviction of his immortality. The feeling that it would be impossible for him to die was associated with a strong sense of participation in a nature both enduringly material, therefore immortal, and at the same time enduringly spiritual, therefore also immortal, though in a different way. In this poem, as in so many others by Wordsworth – "The Boy of Winander," the Matthew poems, and "The Ruined Cottage," for example – the speaker confronts the fact of his own death by confronting the death of another. He speaks as a survivor standing by a grave, a corpse, or a headstone, and his poem takes the form of an epitaph.

The second stanza of "A Slumber Did My Spirit Seal" speaks in the perpetual "now" of a universal knowledge of death. The speaker knows his own death through the death of another. Then Lucy seemed an invulnerable young "thing;" now she is truly a thing, closed in on herself like a stone. She is a corpse, without senses or consciousness, unable to feel any touch, unable to move of her own free will, but unwillingly and unwittingly moved by the daily rotation of the earth.

The structure of the poem is temporal. It is also "allegorical" in the technical sense in which that term is used by Walter Benjamin or by Paul de Man. The meaning of the poem arises from the interaction of two emblematic times. These are juxtaposed across an intervening gap. They are related not by similarity but by radical difference. The ironic clash between the two senses of "thing" is a miniature version of the total temporal allegory which constitutes the poem.

The play on the word "thing" exists, it happens, also in German. Two curious passages in Martin Heidegger's work will perhaps help to understand it better in Wordsworth. The first is in a passage in "*Der Ursprung des Kunstwerkes*" ("The Origin of the Work of Art"), in which Heidegger is giving examples of times when we do or do not call something a "thing":

> A man is not a thing. [*Der Mensch ist kein Ding.*] It is true that we speak of a young girl who is faced with a task too difficult for her [*eine ubermassige Aufgabe*] as being a young thing, still too young for it [*eine noch zu junges Ding*], but only because we feel that being human is in a certain way

missing here [*hier das Menschsein in gewisser Weise vermissen*] and think that instead we have to do here with the factor that constitutes the thingly character of things [*das Dinghafte der Dinge*]. We hesitate even to call the deer in the forest clearing, the beetle in the grass, the blade of grass a thing. We could sooner think of a hammer as a thing, or a shoe, or an ax, or a clock. But even these are not mere things [*Aber ein blosses Ding sind auch sie nicht*]. Only a stone, a clod of earth, a piece of wood are for us such mere things.

Strangely, though perhaps in response to a deep necessity, Heidegger gives almost exactly the same list of mere things as Wordsworth. His young girl, stone, clod of earth, piece of wood, correspond to Wordsworth's Lucy, rocks, stones, trees, and the earth itself. Moreover, Heidegger, certainly not known for his attention to the sexual aspect of things, finds himself of necessity, in his account of the uses of the word "thing," introducing the fact of sexual difference. A young girl is a thing because something is missing in her which men have. "A man is not a thing." This something missing makes her "too young for it," too young for the burdens of life. She is too innocent, too light.

This lightness of the maiden thing, which makes a young girl both beneath adult male knowledge and lightheartedly above it, appears in another odd passage in Heidegger, in this case in *Die Frage nach dem Ding* [*What is a Thing?*]. Heidegger first recalls the story in Plato's *Thaetetus* about the "goodlooking and whimsical maid from Thrace" who laughed at Thales when he fell down a well while occupied in studying the heavens. In his study of all things in the universe, "the things in front of his very nose and feet were unseen by him." "Therefore," says Heidegger in commentary on Plato's story, "the question 'What is a thing?' must always be rated as one which causes housemaids to laugh. And genuine housemaids must have something to laugh about [*Und was eine rechte Dienstmagd ist, muss doch auch etwas zum lachen haben*]." The question, "What is a thing?", which is the question implicit in "A Slumber Did My Spirit Seal," would be a laughable non-question to Lucy. She would not understand it because she *is* a thing. Being a thing makes her both immeasurably below and immeasurably above laughable man with his eternal questions. By dying Lucy moves from the below to the above, leaving the male poet in either case in between, excluded, unable to break the seal.

As the reader works his or her way into the poem, attempting to break its seal, however, it comes to seem odder than the account of it I have so far given. My account has been a little too logical, a little too much like Thales' account of the universe, an analogical oversimplification. For one thing, the speaker has in fact not died. Lucy, it may be, has achieved immortality by joining herself to the perpetual substance of earth, which cannot die, as Wordsworth very forcefully says at the beginning of Book V of *The Prelude*. The speaker by not dying remains excluded from that perpetual vitality. His immortality is the bad one of a permanent empty knowledge of death and a permanent impossibility of dying. The "I" of the first stanza ("I had no human fears") has disappeared entirely in the impersonal assertions of the second stanza. It is as though the speaker had lost his selfhood by waking to knowledge. He has become an anonymous impersonal wakefulness, perpetually aware that Lucy is dead and that he is not yet dead. This is the position of the survivor in all Wordsworth's work.

Moreover, an obscure sexual drama is enacted in this poem. This drama is a major carrier of its allegorical significance. The identification of this drama will take the reader further inside. As we know from *The Prelude* as well as from the Lucy poems, nature for Wordsworth was strongly personified. It was, oddly, personified as both male and female, as both father and mother. The earth was the maternal face and body he celebrates in the famous "Infant Babe" passage in the earliest version of *The Prelude*, written also in Goslar in 1798:

> No outcast he, bewilder'd and depress'd;
> Along his infant veins are interfus'd
> The gravitation and the filial bond
> Of nature, that connect him with the world.

Nature was also, however, in certain other episodes of the earliest *Prelude*, a frightening male spirit threatening to punish the poet for wrongdoing. The poem "Nutting," also written at Goslar, though not later incorporated into *The Prelude*, brings the two sexes of nature together in the astonishing scene of a rape of female nature which brings the terror of a reprisal from another aspect of nature, a fearsome male guardian capable of revenge.

Wordsworth's mother died when he was eight, his father when he was thirteen. His father's death and Wordsworth's irrational sense of guilt for it are the subject of another episode of the two-book *Prelude*, another of the "spots of time." His mother's death, however, is curiously elided, so that the reader might not even be sure what the poet is talking about:

> For now a trouble came into my mind
> From obscure causes. I was left alone . . .

The death of Wordsworth's mother hardly seems an "obscure cause" for sorrow, and yet the poet wants to efface that death. He wants to push the source of the sorrow of solitude further back, into deeper obscurity. In the Lucy poems the possession of Lucy alive and seemingly immortal is a replacement for the lost mother. It gives him again that direct filial bond to nature he had lost with the mother's death. It perhaps does not matter greatly whether the reader thinks of Lucy as a daughter or as a mistress or as an embodiment of his feelings for his sister Dorothy. What matters is the way in which her imagined death is a re-enactment of the death of the mother as described in *The Prelude*.

The re-enactment of the death of the mother takes a peculiar form in "A Slumber Did My Spirit Seal," however. This poem, and the Lucy poems as a group, can be defined as an attempt to have it both ways, an attempt which, necessarily, fails. Within his writing, which is what is meant here by "Wordsworth," the poet's abandonment has always already occurred. It is the condition of life and poetry once Wordsworth has been left alone, once he has become an outcast, bewildered and depressed. His only hope for re-establishing the bond that connected him to the world is to die without dying, to be dead, in his grave, and yet still alive, bound to maternal nature by way of a surrogate mother, a girl who remains herself both alive and dead, still available in life and yet already taken by Nature. Of course this is impossible, but it is out of such impossibilities that great poems are made.

Wordsworth's acting out of this fantasy is described in an extraordinary passage by Dorothy Wordsworth. This is her entry in the "Grasmere Journals" for 29 April 1802, three and a half years after the composition of "A Slumber Did My Spirit Seal":

> We then went to John's Grove, sate a while at first. Afterwards William lay, and I lay in the trench under the fence – he with his eyes shut and listening to the waterfalls and the Birds. There was no one waterfall – it was the sound of waters in the air – the voice of the air. Williams heard me breathing and rustling now and then but we both lay still, and unseen by one another. He thought that it would be as sweet thus to lie so in the grave, to hear the *peaceful* sounds of the earth and just to know that our dear friends were near.

"A Slumber Did My Spirit Seal" dramatizes the impossibility of fulfilling this fantasy, or rather it demonstrates that it can only be fulfilled in fantasy, that is, in a structure of words in which "thing" can mean both "person" and "object," in which one can have both stanzas at once, and can, like Lucy, be both alive and dead, or in which the poet can be both the dead–alive girl and at the same time the perpetually wakeful survivor. To have it as wordplay, however, is to have it as the impossibility of having it, to have it as permanent loss and separation, to have it as the unbridgeable gap between one meaning of the word "thing" and the other.

In "A Slumber Did My Spirit Seal" this simultaneous winning and losing, winning by losing, losing by winning, is expressed in a constant slipping of entities across borders into their opposites. As a result the mind cannot carry on that orderly thinking which depends on keeping "things" firmly fixed in their conceptual pigeon-holes. Lucy was a virgin "thing." She seemed untouchable by earthly years, that is, untouchable by nature as time, as the bringer of death, as death. The touch of earthly years is both a form of sexual appropriation which leaves the one who is possessed still virgin if she dies young, and at the same time it is the ultimate dispossession which is death. To be touched by earthly years is a way to be sexually penetrated while still remaining virgin.

The speaker of the poem rather than being the opposite of Lucy, male to her female, adult knowledge to her prepubertal innocence, is the displaced representative of both the penetrated and the penetrator, of both Lucy herself and of her unravishing ravisher, nature or death. The speaker was "sealed," as she was. Now he knows. He is unsealed, as she is. To know, however, as the second stanza indicates, is to speak from the impersonal position of death. It is to speak as death. Death is the penetrator who leaves his victim intact, unpierced, but at the same time wholly open, as an unburied corpse is exposed, open to the sky, like rocks and stones and trees. The speaker's movement to knowledge, as his consciousness becomes dispersed, loses its "I," is "the same thing" as Lucy's death. It finds its parable in that death.

Whatever track the reader follows through the poem he arrives at blank contradictions, These contradictions are not ironic. They are the copresence of difference within the same, as, for example, time in the poem is not different from space but is collapsed into the rolling motion of the earth, or as Lucy in her relation to the speaker blurs the difference of the sexes. Lucy is both the virgin child and the missing mother, that mother earth who gave birth to the speaker and has abandoned him. Male and female, however, come together in the earth, and so Lucy and the speaker are "the same," though the poet is also the perpetually excluded difference from Lucy, an unneeded increment, like an abandoned child. The two women, mother and girl child, have jumped over the male generation in the middle. They have erased its power of mastery, its power of logical understanding, which is the male power *par excellence*. In expressing this, the poem leaves its reader with no possibility of moving through or beyond or standing outside in sovereign control. The reader is caught in an unstillable oscillation unsatisfying to the mind and incapable of being grounded in anything outside the activity of the poem itself.

"A Slumber Did My Spirit Seal" shimmers between affirming male mastery as the consciousness which survives the death of the two generations, mother and daughter or sister, and *knows*, and lamenting the failure of consciousness to join itself to the dead mother, and therefore to the ground of consciousness, by way of its possession of the sister or daughter. On the one hand, he does survive; if he does not have possession or power, he has knowledge. On the other hand, thought or knowledge is not guiltless. The poet has himself somehow caused Lucy's death by thinking about it. Thinking recapitulates in reverse mirror image the action of the earthly years in touching, penetrating, possessing, killing, encompassing, turning the other into oneself and therefore being left only with a corpse, an empty sign.

Lest it be supposed that I am grounding my reading of the poem on the "psychobiographical" details of the poet's reaction to the death of his parents, let me say that it is the other way around. Wordsworth interpreted the death of his mother according to the traditional trope identifying the earth with a maternal presence. By the time we encounter her in his writing she exists as an element in that figure. His life, like his poetry, was the working out of the consequences of this fictitious trope, or rather of the whole figurative system into which it is incorporated. This incorporation exists both in Wordsworth's language and in the Western tradition generally, both before and after him. To put this as economically as possible, "A Slumber Did My Spirit Seal," in the context of the other Lucy poems and of all Wordsworth's work, enacts one version of a constantly repeated Occidental drama of the lost sun. Lucy's name of course means light. To possess her would be a means of rejoining the lost source of light, the father sun as *logos*, as head power and fount of meaning. As light she is the vacant evidence that that capital source seems once to have existed. Light is dispersed everywhere but yet may not be captured or held. It is like those heavens Thales studied. To seek to catch or understand it is to be in danger of falling in a well. The fear of the death of Lucy is the fear that the light will fail, that all links with the sun will be lost, as, in "Strange Fits of Passion," another of the Lucy poems, the setting of the moon, mediated female image of the sun, makes the poet–lover fear Lucy's death:

> "Oh mercy!" to myself I cried,
> "If Lucy should be dead."

The fulfillment of that fear in her actual death is the loss both of light and of the source of light. It is the loss of the *logos*, leaving the poet and his words groundless. The loss of Lucy is the loss of the poet's female reflex or Narcissistic mirror image. In the absence of the filial bond to nature, this has been the only source of his solid sense of selfhood. In one version of the Narcissus story, Narcissus' self-love is generated by the hopeless search for a beloved twin sister, who has died. For Wordsworth, "The furiously burning father fire" (Wallace Stevens' phrase) has sunk beneath the horizon, apparently never to return. In spite of the diurnal rotation of the earth that earth seems to have absorbed all the light. Even the moon, reflected and mediated source of sunlight at night, and so the emblem of Lucy, has set. The consciousness of the poet has survived all these deaths of the light to subsist as a kind of black light. His awareness is the light-no-light which remains when the sun has sunk and Lucy has died, when both have gone into the earth.

This loss of the radiance of the *logos*, along with the experience of the consequences of that loss, is the drama of all Wordsworth's poetry, in particular "A Slumber Did My Spirit Seal." In the absence of any firm grounding the poem necessarily takes on a structure of chiasmus. This is the perpetual reversal of properties in crisscross substitutions I have tried to identify. The senses of the poem continually cross over the borders set up by the words if they are taken to refer to fixed "things," whether material or subjective. The words waver in their meaning. Each word in itself becomes the dwelling place of contradictory senses, as though host and parasite were together in the same house. This wavering exceeds the bounds of the distinction between literal and figurative language, since literal ground and figurative derivative change places too within the word, just as do the other opposites. This wavering within the word is matched by an analogous wavering in the syntax. That in turn is matched by the large-scale relation of going and coming between the two stanzas. Each of these waverings is another example of the disparate in the matching pair which forbids any dialectical synthesis. The tracing out of these differences within the same moves the attention away from the attempt to ground the poem in anything outside itself. It catches the reader within a movement in the text without any solid foundation in consciousness, in nature, or in spirit. As groundless, the movement is, precisely, alogical.

This explanation of Wordsworth's little poem has led me seemingly far away from a sober description of the state of contemporary literary study. It is meant, however, to "exemplify" one mode of such interpretation. In a passage in *The Will to Power* Nietzsche says: "To be able to read off a text as a text without interposing an interpretation is the last-developed form of 'inner experience' – perhaps one that is hardly possible." If it is hardly possible, it may not even be desirable, since interpretation, as Nietzsche also elsewhere says, is an active, affirmative process, a taking possession of something for some purpose or use. In the multitudinous forms of this which make up the scene of literary study, perhaps the true fork in the road is between two modes of this taking possession, two modes of teaching literature and writing about it. One mode already knows what it is going to find. Such a mode is controlled by the presupposition of some center. The other alternative mode of reading is more open to the inexhaustible strangeness of literary texts.

This enigmatic strangeness much literary study busily covers over. The strangeness of literature remains, however. It survives all attempts to hide it. It is one of the major correlatives of the human predicament, since our predicament is to remain, always, within language. The strangeness lies in the fact that language, our Western languages at least, both affirm logic and at the same time turn it on edge, as happens in "A Slumber Did My Spirit Seal." If this is the case, the alternative mode of literary study I have tried to exemplify both can and should be incorporated into college and university curricula. This is already happening to some extent, but, as I see it, the development of programs for this, from basic courses in reading and writing up to the most advanced graduate seminars, is one task in humanistic studies today.

Postscript 1984★

Reading Meyer Abrams' "Construing and Deconstructing" and trying to remember what was going on in my mind when I was writing "On Edge," now five years ago, I do not quite want to say what Thomas Hardy said of *Tess of the d'Urbervilles*: "*Melius fuerat non scribere*. But there it stands." Though I would not write "On Edge" in the same way today, I am glad I wrote it, and in any case, there it stands. As with any piece of writing, the passage of time has detached it more and more from its author, who is no longer quite the same person. Perhaps he was made a somewhat different person by the act of writing it. "On Edge" must now in any case make its own way in the world, as a fatherless orphan who can only go on saying the same thing, over and over, in answer to any questions, such as those Meyer Abrams puts to it.

The situation of literary studies in the United States today, moreover, is markedly different from what it was in 1979. It is my impression that Meyer Abrams is now trying to come to terms with a *fait* largely *accompli*. A good bit at least of what I hoped for then has now occurred, namely the widespread assimilation of new rhetorical methodologies into normal practice in the study and teaching of literature in America. The frontier or edge of literary study has moved on to a different location, a new asking of questions about the relation of literature to history and to society in the light of recent rhetorical and linguistic insights. For better or for worse, the study of literature in the United States has been permanently altered by structuralist and poststructuralist

---

★ This postscript was added for the reprinting of this essay in *Romanticism and Contemporary Criticism*, Morris Crups and Michael Fischer, eds (Ithaca, New York: Cornell University Press, 1986), and is a response to comments made by Meyer H. Abrams, available in the book cited.

methods. Not that there is not still opposition, but that opposition has gone into a new phase, I suppose predictable, but nonetheless deplorable; I mean a phase of irrational polemic, sometimes by distinguished older scholars who apparently feel so threatened by these new directions of literary study that they are willing to abandon all traditions of scholarly accuracy and responsibility in order blindly to attack what they appear to have made no attempt to understand. Meyer Abrams by no means belongs in that category. He has read Derrida and me with great care. His essay has considerable importance as one of the most serious and detailed attempts by a scholar–critic of a different set of commitments to come to terms with so-called deconstruction. With Meyer Abrams one can differ and still talk, and all honor to him and to his essay for that.

My reply, though I am sure my claim that he has not entirely understood deconstruction will not fill him with delight, is meant nevertheless to keep the door open for further dialogue between us, and between people like him and people like me. I have attempted especially to try to answer the question of why Abrams and I, two literary scholars brought up in somewhat the same tradition and both with presumably some competence as readers, nevertheless read Derrida so differently and why we read "A Slumber Did My Spirit Seal" so differently. I find that a puzzling question. I think I have found the answer to it, an answer that lies not in the highfalutin altitudes of pure literary theory but in the lowlands of basic and instinctive orientation toward language, literary or otherwise.

Controversy and polemics in literary study rarely accomplish much. Neither side is likely to cover itself with glory, and much foolishness may be spoken. Nevertheless, the stakes are high enough in this case perhaps to justify a brief response to Abrams' essay. Though I am of course grateful to him for the careful attention he has given to an essay of mine and to a selection of the work of Derrida, he nevertheless seems to me a striking example of the way a man can be learned, distinguished, generous and open minded, at least to a degree, and yet, in this case at least, miss major points in the texts on which he is commenting. Something could be said about more or less every line or sentence of Abrams' essay, something, it seems to me, identified as slightly askew in his formulations and conclusions. In the interests of brevity I shall first identify several less than pervasive though by no means insignificant points of misunderstanding or errancy and then move quickly on to the fundamental misunderstanding which underlies Abrams' whole essay.

First smaller point: I am much troubled by the remarks toward the end of Abrams' essay about the way young people today use so-called deconstructive methods because they produce new and publishable readings and are a way of getting ahead in the academic world, getting promotion and tenure, etc. Abrams here seems to me, if I may say so, shockingly cynical. He shows an amazing lack of confidence in the intellectual integrity of the young people in our profession. Surely he knows that good work was never yet done with that kind of motivation. The only hope in literary study and teaching is to say it like it is as one sees it. Of those sentences in Abrams' essay one can certainly say: *melius fuerat non scribere.*

Second point: Abrams' discussion of Derrida, though it makes a somewhat wider sweep through his writings than many more reductive accounts of it do, is nevertheless primarily based on quite early work, especially *De la grammatologie* and other early essays. Though Derrida would not, I think, by any means repudiate what he wrote then, he has of course published many books and essays since. His new work should surely now form the essential context for any reading of what he wrote earlier, and the early work itself can hardly be understood in isolation from the context of the relation of Derrida's first books to Husserl, to Heidegger, and even to Sartre or to French existentialism of that time generally. If Abrams wanted to make a more solidly based assessment of the implications of Derrida's work for literary study, it might have been better to discuss *Glas*, or *La carte postale*, or *Signéponge*. The same thing might be said in a somewhat different way of his treatment of my essay. Though, as I have said, I am grateful for the careful attention he has given my discussion of "A Slumber Did My Spirit Seal," it seems to me a shaky use of synecdoche to make it stand for my work in general or for American deconstructive criticism in general, in its presumed deviation from Derrida. Abrams' generalizations here are built on an excessively fragile foundation.

Final preliminary point: Abrams often talks as if he thinks it is being claimed that so-called deconstruction is a wholly new and unheard of mode of interpretation, based on new insights into language, something that has never been done before. Nothing could be further from the truth. What is being claimed, rather, is that deconstruction is only the current version of a long tradition of rhetorical study going back especially to the Greeks, though to some degree to an aspect of Greek thought that has tended to be obscured or effaced – even by the Greeks themselves, as by Plato. Good writers and good readers have always known what deconstruction knows, for example about figurative language. What Abrams calls his own "oldreading" is in fact the Johnny-come-lately. It is based on a quite recent set of assumptions about literary interpretation, assumptions narrowly circumscribed within a certain historical situation, that of nineteenth- and twentieth-century humanism in literary study. Like so-called aestheticism, of which it is the mirror image or twin, this humanism tends to sequester literary texts from fundamental ontological, metaphysical, or religious questions.

Now the most important point: The major misunderstanding in Abrams' essay might be approached by way of his title, "Construing and Deconstructing." If these two terms are translated into their more traditional equivalents, Abrams' title would be "Grammar and Rhetoric," that is, the names of two of the three branch-roads of the medieval trivium, the third being logic. Abrams' error is the aboriginal one of assuming that the grammar of a language, for example the language of Wordsworth's little poem, is a first and fundamental level of easily identifiable meaning to which figurative language, the deviant realm of tropes, is added as a nonessential second layer open to what Abrams, in a nice little play of double meaning of his own, calls "over-reading." First there is under-reading, or the construing of plain grammar, and then, if you happen to want it (though why should you?) there is over-reading, the interpretation of figures, what is sometimes called deconstruction. The latter is a kind of supererogatory fiddling with the text. It is altogether dependent, to boot, on the fact that the deconstructer has first performed, like every other reader, the under-reading of the text, that construing of its plain sense which all competent readers spontaneously and successfully accomplish.

The claim of the tradition to which Derrida and I belong is that this is a false picture both of language and of the process of good reading. The major presupposition of deconstruction and of the long tradition to which it belongs is that figurative language goes all the way down, so to speak. It is not something added on top of an easily construable grammar. The language of poems, novels, philosophical texts, or of any other genre, for example literary criticism, is not like that honey pot with which Pooh in A. A. Milne's story fears he may have baited the trap for heffalumps, honey on top, product of the sweet flowers of rhetoric, and cheese at the bottom, the plain food of literal language. Language is honey all the way to the bottom, and the bottom is a long way down. All language is irreducibly and fundamentally figurative, as in my play on words for bottom or ground here. All good reading is therefore the reading of tropes at the same time as it is the construing of syntactical and grammatical patterns. Any act of reading must practice the two forms of interpretation together. This means that there is no such thing as that plain under-reading which Abrams hypothesizes. With the collapse of this hypothesis Abrams' whole argument against deconstruction, his aberrant reading of it, as well as his proposal of an alternative pedagogy, falls to the ground. There is only and always, from the beginning, one form or another of over-reading, the reading of grammar and tropes together, more or less adequately.

One evidence of the nonexistence of the grammatical under-reading Abrams imagines is the wild diversity of "first readings" of any given text one gets from so-called competent readers. Abrams presents, almost in spite of himself, one example of this in his brief discussion of previous commentary on "A Slumber Did My Spirit Seal." Anyone who has followed the history of the interpretation of any major works in the canon of Western literature, even the most apparently "simple" ones, will have encountered other versions of this diversity. What Abrams really means by "we under-readers who start and stop with the plain sense everyone can agree on" is "I, Meyer Abrams, and those I can persuade to accept my reading." The evidence against the notion of a broad agreement on the plain construed sense of literary works is overwhelming.

Any good reader confronted with the words of "A Slumber Did My Spirit Seal," as Abrams cites it at the end of his essay, will be assailed by a swarm of questions, not by any means faced with a clear, spontaneously generated, construed meaning on the basis of which he can execute arabesques of irresponsible or ungrounded "over-readings." Some of these questions are "grammatical": e.g., why does the poem say "did . . . seal" rather than use the simple past tense, "sealed"? Some are "rhetorical" or have to do with tropes: e.g., what does it mean to say someone's "spirit" "slumbers"? what does it mean to say that someone's "spirit" (whatever *that* means in this case) is "sealed"? does it mean as an envelope, or as with a bit of wax, or as a tomb, or as someone's lips are "sealed," or what? All these enigmas are on the same level, so to speak. Each enters into the others, is intertwined with them, so that one cannot be "solved" without the others. Their failure to form a hierarchy forbids the certain establishment of that plain sense or under-reading which Abrams wants to make the basis of literary study.

All the other conclusions of Abrams' essay are vitiated by the insubstantiality of his initial premise, in particular his way of reading deconstructive texts by Derrida and by me, his questioning of my placing of "A Slumber Did My Spirit Seal" in a wide context of passages by Wordsworth and by others, and his picture of a proper pedagogy as beginning with construing or grammar and then going on, for very advanced students, to deconstruction, that is to rhetoric as the understanding of tropes.

The whole effort of deconstructive criticism has been to demonstrate, patiently, over and over again, with many different texts of different sorts – poems, novels, philosophy, criticism, prefaces, and so on – the exact opposite of what Abrams wants to say, namely to demonstrate that the plainest grammatical sense is already turned aside from itself by tropes of one sort or another. Far from building his reading of Rousseau on an under-reading which everyone accepts, Derrida wants to show both that a specific reading, namely the "logocentric" one, is inevitable for any reader at any time in our culture and at the same time that such a reading always contains the traces, vestiges, or latent indications of another reading undoing the first. Deconstruction displaces or reorients that metaphysical reading by following those traces and thereby placing the logocentric reading in a different context. This new context turns the logocentric reading into something other than itself. This procedure shows that the logocentric reading is something far different from the solidly based under-reading Abrams presumes it to be, namely that it is but one strand in a complex fabric.

As for what Abrams says about my initial paraphrase of "A Slumber Did My Spirit Seal," I am sorry to say that he has missed the point of what I was trying to do, and for a reason which may have a profound significance for the differences between us. My initial paraphrase was meant to be ironic, that is, to display its manifest inadequacy, as a way of preparing for the attempt later on to account for this inadequacy and to try to repair it. The reader was meant to recognize that there is something strangely incomplete or lacking in such an account of the poem and to expect something more as an attempt to repair that incompleteness. As someone has said, there should be a mark of punctuation for irony.

On the question of context: Abrams assumes that there is a solid context for the reading of detached texts, such as a short lyric poem like "A Slumber Did My Spirit Seal," in the grammatical competence of any reader or speaker of the language in which it is written. Derrida knows French, therefore he can read Rousseau, just as any other Frenchman can. I know English, so what's my problem with "A Slumber Did My Spirit Seal"? If Derrida and I are right, and we are, about the enigmas introduced into even the most apparently simple passage by its permeation or pervasion by figurative language, one of the effects of this is to make each piece of language idiosyncratic, idiomatic, the generator of an idolect of its own. It follows from this that the presumed sufficient context in standard French or English is an illusion.

We need in such an emergency all the help we can get. One such help is other "similar" passages in the same writer or in other writers, in a widening field which, as Derrida puts it, can never be "saturated," and which of course creates as many problems as it solves, especially by way of what is problematic about that "similarity." In what way, exactly, do the so-called Lucy poems form a group? I agree with Abrams that this is a problem, but I do not think the problem can be solved by pretending there is no relation among them. The other "similar" passages will not "solve" the enigmas, which are in any case insoluble in the sense of being incapable of being untied, made clear once and for all, but the analogues will perhaps assist the reader in catching a glimpse of what is heterogeneous, incommensurate, idiolectal, idiomatic, or even "idiotic" (in the sense of being unconstruable) in the text at hand. All this depends, of course, on the capacity to see it as, on the first and most immediate level, strange, puzzling, lacking in transparency of meaning.

Finally, on the question of pedagogy: As I have already hinted, it would follow from the pervasion of grammar by rhetoric which deconstruction patiently demonstrates, that Abrams' model for teaching is an impossibility. He imagines that it is possible to teach novices first "to write texts that will say, precisely and accurately, what they mean, and to construe, precisely and accurately, the texts that they read." Then possibly, at some much later stage, in advanced seminars, as an unnecessary frill, the "equilibristic art" of deconstruction might be taught. Alas, this will not work. There is no grammar without rhetoric, as teachers of composition have always known, and as they are finding out again in different ways today. Students will learn neither to write well nor to read well unless they are taught both grammar and rhetoric together from the beginning. That this makes difficulties for the devising of curricula in composition and in literature (and for the training of teachers of both) I would be the last to deny, but so have recent advances in physical and biological knowledge made great problems for the teaching of those disciplines. The difference is that the inherence of tropes, including the trope of irony, in ordinary as well as in literary language has been known since Plato and the Greek rhetoricians. To say that rhetoric or the knowledge of tropes should not be taught from the beginning, along with grammatical competence, in courses in composition and reading is like saying schools should first teach that the sun moves around the earth or that lice are bred from human sweat, and then let a few advanced students know it is not so simple.

There is no help for it. If language is "perfidious," to use Abrams' somewhat invidious word, then students even at the most preliminary level should be told this truth, just as beginning courses in biology or physics must try to explain the latest knowledge of genetics or of particle physics. That there are special difficulties in using language to explain language, as a teacher of composition or rhetoric must do, there can be no doubt, but there is no alternative but to try. Once more I think Abrams is surprisingly condescending both to teachers of composition and reading and to their students in suggesting that they will necessarily fail in this attempt.

I conclude by asking again why it might be that there is such a great gulf between Abrams and me in what happens when we first encounter something like those eight lines of "A Slumber Did My Spirit Seal" he cites at the end of his essay as the final challenge to deconstruction. What I have said already about his failure to identify the trope of irony in my essay may give the clue. I am reminded of the passage in George Eliot's *Daniel Deronda* describing Gwendolen's blindness to religious experience and to economic or political knowledge:

> She had no permanent consciousness of other fetters, or of more spiritual restraints, having always disliked whatever was presented to her under the name of religion, in the same way that some people dislike arithmetic and accounts: it has raised no other emotion in her, no alarm, no longing; so that the question whether she believed it had not occurred to her, any more than it had occurred to her to inquire into the conditions of colonial property and banking, on which, as she had had many opportunities of knowing, the family fortune was dependent. (chapter 6)

Just as, so I have gradually come to believe, there are people learned, sensitive, and intelligent for whom metaphysical or religious questions are nonquestions, or people, also learned, sensitive, and intelligent, for whom social or political questions are nonquestions, so it may be that there are people who have a blind spot in the area of recognizing the strange things tropes do to a given piece of language. This may especially appear in an insensitivity to irony, which is like failing to see the point of a joke. Nothing is more annoying than to be told one has not seen that a joke is a joke, an irony an irony. Disagreements about the way to take a possibly ironic passage are likely to give rise to the bitterest and most acrimonious controversies, such as those I began this postscript by deploring. Something of this sort, nevertheless, may be the cause of the fissure or cleft between Meyer Abrams and me, though I continue to hope that he will come over to my side of the chasm. Perhaps it is the fissure between all under-readers and all over-readers, though I should prefer to make it a distinction between worse and better reading as such, for example of "A Slumber Did My Spirit Seal."

Questions and answers

Question: You seem to make two different claims for deconstruction, one soft and the other hard. The soft claim seems to be that deconstruction is simply an attempt to test or question the weight-bearing capacity of the ground assumed by a text. The hard claim seems to be the conclusion that the ground in each case can't bear the weight imposed on it. I think that a critic of deconstruction like Walter Jackson Bate wouldn't oppose the first notion; he's not against testing or questioning texts. But it's the second notion that alarms him.

Answer: I agree. The second part is the specifically skeptical aspect of deconstruction that does annoy and alarm people like Professor Bate. My answer to that would be to say to him or to anyone else, let's look at the works together. Let's read them together and do that testing, and we'll see whether you can persuade me that the ground of a text does bear the weight. That's what I mean by the claim that deconstruction is simply good reading and that the best places for discussing deconstruction are to be found in shared acts of reading, not in pure theory. In the latter, untested preconceptions about what goes on in Kant or Wallace Stevens, for example, move very easily into polemical statements.

Question: If Bate read further into deconstruction, don't you think that he would find comfort in the obvious conservatism that has developed there? It seems to me that the conclusion to your questioning is predetermined; that is, you already know that literature won't sustain the meanings imposed on it. But faced with that fact you finally develop the conservative argument that since there's no way in which you can justify *any* map of literary history, for example, you're justified in holding on to the map you've got. Do you think that deconstruction consequently shelters academic and intellectual conservatives who in a previous era would have been New Critics?

Answer: I don't agree that my conclusions are predetermined. I'm still looking and would be glad to find solid ground to stand on. As for the map of literary history, I believe a new one on the basis of new developments is possible. Drawing that map is a major task today. Insofar as deconstruction is simply good reading or careful reading, then it is a form of reading in general of which the New Criticism was another form. Unlike the New Critics, deconstructionists argue that you can't take it for granted that a good work of literature is going to be organically unified. Deconstruction sees irony as not necessarily (or perhaps ever) a trope of determinable meanings (saying one thing and meaning another identifiable thing) and puts more emphasis than Brooks did on such problematic tropes, however much interest he took in them. Deconstruction is more Empsonian or Burkean than Brooksian. I would say that it's all there in Kenneth Burke and Empson: you don't need Derrida if you have read Burke. Derrida has, however, applied notions about language like Burke's to a larger variety of works. He is interesting to me not only as a theorist but also as a reader.

Question: Sometimes you seem to be suggesting that a poem is a speech act, in which case it would follow that we need to consider the situation of the poem as we read it. If the poem is a speech act, then how do you justify your analysis of "parasite" and "host," for example, where you take these words back to their origins and thus ignore the context of the texts in which they appear?

Answer: In my view, words retain some of their historical force in whatever situation they're used. Therefore the poem is not for me a vacant place given meaning by one or another community of readers, as it is for Stanley Fish. The poem has power, even dangerous power, over me when I read it. One of its powers is the inhabitation in words of some aspect of historical meaning. I stand by my history of "parasite" and "host," though it was meant to some degree to be playful. I was trying to show that these words tend to liberate, in a canny user of them like Shelley, not their whole history but a significant part of it. Arguing from etymologies, as Heidegger, for example, does, is dangerous because there may have been a break in the history of a word's meaning. That history is not all necessarily preprogrammed in the word's root. On the other hand, I don't think a word is entirely defined by its situations; it is not a blank sound or mark to which I give meaning freely or because I belong to some interpretative community. Literature is always full of surprises for even the halfway good reader.

Question: In "The Function of Rhetorical Study at the Present Time," you say that you think it's more important to read Shakespeare, Spenser, and Milton than Borges or Virginia Woolf, and in another place you state that it's important to read "the best" literature. What criteria or resources does deconstruction offer to help us determine the "best" literature?

Answer: I originally made that remark at a meeting at Texas A & M before a gathering of chairmen of departments of English. I was trying to affirm the conservative side of my position. I meant there's too much attention paid to modern literature. I picked Virginia Woolf as a writer whom you can spend too much time studying, however important she is. One needs to know what she knew, including all those male writers she has such an uneasy relation to in *A Room of One's Own*. Although I think that Virginia Woolf is important, I also think that one shouldn't only read twentieth-century literature. Deconstruction is conservative as far as the canon goes. There's been relatively little fiddling with the canon on the part of the deconstructionists, though even slight rearrangements, for example putting Hegel side by side with Genet, as Derrida does in *Glas*, may have more than trivial consequences. There's a rereading of the canon by the deconstructionists, but the people that we read are essentially the ones that everybody else reads. Because the canon is pretty well taken for granted in deconstruction, this particular form of criticism hasn't discovered all that many great writers whom nobody else had noticed. Derrida, for example, teaches philosophy. He teaches mostly the central canon of major philosophers, Plato, Leibniz, Descartes, Kant, Hegel, Heidegger, just as any other historian of philosophy would do.

Question: Suppose you were a student whose education stopped about 1965. You knew about the New Criticism, rhetorical criticism, and reader-response criticism, but nothing about deconstruction. If you were such a student, how would you read a poem differently from the way you do now? What would you fail to see in it that you think you can now see?

Answer: Nothing, if I had been a good reader. That's what I mean when I say that you don't need Derrida or deconstruction if you have not so much Brooks and Warren as Empson and Burke, that side of the New Criticism that's slightly more radical in its view of figures of speech and so on. I would also say, however, that by putting in question the assumption that a good literary work is going to be organically unified, deconstruction has freed me to deal with aspects of works which are not easily assimilated on the assumption of unity. The deconstructionist critics have called attention to the special power of catachresis, a figure of speech, if you can call it that, to which the New Critics did not pay much attention. (Derrida's "White Mythology" is of course a key text here.) Catachresis and prosopopoeia have been important in my recent work. They are limits where rhetorical analysis of literary texts based on the opposition between literal and figurative languages breaks down and where there may be a glimpse, as in the wink of an eye, of something beyond language. That "something," it may be, forbids language, the language of poems for example, to "come clear." Catachresis and prosopopoeia converge, as in "face of a mountain," but have different temporal orientations, catachresis toward the present and toward the "making present" by naming of what would otherwise slip away, prosopopoeia toward the past, the invocation of the absent, inanimate, or dead by giving it the mask of personification, speaking to it or of it as though it were a living person: "Ye knew him well, ye cliffs and islands of Winander." As my example shows, apostrophe and prosopopoeia are of course closely connected. I have tried to work some of this out in *The Linguistic Moment*.

Question: But I would say that in *The Linguistic Moment* you give an organic reading of Yeats' "Nineteen Hundred and Nineteen." By showing that there's disorder in each of the individual parts of the poem, you suggest that the poem consistently creates an image of disorder. I am consequently still not sure what is new about your reading.

Answer: What you say is based on a misunderstanding of the opposition between an "organically unified" reading and a deconstructionist one. A deconstructionist reading can be quite specific about the particular ways a given poem, say Yeats' "Nineteen Hundred and Nineteen," does not hang together or cohere, is heterogeneous, defies the unifying power of logical reason, the logos, without thereby making for an organically unified reading. Nor does such a reading mean that it's a free-for-all, that one is free to make any reading whatsoever of the poem. I would say that I think my reading of Yeats' poem is right, that all right-thinking people will come, given enough time, to my reading. When one speaks of undecidability as a feature of deconstructive criticism, one doesn't mean a free-for-all but a very precise identifiable movement back and forth among possibilities, each of which can be articulated phrase by phrase. My notion is that a poem has a coercive effect on any reader and on any reading, even an inadequate one. Even the most evasive paraphrase contains latently the meanings it tries to suppress, for example Abrams' reading of "A Slumber Did My Spirit Seal." The exemplary statement of this is in Paul de Man's foreword to Carol Jacobs' *The Dissimulating Harmony*. To de Man's statement I give my entire allegiance. Here are his words, if I may be allowed, belatedly and in his memory, to read them into the record:

> Understanding is not a version of one single and universal Truth that would exist as an essence, a hypostasis. The truth of a text is a much more empirical and literal event. What makes a reading more or less true is simply the predictability, the necessity of its occurrence, regardless of the reader or of the author's wishes. "Es ereignet sich aber das Wahre" (not *die Wahrheit*) says Hölderlin, which can be freely translated, "What is true is what is bound to take place." And, in the case of the reading of a text, what takes place is a necessary understanding. What marks the truth of such an understanding is not some abstract universal but the fact that it has to occur regardless of other considerations . . . it is not a matter of choice to omit or to accentuate by paraphrase certain elements in a text at the expense of others. We don't have this choice, since the text imposes its own understanding and shapes the reader's evasions. The more one censors, the more one reveals what is being effaced. A paraphrase is always what we called an analytical reading, that is, it is always susceptible of being made to point out consistently what it was trying to conceal.

Question: I'm always surprised when you talk about the coerciveness or independent status of the poem. How can you exempt the poem from the skepticism in deconstruction that seems to undermine every other presence?

Answer: I need something to hang on to or to stand on. It's those words on the page. They are not so much "presence" as what Mallarmé calls "une apparence fausse de présence." In giving that nonpresent presence irresistible power I'm testifying to my experience with literature, which is that I can't make George Eliot's *Middlemarch* or Stevens' "The Rock" mean anything that I want it to mean. Such a text that has coercion over me may be complicated, heterogeneous, enigmatic, but that doesn't make it disappear or free me to make it mean anything I want. This fact preserves the possibility of saying to somebody, "You're wrong in this case." Luckily, since a teacher needs to feel able to say that. This power of the text over its readers also opens up the possibility of dialogue among readers in which you could actually work out whether somebody was right or wrong. It follows that the real way to get at Derrida – it would be hard to do – would be to try to demonstrate that he is wrong about Plato or Ponge or Hegel, that his readings are wrong. This would be far more to the point than arguing in a vacuum about his "theories."

Question: How does Frye's theory of archetypes fit in with your view of deconstruction?

Answer: For Frye, archetypes tend to be thought of as preceding or exceeding any of their embodiments. Therefore, though Frye's theory is not openly Jungian, he nevertheless suggests that there is a reservoir of archetypes somewhere, and that they have to reappear out of some place. For me or for Derrida, the patterns exist only in their embodiments; there is no *ur* example. There is no origin other than a movement of differentiation. Frye has not been much talked about or criticized by deconstructionists as far as I know, but in "Structure, Sign, and Play" Derrida explicitly criticizes a nostalgia for an original happy savage state in Lévi-Strauss. In the Lévi-Straussian or structuralist anthropological view of myth, you have two, three, five, a dozen, a hundred different examples of the myth you have gathered, and it looks as if they bend back toward some original myth of which they are all representative, though Lévi-Strauss correctly sees that as an anaclastic illusion. Frye sometimes seems to yield to that illusion.

Question: M. H. Abrams has used your essay "On Edge" to make a sharp distinction between Derrida's linguistic philosophy and the use made of it in American deconstructive criticism. Do you see any grounds for distinguishing between your literary criticism and Derrida's philosophy?

Answer: I should hope there would be a difference! On the other hand it would be a mistake to assume too easily that American deconstruction is necessarily all that tame or conservative. Profound changes in curriculum and departmental organization are already beginning in American colleges and universities as a result of deconstruction. Your question has been raised by people quite different from Abrams in orientation. For example, Rodolphe Gasché in an essay in *Glyph* makes the point rather aggressively that Derrida belongs to a certain European context, that he is genuinely revolutionary in that context, that he is a philosopher, not a literary critic, and that when he is appropriated in the United States primarily by literary critics and for the purposes of reading, he is tamed and made more conservative. The people who do this kind of criticism in America, moreover, tend to be in élitist institutions, say some of our critics, and therefore uphold the status quo, vote conservatively, and so on. Deconstructionists find themselves in the strange situation of being attacked by both sides: by conservatives like Bate and Wellek and Gerald Graff for being nihilistic and by Marxists for not changing the institution one iota. On the one hand we do nothing, on the other are violent anarchists. I don't see how our opponents can have it both ways. In fact both are grievously in error. I would agree that there is a change when you move from one institutional context to another. Derrida, it is true, is supposed to be a philosopher, and most of the people in America who do this kind of criticism are literary critics, though Derrida's influence on philosophy proper in America is beginning to be strongly felt. This fact is resisted and deplored by philosophers like Searle. On the other hand, I do think that Gasché is wrong in ignoring the fact that Derrida is primarily a reader of pieces of language and that among the things that he has read are works of literature. It's not necessarily the case, then, that a critic of literature must be less radical than Derrida. It's not intrinsic in the transfer that deconstruction must be weakened over here. Changed, yes, but after all Derrida teaches at Yale a few weeks each year and lectures widely in the States. At least to that degree his activity is transferred to the United States.

Question: You no longer feel that there is any sort of interaction between the self and language?

Answer: I'm skeptical about whether you can think of the self as something inside me like a grain of sand, as Yeats put it, something like a definite hard object. It seems to me that the self is a function primarily of language rather than a preexistent given which uses language. Language is prior to selfhood rather than the other way around, though the latter is what Georges Poulet, along with so many other distinguished critics, appears to think. Once you see the self as generated by language, then selfhood becomes much more varied, precarious, and complicated. I agree with Nietzsche here. He defines the self as a congeries of warring selves. The issue of selfhood is of great importance in the criticism of fiction. It is traditional to assume that a good work of fiction is going to present characters each of whom has a total unity. It seems to me, on the contrary, that one of the major things the tradition of realistic fiction does is to put that notion of selfhood in question. A marvelous example of this is Meredith's *The Egoist*. Clara Middleton discovers that though her act of promising to marry Willoughby presupposes a fixed and unified self on the basis of which promises can be made, she does not in fact have such a self. She is rather "a multitude of flitting wishes." It's not, then, that there's necessarily no such thing as selfhood but that it cannot be taken for granted. The nature of selfhood is one of the things that literature makes problematic or about which literature raises questions.

Question: But in "The Function of Rhetorical Study at the Present Time" you suggest that calling into question the notion of the self eventually affirms the self.

Answer: Well, the self is a hard thing to do without – almost impossible, in fact, even in the most practical sense. Suppose I could say that yesterday I signed that promissory note or took out that mortgage but I'm not the same person today that I was yesterday, so you can't hold me to the mortgage payment. Obviously that would cause great problems. It seems like a trivial example, but our whole social life depends on the possibility of holding somebody to promises and commitments that presuppose you're somehow the same person from day to day and from year to year. It's a serious business, this question of self, not just a theoretical speculation. This is why I think it's better that questions about it should be raised in a relatively safe area like novels rather than in other areas. That is one of the things we need novels for, to assuage our anxiety about a subject by allowing questions to be raised about it and perhaps to lead us, as *The Egoist* does, to a happy ending, thereby calming our fears. In *The Egoist* the idea of selfhood as a fixed, preexisting thing is replaced by a much more precarious notion of selfhood, a notion which would be a little harder to live with if it were widely accepted.

Question: But doesn't deconstruction, in practice, affirm the self that it wants to question?

Answer: Yes, though perhaps in a form which is slightly shaken or transformed. Nietzsche is a good example of this. Book III of *The Will to Power* is one of the most powerful puttings into question of the notion of selfhood I know. Nietzsche argues subtly and overtly that there is no such thing as the self, that it is just a changing set of functions, linguistic conventions, etc. But notice the way Nietzsche says this: "*I hold [Ich halte]* that there's no such thing as the self." He cannot perform the activity of deconstructing the self without at the same time affirming it. It is a splendid example of your point.

Question: Where do you see literary study going in the immediate future? Are significant further changes likely to take place?

Answer: I think the frontier or border on which we stand now is very different from our situation five years ago when I wrote "On Edge: The Crossways of Contemporary Criticism." We stand at a different crossroads and have different choices to make. The assimilation of poststructuralist modes of criticism into college and university curricula for which I called then has to a considerable extent occurred or is occurring. The danger now is that deconstruction might petrify, harden into a dogma, or into a rigid set of prescriptions for reading, become some kind of fixed method rather than a set of examples, very different from one another, of good reading. I see the frontier of literary study at the present time as involving the genuine assimilation of the lessons of deconstruction (no easy matter, involving as it does the careful reading of the work of de Man, Derrida, *et al.*) and then requiring us to move on as they are (or rather as Derrida is and as de Man was in work done shortly before his death) toward the difficult questions of what these new developments mean for ethics, for the institutionalizing of literary study, and for the broadest and most fundamental questions of literary history, of history as such, of social policy and social organization, of the role of literature in society. The stakes here are enormous. The most prudent and careful as well as the most courageous work of thought will be necessary, but if literature, as a mode of the aesthetic, is to have the role allotted to it by Kant, and ever since Kant, as the bridge between epistemology and ethics, the new developments in literary study have important implications not only for the bridge but for those realms the bridge is supposed to join. So we may be not so much at a frontier or at a crossroads as standing on a bridge – a bridge, moreover, that has received in recent years a new testing, shaking, or solicitation.

12

The function of rhetorical study at the present time

The new statement is always hated by the old, and, to those dwelling in the old, comes like an abyss of scepticism. But the eye soon gets wonted to it, for the eye and it are effects of one cause; then its innocency and benefit appear, and presently, all of its energies spent, it pales and dwindles before the revelation of the new hour.

Emerson, "Circles"

What is the present relation between literary theory and pedagogy in American colleges and universities? Most professors in departments of literature still assume that their chief responsibility is teaching students how to read "primary texts." The context or situation in which that duty is performed, however, has changed radically from what it was thirty years ago. The old consensus in literary studies in the United States, such as it was, has been challenged in manifold ways. There is now, for example, widespread disagreement about just what those "primary" texts ought to be and about just how they ought to be organized in courses and curricula. At the same time, as everyone knows, there has been a spectacular proliferation of powerful and incompatible "critical theories": structuralist, semiotic, Lacanian, Marxist, reader-response, deconstructionist, New Historicist, and so on.

In such a situation the relation of "theory" to "example" is fundamentally changed. Changed also is the relation of theory to the act of reading the example, as well as the relation of that whole process to what may be called, by a kind of shorthand, "history." I mean here by "history" something assumed to be radically different from either theory or literary texts. History takes place in the real world of flesh and blood men and women carrying on their daily lives. We might mean by history in this sense something that occurred either in the past or now, when, as we say, "history is being made every day." I believe we tend to think these days of the historical as violent, as involving suffering. The downing of Korean Flight 007 is more likely to come to mind as an example of a historical happening than the "blameless" lives of an insurance salesperson in Topeka, Kansas, and his or her spouse and children.

All reading and teaching of literature is theoretical. This is so in the strict sense that any sort of reading and teaching of literature presupposes all sorts of assumptions about what literature is and about how it should be read. I mean by "literary theory" here the shift from the hermeneutical process of identifying the meaning of a work of literature to a focus on the question of how that meaning is generated. When there is a general consensus about literary theory, for example at the time the New Criticism was more or less universally accepted in the United States, theory tends to be effaced, latent, presupposed; one just goes to work doing or teaching "close reading." When a multitude of conflicting critical theories call for attention, however, and when in addition there is confusion over the canons and the curricula of literature, as at the present time, then literary theory, rather than being something that can more or less be taken for granted, becomes overt, exigent, even, some would say, strident. Theory tends to become a primary means of access to the works read. These works now tend to be redefined as "examples" demonstrating the productive effectiveness of this or that theory.

In such a situation, literary theory even tends to become a primary object of study in itself, as in that ever-increasing number of courses and programs these days in critical theory as such, sometimes treated historically, sometimes as a matter of current concern. The "examples" read, at the same time, are no longer so often drawn from an established canon arranged in traditional canonical ways, for example by genre and historical period. The result is that the examples read are likely to be subordinated to theory in the sense that the example is read as a more or less arbitrary choice among innumerable possible ones of a theoretical concept that claims universal applicability. The teacher teaches the student to read the example in a certain way. The implicit claim is that everything should be read analogously. What is taught is a universal way of reading and its accompanying explicit and self-conscious theory, not the works in an agreed-upon canon read in canonical ways as having established meanings and as transmitting from the past agreed-upon cultural values. The place of those established meanings and enshrined values is more and more taken by theory itself.

Seen from this perspective, the function of theory is to liberate us from ideology, even from the ideology of theory itself. Critical theory performs an ethical and political act. It has institutional and social force. Critical theory is, then, no longer "merely theoretical." Rather it makes something happen by disabling the power of the works read to go on proliferating the ideology that traditional canonical or thematic readings of it have blindly asserted, often without even being aware that they are merely thematic or are ideologically determined. Critical theory, seen from this point of view, earns its label of "critical." It becomes within our educational institutions one of the most powerful and indispensable means of unmasking ideological assumptions.[1]

That our profession is undergoing unusually rapid changes no one can doubt, especially those of us who find ourselves chairs of departments of English. The pressures are coming from various directions. Chairs must often feel themselves to be at the confluence of contradictory winds of change, blown here and there like a tumbleweed. A chair's response may be to make himself or herself as much like a rock as possible, stolid and imperturbable. The point of this paper is to assert that this is the wrong strategy.

The changes are coming from society, in one direction, and from within the discipline itself, in the other. Although they appear to be contradictory or to make contradictory demands on departments and on chairs and governing committees, I argue that this is not so and that the present situation offers us an opportunity to revitalize literary study as well as the study of expository writing.

These changes are well known to all chairs of departments of English these days. What is not so clear is the right responses to them. I have sometimes found myself agreeing with those who foresee the atrophy and perhaps eventual disappearance of traditional departments focused on English literary history. After all, such departments, whose main business is the interpretation of major English and American works, from *Beowulf* and Chaucer to Wallace Stevens or Robert Frost, have existed in something like their present form for less than a hundred years. Before that, major universities did without them. They could cease to exist, and the academies would do without them again. Literature departments could become small and marginal, as have departments of classics. Their place could be taken by large and vigorous pragmatic programs in expository writing.

I now no longer think this is at all likely, or at least not likely unless the professors of literary history and interpretation remain inflexibly committed to maintaining things as they are or have been. The analogy with classics is a false one. Whatever the virtues of Greek and Latin as the languages of major literatures or as the basis for so many centuries of prolonged masculine puberty rituals, these languages are not what we converse and write in today. Some form of English is. The study of the great works of English, not to speak of American, literature will remain fundamental, for its models of good writing, if for no other reason.

The worst catastrophe that could befall the study of English literature would be to allow the programs in expository writing to become separate empires in the universities and colleges, wholly cut off from the departments of English and American literature. That this would be a catastrophe for the professors of literature there can be no doubt. Deans, provosts, and presidents these days are a little dubious about the function of the study of literature. In fact many of them have always been dubious. They have tended to assume that the real function of departments of English is to teach good writing. Good writing they understand, or think they do, and are willing to fund. They are much less willing to fund the study of literature, particularly if the enrollments in courses in Chaucer, Milton, and Wordsworth go down markedly. Departments of English that cut themselves off from expository writing will, one can predict, be punished for it. They will atrophy in the way we fear. My ears still ring with the heartfelt exclamation I heard a vice-chancellor at a distinguished state university make in response to a department of literature he thought was not shouldering the burden of expository writing: "I'll starve 'em out!"

On the other side, I am persuaded that programs in expository writing stand to lose much if they are cut off from departments of English literature. This belief rests on a simple premise. Learning to write well cannot be separated from learning to read well. The good departments of English literature have never had as their central mission anything other than teaching how to read well. All the "theory," all the facts of literary history, all the establishing of texts, and so on, have always been ancillary.

I do not minimize the difficulties involved in keeping expository writing and the study of literature together. Nor do I minimize the changes that will be necessary in the present structure of programs in literature, from basic courses for freshmen and sophomores on through the most advanced graduate seminars. I view the development of integrated programs in reading well and in writing well as the major challenge to our profession at the present time.

"Rhetorical study" is the key to this integration. I have the impression that much more has been done already on the side of expository writing than on the side of the study of reading or interpretation. The teaching of writing and reading in high schools, like the teaching of foreign languages, has, I believe, improved in the last decades more than one may think and more than the statistics may yet show. It seems likely to improve even more. Gradually, students will come to college better able to read and write than they have been in the past. Meanwhile, under the pressure of immediate practical need, a large number of teachers all over the country are working out programs in expository writing for this or that college or university. These programs will no doubt gradually be refined until they more or less work, though one should not underestimate the number of failures and inadequacies, many of them almost certainly due at least in part to the unwillingness of legislators, trustees, and administrators to believe how much it costs to do a good job of teaching writing. There will always also be the attempt to fund expository writing at the expense of programs of literature. At the same time, a large and valuable literature on expository writing is developing – not only textbooks of all kinds but an impressive body of theoretical, empirical, and statistical work. Part of the strength of this work is that its authors have, far more than many teachers of literature, quietly accepted and assimilated that transformation in the state of the discipline which I described above. That transformation, of course, has been motivated in good measure by developments in modern linguistics. I am thinking, for example, of what is sometimes called the "paradigm shift" from a referential or mimetic view of language to an active or performative one. People involved at the frontier of this exciting new branch of the broader discipline of English language and literature have the air of persons doing something justifiable and good, while teachers of literature sometimes seem to me to have a furtive and guilty air, as though they were doing something not altogether justifiable in the present context.

It remains for the teachers of literature to catch up and to regain their own sense of frontier excitement. My instincts are strongly preservative or conservative. Nevertheless, I do not believe that an appeal for maintaining traditional humanistic values as a defense of the status quo in literature programs washes well these days, either with students or with the holders of the purse strings, the deans and provosts. I am not at all sure those who go on affirming these pieties believe in them any longer in the old way; sometimes the affirmations sound a bit defensive. Do not misunderstand me. I agree that the study of literature should focus on an exploration of those values. Moral, metaphysical, and religious questions remain the most important ones, in literature as in life, and one of the best places in which to gain an understanding of them is in the masterworks in one's native tongue. The affirmation of humanistic values, however, needs to be accompanied, in the teaching of literature at any rate, by an adequate reading of those texts. Moreover, any defense of literature on the basis of its affirmation of values must be combined these days, I am convinced, with the defense that says one cannot write well, even write a good business letter or scientific report, unless one can read well the best that has been thought and said in our language.

I have said that the key to the integration of reading and writing is "rhetorical study." Rhetoric has been a two-branched discipline ever since the Greeks. On the one hand, it is the study of persuasion, of how to do things with words. On the other hand, it is the study of the way language works. In particular, it is the study of the function of tropes, the whole panoply of figures, not just metaphor, but metonymy, synecdoche, irony, metalepsis, prosopopoeia, catachresis – the works. It would oversimplify to say that the study of rhetoric as persuasion belongs to expository writing while the study of figurative language belongs to programs in literature. Nevertheless, the relative emphases go in those directions. What is the teaching of writing but the teaching of how to do things with words? This is particularly true for those teachers for whom the paradigm shift from a mimetic to a performative view of language has occurred. What is the teaching of reading but the teaching of the interpretation of tropes? I suspect, however, that the theory and practice of the teaching of expository writing – as sophisticated as they are – are still inhabited and inhibited to some degree by the mirage of straightforward referential language. Good writing, it is still often thought, is calling a spade a spade. On the one hand, such teaching might still have something to learn from those recent developments in literary study that are focused on the problems of figurative language. On the other hand, it is by no means fully accepted by all teachers of literature that the center of our discipline is the teaching of reading and that the center of that is expertise in handling figurative language. Moreover, the question of the performative or persuasive power of language has had an increasing role recently in new theories of reading – for example, in reader-response criticism. Even so, a recognition that all language, even language that seems purely referential or conceptual, is figurative language and an exploration of the consequences of that view for the interpretation of literature represent, it seems to me, one of the major frontiers of literary study today. Most of the new forms of criticism I named earlier – semiotic, Structuralist, Lacanian – not only depend in one way or another on recent theories of language but also recognize in one way or another that the center of literary interpretation is the study of tropes.

Among these kinds of criticism, the form called "deconstruction" – for example, the work of Jacques Derrida and Paul de Man – has especially concerned itself with questions about figurative language. "Deconstruction" is not, as it is sometimes said to be, nihilism or the denial of meaning in literary texts. It is, on the contrary, an attempt to interpret as exactly as possible the oscillations in meaning produced by the irreducibly figurative nature of language. One of the attractions, for me, of such criticism at the present time is that it promises that integration of expository writing and the study of literature which I believe is the main task facing our profession at the moment. To speak from my own limited experience, such programs as the Literature Major at Yale, and such courses as "Daily Themes," resurrected at Yale by John Hollander, are beginning to make a concentrated effort to develop elaborated curricula combining rhetoric in its two senses. In the fall of 1979 Seabury Press published *Deconstruction and Criticism*, a book by a group of teachers at Yale that attempted to indicate and exemplify, with special reference to Shelley, the direction these new modes of interpreting literature might take. At many of the colleges and universities where I have lectured, I have found young teachers who have been deeply influenced by this form of criticism. Such teachers are beginning in a thoughtful way to work out its consequences for the organization of courses and curricula in English literature.

That the consequences could be substantial changes in the current organization of programs in literature there can be no doubt. I shall conclude this paper by trying to indicate two of these consequences, one affecting our sense of the organization of literature into periods, the other indicating the need for a definition of genres by function rather than by form. My analysis is also meant to exemplify the form of criticism I have just been talking about, as it might be applied not to works of literature themselves but to the conceptualizations by which they have been traditionally organized.

*

One day he showed me, in confidence and out of vainglory, the cabinet where he kept his letters from women. It was a tall piece of furniture, impressive beneath its bronze appliqués, and was provided with a hundred little drawers.

"Only a hundred!" I exclaimed.

"The drawers are subdivided inside," Damien replied, with the solemnity that never left him.[2]

[Mr Brooke:] "But now, how do you arrange your documents?"

"In pigeon-holes partly," said Mr. Casaubon, with rather a startled air of effort.

"Ah, pigeon-holes will not do. I have tried pigeon-holes, but everything gets mixed in pigeon-holes. I never know whether a paper is in A or Z."[3]

The word "periodization" suggests an act: the act of dividing literary history into segments, framing it or pigeonholing it, so to speak. We write of medieval literature, the neoclassical period, the baroque, the eighteenth century, Romanticism, the Victorian period, the Pre-Raphaelites, the late Victorians, Modernism, post-Modernism, and so forth. By what right, according to what measure, guided or supported by what reason, is this framing performed? What justifies it, as one justifies a line of type, rules it, and keeps it from straggling all down the page? Is periodization a free positing or the referential recording of a knowledge? Is it a performative *Setzen*, which makes what it names, or is it a scientific *Erkennen*, which names what is already there? Is it an invocation, an injunction ("Let the Victorian period be!"), or a neutral description ("The Victorian period is")?

The problematic of periodization, it is easy to see, is a particularly complex form of the problematic of naming, as when parents or church or civil authorities name a baby, or when the corpus of an author's work is labeled with the name of the supposed author ("I am reading Shelley"), or when a text is given a title by the author or by others, perhaps by his survivors ("The Triumph of Life"). The complexity in regard to period names lies partly in the evident hetereogeneity of the "facts" supposed to be gathered under the single name. How can "Victorian literature" label a unity in the same way that the word "Tennyson" presumably does, or "Ulysses"? My last example, however, is already a pun. Do I mean Tennyson's poem or Joyce's novel? Should I have italicized the word instead of putting quotation marks around it? How can two works, each with its own self-enclosed uniqueness, have the same title? Does the chronologically later title necessarily allude to the earlier, quote it? The problem here is the reverse of that of twins. If twins are indeed "identical," doubles, should they not have the same name, not Shem and Shaun or Jacob and Esau, but Shem One and Shem Two, Esau and Esau, or Jacob and Jacob?

The special complexity of period naming enters by way of the necessary incorporation into its problematic of all the issues involving history and literary history. Does literary history exist, in the sense of an orderly narrative and causal sequence, readable, comprehensible by the imaginative reason? Or is it no more than a vast shifting fabrication, made up after the fact by the historians? If literary history exists, is the specificity of a literary period some self-enclosed uniqueness, or perhaps imposed from outside time by occult spiritual forces? Or is it the result of an orderly and inevitable development from the period before, determined by its predecessor, forecast perhaps by some predictable negative reaction, the son killing the father but even in doing so being ruled by him, Romanticism following Neo-classicism, the post-Modern the Modern, as the night the day, or day night? Is it, as my last figure suggests, and as some historians have argued, a matter of natural rhythms? Are literary periods part of nature, like the circuits of the sun and the moon, the turn of the seasons, the rise and fall of the tides? Such a view might justify all our habitual metaphors of genesis, growth, and development from period to period in literary history. Or is the specificity of each period a matter of a particular social structure, a particular assemblage of material means of communication, production, distribution, and consumption? Is Victorian literature a result of the railroad and the proliferation of printed periodicals, or, to put the question another way, is it a result of the absence of television?

The problem of period names, in short, is metaphysical through and through, for periodization involves the whole network of assumptions about beginning, causality, end, and ground that makes up the fabric of

Occidental metaphysics, that fabric which has bound together Western culture since Plato's precursors and the Old Testament prophets, our bifurcated heterogeneous "genesis." To put the validity of period names in question is therefore an intrinsic part of what is sometimes today called "The deconstruction of metaphysics," though such putting in question has of course always been a part of metaphysics, as a parasite within the host. Deconstruction is not itself period-bound. It is part of any period in our history.

The problematic of period names includes the following issues, among others: Who has the right to name the period? Must a genuine period name be given by those living within the period, or can a period be recognized and named only after the fact. Is the name, in other words, inside or outside the borders of the period itself? This question, as can be seen, is a version of the question whether the title of a work of literature is part of the work or affixed from the outside as an arbitrary and perhaps falsifying label. Does the name of a period indicate its intrinsic essence, its very being, or is it a convenient fiction? Is "P. B. Shelley" really "P. B. Shelley," or has someone exercised his or her will to power over him by giving him a name foreign to what he really is? If its very being is the source of a given period label, is that label grounded in some transcendent or supernatural power that orders history and literary history, or is it immanent within history itself?

It is easy enough to claim to reject both of these last alternatives as obfuscations, one form or another of the mystification of the zeitgeist, though I believe some implicit or unthought-through acceptance of one or the other is more deeply ingrained than one might think. It is also easier to dismiss the dialectical–material, natural, and history-of-ideas explanations than really to free oneself of their assumptions. Even if one accepts the notion that period names are fictions through and through, baseless performatives, one would need to explain their complex function in the institutionalized study of literature – for example, in American colleges and universities. That function has to do with matters of political, academic, and spiritual "power," if there is such a thing. It has to do with the organization of courses, curricula, programs, catalogs, the placement of books in libraries, scholarly and critical journals, professional organizations and meetings, the structure of ranks within departments of English, French, German, and so forth, the making and not making of academic careers. Someone invents the term "post-Modernism," and behold! a new discipline springs up, with journals, courses, jostlings for prestige, and so on. The pigeon-holing by periods, moreover, differs more than one might at first think from department to department within the same university, from university to university, college to college, and from country to country in the West. "Modern

English Literature" at the University of Zürich, for example, is everything after Shakespeare, whereas "Modernism" at Yale begins about 1890, as far as I can tell. Period terms are translatable from one Occidental language and institution to another, but not wholly so. They are both translatable and untranslatable, like any terms that one tries to move from one "natural language" to another.

One way to see the complexities of what might be meant by calling period names fictions is to observe that they are all figures of speech. They are therefore open to tropological analysis. An amazing potpourri of forms of figuration, in fact, is to be found in the period names we have. All are to be placed somewhere on the metaphor–synecdoche–metonymy axis, but just where would lead in each case to a different set of implications. Every period name is in one way or another a synecdoche, a part taken as representative of the whole. The question is whether the chosen part is genuinely similar to the whole, metaphorically valid, or whether it is a mere contingent metonymy, a piece of a heterogeneous mixture chosen arbitrarily to stand for the whole or to make a mélange without intrinsic unity seem like a whole.

Each period name begs innumerable questions about the nature of the period. Each is a strategic interpretation, for "political" purposes, according to one or another mode of figurative reduction. The incoherence of period names is striking, and to unfold the implications of any one would demand a long analysis. The analysis would tend to dissolve the unity and historical uniqueness of the period in question, as A. O. Lovejoy's celebrated analyses of Romanticism reduce it to a heterogeneous collection of "romanticisms," or as Paul de Man's discussion of "Modernism" shows it to be a concept by no means unique to a single period but a recurrent ever-repeated self-subverting move in each period's sense of itself in relation to previous periods. If de Man is right the term "post-Modern" is a tautology or an oxymoron, since no writer or critic ever reaches the modern, in the sense of the authentically self-born, much less goes beyond it. The "modern" is the always-already and the always not-yet of periodization.

I have said that each period term demands a long analysis, but in a moment one can see that several ("Renaissance," "Neo-classicism," "Pre-Raphaelitism") involve the notion of repetition. In each of these the specificity of the period defines itself or is defined as the recurrence, whether genuine or in parody, of an earlier period. The word "classicism" itself implies classification or pigeonholing, that affirmation of male mastery over the muse of history in all her elusive documentary incarnations. Some period names seem scrupulously neutral or merely chronological ("the eighteenth century"), but chronological classification is of course once more a metaphysical notion, calling up inevitably ideas of historical causation. Other period terms describe in figure a stylistic feature ("the baroque"). Both "the baroque" and "the Renaissance" imply an assimilation of the period to nature. The baroque is rough, like an irregular pearl, and in the Renaissance the classical world was self-born, born anew. Other period names label the period metonymically with the name of its monarch ("Victorian," "Edwardian"). Others ("Romanticism," "Modernism") involve a complex interpretation of previous periods, as well as a double contradictory claim that the period in question is unique and novel and that the quality in question is universal and recurrent. The coming to consciousness of literature as literature in the German Romantics, especially in Friedrich Schlegel, is exemplary here, as Phillipe Lacoue-Labarthe and Jean-Luc Nancy have admirably argued.[4]

As an example of the way a period name is an archival function, a necessary hypothetical fiction, and a strategic performative, operating inside the body of literature it labels but at the same time imposed from the outside and maintained for some purposeful taking possession, I shall, in conclusion, discuss briefly the term "Victorian fiction." According to one pigeon-holing, the term "Victorian fiction" is a subtitle within the larger title "realistic fiction"; according to another it is a subdivision of "the Victorian period."

"Realistic fiction" has as perhaps its most salient characteristic the ability to create the powerful phantasms of personalities. The reader feels he knows Elizabeth Bennet, Dorothea Brooke, Plantagenet Palliser, Michael Henchard, and Joe Christmas in the same way he knows his friends or relatives. Perhaps he knows them even better. One of the powerful attractions of reading novels (when this activity was a central feature of our culture, as it probably no longer is) was the way they seemed to give an even more intimate access to the mind and heart of another person than the reader could ever feel himself to have in "real life." Nevertheless, the feeling that one is encountering a "character," a "person," "another self" is demonstrably an illusion, both in the novel and in real life. It is as much an illusion as the other basic concepts of Occidental metaphysics, with which it is inextricably connected. Moreover, if the realistic novels of the last four hundred years have strongly reinforced the illusion of selfhood, they have at the same time constantly and explicitly deconstructed that illusion. They have shown it to be the result of a misinterpretation, the misreading of signs.

There is no "real novel," however, from *Don Quixote* to *Ulysses*, *The Waves*, or even *L'Innomable*, that does not create in two ways the powerful illusion of characters. One is the illusion of the character of the narrator. The narrator seems to be a man (or woman) speaking to us.

There is an almost irresistible temptation to think of the narrative voice as that of the author. The second illusion is that of the characters in the story. They seem to be men and women like ourselves. This positing of two forms of character is a distinguishing feature of novels as such, or perhaps of narrative as such, since who would deny these illusions, *mutatis mutandis*, to fairy tales, to Norse sagas, or *The Odyssey*?

The function of novels within the community of their readers may by hypothesis be said to be circular. Each culture, as well as each period of that culture, has its own complex presuppositions about selfhood. An example would be the relatively fixed notion of selfhood in England, perhaps reinforced by certain aspects of Protestantism, as against the relatively fluid feeling for character in France. Novels reinforce and partly create these presuppositions in each community of readers – or did during the period the novel reigned as a major genre. Readers go to a novel to be reassured, to encounter characters "like themselves." They read the novel according to their presuppositions about selfhood, so that, confronted by the characters on the page that have the magic power to generate the illusion of character, they are like a child with a hobbyhorse, not like the "savage" at the cinema. Once that interpretation has been made, however, once they have yielded to the illusion of knowing Pip, Lord Jim, Elizabeth Bennet, or Dorothea Brooke, following their lives through as they follow the text through, knowing them better and better, knowing them intimately from within, they turn the line around and interpet their neighbors and themselves according to the models they have encountered in novels. They people the world with Willoughbys, Claras, and Dorotheas. In this way nature imitates art. England after 1836 begins to be filled with Dickensian characters, even with people who feel themselves to be Dickensian characters.

The novel, then, has had a powerful, perhaps indispensable, social function during its reign. The fictions of character and the characteristic life lines of characters that it sustains and creates have formed one of the fundamental cohesive forces keeping each community of readers together. A community may be defined as a group of people who live by the same fictions, the same simplifications, the same hypostatized figures posited as substances. The novel has helped to make and maintain such communities.

This function of the novel seems clear enough, but what is the function of the contrary aspect of each work of fiction, its putting in question of the notions of character from which it derives its benign power to buttress society? This disintegrating would seem to be not only antisocial but even auto-destructive, since it demolishes the illusion of character on which the novel's power and function depend. This autodeconstruction reduces the readers of a given novel to the state of children who have outgrown their toys and see the sticks and yarn behind the hobbyhorse. Why is this dissolution of its own fundamental fiction as constant a feature of realistic fiction as the creation of the fiction of character in the first place?

I suggest that the function is apotropaic. It is a throwing away of what is already thrown away, in order to save it. It is a destroying of the already destroyed, in order to preserve the illusion that it is still intact. All men and women living within a culture accepting a certain notion of character have an uneasy feeling that their belief in character, even their belief in their own characters, may be confidence in an illusion. The function of the self-deconstructive aspect of novels would then be to assuage this covert suspicion by expressing it overtly, in a safe region of fiction. Character is thus triumphantly reaffirmed in the face of its being put in question, even if that reaffirmation may be no more than the persistence of that deconstructing voice, the voice of the narrator who says "I am I," and who goes on saying "I am I" even when he has demonstrated that there is no "I," or the persistence of the character who says, "I have and am no I."

My hypothesis, then: the novel as the perpetual tying and untying of the knot of selfhood works, in the psychic economy of the individual and of the community, to affirm the fiction of character by putting it fictionally in question and thus short-circuits a doubt that, left free to act in the real social world, might destroy both self and community. Belief in the subject, in character, is thereby precariously maintained by the novel over the abyss of its dismantling. Is not the positing of the subject necessary to the positing of its fictionality, in a perpetual torsion of nay saying and yea saying, of nay saying that cannot be said without the yea saying its saying unsays? The novel demonstrates, in a "safe" realm where nothing serious is at stake, the possibility of maintaining the fiction of selfhood in the teeth of a recognition that selfhood is a fictive projection, an "interpretation" not a fact, and is always open to being dissolved by a contrary interpretation – for example, that of the multiplicity or the nonentity of the ego. The novel is an instrument, a production of its society that has a certain function within the psychic economy of that society. It is not a mimetic copy of something that could do perfectly well without the copy. Nor is it the creation of a supplementary alternative "world" with no relation, other than that of accurate mirroring, to the real social world.

The same linguistic materials – or their approximate translations from country to country, language to language, dialect to dialect, century to century – have always been available within the Occident, since its "dawn," to use another familiar figure from nature. In a period of less than three thousand years there have not been enough changes in our

Western languages or even enough changes in our means of production, consumption, and living together to make the sequence of periods more than a series of permutations of the same materials. The specificity of a period lies in the special way these materials are put together at a given time and in a given place, for example in Victorian England. It lies also in the special function these materials so selectively organized have in that particular country and time, or within a particular class in that country. I have taken as my example "Victorian fiction." There is nothing in that whole body of novels in the way of technique, conventions, themes, assumptions about character, society, and so on that is unique to the period. All have clear parallels earlier and later. Nevertheless, Victorian fiction is different in the proportion of the mixture, so to speak, and in the function that the novels as physical objects, works printed in book or periodical form, had in the culture for which they were produced.

It is therefore legitimate to speak of "the Victorian novel" or even of "the Victorian period." Yes, Virginia, there is a Victorian period. It has the same kind of existence as does Santa Claus. The Victorian period is the result of many performative acts of language bringing together a fiction that exists, but never as present or as presence. If this is so, this fact should have certain consequences for the organization of departments, courses, curricula, careers, for all those pigeonholings, runnings, and followings of paths that make up the phantasmal mappings and boundaries by which the study of literature is institutionalized.

Not least of these mappings would be a result of the recognition that the function of Victorian novels for the Victorians and their functions for us should not be assumed to be the same. In that effort of integrating programs in reading and in writing I have been advocating here the central question would be not "What function did these Victorian novels have for the Victorians" but "What is the function, the efficacy, of Victorian novels here and now, in this particular context?" That there is still a function it has been the whole purpose of this essay to argue.

If my discussion of the figures of periodization and of the performative function of Victorian novels exemplifies the two branches of rhetoric described earlier, it hardly constitutes a detailed plan for those curricular changes in the study of literature I think necessary. These should in any case occur gradually from within. The traditional historical organization by periods and genres should be dismantled only when we are sure we have alternatives that will be better. Much is gained, even for creative teaching, by having a firm rubric like "Victorian fiction" within which to teach, rather than having to invent the whole syllabus from the ground up every time one presents a course. It is also true, however, that the rubrics may no longer fit in the contexts in which the teaching of literature functions or correspond to the teacher's insights into how reading should be taught. In such circumstances, the old rubrics should probably go.

The exact form the new courses and curricula will take is hard to predict, but there will undoubtedly be some breaking down of the old pigeonholing by periods and genres, more attention to the problems of interpreting nonfictional prose (philosophical and critical texts) along with plays, novels, and poems. There will also probably be a recognition that the problems of interpretation – for example, the decisive function of figurative language in making meaning heterogeneous or undecidable – cut across period lines and generic lines. The methods used to read a passage by Locke, or an essay by Kenneth Burke or William Empson, must be similar to those used to read Shelley or Dickens. The newly organized courses are likely to find it necessary to include texts in other languages, probably to be read in translation, at least in the undergraduate curriculum. It will be necessary to pay some attention to the original languages, however, and to the problems of translation. If Montaigne, Rousseau, Diderot, Goethe, Kleist, or Nietzsche are to be taught, the inadequacies of any translations must somehow be confronted in the teaching. Such new courses will probably best be developed by young teachers who have been influenced by the new modes of thinking in expository writing and in the interpretation of literature. It is these teachers who must respond to the immediate needs of their students and of the institutions where they teach. Some utopian planning and theorizing, however, may also be helpful. Though many articles, essays, and even books applying the new modes of criticism to English and American texts already exist, the new teaching of literature does not yet have its *Understanding Poetry* or its version of the Norton *Anthology*. These would be textbooks trying to work out the practical consequences for introductory courses of assuming that a good work of literature may be a heterogeneous assemblage rather than an "organic unity," that the key to understanding it is a sophistication in the interpretation of figures, and that its function may be more performative than mimetic. A period of rapid change in a discipline has its excitements and challenges. Of these we may expect to have plenty in the next decades.

Notes

1. The essay that follows was originally presented at Texas A & M at a summer conference of the Association of Departments of English; it was printed in a special issue of the *ADE Bulletin*, 62 (Sept.–Nov. 1979), *The State of the Discipline: 1970s–1980s*. Permission to reprint this essay is gratefully acknowledged. I am using here the somewhat altered version of the essay reprinted in 1988 in *Teaching Literature: What is needed now*, James Engell and David Perkins, eds, *Harvard English Studies 15* (Cambridge, Mass., 1988),

pp. 87–109. The changes were to make the essay correspond better to my present convictions – for example, by the omission of a sentence about the canon – but the essay is still marked by its original occasion and by the time of its writing. As for the canon, I would now say that no canon is absolute. Each is an aspect of particular historical, ideological, political circumstances, both causer and caused, maker of history and made by it. Changes in the canon can come in two ways, however: by the addition of new works or the dropping of old ones, and, on the other hand, by new, noncanonical readings of old canonical works; for example, the challenging new feminist readings of Milton or of Victorian fiction.
2. Colette, *The Pure and the Impure*, tr. Herma Briffault (New York, 1967), p. 42.
3. George Eliot, *Middlemarch*, (New York, 1977), bk. I, ch. ii.
4. Phillipe Lacoue-Labarthe and Jean-Luc Nancy, *L'absolu littéraire: Théorie de la littérature du romantisme allemand* (Paris, 1978).

13

English romanticism, American romanticism: what's the difference?

The claim that there is a distinct species of literature in America, as the American robin differs from the English robin, has a long tradition. The notion that American romanticism differs essentially from English romanticism is vigorously present in Emerson and in Whitman, as well as in multitudes of lesser writers, critics, and orators in mid-nineteenth-century America, for example in those speech-makers Dickens parodies in the splendid rhetoric of the Honourable Elijah Pogram in *Martin Chuzzlewit*:

> "Our fellow-countryman is a model of a man, quite fresh from Natur's mould!" said Pogram, with enthusiasm. [Pogram is speaking of a certain unsavory Mr Chollop.] "He is a true-born child of this free hemisphere! Verdant as the mountains of our country; bright and flowing as our mineral Licks; unspiled by withering conventionalities as air our broad and boundless Perearers! Rough he may be. So air our Barrs. Wild he may be. So air our Buffalers. But he is a child of Natur', and a child of Freedom; and his boastful answer to the Despot and the Tyrant is, that his bright home is in the Settin Sun." (*Martin Chuzzlewit*, ch. 34)

It is easy to understand the appeal of such a declaration of independence for the American ethos and for the literature which expresses it. This claim is heard on many sides today. The chorus is likely to get louder and more numerous. Authenticity in a work of literature derives from its originality, its freshness, its distinctiveness. A valid work must represent a fresh start. It must make it new and make it better than it has ever been made before. Elijah Pogram's great work, the Pogram Defiance, "defied the world in general to com-pete with our country upon any hook; and devellop'd our internal resources for making war upon the universal airth" (*ibid.*). If American romanticism can be shown to be a derivative, a pale offshoot of English romanticism or of European romanticism generally, moon to its sun, its claims to force and validity are greatly weakened. American literature needs to show that it has followed the westering sun and the westering of civilization. It must be nearest the sun, or it must be the sun, shedding light and power everywhere. As Harold Bloom observes in *Agon*, "Whitman could identify himself . . . with the sun, once even asserting . . . that he could send forth sunrise from himself."[1]

This need to affirm uniqueness and an independent history for American romanticism is perhaps especially strong again today. The reasons for this are evident. It can be said without cynicism that departments of American studies and specialists in American literature need to justify their existence. At a time when the role of Britain on the stage of world history is getting smaller and smaller, while the United States is a super-power with the fate of the world in its hands, it seems ridiculous to have a literature here which is a mere branch or twig of the Royal Oak, especially of an oak so feeble and so superannuated. In the conservative political climate of this particular moment there is a great need to be able to believe in a special and separate form of romanticism in America in order either to support or to attack the reigning ideology. In either case the appeal is to what is essentially American as opposed to various forms of unAmerican activity. We need to be able to match Emily Dickinson or Whitman, Stevens or Faulkner, against Shakespeare, Wordsworth, Dickens, or Yeats, and we need to be able to say that our American authors have special qualities not found elsewhere.

Moreover, powerful methodologies imported from abroad threaten the integrity of our homegrown or homemade traditions of interpretation, for example American pragmatism. These foreign imports threaten our need to believe that we can go it alone. Why do we need Derrida, Lacan, or Adorno, or even Marx and Nietzsche, when we have Emerson, William James, Dewey, and Kenneth Burke?

Which of us can say he does not respond to the appeal of this assertion and share the assumptions behind it? The current vogue of Richard Rorty's powerful *Mirror of Nature* is an example of this appeal. Harold Bloom's recent *Agon* gives the most vigorous polemical expression to what his "Coda" calls "The American Difference in Poetry and Criticism." The central purpose of this admirable book is to persuade the reader that the tradition of Whitman, Dickinson, Crane, Stevens, Ashbery, Merrill, and Ammons is essentially different both from British and from continental poetic traditions, just as the criticism or philosophy of Emerson, Peirce, James, and Burke is different from anything in England or on the continent:

> We *do* have a national criticism [writes Bloom], as we have had a national poetry since Whitman and Dickinson. There is an American or non-Hegelian Negative, and it is indebted to Emerson for having pioneered a diachronic rhetoric. . . . From Emerson himself through Kenneth Burke,

the American tradition of criticism is highly dialectical, differing in this from the British empirical tradition that has prevailed from Dr Johnson to Empson. But this American tradition precisely resembles Whitmanian poetry, rather than the Continental dialectics that have surged from Hegel through Heidegger on to the contemporary Deconstruction of Jacques Derrida and Paul de Man. . . . The American critic, here and now, in my judgment, needs to keep faith both with American poetry and the American Negative, which means one must not yield either to the school of Deconstruction or to the perpetual British school of Common Sense. Our best poets, from Whitman through Stevens to Ashbery, make impossible and self-contradictory demands upon both their readers and themselves. I myself urge an antithetical criticism in the American grain, affirming the self over language, while granting a priority to figurative language over meaning. The result is a mixed discourse, vatic perhaps, and at once esoteric and democratic, but that is the burden of American tradition. (*Agon*, 19, 335–6)

Bloom a little too much here wants to have the cake of his fun with what he calls, alluding to a certain T-shirt, the "Deconstruction Road Company," while at the same time eating the cake in the form of assimilating the insights of deconstruction into the priority of figurative over literal language. In any case, the doctrine of his book is heady stuff, and it is hard to keep one's head when assessing it, particularly when one is oneself one of the objects of the polemic, and particularly when the localized reading of American literary history is so strongly reinforced by those broader ideological currents I mentioned earlier and by its appeal to our pragmatic American desire for mastery over language, our desire to ask of a text, as Bloom puts it, not "Am I getting this poem right?" but "What is it good for, what can I do with it, what can it do for me, what can I make it mean?" (*Agon*, 19). "You should just shrug," says Bloom, "when they tell you finally that it is a right reading" (*Agon*, 20). This is tremendously attractive, and not just to untrained students. If all reading is misreading, and if the strongest reader is the one most expert in misprision, why should I not do as Bloom does, or says he does, and make the text mean what I like, in spite of the fact that, for example, Stanley Fish's current work on interpretative communities argues persuasively for the difficulty or even impossibility of doing this. When I seem freest, most asserting the powers of the strong self over language, I may be most the unwitting spokesman for ideological currents drifting around in the circumambient air. Though it may be impossible not to speak in the name of some interpretative community or other, one would wish to be as self-conscious about this as possible, and so I raise my head above the Bloomian rhetoric and ask: How would one go about testing the theory that American romanticism is different?

There are, it seems to me, four possible theoretical presuppositions supporting an argument for the uniqueness of American romanticism. Though they are hardly compatible with one another, they tend to appear together in a contradictory mix. All are present implicitly or explicitly in Bloom's *Agon*. All are present, though in different proportions, in my passage from *Martin Chuzzlewit*.

First possibility: It can be argued that poetry arises from nature, from climate. Our flora and fauna, our landscape, the names for all our birds, beasts, mountains, and rivers, are different, therefore the poems of our climate will be different. We have bears, buffaloes, the Rocky Mountains and the Great Plains, wild asters and Black-eyed Susans,

> Deer walk upon our mountains, and the quail
> Whistle about us their spontaneous cries;
> Sweet berries ripen in the wilderness . . .[2]

How can our poetry be expected to be like that of Wordsworth or Tennyson?

Second possibility: We are children not only of nature but also of freedom. Our democratic social structures, not only on the large scale but also in the fine grain of day to day personal intercourse, differ from those of old Europe, land of the despot and the tyrant. Consequently our poetry will also differ. It will be at once democratic and esoteric or élitist, since it will be a democratic agon of warring élites, none able to master all the others. What we need in order to show the uniqueness of American romanticism and American criticism is a sociologically based interpretation of both.

Third possibility: It can be argued that though American romanticism is based on European sources, as Emerson's work, for example, is conspicuously derived from Swedenborg, Plato, English and German romanticism, and so on, nevertheless American romanticism represents a distinct *clinamen*, a swerve from these sources. Like father, unlike son. The law of misprision or strong misreading would lead us to expect American romanticism to be different, though Bloom's claim for a relatively smooth continuity and homogeneity from Emerson to Whitman to Crane to Stevens and beyond seems to contradict his major insight into literary history. This insight is the notion that though literature is made of literature and not as a reflection of nature or of social conditions, the line from one work to another is twisted, oblique, angled. The uniqueness of American romanticism, this third theory would argue, arises from this divergence.

The fourth possibility is one version or another of the doctrine of continued inspiration, a familiar part of our American Protestant tradition, but familiar in English romantic poetic theory too from

Shelley to Yeats. As Yeats puts this: "Solitary men receive, as I think, the creative impulse from the lowest of the Nine Hierarchies, and so make and unmake mankind, and even the world itself, for does not 'the eye altering alter all'?"[3] The authenticity and authority of poetry, this argument would run, comes in one way or another from some direct access to transcendent sources. Each poet starts afresh and rejects all who have come before in the name of a new inspiration. Bloom's "Gnosticism" is of course a version of this, and he correctly demonstrates its presence for example in Emerson. By Gnosticism, says Bloom, "I mean a timeless knowing, as available now as it was then. . . . Gnostic freedom is a freedom for knowledge, knowledge of what in the self, *not* in the psyche or soul, is Godlike, and knowledge of God beyond the cosmos" (*Agon*, 4). Bloom cites the Emerson of *Self-Reliance* on this:

> Yet see what strong intellects dare not yet hear God himself unless he speak the phraseology of I know not what David, or Jeremiah, or Paul. We shall not always set so great a price on a few texts, on a few lives. . . . When we have new perception, we shall gladly disburden the memory of its hoarded treasures as old rubbish. When a man lives with God, his voice shall be as sweet as the murmur of the brook and the rustle of the corn.

How can our American romanticism not be unique if it arises out of the direct voice of God speaking afresh within the self of each new poet?

These four theories may be reconciled, in spite of their incompatibility, but only by establishing a hierarchy putting one at the top as the arch-explanation governing the others. The freshness of nature, for example, may be seen as Emerson sees it, that is, as the model for the poet–prophet's openness to the divine inspiration of the present moment. The poet, like a flower, must be cut off from the past and its wornout scriptures in order to be open to the supernatural influxes of the present. The uniqueness of American political and social democracy in turn may be caused, according to a certain form of material determinism, by the special qualities of our climate, and though our poets may necessarily use materials from the old-world writers, their swerve from English or continental romanticism is determined by their independent inspiration. The notion of continued and continually unique inspiration tends to affirm itself implicitly or explicitly as the top of the hierarchy. Bloom is more and more openly a religious writer, as much as René Girard, for example, though his Gnosticism is of course very different from Girard's Roman Catholicism. There is of course nothing wrong with this, but the relation between literary criticism and religious belief still seems to me extremely problematic and complex. It can be said that there is an almost irresistible temptation for literary critics to talk about everything else under the sun except literature.

The fact that all four of these supports for the theory that American romanticism is unique tend to be appealed to at once, in spite of their incoherence with one another, should put interpreters on guard. It should perhaps send them back to the texts to see if in fact there is evidence that any one of the four or some combination, however contradictory, actually operate to make an "American difference" in poetry and criticism. Let me take as example the almost universal image of the liminal margin of the shore, whether seashore, lakeshore, or riverbank. Almost any writer in both English and American romanticism would provide examples of this motif. Any knowing reader can immediately think of a superabundance of examples. Moreover, most readers would agree that the image is important in the work of the poets in question, and most would agree that its interpretation in each case would expand to include all that is deepest and most problematic in the work of the poet. The image of the shore tends to be associated in each case with images of lines, whether as edges or as paths leading from here to there, and with images of circles receding out to the horizon's bound.

Think, for example, of the dreamer in Book Five of *The Prelude*, "seated in a rocky cave/By the sea-side" (ll. 58–9), or of the passage in the first "Essay upon Epitaphs" beginning "Never did a child stand by the side of a running stream"[4]; or of Keats' "Bright Star," with its "moving waters at their priestlike task/Of pure ablution round earth's human shores" (ll. 5–6); or of the dreamer in Shelley's "The Triumph of Life," "beneath the hoary stem/Which an old chestnut flung athwart the steep/Of a green Apennine": "before me fled/The night; behind me rose the day, the deep/Was at my feet, and Heaven above my head" (ll. 24–8); or of the poems of Matthew Arnold with their many (and not wholly consistent) uses of the image of the shore, for example "Dover Beach," with its echoes of Sophocles, Senancour, and, surely, Keats' "Bright Star": "The Sea of Faith/Was once, too, at the full, and round earth's shore/Lay like the folds of a bright girdle furled./But now I only hear/Its melancholy, long, withdrawing roar" (ll. 21–5); or, to turn to American writing, of the line that goes from the circling shore of Thoreau's Walden Pond to Emerson's poem, "Seashore," to Whitman's "Out of the Cradle Endlessly Rocking," to Stevens' "The Idea of Order at Key West," to Ammons' "Corson's Inlet."

There is of course not time here to explore all these examples in detail. My claim is that if this were to be done, it could be demonstrated not only that the image of the shore is in each case an inextricable part of the whole system of thought and imagery in the writer in question but that in each case the use of the image is at once constrained by traditional linguistic patterns which are much larger than something so small and local as English or American romanticism, and at the same time to some degree idiosyncratic, different from the use of the image in any of its "sources" or in any of the immediately adjacent writers in the same country. It is the task of criticism both to identify the relation of a given use of such an image to the larger recurrent linguistic paradigms going back to the Greeks and the Bible and at the same time to identify the specificity of a given use, its difference from all those immediately around it, even those alleged to be its immediate "source." A formulation by Jacques Derrida in "White Mythology" is exemplary here:

> It goes without saying that it will not do here to suppose some homogeneous continuum (tradition constantly referred back to itself, whether the tradition of metaphysics or that of rhetoric). However, we must pay attention to the more lasting constraints of this kind (which have had their effect through the systematic links of a very long chain); we must take the trouble to delimit their general functioning and the limits of the effects: otherwise we should risk mistaking the most derivative effects for the original characteristic of a hastily identified configuration, an imaginary or marginal mutation. We should be prey to a precipitate and impressionistic empiricism, concentrating on alleged differences which would in fact be mainly linear and chronological breaks. So should we step from discovery to discovery, each step marking a break! . . . Here we are led back to the program, not yet spelled out at all, of a new problematic of signatures.[5]

The notion of an American difference in poetry or criticism is an example of the fallacy of misplaced concreteness. It is at once too general and too specific. It ascribes a unity and a reified existence to an entity (American romanticism) which is a fictitious creation of the critic, made by ignoring all sorts of differences from one text to another. At the same time it is not general enough to recognize that all the texts in both English and American romanticism are permutations of linguistic materials at least two and a half millenia old. No doubt local conditions, including at least the first three of my hypothetical causes of uniqueness, contribute to the specific form the permutation takes in a given case. No doubt also there are many breaks in the fabric, rents in the continuity of the tradition, leaps forward which are at the same time leaps backward to a configuration not immediately antecedent but perhaps centuries old.

Let me take in conclusion as one small example of this the relation between Stevens' "The Idea of Order at Key West" and the poem it surely to some degree echoes, Emerson's "Seashore." Stevens revises or tropes Emerson, twists him or goes him one better. In doing so he produces an antithetical version of the motif of the shore. Emerson's "Seashore" is a rather straightforward confrontation of the force of man by the force of the sea, with the portals of the sea ("I unbar the doors," says Emerson's sea) leading to other shores or to the activity of imagination engendered by the sea ("A few rods off he [man] deems it [the ocean] gems and clouds."). In Stevens' "The Idea of Order at Key West" Emerson's doors become the "fragrant portals, dimly starred," and a voice speaks which is neither man's voice nor the sea's voice, though it is born of "the grinding water and the gasping wind." This voice leads beyond any horizon, beyond any New Haven on the other side. It is a voice which "made/The sky acutest at its vanishing."

For Emerson, for example in "Circles," the self remains fixed as a center at the center:

> Yet this incessant movement and progression which all things partake could never become sensible to us but by contrast to some principle of fixture or stability in the soul. Whilst the eternal generation of circles proceeds, the eternal generator abides. That central life is somewhat superior to creation, superior to knowledge and thought, and contains all its circles.[6]

Emerson's "Seashore" is relatively univocal, capable, more or less, of being given a single determinate, unified interpretation, whatever may be the case with the rest of Emerson's writings. Emerson's poem is a dialogue of subject and object in which subject triumphs over object by ascribing its own voice and values to the sea. The sea speaks in Emerson's poem, but it speaks for the humanistic meanings of the sea, even for those artistic meanings man projects into the sea. The poem expresses the way man makes the sea the figure for his aspiration beyond what he is and where he is: "I make some coast alluring," says the sea, "some lone isle,/To distant men, who must go there, or die."

In "The Idea of Order at Key West," on the contrary, full of echoes though it is of Emerson's poem, the dialogue between man and the sea remains an unresolved interchange. The poem is dialogical in Bahktin's sense. It is subject to two different *logoi*, or sources of meaning, the human voice and the inhuman one. The poem asserts on the one hand, in subtle and elided ways, the traditional metaphysical idea of a *logos* behind or beneath both mind and sea, transcendent and immanent at once, their common rhythm, ratio, measure, voice, reason, being, and ground, their "genius," as the poem puts it. At the same time the poem deconstitutes that affirmation by asserting in the same words a humanistic perspectivism often assigned to Stevens as the one thing he believed and said.

Emerson, in "Seashore" at least, presents a regressive or reductive reading of romanticism. He reduces it, as do some twentieth-century interpretations of Wordsworth and Coleridge, of Shelley and Keats, or of Stevens himself, to a mere dialogue of subject and object. Stevens goes deeper, but his doing so, as can be shown, is more a revival of the complex uncertainties present in one way or another from the Greeks on down in the concept of *logos* than anything new given birth under our westering sun. The fundamental undecidability of "The Idea of Order at Key West" is carried by an intricate network of words and figures in the poem translating the play of meanings in the Greek word *logos* and in associated words like *eidos* and *poeisis*. Each key term of the poem introduces one more way of expressing the impossibility of deciding whether the making mind and voice of the singer by the sea discovers in her making an order already there but hidden, until she sings, in the meaningless plungings of the water and in the inarticulate gaspings of the wind, or whether she imposes order on what is intrinsically without it.

I conclude with the assertion that each poem, essay, or work of fiction in English and American romanticism, or each isolatable passage from any one of these, is a node or intersection in an overdetermined network of associations, influences, constraints, and connections, often connections leaping far over chronological or geographical contiguity, and stretching out in all directions, before, behind, on all sides. These nodes or intersections are both too specific and too impersonal, unsigned, to be incorporated into generalizations at the level of claims that there is an American difference in poetry and criticism. Each must be patiently untangled and interpreted for itself, and the interpreter must do his best to resist the almost irresistible lure of premature generalization.

Our own American Henry James (or is he England's Henry James?) has in a familiar passage in the Preface to *Roderick Hudson* given a splendid model for this complexity of any cultural form, for example of a literary text. James is writing about the novelist's art, but what he says may be taken also as a parable of the critic's double responsibility. His need is to be faithful to the specificity of the text he interprets while honoring also the fact that this specificity lies in the innumerable relations of that text to the immense web of its manifold contexts. The interpreter too is as much inextricably woven into this context as is the writer. He cannot by any effort extricate himself and survey the whole from without. He too is constrained in what he can see and say by his placement within the web:

> The very condition of interest [writes James] [is] . . . the related state, to each other, of certain figures and things. To exhibit these relations, once they have all been recognized, is to "treat" his idea, which involves neglecting none of those that directly minister to interest; the degree of that directness remaining meanwhile a matter of highly difficult appreciation, and one on which felicity of form and composition, as a part of the total effect, mercilessly rests. Up to what point is such and such a development *indispensable* to the interest? What is the point beyond which

it ceases to be rigorously so? Where, for the complete expression of one's subject, does a particular relation stop – giving way to some other not concerned in that expression?

Really, universally, relations stop nowhere . . .[7]

Notes

1. Harold Bloom, *Agon: Towards a Theory of Revisionism* (New York, Oxford, 1982), p. 333.
2. Wallace Stevens, "Sunday Morning," ll. 114–16.
3. W. B. Yeats, "The Symbolism of Poetry," *Essays and Introductions* (London, 1961), pp. 158–9.
4. William Wordsworth, *Poetical Works*, T. Hutchinson and E. de Selincourt, eds, (London, 1966), p. 729.
5. Jacques Derrida, "White Mythology," *New Literary History*, VI, No. 1 (Autumn 1974), p. 30; for the French original see *Marges* (Paris, 1972), pp. 274–5.
6. Ralph Waldo Emerson, "Circles," *Essays: First Series* (Boston and New York, n.d.), p. 318.
7. Henry James, "Preface," *Roderick Hudson*, Sentry Edition (Boston, 1877), pp. xiv–xv.

14

Composition and decomposition:

Deconstruction and the teaching of writing

My topic is the relation between writing and reading, or between the teaching of writing and the teaching of reading. In what ways do they, or might they, facilitate one another or inhibit one another? The title of this essay might have been "Rhetoric and Rhetoric," or "The Trivium: Where Three Roads Cross," the latter with a memory that it was at such a triple fork that Oedipus killed Laius. Is one rhetoric, rhetoric as analysis, the study of tropes, the oedipal murderer of the other rhetoric, rhetoric as persuasion, as synthesis, as the effective composition of essays or the composition of effective essays, writing with a purpose? The trivium, in medieval education, comprised grammar, logic, and rhetoric. It was preliminary or propaedeutic to the quadrivium: arithmetic, geometry, astronomy, and music, the finishing touches to a liberal arts education. The seven form a sequence. It is impossible to go on to the second group until you have mastered the first, though the image of the three meeting roads suggests that the elements of the trivium are somehow inextricably connected, as in turn are those of the quadrivium, where four roads cross. In any case, if students come to college these days not knowing grammar, we must begin there before we can go on to logic or dialectic and then to rhetoric, much less hope to attain to harmony and the music of the spheres.

It might seem that from the point of view of either pedagogy it would be better for each to go it alone. The teaching of writing, it might be said, has established itself anew as an important separate discipline, with its independent institutionalization in the form of professional societies, meetings, journals, a hierarchy of distinguished practitioners, and so on. This new or reborn discipline has a double strength. It founds itself on the most advanced twentieth-century scientific or quasi-scientific discoveries about the nature of language and the nature of composition, the processes whereby writing is generated and revised. In addition it has the most urgent practical necessity and pragmatic grounding: daily contact with writing samples from thousands of students. The emphasis can happily be on *praxis* as opposed to *theoria*. Such theory as there is is immediately testable in practice. The discipline is required to appropriate only as much theory as it needs and as works, while bad ideas can fairly easily and quickly be shown not to work and can be hooted out of court. When one adds to this the strong public and institutional support for the teaching of writing, one has what seem almost ideal conditions for the flourishing of an independent discipline. It is not surprising that just this is happening in many places. Independent departments or programs in composition are beginning to overshadow the adjacent departments of English literature in size, strength, and funding.

By contrast, programs in literature seem, in some colleges and universities at least, increasingly marginal and detached from present conditions. Their enrollments and numbers of majors are declining. Peter Demetz, in a recent essay based on his experience as president of the Modern Language Association and as chairman of the MLA Commission on the Future of the Profession, reports that from 1969 to 1979 the number of college freshmen choosing to major in English declined from 6.1 per cent of the women and 1.1 per cent of the men to 1.2 per cent of the women and 0.6 per cent of the men. Demetz cites a report of the National Council on Education predicting that by 1986–7 the percentage of BAs in English and American literature will reach a low of 2.7 per cent of all degrees awarded.[1] By contrast, of course, programs in writing have proliferated and are flourishing even where, as at Yale, there is no "writing requirement." Teachers of English literature seem to have been relatively less able than teachers of composition to accommodate themselves to current social, economic, and ideological realities. Teachers of literature may either remain stubbornly stuck in traditional canons and methods of teaching or allow themselves to become victims of the merely fashionable and often spuriously "relevant" in the attempt to attract students. Moreover, these days departments of English literature are often the locus of rarefied battles among competing theories of criticism, mostly foreign imports – Lacanian psychoanalysis, structuralism, semiotic Marxism, phenomenology, so-called deconstruction, and so on. These may seem to have almost nothing to do with the practical business of teaching English literature, much less with teaching English composition. Many or even most of the teachers of literature in such departments are in any case indifferent or downright hostile to these theories and seek to minimize their influence. Teachers of composition would seem to do well to leave the literary theorists to their monastic disputes and the departments of English to the general disarray or glum conservatism of their enterprise.

On the other hand, it is not altogether clear that theory can so blithely be separated from practice. Their relation is a complex one – neither safe separation, nor smooth transition, nor easy overlapping or meshing. It seems that the teaching of composition is primarily a practical matter. Writing well is learned gradually as an acquired habit, like speech itself. On the other hand, composition handbooks are full of theoretical statements, not only about language, but also about the ethical, ideological, and even political matters that are inextricably connected with assumptions about language. Even the most immediate practical advice to a student about his writing has such implications. Such advice or instruction is not innocent. It is not evident that it is good either for the student or for the teacher to remain innocent of this lack of innocence. It is not clear, either, that *praxis* can, in any case, really be taught in detachment from the *theoria* it presupposes, unless we think students can learn to write blindly, by rote, whereas it appears our aim should be to teach them to use language freely as a means to some end, to write effectively and for a purpose. Most teachers of composition no doubt find themselves again and again in the somewhat embarrassing situation of teaching not just grammar and rhetoric but also logic, ethics, politics, even something of theology and the music of the spheres.

At the other extreme, even those rarefied debates about literary theory have practical implications for the teaching not just of reading but of writing. Such debates have their correlates in the day-to-day practices of writing and the teaching of writing. Much might be gained by trying to bring these correlations into the open. As Paul de Man put this in a recent essay, if "the disputes among literary theorists more and more appear to be like quarrels among theologians, at the furthest remove from any reality or practicality," at the same time "disputes among theologians, for all their abstruseness, have in fact very public equivalents: how is one to separate the disputations between nominalists and realists in the fourteenth century from 'the waning of the Middle Ages?'" In the same way, the "nearly imperceptible line" between a semiotician and grammarian of poetry like Michael Riffaterre and a theoretician of rhetoric like de Man may, as de Man says, "be inextricably intertwined with the 'waning' of modernity."[2] That is to say, it may be closely associated with the social and ideological situation within which the teaching of writing takes place today. If this is the case, anything that can be done to effect a rapprochement between literary theory and the teaching of writing would be all to the good. The theorists of literature would do well to face the practical implications for the teaching of writing as well as for the teaching of reading of their theories, and the teachers of writing would do well to be as clear as possible about the theoretical assumptions of what they do.

This makes a strong argument for not detaching programs in

composition from departments of English. The teaching of reading and the teaching of writing must go hand in hand. Writing disabilities are no doubt evidence of corresponding reading disabilities, and the latter may be even harder to detect and remedy. Failures in grammar or idiom are there on the page of a writing sample, relatively easy to spot if not to help the student correct, while the strange things that may go on in students' minds when they read a page of Milton, of Jane Austen, or of Stevens, not to speak of the newspaper or of a textbook in political science, are more difficult to bring into the open, much less ameliorate.

Nevertheless, reading is itself a kind of writing, or writing is a trope for the act of reading. Every act of writing is an act of reading, an interpretation of some part of the totality of what is. That totality is not a set of nonlinguistic objects but a field of signs to be read, which means to have more signs added to them by the new composition. If reading and writing are so intimately connected, the teachers of writing have as much to gain from making sure their colleagues in literature have taught students the rudiments of reading (if only we were sure these days what that might mean) as the teachers of literature have to gain from having the art of writing correctly and persuasively well taught (assuming we know what that might mean). As a matter of fact, much of the actual teaching of reading goes on in courses in composition. In any case, any artificial detachment of one from the other will be a disaster for both disciplines.[3]

In spite of these associations, reading and writing seem in many ways to be antithetical activities, as their names suggest. Writing is composition, putting words together in the right order so they will produce a certain effect on the reader or accomplish a certain end. This is rhetoric as persuasion. It works by synthesis. Reading, on the other hand, is decomposition, deconstruction, the analysis or untying of the links that bind a piece of language together so that the reader can see how it works and make sure he has grasped its meaning correctly. The act of reading well seems, then, to go in the opposite direction from the act of writing well. Reading is not rhetoric as putting together, composition, but rhetoric as taking apart, the study of tropes, decomposition. It is easy to see, however, that no skillful composition is possible without that prior act of decomposition practiced through reading models of composition by others. I learn to make a chair by studying the way another man has made a chair, and this probably means taking his handiwork apart to see in detail how he did it. There is no learning to write well without a concomitant learning to read well. There is no help for it. Those involved in programs in writing either must make sure that reading is being well taught by their colleagues in literature or must teach reading themselves. Of what would good teaching of reading consist?

Among the most powerful and challenging techniques of reading today is the one called "deconstruction." Sentences of the form "Deconstruction is so and so" are a contradiction in terms. Deconstruction cannot by definition be defined, since it presupposes the indefinability or, more properly, "undecidability" of all conceptual or generalizing terms. Deconstruction, like any method of interpretation, can only be exemplified, and the examples will of course all differ. By deconstruction I mean reading as it is practiced by Jacques Derrida, Paul de Man, and myself, along with an increasing number of others in this country and abroad.[4] A large number of teachers and critics are pursuing the renewal of this rhetoric of reading along parallel but not always convergent or superposable lines. A new undergraduate major at Yale, the literature major, is devoted, in part at least, to developing a reading and writing curriculum from freshman and sophomore courses on up to introduce students to the renewed development of a rhetorical analysis of texts. Other colleges and universities are developing similar programs. I speak of deconstruction as if it were one special technique of reading, but in fact deconstruction is a currently fashionable or notorious name for good reading as such. All good readers are and always have been deconstructionists.

To take a little further my claim that the two forms of rhetoric, rhetoric as persuasion and rhetoric as knowledge of tropes, have always gone hand in hand, along with my argument that all good readers are deconstructionists, I must mildly take issue with an assertion made by Winifred Horner in her admirable introduction to the volume in which this essay originally appeared. She says that there was in the eighteenth century "a shift in emphasis in the general thrust of language study from the creative act to the interpretative act." Broadly speaking, this seems a fair sketch of the history of rhetoric, but the double or bifurcated definition of rhetoric of course goes back to the Greeks. As Horner herself observes, the taxonomy of tropes is almost all the work of the Greeks. Our "proper" English words for the various figures of speech – metaphor, metonymy, hyperbole, irony, apostrophe, prosopopoeia, parable, parabasis, and the rest – are still the Greek ones. This has a profound historical and linguistic significance, as does the fact that all the proper names for the tropes are themselves tropes, though there is not space here to discuss the latter fact in detail. The eighteenth-century Scottish development of rhetoric as the study of reading and of tropes was, like the Renaissance English one with Puttenham and others, more a revival of a Greek discipline than an innovation. Moving to the renewal of tropological study in our century, one can say that it is not an accident that Friedrich Nietzsche, one of the founding fathers of the modern version of rhetoric as the study of tropes, was a classical philologist.

Nietzsche offered in the winter term of 1872–3 at Basel a course on classical rhetoric, not as the art of persuasion but as the taxonomy of figures of speech.[5] Here, as in so many other areas of thought, the Greeks had names for it, plus all the accompanying concepts, and the best we can hope is to reach back up again to where they had already been, with perhaps some slight additional tropes, twists, or turns of our own.

The presence of both forms of rhetoric can already be seen in Plato and Aristotle. It is true that Plato in the *Gorgias* and in the *Phaedrus*, speaking of course through Socrates, seems to consider rhetoric primarily as the study of means of persuasion, licit or illicit. Plato attacks rhetoric primarily on the grounds that it is not an art but a "habitude," a "routine" (*empeiria*), a species of "flattery" (*kolakeia*), a "semblance of a part of politics."[6] To call something a semblance (*eidolon*) is about the worst thing Plato can find to say about it, and calling a rhetorician a semblance links the rhetorician with the Sophist, who is in *The Sophist* condemned as a semblance of the wise philosopher. The rhetorician is a mere phantom of the true political orator because his power of persuasion is not based on genuine knowledge of justice – what is good for the soul – any more than a cook's concoctions are based on medical knowledge of what is good for the body. This seems to put rhetoric firmly on the side of composition and to define it as a skill in persuasion, a base and baseless skill at that. But when Plato has Socrates in the *Phaedrus* define a kind of rhetoric that is a genuine art and not a routine and that must therefore be guided by true knowledge, he gives as the broadest definition of that knowledge a gift for division and combination. If you want to be a true rhetorician, you "must know the truth about the subject that you speak or write about; that is to say, you must be able to isolate it in definition, and having so defined it you must next understand how to divide it into kinds, until you reach the limit of division."[7] So much for division, which should govern the composition of a good piece of writing or speaking. Combination, on the other hand, is the assertion of resemblance between things unlike or not identical. It includes, in fact, the whole region of tropes. Plato (or Socrates) sees this as primarily a resource of the false rhetorician who seeks to persuade his hearers that the false is true, the true false. Here what is needed is skill at analysis, skill in detecting false resemblances – in short, reading defined as decomposition or demystification, what today is called deconstruction. Plato too is a deconstructionist before the fact, and his discussion of rhetoric in the *Phaedrus* contains a program for the study of both kinds of rhetoric.

The same may be said for Aristotle. The basic resources of rhetorical or argumentative persuasion are in Aristotle's *Rhetoric* said to be the example and the enthymeme. The example is a truncated form of inductive logic, the enthymeme, of deductive logic. Both in fact are tropes, figures of speech. Example is a synecdoche, part for whole and then applied to another part, with all the problems belonging to that trope, and the enthymeme is defined as an incomplete syllogism, that is, once more argument by similitude or trope, since the syllogism is a formally stated proportional metaphor.[8]

I turn now to a much later example of how inextricably involved in one another the two kinds of rhetoric are. In a well-known passage in *Middlemarch*, George Eliot observes that "we all of us, grave or light, get our thoughts entangled in metaphors, and act fatally on the strength of them" (book 1, ch. 10). "Entangled": it is of course itself a metaphor, and so an example of what the sentence affirms. Somewhat less well known is a wonderfully witty and penetrating passage in *The Mill on the Floss* (book 2, ch. 1) about poor Tom Tulliver's sufferings in school at the hands of Mr Stelling. The passage has to do with an example of the general doctrine about metaphor enunciated later in *Middlemarch*. It is an example especially appropriate here, since it has to do with the way fatal errors in pedagogical theory are the result of committing the aboriginal linguistic error of taking a figure of speech literally. In this case the figure is the one saying the mind is like a field that needs to be plowed and harrowed by grammar and geometry. This metaphor has been preceded by one describing teaching as "instilling" information into the mind of the student. It is followed by three others, that of the mind as an intellectual stomach, and those of the mind as a blank sheet of paper and as a mirror. As George Eliot's narrator ironically exclaims: "It is astonishing what a different result one gets by changing the metaphor!"

A full reading of this admirable text would take up far more space than I have. The passage is a miniature treatise on rhetoric as reading, as well as a little anthology of the basic tropes of the Western tradition. It speaks of the activity of reading, manifests a model of that activity, and invites us to read it according to the method it employs. In all these ways it is exemplary of that form of reading I am calling "deconstructive," or of reading as such. Though good reading does not occur as often as one might expect or hope, it is by no means confined to any one historical period and may appear at any time, perhaps most often in those readers, like George Eliot, who are also good writers, masters of composition. The deconstructive movement of the passage in question is constituted by proffering and withdrawing one metaphorical formulation after another. Each metaphor is dismantled as soon as it is proposed, though the sad necessity of using metaphors is at the same time affirmed.

Far from suggesting that metaphor may be opposed to literal or to conceptual language as an external adornment that might be removed, leaving the naked literal names or concepts, George Eliot sees metaphor as unfortunately an intrinsic part of language. It is not by any means to be stripped away from any discourse or argument, even the most unadorned. The only cure for metaphor is another metaphor, but that new metaphor only inoculates you with a somewhat different disease. As George Eliot says of this lamentable linguistic predicament: "It was doubtless an ingenious idea to call the camel the ship of the desert, but it would hardly lead one far in training that useful beast. O Aristotle! if you had had the advantage of being the 'freshest modern' instead of the greatest ancient, would you not have mingled your praise of metaphorical speech as a sign of high intelligence, with a lamentation that intelligence so rarely shows itself in speech without metaphor – that we can so seldom declare what a thing is, except by saying it is something else?"[9]

The camel as ship of the desert is not just an example of metaphor. It is a metaphor of metaphor, that is of transfer or transport from one place to another. This is not only what the word "metaphor" etymologically means, but also what metaphor does. If Puttenham's far-fetched Renaissance name for metalepsis is "the Far-fetcher," he calls metaphor the "Figure of Transport." Metaphor gets the writer or reader from here to there in his argument, whether by that "smooth gradation or gentle transition to some other kindred quality" of which Wordsworth speaks in *Essays upon Epitaphs*,[10] echoing the Socrates of the *Phaedrus* on "shifting your ground little by little,"[11] or by the sudden leap over a vacant place in the argument of which George Meredith writes: "It is the excelling merit of similes and metaphors to spring us to vault over gaps and thickets and dreary places."[12] Pedagogy is metaphor. It takes the mind of the student and transforms it, transfers it, translates it, ferries it from here to there. A method of teaching, such as Mr Stelling's, is as much a means of transportation as a camel or a ship. My own "passages" from Plato and Eliot are synecdoches, parts taken from large wholes and used as figurative means of passage from one place to another in my argument.

The sentence about the camel brings into the open the asymmetrical juxtaposition between the opposition of literal and figurative language, on the one hand, and the opposition of practice and theory on the other. The reader may be inclined to think they are parallel, but this probably depends on a confusion of mind. One thinks of literal language as the clear, nonfigurative expression of ideas or concepts, for example, "the abstract" concepts of grammar, such as the relation between cases and terminations in the genitive or the dative that Tom Tulliver has so much trouble learning, just as a modern student of English composition has trouble learning the rules of English grammar. At the same time one thinks of literal language as the act of nonfigurative nomination, calling a spade a spade and a camel a camel, not a ship. We tend to think of figure as being applied at either end of the scale from abstract to concrete as an additional ornament making the literal expression "clear," more "vivid," or more "forceful." As George Eliot's sentence makes "clear," however, the trouble with theory is not that it is abstract or conceptual but that it is always based on metaphor – that is, it commits what Alfred North Whitehead calls the "fallacy of misplaced concreteness."

If it is true, as both Whitehead himself and such literary theorists as William Empson and Kenneth Burke aver in different ways, that original thinking is most often started by a metaphor, it is also the case that each metaphorically based theory, such as the alternative pedagogical theories George Eliot sketches out, has its own built-in fallacious bias and leads to its own special form of catastrophe in the classroom. If a camel is not a ship, the brain is neither a field to plow nor a stomach nor a sheet of paper nor a mirror, though each of these metaphors could, and has, generated ponderous, solemn, and intellectually cogent theories of teaching. Neither theory nor literal meaning, if there is such a thing (which there is not), will help you with that camel. As soon as you try to tell someone how to manage one you fall into the theory – that is, into some metaphorical scheme or other. The opposition between theory and practice is not that between metaphorical and literal language, but that between language, which is always figurative through and through, and no language – silent doing. If the praxis in question is the act of writing, the habit of writing well, it can be seen that there are going to be problems in teaching it, more problems even than in teaching someone how to drive a camel or make a chair. That the terms for the parts of a chair are examples of those basic personifying catachreses whereby we humanize the world and project arms and legs where there are none may cause little trouble as the apprentice learns from watching the master cabinetmaker at work, but it might cause much trouble to someone writing about chairs.

The task, most people would agree, is not to teach students in writing courses grammatical theory, but to make each student pass somehow from a condition in which he or she cannot write well to a condition in which he or she can write well. First the student cannot write well and later he or she can. To make this happen is perhaps more difficult than to make that camel pass through a needle's eye. No theoretical metaphor helps much in thinking about this strange transition or carrying over, much less in making it happen. What goes on in the student's mind, whether it is plowed and harrowed, or digests the practical rules of good writing, or has them "instilled" by a process of slow dripping, or is inscribed with them, or reflects them, is in a way irrelevant. It is an adjacent matter of theoretical speculation. What counts is the practical results, the words a given student puts down on paper, and yet what is said to the student or what he reads seems to have something to do with this transition.

So far I have emphasized the insight into the fundamentally figurative character of language in rhetoric as reading, as decomposition, whether that rhetoric is ancient, Victorian, or contemporary deconstructionist. My argument is that if both teachers and students of rhetoric as composition do not aim to become as good readers as Plato, George Eliot, or Derrida, as wise in the ways of tropes, they will not learn to be good teachers or practitioners of writing either. It follows that good courses in rhetoric as reading must always accompany programs in composition, not only in preparation for reading Shakespeare, Milton, Wordsworth, and Wallace Stevens, but as an essential accompaniment to courses in writing. I suspect that the impetus for this new direction in the teaching of reading may come or is coming from the teachers of composition themselves, out of the pressures of their practical encounters with students of writing, but we must make sure we base our rhetoric as reading on the deepest possible knowledge of what good reading would be. Present-day rhetoricians' questioning of teaching on the assumption that figures of speech are or should be ornaments added to a literal base of discourse is of course inextricably associated with a set of other questionings: a questioning of the idea that a preexisting, unified self uses language as a tool of expression, writing with a purpose; a questioning of the idea that writers have their argument clearly in mind first and then copy that mental argument in words, refining it in revision to a closer and closer correspondence to the original;[13] a questioning of the idea that a good piece of writing must or can be "organically unified"; a questioning of the paradigm of "realism" that assumes good writing is to be tested by its correspondence to some external reality. Exploring each of these in its relation to the teaching of both reading and writing would require a separate essay, but the "command of metaphor" in this area too is the key that opens all these doors. Once students of rhetoric in both senses acquire this mastery, all else follows.

On the assumption that this is the case, I shall turn briefly in conclusion to a group of widely used textbooks of composition to see what they have to say about metaphor or figures of speech generally.[14] To analyze the rhetoric and the latent or unthought-out (*impensé*, as the French say) ideology of these textbooks, their subtexts, undertexts, or underthoughts, would be a long work. I limit myself to what they say explicitly about metaphor. I have been somewhat surprised by the way most (though not quite all) of them repeat what I should have thought by now would be well-exploded assumptions about the role of figures of speech in good writing. The same figurative terminology for this (the words "vivid" and "concrete" for example) is repeated from textbook to textbook. Or, more precisely, recognition of the constitutive power of figurative language and of the way it is inextricably part of any piece of writing is mingled with many unfortunate vestiges of a set of systematically connected fallacies or received ideas about metaphor. Perpetuating these can in no way help students learn to write. Far from it. Nor can it help students as readers if, for example, they are taught in writing courses to expect metaphor to be a nonessential element in a dialogue of Plato, a novel by George Eliot, or an article in the daily paper.

One of the books I have consulted says nothing at all in any extended way about figures of speech.[15] It is lacking the ritual section present in most handbooks of composition defining metaphor, simile, "dead" metaphor, and "mixed" metaphor and giving hints for their use or avoidance. Perhaps omitting this is a good thing. At least it does not mislead students by telling them something mistaken. This strategy has the disadvantage, however, of suggesting by omission that figurative language is not much of a problem for the novice writer.

Most other textbooks of composition I have consulted are not so shy of giving definitions and advice. One book, for example, though early on it intelligently urges the use of analogy or metaphor as a means of "discovering new ideas about your topic," later on takes this back by making what seems to be an extraordinarily odd and unworkable suggestion: "In general, it is best to avoid metaphor in philosophy papers."[16] Most of the textbooks, including this one, accept without question the opposition between "abstract ideas," on the one hand, and visible, solid figures on the other. Metaphor is good because it "makes a picture," is "clear" or "concrete," and therefore is "fresh" and has "force," though all it does is to "illustrate" an idea that remains essentially the same after its illustration. The idea is only more visible, brought more into the open, solidified out of its impalpability, like a cement block. "A figure of speech should be fresh, clear, and should make an image for the reader," says one book. "The purpose of the figure of speech is to create a picture, to make an idea clear and forceful through comparison."[17] "[A] figure of speech," says another book, "is an effective way to make the abstract concrete. . . . The analogy . . . pictorializes the argument by likening the process to something every reader will both understand and feel."[18]

A third book presents a more or less complete repertoire of all these *idées reçues*:

[Metaphors are] the most useful way of making our abstractions concrete. . . . Metaphors illustrate, in a word, our general ideas. . . . Almost all our words are metaphors, usually with the physical picture faded. *Transfer* itself pictures a physical portage. . . . But mercifully the physical facts have faded – transfer has become a "dead metaphor" – and we can use the word in comfortable abstraction. . . . The metaphor, then, is your most useful device. It makes your thought concrete and your writing vivid. . . . But it is dangerous. It should be quiet, almost unnoticed, with all details agreeing, and all absolutely consistent with the natural universe.[19]

Another textbook, my final example, is the most explicit of those I have consulted in opposing literal to figurative language and in defining metaphor as something optional that may be added after the fact by daring students to a literal discourse existing before any metaphor. The author of this text has a splendid sense of the latent or not so latent comedy in mixed metaphor, but his way of dealing with this is to recommend avoiding metaphor altogether or using it in a wary and deliberate way. His advice reminds me of the creative writing student Mary McCarthy overheard saying she had finished writing her story for the week but "had to go back and put the symbols in":

> Because metaphors and similes usually compress meaning into a minimum of words, they are best attempted after a first draft has given you sufficient control over your *literal* (nonfigurative) meaning. Think of the search for apt images as an optional, potentially fruitful part of the revising process. I say "optional" because some young writers, still engrossed in trying to master principles of effective sentence structure, feel understandably reluctant to carry an extra burden; for a while at least, they can be satisfied if they have weeded out formulaic language and achieved a good measure of concreteness. To insist that they sprinkle their papers with figures of speech would be like asking an intermediate swimming class to concentrate on perfecting the racing turn.
>
> . . . Figurative language, then, is as tricky as it is useful. When you intend an abstract meaning, you have to make sure that your dead metaphors stay good and dead. And when you do wish to be figurative, see whether you are getting the necessary vividness and consistency. If not, go back to the literal statement; it is better to make plain assertions than to litter your verbal landscape with those strangled hulks.[20]

Crews has an interesting account of how he arrived at the figure of the racing turn (after deliberately considering and rejecting three other metaphors).[21] I doubt that this is in fact the way metaphors most commonly get into pieces of writing, good or bad. It would be useful to have broader empirical studies of this, but, lacking these, one may be permitted to guess that the choice of metaphors is usually much more constrained and involuntary, even in those who, like Aristotle's good poet, have that command of metaphor that is the mark of genius. In the passages from Crews I have cited, what about "fruitful," "weeded out," "good measure," "concreteness," "sprinkle," "dead," and that "landscape" "littered" with "strangled hulks"? Were they all the result of clearheaded choice among alternatives? Are they dead metaphors, safely dead; cliché metaphors, tamed, therefore legitimately used without much thought for their consistency with one another (there seems to be some measure of concrete in that weedy garden); mixed metaphors; or figures carefully chosen for their force, clarity, concreteness, and so on? Or are they a kind of ironic in-joke for teachers and shrewd students, strangled hulks of mixed metaphors deliberately left littering the landscape of Crews' prose? Since "strangled hulk" is taken from one of Crews' examples of mixed metaphor (188), it seems that the latter may be the case. In any case, the system of mistaken assumptions about metaphor in these various textbooks may be easily identified. This system includes (1) the idea that metaphor is a detachable part of language, something supplemental, adventitious, or external to a given argument, something the argument could do without and still remain the same argument, a matter of free choice, "optional"; (2) the idea that metaphor may be defined by opposition to some presumed literal language, whether "concrete" or "conceptual"; (3) the idea that a metaphor should be primarily "illustrative," that is, that it should function to make ideas that can in fact be expressed accurately without it more "vivid," "clearer," more "concrete," more "compressed," though without of course essentially changing the idea; (4) the assumption that the logic of metaphor is the logic of mimetic realism – that metaphor must "picture" the real physical world accurately and consistently; (5) the notion that there is such a thing as a "dead metaphor," a harmless fossilized remnant of the etymological origin of abstract words, the belief that these dead metaphors can be counted on, if they are handled right, to remain safely dead, and the conviction that they should remain safely dead; (6) the idea that a student should first write his essay out in entirely literal language, free of all metaphorical adornment, and then, if he dares, go back and add appropriate metaphors, though this is really a matter for advanced students, since metaphors are "dangerous" and should be used sparingly – a little pepper goes a long way; (7) the idea that figures of speech generally may be subsumed under the category of metaphor or analogy. Though simile as a special case of metaphor is usually mentioned, and personification is often identified, these handbooks, with rare exceptions, do not think it necessary to say anything about metonymy or synecdoche, much less about irony, metalepsis, catachresis, chiasmus, or any of the other tropes that the new rhetoric of reading has found it necessary to discriminate. Finally, there is (8) the assumption that information or advice about the use of figurative language is in any case a marginal part of the teaching of writing and can be tucked away somewhere in a paragraph or two as a minor subcategory of "diction." As Jacques Derrida has noted in "White Mythology," the tradition of treating metaphor this way in handbooks of rhetoric goes back at least to Aristotle.[22]

It will be apparent from what I have already said about Plato, Aristotle, and George Eliot that I consider these assumptions false to the actual nature of language and therefore an inadequate basis for the teaching of writing. Metaphors are not like the racing turn. They are the universal medium in which the writer – novice, intermediate, and advanced – must learn to swim. The pervasively figurative nature of language is the "destructive element" in which, to borrow Stein's advice in *Lord Jim*, all writers must "immerse" themselves in order to swim at all. The "dream" into which we are all born is figurative language itself. Within this dream we must live, and those who try to climb out into the open air of nonfigurative language or out of language altogether will surely drown. "Yes!" says Stein.

> Very funny this terrible thing is. A man that is born falls into a dream like a man who falls into the sea. If he tries to climb out into the air as inexperienced people endeavour to do, he drowns – *nicht wahr?* . . . No, I tell you! The way is to the destructive element submit yourself, and with the exertions of your hands and feet in the water make the deep, deep sea keep you up.[23]

The authors of these handbooks, along with most teachers of composition, would no doubt say, truthfully enough, that they know all this already, but that it is impossible, impractical or ineffective to try to teach this to beginning college students. Many such students are only marginally literate and may have drastic "writing disabilities," as they say. It would only make things worse to try to explain figurative language to them. As I have already suggested, the relation between theory and practice is by no means straightforward. Any theory is like that dream Stein recommends we should follow and follow again, "*ewig – usque ad finem,*" though it is not clear that every theory rigorously followed would not lead to some catastrophe. There is always an otherness of theory to itself and therefore an incommensurability of theory and any application of it. To put this another way, empirical studies of the relative effectiveness of different theories of teaching writing are not altogether reassuring. They suggest that students will get somewhat better whatever the teacher does, perhaps through sheer *praxis*. One learns to write by writing. On the other hand, I am enough of a believer in the reasonableness of things to suspect that a thoroughly vitiated theory may come in one way or another to inhibit or vitiate practice. To teach students the doctrine about figures I have found in these textbooks is like limiting classes in sex education to tales about the birds and bees or like assuming in teaching young medical students that though the human body is in fact an organism it is simpler and more workable to tell students it is a wind-up mechanism.

Teachers of writing and reading should take heart from the teachers of mathematics, biology, and physics. Far from trying to hide from students the complexities of new developments in these disciplines, they have gone to work to teach the "new math" from grade school on and to develop appropriate introductory courses teaching new discoveries in genetics and nuclear physics. I believe we should all go to work together, teachers of reading and teachers of writing in cooperation, to do something of the same sort for our disciplines. We should take the most advanced insights into language from both sides and attempt to work out commensurate pedagogies. To some degree this is already happening. The book in which this essay originally appeared is one evidence of the widely felt need for such cooperation. What a "deconstructive" textbook of freshman writing would be like I am not sure, though it would certainly have more and different material on figurative language. Probably the term "deconstruction" has in any case outlived its polemical usefulness as a slogan and should be dropped in such a book. The difficulty of writing such a textbook is not an argument against trying to do it, any more than it is in the analogous situations in biology and physics. In any case, insofar as the teaching of composition suggests that the student should write a literal version first and perhaps add metaphors later; insofar as it still assumes that figures are adventitious adornment; insofar as it assumes that the writer has the ideas before he or she writes them down and that revision is a matter of achieving closer and closer approximation to some pre-existent model, whether in the mind of the writer or in some preliminary outline; insofar as it assumes that a good piece of writing should be or can be univocal, wholly unified, it still has much to learn from that form of the rhetoric of reading called at the moment, for better or worse, deconstruction. Insofar as teachers of reading still assume that reading is a passive, objective act and not itself another scene of writing; insofar as they assume that reading is a matter of identifying the literal, thematic sense of the text, its representation of some extralinguistic state of affairs; insofar as they think they can go on blithely teaching the great authors in the canon of English literature as though nothing had happened to the basic literacy of college students, they need to learn from the experience of teachers of composition, or at least from that cooperative teaching of writing and reading I have dared to hope for here.

Notes

1. Peter Demetz, "An Inarticulate Society," *Yale Alumni Magazine and Journal* 45, no. 2 (November 1981): 16, and see also "Recommendations of the Commission on the Future of the Profession," in *Profession 81* (New York, 1981), pp. 1–5, especially recommendation 3, to which this present essay may be said to be a response.
2. Paul de Man, "Hypogram and Inscription: Michael Riffaterre's Poetics of Reading," forthcoming in *Diacritics*.
3. I am glad to find support for this belief not only in the third recommendation of the MLA Commission, referred to in note 1 above, but also in an accompanying essay by Wayne Booth, "The Common Aims That Divide Us: Or, Is There a 'Profession 1981'?" in *Profession 81*, 13–17.
4. Though a large part of the work of Derrida and de Man would be relevant to the topic of the rhetoric of reading, two works are especially important, Derrida's "White Mythology: Metaphor in the Text of Philosophy," tr. F. C. T. Moore, *New Literary History* 6, no. 1 (Autumn 1974): pp. 6–74, originally "La mythologie blanche (la métaphore dans le texte philosophique)," *Poétique*, no. 5 (1971): pp. 1–52, reprinted in *Marges* (Paris, 1972), pp. 247–324; and de Man's *Allegories of Reading: Figural Language in Rousseau, Nietzsche, Rilke, and Proust* (New Haven, London, 1979).
5. See Friedrich Nietzsche, *Gesammelte Werke* (Munich, 1922), 5:285–319, and Friedrich Nietzsche, "Rhétorique et language," tr. Philippe Lacoue-Labarthe and Jean-Luc Nancy, *Poétique*, no. 5 (1971): pp. 99–142.
6. *Gorgias*, 462c, 463b, and 463d, tr. W. D. Woodhead, *Plato: The Collected Dialogues*, Edith Hamilton and Huntington Cairns, eds, Bollingen Series 71 (Princeton, 1973), pp. 246, 247.
7. *Phaedrus*, 1, 277b, tr. R. Hackforth, *Collected Dialogues*, p. 522.
8. *Rhetoric*, 1356b, tr. Lane Cooper (New York, London, 1932), p. 10, and see also *Rhetoric*, 1395b ff., pp. 154 ff.; on proportional metaphor see Aristotle. *On the Art of Poetry*. 1457b, tr. S. H. Butcher (Indianapolis, 1975), p. 28.
9. See Aristotle, *On the Art of Poetry*, 1458b, p. 31: "But the greatest thing by far is to have a command of metaphor. This alone cannot be imparted by another; it is the mark of genius."
10. William Wordsworth, *The Prose Works*, W. J. B. Owen and J. W. Smyser, eds, (Oxford, 1974), 2:81.
11. *Phaedrus*, 262a, p. 507.
12. George Meredith, *One of Our Conquerors* (New York, 1906), chap. 18.
13. For a valuable corrective of this paradigm see Nancy Sommers, "Revision Strategies of Student Writers and Experienced Adult Writers," *College Composition and Communication* 35 (1980): pp. 378–88, and for an inside discussion of the relevance of "deconstruction" to the teaching of reading and writing, see Jasper Neel, "Writing about Literature (or Country Ham)," in *Publishing in English Education*, Stephen N. Judy, ed. (Montclair, N.J., 1981).
14. I have examined the following: Sheridan Baker, *The Complete Stylist and Handbook*, 2d ed. (New York, 1980); Frederick Crews, *The Random House Handbook*, 3d ed. (New York, 1980); Elaine P. Maimon, Gerald L. Belcher, Gail W. Hearn, Barbara F. Nodine, and Finbarr W. O'Conner, *Writing in the Arts and Sciences* (Cambridge, Mass., 1981); James M. McCrimmon, Susan Miller, and Webb Salmon, *Writing with a Purpose*, 7th ed. (Boston, 1980); Dean Memering and Frank O'Hare, *The Writer's Work: Guide to Effective*

Composition (Englewood Cliffs, N.J., 1980); Robert Scholes and Nancy R. Comley, *The Practice of Writing* (New York, 1981).
15. Scholes and Comley, *Practice of Writing*.
16. Maimon et al., *Writing in the Arts and Sciences*, pp. 27, 200–1.
17. Memering and O'Hare, *Writer's Work*, p. 350.
18. McCrimmon, Miller, and Salmon, *Writing with a Purpose*, p. 167.
19. Baker, *Complete Stylist*, pp. 191, 192, 195.
20. Crews, *Random House Handbook*, pp. 186, 189.
21. Ibid., pp. 186–7.
22. "White Mythology," 30 ff.
23. *Lord Jim* (London, 1948), ch. 20.

15
Constructions in criticism

My contribution to the topic of this issue of *boundary 2** is a reflection on what seems to me an important feature of the present state of humanistic study, perhaps of humanistic study at any time. This is the tendency to ground such study on theoretical work from outside the strict domains of the humanities. Whether that external grounding is in anthropology with Lévi-Strauss, or in psychoanalysis, with Freud or Lacan, or in scientific linguistics, with Saussure or Chomsky, or in political economy, with Marx, the problem is the same, or at least analogous. What is needed is a solid ground on the basis of which humanistic study can be carried on, for example the interpretation of a novel or poem. In order for this to occur a canonical or unequivocal reading of the extra-humanistic text tends to be assumed. When humanists who happen to be also good readers turn to Lévi-Strauss, to Freud, Lacan, Saussure, Chomsky, or Marx, however, they find that the grounding text is just as problematic as the literary text they want to use it to explain. The "scientific" or extra-humanistic text turns into a literary text. It has, for example, the same features of dependence on figurative language as characterizes poems or novels. Humanists may become permanently lost in the labyrinthine corridors of the extra-humanistic grounding text whose meaning they need to be able to take for granted in order to get on with their own proper work. I take, somewhat arbitrarily, as one example of this, the work of Sigmund Freud. My passages from Freud come from *Studies on Hysteria* (1893–5), from *The Interpretation of Dreams* (1900), from "Dora" (1905), and from a little paper published late in Freud's life, "Constructions in Analysis" (1937).

The situation of a practicing analyst reading a text by Freud and the situation of a literary critic are very different. Analysts presumably seek in Freud assistance in their own practical clinical work. Their business is to cure patients, a serious business, even sometimes a life or death business. The analyst, I should think, would seek in Freud examples of clinical practice or models for it, or would seek hypotheses about mental life or about ways to cure mentally ill patients. Freud gives directions for such use of his work toward the end of "Constructions in Analysis

---

* Where this essay originally appeared.

[*Konstruktionen in der Analyse*],"[1] after he has proposed, in a seeming digression from the main theme of the essay, the theory that delusions and hallucinations contain "a fragment of historical truth [*ein Stück historischer Wahrheit*]" or a "kernel of truth [*Wahrheitskerns*]" (*SE*, XXIII, 267–8; *GW*, XVI, 54, 55): "It would probably be worth while to make an attempt to study cases of the disorder in question on the basis of the hypotheses that have been here put forward [*nach den hier entwickelten Voraussetzungenen studieren*] and also to carry out their treatment on those same lines" (*SE*, XXIII, 267; *GW*, XVI, 55). Freud's theory of delusions, like his theory of the efficacy of constructions, might work or it might not work, but in any case it would be open to empirical testing. Its value is in its practical efficacy, not in its theoretical beauty or even in its truth, though Freud's "Constructions in Analysis" is throughout governed by the authority of the concept of truth, as when he says delusions collective or individual contain a kernel or a fragment (the two figures are not quite the same in implications) of truth.

The situation of literary critics reading Freud is quite different. Their situation is freer, more frivolous, since surely matters of life and death are not at stake in the reading of a poem or a novel. Or are they? They seek in Freud, presumably, a solid theoretical ground for the enterprise of interpreting works of literature. The search for grounds for literary interpretation in extra-literary texts, in Marx, Nietzsche, Heidegger, or Derrida, as well as, conspicuously, in the work of Freud, is a distinguishing feature of current literary criticism, though one of course not altogether unheard of before the twentieth century.[2] The situation merits thought. Why is it that literary criticism cannot provide its own intrinsic grounds for its own enterprise, as other disciplines presumably do?

The use of Freud by literary critics is exemplary here. Such appropriation of Freud, it seems to me, goes implicitly or explicitly by way of an analogy: The interpretation of a literary text is like the treatment of a patient. This analogy goes both ways, and the figure is of course Freud's own, as for example in "Dora" ("Fragment of an Analysis of a Case of Hysteria"), when he says a transference is a new edition of an old text. Since Freud's word for transference. *Übertragung*, is also, along with *Übersetzung*, one of the common German words for "translation," the figure of transference as a new edition, perhaps revised, of an old text is already in a sense latent in the word Freud chooses: "What are transferences [*Übertragungen*]? They are new editions or facsimiles of the impulses and phantasies which are aroused and made conscious during the progress of the analysis; but they have this peculiarity, which is characteristic for their species, that they replace some earlier person by the person of the physician. . . . Some of these transferences have a content which differs from that of their model [*Vorbilde*] in no respect whatever except for the substitution [*Ersetzung*]. These then – to keep to the same metaphors [*Gleichnisse*] – are merely new impressions or reprints. Others are more ingeniously constructed; their content has been subjected to a moderating influence – to *sublimation*, as I call it – and they may even become conscious, by cleverly taking advantage of some real peculiarity in the physician's person or circumstances and attaching themselves to that. These, then, will no longer be new impressions, but revised editions" (*SE*, VII, 116; *GW*, V, 279–80). The patient, however, as Freud says, is only metaphorically a text, however far one can go with the figure that says the analyst's work is like the interpretation of a poem. The analysand is in fact a flesh and blood person, the incarnation of signs as symptoms – paralysis, vomiting, aphonia, stuttering, dizziness, a persistent cough, delusions, or whatever. The literary critic confronts a real text, black marks on a page that can never suffer or answer back or dismiss the critic, say a final no to him, as Dora did to Freud. To put this another way, that is, by reversing the metaphor, it does not make sense, except metaphorically, to say that the critic "cures" the text by interpreting it, though I have myself, following the lead of Wallace Stevens, used just that metaphor.[3]

The function of metaphor, transference, carrying over, in all these transactions, is what seems most problematical both in Freud's "Constructions in Analysis" and in the use of it by literary critics. What is at stake when a literary critic grounds his work in a translated or transposed procedure from the realm of mental illness and its cure? What is at stake when I read Freud not in German but translated, transposed into Strachey's English? What is at stake when Freud, in the essay "Constructions in Analysis," uses, as if by an unavoidable necessity, a whole series of not quite compatible metaphors to describe the procedure of construction whereby the analyst takes the raw material [*Materialien*] he has elicited from the patient – fragments, ideas, feelings – translates them back into evidence of the repressed material and puts it all together as a coherent story, account, or narrative, "a picture of the patient's forgotten years that shall be alike trustworthy and in all essential respects complete [*ein zuverlässiges und in allen wesentlichen Stücken vollständiges Bild der vergessenen Lebensjahre des Patienten*]" (*SE*, XXIII, 258; *GW*, XVI, 44)? The metaphors in "Constructions in Analysis" include the figure of the coin game of heads and tails in relation to its protocols or rules, the metaphor of the archeologist's work of reconstruction, the metaphor comparing construction to delusions or hallucinations, and the metaphor of construction or reconstruction itself. What is their status? Why does Freud need so many of them, and such diverse ones? What is their truth value?

Here an important difference between the situation of the analyst in relation to Freud's essay and the situation of the literary critic may be noted. The analyst might be imagined as abstracting the embedded clinical hypotheses from the essay and testing them in practice, as Freud incites them to do. Literary critics are in the quite different situation of attempting to base or ground their interpretation of one text on another text. First they must be sure that they have read the grounding text with the same sophistication they would apply to any literary text. The ground is of the nature of the superstructure to be built on it, and that ground, in the case of Freud at least, characteristically gives way and reveals itself to be no solid ground but yet another text open to a perhaps interminable interpretation, with an indefinite postponement of the moment when we could stand firmly on Freud and on that basis begin the solidly grounded interpretation of literary texts proper which was our original goal.

The moment this slippage or abyssing occurs in "Constructions in Analysis" is the first paragraph of the third section:

> The path that starts from the analyst's construction ought to end in the patient's recollection; but it does not always lead so far. Quite often we do not succeed in bringing the patient to recollect what has been repressed. Instead of that, if the analysis is carried out correctly, we produce in him an assured conviction of the truth of the construction which achieves the same therapeutic result as a recaptured memory. The problem of what the circumstances are in which this occurs and of how it is possible that what appears to be an incomplete substitute should nevertheless produce a complete result – all of this is matter for a later enquiry. (*SE*, XXIII, 265–6; *GW*, XVI, 52–3)

Here Freud recognizes an extraordinary fact. A construction, reconstruction, or projection which is never confirmed by memory, what Freud calls "an incomplete substitute [*ein . . . unvollkommener Ersatz*]" nevertheless may "produce a complete result [*die volle Wirkung tut*]" (*SE*, XXIII, 266; *GW*, XVI, 53). It is not without significance that consideration of this strange fact is, once more, as so often before in Freud's work, postponed to the future: "all of this is material for a later enquiry [*das bleibt ein Stoff für spätere Forschung*]," or as the manservant in Nestroy's *Der Zerrissene* habitually puts this: "It will all become clear in the course of future developments" (*SE*, XXIII, 265; *GW*, XVI, 52), Freud's little essay is governed by the "authority [*Autorität*]" (*SE*, XXIII, 262; *GW*, XVI, 48) of the concept of truth [*Wahrheit*], truth as correspondence between the analyst's constructions or reconstructions and the repressed memories or "forgotten events [*vergessenen Geschehens*]" (*SE*, XXIII, 263; *GW*, XVI, 50), truth as revelation or bringing to light: "It depends only upon analytic technique whether we shall succeed in bringing what is concealed to light (*das Verborgene vollständig zum Vorschein zu bringen*" (*SE*, XXIII, 260; *GW*, XVI, 46). What kind of truth is it which is efficacious even if it cannot be tested by a yes or no? Is it not just that truth according to the "famous principle [*nach dem berruchtigten Prinzip*]: 'Heads I win, tails you lose'" (*SE*, XXIII, 257; *GW*, XVI, 43) which Freud begins by repudiating, truth without negation, or as all negation, truth as yes and yes, or as no and no, hence not computable, accountable, or reconstructable by any binary logic, truth indefinitely postponed?

The extraordinary development of Freud's thought proceeds by sudden discontinuous leaps, transformations, reworkings, reversals, tireless theoretical experimentations with new models for thinking about the mind or for organizing recalcitrant psychic data. The trajectory of this development has often been charted, for example in terms of Freud's relatively early "discovery" that the sexual traumas of his hysterical patients, as he came to think, were most often imaginary, not real, or in terms of the great reversal around 1919, the time of "The Uncanny" and *Beyond the Pleasure Principle*. Another mapping can be made in terms of a crucial change in Freud's use of the figure of the labyrinth already introduced in my first paragraph here. The passages in question will also show that the question of the truth, on the one hand, and the therapeutic efficacy, on the other, of what Freud calls "constructions" had already been an issue in Freud's earliest work. If Freud's work is marked by notorious reversals, it has also a profound continuity in his anxiety about the truth value of those "constructions."

A spectacular sequence of pages in the fourth and final section of *Studies on Hysteria (Studien über Hysterie)* (1893–5), "The Psychotherapy of Hysteria," presents a series of versions of the figure of the labyrinth. These pages constitute one of Freud's first great methodological meditations. Freud's versions of the labyrinth add up to a theoretical model of admirable complexity. His basic image is of complicated spatial patterns of tangled labyrinthine lines surrounding, coming from, and returning to, what Freud calls the "pathogenic nucleus." By the proper procedures it is possible to follow the lines, reach this nucleus, bring it to the surface, extirpate it, and so cure the patient. The nucleus is of the same nature as the lines which lead to it. The whole maze could be mapped. It is in fact mapped by the analyst as he pieces his bits of data together to make a complete design. He thereby triumphantly reaches the center and returns from it with his prize, like Marlow bringing Kurtz back from the heart of darkness, or like Orpheus returning with Eurydice.

There is a crucial change from this to a famous passage in *The Interpretation of Dreams (Die Traumdeutung)* (1900) which uses a version of the same figure, in this case the mushroom mycelium. In the later passage Freud speaks of the center as something which can by no means be reached by following lines from the periphery. The center is now seen as something wholly heterogeneous to the tangle surrounding it. It is therefore unmappable by any species of cartography. Matters are not quite so simple as this, however, as they rarely are with Freud. It is worth following in detail the passages in *Studies on Hysteria* to see how latent or overt contradictions there prepare for the fuller insight expressed in *The Interpretation of Dreams*. The question of the relation between latent and overt is in fact what is at stake.

The psychic structure of the hysteric and the procedure used to reach the pathogenic nucleus and bring it to the surface are described not in one coherent figure but in a series of not quite compatible ones. Freud is not unaware of this fact. He calls readers' attention to it, in case they have not noticed it for themselves. It is one of those splendid moments in which Freud draws himself up and interrogates his own enterprise. There is another such in *Beyond the Pleasure Principle*, beginning, "It may be asked whether and how far I am myself convinced of the truth of the hypotheses that have been set out in these pages" (*SE*, XVIII, 59). In *Studies on Hysteria* Freud inserts a parenthetical paragraph both calling attention to his procedure and attempting to explain away its peculiarities. It is a version of what I call "the linguistic moment."[4] Freud calls attention to the verbal means by which he is saying what he is saying and also to the means (they are the same) by which he is reaching that pathogenic nucleus and freeing it. The medium is figurative language or, rather, multiple contradictory figures. If this medium is unsound as a means of traversing the space in question and reaching its organizing center, then the whole enterprise is put in doubt, as is the presupposition that the center is of the same nature (homogeneous and not allergenic) as the paths or threads (figures here for figurative language itself) used to reach it:

> (I am making use here [says Freud] of a number of similes, all of which have only a very limited resemblance to my subject and which, moreover, are incompatible with one another. I am aware that this is so, and I am in no danger of over-estimating their value. But my purpose in using them is to throw light from different directions on a highly complicated topic which has never yet been represented. I shall therefore venture to continue in the following pages to introduce similes in the same manner, though I know this is not free from objection.) (*SE*, II, 291; *GW*, I, 295)

This is a curious passage in many ways. None of his similes (*Gleichnissen*), says Freud, has more than "a very limited resemblance [*eine recht begrenzte Ähnlichkeit*]" to what it names. What does this mean, a limited resemblance? Limited in what way, by being a distorted picture, or by being an allotropic trope, turning away from what it names and leading away from it in its otherness? The similes, moreover, says Freud, are incompatible with one another. They cannot be reconciled in one single picture or map, however complicated a one. They are used in their heterogeneity "to throw light from different directions [*von verschiedenen Seiten hier zu veranschaulichen*]" on something, "a highly complicated topic which has never yet been represented [*ein höchst kompliziertes und noch niemals dargestelltes Denkobjekt*]." Just because this "object of thought" has never yet been represented would not seem sufficient reason for not representing it directly or literally, giving a photograph of this hitherto unknown place, so to speak. It seems that this place, perhaps because of its obscurity or complexity, perhaps because it has never been "represented" before and so lacks a proper name in any language, perhaps because it could by no means, at any time or place, ever be represented except tropologically, must, at least for now, be presented in figures. Freud's figure for this is the projecting of light from different directions on a dark object or place, a midnight crossroads. Each light source perhaps reveals a new aspect of the place. If so, perhaps their figurative nature (the fact that each taken alone bears only a limited resemblance to its object) will be cancelled out. Perhaps a full multi-dimensional picture of the object will be produced, like those super-imposed slightly different images that create stereoscopic vision. Perhaps. In any case, all Freud's later work is commanded by this necessity of multiple figurative models, each replacing the last but not wholly disqualifying it. In this passage, having raised these questions about his own procedure, a procedure which not only uses figures but can only be described in figure, Freud says he is going to go on using similes in the same way, even though he recognizes the objections that can be raised. He has himself raised them. He is like a man saying he has transgressed and is going to go on transgressing: "*Ich kann nicht anders.*" Such transgression is the only way to go forward on these roads.

What are the figures Freud uses? In what way are they of limited resemblance to what they name? How are they incompatible with one another? All the figures are graphological or, as Freud says, "pictorial [*bildlich*]" (*SE*, II, 288; *GW*, I, 291), though the German word here can also mean simply "figurative." The form taken by the sequence of figures is not merely that of linear juxtaposition, nor exactly "concatenation," to use one of the figures Freud employs, but an odd sort of addition which is at the same time subtraction. The series is not a dialectical sequence leading by negation to a synthetic sublation. It is rather as if Freud said, "it is this. No, it is not this, but it is really that, though it is also still this. No, it is not that, but it is really this other image, though still the other two," and so on. What is at stake, it will be remembered, is the structure of consciousness and of what is excluded from consciousness. This is defined by Freud as a system of remembering and forgetting. The question is what route the doctor must follow to reach "the pathogenic psychical material which has ostensibly been forgotten [*das pathogene psychische Material, das angeblich vergessen ist*]" (*SE*, II, 287; *GW*, I, 290), so that it can be remembered and so extirpated, like a foreign body. This formulation already seems odd, when one thinks about it. It means that remembering, for hysterical patients, is a means of forgetting, of wiping the slate clean, so that the forgotten memories can no longer be "pathogenic": "The patient is, as it were, getting rid of [the memory picture] by turning it into words" (*SE*, II, 280; *GW*, I, 283). The power of doing harm of these memories depends on their not being accessible to consciousness. It depends on their being "forgotten," and yet, says Freud, though this pathogenic psychical material "is not at the ego's disposal and . . . plays no part in association and memory, nevertheless in some fashion [it] lies ready to hand and in correct and proper order [*in richtiger und guter Ordnung*]" (*SE*, II, 287; *GW*, I, 290). It is there and not there, and it is in the correct order. The latter fact is important because it determines the possibility of reaching the center. Only if all the material remains in proper sequence, in line, can it be followed backward to its source.

Freud, however, raises a question about this a moment later: "Whether this impression [that the material 'in some fashion lies ready to hand in correct and proper order'] is justified [*berechtigt ist*], or whether in thinking this we are not dating back [*zurückverlegt*] to the period of the illness an arrangement of the psychical material which in fact was made after recovery – these are questions which I should prefer not to discuss as yet, and not in these pages" (*SE*, II, 287; *GW*, I, 291). Freud was for the rest of his career both raising these questions and postponing a definitive answer to them. The reader will see what is at stake here. Only if the material is at hand and in the proper order can the pathogenic material be reached by following its line. On the other hand, if the order is created after the fact, by the analysis itself, then what is reached by following that order may be factitious, a "construction." It may be a mirage or fiction generated by the pattern the psychotherapist has made. The attainment of a clarified order bringing everything into the open is "recovery." What is brought into the open, however, in this second possibility, is something the therapist and his patient have made, not something pre-existing the analysis. It exists like the imaginary center of gravity of a ring, or like the second focus of a planetary ellipse.

Assuming that the order was there in the first place, its form must be given an increasingly complicated description, as figure is traced over figure. Each trope does not so much cancel the one before as reveal its inadequacy, its need for a supplementary figure. For one thing, as Freud says, in most cases there is not a single pathogenic nucleus, but "*successions* of *partial* traumas and *concatenations* of pathogenic trains of thought [*Reihen von Partialtraumen und Verkettungen von pathogenen Gedankengängen*]" (*SE*, II, 288; *GW*, I, 291), and not "a *single* hysterical symptom, but a number of them, partly independent of one another and partly linked together [*verknüpft*]" (*SE*, II, 287; *GW*, I, 291). The origin is not single, but a chain, a succession, and it culminates not in a single symptom but in several. These symptoms are, moreover, partly linked and partly separate, whatever *that* may mean. Saying this is a characteristic taking with one hand and giving away with another. It invites the reader to think in terms of the spatial images of chains and links and trains and concatenations, while at the same time cutting those links, reminding the reader that they were not really there, or only partly there, or only there in figure.

If what is at either end of the labyrinth, the trauma at the center and the symptom out in the broad daylight, are multiple, and if the multiple elements of each are ambiguously connected, the line from the periphery to the center through all the corridors of the maze is no less multiple and takes no less ambiguous a form.

The first image Freud proposes is that of an "unmistakeable linear chronological order [*Erstens ist eine lineare chronologische Anordnung unverkennbar*]" (*SE*, II, 288, *GW*, I, 292). Each line of memories leads back through time to the nucleus. This nucleus is now spoken of for convenience as simple, though Freud has already told the reader it is in fact multiple. This arrangement of materials belonging to the same "theme" is first thought of as a series of separate items "like a file of documents, a packet, etc." (*SE*, II, 289; *GW*, I, 292).

In the next paragraph, however, and indeed in all the following pages, the memory is figured as a path or as a thread. The image of discrete elements arranged in a "file," with spaces between, like dominoes is replaced by the image of a line. It is as though what had been secondary, the relation of similarity between items belonging to the same theme, now becomes primary. The material itself is now thought of as those lines or as paths of relationship. The effect, it is easy to see, is to lead the reader to forget how problematic the relation of analogy between one memory and another within the same thematic file might be. The relation of analogy or of logical connection is now all there is. The items in their separateness have dissolved in the line or track of which they are part. The articulation between one thing and another becomes the things, or the things are their power of articulation.

The next step in the development confirms this. Freud first identifies a second kind of arrangement of themes, that of strata, each "characterized by an equal degree of resistance," arranged in concentric circles, as in a circular maze, around the nucleus, with greater and greater resistance to being remembered or encountered, as doctor and patient get closer and closer to the center. He then goes on to describe a third kind of arrangement, one "according to thought-content, the linkage made by a logical thread which reaches as far as the nucleus and tends to take an irregular and twisting path, different in every case" (*SE*, II, 289; *GW*, I, 293). What Freud here calls "logical" is in fact analogical, as the specific analyses show. It is figurative similarities, what Freud was later to call "condensations" and "displacements," metaphors and metonymies, which allow the analyst to slide along the line by the detection of hidden connections. These may move laterally from one thematic file to another, though they always work in this roundabout way toward the center. In this case too the longest way round is the shortest way home. While the first two forms of organization, says Freud, "would be presented in a spatial diagram by a continuous line, curved or straight, the course of the logical chain would have to be indicated by a broken line which would pass along the most roundabout paths from the surface to the deepest layers and back, and yet would in general advance from the periphery to the central nucleus, touching at every intermediate halting place – a line resembling the zig-zag line in the solution of a Knight's Move problem, which cuts across the squares in the diagram of the chess-board" (*SE*, II, 289; *GW*, I, 293). The broken line may be called "logical," but its leaps are more figurative than conceptual, since it jumps from theme to theme by connections of analogical relationships. The movements of the analyst along this logical/analogical line are not only like a knight's move in chess but also like the movements of a player in a game in which the trick is to retrace every track in a labyrinthine pathway with the least overlapping or retracing. The analyst, like such a player, is not permitted to move further in toward the center until all the paths in a given peripheral stratum are followed through exhaustively.

The definition of this effort of exhaustive inventory is assisted by the next modification of his figure Freud proposes. The lines do not in fact remain separate, particularly as they approach the nucleus. A given bit of line is made of the superimposition of several lines. It may therefore be, as Freud says in one of his earliest expressions of this concept, "overdetermined [*überbestimmt*]" (*SE*, II, 290; *GW*, I, 294): "The logical chain corresponds not only [*nicht nur*] to a zig-zag, twisted line, but rather [*sondern vielmehr*] to a ramifying system of lines and more particularly to a converging one. It contains nodal points at which two or more threads meet and thereafter proceed as one; and as a rule several threads which run independently, or which are connected at various points by sidepaths, debouch into the nucleus. To put this in other words, it is very remarkable how often a symptom is determined in several ways, is 'overdetermined'" (*SE*, II, 290; *GW*, I, 293–4). "Not only . . . but rather" – this odd antithesis is a good expression of the mode of relationship among Freud's various metaphors. It is not either/or and not both/and either, but a strange relation in which the new figure contradicts the first but even so does not displace it: "not only" "but rather." The relationship among figures is in fact itself analogical or figurative. Freud's language is of the nature of the mnemonic material itself. It is obliged to articulate itself in the same paradoxical way, since it is not a matter of describing something literal in figures but of finding the necessarily multiple and contradictory figures for something itself strangely figurative, the mental activity of the hysterical patient. I say "strangely" because the thought of the patient exists, at the level of consciousness at least, only in figures, for example in the hysterical symptoms themselves, which are tropes of substitution for the traumatic nucleus. Freud's figures are figures for figuration, analogies for the activity of analogy, in a *mise en abyme* which both opens the chasm of an infinite regress and at the same time fills it with all these images, maze superimposed on maze.

Having provided this sequence of "not only but rathers" for the lines to the center, Freud then proceeds to speak in the same ambiguous way about the nucleus itself, again in a sequence of not quite compatible metaphors. He has been talking, he says, as if the "pathogenic material" were like a foreign body and of the treatment of it as if it were like the removal of such a body from living tissue – the excision of a splinter, a bullet, or a tumor. Now we can see, he says, "where this comparison fails [*worin dieser Vergleich fehlt*]" (*SE*, II, 290; *GW*, I, 294). The foreign body is connected, and in an odd way, with the surrounding tissue. It is part of it and yet not part of it. There is never any clearly marked boundary line, with the healthy psyche on this side and the pathogenic nucleus on the other. All one can say is that the more one penetrates the more purely pathogenic what one encounters is. Once more the topographical figure is both necessary and inadequate. It must of necessity be used in order to demonstrate its own inadequacy, its failure to figure what Freud is at the same time unable to express in any way except as figures that fail. "Our pathogenic psychical group, on the other hand," says Freud, "does not admit of being cleanly extirpated from the ego. Its external strata pass over in every direction into portions of the normal ego; and, indeed, they belong to the latter just as much as to the pathogenic organization. In analysis the boundary between the two is fixed purely conventionally, now at one point, now at another, and in some places it cannot be laid down at all. The interior layers of the pathogenic organization are increasingly alien to the ego, but once more without there being any visible boundary at which the pathogenic material begins" (*SE*, II, 290; *GW*, I, 294–5).

Here is another case of the "not only . . . but rather." The reader can see that Freud's difficulty comes from the impossibility of representing as the mapping of a set of spatially organized objects, joined by paths, and divided by walls and boundaries, what in fact has the nature of the psyche and the nature also of what is inextricable from the psyche, namely signs. The pathogenic nucleus is entirely unlike the conscious ego, and yet it is not entirely unlike it, since no sharp dividing line between the two can be found. In order for the psychoanalytical hypothesis to be valid, it must be possible, beginning with data present to the consciousness of the ego, to move through that to something which is altogether alien to it. Yet if the two are wholly heterogeneous this would be impossible. There would be an opaque wall between the two. The penetration of this wall can take place only by way of something which is figured by the topographical analogy and which yet transcends it. It can take place only by way of that similarity between dissimilars which is analogy itself, with the strange difference that the pathogenic nucleus is something that exists, for the conscious ego at least, only in figure. All Freud's work, from one end to the other, explores the question of what sort of thing it is which can exist only in figure or only as figure. Such a thing can be explored only through figure, as Freud even so early as the *Studies on Hysteria* already knew.

Having rejected the figure of a foreign body within the ego which might be extirpated, Freud goes on to propose yet another figure, that of an infiltrate; "In fact the pathogenic organization does not behave like a foreign body, but far more like an infiltrate. In this simile the resistance must be regarded as what is infiltrating. Nor does the treatment consist in extirpating something – psychotherapy is not able to do this for the present – but in causing the resistance to melt and in thus enabling the circulation to make its way into a region that has hitherto been cut off" (*SE*, II, 290–1; *GW*, I, 295). Freud's expression here is again in more than one way odd. First he says the pathogenic material is like an infiltrate, that is, like something which has power to cross cellular boundaries, permeate membranes, and gradually pervade the whole region around it within which it was originally a localized alien block, globe, or orb. Then Freud contradicts this and says it is the resistance which must be regarded as infiltrating. This seems to mean that what spreads out from the pathogenic nucleus is not the pathogenic material itself but the resistance to its being uncovered. If it were to be encountered face to face it would be deprived of its pathogenic power, its power, that is, to manifest itself at the surface in disabling hysterical symptoms – paralysis, vomiting, blindness, or whatever. The resistance, however, is not only a wall forbidding access to the center of the maze. It is far rather a displaced sign of the nuclear trauma. In this it is not different from the hysterical symptoms themselves. The latter are displacements and condensations hiding the original trauma, and yet revealing it if the analyst is clever at interpreting tropes. Paralysis, for example, may stand for the forbidden act performed or wished to be performed by that limb.

My image of the opaque wall in fact appears in Freud's own language. "The account given by the patient sounds as if it were complete and self-contained. It is at first as though we were standing before a wall which shuts out every prospect and prevents us from having any idea whether there is anything behind it, and if so, what. But if we examine with a critical eye the account the patient has given us without much trouble or resistance, we shall quite infallibly discover gaps and imperfections in it. . . . [T]he physician will be right in looking behind the weak spots for an approach to the material in the deeper layers and in hoping that he will discover precisely there the connecting threads for which he is seeking . . ." (*SE*, II, 293; *GW*, I, 297–8). Here again is a "not only . . . but rather." It is another topographical figure which is incoherent as figure because it figures what can never be given in figure, except contradictorily, namely the activity of figuration itself. Here the analyst encounters a wall which is not really a wall, or not only a wall, but rather a gap, and not only a gap but rather a thread leading into the interior. A wall which is a gap which is a thread could not exist as a physical thing, but it is an admirable definition of a covert sign. Such a sign hides what it signifies and yet gives clues to it which may be followed to that hidden significance. Such signs are the apparently impenetrable wall of the resistance, and yet at the same time they are the fissure through which the secret may be revealed. Freud says psychotherapy as yet cannot extirpate the nucleus. Does this mean extirpation might be conceivable? In any case therapy can now only cause the resistance to melt by interpreting the signs, that is, by turning the wall into a narrow defile, the defile into a thread, the thread into a path which when opened up will allow the light of consciousness to penetrate and circulate freely, like blood into a part of the body which has been cut off from circulation, so curing the patient.

The image of the "defile [*Enge*]" (*SE*, II, 291; *GW*, I, 295) is used a little earlier in a passage which contradicts the general orientation of Freud's series of images. Most of the time throughout these pages Freud speaks as though the activity of the physician were one of penetration. His movement is not an escape from the labyrinth by following Ariadne's thread, but the following of that thread through passageway after passageway and through one narrow fissure after another until the center is reached, the Minotaur confronted: "We must get hold of a piece of the logical thread, by whose guidance alone we may hope to penetrate to the interior" (*SE*, II, 292; *GW*, I, 297). In a passage on the defile of consciousness Freud reverses this image and speaks as though the physician not only penetrated but rather dragged material in broken segments out through a narrow crack into the light of day where it can be reconstructed as a map of the interior. Once again this reversal makes sense only if the material is seen as being always of the nature of signs. To penetrate to the interior, encountering sign after sign and interpreting them one by one, is the same thing as bringing those signs out in the open and putting them together to make a total pattern, the topographical layout of the labyrinth. If the material from the depths always emerges "filed" in reverse chronological order, it comes out through the narrow "defile" of consciousness, though this pun exists only in the English translation, not in the German original. The gap of this defile is defined by the fact that only one memory at a time can be present to consciousness. The doctor must draw the camel through this needle's eye in pieces and then reconstruct the whole animal again on this side of the needle. The paragraph explaining this is an admirable example of the young Freud's figurative imagination. He piles figure on figure to express what can be given only in figure and yet is falsified by every figure:

> If it were possible, after the case has been completely cleared up, to demonstrate the pathogenic material to a third person in what we now know is its complicated and multidimensional organization, we should rightly be asked how a camel like this got through the eye of the needle. For there is some justification for speaking of the "defile" of consciousness [*Enge des Bewusstseins*]. The term gains meaning and liveliness for a physician who carries out an analysis like this. Only a single memory at a time can enter ego-consciousness. A patient who is occupied in working through such a memory sees nothing of what is pushing after it and forgets what has already pushed its way through. If there are difficulties in the way of mastering this single pathogenic memory – as, for instance, if the patient does not relax his resistance against it, if he tries to repress or mutilate it – then the defile [*der Engpaß*] is, so to speak, blocked. The work is at a stand-still, nothing more can appear, and the single memory which is in process of breaking through remains in front of the patient until he has taken it up into the breadth of his ego. The whole spatially-extended mass of psychogenic material is in this way drawn through a narrow cleft [*eine enge Spalte*] and thus arrives in consciousness cut up, as it were, into pieces or strips. It is the psychotherapist's business to put these together once more into the organization which he presumes to have existed [*die vermutete Organisation*]. Anyone who has a craving for further similes [*Vergleichen*] may think at this point of a Chinese puzzle [*ein Geduldspiel*]. (*SE*, II, 291; *GW*, I, 295–6)

"Anyone who has a craving for further similes" – Freud both offers simile after simile and yet discounts them all. He does this both by giving so many in incoherent multiplicity and by the explicit ironic refusal to "overestimate their value." You can have as many as you like, he says, but do not think I take any of them too seriously, just as I only describe the total pattern I make of all those cut-up strips as an organization which I "presume" to have existed. The map can only be matched with another map, in a sign/sign relation. It cannot be matched with what is mapped in a sign/thing relation, since direct access to that "thing" is impossible. Moreover, there is no affirmation made by Freud in the whole series of paragraphs which is not reversed or contradicted, without having been withdrawn. The pathogenic material and the sequence of signs, memories, and symptoms leading to it is not only a continuous file of documents but rather a series of strata, and not only a series of strata but rather a thread, chain, or path which leads zig-zag through the whole labyrinth to the center, and not only a zig-zag path but rather a ramifying system of lines which converge at certain nodes and overlap or become one, and these threads are not only "logical" but rather always "analogical," so that the line moves by overlapping condensations and side-stepping displacements from file to file, and the center of this system is usually not only one but rather two or more, and it is not only a foreign body but rather something which has so infiltrated the ego that no frontier between foreign land and homeland, uncanny and canny, can be found, and the exploration is not only a penetration but rather a bringing to the surface of bits of material drawn through a narrow gap which is rather a wall, and the center is not only something objectively there but rather something which can never be encountered directly but rather pieced together after the fact and so is never verifiable, in a virtually unending series of "not only but rathers."

Why is it that Freud, for all his confidence, at the beginning of his career at least, in the objective existence of the pathogenic nucleus causing mental disorder, cannot avoid putting that existence in question, even in the *Studies on Hysteria*? He puts it in question by demonstrating repeatedly that it cannot be named literally, but only in figures that always break down and fail to figure adequately what they "represent." Why must Freud ultimately recognize that the center of the labyrinth of the mind is a place that can by no means, not even by figurative ones, be placed or named? The ultimate direction toward which Freud's exploration of his topographical figures in the *Studies on Hysteria* is leading is given not in this early book but in a more celebrated passage in *The Interpretation of Dreams*. Here Freud affirms that in a structure of this sort there is a center which can never be reached or identified. This center is the source of the ramifying labyrinthine growth, yet it can never have any light shed on it:

> Even in the best interpreted dreams, there is often a place that must be left in the dark, because in the process of interpreting one notices a tangle [*ein Knäuel*] of dream-thoughts arising which resist unravelling but has also made no further contributions [*keine weiteren Beiträge*] to the dream-content. This, then, is the navel of the dream, the place where it straddles the unknown [*dem Unerkannten aufsitzt*]. The dream-thoughts, to which interpretation leads one, are necessarily interminable [*ohne Abschluß*] and branch out on all sides into the netlike entanglement [*in die netzartige Verstrickung*] of our world of thought. Out of one of the denser places of this meshwork [*Geflechts*], the dream-wish rises like a mushroom out of its mycelium. (*GW*, II/III, 530)[5]

The image here has at least a "limited resemblance" to those in the *Studies on Hysteria*, except that now Freud clearly recognizes that the center must necessarily remain unknown. It is impossible to give, whether literally or in figure. As a result, the dream-thoughts are a trap or netlike entanglement which can never be successfully unravelled. This is both because it branches out interminably in all directions and because its source can never be identified. The source is the origin of the net of dream-thoughts. Though it has made no further contributions to the dream-content beyond generating them in the first place, as mycelium generates mushroom, that initial contribution is enough to make the dream-thoughts an impenetrable and interminable entanglement. Within this net the interpreter may remain permanently trapped.

I conclude this brief trajectory through a few passages within the vast maze of Freud's writings by returning to my beginning. The work of Freud, like that of any other "extra-humanistic" writer, cannot be used as the base of interpretation in the humanities without being read and without being tested, so to speak, for its reliability as ground. When this act of reading is performed, Freud's writing turns out not to be a firm support on the basis of which further properly humanistic studies may be made. Freud's work turns out itself to invite an interminable interpretation, or at any rate an interpretation whose end cannot be foreseen and certainly has not yet been reached. The presumed ground becomes itself an object of anxious interrogation of the same sort we apply to a poem or a novel. When this happens, the reassuring distinction between scientific and humanistic texts breaks down, leaving the humanist once more with only his unaided powers as a reader to guide him.

Notes

1. Sigmund Freud, *Gesammelte Werke*, XVI (London, 1942), pp. 43–56; English tr. James Strachey, *The Complete Psychological Works*, Standard Edition, XXIII (London, 1953), pp. 255–69. Further references to Freud's writings will be to

these editions, identified as *GW* and *SE* respectively, followed by the volume and page numbers.
2. The use of philosophical texts as a ground for literary study is not quite the same as the use of "scientific" ones, since philosophy is normally thought of as one of the humanities, but it is not altogether different either, since philosophy makes claims of truth-telling not unlike those of psychoanalysis, linguistics, or anthropology.
3. See J. Hillis Miller, "Stevens' Rock and Criticism as Cure," *The Georgia Review*, XXX, pp. 5–31, 330–48.
4. This essay was originally conceived as part of a book with that title, published in 1987 by Princeton University Press. It was omitted there for lack of space.
5. In this case I am using the translation of Samuel Weber in *The Legend of Freud* (Minneapolis, 1982), p. 75, both because it follows the original more closely and to call attention to Weber's admirable book and penetrating analysis of this passage. Strachey's translation is at *SE*, V, p. 525. For an excellent discussion of Strachey's translation of Freud and of his influence on the history of the psychoanalytical movement see Darius Ornston, "Strachey's Influence: A Preliminary Report," *International Journal of Psycho-Analysis*, LXIII (1982), pp. 409–26. There is no doubt, alas, as Ornston's essay persuasively indicates, that to find out what Freud really said one must read him in German.

16

The search for grounds in literary study

You ask me in what I think or have thought you going wrong: in this: that you would never take your assiette as something determined final and unchangeable for you and proceed to work away on the basis of that: but were always poking and patching and cobbling at the assiette itself –
> Matthew Arnold, *Letters to Clough*[1]

. . . perhaps one is a philologist still, that is to say, a teacher of slow reading [*ein Lehrer des langsamen Lesens*].
> Friedrich Nietzsche, "Preface" to *Daybreak*[2]

Is it legitimate to see works of literature as in one way or another interrogations of the ground, taking ground in the sense of a sustaining metaphysical foundation outside language, outside nature, and outside the human mind? The role granted to poetry or to "literature" within our culture and in particular within our colleges and universities today is curiously contradictory. The contradiction is an historical inheritance going back at least to Kant and to eighteenth-century aesthetic theory or "critical philosophy." The tradition comes down from the enlightenment through romantic literary theory and later by way of such figures as Matthew Arnold (crucial to the development of the "humanities" in American higher education) to the New Criticism and the academic humanism of our own day. On the one hand the enjoyment of poetry is supposed to be the "disinterested" aesthetic contemplation of beautiful or sublime organic forms made of words. It is supposed to be "value free," without contamination by use of the poem for any cognitive, practical, ethical, or political purposes. Such appropriations, it is said, are a misuse of poetry. According to this aestheticizing assumption one ought to be able to read Dante and Milton, for example, or Aeschylus and Shelley, without raising either the question of the truth or falsity of their philosophical and religious beliefs, or the question of the practical consequences of acting on those beliefs. Cleanth Brooks, for example, in

263

a recent essay vigorously reaffirming the tenets of the New Criticism, presents *Paradise Lost* as a case in point:

> Milton tells us in the opening lines of *Paradise Lost* that his purpose is to "justify the ways of God to men," and there is no reason to doubt that this was what he hoped to do. But what we actually have in the poem is a wonderful interconnected story of events in heaven and hell and upon earth, with grand and awesome scenes brilliantly painted and with heroic actions dramatically rendered. In short, generations of readers have found that the grandeur of the poem far exceeds any direct statement of theological views. The point is underscored by the fact that some readers who reject Milton's theology altogether nevertheless regard *Paradise Lost* as a great poem.[3]

On the other hand, literature has been weighted down in our culture with the burden of carrying from generation to generation the whole freight of the values of that culture, what Matthew Arnold called "the best that is known and thought in the world."[4] Cleanth Brooks elsewhere in his essay also iterates this traditional assumption about literature. Walter Jackson Bate, in a recent polemical essay, sees specialization, including the New Criticism's specialization of close reading, as greatly weakening the humanities generally and departments of English in particular. Bate regrets the good old days (from 1930 to 1950) when departments of English taught everything under the sun but reading as such, in a modern reincarnation of the Renaissance ideal of *litterae humaniores*. The literature components of the humanities in our colleges and universities, and departments of English in particular, have with a good conscience undertaken, after hurrying through a soupçon of rhetoric and poetics, to teach theology, metaphysics, psychology, ethics, politics, social and intellectual history, even the history of science and natural history, in short, "Allerleiwissenschaft," like Carlyle's Professor Diogenes Teufelsdröck.[5]

The implicit reasoning behind this apparently blatant contradiction may not be all that difficult to grasp, though the reasoning will only restate the contradiction. It is just because, and only because, works of literature are stable, self-contained, value-free objects of disinterested aesthetic contemplation that they can be trustworthy vehicles of the immense weight of values they carry from generation to generation uncontaminated by the distortions of gross reality. Just because the values are enshrined in works of literature, uninvested, not collecting interest, not put out to vulgar practical use, they remain pure, not used up, still free to be reappropriated for whatever use we may want to make of them. Has not Kant in the third critique, the *Critique of Judgment*, once and for all set works of art as reliable and indispensible middle member

(*Mittelglied*), between cognition (pure reason, theory, the subject of the first critique) and ethics (practical reason, praxis, ethics, the subject of the second critique)? And has not Kant defined beauty, as embodied for example in a poem, as "the symbol of morality [*Symbol der Sittlichkeit*]"?[6] Both Bate and René Wellek, the latter in another outspoken polemical essay with the nice title of "Destroying Literary Studies," invoke Kant, or rather their understanding of Kant, as having settled these matters once and for all, as if there were no more need to worry about them, and as if our understanding of Kant, or rather theirs, could safely be taken for granted: "Why not," asks Bate, "turn to David Hume, the greatest skeptic in the history of thought . . . and then turn to Kant, by whom so much of this is answered?" (52); "One can doubt the very existence of aesthetic experience," says Wellek, "and refuse to recognize the distinctions, clearly formulated in Immanuel Kant's *Critique of Judgment*, between the good, the true, the useful, and the beautiful."[7] So much is at stake here that it is probably a good idea to go back and read Kant for ourselves, no easy task to be sure, in order to be certain that he says what Bate and Wellek says he says.

When Matthew Arnold, the founding father, so to speak, of the American concept of the humanities, praises the virtues of disinterested contemplation, he is being faithful to the Kantian inheritance, no doubt by way of its somewhat vulgarizing distortions in Schiller. It was, and is, by no means necessary to have read Kant to be a Kantian of sorts. Arnold's full formulaic definition of criticism, in "The Function of Criticism at the Present Time" (1864), is "a disinterested endeavour to learn and propagate the best that is known and thought in the world."[8] He speaks elsewhere in the same essay of the "disinterested love of a free play of the mind on all subjects, for its own sake."[9] When Arnold, in a well-known statement in "The Study of Poetry" (1880) which has echoed down the decades as the implicit credo of many American departments of English, says: "The future of poetry is immense, because in poetry, where it is worthy of its high destinies, our race, as time goes on, will find an ever surer and surer stay," he goes on to make it clear that poetry is a "stay" just because it is detached from the question of its truth or falsity as fact. Poetry can therefore replace religion when the fact fails religion. Poetry is cut off from such questions, sequestered in a realm of disinterested fiction. Just for this reason poetry is a "stay," a firm resting place when all else gives way, like a building without a solid foundation. "There is not a creed which is not shaken," says Arnold in his melancholy litany,

> not an accredited dogma which is not shown to be questionable, not a received tradition which does not threaten to dissolve. Our religion has

materialized itself in the fact, in the supposed fact; it has attached its emotion to the fact, and now the fact is failing it. But for poetry the idea is everything; the rest is a world of illusion, of divine illusion. Poetry attaches its emotion to the idea; the idea *is* the fact.[10]

The image here is that of a self-sustaining linguistic fiction or illusion which holds itself up by a kind of intrinsic magic of levitation over the abyss, like an aerial floating bridge over chaos, as long as one does not poke and patch at the assiette. This bridge or platform may therefore hold up also the ideas the poem contains and the readers who sustain themselves by these ideas.

Arnold had this double or even triple notion of the staying power of poetry already in mind when, in 1848 or 1849, many years before writing "The Study of Poetry," he wrote to Arthur Hugh Clough: "Those who cannot read G[ree]k sh[ou]ld read nothing but Milton and parts of Wordsworth: the state should see to it. . . ."[11] Most Freshman and Sophomore courses in American colleges and universities in "Major English Authors" are still conceived in the spirit of Arnold's categorical dictum. The uplifting moral value of reading Milton and parts of Wordsworth, so important that it should be enforced by the highest civil authority, is initially stylistic. Arnold opposes the solemn, elevated, composing "grand" style of Homer, or, failing that, of Milton and parts of Wordsworth, to the "confused multitudinousness" (*ibid.*) of Browning, Keats, and Tennyson, the romantics and Victorians generally, excepting that part of Wordsworth. The occasion of Arnold's letter to Clough is the devastating effect on him of reading Keats' letters: "What a brute you were to tell me to read Keats's Letters. However it is over now: and reflexion resumes her power over agitation" (96). From Keats Arnold turns to the Greeks, to Milton, and to those parts of Wordsworth to subdue his inner agitation as well as to protect himself from the agitation without.

Only secondary to the sustaining effect of the grand style as such are the "ideas" expressed in that style. A writer, says Arnold, "must begin with an Idea of the world in order not to be prevailed over by the world's multitudinousness" (*ibid.*, 97). The Idea, so to speak, is the style, or the style is the Idea, since the grand style is nothing but the notion of composure, elevation, coherence, objectivity, that is, just the characteristics of the grand style. This combination of grand elevated style and presupposed, preconceived, or pre-posited grand comprehensive Idea of the world (never mind whether it is empirically verifiable) not only composes and elevates the mind but also fences it off from the confused multitudinousness outside and the danger therefore of confused multitudinousness within. The latter, Arnold, in the "Preface" of 1853, calls "the dialogue of the mind with itself."[12] He associates it especially with the modern spirit, and fears it more than anything else. It is the dissolution of the mind's objectivity, calm, and unity with itself. This composing, lifting up, and fencing out through literature takes place, to borrow from one of the authors Arnold tells us exclusively to read, as God organizes chaos in the work of creation, or as Milton, at the beginning of *Paradise Lost*, prays that his interior chaos, likened to the unformed Abyss, may be illuminated, elevated, impregnated, and grounded by the Holy Spirit or heavenly muse: "Thou from the first/ Was present, and with mighty wings outspread/Dove-like satst brooding on the vast Abyss/And madst it pregnant: What in me is dark/ Illumine, what is low raise and support" (*Paradise Lost*, I, 19–23).

It is only a step from Kant's image in paragraph 59 of the *Critique of Judgment* of art or poetry as *hypotyposis* [*Hypotypose*], indirect symbols of intuitions for which there is no direct expression,[13] to Hegel's assertion that sublime poetry, like parable, fable, and apologue, is characterized by the non-adequation and dissimilarity between symbol and symbolized, what he calls the *Sichnichtentsprechen beider*, the non-correspondence of the two.[14] It is only another step beyond that to I. A. Richards' assertion, in *Principles of Literary Criticism*, with some help from Jeremy Bentham's theory of fictions, that the function of poetry is to produce an equilibrium among painfully conflicting impulses and thereby to provide fictive solutions to real psychological problems. Another step in this sequence (which is not even a progression, radicalizing or deepening, but a movement in place), takes us to Wallace Stevens' resonant formulation in the *Adagia* of what all these writers in somewhat different ways are saying: "The final belief is to believe in a fiction, which you know to be a fiction, there being nothing else. The exquisite truth is to know that it is a fiction and that you believe in it willingly."[15]

Proof that Matthew Arnold still plays an indispensable role within this sequence as the presumed base for a conservative humanism is a forceful recent article by Eugene Goodheart, "Arnold at the Present Time," with accompanying essays and responses by George Levine, Morris Dickstein, and Stuart M. Tave.[16] As is not surprising, the oppositions among these essays come down to a question of how one reads Arnold. If Goodheart grossly misrepresents "deconstruction" and the sort of "criticism as critique" I advocate (which is not surprising), he is also a bad reader or a non-reader of Arnold. Goodheart takes for granted the traditional misreading of Arnold which has been necessary to make him, as Goodheart puts it, "the inspiration of humanistic study in England and America" (451). Levine, Dickstein, and Tave are, it happens, far better and more searching readers of Arnold. Adjudication of differences here is of course possible only by a response to that call, "Back to the texts!," which must be performed again and again in literary study. Nothing previous critics have said can be taken for granted, however authoritative it may seem. Each reader must do again for himself the laborious task of a scrupulous slow reading, trying to find out what the texts actually say rather than imposing on them what she or he wants them to say or wishes they said. Advances in literary study are not made by the free invention of new conceptual or historical schemes (which always turn out to be old ones anew in any case), but by that grappling with the texts which always has to be done over once more by each new reader. In the case of Arnold the poetry and prose must be read together, not assumed to be discontinuous units or an early negative stage and a late affirmative stage negating the earlier negation. Far from offering a firm "assiette" to the sort of humanism Goodheart advocates, such a careful reading of Arnold will reveal him to be a nihilist writer through and through, nihilist in the precise sense in which Nietzsche or Heidegger defines the term: as a specifically historical designation of the moment within the development of Western metaphysics when the highest values devalue themselves and come to nothing as their transcendent base dissolves:[17] "There is not a creed which is not shaken, not an accredited dogma which is not shown to be questionable, not a received tradition which does not threaten to dissolve." "I am nothing and very probably never shall be anything," said Arnold in one of the letters to Clough.[18]

A house built on sand, in this case a humanistic tradition built on the shaky foundation of a misreading of Matthew Arnold, cannot stand firmly. To put this another way, the affirmations of Goodheart, Bate, Wellek, and others like them participate inevitably in the historical movement of nihilism ("the history of the next two centuries," Nietzsche called it)[19] which they contest. Most of all they do this in the act itself of contestation. "The question arises," says Heidegger in the section on nihilism in his *Nietzsche*,

> whether the innermost essence of nihilism and the power of its dominion do not consist precisely in considering the nothing merely as a nullity [*nur für etwas Nichtiges*], considering nihilism as an apotheosis of the merely vacuous [*der blossen Leere*], as a negation [*eine Verneinung*] that can be set to rights at once by an energetic affirmation.[20]

In a brilliant essay on "The Principle of Reason: The University in the Eyes of its Pupils,"[21] Jacques Derrida identifies the way the modern university and the study of literature within it are based on the domination of the Leibnizian principle of reason, what in German is called *der Satz vom Grund*, the notion that everything can and should be accounted for, *Omnis veritatis reddi ratio potest*, that nothing is without reason, *nihil est sine ratione*. Following Nietzsche and Heidegger, Derrida also argues that so-called nihilism is an historical moment which is "completely symmetrical to, thus dependent on, the principle of reason" (15). Nihilism arises naturally and inevitably during a period, the era of technology, when the principle of universal accountability holds sway in the organization of society and of the universities accountable to that society. "For the principle of reason," says Derrida, "may have obscurantist and nihilist effects. They can be seen more or less everywhere, in Europe and America, among those who believe they are defending philosophy, literature and the humanities against these new modes of questioning that are also a new relation to language and tradition, a new affirmation, and new ways of taking responsibility. We can easily see on which side obscurantism and nihilism are lurking when on occasion great professors or representatives of prestigious institutions lose all sense of proportion and control; on such occasions they forget their principles that they claim to defend in their work and suddenly begin to heap insults, to say whatever comes into their heads on the subject of texts that they obviously have never opened or that they have encountered through a mediocre journalism that in other circumstances they would pretend to scorn" (15). Obviously much is at stake here, and we must go carefully, looking before and after, testing the ground carefully, taking nothing for granted.

If such a tremendous burden is being placed on literature throughout all the period from Kant to academic humanists of our own day like Bate and Goodheart, it is of crucial importance to be sure that literature is able to bear the weight, or that it is a suitable instrument to perform its function. The question is too grave for its answer to be left untested. To raise the question of the weight-bearing capacities of the medium of poetry is of course not the only thing criticism can do or ought to do, but I claim it is one all-important task of literary study. The question in question here is not of the thematic content of, or the assertions made by, works of literature but of the weight-bearing characteristics of the medium of literature, that is, of language. It is a question of what the language of poetry is and does. Is it indeed solid enough and trustworthy enough to serve, according to the metaphor Kant proposes at the end of the introduction to the *Critique of Judgment*, as the fundamentally necessary bridge passing back and forth between pure cognition and moral action, between *theoria* and *praxis*? "The realm of the natural concept under the one legislation," says Kant,

> and that of the concept of freedom under the other are entirely removed [*gänzlich abgesondert*] from all mutual influence [*wechselseitigen Einfluss*] which they might have on one another (each according to its fundamental laws) by the great gulf [*die grosse Kluft*] that separates the supersensible from phenomena [*das Übersinnliche von den Erscheinungen*]. The concept of freedom determines nothing in respect of the theoretical cognition of

nature, and the internal concept determines nothing in respect of the practical laws of freedom. So far, then, it is not possible to throw a bridge from the one realm to the other [*eine Brücke von einem Gebiete zu dem andern hinüber zu schlagen*].[22]

Art or the aesthetic experience is the only candidate for a possible bridge. The whole of the *Critique of Judgment* is written to test out the solidity, so to speak, of the planks by which this indispensable bridge from the realm of knowledge to the realm of moral action might be built, across the great gulf that separates them. If the "beauty" of the work of art is the sensible symbol of morality, it is, on the other hand, the sensible embodiment of the pure idea, what Hegel was to call, in a famous formulation, and in echo of Kant's word *Erscheinungen*, "the sensible shining forth of the idea [*das sinnliche 'scheinen' der Idee*]."[23] As Hegel elsewhere puts it, "art occupies the intermediate ground between the purely sensory and pure thought [*steht in der 'Mitte' zwischen der umittelbaren Sinnlichkeit und dem ideellen Gedanken*]" (ibid., I, 60, my trans.). Whether Kant or Hegel establish satisfactorily the solidity of this ground, its adequacy as a bridge, is another question, one that a full reading of Kant's third *Kritik* and of Hegel's *Ästhetik* would be necessary to answer. That the answer is affirmative does not go without saying, nor of course that it is negative either. Others are at work on this task of re-reading Kant and Hegel.

The sort of interrogation for which I am calling is neither a work of "pure theory" nor a work of pure praxis, a series of explications. It is something between those two or preparatory to them, a clearing of the ground and an attempt to sink foundations. It is "criticism" in the fundamental sense of "critique," discriminating testing out, in this case a testing out of the medium of which the bridge between theory and practice is made. If criticism as critique is between theory and practice, it is also neither to be identified with hermeneutics, or the search for intentional meaning, on the one side, nor with poetics, or the theory of how texts have meaning, on the other side, though it is closely related to the latter. Critique, however, is a testing of the grounding of language in this or that particular text, not in the abstract or in abstraction from any particular case.

If this sort of investigation of the weight-bearing features of language is often an object of suspicion these days from the point of view of a certain traditional humanism, the humanism of *litterae humaniores*, it is also under attack from the other direction, from the point of view of those who see the central work of literary study as the reinsertion of the work of literature within its social context. The reproaches from the opposite political directions are strangely similar or symmetrical. They often come to the same thing or are couched in the same words. It is as if there were an unconscious alliance of the left and the right to suppress something which is the bad conscience of both a conservative humanism and a "radical" politicizing or sociologizing of the study of literature. A specific problematic is associated with the latter move, which attempts to put literature under the law of economy, under the laws of economic change and social power. I shall examine this problematic in detail elsewhere,[24] but it may be said here that the most resolute attempts to bracket linguistic considerations in the study of literature, to take the language of literature for granted and shift from the study of the relations of word with word to the study of the relations of words with things or with subjectivities, will only lead back in the end to the study of language. Any conceivable encounter with things or with subjectivities in literature or in discourse about literature must already have represented things and subjects in words, numbers, or other signs. Any conceivable representation of the relations of words to things, powers, persons, modes of production and exchange, juridical or political systems (or whatever name the presumably non-linguistic may be given) will turn out to be one or another figure of speech. As such, it will require a rhetorical interpretation, such as that given by Marx in *Capital* and in the *Grundrisse*. Among such figures are that of mimesis, mirroring reflection or representation. This turns out to be a species of metaphor. Another such figure is that of part to whole, work to surrounding and determining milieu, text to context, container to thing contained. This relation is one variety or another of synecdoche or of metonymy. Another figure of the relation of text to social context is that of anamorphosis or of ideology, which is a species of affirmation by denial, abnegation, what Freud called *Verneinung*. Sociologists of literature still all too often do no more than set some social fact side by side with some citation from a literary work and assert that the latter reflects the former, or is accounted for by it, or is determined by it, or is an intrinsic part of it, or is grounded in it. It is just in this place, in the interpretation of this asserted liaison, that the work of rhetorical analysis is indispensable. The necessary dialogue between those practicing poetics or rhetoric and sociologists of literature has scarcely begun. Conservative humanists and "radical" sociologists of literature have this at least in common: both tend to suppress, displace, or replace what I call the linguistic moment in literature.[25] Here too, however, denegation is affirmation. The covering over always leaves traces behind, tracks which may be followed back to those questions about language I am raising.

Kant, once more, in the "Preface" to the *Critique of Judgment* has admirably formulated the necessity of this work of critique:

> For if such a system is one day to be completed [*einmal zu Stande kommen soll*] under the general name of metaphysic . . . , the soil for the edifice

[*den Boden zu diesem Gebaude*] must be explored by critique [*die Kritik*] as deep down as the foundation [*die erste Grundlage*] of the faculty of principles independent of experience, in order that it may sink in no part [*damit es nicht an irgend einem Teile sinke*], for this would inevitably bring about the downfall [*Einsturz*] of the whole. (Eng. 4; Ger. 74–5)

Elsewhere, in the *Critique of Pure Reason*, the same metaphor has already been posited as the foundation of the edifice of pure thought:

But though the following out of these considerations is what gives to philosophy its peculiar dignity, we must meantime occupy ourselves with a less resplendent [*nicht so glänzenden*], but still meritorious task, namely, to level the ground, and to render it sufficiently secure for moral edifices of these majestic dimensions [*den Boden zu jenen majestätischen sittlichen Gebäuden eben und baufest zu machen*]. For this ground has been honeycombed by subterranean workings [*allerlei Maulwurfsgänge*: all sorts of mole tunnels: Smith's translation effaces the figure] which reason, in its confident but fruitless search for hidden treasures has carried out in all directions, and which threaten the security of the superstructures [*und die jenes Bauwerk unsicher machen*].[26]

Which is critique? Is it groundbreaking to be distinguished from mole-tunneling and a repair of it, as the second quotation claims, or is critique, as the first quotation affirms, the work of tunneling itself, the underground search for bedrock which in that process hollows out the soil? Does this contradiction in Kant's formulations not have something to do with the fact that Kant uses a metaphor from art, or to put this another way, throws out a little artwork of his own in the form of an architectural metaphor, in order to define the work of criticism which is supposed to be a testing out of the very instrument of bridging of which the definition makes use? This is an example of a *mise en abyme* in the technical sense of placing within the larger sign system a miniature image of that larger one, a smaller one potentially within that, and so on, in a filling in and covering over of the abyss, gulf, or *Kluft* which is at the same time an opening of the abyss. Such a simultaneous opening and covering over is the regular law of the *mise en abyme*.

Have I not, finally, by an intrinsic and unavoidable necessity, done the same thing as Kant, with my images of bridges, tunnels, bedrock, pathways, and so on, and with my strategy of borrowing citations from Arnold, Kant, and the rest to describe obliquely my own enterprise? This somersaulting, self-constructing, self-undermining form of language, the throwing out of a bridge where no firm bedrock exists, in place of the bedrock, is a fundamental feature of what I call critique. Groundleveling, it appears, becomes inevitably tunneling down in search of bedrock, as, to quote Milton again, beneath the lowest deep a lower deep still opens.

I end by drawing several conclusions from what I have said, and by briefly relating what I have said to the question of genre. The first conclusion is a reiteration of my assertion that the stakes are so large in the present quarrels among students of literature that we must go slowly and circumspectly, testing the ground carefully and taking nothing for granted, returning once more to those founding texts of our modern tradition of literary study and reading them anew with patience and care. To put this another way, the teaching of philology, of that "slow reading" or *langsamen Lesen* for which Nietzsche calls, is still a fundamental responsibility of the humanities, at no time more needed than today. Second conclusion: Disagreements among students of literature can often be traced to often more covert disagreements about the presupposed ground of literature – whether that ground is assumed to be society, the self, language, or the "thing." One of these four presuppositions may be taken so for granted by a given critic that he is not even aware that it determines all his procedures and strategies of interpretation. Much will be gained by bringing the fundamental causes of these disagreements into the open. Third conclusion: Though the intellectual activity of ground-testing and of testing out the very idea of the ground or of the principle of reason, through slow reading, has a long and venerable tradition under the names of philology and of critical philosophy, nevertheless such testing has a peculiar role in the university. It is likely to seem subversive, threatening, outside the pale of what is a legitimate activity within the university, if research within the university, including research and teaching in the humanities, is all under the sovereign and unquestioned rule of the principle of reason. Nevertheless, moving forward to the necessary new affirmation and the new taking of responsibility for the humanities and within the humanities depends now, as it always has, on allowing that interrogation to take place.

This new taking of responsibility for language and literature, for the language of literature, which I am calling critique, has, finally, important implications for genre theory or for generic criticism. What I have said would imply not that generic classifications or distinctions and the use of these as a guide to interpretation and evaluation are illegitimate, without grounds, but that they are in a certain sense superficial. They do not go all the way to the ground, and the choice of a ground (or being chosen by one) may be more decisive for literary interpretation than generic distinctions and even determine those generic distinctions and their import. It is only on the grounds of a commitment to language, society, the self, or the "it," one or another of these, that generic distinctions make sense and have force. The choice of a ground determines both the definition of each genre and the implicit or explicit hierarchy among them. It is possible, it makes sense, to say "This is a lyric poem," or

"This is a novel," and to proceed on the basis of that to follow certain interpretative procedures and ultimately to say, "This is a good lyric poem," or "This is a bad novel." Nevertheless, it is possible and makes sense to do these things only on the grounds of a prior commitment, perhaps one entirely implicit or even unthought, to founding assumptions about the ultimate ground on which all these genres are erected as so many different dwelling places or cultural forms for the human spirit to live in and use.

Beyond that, it might be added that what I am calling critique, in its double emphasis on rhetoric as the study of tropes, on the one hand, in a work of whatever genre, and, on the other hand, on the way any work of literature, of whatever genre, tells a story with beginning, middle, end, and underlying *logos* or *Grund* and at the same time interrupts or deconstructs that story – this double emphasis tends to break down generic distinctions and to recognize, for example, the fundamental role of tropes in novels, the way any lyric poem tells a story and can be interpreted as a narrative, or the way a work of philosophy may be read in terms of its tropological patterns or in terms of the story it tells. Much important criticism today goes against the grain of traditional generic distinctions, while at the same time perpetuating them in new ways in relation to one or another of my four grounds, just as many important works of recent primary literature do not fit easily into any one generic pigeon-hole.

Notes

1. *The Letters of Matthew Arnold to Arthur Hugh Clough*, H. F. Lowry, ed., (London, New York, 1932), p. 130.
2. Friedrich Nietzsche, *Daybreak: Thoughts on the Prejudices of Morality*, tr. R. J. Hollingdale (Cambridge, 1982), p. 5, trans. slightly altered; German: Friedrich Nietzsche, *Morgenröte*, "Vorrede," *Werke in Drie Bänden*, Karl Schlecta, ed. (Munich: Carl Hanser Verlag, 1966), 1016. Further citations will be from these editions.
3. Cleanth Brooks, "The Primacy of the Author," *The Missouri Review*, 6 (1982), p. 162. The passage by Brooks is cited again and discussed in more detail in Chapter 21, below.
4. Matthew Arnold, "The Function of Criticism at the Present Time," *Lectures and Essays in Criticism, The Complete Prose Works*, R. H. Super, ed., III (Ann Arbor, 1962), p. 270.
5. See Walter Jackson Bate, "The Crisis in English Studies," *Harvard Magazine*, 85, No. 1 (1982), pp. 46–53, esp. pp. 46–7. For a vigorous reply to Bate's essay see Paul de Man, "The Return to Philology," *The Times Literary Supplement*, No. 4, 158 (10 December 1982), 1355–6.
6. Immanuel Kant, paragraph 59, "Of Beauty as the Symbol of Morality," *Critique of Judgment*, tr. J. H. Bernard (New York, 1951), p. 196; German: *Kritik der Urteilskraft, Werkausgabe*, Wilhelm Weischedel, ed., X (Frankfurt am Main, 1979), p. 294.

7. René Wellek, "Destroying Literary Studies," *The New Criterion* (December 1983), p. 2.
8. Matthew Arnold, "The Function of Criticism at the Present Time," p. 282.
9. *ibid.*, p. 268.
10. Matthew Arnold, "The Study of Poetry," *English Literature and Irish Politics, The Complete Prose Works*, R. H. Super, ed., IX (Ann Arbor, 1973), p. 161.
11. *Letters to Clough*, p. 97.
12. Matthew Arnold, *Poems*, Kenneth Allott, ed. (London, 1965), p. 591.
13. See Kant, *Critique of Judgment*, eds. cit.: Eng., pp. 197–8; Ger., pp. 295–7.
14. G. W. F. von Hegel, *Aesthetics: Lectures on Fine Art*, tr. T. M. Knox, I (New York, 1975), p. 378; *Vorlesungen über die Ästhetik*, I (Frankfurt am Main, 1970), p. 486.
15. Wallace Stevens, *Opus Posthumous* (New York, 1957), p. 163.
16. "The Function of Matthew Arnold at the Present Time," *Critical Inquiry*, 9 (1983), pp. 451–516. Goodheart's essay, "Arnold at the Present Time," is on pp. 451–68.
17. See Friedrich Nietzsche, "European Nihilism," *The Will to Power*, tr. Walter Kaufmann and R. J. Hollingdale (New York, 1968), pp. 5–82. These notes are dispersed in chronological order with the other notes traditionally making up *Der Wille zur Macht* in Nietzsche, "Aus dem Nachlass der Achtzigerjahre," *Werke in Drei Bänden*, III, pp. 415–925. See also Martin Heidegger, "Nihilism," *Nietzsche*, tr. Frank A. Capuzzi, IV (San Francisco, 1982); German: *Nietzsche*, II (Pfullingen, 1961), pp. 31–256; 335–98.
18. *Letters to Clough*, p. 135.
19. *The Will to Power*, p. 3.
20. Heidegger, "Nihilism," *Nietzsche*, IV, p. 21; German: *Nietzsche*, II, p. 53.
21. Tr. Catherine Porter and Edward P. Morris, *diacritics*, 13 (1983), pp. 3–20.
22. Kant, *Critique of Judgment*, Eng., p. 32; Ger., p. 106.
23. Hegel, *Ästhetik*, I, 151, my translation.
24. In "Economy," in *Penelope's Web: On the External Relations of Narrative*, forthcoming.
25. A book on nineteenth- and twentieth-century poetry with that title is forthcoming from Princeton University Press.
26. Immanuel Kant, *Critique of Pure Reason*, tr. Norman Kemp Smith (New York, 1965), pp. 313–14; German: *Kritik der reinen Vernunft*, A (1781), p. 319; B (1787), pp. 375–6, *Werkausgabe*, ed. cit., III, pp. 325–6. For a discussion of the image of the mole in Kant, Hegel, and Nietzsche see David Farrell Krell, "*Der Maulwurf: Die philosophische Wühlarbeit bei Kant, Hegel und Nietzsche*/The Mole: Philosophic Burrowings in Kant, Hegel, and Nietzsche," *Boundary 2*, 9 and 10 (Spring/Fall, 1981), pp. 155–79.

17

Gleichnis in Nietzsche's *Also Sprach Zarathustra*

I

What is the difference between approaching Nietzsche from the point of view of a literary critic, as I do here, and approaching him from the point of view of a philosopher? Is it possible or proper to speak in any case of "approaching" Nietzsche from one direction or another, as though he were that "powerful pyramidal rock not far from Surlei [*mächtigen pyramidal aufgetürmten Block unweit Surlei*],"[1] locus of the coming to Nietzsche of the idea of the eternal return? It seems as if there ought to be a fundamental difference between reading Nietzsche from the perspective of philosophy and reading him from the perspective of literary criticism, a distinct and uncrossable fissure between one way of talking about him and the other. Yet the closer one gets to a text by Nietzsche or indeed to a text by any other philosopher, the more the seam vanishes in a single demand or requirement for what Nietzsche calls in the preface to *Daybreak*, "philology" or the teaching of "slow reading [*langsamen Lesens*]."[2] Good reading, slow reading, does not occur all that often. It is as likely to occur on one side of the fissure as on the other.

Nevertheless, there are certain identifiable institutionalized or conventional differences between the discourse of the literary critic and the discourse of the philosopher. These might be identified as the differing contexts in which a text read is placed and as the kinds of questions asked of it. In this essay, rather than placing Nietzsche in the context of, say, Schopenhauer, Hegel, or the Pre-Socratics, in one direction, and Heidegger, in the other, as I imagine a philosopher doing, I shall place him in the context of authors more usually taught in courses in literature: Carlyle and Maurice Blanchot, along with Kierkegaard, who is a borderline case. In addition, I shall ask questions of passages in *Thus Spoke Zarathustra* and *Ecce Homo* which come not from the direction of analysis of the meaning and coherence of concepts, as I imagine (perhaps naïvely) a philosopher might do, but from the direction of narrative theory and the theory of tropes, provinces usually thought to be occupied by students of literature.

The basic idea of *Thus Spoke Zarathustra* is the thought of the eternal return, with its associated presupposition of the idea of the death of God. In *Ecce Homo* Nietzsche calls "the idea of the eternal recurrence [*der Ewige-Wiederkunfts-Gedanke*]" "the fundamental conception of this work [*die Grundkonzeption des Werks*]" (*E*. 295; *G*, 1128). In "On the Vision and the Riddle [*Vom Gesicht und Rätsel*]," the crucial section on the eternal return in the third part of *Zarathustra*, Nietzsche, or rather Zarathustra, speaks of it as "my abysmal thought [*meinen abgründlichen Gedanken*]" (*E*, 269; *G*, 408). The thought of the eternal return is at once fundamental, a solid ground or grounding [*Grund*] for further thought or for the writing of *Thus Spoke Zarathustra*, and at the same time it is groundless, abysmal [*abgründlich*], a bottomless gulf. It is an abyss which is at the same time a ground. My literary critical questions are the following. First question: Why is it appropriate for this thought to be expressed in the form of a fictional narrative in which Nietzsche projects himself into an imaginary protagonist, namely Zarathustra, and then doubles that protagonist with a narrator or witness who reports what Zarathustra said and did, as the gospel-makers reported the doings and sayings of Jesus? What is the relation of necessity between the thought and the form, if there is one? Second question: Why is parable (*Gleichnis*) the appropriate genre for Nietzsche's fictional protagonist to use as the means of expressing the "most abysmal idea" (*Ecce Homo, E*, 306; *G*, 1136), the idea of the eternal return?

I shall attempt to answer these questions first by placing *Zarathustra* in the context of other works of similar narrative form in the nineteenth century and then by way of a discussion of the chapter on *Thus Spoke Zarathustra* in *Ecce Homo*, especially the third section of that chapter, and two sections of *Zarathustra* itself, both from the third part, "On the Vision and the Riddle" and "The Return Home [*Die Heimkehr*]." First I shall place Nietzsche in the context of two authors of the nineteenth century who wrote works similar in form to *Zarathustra*, Carlyle and Kierkegaard.

II

Nietzsche labels Carlyle "a typical romantic," not high praise from him.[3] It is a conspicuous feature of romanticism, taking that term in the broadest sense as a name for virtually the whole of European and American literature and philosophy since Kant, that secular writing tends to replace religious writing or to arrogate to itself the function once ascribed only to Scripture, to the Bible. This function includes utterance of transcendent truth or absolute truth and the bringing of salvation to the individual. Matthew Arnold spoke for this historical shift when he said, in a notorious pronouncement, that as the facts more and more fail religion, poetry will more and more come to take its place as man's support and stay:

> Our religion has materialised itself in the fact, in the supposed fact; it has attached its emotion to the fact, and now the fact is failing it. But for poetry the idea is everything; the rest is a world of illusion, of divine illusion. Poetry attaches its emotion to the idea; the idea *is* the fact. . . . More and more mankind will discover that we have to turn to poetry to interpret life for us, to console us, to sustain us. Without poetry, our science will appear incomplete; and most of what passes with us for religion and philosophy will be replaced by poetry.[4]

If poetry is indeed replacing religion during this period, one of the ways this happens is in the adaptation of Biblical modes of narration in secular literature. An obvious aspect of the Biblical way of expressing absolute truth and bringing salvation, especially of the Biblical way in the words of Jesus himself in the New Testament, is the use of that form of indirection which is called allegory or, more precisely, parable. A parable is a little realistic story about ordinary people in ordinary domestic or communal situations which does not mean what it says but stands for some other thing, a religious truth which is said by means of the parable, but said indirectly. A group of important works in the period I have, following Neitzsche, called "romantic" borrows from the Bible this method of parabolic narrative. Among these might be listed Kierkegaard's *Either/Or*, Nietzsche's *Thus Spoke Zarathustra*, and Carlyle's *Sartor Resartus*.

All these works, and their authors, share certain features. These can perhaps best be identified as secular permutations of the central Biblical personage and that central New Testament literary form of parable. If all priests or ministers are representatives of Christ, vicars of Christ, the central figures of these secular works, in however indirect or ironic a fashion, all play a priestlike or even Christ-like role. The authors of these books, Kierkegaard, Carlyle, and Nietzsche, were all in one way or another trained for the ministry or came from families where that was the usual vocation. All three lost that vocation and shifted to writing philosophical literature as a substitute vocation. Each was in one way or another what is called a "failed priest." Though Kierkegaard took a degree in theology he never became a pastor, but became a writer instead. Kierkegaard's religious vocation and its strange relation to what he called his "aesthetic works," of which *Either/Or* is perhaps the greatest, is well known. It is spelled out in detail in *The Point of View for My Work as an Author*, written in 1848, but published in 1859, four years after Kierkegaard's death. There Kierkegaard says:

But from the point of view of my whole activity as an author, integrally conceived, the aesthetic work is a deception, and herein is to be found the deeper significance of the use of pseudonyms. A deception, however, is a rather ugly thing. To this I would make answer: One must not let oneself be deceived by the word "deception." One can deceive a person for the truth's sake, and (to recall old Socrates) one can deceive a person into the truth. Indeed, it is only by this means, i.e., by deceiving him, that it is possible to bring into the truth one who is in an illusion.[5]

Carlyle of course studied for the ministry for five years at the University of Edinburgh (from 1809 to 1814), but then lost his faith and his vocation, becoming a writer instead. The Herr Professor Teufelsdröckh of *Sartor Resartus* shadows forth symbolically or "hieroglyphically," as Carlyle would say, Carlyle's conception of the way the vocation of writing can be a displacement of the vocation of minister. Nietzsche's father was a Lutheran pastor, and though he was trained as a classical philologist, his students during the brief period he was a professor at Basle were apparently as much from the faculty of theology as from classics. Nietzsche's *Ecce Homo*, published, like Kierkegaard's *The Point of View for My Work as an Author*, posthumously, shows how much Nietzsche identified his vocation as writer with the vocation of preacher or even with the vocation of Christ himself. The concept of the Anti-Christ is obviously the reciprocal of the concept of Christ as the Messiah and impossible without it.

All three writers had conversion experiences: Kierkegaard's on 19 May 1838 at 10:30 a.m., spoken of in his journal as an "indescribable joy,"[6] and the only one of the three which is strictly speaking a conversion to Christianity as such, Carlyle's in Leith Walk in Edinburgh, probably in the summer of 1822, and Nietzsche's in Sils Maria, on a walk high in the Engadine, when he had his revelation of the "eternal return."

For all three of these writers, it may be noted parenthetically, a crucial turning point in their personal lives, and one somehow associated with their vocation as writers, was a love affair that failed. In Carlyle's case it was his early love for Margaret Gordon, afterwards Lady Bannerman, perhaps adumbrated in *Sartor Resartus* in that doomed love for Blumine which is the decisive turning point in Teufelsdröckh's personal life, leading to the wanderings which lead in turn to the "Everlasting Yea" and to his God-given vocation as a writer. In Kierkegaard's case it was the tragically broken engagement to Regina Olsen which, as Kierkegaard said, "made him a poet" (*ibid.*, xv). In Nietzsche's case, his unfulfilled love for Cosima Wagner is the central event in his own private mythology. It is shadowed forth, for example in the *Dionysus-Dithyramben* and even in the last postcards he wrote in his madness, as a repetition of the myth of Dionysus, Ariadne, and Theseus, with

Nietzsche himself as Dionysus, Cosima as Ariadne, and Richard Wagner as the villainous forgetful Theseus. There would be much more to say about this motif of the failed love affair and its relation to the theme of a calling to be a secular writer as a displacement of a rejected vocation as a Christian minister. This motif calls attention to the way the romantic paradigm I am identifying is the reverse mirror image or secular parody of such religious allegories as *Le Roman de la Rose, La Divina Commedia,* or *Sir Gawain and the Green Knight,* where the lady is a symbolic means of access to heaven. For Carlyle, Kierkegaard, and Nietzsche, or their fictional protagonists, the failure of love is associated obscurely or directly with the failure of an overt religious vocation. The fiasco or catastrophe of love makes the person a writer and defines his writing as a displacement or reversed mirror image of religious allegory or parable. On the other hand, Christ himself was celibate, held himself aloof from women, as is made most explicit in the story of Mary Magdalene. The priests of the Roman Catholic Church, Christ's vicars, imitators of Christ, "AfterChrists," as Gerard Manley Hopkins puts it, are celibate too. Zarathustra or Nietzsche, Teufelsdröckh, Kierkegaard or his pseudonymous spokesmen could be as much practicing an *imitatio Christi* as refusing it in their rejection of an intimate liaison or tie to an earthly person in favor of that other ligature of religious obligation. Christ bid those who believed in him to leave father and mother, wife and children, and all family ties in order to follow him: "If any one comes to me and does not hate his own father and mother and wife and children and brothers and sisters, yes, and even his own life, he cannot be my disciple" (Luke 14:26). I resist the temptation of a longer detour into this topic to return to my primary focus, which is to try to define more exactly the mode of literature all three of these writers then composed, after the failure of love and the refusal of direct religious vocation.

I have said that this mode is the reversed mirror image of religious parable. In each of these works the author, rather than speaking directly in his own voice and as himself, invents an elaborate fictional narrative machinery and projects what he has to say into various fictional characters, a fictional narrator, and a fictional protagonist or protagonists. The work may be published anonymously or pseudonymously, thereby removing it even further from being the direct expression of its author. Carlyle's elaborate narrative concoction of an English editor of the papers of an eccentric German professor and ostensible author of *Sartor Resartus* is matched by Kierkegaard's invention of a certain Victor Eremita who has found documents, deciphered, and published them. These papers are supposed to have been written by two further fictional characters, "A," an aesthetic man, and "B," a magistrate, a representative of the ethical stage of human life. The *Diary of a Seducer,* in turn, is not by

A but said to be edited by him, so this part of the book is a fiction within a fiction within a fiction, or, as Victor Eremita says in his "preface," "one author seems to be enclosed in another, like the parts in a Chinese puzzle box."[7] Nietzsche in his turn in *Also Sprach Zarathustra* invents a narrator who reports the oracular sayings of another invented character, Zarathustra. The narrator's relation to Zarathustra is like the relation of Matthew, Mark, or Luke to the sayings of Jesus in the Synoptic Gospels.

All of these works are characterized in one way or another by an ostentatious exuberance of style, a style which calls attention to itself by its eloquence, its rhetoric, its openly figurative or parabolic quality. Even within the narrative fiction of each work what is said is not said directly but in enigmatic figure. We go to all three works to find the most complete expression of the truth the author wanted to convey to his readers, but all three are characterized in one way or another by that most dangerous of rhetorical devices, hyperbolic irony or ironic hyperbole. This is dangerous because it undercuts or renders problematic the truth-value of everything that is said. The local irony in the style is associated with the large self-deconstituting narrative structure of fiction within fiction or of what Jacques Derrida calls "double invagination."[8] Whatever is said within the work or even in a preface or appendix, though it may seem to give the reader the solid ground she needs on the basis of which to interpret the work, may be said ironically and so makes itself wavering, uncertain, a quicksand, no solid base. It is Teufelsdröckh's irony, his "underground humours and intricate sardonic rogueries," repeatedly called attention to by his poor hard-working literalist English editor, in green spectacles, which more than any other feature of Teufelsdröckh's style makes the editor suspicious of his veracity and determined not to become one more fool among those fools who have taken Teufelsdröckh with absolute seriousness: "Of one fool, however, the Herr Professor will perhaps find himself short."[9]

All three of these works, modeled though they may be on one form or another of continuous narrative, such as that of an ordinary novel, conspicuously deviate from such smooth narrative continuity. *Either/Or* and *Thus Spoke Zarathustra*, like *Sartor Resartus*, are notably discontinuous works, islands or stepping stones in a murky chaos, to use the editor's figure in *Sartor*, from one to another of which the reader must leap. They start and stop, and start again, continuously burning up the material they present and needing to make a new beginning with new materials. Each, finally, has as its most salient feature, the feature to which all the others are subsidiary, the evident intention to convey to its readers, by these indirect, fictional, ironic, puzzling means, an absolute, transcendent truth, the truth most necessary to the reader's salvation. It is a truth which is a substitute for traditional religious truth and promises to serve the same function. The authors of all these works in one way or another claim to know something we do not know, something it will be extremely difficult to convey to us and yet something it is of the utmost importance that we understand and accept. In all these characteristics the three works I am setting side by side are a secular appropriation of the method of the parables of Jesus in the Gospels. To a comparison with these I now turn.

Henry Alford, a Victorian Dean of Canterbury and editor of a still standard edition of the Greek New Testament published in 1873, defined a parable as "a serious narration within the limits of probability, of a course of action pointing to some moral or spiritual truth; and [it] derives its force from real analogies impressed by the Creator of all things on his creatures." Alford goes on to say that therefore only Christ can dare teach in parables, whereas the secular parables of mere men "would be in danger of perverting instead of guiding aright," since "we do not, as He did, see the inner springs out of which flow those laws of spiritual truth and justice which the Parable is framed to elucidate."[10] Why did Christ speak parabolically rather than directly of those inner springs, the "mysteries of the kingdom of heaven" (Matthew 13:11)? This was of course just the question the disciples asked him: "Why speakest thou unto them in parables?" Christ's answer is the best guide we have to the nature and function of this strange form of literature in its sacred or scriptural form: "Because it is given unto you to know the mysteries of the kingdom of heaven, but to them it is not given. For whosoever hath, to him shall be given, and he shall have more abundance: but whosoever hath not, to him shall be taken away even that he hath. Therefore speak I to them in parables: because they seeing see not; and hearing they hear not, neither do they understand" (Matthew 13:10–13). I have elsewhere discussed the way the parables are about parable, about the dissemination of the word, and the terrifying paradox of the parables of Jesus in its relation to this fact.[11] The parables say the truth, but if you are not already fertile ground for the word, the parables will only darken your understanding further. They will take away even what little understanding you have. Nevertheless, the indirect mode of parable is the proper one for Christ's teaching to the particular auditors he has. Christ is the Word of God personified, incarnated as a man. He has direct knowledge of all the analogies between created, visible, tangible things and the invisible, intangible, spiritual mysteries of the kingdom of heaven. These analogies are fixed immutably by God in the act of creation. They have stood since the foundation of the world and will stand until the last trump abolishes that creation. Since what his auditors know already is those earthly things, the facts of daily life, of sowing and reaping, fishing, wine and oil making, domestic life within the home, Christ the

Word's only way to disseminate the Word is indirectly, by speaking of it parabolically, for those who have ears to hear, in terms of those familiar matters of domestic economy which are intrinsically analogous to the unseen mysteries of the kingdom of heaven.

The situation of Carlyle, Kierkegaard, and Nietzsche or their imaginary spokesmen, Teufelsdröckh, "B," or Zarathustra is very different. They are in the situation of the auditors of Christ's parables, not Christ himself, as their refusal of direct religious vocation testifies. They think they have insight by way of earthly things into the spiritual truths for which those things stand. If so, they are authorized to speak parabolically or, as Teufelsdröckh's Editor says, "hieroglyphically," but that authority is always uncertain, secular rather than sacred. It is thrown out from down here toward the truth up there it would express, not spoken as Christ speaks, from the heart of truth, as the Truth, the Word, the Logos. Moreover, the parables of Jesus are grounded in stories which are given as historically true, as grounded in the real social life of the people to whom he speaks, while the parables of Carlyle, Kierkegaard, and Nietzsche are openly fictional. They are about people who never existed and are grounded only in the most indirect ways on historical or biographical realities. Finally, and perhaps most crucially, the theories of language underlying sacred and secular parable are radically different.

III

What, exactly, then, is Nietzsche's theory of the language of parable? The chapter on *Zarathustra* in *Ecce Homo* expresses Nietzsche's sense that *Also Sprach Zarathustra* was given to him in an act of inspiration, or at any rate would have seemed so to him "if [he] had the slightest residue of superstition [*Aberglauben*] left in [his] system" [*E*, 300; *G*, 1130). One sign of this sense of inspiration is the way all objective things present themselves as metaphors and those metaphors as the vehicles of transobjective truth. Here is the passage:

> The concept of revelation [*Offenbarung*] – in the sense that suddenly, with indescribable certainty and subtlety, something becomes *visible*, audible, something that shakes one to the last depths and throws one down – that merely describes the facts. One hears, one does not seek; one accepts, one does not ask who gives; like lightning, a thought flashes up, with necessity, without hesitation regarding its form – I never had any choice.
> ... – The involuntariness of image and metaphor [*des Bildes, des Gleichnisses*] is strangest of all; one no longer has any notion of what is an image or a metaphor: everything offers itself as the nearest, most obvious, simplest expression. It actually seems, to allude to something Zarathustra says, as if the things approached and offered themselves as metaphors [*sich zum Gleichnis anböten*] ("Here all things come caressingly to your discourse

[*hier kommen alle Dinge liebkosend zu deiner Rede*] and flatter you; for they want to ride on your back. On every metaphor you ride to every truth [*Auf jedem Gleichnis reitest du hier zu jeder Wahrheit*]. . . . Here the words and word-shrines of all being [*alles Seins Worte und Wort-Schreine*] open up before you; here all being wishes to become word, all becoming wishes to learn from you how to speak [*alles Sein will hier Wort werden, alles Werden will von dir reden lernen*]"). (E, 300–1; G, 1131–2.)

There are two distinct figures for the act of figuration here. The word Kaufmann here translates as "metaphor" (*Gleichnis*) is given by him as "parable" in his translation of what Nietzsche is citing, *Zarathustra*, III, "The Return Home": "On every parable you ride to every truth."[12] The German word *Gleichnis* means both "metaphor" and "parable." It is the word Luther uses to name the parables of Jesus in the New Testament. The passage from *Ecce Homo* associates the parabolic with a certain form of figure (whether as *Bild* or as *Gleichnis*), and with a certain form of narrative. Parabolic metaphor is also explicitly identified by Nietzsche with the language of apocalypse or revelation. The "inspiration" which gave birth to *Zarathustra* in a strange combination of freedom and involuntary submission to another voice speaking through the writer ("one could hardly reject altogether the idea that one is merely incarnation, merely mouthpiece, merely a medium of overpowering forces" [*Ecce Homo E*, 300; *G*, 1131]), was a lifting of veils, an opening up, *Offenbarung*, of the depths, so that what had before been invisible and inaudible now is seen and heard. Nietzsche is no longer one of those who having eyes sees not and ears but neither hears nor understands. The words and word-shrines of being open up before him. Things become words and the words are as it were the sacred enclosures containing "being," the underlying ground of all things. For the inspired Nietzsche these words as concealing husks open up to reveal what they have kept hidden.

How does this revelation or apocalypse through parable, in Nietzsche's view, occur? It happens through a certain transformation of ordinary things into figure or image which is of the essence of parable. One might ordinarily think of metaphor as a voluntary operation. One knows the literal word and substitutes a metaphorical one for vividness or point or whatever, in full awareness that it is transferred from another realm. The ship does not "plough" the waves, but the poet speaks of the ship's movement by means of this figure. In the case of the "gale [*Sturm*]" of inspiration which "gave" Nietzsche *Zarathustra* the act of figuration was very different from this. It was, for one thing, wholly involuntary. Things approached and offered themselves as metaphors or as parables. The things themselves as they were perceived were instantly transformed into parables. Things as seen, heard, or felt were instantly changed into words and those words into the expression of a parabolic meaning. There is in fact in what Nietzsche describes a total breakdown or obliteration of the two fundamental distinctions necessary to the analysis in traditional rhetoric of metaphor: the distinction between word and thing and the distinction between literal and figurative language. The things became instantly words and those words were not transported from afar to be the vehicle of a metaphoric meaning, doubling for some displaced literal word, but were "near," "simple," "obvious." Every thing offers itself as the nearest, most obvious, simplest expression, that is, the things themselves as metaphor appear as just like a literal word, so that in the state of inspiration "one no longer has any notion of what is an image or a metaphor." Another way to put this extraordinary linguistic experience would be to say that in it the things themselves are catachreses, the unique and indispensable expression of a truth which can be said in no other way. Such expressions are neither literal nor figurative but beyond that distinction.

This mode of expression is essential to parable and will allow a distinction to be made between allegory, at least some modes of allegory, and parable. In allegory the narrative personifications stand for abstractions which could be expressed discursively, as Spenser's Orgoglio is pride and pride is a moral sin open to conceptual definition and analysis. At least it might be possible to read *The Faerie Queene* in this way. In parable the realistic narrative is the vehicle of a meaning, the magical opening up of a meaning which is incapable of being expressed in any other way. Commentary on a parable can only in one way or another repeat it, that is, present itself as another parabolic expression. The words are the shrines or protective coverings, frames, of a truth which only they have in charge.

I have said that at the deepest level Nietzsche's concept of parable is expressed in two images, that is to say in terms of parables or *Gleichnissen*, according to the law just enunciated that one may speak only parabolically about parable. The two figures are reversed mirror images of one another. In Nietzsche's covert little parable, Nietzsche the parabolist of Zarathustra is Dionysus to whom things come crowding around as caressing, flattering, beseeching animals asking to ride on Dionysus' back: "Here all things come caressingly to your discourse; for they want to ride on your back." This figure then instantly reverses. The things-become-words are now animals on whose backs Nietzsche–Dionysus "rides to every truth." This strangely reversible image is of course a figure for the figure of metaphor. The word metaphor means "transport." A *metaphora* in modern Greek is a truck on which you might send your luggage or other valuables from here to there. A metaphor is a means of transportation, the vehicle of its meaning, the tenor, but in order for the metaphor to become the vehicle on which the inspired poet might ride to truth, the poet has first himself to be the vehicle, the broad back on which all things ride as language. The breakdown of the distinction between literal and figurative language, tenor and vehicle, occurs in that reversal or chiasmus. The carrier becomes the carried. The hidden truth is opened up or reached in a moment of "transport" in another sense, transport in the sense of mystagogic insight, elevation, revelation. It is necessary, in Nietzsche's little parable, first to carry all things on one's back before one can make all things the means of a transportation going far beyond the near, the simple, and the obvious.

Franz Kafka, it will be remembered, said of the night during which he finished his first great story, *The Judgment*, that many times during that night he carried the whole world on his back. Whether the story, parabolic record of his act of transportation, then carried Kafka "to every truth" is another question, but one may say that at least it was a discovery of the reasons why it is impossible to "go over."[13]

IV

Here, then, are an identification of the narrative mode of *Thus Spoke Zarathustra* and an identification of Nietzsche's theory of parable or *Gleichnis*. This returns us to my initial questions. Why is it proper or necessary that the abysmal and at the same time fundamental thought, *abgründlich* and *gründlich* at once, the thought of the eternal recurrence, should be expressed in just this narrative mode and in just that peculiar use of figurative language characteristic of parable? To answer this question it is necessary, with the help of Nietzsche's expression in these modes, to try to understand just what Nietzsche's thought of the eternal recurrence is. I turn to what is perhaps the crucial expression of that thought, "Of the Vision and the Riddle." The context of Nietzsche's formulation is complex. Not only is there a double parable, a riddling vision followed by a visionary riddle, Zarathustra's mountain climb to the gateway named "Moment" carrying the dwarf, embodiment of the spirit of gravity, followed by Zarathustra's vision of the shepherd choking on the snake. The two parables are told by Zarathustra to auditors on board a ship which has come from afar and is going yet farther, so the narrative motif of the journey toward mountain heights is contained within the narrative motif of the sea journey.

The reader might be tempted to think the first parable, that of the gateway named "Moment," is a vision, the parable of the shepherd and snake the riddle, but Zarathustra defines both of them as visions which are riddles, and he affirms that they form a single unit, two in one. "To you alone," he says to the sailors, "I tell the riddle that I *saw*, the vision of the loneliest (*euch allein erzähle ich das Rätsel, das ich sah, – das Gesicht des*

Einsamsten]." And later, speaking again to the sailors, this time perhaps speaking especially of the shepherd and the snake, Zarathustra explicitly uses the term parable [*Gleichnis*]: "Guess me this riddle that I saw then, interpret me the vision of the loneliest. For it was a vision and a foreseeing. What did I see then in a parable? [Was *sah ich damals im Gleichnisse?*]" (E, 271–2; G, 410). Here is the central passage of the first half of the vision, Zarathustra's words to the dwarf, as he reports them to the sailors:

> "Behold this gateway, dwarf!" I continued. "It has two faces. Two paths meet here; no one has yet followed either to its end. This long lane stretches back for an eternity. And the long lane out there, that is another eternity. They contradict each other, these paths; they offend each other face to face; and it is here at this gateway that they come together. The name of the gateway is inscribed above: 'Moment.' But whoever would follow one of them, one and on, farther and farther – do you believe, dwarf, that these paths contradict each other eternally?"
>
> "All that is straight lies," the dwarf murmured contemptuously. "All truth is crooked; time itself is a circle."
>
> "You spirit of gravity," I said angrily, "do not make things too easy for yourself! Or I shall let you crouch where you are crouching, lamefoot; and it was I that carried you to this *height*.
>
> "Behold," I continued, "this moment! From this gateway, Moment, a long, eternal lane leads *backward*: behind us lies an eternity. Must not whatever *can* walk have walked on this lane before? Must not whatever *can* happen have happened, have been done, have passed by before? And if everything has been there before – what do you think, dwarf, of this moment? Must not this gateway too have been there before? And are not all things knotted together so firmly that this moment draws after it *all* that is to come? Therefore – itself too? For whatever *can* walk – in this long lane out *there* too, it *must* walk once more.
>
> "And this slow spider, which crawls in the moonlight, and this moonlight itself, and I and you in the gateway, whispering together, whispering of eternal things – must not all of us have been there before? And return and walk in that other lane, out there, before us, in this long dreadful lane – must we not eternally return?" (E, 269–80; G, 408–9)

The gateway is named not "Present" or "Presence" but "Moment [*Augenblick*]," the blink of an eye. The pathways leading from it before and after are eternal [*eine Ewigkeit*]. They neither lead to any beginning, in one direction, nor to any ending, in the other, nor do they form a temporal circle, even an infinite one, the ouroboros or snake with his tail in his mouth. This, I take it, is the meaning of the riddle of the shepherd who is being choked by the snake in his throat. He is liberated only when he rejects the assumption that there must be some origin, end, or ground by biting off the head of the snake and spewing it forth. This rejection of logocentric thinking transforms the shepherd into the overman, the *Übermensch*: "The shepherd, however, bit as my cry counseled him; he bit with a good bite. Far away he spewed the head of the snake – and he jumped up. No longer shepherd, no longer human – one changed, radiant, *laughing!* [*ein Verwandelter, ein Umleuchteter, welcher* lachte!] Never yet on earth has a human being laughed as he laughed!" (E, 272; G, 410). Time in Zarathustra's visionary parable of the eternal return has neither origin nor end, nor even any common measure or ground, any *logos* in the form of the presence of the present. Though the past and the future contradict each other [*widersprechen sich*], offend each other [*stoßen sich*], across the barrier which is no barrier of the open gateway marked *Augenblick*, nevertheless the past is the already happening of the future and the future the eternal repetition of what has already happened in the past.

Moreover (and this is of the utmost importance here), the so-called "present" moment is also taken up into this intricate perpetually reversing knot. The presence of the present is emptied out of the moment too, since it too has happened innumerable times before and will happen innumerable times again. The moment is not presence but image, repetition, simulacrum, nor is it modeled on any past or future which was ever present. The *Augenblick* draws past and future into itself, it draws the future after itself, and it draws even itself through itself, in a knot made of a perpetually reversing repetition without ground in any *logos*: "And if everything has been there before," asks Zarathustra, "– what do you think dwarf, of this moment? Must not this gateway too have been there before? And are not all things knotted together so firmly that this moment draws after it *all* that is to come? Therefore – itself too? [*Und sind nicht solchermaßen fest alle Dinge verknotet, daß dieser Augenblick alle kommenden Dinge nach sich zieht? Also – sich selber noch?*]" (E, 270; G, 409).

Nietzsche's difficult thought of the eternal return involves the repudiation of the traditional logocentric idea of a time oriented around the presence of the present, so that the past is what was present but is no longer so, and the future a present to be. In place of that concept Nietzsche puts the notion of a present moment which is never present but is the interruption without interruption (like an open gateway) of a past which was never present and which already repeats a future which, on the other side of that non-present screen of the present, will repeat the past in the eternal return of the same which is always different, since it is governed by no original word on the basis of which the sameness of the eternal return could be measured.

It will now easily be seen what are the answers to my initial and guiding questions. A fictional protagonist, modeled on no real historical original, and the literary form of parable, which gives in figure what could in no way be given literally, are both extended modes of that figure-no-figure called catachresis. A catachresis is a figurative name for that which has no literal name. Since literal naming presupposes somewhere the presence of the present, only a form of expression suspending the possibility of literal naming would be appropriate for that "most abysmal thought," the thought of the eternal recurrence, in which, as Maurice Blanchot puts it in *Le pas au delà*, everything returns, "*except* the present, the possibility of presence. [*Qu'est-ce qui reviendra? Tout*, sauf *le présent, la possibilité d'une présence.*)"[14]

I shall stop here, though, like Zarathustra, somewhat in fear "of my own thoughts, and the thoughts behind my thoughts [*meinen eignen Gedanken und Hintergedanken*]" (E, 270; G, 409), for does not the thought of the eternal return also return eternally, drawing behind it all of the future and moving forward toward a past which has displaced itself into the future, waiting there for me or for anyone else to think it again?

Notes

1. Friedrich Nietzsche, *Ecce Homo* (with *On the Genealogy of Morals*), tr. Walter Kaufmann (New York, 1967), p. 295. German: Friedrich Nietzsche, *Werke in Drei Bänden*, Karl Schlechta, ed. II (Munich, 1966), p. 1128. Further references to *Ecce Homo* will be to these editions, the English translation identified as "*E*," followed by the page number, the German as "*G*," followed by the page number. (See also note 12.)
2. *Daybreak: Thoughts on the Prejudices of Morality.* tr. R. J. Hollingdale, (Cambridge, 1982), p. 5. German in *ed. cit.*, I, p. 1016.
3. *Ein typischer Romantiker*, in *Götzen-Dämmerung. ed. cit.*, II, p. 997.
4. "The Study of Poetry," in *English Literature and Irish Politics, The Complete Prose Works*, R. H. Super, ed., IX (Ann Arbor, 1973), pp. 161–2.
5. Søren Kierkegaard, *The Point of View for My Work as An Author*, tr. Walter Lowrie (New York, 1962), pp. 39–40.
6. Cited by Lowrie, *op. cit.*, p. xxiii.
7. S. Kierkegaard, *Either/Or*, tr. David F. Swenson, I (New York, 1959), 9.
8. "Living On: Border Lines," in *Deconstruction and Criticism*, Harold Bloom et al. (New York, 1979), pp. 97 ff.
9. Thomas Carlyle, *Sartor Resartus: The Life and Opinions of Herr Teufelsdröckh* (Indianapolis, New York, 1937), p. 203.
10. I have discussed Alford's theory of New Testament parable at greater length in "Parable and Performative in the Gospels and in Modern Literature," in *Humanizing America's Iconic Book*, Gene M. Tucker and Douglas A. Knight, eds, (California, 1982), pp. 5–71.
11. In the essay cited in note 10 above.
12. *Thus Spoke Zarathustra*, tr. Walter Kaufmann, *The Portable Nietzsche*, (New York, 1954), p. 295. For the German see *ed. cit.*, II, 432. Henceforth the English translation will be identified as "*E*," followed by the page number in

this edition, the German as "G," followed by the page number in this edition. (See also note 1.) See my *The Linguistic Moment* (Princeton, N.J., 1985), pp. 424–33, for a fuller reading of Nietzsche's "Of the Vision and the Riddle," discussed briefly in section IV of this essay.
13. *Von den Gleichnissen* ("On Parables"), in *The Great Wall of China: Stories and Reflections*, (New York, 1946), p. 258.
14. Maurice Blanchot, *Le pas au delà*, (Paris, 1973), p. 27.

18

How deconstruction works

> Shee as a veil down to the slender waist
> Her unadorned golden tresses wore
> Dissheveld, but in wanton ringlets wav'd
> As the Vine curls her tendrils, which impli'd
> Subjection . . .
>
> Milton Paradise Lost, IV, 304–308

Deconstruction is by no means just one more "method" of reading. It is a transformation of ways of thinking and doing that coincides with wide-ranging changes going on in Western societies today. Deconstruction therefore has many dimensions – institutional and pedagogical, familial and sexual, political and juridical, even theological and scientific.

All of these dimensions are involved when I, for example, read Book IV of Milton's *Paradise Lost* and come upon the phrase "as the Vine curls her tendrils." The phrase occurs in a 100-line passage of extraordinary beauty describing Satan's first view of Eden, and within that of the Garden of Paradise, and within that of Adam and Eve: "Two of far nobler shape erect and tall." Adam's "Hyacinthin Locks" do not fall below his shoulders, but Eve's hair falls as a veil to her waist.

The passage describing Eden has both moved and troubled many readers, among them John Ruskin and William Empson. Milton's language, here as so often, goes against the apparent intention of his argument, so that it is impossible to say decisively that it says only this or that.

On the one hand, Milton tries to incorporate Eve within the general economy of creation, to say that like Adam she is still unfallen and free to fall or not. Although in her, as in Adam, "the image of thir glorious Maker shon," they are "Not equal, as thir sex not equal seemd"; she is made for subjection to Adam and to God through Adam: "Hee for God only, shee for God in him."

On the other hand, the echo in "the Vine curls her tendrils" of an earlier description of Eden – of "umbrageous Grots and Caves/Of cool recess, ore which the mantling Vine/Lays forth her purple Grape, and gently creeps/Luxuriant" – places Eve in the general disheveled and

293

untamable luxuriance, or "wantonness," of Nature. This wantonness is a figure for the luxuriance of Milton's poetic power, present here in what Ruskin called the "pathetic fallacy" of personifying inanimate nature. Eve's disheveled wantonness means that she has in effect already fallen when we (and Satan) first see her, whatever Milton may say about those tendril curls implying subjection. This makes it impossible to include her in the general scheme of creation – in fact, it puts her above Adam or outside his control and identifies her with Milton's independent power of poetry. Eve's curling tendrils imply independence as well as subjection.

Within the phrase "as the Vine curls her tendrils" is the interference of one meaning with another, of figuration with theology, independence with subjection. A critic who is not a deconstructer might reconcile the diversity in the phrase or in the poem by finding an "organic unity," or by subordinating one meaning to another, or by absorbing the divergent meanings. Such a critic might, for instance, argue that Eve's disheveled wantonness is only a momentary suspension of the harmony of creation (and of Milton's poem), that this deviation is corrected when Eve turns back to Adam and to God through Adam.

In a deconstructionist reading, the two meanings are asymmetrical and irreconcilable, like rhetoric and logic. Such doubleness is only one of the things deconstruction finds in texts. To identify such an interference in the words is far from implying that the reader is free to make the phrase mean anything he or she likes.

19

President's column

(i) Responsibility and the joy of reading

My first responsibility as president of the MLA is the task of writing this little essay for the *Newsletter*. I start with a question about responsibility: To whom or to what am I responsible as a teacher of literature? After that I'll get to joy, the joy of reading.

No doubt the MLA has responsibility primarily for what might be called the institutional side of our profession. So a new president might well choose, among things of importance that have happened at the MLA during the last year, to write about the choice of a new executive director, Phyllis Franklin, or about the MLA's role in challenging the nomination of Edward Curran as director of the National Endowment for the Humanities, or about the move of MLA headquarters to 10 Astor Place. Or I might celebrate all the things the MLA does for the institutional side of our professional lives: the annual convention, or the *Job Information List* and the services of the annual convention to job seekers, or the annual *Bibliography* or our activities to improve the conditions of teachers of composition, languages, and literature on part-time or one-year appointments, or the conference being planned for summer 1987 by the English Coalition, of which the MLA is a part, to reconsider the English curriculum from grade school to the graduate level. Or I might reiterate the continuing commitment of the MLA to affirmative action and to a strong role for the interests of all our members, through such bodies as the Committee on Academic Freedom, the Commission on the Status of Women in the Profession, the Commission on Foreign Languages, Literatures, and Linguistics, or the Commission on the Literatures and Languages of America. Or I might take note of a major change in *PMLA*, the appointment of John Kronik of Cornell as the first editor of *PMLA* who is not also the executive director of the association.

I might indeed do all that, But after the last paper has been read at the convention, the last vacancy filled, the last item listed in the *Bibliography*, the last essay published in a given year of *PMLA*, a question still remains: Exactly what is all this vast institutional and professional activity supposed to aid or "facilitate"? I suggest that one answer to that question, perhaps the bottom-line answer, is that it is all for nothing unless it

295

supports the activity of reading. I mean, initially, the reading of the teacher, not the reading of the student. How can we teach reading if we are not readers ourselves? And I suggest that real reading, when it occurs, which may not be all that often, is outside the institution, allergic to institutionalization, private, solitary. I suggest, finally, that real reading, when it occurs, is characterized primarily by *joy*, the joy of reading.

What do I mean by the joy of reading? The *OED* defines *joy* as "a vivid emotion of pleasure arising from a sense of well-being or satisfaction; the feeling or state of being highly pleased or delighted; exultation of spirit; gladness, delight." The word of course has sensual and erotic overtones, as in "the joy of cooking," or "I wish you all joy of the worm." It is associated with cognate words like *delight, pleasure, ecstasy, exultation*. To speak of the joy of reading will remind some of Roland Barthes' *plaisir du texte*.

But I have in mind more specifically the powerful uses of the word in the Romantic period, not only Schiller's "Ode to Joy" but Coleridge's "Dejection: An Ode," where the "shaping spirit of Imagination" gives that "Joy" which is "Life, and Life's effluence, cloud at once and shower," "the spirit and the power/Which wedding Nature gives to us in dower/A new Earth and new Heaven." And I have in mind Wordsworth's "Surprised by joy – impatient as the wind," where a sudden inrush of joy can make the poet forget even the sorrow of his daughter's death and turn instinctively to "share the transport" of his joy with her, forgetting that she is "deep buried in the silent tomb." For me, the joy of reading, when it comes, is something like Wordsworth's sudden joy: surprising, unpredictable both in its nature and in its possible effects, a break in time, in that sense anarchic, a dissolution of pre-existing orders, the opening of a sense of freedom that is like a new earth and a new heaven, an influx of power. The joy of reading is in this sense apocalyptic. It has to do with transfiguration and the end but also has to do with a momentary lapse of the fear of death.

I open, for example, a volume of Francis Ponge I have at hand. Ponge is an author I have no responsibility to write about or teach. What I read by Ponge, those strange poems that "take the side of *things*," gives me that joy of reading. No doubt this is partly because of my freedom from obligation toward Ponge or to teach Ponge. "Puisque tu me lis, cher lecteur," says Ponge, "donc je suis; puisque tu nous lis/(mon livre et moi), cher lecteur,/donc nous sommes (toi, lui et moi)." I am, at least in part, because I read, and that is the widest import of the joy of reading.

Our professional vocation, with all its responsibilities, begins and ends in that joy of reading. It is a joy that is only with difficulty institutionalized, if it can be institutionalized at all. All our meetings, commissions, publications, and so on are for the sake of that. Our primary responsibility is to that. I would alter Yeats' "in dreams begins responsibility" to say, "in reading begins responsibility." Now I am not so naive as to think that reading is ever altogether solitary, that the reader is ever cut off from all his or her context of familial, community, departmental, institutional, even national or historical reponsibility. If writing, for Henry James in the preface to *The Golden Bowl*, is part of the "conduct of life," and if he defines the conduct of life as "things done, which do other things in their turn," reading too, I claim, is part of the conduct of life in this sense. It is a thing done that does other things in its turn. Institutional and professional responsibility, the responsibility to teach and to write, to read all those manuscripts and to serve on all those committees, begins when the act of reading turns outward and does other things in its turn.

About those other forms of responsibility I may say something in a future *Newsletter*, but here and now I want to affirm that our primary professional and vocational responsibiity is to the impatience, transport, and surprise of the joy of reading.

(ii) *Responsibility and the joy(?) of teaching*

In the last president's column, in the Spring 1986 *Newsletter*, I raised the question of the responsibilities of the teacher of language and literature. To whom or to what are we primarily responsible when we write about, read, or teach literature? I concluded that our professional vocation, with all its responsibilities, to students, to colleagues, to our institutions, to the various communities to which we belong, begins and ends with what I called the joy of reading. The joy of reading is a sense of insight, freedom, and power that comes, when it comes, always as a somewhat surprising and unpredictable effect of reading. We can never know just what is going to happen when we read. That act of reading, I said, then turns outward and does other things in its turn. In that sense it is part of what Henry James, echoing Emerson and speaking of writing rather than of reading, called "the conduct of life."

This column takes up the most immediate and direct of those doings resulting from reading: teaching. The first thing that reading "does in its turn" is bring about another act of language. Those new words may be no more than the silent and almost inarticulate commentary we add as marginal response when we read. This commentary first enters the realm of efficacious conduct, for most of us, when we teach what we have read.

But is there a joy of teaching? The truth is that, for me at least, teaching is by no means always an unmitigated joy. Joy of reading, yes. But teaching is often a hazardous and unsatisfactory activity. Whether we are prepared or unprepared the class may go well or ill, for reasons that are not always easy to understand or to explain to oneself. Nothing is more disheartening than a class that inexplicably "bombs." It can ruin your whole day, and decades of teaching experience are no guarantee against that happening.

But the joy of teaching, when it comes, is exhilarating. A student makes a comment or asks a question that leads the teacher to see something new in the poem, novel, or whatever it is she or he is teaching. Some unexpected insight comes to the teacher in the midst of the class hour. In either case teaching suddenly becomes no longer the presentation of something the teacher already knew when the class began. It becomes rather an active process of invention or discovery. Such teaching is an inaugural event in itself, like the original reading on which the teaching is based. Teaching too brings something new into the world.

It will be seen that I do not think of teaching as simply the transmission to the students of knowledge already fully possessed by the teacher. The teacher is not a colorless medium or relay station by means of which a message is carried over from here (the library or the archives or "the tradition") to there (the students' minds). This is true even though one of the primary duties of the teacher is to make manifest "historical and philological facts as the preparatory condition for understanding," to borrow Paul de Man's phrasing in his already classic essay "The Resistance to Theory." Teaching, in fact, is not oriented entirely toward the students, responsible exclusively to them. Teaching, as de Man says, is not a species of therapy or counseling, nor is it, according to an even more venerable figure, a species of midwifery, a maieutic procedure that elicits the birth in the students of something they obscurely knew already but did not know they knew. Teaching is rather primarily responsible to the texts being "read in class" or to the "material" or the "things" presented.

Another way to put this is to say that teaching is a prolongation, extension, or modulation of that first, virtually solitary act of reading that I celebrated in my earlier column. Even that solitary and mute reading, as I have said, is already accompanied by an at least rudimentary ground bass of commentary, an implicit scribbling in the margin. The chief thing, along with the indispensable scholarly and philological information, that the teacher displays to her or his students is a method of reading in action. This formulation must not be misunderstood. The phrase "in action" emphasizes the way neither "method" nor "theory" amounts to much when it is taught as such, detached from the activity of reading this or that particular text. Theory and method arise from reading, if they are to have force. The act of reading, when it occurs, which may not be as often as we would like to think, is more often the severe modification or even disconfirmation of presupposed theory and method than their peaceful ratification. The new theory that comes out of reading, moreover, may by no means be altogether compatible with that philological and scholarly knowledge, received from the tradition, the teacher began by accepting the responsibility to pass on to his or her students. This would follow as an inevitable consequence if reading has those qualities of surprise and inaugural novelty I claim it has. The reader rarely finds in those venerable poems, novels, or plays just what he or she has been led to expect to find there.

This fact has important consequences for teaching. It means that, contrary to what is often assumed, teaching is not primarily an interpersonal transaction oriented toward an interchange between teacher and students. The teacher is, rather, oriented primarily toward the text, primarily responsible to that, obligated in what he or she says to that, responsive to that. Though there can be no doubt that the successful teacher has an obligation not only to tell it like it is but to make that telling as clear as possible to the particular group of students in that particular class, nevertheless students are not so much partners in an intersubjective relation as the witnesses or overhearers of an activity of reading that is the teacher's interaction with the text at hand taking place before their eyes and ears, so to speak. I have at any rate learned most from those teachers in whom that responsibility to the text was displayed as a current event.

It also follows from what I have been saying, finally, that the teacher's authority by no means comes from her or his "personality" or from the possession of some unique method of reading that is validated by the personal "I" or by the authority of some "community of readers" to which she or he belongs, along with its attendant methods of interpretation. The teacher's authority, when she or he has it, comes from an impersonal response to the work being read, a response that transcends the "I." It is not the subjectivity of the teacher that is obligated to the work but an impersonal power of reading that he or she shares, to some extent, with all other readers of the same work. Hence the possibility of teaching literature, if it is possible. Teaching is an interlinguistic transaction, not an intersubjective one. It is a reaction necessitated by an implacable demand made by the language of the work on its reader and manifested in its turn by the teacher to his or her students. The joy of teaching, when it occurs, arises from the teacher's formation of new insights into the work on the spot, through the act of trying to explain it to students.

(iii) The obligation to write

In two previous *Newsletters*, I wrote brief essays entitled "The Joy of Reading" and "The Joy (?) of Teaching." (The question mark in the second title indicates that the idea that teaching is always or even primarily joyful is problematic.) In those essays I claimed that reading and teaching are not imposed from without, as social, professional, or institutional responsibilities. They are, rather, the consequences of an interior and linguistic imperative. The obligations to read and to teach come from language, from the poems, novels, and plays we read and teach. They come as almost irresistible compulsions, in the form of "Thou must."

The third and last topic completing the repertoire of our professional responsibilities is, of course, writing. As I did with the other two obligations of our profession, I want to argue that writing is only apparently a merely institutional or conventional responsibility, imposed on us from the outside by chairpersons and administrators or by an absurd tradition that says "publish or perish." Writing, I claim, is in fact intrinsic to the vocation that begins with the more or less private joy of reading. Writing too remains rooted in that solitary transaction with the words on the page. The insistence on measuring our professional worth by our bibliographies, the demand that we write and publish to get tenure and "advance in the profession," is only the extrinsic and in a certain sense contingent institutionalization of an intrinsic compulsion to write. That compulsion remains private and obscure because it comes from reading.

It seems at first difficult to argue persuasively that writing scholarship or criticism is an intrinsic obligation in the same way that reading and even teaching are. Surely reading and teaching do not demand to be completed by writing! We all know, or think that we know, strong and original readers, brilliant teachers, who have never, or hardly ever, lifted pen to paper or fingers to the word processor's keyboard. The need to write seems another matter or métier entirely. It seems to be something present sporadically here and there in some readers and teachers but by no means present as a genuine vocation in all of them. Nevertheless, I claim that reading and teaching are completed only by writing. The obligation to write is as strong as the obligations to read and to teach, for those who have a vocation for reading and teaching.

In fact, strange as it may seem, the most difficult thing for the reader and teacher is, paradoxically, not to write, as Maurice Blanchot argues in *L'écriture du désastre*: "Que d'efforts pour ne pas écrire, pour que, écrivant, je n'écrive pas, malgré tout – et finalement je cesse d'écrire, dans le moment ultime de la concession. . . ." (How many efforts in order not to write, in order that, writing, I should not write, in spite of everything – and finally I cease to write, in the ultimate moment of concession. . . .) Strange words! No doubt they have a different meaning within the intricate fragmentary argumentation by aphorism of *L'écriture du désastre*, and a different meaning for a "primary" writer like Blanchot from the meaning I give to them in relation to the more humble métier of "secondary" writing as you or I might be obligated to practice it. Nevertheless, what writer could have demonstrated more strikingly than Blanchot has, in all those hundreds of review essays written over the past decades, the necessary connection between reading and writing about what we read? And what writer could have made more problematic that distinction between "primary" and "secondary" writing, without in any way denying that *La folie du jour* is a "récit" and *L'écriture de désastre* is something else, perhaps "criticism" or "literary theory"?

It is a commonplace these days to observe that the act of reading is always accompanied by secondary acts of language. As we read we compose, without thinking about it, a kind of running commentary or marginal jotting that adds more words to the words on the page. There is always already writing as the accompaniment to reading. The actual writing down of that involuntary ground bass of commentary in a form that is readable by others, publishable, assimilable by one or another of the professional communities to which we belong, may be said to be accidental. It may happen or it may not happen. What we cannot prevent, what *must* happen, is the first writing that is inseparable from reading. Blanchot might call this "writing without writing."

This "first writing" is fundamentally heterogeneous and problematic. On the one hand it is a rudimentary assimilation of what we are reading to what we already know. We make what we read accord with the assumptions, norms, and codes of the "community of readers" to which we happen to belong. The "first writing" of this sort is an assertion of mastery over what is strange, idiomatic, unfamiliar, unassimilable in what we are reading. Writing about what we read in this mode is apotropaic. It wards off the threat in what we are reading by turning it into what we have already read and already know. When this kind of "first writing" is actually written down, published as an essay in a journal, as a review, as a chapter in a book, it becomes part of that vast enterprise of rationalizing appropriation, of making regular, comprehensible, usable, familiar, ready for the archives that is the essence of the modern research university.

On the other hand, however, that "first writing," that involuntary accompaniment of reading, is not so much a response to what is unfamiliar and eccentric in the work as a response to what the strange and eccentric in the work itself responded to. Henry James, in the preface to *The Golden Bowl*, speaks of that splendid effort of critical or "secondary" writing, the prefaces to the New York edition of his work, not as a response to his novels and stories themselves, when he reread them, but as the result of renewed access to what called them into being.

This he calls the "thing" the story is about, the "matter" of the story. He figures this "matter" or "thing" as a blank wall on which a shadow is cast or as limitless "fields of light" or as a shining expanse of untrodden snow.

Mixed with the apotropaic act of covering over in the "first writing," scribbled so to speak in invisible ink in the margin of the book we read, there is something else, a submission to what the work itself submitted to. This submission dispossesses the reader, appropriates him or her, rather than yielding itself to rationalizing appropriation. This too carries over into the essay, chapter, or review, in spite of our best efforts to conceal it. Such carrying over gives, perhaps, the chief interest and value to what we write.

On the other hand (again), it would no doubt be a piece of foolishness to imagine that either what is eccentric, idiomatic, and unassimilable in what we read or what is eccentric, idiomatic, and unassimilable in what we write about what we read is adequate to the "matter" or "thing" to which both respond, adequate in the sense, to use another of James' metaphors, that a silhouette matches a shadow on the wall. This perpetual inadequacy tends to blur the distinctions not only between "primary" and "secondary" writing but also between the two kinds of secondary writing, the one that covers over and wards off and the one that seems faithful to the strangeness in primary writing. Moreover, in spite of the implications of my metaphors (or James'), the "matter" of either the "primary" or the "secondary" text is not something outside language, extrinsic to it. As I began by saying, the obligation to write is intrinsic to language, part of our transaction with it and of its transaction with us.

To succeed in ceasing to write, as Blanchot would wish to do, would be the only way to escape from the double bind of a categorical obligation to write what always turns out to be an inadequate response to that demand. As Blanchot recognizes, however, we cannot achieve not writing by a simple refraining or by a simple act of will. The obligation to write remains a fundamental part of our everyday practice of our profession, intrinsic to it, not accidentally imposed from without. It coexists with the joy of reading and with the more intermittent joy of teaching as the third and by no means least of the main features of our vocation.

(iv) *The future for the study of languages and literatures*★

In earlier columns I have written about the intrinsic activities of our vocation: reading, teaching, and writing. The other things we do, serving on committees or as administrators, advising students, writing letters of recommendation for students and colleagues, and so on, seem to me, important as they are, ancillary to those main activities. They are ways, for the most part, we help others get on with our common business. In this last of my presidential columns I shall say something about our future as I see it. I mean by this the context in which reading, teaching, and writing about languages and literatures will be carried on in the United States in the coming years. Prophecy is perilous, but I see the present moment and the next couple of decades as a time of special hope, opportunity, and challenge for us.

Most of us know through immediate experience how the placement of what we do within colleges and universities and within society has changed in recent years. Several factors seem to me of special importance. Demographic and actuarial facts presage increased numbers of students in the 1990s and an unusually rapid turnover in teaching staff. A large number of senior professors will retire in the mid-nineties. Their departure will provide a great opportunity for renewal and change, for taking new directions. It will also require courage and foresight on the part of those making all those appointments and tenure decisions. If we do not figure out what we want to do with our profession, someone else will figure it out for us.

The courage and foresight I have mentioned will require seeing clearly what is new about our situation. Among the most important of these novelties are the following: (1) The United States is becoming a multilingual and multiracial country, a country in which, for increasing numbers of our citizens, English is a second language. We are becoming in new ways a country of many overlapping cultural heritages. Making decisions about how to deal with this pluralism in our culture will be a major responsibility for public policy in the coming years; it will be our responsibility, as teachers of the modern languages, to make sure our voice is heard by those making these decisions. (2) The United States is more and more becoming a country in which, for better or for worse (and it is not necessarily all for the worse), our common culture is primarily determined not by the reading of books, canonical or otherwise, but by the domination of the mass media: television, cinema, popular music. There is no use simply deploring this trend. We must think through its implications and take advantage of it. (3) The function of colleges and universities as institutions within our society is changing with unusual rapidity. It is changing especially, for example, by way of the rapid increase in cooperative research sponsored not by governmental agencies but by industries, especially high-tech industries like

---

* Some ideas in this presidential column are elaborated in the final essay in this volume, "The Function of Literary Theory at the Present Time."

computer technology and biotechnology. This situation may seem far from the teaching of languages and literatures, but it is going to have decisive effects on what we do. (4) The women's movement is having incalculable effects on our society. Among these are major changes in the curriculum, the canon, and procedures in the study of languages and literatures.

Exactly what differences ought these changes to make in *what* we read, teach, and write about and in *how* we do those things? I see two clear differences. The first is a major alteration in the canon of what we read, teach, and write about and in how these texts are organized in curricula, in class reading lists, and in the contents of books and articles. The second is a new centrality of literary theory to our enterprise. This interest is not merely fashionable. It responds to a deep intellectual need. Literary theory is the indispensable bridge allowing movement back and forth among the various canons and curricula and allowing also for the use of many different sorts of texts to accomplish that primary responsibility of teaching good reading, critical thinking, and accurate, forceful writing. Our main business in the coming years will be to teach people to read – to read all the signs, including those of the newspaper and of the mass culture surrounding us, as well as those signs inscribed on the pages of the old canonical books. In the coming years an informed citizenry in our democracy will be one that can read and think clearly about all the signs that at every moment bombard us through eye and ear. Figuring out the best ways to ensure the existence of this citizenry will be a great responsibility but also an exhilarating opportunity.

20

The imperative to teach

The questions ask: Who or what (today) calls on us to teach? Does that demand lay out a clear road for us to follow? Is that road, if there is one, "under construction," that is, I take it, is it in the midst of a social or historical process into which we as teachers or students might intervene, taking a hand in the work of construction? Is that road, if there is one, a one-way street, *Einbahnstrasse*, presumably in that case going straight from the teachers to the students, with "Do Not Enter" marked at the other end, to keep the students from driving the wrong way, in defiance of the authority of the teacher?

The questions can be extrapolated a little, perhaps down the one-way street that waits to be traversed, showing me the way to go: Is teaching a contingent addition to "literary study," or to "humanistic study" generally? Or, to put it more simply, does reading, the reading of a poem, a novel, or a philosophical text, for example, require teaching it or lead inevitably to teaching it?

It would seem not. It would seem that the teaching of literature or philosophy is a contingent and somewhat artificial addition to reading. It is something added on by the accidental requirements of the institutions some readers happen to be hired by. We are hired to teach and so we teach. The circumstances of that teaching are open to all sorts of empirical, sociological, and historical investigations, for example, study of the development of higher education in the United States, the place of the humanities within that, difference in demands made on teachers by public and private institutions, differences between the demands on teachers of literature *today* and those made in one or another *yesterday*, differences between the role of teaching in the humanities and the role of teaching in the social sciences and sciences, and so on. It might be shown, for example, that literary study in the university, at least in this country, is much more difficult to imagine *without* teaching than is, for example, the study of economics or astrophysics. Our society in general seems to have an uneasy conscience about supporting people or supporting them for long to do humanistic study entirely detached from teaching, whereas a postdoctoral researcher within the university in physics or biology may be more or less free of teaching for relatively prolonged periods.

At the same time one feels, or one may feel, that this demand for teaching made on humanists in the university does not have anything intrinsic or essential to do with reading. It may be because reading as such is so detached from "the real world," as opposed to research in science, with its presumed "applied" usefulness, that our society feels reading literature or philosophy can only be justified if it is firmly attached to the social and socializing activity of teaching, the passing on and reinforcing of the "values" of that society through the teaching of canonical interpretations of canonical works. This need to justify reading through teaching of a socially useful kind may explain why there is so much resistance or hostility to modes of reading and teaching in the humanities which conspicuously do not fulfill that demand.

All this, as I said, is open to empirical study by historians and sociologists of our institutions and professions. Such study would take it for granted that the demand or call for teaching, *l'appel à l'enseignement*, comes "today" from our technological, industrial or "post-industrial," "post-modern" society. It comes relayed by way of one of the most powerful institutions of such a society, the modern "research university," now in the midst of a major shift. This is the shift from support primarily by government agencies to support increasingly by industry, by pharmaceutical companies, for example, or by bio-genetic laboratories, or by computer corporations.

Such an answer to the question of who or what gives the call to teaching would itself be a mode of sociological, even "scientific," research. It can and should be accomplished, as part of that general program of rationalizing appropriation, even of its own procedures, protocols, and assumptions, that fundamentally characterizes the modern university and gives it its reason for being.

The problem with doing this is that it would be barking up the wrong tree, like all attempts to assimilate the study and teaching of literature and the other humanities to the demands of sciences, in the sense that we might think of the humanities as part of "the human sciences." The irresistible call to teach literature comes not from the institution within which the teaching takes place but from reading itself. I mean by this that the command to teach is a purely linguistic call inscribed within works of literature or philosophy (or indeed within any other texts when they are taken as "texts"). This call comes neither from any transcendent source, nor from any subject or subjectivity, for example that of the author or reader, nor from society and its institutions – universities, departments, curricula, programs, courses – however compelling or even coercive those may be. The call, the imperative to teach, does not come from anywhere but from within the text itself.

The text demands that the reader go outside the text to attempt to verify its referential and performative validity, that is, to find out whether it tells the truth and whether it can be efficacious in helping us and our students in living our lives, in making judgments and decisions "in the real world." As Werner Hamacher has observed, it is not one's mother or grandmother, as representatives of social and institutional authority, who beseech the reader to go outside, as Marcel's grandmother, in Proust's novel, begged him to do. It is the text itself that exhorts the reader to stop reading.

Teaching is one of the most important ways to respond to that imperative to go outside the text. Contrary to what is often assumed, it is rhetorical reading, or, to give it another name, "deconstructive reading," which, more than hermeneutic, semiological, or sociological ways of reading, most urgently and consistently recognizes and responds to this intrinsic demand of works of literature or philosophy not only to be read but to be tested for their referential verity and their functional efficacy. This demand can in no way be resisted by trying to sequester the text in one way or another from that "real world," for example, by trying to see it as a free play of signifiers detached from all questions of reference. Teaching, as one response to that demand, would and does take place even where there is no institution to sanction it.

Teaching, it follows, is not primarily communication or dialogue or group therapy. It is the public expression or allegory (in the etymological sense of saying something other than itself out where people can hear, in the *agora*) of the act of reading. Further problems begin, however, to put it mildly, when the act of teaching brings into the open the impossibility of verifying either the referential validity of the text or being certain of what it makes happen or whether what it makes happen is what one would or should want to happen (though one can be sure, or almost sure, that reading makes *something* happen). The impossibility of distinguishing for certain between literal and figurative language in the text, that is to say, the interference of rhetoric in grammar and logic, does not mean that no text is truthfully referential but that neither reader, nor teacher, nor student, whatever his or her location along that one-way or two-way street, can ever be certain whether or not the text is truthfully referential. The celebrated "unreadability" of literary or philosophical texts, of texts in general, does not mean that the reader or teacher can have absolutely certain negative knowledge of the text's lack of referential and performative validity. It means that the reader or teacher can never be sure whether or not the text is truthfully referential and vividly performative or not. It may be or it may not be. There is no way to tell for sure, and the reader-teacher is suspended in the extreme discomfort of responding to an imperative call which at the same time he or she is altogether unable to fulfill.

That intolerable discomfort, "worse than madness," is one reason the attraction of an achieved negativity is perhaps the most dangerous temptation of literary study today, or at any time, since it seems to promise escape from a painful uncertainty and in addition because the thematic assertions of canonical literary works seem so strongly to present a negative knowledge, the demystification of every illusion through the reading of Wordsworth, or Dickens, or Melville, or Wallace Stevens, Proust, Rilke, or Homer, Sophocles, or Virgil, for that matter.

No, all we can learn to know as readers is that we do not yet know for sure one way or the other, and that we are unable to devise rules whereby validity could be certainly tested. It is this unfortunate and dismaying lack of methods of valid testing in literary study which forbids assimilating it into that general enterprise of rationalizing and validating which, as I said, defines the modern university. The teaching of literature is therefore at once the response to a demand made by literature itself and at the same time the demonstration, again and again, in public, before the students, of the impossibility of responding adequately to that demand. Though the teaching of literature is not dialogue but the making public of acts and procedures of reading, there is no reason why remarks made by students in class or papers presented by them should not be teaching too, or do exactly the same thing the teacher's discourse does. Teaching is, in that sense at least, a two-way street. The teaching of literature (and other "humanistic texts") is, nevertheless, as many people are uneasily aware, an anomaly or odd man out in the modern university. This may explain the urgency of various attempts to assimilate it. The teaching of literature, in fact, is neither a one-way street nor a two-way street, but a permanent impasse, or a road impassable for an indefinite time while it is "under construction." It might always have, at the beginning of the way it lays out, that sign one sees in England where roads are under construction: "Road Up!" Or, the sign might say, "You can't get there from here." This unbuilt and perhaps unbuildable construction project might have as motto Kafka's aphorism: "There is a goal but no way. What we call the way is only wandering."

This does not mean that the teaching of literature and other humanistic texts does not and cannot occur. Far from it. Teaching happens all the time, I am happy to say. But it happens as the patient, iterated, and reiterated demonstration, out there in the open, whatever the teacher may think he or she is doing, of the impasse I have tried to define.

21

Presidential Address 1986.

The triumph of theory, the resistance to reading, and the question of the material base

Alles Faktische schon Theorie ist.

                                                            Goethe

As befits a celebration of reading, I begin by reading a passage. I read it in the context of our situation here and now, in December of 1986, gathered in New York City, bound together by our shared profession as readers of literature, writers about literature, and teachers of literature and of the good writing that only good reading makes possible. It comes from "The Destruction of Tenochtitlan," a section of *In the American Grain*, William Carlos Williams'[1] great book about America. *In the American Grain* is a major work of what is these days called "cultural critique." The passage describes Montezuma's capital, one of the high points of world civilization, destroyed by Cortez almost overnight, in the name of European values:

> Streets, public squares, markets, temples, palaces, the city spread its dark life upon the earth of a new world, rooted there, sensitive to its richest beauty, but so completely removed from those foreign contacts which harden and protect, that at the very breath of conquest it vanished. The whole world of its unique associations sank back into the ground to be reënkindled, never. Never, at least, save in spirit; a spirit mysterious, constructive, independent, puissant with natural wealth; light, if it may be, as feathers; a spirit lost in that soil. (32)

This passage expresses with great power and an appropriate pathos the concept of American history underlying the whole of *In the American Grain*. That concept depends on the opposition between two kinds of culture. On the one hand, there is Montezuma's Tenochtitlan or, parallel to that, the culture of the indigenous American Indians generally or, another parallel, Père Sebastien Rasles' receptive response to the Indians and to the American ground beneath them. Rasles, a late seventeenth-, early eighteenth-century Jesuit missionary to the Indians in what is now the state of Maine, is one of the heroes of *In the American Grain*.

On the other hand, there are most of the Europeans who conquered America. Fearful or ignorant of the inherent virtue of the land they confronted here, they superimposed an alien culture on the American ground. Williams' examples include Cortez, who destroyed Tenochtitlan; the New England Puritans, who massacred the Indians and established the self-righteous religion and politics that determined American ideology; and Benjamin Franklin, who praised a niggling calculation of narrow gain. These are the bad guys in Williams' story of American history.

Praising Rasles' *Lettres édifiantes*, Williams says:

> Contrary to the English, Rasles recognized the New World. It stands out in all he says. It is a living flame compared to their dead ash. . . . Reading his letters, it is a river that brings sweet water to us. THIS is a moral source not reckoned with, peculiarly sensitive and daring in its close embrace of native things. His sensitive mind. For everything his fine sense, blossoming, thriving, opening, reviving – not shutting out – was tuned. . . . In Rasles one feels THE INDIAN emerging from within the pod of his isolation from eastern understanding, he is released AN INDIAN. (120–1)

Williams here prescribes not only what a proper culture is like but what stance an outsider should take toward it. A proper culture is like Tenochtitlan: rooted in the ground. It is responsive to a furtive indigenous spirit or spark hidden in the American grain, secreted in its very substance. A proper culture embodies that hidden essence, draws it up out of the ground and makes it visible in buildings, institutions, laws, values, habits, arts, artifacts, ways of production, circulation, and consumption – all the paraphernalia of culture. An outsider should approach such a culture with the reverent respect and openness of Père Rasles and attempt to preserve and open still further the flower that stems from its roots: "to create, to hybridize, to crosspollinize. . . . It is the sun" (Williams, 121). The metaphor here is traditional. Père Rasles is the sun. The indigenous Indian culture is the ground. The sun draws what is hidden in the ground out into the open, to flower there, no doubt as a heliotrope.

Looking at the written records of American history, Williams himself repeats Rasles' reverence in touch. He attempts to open himself to them and, as he says in his headnote, "to draw from every source one thing, the strange phosphorus of the life, nameless under an old misappellation" (v). Proper naming is performative. It is revelation. It brings the hidden spark or spirit back into the open.

Good reading or good criticism repeats in its turn what Williams repeated from Rasles' *Lettres édifiantes*. Good reading also is productive, performative. Naming the text rightly, it brings the strange phosphorus of the life, what Williams elsewhere calls "the radiant gist," back once more above ground. Criticism makes that gist available for present use.

Williams' main example of the contrary attitude and procedure is the New England Puritans. Frightened to death of the reality of the New World, they decimated the Indians, killed Père Rasles, and imposed on the New World a superficial, alien culture. It was a culture brought in from abroad, a culture with no roots in the American grain. The result was that the radiant gist "sank back into the ground, to be reënkindled never". Those New England Puritans, says Williams,

> must have closed all the world out. It was the enormity of their task that enforced it. Having in themselves nothing of curiosity, no wonder, for the New World – that is nothing official – they knew only to keep their eyes blinded, their tongues in orderly manner between their teeth, their ears stopped by the monotony of their hymns and their flesh covered in straight habits. (112)

Strong words, those. For Williams the tragedy of American history is that the Puritan attitude has triumphed everywhere and in manifold ways over the attitude of Père Rasles. Instead of being deeply embedded in our natural environment, in its deep furrowed structure or grain, our culture has destroyed that environment or covered its surface. "It is an immorality," says Williams, "that IS America. Here it began. You see the cause. There was no ground to build on, with a ground all blossoming about them – under their noses" (114).

What can one say, here and now, today, about this opposition between two kinds of culture and about the resulting narrative of American history to which it leads? Is it sentimental balderdash, a kind of homegrown spontaneous Heideggerianism without benefit of Heidegger's critical rigor? Williams' "radiant gist" is perhaps no more than an American version of what Heidegger means by "occulted Being." The two would be saying in somewhat different ways that the history of the West is the history of the forgetting of Being. The triumph of modern technology is the present culmination of this forgetting. Technology includes of course the typewriter (which Heidegger hated – what would he have thought of the word processor?), as well as the jet plane, the computer, the communications satellite, and the atomic bomb. One might ask the question another way: Is Williams' radiant gist no more than a strange version of a now exploded Cratylism, the stubborn belief that the phenomenality of words somehow naturally corresponds to the essence of things? For Williams it would be not so much the magic of a similarity between words and things as the magic of a performative power of words over the deep essence hidden within things. I have elsewhere shown the heterogeneity of Williams' concept of "the strange phosphorus of the life, nameless under an old misappellation." This heterogeneity is not an oscillation between thinking of that life as some kind of spirit and thinking of it as some kind of material fire. Those notions are both within logocentric metaphysics. No, the heterogeneity at issue is the opposition between thinking of the life, or ground, as in one way or another extralinguistic and thinking of it as brought into existence by the posing of its name.

Whether we view Williams' notion of the radiant gist as a deep insight or as an unfortunate residue of mystified religiosity, his formulations have the virtue of forcing us to recognize that all meanings have a material base – cultural meanings as well as meanings embodied in written or printed texts. We ignore that base at our peril. Williams, moreover, presents with great force two antithetical concepts of the way cultural meaning may relate to its material base. It is the force of parabolic embodiment in personages and narratives drawn from the "original sources," from the texts of American history, Cotton Mather's *Wonders of the Invisible World*, Rasles' *Lettres édifiantes*, Franklin's *Poor Richard's Almanac*, and the rest. On the one hand, cultural meaning may grow naturally from meanings secretly inherent in the base, so that the culture is in magical correspondence with the matter of which it is constructed. On the other hand, it may be imposed arbitrarily as a kind of free-floating surface, as, for example, words apparently have exactly the same meaning on whatever material they are imprinted. The matter given cultural meaning is indifferent. A culture is universally transferable or translatable from country to country, from continent to continent, from climate to climate, without loss or change. As the blank sheet of paper is an indifferent matrix on which anything can be written, so the new tongue and all its attendant circumstances can be made to speak anything whatever.

Williams, correctly, sees that "cultural critique" fundamentally and necessarily concerns the relation between material base and ideological superstructure. Surely this is a frontier topic in literary study today, as well as a focal point of controversy.

Williams wants meaning or value to have the possibility of being not arbitrary, conventional, or simply positional but responsive to a potentiality for meaning that is already there, in the ground, waiting to be embodied in all the facets of culture. He sees America, correctly again, as the denial of this responsiveness. The American grain is, paradoxically, not grainy. The possibility that the initial decree of signification is arbitrary, rather than based on a potentiality of signification already there, has haunted American writers throughout the nation's literary history – for example, the Melville of "The Encantadas," or the

Hawthorne of the remarkable preface to *Mosses from an Old Manse*, or the Henry James of the early book on Hawthorne, with its celebrated passage about the superficiality of American culture.

I began by saying I was going to "read" the passage from *In the American Grain* in the context of our present situation, here and now, in the study and teaching of language and literature. What is that situation? It requires a double definition. I begin with the first. As everyone knows, literary study in the past few years has undergone a sudden, almost universal turn away from theory in the sense of an orientation toward language as such and has made a corresponding turn toward history, culture, society, politics, institutions, class and gender conditions, the social context, the material base in the sense of institutionalization, conditions of production, technology, distribution, and consumption of "cultural products," among other products. This trend is so obvious everywhere as hardly to need description. How many symposia, conferences, scholarly convention sessions, courses, books and new journals recently have had the word *history*, *politics*, *society*, or *culture* in their titles?

The shift from language to history has been so sudden, so widespread, so spontaneous, as hardly to be explicable by any single cause. It must have been overdetermined. No man or woman of goodwill can fail to sympathize with most of the motives behind this change: the impatience to get on with it, that is, not to get lost in the indefinite delays of methodological debates but to make the study of literature count in our society, lest the activity of patient reading be sequestered from the pressing demands of our situation. The shift to history and politics comes in response to a demand that arises not so much from without as from within, a demand imposed by ourselves on ourselves. It is a demand to be ethically and politically responsible in our teaching and writing, to grapple with realities rather than with the impalpabilities of theoretical abstractions and barbarous words about language, such as the names of figures of speech. As I said, I have great sympathy for this shift, but not when it takes the form of an exhilarating experience of liberation from the obligation to read, carefully, patiently, with nothing taken for granted beforehand. I include in this obligation the scrupulous reading of the texts of theory.

Among the factors accounting for this change from language to history is no doubt one form or another of what Paul de Man calls "the resistance to theory."[2] By "theory" I mean the displacement in literary studies from a focus on the meaning of texts to a focus on the way meaning is conveyed. Put another way, theory is the use of language to talk about language. Put yet another way, theory is a focus on referentiality as a problem rather than as something that reliably and unambiguously relates a reader to the "real world" of history, of society, and of people acting within society on the stage of history.

One understands the reasons for this resistance to theory. They no doubt include not only the impatience I have mentioned and the desire to be active in the real world but also a profound and instinctive distaste for the way linguistic theory, the theory of rhetorical reading or of deconstruction, has developed, a belief (quite mistaken) that it has become lost in endless sterile concern with the play of language, that it is élite, reactionary, apolitical. What most interests me just here, however, is the way the attacks on theory in the sense of the conceptual presuppositions of rhetorical reading or deconstruction take nearly identical forms whether they come from the left or the right. Both sides resort to moral or moralistic denunciation. From the left come cries that it is immoral not to be concerned with history, with society, with the real conditions of men and women in society. It is immoral to get lost in the sterile meanderings of language playing with itself. From the right come cries that it is immoral to shift from a thematic concern with literature, a study of the way literature expresses the values of our culture, to a nihilistic and "radically skeptical" concern with language, to get lost in the sterile meanderings of language playing with itself. The word *sterile*, used in the attacks from both sides as an epithet defining theory, carries a large sexual freight. The implication is that theory is narcissistic, even self-abusive. Theorists are impotent while the opponents of theory on both the left and the right are men and women of power. They make things happen in the real world in a way whose model is procreation – either male or female reproduction.

While the attacks from the right are more likely to repeat long-exploded clichés that seem to have their source in the banalities of the mass media, the left and the right are often united in the polemical terminology they use and in their misrepresentation, their shallow misunderstanding, and their failure to have read what they denounce or their apparent inability to make out its plain sense. This similarity may lead the dispassionate spectator to suspect that the differentiation between left and right may be itself a figure, a piece of ideological mystification, masking an actual identity of philosophical or theoretical presuppositions, though they are used to justify very different political and institutional programs. I said "dispassionate." Feelings run high in this region. This is no doubt a symptom of the big stakes involved. It takes a strong head to keep one's intellectual balance amid such a cacophony of competing voices.

There is in any case sometimes little basis for choosing between Walter Jackson Bate, René Wellek, Eugene Goodheart, John Searle, and Nathan Scott on the right and, on the left, Jeffrey Mehlman, the editors of

Representations who ran an essay of his as the lead piece, and even my good friends Frank Lentricchia and Edward Said. I mention Lentricchia and Said because, though their work ranks among the most serious and reponsible attempts from the left to come to terms with deconstruction, they still often seem bewitched by some of the misreadings I have mentioned. Neither Derrida nor de Man has ever sequestered his enterprise from politics or history. Quite the reverse. Each has in somewhat different ways insisted all along that one cannot fail to be engaged in history and in political action. Both see humanistic study and literary theory as active interventions in history and politics. What is at issue is the role of language in this engagement and that question of the material base on which I am focusing here.

The misrepresentation of what Derrida or de Man says about history, politics, and the positive role of the humanities would be incredible if it did not so patently derive from the anxiety of the accusers. Both the right and the left are united in their instinctive or irrational opposition to an illocutionary or positional theory of language, the right from the vantage point of an aesthetic view of literature and in the name of humanistic values, the left from the vantage point of a commitment to history and the material base. Both need to point the finger of blame against theory to avoid thinking through the challenge theory poses to their own ideologies. One understands their unwillingness to face this challenge, their resistances even to comprehending it. Nevertheless, this blind refusal to read flouts the minimal obligations of our profession. I have been working lately on what I call "the ethics of reading." If that phrase means anything, it must have something to do with respecting any text discussed, with accepting an obligation to read – to read carefully, patiently, and scrupulously, under the elementary assumption that the text being read may say something different from what one wants or expects it to say or from what received opinion says it says. The blatant and consistent violation of this basic ethical obligation is another major symptom that much is at stake here. Though many factors are involved, surely one of the most crucial is the question of what is meant by the material base of culture, of history, of language, or of sign systems generally.

So much for now for the shift to history and for the role of the resistance to theory as one factor in that shift. The second aspect of recent changes in literary study is a little less evident or a little less frequently recognized. In an apparently paradoxical or even senseless contradiction of the reorientation away from theory toward history and cultural critique, there has been a simultaneous and almost universal triumph of theory. What I mean by *that* will take a little more explanation. In a series of brief essays for the *MLA Newsletter* over the past year I discussed first the primary obligations of our vocation – reading, teaching, and writing – and then said something about the present and future of our profession. I see that present and immediate future as shaped by several developments: (1) demographic and actuarial changes will mean many new positions for teachers of language and literature in the mid-nineties; (2) the country is becoming increasingly multilingual and multiracial; (3) our common culture, however much we might wish it were not so, is less and less a book culture and more and more a culture of cinema, television, and popular music; (4) the relation of colleges and universities to an increasingly "high-tech" society is rapidly changing through a new emphasis on cooperative research with industry (this immediate and local change in the way colleges and universities as social institutions are related to society is of course part of much broader changes, including the internationalization of finance and technology and the creation of new transnational regions for this – for example, the "Pacific rim"); (5) the women's movement has made decisive and permanent changes in the way literature is studied; (6) a new concern for reassessing the function and efficacy of undergraduate education, as in the latest Carnegie report, by Ernest Boyer, and in the Smelser report on lower-division education within the University of California system; (7) instead of a single stable literary canon or set of canons, one for each of the national literatures, we now have an array of overlapping and much more fluid canons, often determined by cross-disciplinary orientations and including various kinds of "nonliterary" works side by side with traditional literary ones; (8) a new centrality in literary studies of theory accompanies the new importance of interdisciplinary studies like comparative literature, women's studies, programs in Afro-American literature, cultural studies, film studies, and critical theory as such.

These factors taken together form the context within which we will do our reading, teaching, and writing in the coming decades. Much could be said about each of these interrelated factors – for example, about the somewhat unexpected implications of a more or less purely instrumental concept of the teaching of foreign languages, especially the less commonly taught languages. By "instrumental" I mean the idea that the country's need to carry on business and diplomacy around the world is the primary reason for teaching languages. This notion is curiously in league ideologically with movements to declare English the official language, to abolish bilingual education, and to impose a common canon of works primarily in English literature or in English translation throughout our schools and colleges, from one end of the nation to the other – to establish the same curriculum in the inner city, in the affluent suburbs, in the rural midlands, and in the South. Both the notions of the canon and the instrumental notion of language study presuppose the idea that translation from one language to another involves no essential loss. This belief in turn rests on a deeply American assumption about the relation of the superstructure of meaning to the material base, here the phonic, semantic, and syntactic particularity of a given language, its nitty-gritty or grain.

The MLA, primarily through the office of the executive director, is currently undertaking five initiatives to intervene actively in these areas. One is the attempt to see what role, if any, the association should have in the new Foreign Language Institute being set up by Richard Lambert with significant foundation support at The Johns Hopkins University School of Advanced International Studies in Washington. Another is the MLA's active participation in preliminary planning for a possible Federal Endowment for Foreign Languages. This possibility of course depends on actions by Congress, but it is of the utmost importance that we have a voice in these deliberations. A third is the association's participation, through the English Coalition and in collaboration with the other major national professional organizations for teachers of English, in planning a major national conference on the teaching of English, to be held with generous foundation sponsorship at Wye Plantation in Maryland next July. A fourth depends on the votes first of the Delegate Assembly and then of the MLA membership; it would involve the MLA's taking some position against the movement to declare English the official language of the United States. The fifth consists of tactful and diplomatic moves to persuade the NEH to support projects involving literacy, composition, and problems of reading pedagogy.

As I have noted, there is much one might say about all these factors and about all these current initiatives, but I want to concentrate on the turn to history and the simultaneous triumph of theory. What do I mean by "the triumph of theory"? The triumph is evident in the violence and irrationality of the attacks on theory, which would not be attacked if it were not active and threatening. In "The Resistance to Theory," that already classic essay of 1979, Paul de Man argues that the opposition always takes local, contingent, one might say "historical" forms, for example in the polemical field of literary study in the United States today, as I have tried, polemically, to identify it. But for de Man the resistance to theory is more seriously an intrinsic, perennial aspect of theory itself. If the resistance to theory is the resistance to reading, theory is itself the resistance to theory, therefore a resistance to the reading it advocates. This is even true for text-oriented rhetorical theories of reading like the one I am here proposing.

This deeper form of the resistance to theory, deeper in the sense of being within theory itself, is not something contingent or historical, located in one particular place and time. It is a human and linguistic universal. The resistance to theory, however, takes different forms in different times and places, and though that resistance is still very much around in 1986, it has changed strikingly since 1979. The resistance to theory as the resistance to reading has now taken the strange form of the almost universal triumph of theory. I offer as one example of that the recent program of the Midwest Modern Language Association, which met in Chicago this past November. Almost all the papers, panels, and sessions of that convention were overtly and one might say aggressively theoretical. Even papers that were in fact old-fashioned positivistic literary history were dressed up in titles that made them sound theoretical.

Another example of the triumph of theory is the development of feminist literary studies. This development has had a tremendous and irreversible effect on the way literature is studied and taught, on the curricula and canons of literary studies. The women's movement is no doubt methodologically diverse, even heterogeneous, but it has been from the beginning not only politically motivated but theoretically exigent through and through.

No doubt many members of the MLA are going on doing what they have always done, important work in biography, historical research, bibliography, editing, and so on, activities that seem remote from "theory" in the current sense. But these essential archival responsibilities of our profession are now defined by the context of the triumph of theory within which they are carried on. Many of these activities have been reoriented, for example, toward the recovery of the biographical and bibliographical facts about works written by women or blacks.

Even the most conservative scholars have been forced to take account of theory by the immense proliferation of activities associated with it, by the constant need to make evaluations of younger colleagues who "do theory," by the tremendous increase in overtly theoretical works and professional activities: courses, essays, books, collections of essays, new journals, old journals transfigured, handbooks, guides, critical-theory groups, programs in critical theory, conferences, symposia, new positions designated for theory, new publishing programs, and so on. Nothing that is said about the end of theory, for example by advocates and practitioners of the so-called new historicism who claim that they have gone beyond theory and back to solid, atheoretical historical research, can obscure that fact. By a familiar paradox, in the present context such declarations against theory or such claims to be atheoretical end by being obviously theoretical statements, and abstract theoretical statements at that. They are abstract in the sense of being performative or positional claims, speech acts of the particular kind called denegations, rather than reasoned empirical arguments. They say, "I am not a theorist," which we know is a theoretical statement. The rejection of theory today can only take place in the context of the whole history of structuralist and poststructuralist theory – Saussure, Benjamin, Bakhtin, Lacan, Foucault, Barthes, Irigaray, Althusser, Fish, Jameson, Bloom, Derrida, de Man, and the rest. This context has changed once and for all the background against which individual acts of reading, teaching, or writing will henceforth be performed. History is not reversible, though it may certainly be reread. Its irreversibility is evident in the way the resistance to theory today is overtly and inescapably theoretical.

Why is this? Why is it that here and now, in literary studies in America, critical theory dominates the scene? Many factors are no doubt involved. Nevertheless, the triumph of theory is not to be accounted for straightforwardly, by even the most exhaustive inventory of the material or ideological conditions of our culture that might have made it predictable. Nor is it simply random, a result of the lawless blowing of the winds of fashion that brings now one habit of mind now another into dominance. The aleatory and determined that are opposed in explanations of cultural change are, of course, one of the binary pairs that contemporary theory has decisively rethought and strategically displaced.

The triumph of theory, like the turn to history, responds to complex motivations and forces, interior and exterior, especially in the younger members of our profession as they find themselves located here or there, in "concrete" teaching and professional situations. Among those motivations and forces are the technological, institutional, and economic changes I mentioned earlier. These make possible, among other things, the extremely rapid circulation of new work, through photocopies and tape recordings of lectures and interviews, and jet-plane travel to distant conferences and symposia. Another factor is increasingly rapid translation; European works of theory may even be published in English translation in the United States before they have been published in the language in which they were written. America has become the center of technological and economic "power," if I may dare to use that word. Although literary theory may have its origin in Europe, we export it in a new form, along with other American "products," all over the world – as we do many of our scientific and technological inventions, for example, the atom bomb. Theory is exported to Japan, to Australia, to South America, to China, back again to Europe, almost everywhere. In each new environment and language it is displaced, transformed, or translated once more in an ever-proliferating heterogeneity.

But the triumph of theory in the United States in the particular forms it has taken no doubt has something to do as well with the notorious thinness of our culture that Hawthorne, James, and then Williams in *In the American Grain* have identified. By thinness I mean the strange way in which our civilization has been powerfully imposed over an incommensurate material substratum. As a newcomer to California from New England, I have of course been made especially aware of this, not because California is different from New England in this respect, but because this general feature of American culture is easier for an outsider to a particular region to see. I take as my allegorical emblem of this aspect of America the magnificent new Orange County Performing Arts Center, a few miles from where I now live. It was built in a few months on what had been a bean field and before that a semidesert. In that littoral semidesert lived for two thousand years a group of peaceful Indians called Gabrielinos. Of course that was not their real name. It was a name imposed by the Europeans. They were, paradoxically, named after the Spanish mission of San Gabriel established to convert them. Most of the so-called Gabrielinos vanished within fifty years after the Spanish came. The site of the Orange County Center could not even have been a bean field without artificial irrigation, any more than it can be a center for the performing arts without importing artists, at great expense, from all over the world. This is no different from what the Metropolitan Opera in New York was doing fifty years ago and is still doing today, nor is it different from that peculiar superficiality that James identified in Hawthorne's notebooks and in the New England of Hawthorne's day.

European culture, Rowland Mallet tells Mary Garland in James' first novel, *Roderick Hudson*,[3] is immemorial, complex, and accumulated: "All these things," he says of the Roman scene around them, "are impregnated with life; they're the results of an immemorial, a complex and accumulated, civilisation" (334). Our American civilization is the negation of that statement. We can remember its beginnings. It is recent, datable, relatively simple. It has not been accumulating long enough to be thick on the ground. The result is that a fissure is evident between the material base and the life that here does not so much impregnate things as lie on their surface. All cultural life, all human meaning, must have a material base. There must be some thing or matter that is made into the signs of that life. In America the arbitrariness of the decree that makes things into the bearers of significance, matter into signs, shows through. That arbitrariness is hard to "see," theoretically. It may be the human condition to erase the material base, to forget it, to do anything to avoid seeing it. But some fleeting glimpse of it at least as a problem is being forced on us by the very triumph of our technology, as little bits of the old bean field still stick out here and there in odd corners of the site of the Orange County Performing Arts Center.

It is our luck or our unluck – our chance, one might say – that this universal structure is forcing itself on our attention through the peculiar conditions of our culture. The triumph of theory in literary studies is one aspect of that culture. Gertrude Stein's notorious aphorism about Oakland is true also of America in general: "There's no there there." California's lack of presence is the future, even the immediate future, of all America and, if Hawthorne and James were right, it is our past too. It might be better to say that in America the not there of the material base is conspicuously incompatible with the not there of the culture that floats on top of it, fragile and insubstantial, like a stage set or like the eclectic postmodern architecture of that admirable Orange County Performing Arts Center.

The triumph of theory in American literary studies corresponds to the structure I have been identifying. It too reflects an evident incommensurability between the sign system and its material base. Here the term *material base* has to be given a wide and problematic reference. It names the base of the particular texts or other significant entities for which the theory purports to account. The awkward synecdochic relation of example to concept in literary theory is one version of this structure. But the base in question is also the day-to-day life of those who are writing the theory, their social, class, institutional, professional, familial situations. The material base is also the somatic symptoms, the body that may become the locus of a sign or a sign system, the substance on which something is written.

The material base includes in addition the one time only of each unique act of reading, the here and now of the man or woman with the book in hand. By speaking of the "one time only" of each act of reading, I mean to emphasize what is accidental, unpredictable, contingent, and radically inaugural in each act of reading. I happen to pick up a certain book in a certain place and at a certain time, in the midst of certain circumstances of my life. However socially controlled or institutionalized this act of reading may seem, it may change the course of my life in unpredictable ways, ways not explicable by the context of the reading, including previous readings of the book by myself or others. The material base includes, finally, those books, articles, computers, tape recorders, copiers, and so on that are the physical means used to proliferate the theories, to translate them from here to there, all over the country and then all over the world. An example is the way I sit here at this moment, here and now, keying this address into my Leading Edge, made in South Korea, with the help of the *Nota Bene* word-processing program. Such tools are our strange new versions of Hegel's "this piece of paper on which I am now writing the *Phenomenology of Spirit.*"

Just here, however, I must attempt to say as clearly as I can the most difficult part of what I have to say. I have so far presupposed that the distinction between the material base and the signs that are, so to speak, inscribed on it is an unambiguous opposition. This opposition is a theoretical concept that anyone can see and accept, according to the etymological meaning of theory as a clear seeing or a seeing through. But this concept is in fact so obscure that I would say a frontier topic for literary study these days is precisely that distinction between base and superstructure. One might say that the triumph of theory is the covering over of that problem, or, put another way, that the triumph of theory is the resistance to reading, a resistance so successful as to be an erasure or forgetting of the material base in question. In literary study the first material base is the words on the page in the unique, unrepeatable time of an actual act of reading. Other sorts of cultural study begin with the confrontation of other forms of material inscription: paintings, artifacts, buildings, bits of barbed wire, or whatever. The importance of the problem of the material base shows that an apparently abstract, purely "theoretical" issue may have decisive institutional and political consequences, since our collective stance on this issue largely determines the way humanistic study and teaching are carried on.

Just what do I mean by saying that the triumph of theory is the resistance to reading in the sense of forgetting that we have even forgotten the materiality of any inscription? A full expression of this point would take more space than I have. It would require a patient, vigilant, and wary rereading of Hegel on sense certainty; Marx on the material base, language, ideology, and money; Nietzsche on language, consciousness, and "facts"; Saussure on the arbitrariness of the sign; and certain key texts by Derrida and de Man: Derrida's "White Mythology" and his admirable recent book on Paul Celan, *Schibboleth*, de Man's "Resistance to Theory" and his "Hypogram and Inscription,"[4] a crucial essay, from the point of view of this topic, on Michael Riffaterre.

I shall, however, speak as briefly and as clearly as possible about what is essential here. The notion of the material – far from being a base, root, the ground of reality, something unambiguously opposed to the impalpabilities of language play or theoretical abstraction – is itself an extremely problematic concept in any discourse in which it appears, including mine so far, even though it may have a necessary place in any discourse about culture or history. That is why I spoke of my example of the Performing Arts Center as an "allegorical emblem." The uncriticized notion of the material base is ideological through and through. It is part of Western metaphysics or of logocentrism. It is the specular reflection of idealism, not something outside it. This is conspicuously so when the material base is taken as the ultimate rock of appeal to set against various forms of so-called idealism, ideology, or superstructure. Another way to put this is to say that political action taken in the name of an appeal to the material base is "based" on a speech act that is illocutionary, positional, performative, not constative, though like all political action it makes constative claims.

Put in yet another way, "materiality," or "the material," or "the material base" is a catachrestic trope, side by side with others, for what can never be approached, named, perceived, felt, thought, or in any way encountered as such, though it is the hidden agent of all those phenomenal experiences. The word *materiality* gives us possession of what it names but only by erasing the named object. What *materiality* names can never be encountered as such because it is always mediated by language or other signs, as Hegel and Marx, each in his own way, recognized. The concept of the material is therefore not a solution but a problem. The patient, careful thinking through of this problem is a major task of literary theory and of cultural critique today.

To begin this thinking, we must scrupulously distinguish phenomenality from the material. We have no difficulty getting direct access to phenomenality. We live within it. Consciousness is phenomenality. But since, as Hegel saw, consciousness speaks, so that consciousness is linguistic through and through – always, already, from the start – we are forbidden ever to have direct access to what the word *materiality* names or nicknames. We can know the material only through names or other signs.

A passage from Mikhail Bakhtin's "Notes," as translated in *Bakhtin: Essays and Dialogues*,[5] may help to make this point clear: "The names of things are also sobriquets. Not from the thing to the word, but from the word to the thing; the word gives birth to the thing" (Morson, 182). No name is "proper." All names, proper or common, are sobriquets, nicknames, figurative substitutes for proper names that can never be given and that cannot exist. *Sobriquets, nicknames* – these are words for what in the language of traditional rhetoric are called "catachreses." A catachresis is a figurative name that is not figurative, because it does not substitute for any literal word that is given or could be given – for example, *leg of a table, face of a mountain, eye of a storm. Gabrielinos* is such a nickname. The giving of the name anticipated the literal vanishing of the Indians. They had already vanished into the white man's name, though, *pace* Williams, their own name for themselves was already such a vanishing. Among the most powerful of such sobriquets, nicknames, or catachreses is *materiality* or *material base* as the name for the whole region of what presumably exists outside language. The concept of the material base involves the area of rhetorical study where the tropes apostrophe, catachresis, and prosopopoeia overlap and diverge. Such mastery of the problem of materiality as is possible will be attained only through the study and understanding of these tropes – no easy task, since the terms necessarily used for the study are bound up with the very thing that is to be studied.

Perhaps the closest we teachers of language and literature can come in our everyday work to glimpsing what we have erased, forgotten, or even forgotten that we have forgotten is in that most ordinary of experiences for the literary scholar, the act of holding a book in one's hand and reading, that is, confronting face to face the materiality of the inscription. The trouble is that the inscription makes the matter invisible once more. We do not see the paper for the words. Another way to put this is to say that reading is always theoretical. Theory, even a theory of the material base, is precisely a clear seeing that turns the material base, this particular piece of paper here and now, into a generalized and generalizable abstraction. The triumph of theory is the resistance to reading in the sense that theory erases the particularity of the unique act of reading, but reading itself is always theoretical in the sense of performing the erasure and forgetting before we know what is happening and without our being able to know. So even the most vigilant and theoretically enlightened reading is the resistance to reading. Nevertheless, a rhetorically sophisticated reading is our best hope at least of remembering that we have forgotten and that we must forget. For this reason I affirm that the future of literary studies depends on maintaining and developing that rhetorical reading which today is most commonly called "deconstruction."

I conclude by addressing some respectful suggestions to the critics and antagonists of deconstruction on the so-called left and the so-called right. To those of the right I say that deconstruction by no means destroys literary studies, nor has it caused or exacerbated some crisis in English studies or in humanistic studies generally. On the contrary, deconstruction and literary theory generally are the only way to respond to the actual conditions – cultural, economic, institutional, and technological – within which literary study is carried on today. Literary theory is the only way to avoid the sequestering of literature within an aestheticism of "organic form" that deprives the study of literature of any effective purchase on our society. That most traditional of humanistic responsibilities and missions, archival preservation, the remembering and storing up of literature, philosophy, and history, will be performed effectively only if the university remains open to the kind of questioning posed by deconstruction, as well as by other forms of theory. This is true even where that questioning extends to things that seem fundamental to the very foundation of the university.

The university can live only in an atmosphere of open debate, maintaining that freedom of speech, thought, and writing which is one of America's most precious heritages, something without which the university as we know it cannot exist. Among the greatest dangers to the humanities today are attempts to suppress and curtail this freedom. Such attempts are all the more unethical when they are directed against the younger, nontenured members of our profession. I mean all sorts of subtle and not so subtle acts that their older colleagues can perform within the bounds of normal procedure and with a clear conscience: denial of tenure, refusal to hire in the first place, denial of active roles on departmental and university committees, perhaps worst of all refusal to publish essays and books that seem threatening. Here I agree with John Stuart Mill. Truth does not need the protection of any sort of censorship. It will flourish best in an atmosphere of free debate, in teaching and in writing. Any foreclosure of that debate poses a mortal danger to the university. I am for diversity, for heterogeneity in the university, not for a permissive pluralism that says "anything goes," but for a fair and open fight for survival that is not even sure the fittest will survive but recognizes such an open fight as our only hope.

The current argument for foreclosing debate often takes the form of claiming that there is a crisis in English studies or in the humanities generally, that theory is destroying literary studies and that something urgently needs to be done to eliminate the theorists. This idea of a crisis is made up out of the clichés of the mass media and out of the anxiety of those who feel that things are going in the wrong direction in our profession. There is no crisis in the humanities. Quite the opposite. There is, rather, a tremendous vitality, a multiform intellectual energy and healthy diversity in all the fields and modes of our disciplines. This vitality involves vocational commitments that are often touchingly hopeful and even unworldly, the commitment, for example, of the highly talented young students who apply for graduate work in the humanities even without the assurance that there will be enough secure jobs for them, or the dedication of the so-called independent humanistic scholars, who face apparently impossible obstacles. Or there is the tremendous intellectual energy released by the development of women's studies, an energy often blocked and thwarted under the old male-dominated modes of study, canon formation, and curricular organization.

Far from being in a crisis, we are at a moment of great intellectual challenge and opportunity, especially for young scholars, critics, and teachers. They will be taking over the profession during the next decade and making unusually rapid innovations in it, unless their elders prevent them from making the changes necessary in our altered social, economic, and institutional conditions. Our students, with all their increasing racial, linguistic, and cultural diversity, are hungry for what the humanities can give them, but they will not be fooled by promises of amnesty and citizenship in the republic of letters if they just adopt traditional values and study the traditional canon, any more than men are going to talk or coerce women into coming back into the fold of the male-dominated canon and ways of literary study. So, if you are among the conservative members of our profession, I can say that you have everything to gain by being open to literary theory. Theory is essential to going forward in humanistic study today.

If you oppose theory from the so-called left, I say you should make common cause with those who practice a rhetorical study of literature, that is, with the multiform movement called "deconstruction," of which a rhetorical study of literature is one vector of force. Your commitment to history, to society, to an exploration of the material base of literature, of its economic conditions, its institutions, the realities of class and gender distinctions that underlie literature – this commitment will inevitably fall into the hands of those with antithetical positions to yours as long as you hold to an unexamined ideology of the material base, that is, to a notion that is metaphysical through and through, as much a part of Western metaphysics as the idealism you would contest. "Deconstruction" is the current name for the multiple and heterogeneous strategies of overturning and displacement that will liberate your own enterprise from what disables it. Among its tasks is that rereading of Marx in which Andrew Parker, Gregory Jay, and many other brilliant younger scholars are currently involved.

As a matter of fact many young (and not so young) scholars are working less at a frontier than on both sides of the apparent canyon between history and language. They are doing the difficult work of thinking out the relation between language and history. They are trying to see whether or not that canyon is a bottomless gulf, whether bridges can be thrown across, whether shouts can be heard from one side to the other, or whether the canyon itself is illusory, the product of our own confusions. One thing is sure: this gulf may not be bridged, traversed, negotiated, or shouted across by those who are not willing to understand "cultural critique" to mean rigorous and vigilant critique not only of positional theories of language that are (falsely) claimed to be intrinsically reactionary and politically ineffective but also of the concepts of culture, critique, history, and especially, as I have been arguing here, the material base. That base must not be taken for granted as safely outside the range of critique. It must not be presupposed as the transcendent given with which the critique begins. Among those engaged in this work from one position or another, perhaps in the end from wholly incompatible positions, from one side of the canyon or down in its depths (but the more points of entry to this question the better), I name, in no particular order, not only Parker and Jay but also Michael Sprinker, Deborah Esch, Thomas Keenen, Cynthia Chase, John Rowe, Jonathan Arac, Michael

Ryan, Ned Lukacher, Gayatri Spivak, Andrzej Warminski, David Carroll, Suzanne Gearhart, Jean-Luc Nancy, and Philippe Lacoue-Labarthe. Much depends on facilitating their thinking and on allowing it to be institutionally effective, productive, not "merely theoretical." I hail all those I have named and the others not named who are also engaged in this thinking. You are my collaborators in a common task, even when you attack me or my close associates in ways that seem to me perverse or irrational, or even when I feel sure that you have "got it wrong" in what you say about the material base and the ideological superstructure.

I conclude by saying that our main professional responsibility, at all levels of instruction, remains what it has always been, to teach the basics: reading and the good writing that can only occur if it is accompanied by good reading. The 'rithmetic alone of the three r's we can mostly leave to our colleagues in other disciplines, though even for us some counting and quantifying are often necessary. Reading here includes not only written texts but all the signs that surround and penetrate us, all images visual and sonorous, the evidences of history that are always one form or another of signs to be read: documents, paintings, films, scores, or "material" artifacts. Reading is the common ground on which all of us can meet to fight out our differences, with the texts and other sign systems to be read laid out on the table between us, so to speak. These include the texts of theory.

To teach reading and writing is a tremendous task. Everything conspires against it, including many aspects both of that turn to history and of that triumph of theory I have identified as the chief features on the terrain of literary studies today. Real reading is not just a recognition of the way the rhetorical or tropological dimension of language undermines straightforward grammatical and logical meaning. It is also an attempt, no doubt an impossible attempt, to confront what language itself has always already erased or forgotten, namely, the performative or positional power of language as inscription over what we catachrestically call the material.

Notes

1. William Carlos Williams, *In the American Grain* (New York, 1956).
2. Paul de Man, "The Resistance to Theory," *The Resistance to Theory* (Minneapolis, 1986), pp. 3–20.
3. Henry James, *Roderick Hudson* (New York, 1971).
4. Paul de Man, "Hypogram and Inscription," *The Resistance to Theory* (Minneapolis, 1986), pp. 27–53.
5. *Bakhtin: Essays and Dialogues on His Work*, Gary Saul Morson (ed.) (Chicago, 1986).

22

The ethics of reading

Here are the first two lines of William Carlos Williams' "Young Sycamore," a poem from *Collected Poems 1934*:

> I must tell you
> This young tree . . .

Why *must* the poet tell the reader? What obligation, compulsion, or imperative compels him to speak? What law must he obey? The rest of this little poem of twenty-four short lines does little more, at least so it seems, than describe the tree as it "rises bodily" from its "round and firm trunk" all the way up to the "two/eccentric knotted/twigs/bending forward/hornlike at the top." Nothing could be more commonplace, or, in a sense, more trivial. Such a poem would seem to have little to do with ethical concerns, with individual or social values, or with the urgent need expressed in the opening line. Nevertheless, the poet says, "I must tell you," as though matters of great import were at stake.

Is the demand on the poet to tell a moral one, or is it ontological, perhaps ultimately a religious obligation? Or is it epistemological, a need to pass on an objective knowledge the poet has acquired, perhaps on the assumption that *veritas vos liberabit*, the truth will make you free? Or is it, finally, merely an aesthetic demand, an obligation on the poet to make a beautiful work of art, an object made of words capable of producing disinterested aesthetic pleasure in the reader, freedom in another sense? Much is at stake in the answers we give to these questions. No less is at stake than our commitment to one or another set of presuppositions about the role of literature in individual and social life, as well as in our schools, colleges, and universities. The questions ask why literature should be read and taught and, ultimately, which works, who should teach them, and in what kind of institutional setting.

If the poet has an irresistible compulsion to tell what he has seen or knows, this obligation is passed on in turn to the reader, critic, and teacher. The situation of the teacher in relation to his or her students is

---

The final pages of this essay appeared in a slightly different form in Robert Moynihan's *A Recent Imagining: Interviews with Harold Bloom, Geoffrey Hartman, J. Hillis Miller, and Paul de Man* (Hamden, 1986).

like that of the poet in relation to the reader. The teacher too has seen something, in this case in the poem. He or she too knows something perhaps others do not know and is compelled to pass it on to his or her students. The teacher too is under a moral compulsion, or must be if the teaching is to be of value. All good teaching involves therefore another version of the "I must tell you." Teaching is an ethical situation of the most concrete and particular sort: person to person. The teacher faces the students in the classroom across the open books bearing the text of the poem.

There is, however, it is easy to see, a possible conflict between the teacher's obligation to the poem and his or her obligation to students, to those in authority in his or her institution, to the canon of accepted works, to the canonical interpretation of those works (including canonical readings of noncanonical works), to the curriculum with all its attendant circumstances, of which this particular class and the teaching of this particular poem are parts. Which of these obligations should take precedence over the others in case of a conflict? Suppose the teacher finds something in the poem which differs radically from the expectations implied by the poem's placement in the textbook, in the curriculum, in the canon of "great works"? William Empson, for example, surely a gifted reader, found the theology and attendant morality of Milton's *Paradise Lost* "appalling." If it is "appalling," should the poem be taught? On what grounds could we decide whether or not it is appalling?

Suppose a teacher reaches the conviction that if he or she tells what he or she knows about a particular work to this particular student it will be morally detrimental to that student? Perhaps for most students most of the time this would not be the case, but here is one student on whom, the teacher is convinced, this work, canonical though it may be, will have a bad moral effect. Does the obligation to the poem, to the institution, or to the student take precedence in such cases? It does not go without saying that works of literature, even those everyone agrees are classics, will have a beneficial effect on all those who read them, all of the time, or be socially constructive. One finds the strangest and most unexpectedly dark things said in those great works, for example in Sophocles and the Bible: "Not to be born is best/when all is reckoned in, but once a man has seen the light/the next best thing, by far, is to go back where he came from, quickly as he can" (*Oedipus at Colonus*, ll 1388–90); "For whosoever hath, to him shall be given, and he shall have more abundance: but whosoever hath not, from him shall be taken away even that he hath. Therefore speak I to them in parables: because they seeing see not; and hearing they hear not, neither do they understand" (Matthew 13:12–13). Such statements, even in their full contexts, take some explaining, and one can easily imagine a situation in which even the explaining would not keep them from being dubious in their effect.

From the other direction, what exactly are the moral obligations of those in charge of appropriating money for educational budgets in the humanities, of hiring the teachers, setting curricula, granting tenure, awarding scholarships, fellowships, and research leaves, approving the publication of books and articles, deciding who gets to teach summer seminars, or becomes a fellow of this or that humanities institute? These decisions are not so much a question of saying, "I must tell you," as saying, "You must tell them." Matthew Arnold gave expression to a particularly fierce version of this third kind of "must" (and incidentally took a view of Milton radically different from Empson's) when he wrote, in a letter to his friend Arthur Hugh Clough in 1848 or 1849: "Those who cannot read G[ree]k sh[ou]ld read nothing but Milton and parts of Wordsworth: the state should see to it."

Though we do not have a "state" with this kind of authority, and though the United States is a free country more or less without censorship laws, this does not mean that there may not be a diffuse form of imposition and, on the other hand, of censorship or even of the attempted suppression of certain ideas and attitudes. This kind of censorship may be all the more powerful for being diffuse, not overtly articulated, and not located in any single institution of bureaucratic power. It is rather located in the discreet and tactful decisions of the more or less benign and rarely, if ever, conspiratorial interlocking directorate made up of a relatively small number of people who serve from year to year on countless committees of selection, write countless letters of recommendation and letters concerning promotion and tenure, serve as editors or on advisory boards, and so on. This system works well enough, and I would not have it all that different, perhaps because I have certainly had my share in all these decisions. But I want to stress here that those on these committees and editorial boards have a tremendous moral obligation. It is the obligation to decide, ultimately, what gets published, who teaches, and what gets taught. One way to glimpse the scope of this responsibility is to recognize what a large difference relatively small changes can make: for example, changes in the methodology of literary interpretation such as are conspicuously taking place now or, to give another apparently but probably not really different example, the shift to a greater importance in programs in comparative literature as opposed to those in the national literatures.

Such questions – questions about the value and use of literature, questions about the ethical and political responsibilities of writers, teachers, and those who choose the teachers – are beginning again to be asked after a long period when they were often said to be irrelevant. As

William Beaty Warner has recently written, "There is something new in the winds of criticism. It is a shift in theory and away from theory; it involves both an affirmation or recuperation of the language-centered critical theory of the last fifteen years, as well as a call toward concerns that are social, political, and historical." No doubt such concerns have never ceased to be part of literary study at any time during the modern history of the development of such study. This history is one of the products of the eighteenth-century enlightenment and of the ensuing flowering of romanticism. Social questions were of course a constant concern of Matthew Arnold, a major influence on the development of humanistic study in America. The relation of literature to society was also a central issue for Friedrich Schiller, a strong influence on Arnold. Schiller's *Letters on the Aesthetic Education of Man* transmitted to Arnold a somewhat distorted version of Kant's exploration in the *Critique of Judgment* of the question of whether art could serve as the bridge between epistemology and ethics and be, as he put it, "the symbol of morality." For Schiller, aesthetic experience, including the reading of literature, is on the one hand a self-sufficient realm of interrelated elements, like the figures in a dance. Like a dance, aesthetic experience is its own end. On the other hand, this self-enclosed, nonutilitarian object of aesthetic contemplation offers a powerful model for political and social organization. When Schiller speaks of the "aesthetic state" he means by "state" both "condition" and "political authority." The aesthetic realm was indeed the "symbol" of social and political morality. Free men and women in society act nevertheless in patterned give and take under the constraints of laws as compelling as those of the rules of a dance. Schiller's celebrated metaphor of art as play is by no means so politically innocent as it may at first appear.

The twentieth-century development of literary study in America has continued to contain in one way or another this tension between seeing literature as self-sufficient and detached, the object of disinterested aesthetic contemplation, and, on the contrary, seeing it as capable and indeed obligated to exert political and moral force on the reality of history. The so-called "New Criticism" of the forties and fifties tended to lean toward the first of these options and to sequester the interpretation of poems, novels, or plays from ethical, social, and political questions.

It has no doubt been assumed all along that reading Homer, Shakespeare, or Milton; Hemingway, Faulkner, or Virginia Woolf is an important part of a college education. It is no doubt assumed that such reading will make people better lawyers, doctors, scientists, bureaucrats, businessmen, or soldiers. The exact mode of the transaction or transfer from literary study to vocational activity has nevertheless not often been thought through clearly or made explicit. Perhaps it has been one of those aspects of the college and university curriculum which those in charge have an obscure sense should not be made too explicit. Its happy functioning perhaps depends on being taken for granted or "going without saying." Perhaps we have had a sense that in this area too, as Winnie Verloc puts it in Conrad's *The Secret Agent*, "things don't stand much looking into."

One form this reticence has taken is the programmatic suspension of questions of belief and practical effect in the New Criticism. This suspension has recently been reaffirmed in a vigorous essay by Cleanth Brooks. In this essay Brooks reasserts the tenets of the New Criticism against more recent ways of studying literature:

> Milton tells us in the opening lines of *Paradise Lost* that his purpose is to "justify the ways of God to man," and there is no reason to doubt that this was what he hoped to do. But what we actually have in the poem is a wonderful interconnected story of events in heaven and hell and upon earth, with grand and awesome scenes brilliantly painted and with heroic actions dramatically rendered. In short, generations of readers have found that the grandeur of the poem far exceeds any direct statement of theological views. The point is underscored by the fact that some readers who reject Milton's theology altogether nevertheless regard *Paradise Lost* as a great poem.[1] (162)

All honor to Brooks and to the revolution in the teaching of literature in America, the turn to "close reading," he did so much to bring about! Nevertheless, by detaching *Paradise Lost* so completely from its theological and moral assertions, by putting aside questions about what might happen if someone took *Paradise Lost* seriously and grounded her or his actions on it in the real world of moral and ethical decision, Brooks tends to trivialize the poem. He makes the teaching of *Paradise Lost* vulnerable to those who say it has no necessary place in a modern college curriculum. If *Paradise Lost* is no more than a "wonderful story" and grand painted scenes, could not its function in the classroom be fulfilled just as well, perhaps better, by the screening of a Cecil B. De Mille spectacular, with a cast of thousands? In at least one major midwestern state university, undergraduate courses in Milton are given only about once every three years because there is so little call for them. If the self-subsistent realm of the aesthetic is cut off from epistemology and ethics, if literature becomes primarily valuable as spectacle, as appearance, as "feeling" (as the etymology of "aesthetic" suggests), then this particular human need can be satisfied in far easier ways, for example by television or cinema, and without all that hard work of reading and of learning new vocabulary.

Quite recently, however, the relations of literature to ethics, to history, and to society have once more become a frontier subject in literary study, in books and articles, in new journals recently established, in symposia and colloquia, in the programs of humanities institutes. A new and more sophisticated interest in the sociology of literature, inspired in part by a vigorous and more intellectually cogent American Marxist criticism, is widely influential. This development is much indebted to the work of Michel Foucault. In the United States it is associated with Fredric Jameson, Edward Said, Gayatri Spivak, Frank Lentricchia, and many others. Many of the brightest young minds in literary study today, along with many established older scholars, are turning back in teaching, in writing, in fellowship proposals, to these questions about the relations of literature to history, to moral choice, and to public decision-making. If such questions are again coming to the fore, they are of necessity being asked in a new context. This is not only the context of our present social and political situation, including the situation of education in America, but also the context of those language-centered methods of reading which have been so much the focus of attention over the last forty years. For better or worse, literary study in America will never be the same after structuralism, semiotics, deconstruction, and poststructuralism.

The most challenging or disturbing of these new methods of reading is no doubt so-called "deconstruction." This has been both widely influential and widely attacked. The attacks have come from the left and from the right, both from intellectual conservatives and from self-styled intellectual radicals. From the right, deconstruction is sometimes seen as destroying literary study, while from the left it is attacked as élitist, as in cahoots with the status quo. It is hard to see how it could be both of these at once. Though a rationale for that could be imagined, more likely deconstruction threatens the good conscience of both sides. Deconstruction is the nerve center of the present controversy, the pivot of the shift William Beaty Warner describes. Deconstruction cannot by definition be defined or delimited, since it is fundamentally a recognition of a mobility within language or from one language to another. Certainly it is not to be encompassed by identifying it as merely one mode of reading among others. As Jacques Derrida[2] has recently argued, "deconstruction in America" has manifold aspects and vectors of force – political aspects, ethical ones, religious, technological, academic, professional, and institutional aspects – along with its more restricted role as a procedure in the interpretation of texts, or perhaps rather on the basis of that. In all these areas it has already effected major shifts within the academy and not only within the academy.

To identify briefly the challenges deconstruction has posed will indicate what it is with which the turn back to ethical, political, and historical questions must come to terms. Deconstruction both puts in question some traditional assumptions in the study of literature and proposes new ways of doing such study and of organizing it institutionally. These affirmations are made in the most grounded way possible, namely in the course of new readings of literary and philosophical texts, for example in the books of de Man and Derrida.

Deconstruction has challenged the assumption that a literary work can be accounted for by reference to the originating selfhood of the writer. It has questioned the assumption that literary history, or history as such, is a series of definable "periods" that develop from one to another according to some paradigm of organic growth. (Such metaphors are almost irresistible. I have used them myself here in my account of the "development" of literary studies in America or in speaking of the "flowering" of literary theory or in my suggestion that Kant begat Schiller begat Arnold begat Trilling or, more generally, humanistic study in America. What, exactly, is the mode of transfer, translation, or carrying over involved in each of these transactions?) Deconstruction has, in addition, challenged the assumption that a good work should have or does have a single, determinable, organically unified meaning. It has challenged the assumption that language, including the language of literature, is primarily referential, that it initially names some extra-linguistic state of things and draws its value from its accuracy and force in doing that. Deconstruction, finally, has patiently shown, through the careful reading of a variety of texts both literary and philosophical, that figurative language is not an adventitious flourish added to a literal base, but that language, including the language of literature, is figurative through and through, all the way down to the bottom, so to speak.

Since the knowledge of figures of speech is traditionally part of the study of rhetoric, it can be said that the rearrangement or reconstruction of the teaching of literature proposed by so-called deconstruction is "trivial" in the etymological sense of having to do with the *trivium*, that three-branched road of medieval education in the liberal arts which led from grammar to logic and then to rhetoric. The *trivium* was preliminary to the higher study of the *quadrivium*: arithmetic, geometry, astronomy, and music. Things were somewhat simpler then, but the *trivium* remains basic in a liberal arts education today. Deconstruction, as a renewal of rhetoric in the sense of a study of the role in language of figures of speech, has challenged the claims of both grammar and logic to be able to encompass, contain, and give the law to the tropological dimension of language.

This new form of rhetorical study has often, not surprisingly, been seen as purely negative and threatening, as "the word turned upside down," as evidence of a "crisis in English studies," or even as "destroying literary studies," to cite the titles of three recent vigorous attacks on it, the first by John Searle,[3] the second by Walter Jackson Bate,[4] the third by René Wellek.[5] These essays are striking in their misinterpretation of what they attack. They have a penchant for making the critics they attack say something farcically different from what in fact they have said, or they suppress, as if by inadvertence, the fact that they are not disinterested observers; Searle, for example, has been involved in an exchange of essays with the object of his attack, though he does not mention that in his attack. In such polemics we see distinguished professors from prestigious institutions losing all sense of scholarly responsibility and lashing out blindly at something they have apparently not taken the trouble to read carefully or to understand. These attacks are certainly not examples of the ethics of reading as I am defining it here.

The sources of this unreasoning defensiveness are clear enough and familiar enough. When fundamental changes, changes going all the way down to the bottom, are taking place in a discipline and in the relation of that discipline to the university and to society, then it is likely to seem, to those who feel themselves safely ensconced within the old way of carrying on that discipline, like "a remarkable example of the confusion into which the present age has fallen; of the obliteration of landmarks, the opening of floodgates, and the uprooting of distinctions," to borrow the words of Sir Leicester Dedlock in Dickens' *Bleak House*. For better or worse, however, this new form of the old rhetorical study of literature has already been widely institutionalized, in courses, in departmental curricula, in hiring policies, in new programs in literature, in new journals, and so on. Deconstruction is also beginning to have a strong influence on the study of philosophy in America. Moreover, as I have said, it is this revived rhetoric which is responding to the actual nature and needs of the society within which our colleges and universities function today. It is these new forms of rhetoric and poetics that will lead the way toward that taking of responsibility for language, for literature, and for the role of these in society and history which is called for today.

Now it might be argued that to expose the study of literature to social and ethical concerns is to run the risk of censorship by functionaries who have no understanding of literature or of the aesthetic values enshrined in it. I see the force of this objection and grant that allowing literature to be thought of as active in personal life and in society raises all sorts of dangers of shallow misinterpretation and blind censorship by special interest groups. I make two answers to such objections. One is the fact that there is already, as I have said, a diffuse, often unarticulated and perhaps therefore all the more dangerous form of censorship in all those choices made of who teaches or publishes what. Much might be gained by bringing out into the open the grounds of those choices and by providing occasions for their discussion. The second answer is that the other side of the freedom gained by a purely aesthetic view of literature is the way such a view tends to render literature harmless, useless, a mere superficial adornment of the serious business of preparing for a job or a profession in our technological and industrial society. Students have a way of knowing where the action is. If enrollments in literature courses have gone down drastically in many colleges and universities, if numbers of majors have declined, offerings become thinner, it may be because such courses and majors do not have any longer a clear role in preparing students for private and public life after graduation. It is not that students see their education as purely instrumental. They are too shrewd for that. But they have a sure instinct, for the most part, for what has force, what makes for life. Students may have been able to figure out that the old aesthetic justification does not carry much weight any longer, perhaps never was cogent. It may in fact be used by administrators and others as a way of neutralizing the study of literature, through the very act of paying pious lip service to it. They thereby make sure it will not be likely to have much power or active effect on the lives of students. Meanwhile, the university can get on imperturbably with its real business of performing manifold services to our scientific, technological, and industrialized society, for example by developing and testing out new computer hardware or software, or by providing a place for that growing cooperation between industry and the university which is so much a part of the academic scene today, in short, by fulfilling the general commitment of the university to that universal principle of accounting for everything, the principle of accountability or principle of reason under which the modern university operates. *Nihil est sine ratione*: nothing is without reason.[6] It is in this area, it may be, that the "must" of an imperative obligation constrains the modern university, not in any "I must tell you" involving poetry.

Unless this challenge is faced head-on by asking directly what ethical, social, and political role the study of literature in America might have or should have, the decline in literary study may well continue. Departments of English literature may well once more be reduced to their original role as departments of rhetoric in the sense of English composition. We must dare to ask whether or not the theology of *Paradise Lost* is appalling; whether Sophocles is right about human life and how we should act from day to day if he is; whether George Eliot is right when she says, in *Middlemarch*, "We all of us, grave or light, get our thoughts entangled in metaphors, and act fatally on the strength of them," and what our teaching of language and of literature should be if this is true; and so on for each of the works we choose to teach or have taught. Whatever changes might be brought about by asking these questions, and they would be considerable, it is only by asking and answering them that literature can be given an other than peripheral place in the contemporary college or university. It is because so many teachers are asking such questions, even in defiance of the ideology of literary study in which they may have been brought up, that such study is faring as well as it is these days.

Exactly what in detail the establishment of a new ethics of reading might be like it would be presumptuous of me to try to spell out here. The new role for literary study can only be defined by serious and prolonged discussion involving young and old, conservatives and radicals in literary study, theorists, literary historians, teachers of composition, Marxists, feminists, and the rest. Much intellectual courage and willingness to suspend vested interests would be necessary to make such give and take productive, but the conditions are right to make such productive discussion possible. Let me try, however, to specify the essential outlines of what might be necessary to recover the old urgency of the "I must tell you" in the teaching of literature.

The primary ethical obligation of the teacher of literature is to the work of literature. If there is a conflict between that and the teacher's obligation to students, in one direction, and to the institution, in the other, the obligation to the work takes precedence by an implacable law of reading. Though one can imagine a situation in which a teacher might choose to remain silent about what she has seen in a work by not teaching that work, if she teaches the work at all, she must tell it like it is. The whole sequence of obligations begins with the act of reading and with the call or demand that the work makes on its reader. Good reading means noncanonical reading, that is, a willingness to recognize the unexpected, perhaps even the shocking or scandalous, present even in canonical works, perhaps especially in canonical works, in Homer, Dante, or Shakespeare, in Milton or Wordsworth, even in Matthew Arnold himself, for example in his *Empedocles on Etna* or in those strange books on the Bible he wrote at the end of his life. By a noncanonical reading I do not mean a critical relativism or a placing of meaning in the "reader's response," a freedom to make the work mean anything one likes, but just the reverse. I mean a response to the demand made by the words on the page, an ability, unfortunately not all that common, to respond to what the words on the page say rather than to what we wish they said or came to the book expecting them to say.

Good reading does not occur all that often, not as often as one might perhaps expect or wish. Perhaps it occurs most often in those who are also good writers. Good reading is by no means a direct result of the reader's "theoretical" presuppositions. Literary theory may facilitate or inhibit good reading, but woe to the reader who goes to a work simply to find confirmation of her theory. She will certainly find what she seeks, but she will not have read the work. Good reading is more likely to lead to the disconfirmation or severe modification of a theory than to offer any firm support for it. Reading, not theory, is the one irreplaceable necessity in the teaching of literature. The rare ability to see the object, in this case a poem, a novel, a play, or a work of philosophy, as in itself it really is, to borrow Arnold's phrasing again, is the one thing necessary in the good teacher of literature. The strangest and most surprising things are present in those great books if we have the wit to see them. Those canonized classics remain in the libraries and bookstores, or on our own shelves at home, like so many unexploded time bombs ready to go off when there is the conjunction of the work and the good reader of that work. Such conjunctions make something happen and have their ethical effects, but exactly what these may be can never be certainly predicted in advance.

My second conviction about the new ethics of reading is that its primary obligation will be or ought to be philological. The teaching of literature must be based on a love for language, a care for language and for what language can do. The study of literature must begin with language and must remain focused there. Its primary tools are citation and discussion of that citation. Such study must be a rhetoric and a poetics before it is literary history or a repertoire of the ideas which have been expressed through the centuries in literature. The necessity of this primary focus on language as such is perhaps the most controversial of the assertions I am making here. Perhaps it is too much to expect departments of English and the other modern languages to give up so much of the prerogative to teach everything under the sun but their primary subject matter and to concentrate on their real business of teaching good reading, but since good reading is fundamentally necessary to good writing, such an apparent narrowing of scope would have the great virtue of bringing together the teaching of reading and the teaching of composition. Moreover, it is only on the basis of the knowledge of what language is and what it can do, what we can do with it and what we cannot do with it, that it is possible to move on to those questions I began by asking about the role of literature in private and social morality, in history, and in the making of public policy.

Here, finally, is a third feature of the new ethics of reading as I foresee it: We may rejoice that the United States is well on the way to recognizing that it is a multilingual not a monolingual country. We may rejoice also that impressive advances in the teaching of languages have been made and incorporated into many secondary school curricula. Some students actually come to college now already knowing a second language well. I said earlier that there has been a shift in the center of gravity of literary study away from the national literatures studied separately to one form or another of comparative literature or of interdisciplinary study. The new forms of this, however, would put in question the idea of translatability which was often a presupposition of older forms of comparative literature. Translation is now seen as a problem, a topic of fundamental importance to be studied, not a solution. The new rhetoric and poetics presuppose a fundamental untranslatability from language to language. They might take Walter Benjamin's "Die Aufgabe des Übersetzers" (roughly to be translated as "The Task of the Translator") as a signal text for beginning to understand why this is so, as a fact about language. This does not mean that it is not better to read Homer or Dante, Descartes or Hegel, Tolstoi, Baudelaire, or Benjamin himself in the best translation available (though how would you know it was best?), rather than not read them at all, just as those who do not read Greek should read Milton and parts of Wordsworth. But it does mean that readers can never trust a translation any more than they can trust what a secondary book or a teacher says is going on in a given work of literature or philosophy. If you are to have a hope of finding that out you must read the work yourself, in the original. This obligation of the reader to respond to the demand made by the text remains the primary imperative in the ethics of reading.

Notes

1. Cleanth Brooks, "The Primacy of the Author," *The Missouri Review*, 6.2 (1983), pp. 161–72.
2. Jacques Derrida, "Mnemosyne," *Mémoires for Paul de Man* (New York, 1986), pp. 3–43.
3. John Searle, "The Word Turned Upside Down," *The New York Review of Books*, 27 (Oct. 1983), pp. 74–8.
4. Walter Jackson Bate, "The Crisis in English Studies," *Harvard Magazine*, 85 (1982), pp. 46–53.
5. René Wellek, "Destroying Literary Studies," *The New Criterion* (Dec. 1983), pp. 1–8.
6. Jacques Derrida, "The Principle of Reason: The University in the Eyes of its Pupils," tr. Catherine Porter and Edward P. Morris, *diacritics*, 13 (1983), pp. 3–20.

23

"Reading" part of a paragraph in *Allegories of Reading*

Any reader of Paul de Man's work is likely to be struck by certain aphoristic formulations that seem deliberately provocative in their all-or-nothing generality and in their slightly defiant irony. Examples are the following: "Conceptual language, the foundation of civil society, is also, it appears, a lie superimposed upon an error" (*AR*, 155). "One sees from this that the impossibility of reading should not be taken too lightly" (*AR*, 245). "We never lie as much as when we want to do full justice to ourselves, especially in self-accusation" (*AR*, 269–70). Among such sentences is the one in "Allegory (*Julie*)" that says, "The paradigm of all texts consists of a figure (or a system of figures) and its deconstruction" (*AR*, 205). I want to try here to "read" this sentence and the remaining part of the paragraph in which it appears (it comes in the middle) – in defiance of de Man's demonstration that reading is impossible.

I was led to this attempted act of reading as a preparation for reading what de Man says on p. 206 of *Allegories of Reading* about the necessary ethical moment in all allegories, that is, in all texts, since for de Man all texts are allegories of their own unreadability. "Ethicity," like other forms of reference to the extralinguistic by way of the linguistic, occurs for de Man not at the beginning, as a basis for language, and not at the end, as a final triumphant return to reality that validates language, but in the midst of an intricate sequence. The sequentiality of this sequence is of course only a fiction, a convenience for thinking as a narrative what in fact always occurs in the tangle of an "all at once" mixing tropological, allegorical, referential, ethical, political, and historical dimensions. I have discussed the ethics of reading in de Man elsewhere. Here my focus is on part of p. 205.

De Man has been reading the second preface to *Julie*, which leads him to the assertion that as soon as any document is seen as a text, that is, "questioned as to its rhetorical mode," "its readability is put into question" (*AR*, 204). An example is the way the second preface "puts into question" the readability of *Julie* by indicating that it is impossible to know whether Rousseau made it up or whether it is a collection of "real" letters. In the context of this discussion, de Man draws himself up and makes a series of apodictic statements about the rhetorical makeup of *all* texts. It is a good example of the way the theoretical generalizations he makes always occur within a specific context and have a somewhat different meaning when they are abstracted from that context, even though they affirm their independence of any context in that all-encompassing "all." Here is the series of generalizations that forms the essential preliminary presupposition for de Man's assertions about the ethical moment in reading:

> The paradigm for all texts consists of a figure (or a system of figures) and its deconstruction. But since this model cannot be closed off in a final reading, it engenders, in its turn, a supplementary figural superposition which narrates the unreadability of the prior narration. As distinguished from primary deconstructive narratives centered on figures and ultimately always on metaphor, we can call such narratives to the second (or the third) degree *allegories*. Allegorical narratives tell the story of the failure to read whereas tropological narratives, such as the *Second Discourse*, tell the story of the failure to denominate. The difference is only a difference of degree and the allegory does not erase the figure. Allegories are always allegories of metaphor and, as such, they are always allegories of the impossibility of reading – a sentence in which the genitive "of" has itself to be "read" as a metaphor. (*AR*, 205)

This series of sentences says a mouthful, as they say. Much of the de Man of *Allegories of Reading* is compactly folded together here. The reader who can understand these sentences will have gone a long way toward understanding *Allegories of Reading* as a "whole," though unfortunately the sentences cannot be "understood," if that word applies at all here, without a careful reading of that "whole." The confident absolutist tone of de Man's assertion, with its "all" and "always," is likely to lead the reader who is at all inclined to skepticism to raise questions: "All?" "Always?" Is de Man perhaps guilty of that tyrannical absolutism of the "one" on which Hölderlin pronounced his malediction in an epigram: "Whence comes among men the cursed wish that there should only be the one and that everything should come from the one?" It is a familiar reproach to deconstruction that it finds always the same thing in every text and that it finds, moreover, what the deconstructor has gone to the text expecting to find. Is de Man guilty of this crime? Is it possible not to be guilty of it? Do those who reproach deconstruction in this way mean anything more than that they prefer their own version of the "one" to that of deconstruction? How could one simultaneously respect the particularity of a particular text and at the same time respect the law which that text exemplifies? This is in fact, is it not, just what is always in question in any speculation about ethics, including no doubt the ethics of reading? Each ethical situation, including each act of reading, insofar as it involves ethical judgment or responsibility, is unique, but how can it be truly ethical if it is not in response to an unconditional law? And surely each reader would wish to be ethical in his or her reading![1] De Man is no doubt, like everyone else, faced with the necessity of somehow fulfilling this double obligation, and as for always finding the same thing, I defy any reader to predict beforehand exactly what de Man will find to say about a given text, any more than the reader of Henry James' *What Maisie Knew* can predict exactly what Maisie is going to say and do when she makes the crucial decision of her life. De Man, like Maisie, seems to be subject to a law, in this case a law of reading, to which only he has access.

There is a further problem, related to this one. The use of the terms "metaphor," "narrative," "reading," and "allegory" in the passage I am discussing is idiosyncratic, to say the least. At any rate the terms are puzzlingly opaque when taken out of the context of, for example, the essays elsewhere in *Allegories of Reading* on metaphor in Nietzsche and in Rousseau, and on reading in Proust. When de Man says the paradigm for all texts consists of a figure (or a system of figures) and its deconstruction, the reader must have in mind the radical theory of figure worked out with the help of Nietzsche and Rousseau. For de Man (or for Rousseau and Nietzsche as he reads them) the act of literal denomination is already an (aberrant) metaphor, blindly imposing a word brought from another realm to cover an ignorance that can by no means be turned into certain knowledge. In the example from Rousseau that de Man discusses at length, a primitive man in his fear names another man he encounters a giant, but since the correspondence of outside appearance and inside nature can never be verified, the metaphor remains suspended, aberrant. That error is further compounded when I deliberately invent the conceptual word "man" to cover my initial uncertainty. The word "man" is for de Man a metaphor over another metaphor or, as he puts it in the intransigent formulation I have already cited, "Conceptual language, the foundation of civil society, is also, it appears, a lie superimposed upon an error" (*AR*, 155). It is because all language is made up of metaphors of this sort, or a system of them, that the paradigm for all texts is a figure or system of figures. Since such figures are always unstable, any text "deconstructs" its metaphors at the same time as it asserts them. Deconstruction, as the reader can see from de Man's formulation, is not something the critic does to the text from the outside in the act of "reading" it, but something all texts inevitably do to themselves. It is a built-in fatality of language that any text must not only posit a figure or system of figures but must at the same time dismantle it, bring its aberrancy into the open.

For de Man this process can never be closed off in the triumphant mastery of the text by itself in its revelation of the erroneous figures on which it is built. In the act of deconstructing itself a text commits again another version of the error it denounces, and this means that all texts are a potentially endless series of repetitions of the "same" error only arbitrarily brought to closure. To put this another way, any text is a narrative that has no ending: "A narrative endlessly tells the story of its own denominational aberration and it can only repeat this aberration on various levels of rhetorical complexity" (*AR*, 162). All texts, in de Man's somewhat idiosyncratic nomenclature, are narratives, in the sense that they are the serial presentation, as if it were a story, complete with implied protagonist, narrator, and reader, of what is in fact the synchronic positing and deconstruction of a figure or system of figures. Any figure is deconstructed at the same moment it is posited. The positing contains the deconstruction.

It might be noted in passing here that though the example of the man named a giant is Rousseau's, the fact that the "figure" in question is also implicitly a prosopopoeia, a "disfiguring" of the face and figure of the other, or the ascription of a consciousness like my own or different from my own to an appearance in the perceptional field, prepares for the concentration on the figure of prosopopoeia in de Man's later work, from the essay on Shelley's "The Triumph of Life" on. De Man's work develops, but in retrospect it appears to have a remarkable consistency and focus, though of course that may be an illusion generated by the reader's inveterate habit of making a consistent story out of what may in fact only be a random series. De Man's notion of the impossibility of closing off any text in a final reading, especially any final reading of the text by itself, should give any reader pause who is tempted to see something in de Man's later work, for example, his theory that the fundamental trope of lyric poetry is prosopopoeia, as the teleology of the early post-1950 work. For him no such closure is possible, only the endless repetition of different versions of the same error.

De Man's formulation of this, in the passage I am trying to "read," needs to be looked at closely. The "paradigm" of a figure or system of figures and its deconstruction is spoken of as a "model." Presumably "paradigm" and "model" mean more or less the same thing: a schematic outline of universal applicability within which a limitless variety of different texts may be fitted. Of all of these it may be said that the illumination provided by the act of (self-)deconstruction coincides with a repetition of another version of the linguistic error that the deconstruction denounces. In fact, the deconstruction is at the same time a committing again of the error. This seems to be the logic of the "But since . . ., it engenders" in de Man's formulation. It is because a final reading is impossible, because the closure of a final illumination and mastery of language can never occur, that a secondary narration is superimposed on the first one, a third one on that, and so on, in the endless repetition of different versions of the same cycle: "*But since* this model cannot be closed off by a final reading, *it engenders*, in its turn, a supplementary figural superposition which narrates the unreadability of the prior narration" (my italics). The "unreadability" is not located in the reader but in the text itself, though the text's inability to mastery itself "engenders" in the reader a corresponding inability to master the text.

De Man's rather odd name for this "supplementary figural superposition" is *allegory*. I say "odd" because de Man's use of the word here seems to correspond neither to ordinary usage nor even quite to his own (also at first sight idiosyncratic) definition of allegory in "The Rhetoric of Temporality." Here, again, is the formulation in "Allegory (*Julie*)": "As distinguished from primary deconstructive narratives centered on figures and ultimately always on metaphor, we can call such narratives to the second (or the third) degree *allegories*. Allegorical narratives tell the story of the failure to read whereas tropological narratives, such as the *Second Discourse*, tell the story of the failure to denominate." *Why* can "we" call such second- or third-level narratives *allegories*? In what possible sense or senses is that the right word? Why is it that texts can never "read themselves"? In any case, to speak of the relation between one part of a text and another as its reading of itself or as its failure to read itself would seem to be no more than a transparent trope for the activity of the author in writing the book. Replacing this trope by its commonsense literal meaning displaces the puzzle or even apparent absurdity of what de Man is saying to another level, where its implausibility is even more obvious. Surely an author is in control of what she writes and is able to read what she has written! What fatality is it that forces Rousseau, for instance, in the example de Man gives later on in "Allegory (*Julie*)," to commit again or have Julie commit again another version of the linguistic error (deification of Saint-Preux) she so lucidly denounces and demystifies in letter 18, part III? "In this text," says de Man,

> . . . darkness falls when it becomes evident that Julie's language at once repeats the notions she has just denounced as errors. . . . If this is so, then it can be said that Julie is unable to 'read' her own text, unable to recognize how its rhetorical mode relates to its meaning. (*AR*, 217)

A footnote to this passage convincingly argues that Julie's blindness is not compensated for by Rousseau's lucidity but is, as de Man would say, the allegory of it:

> By the play of notes which allows him to acquire a distancing perspective with regard to Julie, Rousseau may seem to escape from this obfuscation at the expense of his character. But this pattern is anticipated in Julie herself, whose lucidity with regard to her past experience is never in question and

who is capable of the same distance toward herself as Rousseau allows himself towards her, yet remains entirely unable to avert the repetition of her errors. R.'s statement, in the Preface, of helplessness before the opacity of his own text is similar to Julie's relapse into metaphorical models of interpretation at her moments of insight. The manipulation of point of view is a form of infinite regress inscribed within the metaphor of selfhood. (*AR*, 217)

Why this "helplessness"? It seems entirely inexplicable. The most obvious explanation, that it is a defect of memory, is explicitly rejected by de Man. It would be tempting to say that for de Man no one can remember long enough the difficult and painful process of rhetorical deconstruction to avoid committing again the same linguistic mistakes that have just been deconstructed. Certainly the difficulty of remembering the intricate argumentation of one of de Man's essays and making the displacements necessary to apply that argumentation to a different text (supposing someone should want to do such a thing)[2] would support the idea that de Man is talking about a defect of memory, a kind of fatal amnesia perhaps especially likely to occur with insights into the role of language in individual and collective human life so painful as those de Man offers the reader. We have every reason to want to repress and forget. But no, de Man explicitly forbids this interpretation of what he is saying. Julie is entirely lucid with regard to her past experience and Rousseau remembers and understands everything he has written. This comprehensive and comprehending memory nevertheless in no way mitigates the "helplessness," which means that both author and character are unable to avert the repetition of errors that are both remembered and understood. Why is this? It is not too much to say that getting a clear answer to this question is the key to understanding all of de Man's work, if the word "understand" is still in any way appropriate here, since part of de Man's point is that this insight is not open to understanding in the ordinary sense. Even though we can grasp what de Man is saying with total lucidity, we are still helpless before the opacity of the text of de Man's essays, just as Rousseau (or "R.") remains in a state of "helplessness before the opacity of his own text."

The reason for this impotence must be that the fatality in question has nothing to do with the psychological categories of memory, lucidity, insight, and blindness. It is a linguistic necessity that no amount of intelligence, memory, and vigilant insight will avail to avert. The harder I try to remember, even the more successful I am in remembering, the more certain I am to forget. It seems as if my insight must not ever have been "present" in the sense of being a possession within my consciousness in its self-presence. Therefore it is in principle not something I can "remember," nor forget either, for that matter. What de Man says about the failure to read even one's own writing must apply also to me as a reader (which is a metaphor for this essay as an act of reading). It must also apply to de Man himself, which is to say, to de Man's essay, though his work is peculiarly resistant to such demonstrations. What appears an example of self-opacity is often the object of lucid insight elsewhere in the text of *Allegories of Reading*. It would be a bold reader who would try to second-guess de Man and claim to make a move beyond the last move he has already made. He is pretty certain to have been there before and already to have surveyed the topography, mapped the terrain. In this case, de Man's peculiar use of the term "allegory" will help the reader to "understand" the irresistible coercion toward error that de Man sees in human beings' subjection to language.

"We can call such narratives to the second (or the third) degree *allegories*," says de Man. An allegory is therefore for de Man a narrative. It tells a story, but as opposed to primary narratives centered on the deconstruction of metaphor that tell the story of the failure to denominate, allegories tell the story of the failure to read. The term "degree" here is slightly odd, as is the addition in parentheses of "or the third." By "or the third" I suppose de Man means that the deconstruction of the initially asserted figure or system of figures could already be thought of as a second narrative superimposed on the first, so that the allegory of the failure to read can be thought of as already a third narrative posited over the first two, while if the positing of the figure and its deconstruction are thought of as a single story, then the allegory is only the second narrative. As for the word "degree," this makes an important assertion and forestalls what would be a serious mistake, namely thinking of allegories of the impossibility of reading as being fundamentally different in kind from "tropological narratives," which "tell the story of the failure to denominate." No, de Man is anxious to have us understand that the rhetorical ingredients of both kinds of narratives are the same, able to be marked out on the same scale, measurable by the same standards. I take it he means that both kinds of narrative are made of the same universal narrative ingredients of figurative language taken literally and then shown to be aberrant. In one case the story is oriented toward the "real world," the object of "denomination." In the other case, the allegorical narrative at second (or third) degree, the story is oriented toward another story, namely, the story of denomination, but as de Man categorically asserts, "The difference is only a difference of degree and the allegory does not erase the figure." The word "erase" is also important here. It is a word de Man uses occasionally to name an (impossible) obliteration, as when, discussing in the preface to *Allegories of Reading* his use of the now polemically charged word "deconstruction," he says that he got the word from Jacques Derrida, "which means that it is associated with a power of inventive rigor to which I lay no claim but which I certainly do not wish to erase" (*AR*, x). In the present case, to say that the allegory does not erase the figure is a way of asserting the positive side of the linguistic operation called "deconstruction." Deconstruction reaffirms at the same time as it puts in question, which means that the whole chain of positings and putting in question remains unerased to the end, however many new layers of allegorical narrative are superposed on the original figure or system of figures: "the allegory does not erase the figure."

But why should de Man call this second or third degree of narration *allegory*? The appropriateness of the term "allegory" will become apparent if the reader remembers not only the etymology of the word but also the specific definition of it de Man gives in "The Rhetoric of Temporality," now reprinted in the new edition of *Blindness and Insight*. *Allegory*: The word means to say it otherwise in the marketplace, in public, as an exoteric expression of an esoteric wisdom. As in the case of parable, for example, the parables of Jesus in the Gospels, this is a way of revealing it and not revealing it. If you have the key to the allegory, then the esoteric wisdom has been expressed (otherwise), but then you would not have needed to have it said otherwise. If you do not have the key, then the allegory remains opaque. You are likely to take it literally, to think it means just what it says. If you understand it you do not need it. If you do not understand it you never will do so from anything on the surface. A paradox of unreadability is therefore built into the concept of allegory from the beginning.

This is not enough to say, however. For de Man, allegories are always temporal, that is, spread out on a diachronic scale, which is to say that allegories are always narratives. As opposed to symbols, which are synchronic and presuppose the similarity of the symbol and the symbolized within a spatial array, the symbol being a sign, the symbolized a thing, allegories are a matter of before and after, a matter of a sign–sign relation rather than a sign–thing relation. The relation between sign and sign within the allegory is always a matter of distance, difference, and discrepancy. The allegorical sign is unlike the sign it refers to, stands for, or substitutes for. Here is de Man's formulation of all this in "The Rhetoric of Temporality": "In the world of the symbol it would be possible for the image to coincide with the substance, since the substance and its representation do not differ in their being but only in their extension: they are part and whole of the same set of categories. Their relationship is one of simultaneity, which, in truth, is spatial in kind, and in which the intervention of time is merely a matter of contingency, whereas, in the world of allegory, time is the originary constitutive category. . . . It remains necessary, if there is to be allegory, that the allegorical sign refer to another sign that precedes it. The meaning constituted by the allegorical sign can then consist only in the *repetition* (in the Kierkegaardian sense of the term)[3] of a previous sign with which it can never coincide, since it is of the essence of this previous sign to be pure anteriority" (*BI*, 207). More pages of commentary, not entirely relevant here, would be necessary to elucidate that concluding phrase about "pure anteriority." Suffice it to say that de Man means here a pastness that was never present or presence and that therefore can never be reached as such by any remounting of the stream of time, for example, in recollective memory.

In the light of these definitions one can see why *allegory* is the right word for the universal linguistic structure of all texts de Man is describing in "Allegory (*Julie*)," and why all allegories are "always allegories of the impossibility of reading." If the allegorical sign repeats the earlier sign, then it repeats also the error inscribed in that earlier sign, which was always a figure or system of figures and its deconstruction. The error inscribed in the earlier sign is, however, repeated in the allegorical sign in a blind form, that is, in the form of an unrecognizable difference, or in the form of a difference that can be recognized only by those who have the key to the allegory. In that blindness, difference, and discrepancy between one part of the text and another, along the temporal and narrative line, lies the text's inability to read itself. The example de Man gives in this essay is Julie's repetition in her relation to God of the aberrant metaphorical structure she has first yielded to and then lucidly deconstructed when it was applied to Saint-Preux. The impossibility of reading is inscribed in the text in that allegorical relation between Julie's relation to God and her relation to Saint-Preux. De Man's logic seems clear enough, and it is airtight, irrefutable. It is just *because* all texts are a figure or system of figures and its deconstruction followed by a "supplementary figural superposition" "engendered" by the first, but engendered in the form of an allegory, that the story told is the story of unreadability. The new figure or system of figures refers to the first, but in a way that is based on difference and dissimilarity, so that the relation between the second sign and the first sign of which it is the allegory is both necessary, fatal, with the fatality of an unavoidable "engendering," and at the same time blinded, esoteric, not immediately apparent as a new version of the first. As de Man says in the definition of allegory in "The Rhetoric of Temporality," "The relationship between the allegorical sign and its meaning [*signifié*] is not decreed by dogma" (*BI*, 207). There is no available code by which the relationship can be made certain, masterable. It occurs, necessarily, but not in a predictable or rational way. It does not occur in a way based, for example, on the similarity between the allegorical sign and the earlier sign to which it refers. In allegory anything can stand for anything. No ground whatever, subjective, divine, transcendent, nor even that of social convention, supports the relationship. It just happens, by a linguistic or narrative necessity. Just go on talking or writing and you will be sure to narrate allegorically the impossibility of reading your prior narration. Since the allegory repeats the first error in this necessitated and yet not perspicuous way (in spite of the fact that the first error, the taking of a metaphor literally, was clearly deconstructed), this means that this second allegorical figural superposition "narrates the unreadability of the prior narration." It narrates it by showing that all the lucidity of the deconstruction of the first figure or system of figures has not in the least prevented the text from repeating another version of the same error. It is as if it could not remember from one moment to the next its own insights or perhaps were unable to recognize the allegorical similarity in dissimilarity. The supplementary figural superposition narrates the unreadability of the prior narration in the peculiar way allegories have of saying one thing and meaning another. The second part of *Julie* appears to narrate Julie's disenchantment with Saint-Preux and her subsequent turning to God, but what *in fact*, that is, allegorically, Julie's turn to religious devotion means, narrates, tells, is, by the fatality of a necessary engendering, the text's inability to read itself. Julie's failure to be able to "read" her own earlier letters to Saint-Preux (letters that, one would think, ought to prevent her from making the "same" mistake again) is the allegory of what the text is "really about," namely, its inability to read itself. The same thing may be said of Rousseau's inability to read what he has written. This is dramatized in R.'s stubborn refusal to say whether or not he has made up the letters of *Julie*, just as "our" inability to read *Julie*, yours, mine, de Man's, is another allegory of the text's inability to read itself. This intratextual unreadability is what all texts are "really about," the story they all really tell.

All this seems, as I said, clear enough. De Man's lucid formulations are a triumph of his methodological rigor and clarity. He lucidly expresses as knowledge or lucidly expresses knowledge *of* what he calls a perpetual and entirely irremediable "state of suspended ignorance" (*AR*, 19). But is that entirely the case? The reader may still have some nagging doubts, since certain aspects of what de Man says do not quite make sense, not at least from the point of view of ordinary logic and reason. Why in the world is it that a "text" cannot remember in one place what it so penetratingly knew in another place. Why can the text not read itself? The reader may have at this point the feeling that perhaps she has not been able to read de Man, has missed something vital in spite of having pored over and over this brief series of sentences in an attempt to defy de Man's claim that all texts are unreadable. As the beginning of an attempt to answer these troublesome questions, several preliminary observations may be made:

1. As opposed to the deconstructive procedures of Jacques Derrida, with which de Man's work is of course often paired, de Man has a tendency, in spite of the fact that each of his essays is the "reading" of a particular text, to move to levels of absolute generality and to say, for example, that *all* texts narrate the allegory of the impossibility of reading. Derrida, on the other hand, seems more interested in what is irreducibly idiomatic, both in the sense of belonging to a particular language and in the sense of belonging to a particular semantic region, about each one of the terms he interrogates, *différance, hymen, glas, pas*, or whatever – the list gets longer with each new essay he writes. In a recent essay, for example, "Des tours de Babel," Derrida makes a point of the fact that the word "Babel" expresses a general structure in a way that is unique, irreplaceable, "almost untranslatable": "En ce sens il [la tour de Babel] serait le mythe de l'origine du mythe, la métaphore de la métaphore, le récit du récit, la traduction de la traduction, etc. Il ne serait pas la seule structure à se creuser ainsi mais il le ferait à sa manière (elle-même *à peu près* intraduisible, comme un nom propre) et il faudrait en sauver l'idiome"[4] The relationship between the particular example and the universal law it exemplifies seems to be different in de Man from what it is in Derrida.

2. Another (different) way to put this would be to say that language appears to be the ultimate court of appeal for de Man, the place where the buck stops, so to speak. The end point of each of de Man's rigorous argumentations or readings is another demonstration that what appeared to have to do with selfhood or society or history or ontology "really" is another manifestation of the implacable laws of language. This cannot quite be said for Derrida or cannot be said in the same way. There is the difference between them, even though it may be a difference no further away than the two sides of the same coin. It would be a mistake to make too much of the difference at the level of fundamental insight or presupposition between de Man and Derrida. The reader anxious to do that should remember Derrida's assertion in his book on de Man of entire allegiance to de Man's later work as a whole. Even so, it is unlikely that de Man would have written, for example, the following sentences in Derrida's recent book on Joyce, *Ulysse gramophone: Deux mots pour Joyce*, where there is a formulation of something almost prelinguistic that motivates the linguistic and makes it that the word "*oui*" or the word "yes" is presupposed by any act of language, even the first, and so is not a word at all in the ordinary sense. Or at any rate, it is that "place-no-place" of perpetual *différance* where the linguistic and the nonlinguistic converge.

There is always a yes before the first yes: "Le discours sur l'être suppose la responsibilité du *oui*: oui, ce qui est dit est dit, je réponds ou il est répondu à l'interpellation de l'être, etc. Toujours en style télégraphique, je situerai alors la possibilité du oui et du oui-rire en ce lieu oú l'égologie transcendentale, l'ontoencyclopédie, la grande logique spéculative, l'ontologie fondamentale et la pensée de l'être ouvrent sur une pensée du don et de l'envoi qu'elles présupposent mais ne peuvent contenir."[5] Although to say "*oui*" is an act of language, it always presupposes a "*oui*" before the first "*oui*", which can hardly be said to be language in the ordinary sense and to which the first "*oui*" responds, whereas for de Man it appears that there is nothing before language, though there is the darkness of the "other" of language itself within any text (a formulation in which de Man no doubt would have seen the trap of an undeconstructed metaphor in "other": other either as another person or as a name for a transcendental ground).

3. The figure or system of figures on which the passage in de Man I am discussing depends (and which it inevitably uses again even though it has lucidly deconstructed it) is personification, prosopopoeia. This is, as I have said, the trope to which he turns his attention in a series of brilliant essays written after the publication of *Allegories of Reading*. About personification in the passage I am reading there is, however, more to say.

Prosopopoeia has already been de Man's implicit target in the essay that immediately precedes "Allegory (*Julie*)" in *Allegories of Reading*, namely, "Self (*Pygmalion*)." The first person pronoun is used rarely and sparingly by de Man (though we have seen an example in the preface to *Allegories of Reading*). This goes along with an austere rigor that makes his essays sometimes sound as if they were written by some impersonal intelligence or by language itself, not by someone to whom the laws of blindness and the impossibility of reading also apply, as they do to the rest of us. To put this another way, de Man is unwilling, perhaps on principle, to apply overtly to himself the insights into the necessity of error that he nevertheless formulates as universal. The "principle" in question may be the fact that on principle each reader must be blind to his or her own blindness. Attempts to recognize it or to formulate it would be futile gestures, merely compounding the error. This may be an area where it is better to keep silent, as de Man does.

To put this yet another way, de Man clearly recognizes or recognizes clearly that the self is a metaphor, moreover a metaphor without particular authority. Especially does the self not have authority in that attractive form of a return of the self beyond its deconstruction, as the wielder of the instrument of deconstruction. In "Self (*Pygmalion*)" de Man somewhat scornfully gives short shrift to the notion present in Heidegger and in a different way in Paul Ricoeur's interpretation of Freud that "the subject is reborn [beyond its deconstruction] in the guise of the interpreter": "Our present concern is merely whether Rousseau, like Ricoeur's Freud, reclaims a measure of authority for the self, grounded in its ability to understand its own failure to make such a claim" (*AR*, 174, 175). That would appear to describe exactly the authority that de Man seems to claim for himself throughout *Allegories of Reading*, the ironic authority to assert a lucid insight into ignorance, the authority of a self that can assert that the self is only a metaphor. But no, this recuperation of the self beyond its deconstruction is an illusion, another error, no doubt a particularly attractive one to the deconstructive critic, who needs all the comfort she can get and would like to find it in the assurance that "she" is the master of the technique of deconstruction. De Man deprives his readers (and himself) of even this paradoxical survival of the self as a substantial point of authority outliving the demolition of everything else but language, even itself: "From the point of view of truth and falsehood, the self is not a privileged metaphor in Rousseau" (*AR*, 187). Nor is it for de Man himself. What is described in terms of Rousseau, Proust, Nietzsche, or whoever is in fact an impersonal and universal operation of language, spoken of only "*par la commodité du récit*", as "Proust" puts it, in terms of this or that proper name.

Nevertheless the use of some proper name or pronoun, or at least the barely visible traces of some almost effaced prosopopoeia, seems to be another of those irresistible necessities of language, perhaps one of the most important, in the sense of having far-reaching consequences. The presence of this trope in de Man's most impersonal and universalized formulations, such as the ones I am discussing here, in spite of de Man's "deconstruction" of the idea that selfhood is a privileged ontological category, is evidence that he is unable to avoid using it in his own language. It could be said to be the example in my passage of each text's inability to read itself.

How does this occur? A text does not "read itself," except metaphorically. Reading is a word that applies literally only to the activity of some conscious reader, however metaphorical the existence of the self of that reader may be. Although he can scrupulously avoid, for the most part, speaking of himself as an "I" or speaking of the operations performed by the critical texts he has written as products of a masterful subjectivity, all insight and no blindness, nevertheless it seems impossible even for a reader of "de Man's" rigor to avoid talking about the impersonal relations between one part of a text and another as if they were acts involving a self. The text tells the story of its failure to denominate. It brings lucidly into the open like a masterly detective the errors in its own metaphors. Then this narration "engenders," as if it were capable of sexual reproduction, a supplementary figural superposition that narrates its inability, in spite of its deconstructive insight into the aberrancy of its own metaphors, to read itself. This allegory, or narration at the second or third power is a demonstration that reading is impossible. This demonstration remains entirely intratextual, in spite of its applicability to the author, narrator, or critic as readers. It has nothing to do with any of them as selves.

The prosopopoeia in "engenders" is crucial here, since it personifies as a natural temporal process, one with the organic continuity and necessity of conception, gestation, and birth, what is in fact a very different kind of temporal necessity. The metaphorical word "engenders" names an impersonal linguistic necessity, a necessity marked, as de Man's theory of allegory insists, not by organic continuity, but by disconnection, contingency, and dissimilarity. The word "engenders" makes the strange linguistic process de Man is describing sound as if it were a story with beginning, middle, and end corresponding referentially to events in the historical world. In fact, de Man of course wants to affirm the reverse, that the "materiality of history," with all its violence and injustice, is determined not by human will, but by impersonal laws of language over which we have no control and which we cannot even clearly understand, since our understanding always contains a residue of misunderstanding.

The prosopopoeia in "engenders" and in the strange idea that a text reads or fails to read itself is far from innocent. It covers over and gives an appearance of plausibility to what remains, for "me" at least, the inexplicable mystery of why language behaves the way de Man says it does, that is, why it "engenders," by an unavoidable fatality, the two forms of incoherence de Man identifies: the deconstruction of its own fundamental metaphors and then their reassertion in a different, disguised form, but in a form that may still be detected behind the mask of an apparent dissimilarity. Why does language behave as if it were a person? Since language is, as I have said, the court of final appeal for de Man, there seems no answer to this. It does because it does. "The error is not within the reader," says de Man at the end of "Promises (*Social Contract*)." Language itself dissociates the cognition from the act. *Die Sprache verspricht (sich)*: de Man's witty subversion of Heidegger's celebrated formulation means both "language promises (itself)," and "language makes a slip of the tongue, a *lapsus linguae*." "To the extent that is necessarily misleading," he continues, "language just as necessarily conveys the promise of its own truth. This is also why textual allegories on this level of rhetorical complexity generate history" (*AR*, 277). "Generate" here echoes "engenders" in the earlier passage. It insinuates the same idea of a genetic causality, borrowing a term from the conception of history that is being contested to name the very different idea that language, with the unhappy peculiarities de Man identifies, blindly makes history happen as it does happen.

As I said earlier, however, de Man is almost certain to have been there before we arrive and to have anticipated any "deconstruction" of his own text we may perform. The example of that here is the final phrase of the last sentence in the paragraph in "Allegory (*Julie*)" I have been reading. After having asserted that all allegories are "always allegories of the impossibility of reading," de Man adds, apparently as a kind of thought-teasing afterthought, the following, after a dash: "– a sentence in which the genitive 'of' has itself to be 'read' as a metaphor." What, exactly, does this mean? What does it mean to take the word "of," used as a genitive, as a metaphor? There are three "of's" in this sentence: "allegories *of* metaphor," "always allegories *of* the impossibility *of* reading," and presumably de Man's stricture must apply to all. A similar "of" of course appears in the title of the book: *Allegories of Reading*. The reader's first inclination may be to think that de Man is referring to the notorious doubleness of the genitive "of," the way it may go both ways and mean both "out of" and "about or concerning." An allegory of reading is both an allegory about or concerning reading and an allegory that is generated out of the act of reading. It is possible that de Man means that each of these versions of "of" is the metaphor of the other. To say "allegory of reading" or "allegory of the impossibility of reading" is to say simultaneously that a narrative is the oblique or hidden story of the impossibility of reading and to say that the allegory is generated out of the impossibility of reading or that the impossibility is generated out of the act of reading. Such a double reading of the genitive would not, however, be metaphorical at all, since it would leave intact the literal genesis of the allegory from the impossibility of reading the impossibility of reading from the allegory. A metaphor is a substitution, a transfer from one realm where it is legitimate to another realm where it is "only figurative." We know that for de Man all metaphors are always in error, aberrant, the covering over of an irremediable ignorance about what is "really there," for example, what it is really like inside that creature who looks like another me and to whom I give the name first of "giant" and then of "man." When de Man says the genitive "of" must be taken as a metaphor, he must want to break the literal line of generation and make it fictive, aberrant, figural.

In this case, it is clear what must be the metaphorical substitution, as is its motivation clear. To speak with the genitive "of" of "the impossibility *of* reading" or of allegories *of* that impossibility or of "allegories *of* metaphor" is to insinuate within the apparently abstract formulation just that covert prosopopoeia, that affirmation of a natural, organic, generative, genetic causality that I have identified in "engenders" and in the figure of the personified text reading itself. An old, crumbling *Webster's* (1898), the only English dictionary I have here where I am writing this essay, defines "of" as a preposition meaning "from or out of;

proceeding from, as the cause, source, means, author, or agent bestowing. . . . Hence *of* is the sign of the genitive case, the case that denotes production; as, the Son *of* man, the son proceeding from man, produced from man." Old Noah Webster or whatever sons of Noah wrote this entry chose with admirable insight a Biblical example where the capitalized S indicates that the Son of man in question is really Christ, the son of God, divine as well as human, the logos itself or himself, therefore in a sense the father of all mankind, or at least the model on the basis of which God the Father produced all mankind. The example shows that theological issues are never very far from explicit in that genitive "of," along with a metalepsis reversing the order of temporal priority. The genitive "of" involves characteristically an inextricable mixing of metaphysical or theological categories (logos as ground of being), personal and genetic categories (logos as mind, as self, as father or son), and linguistic categories (logos as word or Word).

In any case, to "read" that "of" in de Man's sentence not literally but as a metaphor is to see the whole latent personification governing the passage as an error, an aberrancy. The metaphorical "of" covers a relationship that is not genitive or genetic but linguistic, and for which there is no name. If "of" is a metaphor here, what literal formulation could be substituted for it? No such alternative literal word exists. One may therefore say that the genitive "of" read as a metaphor is, like all primary aberrant failing denominations, strictly speaking a catachresis. It is another example of what de Man elsewhere observes, the overlapping, but not total symmetry, of prosopopoeia and catachresis. The metaphorical, personifying, catachrestic "of" is a placeholder brought in to cover over an irreducible ignorance about why language works as it does work. De Man's enigmatic phrase about reading the genitive "of" as a metaphor shows his awareness of this fact, or his text's awareness, as well as its awareness that the evidence of its own failure to read itself is the covert reintroduction of the category of selfhood that has already been denounced as an aberrant metaphor, without authority.

No doubt de Man's clarity about the impossibility "of" reading, his reading of the impossibility of reading, "engenders" new repetitions of the aberrancy it so clearly identifies, for example, in my persistence in referring to what is only a text, words on the page, as if it were a person, "de Man," with whom I might have a conversation or toward whom I might have ethical obligations.[6] As de Man makes clear on the page following the one I have been trying to read, ethics or "ethicity" is a linguistic necessity or imperative, not a subjective one. "Ethics," says de Man, "has nothing to do with the will (thwarted or free) of a subject, nor *a fortiori*, with a relationship between subjects" (*AR*, 206). Just what is de Man's conception of the necessary ethical dimension of language, and therefore of reading, I have elsewhere attempted to identify.[7]

Notes

1. For an attempt to avoid the totalitarian tyranny of the one in a theory of judging and of justice see J.-F. Lyotard and Jean-Loup Thébaud, *Au juste* (Paris, 1979), and the discussions of Lyotard by various scholars in *diacritics* 14 (Fall 1984) and in *La Faculté de juger* (Paris, 1985).
2. It should be remembered that if this is to be done at all it has to be carried out all the way to the end, or even beyond the end. Nothing could be more futile and feeble than an intermittent or partial application of de Man's insights into language in a critical essay that remains nevertheless in its fundamental procedures blithely thematic, psychologistic, or referential.
3. Whatever *that* means; the allusion to Kierkegaard invites pages of discriminations, which cannot be added here.
4. Jacques Derrida, "Des tours de Babel," in *Psyché: Inventions de l'autre* (Paris, 1987), p. 205. (In this sense it [the tower of Babel] would be the myth of the origin of myth, the metaphor of metaphor, the story of story, the translation of translation, etc. It would not be the only structure to hollow itself out in this way, but it would do this in its own way (itself *almost* untranslatable, like a proper name) and it would be necessary to preserve its special idiom.)
5. Jacques Derrida, *Ulysse Gramophone: Deux mots pour Joyce* (Paris, 1987), p. 132. (Discourse about being supposes the responsibility of the *yes*: yes, what is said is said, I answer or it is answered to the interpellation of being, etc. Still in telegraphic style: I would then situate the possibility of the yes and of the yes-laugh in that region where transcendental egology, the onto-encyclopedia, the great speculative logic, fundamental ontology, and the thought of being open out on a thought of the gift and of the act of sending that they presuppose but cannot contain.)
6. For another reading of "of" as figurative, see the paragraph about "of" in Keats' title, *The Fall of Hyperion*, in de Man's "The Resistance to Theory," *The Resistance to Theory* (Minneapolis, 1986), pp. 16–17.
7. In the chapter entitled "Reading Unreadability: de Man," in *The Ethics of Reading* (New York, 1986), pp. 41–59. This present essay was written in 1985, before the discovery of Paul de Man's early writings and the ensuing outpouring of writings about those writings. My reading of the paragraph in *Allegories of Reading* still seems to me just, and I have made only two changes, necessary for clarification. On p. 158 a reference to de Man's "early work" now reads "early *post-1950* work." The sentence about Derrida and de Man now reads "entire allegiance to de Man's *later* work as a whole." The French version of Derrida's book on de Man, *Mémoires*, will contain an augmented version of his essay on the early writings of de Man, "Like the Sound of the Sea Deep within a Shell: Paul de Man's War," *Critical Inquiry*, 14 (Spring 1988): pp. 590–652. I have had my own say about de Man's early writings and about their relation to his later writings and to "deconstruction" generally in an untitled article in *The Times Literary Supplement*, 17–23 June 1988, pp. 676, 685, and in "An Open Letter to Professor Jon Wiener," forthcoming in a volume of essays on de Man's early writings to be published by the University of Nebraska Press. I add here that the juxtaposition of de Man's early and late writings is a starkly dramatic way to confront the fact that the triumph of Nazi totalitarianism in Germany, the Holocaust, and the Second World War were a decisive transformation of Western culture and even a break in world history. Whatever we say, do, or write, do by writing, thereafter takes place against the background of those events, whether or not we know it or wish it.

This was always true in a special way of Paul de Man's later writings, and now we have a way to know that. It may not be so easy to remember that whatever anyone writes henceforth is also in one way or another inscribed on the same background.

24

Paul de Man's wartime writings

> The new statement is always hated by the old, and, to those dwelling in the old, comes like an abyss of scepticism. But the eye soon gets wonted to it, for the eye and it are effects of one cause: then its innocency and benefit appear . . .
>
> Ralph Waldo Emerson, "Circles"

The violence of the reaction in the United States and in Europe to the discovery of Paul de Man's writings of 1941–2 marks a new moment in the collaboration between the university and the mass media. This is so at least in the United States, where literary theory and literary theorists have hardly been of much interest to the newspapers. It is an extremely instructive moment, one worth much sober reflection.

For the most part, so far at least, it has been a question of journalism all the way. It has also been a question of reading, a question of how one reads what de Man wrote both early and late, a question of what would constitute an accurate and adequate reading of the facts in the case. These facts are almost all written documents. The wartime writings of Paul de Man were published in a student journal, *Les Cahiers du libre examen*, and in two Belgian newspapers, *Het Vlaamsche Land* and *Le Soir*. The outpouring of denunciations of de Man and of so-called "deconstruction" has been, so far, primarily in newspapers, in the *New York Times*, the *Nation*, *Newsweek* and the *Los Angeles Times*, along with some student newspapers, in the United States, and, most recently, the *Village Voice*, in an article full of resentment, malice and undisguised xenophobia; in *La Quinzaine littéraire*, the *Frankfurter Allgemeine Zeitung*, and the *Manchester Guardian* in Europe. Most, though not all, of these attacks have been written by academics who also write journalism. It is as though these professors had somewhat abruptly discovered the power of the press in this area, just as the young de Man discovered the power of the press in wartime Belgium, long before he began the advanced university study of literature as a Junior Fellow at Harvard in the mid-1950s.

Why was the finding of de Man's wartime writings so "newsworthy?" And why has the reporting of them in the mass media given rise to such extraordinary falsifications, misreadings, distortions and selective slanting of quotations, both of what de Man actually said in those writings and of "deconstruction," the mode of interpretation of philosophy, literature and culture with which he came to be associated thirty years later? And why have the falsehoods and distortions taken just the forms they have taken, with just the same errors being repeated from newspaper to newspaper? One of the most scandalous aspects of the whole affair, at least to an outsider to the way journalism apparently works, is that the same errors, the same quotations out of context, the same false characterizations of "deconstruction," are repeated from newspaper to newspaper in the United States, France, Germany, and Great Britain, apparently without any attempt to verify the facts or to read de Man's writings, early or late. One would have thought that in a case of such gravity a little checking of facts and re-reading of the evidence would have been in order, especially on the part of those journalists who are also professors, professionally committed to a sober truth-telling. Liberal newspapers and conservative newspapers have rushed to condemn what they see as a common enemy and they have said almost the same things – the *Nation*, on the one hand, and *Newsweek* and the *Frankfurter Allgemeine Zeitung*, on the other.

No doubt the reasons for this are multiple. They include a suspicion of any new and difficult mode of thought, especially (in the United States) when imported from the Continent; a general hostility to critical theory (but that in itself takes some explaining); the fact that at this moment in history there is widespread concern to identify the last remnants of the Nazi regime and to purify ourselves of them, to cut ourselves off from that period of history and to deny that anything like that could happen again. (False analogies of de Man's "case" with those of Waldheim and Heidegger have of course been made.)

But the strongest motivation for the irresponsible errors and insinuations in these newspaper articles is clear enough. The real target is not de Man himself. He is dead, beyond the reach of attack. The real aim is to discredit that form of interpretation called "deconstruction," to obliterate it, as far as possible, from the curriculum, to dissuade students of literature, philosophy and culture from reading de Man's work or that of his associates, to put a stop to the "influence" of "deconstruction." Beyond that, as the article in *Newsweek* and a later one in the *Wall Street Journal* attacking the English Department at Duke University made clear, the target is literary theory or critical theory generally, for example the so-called "new historicists," or feminist theorists, or students of popular culture, or practitioners of so-called "cultural criticism." The rapid widening of the targets of hostility has been a conspicuous fact.

The argument, implied or overt, goes as follows, in a crescendo of distortions. First error: it is asserted that de Man's wartime writings are fascist, collaborationist, antisemitic through and through, and that he was himself a fascist, collaborator, and antisemite. Second error: de Man's later writings, after 1953, when he became a famous professor, theorist and teacher in the United States – at Cornell, Johns Hopkins and Yale – are asserted to be continuous with the early writings, whether by being a disguised autobiographical apology for them or by continuing to affirm in new and more sophisticated forms the same ideas and commitments. Third error: de Man was a "deconstructionist." All deconstruction must be all of a piece. De Man was a Fascist. Now we know what we have suspected all along: Deconstruction is Fascist. Therefore get rid of it.

All these propositions are false. The facts are otherwise. What is most terrifying in this argument is the way it repeats the well-known totalitarian procedures of vilification it pretends to deplore. It repeats the crime it would condemn.

I have said the facts are far otherwise. Let me try to state them as succinctly and exactly as possible, with a strong recommendation to all who read this and who interest themselves in these questions to read all of de Man's wartime writings (they will soon be published *in toto*), to read de Man's later writings too and those of other "deconstructionists" – and then judge for yourselves. In this matter as in all such matters, there is no substitute for hard reading and for making up one's own mind. This is not a matter where you would want to let the newspapers do your reading and thinking for you.

First fact: de Man was by no means in these early writings totally fascist, antisemitic and collaborationist. The facts are much more complex. De Man was first editor of a student journal of the University of Brussels called *Les Cahiers du libre examen*. This journal defined itself as "democratic, anti-clerical, anti-dogmatic and anti-fascist." Like most newspapers and periodicals in Belgium, it was shut down by the Germans after they occupied Belgium in 1940. De Man then obtained a position as cultural correspondent with a prominent Brussels evening newspaper that had been taken over by collaborationists, *Le Soir*. The job was perhaps obtained through the influence of Paul de Man's uncle Henri de Man, though there is no hard evidence for this that I have seen. Henri de Man was a prominent Belgian socialist who deluded himself into brief collaboration with the Germans. He remained behind to advise the monarchy after the Belgian government fled into exile. After a few months Henri de Man left Belgium for France in November, 1941 and then went into permanent exile in Switzerland in the closing days of the war. He was condemned in absentia by the Belgian authorities after the war. In the general review by the authorities after the war, Paul de Man, on the other hand, was not included among collaborators. He was allowed freely to leave the country when he chose to do so.

Paul de Man wrote some 169 articles for *Le Soir* from December 1940 to November 1942, when he was twenty-one and twenty-two years old. He also published during the same period ten articles for a Flemish journal, *Het Vlaamsche Land*, also under the control of the Germans. These articles are all book reviews, concert notes and general statements about literature and culture. They are a strangely heterogeneous mixture, the work of a brilliant and widely read young man with little formal literary education who clearly enjoys passing judgments pro and con on a wide variety of authors, composers and musicians, and who is prepared to make general pronouncements about the specific character of the different national literatures and about the development of literature in the past and in the future. There is one inexcusable and unforgettable article, "The Jews in Contemporary Literature" (*Le Soir*, 4 March, 1941) written for a special antisemitic section of *Le Soir*, and there is one sentence echoing antisemitic rhetoric in one of the essays in Flemish (*Het Vlaamsche Land*, 20 August, 1942). The essay in *Le Soir* uses the language of antisemitism to argue that the Jews have not corrupted modern European literature, but that European literature has remained fundamentally healthy. European literature, the essay argues, would hardly be weakened at all if all European Jews were put in a separate colony. This is an appalling idea, in itself and in view of what happened so soon thereafter, and it is an appalling untruth, but it must be recognized that this is not the same thing as saying that the Jews are a pollution of Western culture. This latter idea *is* expressed in the articles by other authors published adjacent to de Man's, and this idea is explicitly condemned by de Man as "vulgar antisemitism." "The reality," he says, is "different."

This is an example of a *leitmotif* of all de Man's essays for *Le Soir*, namely a putting in question of received ideas and opinions. Moreover, the same essay, strangely, mentions Kafka along with Hemingway and Lawrence as three great and exemplary modern authors. Other essays (in *Le Soir*, 27 May, 1941; in *Het Vlaamsche Land*, 17–18 May, 1942; and 26–27 July, 1942) praise Proust as a major writer. Did de Man not know Kafka was a Jew, or could the mention of Kafka here be an example of the kind of double-talk one learns to practise under a totalitarian regime? In an essay written at the end of his life de Man, in one of the two references to Leo Strauss in his writings, praises Strauss for having understood "double-talk, the necessary obliqueness of any persecuted speech that cannot, at risk of survival, openly say what it means to say" (*The Resistance to Theory*, p. 107). To suggest that this may explain the oddnesses of de Man's essay on the Jews in no way exonerates him from responsibility for whatever support his essay may have given to the then developing German policy that led seventeen months later to the first deportations of Jews from Belgium to the death camps. But it is important to note that the essay itself is by no means straight party-line antisemitism such as is represented in the attacks on Freud and Picasso in adjacent articles in the same issue of *Le Soir*.

Moreover, it is also important to put the now notorious article on the Jews in Western literature in the context of the other 168 articles in *Le Soir* and to recognize that antisemitism does not recur in them, nor does de Man, as has been asserted in the newspaper accounts, by any means consistently praise collaborationist authors or collaborationist ideas. One article on Charles Péguy, for example (*Le Soir*, 5 June, 1941), praises Péguy's support for the cause of Dreyfus. An antisemite would not have so unequivocally praised a Dreyfusard. Another article attacks with more than a little insolence as ignorant and mistaken a political book by the collaborationist writer Montherlant (*Le Soir*, 11 November, 1941). Just because Montherlant is a polished writer, says de Man, does not mean he knows anything about politics or history. In fact, says de Man, his book is very bad. In another much later article (*Le Soir*, 1 September, 1942), written after the deportations of Jews from Belgium had begun, de Man's discussion of a poem by Hubert Dubois called "Le Massacre des Innocents" seems a clear outcry against those deportations as evidence of "the guilt that has led humanity to the frightful state in which it finds itself at this moment."

These early writings must also be put in the context of the testimony of three people who knew de Man at the time, a colleague at *Les Cahiers du libre examen*, Charles Dosogne; a man linked to the Belgian resistance, Georges Goriély; and another man associated with the Resistance, Georges Lambrichs, later editor of *La Nouvelle nouvelle revue française*. All testify that Paul de Man was not antisemitic, that he was "anything but a collaborator," that he was neither fascist nor pro-Nazi. In the absence of personal testimony on the other side, from those who knew de Man in Belgium during the war, the assertions of these witnesses should carry much weight. I might add here my own testimony that in all the years I knew de Man (from 1966 until his death in 1983) I never heard him utter a single antisemitic word. The evidence suggests that he stupidly wrote the deplorable essay in order to please his employers and keep his job, putting in as much "double-talk" as he dared. According to the letter he wrote to Renato Poggioli when he was a Junior Fellow at Harvard and had been anonymously denounced, he quit writing for *Le Soir* in

November of 1942 when "Nazi thought control" made it impossible for him any longer to express himself freely. This seems to have been the moment when Nazi propaganda control was extended from the political to the cultural parts of *Le Soir*, for which of course de Man wrote and which had until then been free of direct censorship.

Nevertheless, what *is* a crucial fact about the articles for *Le Soir* and *Het Vlaamsche Land*, taken as a whole, and with all proper recognition of their truly heterogeneous character, is the way they allow an understanding of the implicit connection between the article on the Jews and certain nationalist ideas about literature which are present there and which recur in many of the essays that are in no way antisemitic or even explicitly political, just book reviews or concert notes. These are ideas about the specificity of national character and of the literature of each nation, ideas about the power of literature to express directly transcendent truth, and, beyond that, certain ideas about the individual organic development of the literature of each country according to intrinsic laws of its own. The article on "The Jews in Contemporary Literature" depends on the absurd and extremely dangerous notion that there is a specific national and racial character in French literature, a different one in German literature, and that the Jews have yet another specific identity. These ideas about the specificity of the German, French, Spanish, Flemish, Walloon and Dutch national characters recur in essay after essay in which there is nothing at all anti-Semitic or even explicitly political, for example in reviews that praise now-forgotten Belgian novelists or composers for having roots in Belgian folklore or folk music and in the constant concern for the differences in culture between French-speaking and Flemish-speaking Belgium. (De Man himself came from a Flemish-speaking family.)

Now then, what about de Man's later writings and what about "deconstruction" generally? Like his wartime writings, the writings of Paul de Man after he came to the United States and began publishing again in 1953, are heterogeneous. The heterogeneity of the later writings, however, is more a matter of a series of three discernible phases. There is an initial "phenomenological" phase in which the main categories of his criticism are consciousness, intentionality (in the Husserlian sense), and temporality. This phase culminates in *Blindness and Insight* (1971). Far from being a "deconstructionist" in this work, de Man opposes Derrida's reading of Rousseau in a long essay in *Blindness and Insight*. The second phase can be conveniently thought of as initiated by the transitional essay of 1969, "The Rhetoric of Temporality." The work of this period is gathered in *Allegories of Reading* (1979). In this phase the major categories of criticism are linguistic and rhetorical: metaphor, irony, symbol, allegory, the distinction between constative and performative uses of language. In the final phase, initiated with "The Resistance to Theory"

(1982), there is a more overt turn to history, ideology and politics, though a concern for all three is there all along in de Man's post-1953 work. As he asserted in the interview of 4 March, 1983, with Stefano Rosso: "I don't think I ever was away from these problems, they were always uppermost in my mind" (*The Resistance to Theory*, p. 121).

In spite of this developmental diversity, the connection between all de Man's later work and his early wartime writings – for there is a connection, though it is not at all the one the journalists have attempted to find – can best be defined by saying that the special and most urgent targets of all his later work are just those ideas about national character, the independent and organic evolution of each national literature, and so on, that are presupposed in his writings for *Le Soir*, *Het Vlaamsche Land*, and even in what he wrote for *Les Cahiers du libre examen*. De Man later called this whole cluster of ideas "aesthetic ideology." It was the main object of his systematic attack in essay after essay of his writings after 1953, especially but by no means exclusively in the essays of his last years, for example in an important and as yet unpublished seminar on "Kant and Schiller" (1983). But already in 1955, for example, in an essay published in *Monde nouveau* entitled "Tentation de la permanence," de Man sharply criticizes the Heidegger of the later essays on Hölderlin for being tempted by the lure of an ahistorical permanence attained through poetic language.

What is significant and instructive about the presence of this "aesthetic ideology" in de Man's early writings is the confirmation it gives to one of his basic later insights about literature, namely his recognition of the potentially disastrous political implications of apparently innocuous and purely "aesthetic" mistakes in assumptions about the nature of literature and of literary history. This may help to explain the urgency with which he always contested those ideas – in his writing, in his teaching and in his interventions in discussions of papers presented at conferences and symposia. The reading of the early writings *will* help to clarify the importance and the political import of de Man's writings after 1953.

As my account of his early writings has, I hope, made absolutely clear, the phrase "innocency and benefit" in my epigraph from Emerson is by no means meant to apply to de Man's early writings. Both the phrase and the whole citation from Emerson do describe, however, the indispensable usefulness of his later writings and of the work of "deconstruction" generally. For "aesthetic ideology" and the nationalism associated with it have by no means disappeared. They are extremely widespread and powerful in Europe and America today, for example in the xenophobia in the United States that resists literary theory because it is a foreign import. What de Man called "aesthetic ideology" forms an important part of the contemporary tissue of received opinion about literature, national identity and culture, both in the mass media and in the university. It was what I was taught at college and university, and it is what we are all likely to say or think on these topics if we are not vigilant. Which of us can say he or she is free of it? And yet de Man's work and his historical placement shows it is both false and can lead to hideous political and historical consequences.

What I have said about de Man's later work can also be said of "deconstruction" generally. Like his work, "deconstruction" is not one single thing. It is diverse and heterogeneous, with many active aspects, facets and functions, for example in religious studies, in architecture and in legal theory, as well as in philosophical and literary studies. Of "deconstruction" generally the same thing can be said that de Man said of his own work in the "Preface" to the posthumously published *The Rhetoric of Romanticism* (1984): it does not "evolve in a manner that easily allows for dialectical progression or, ultimately, for historical totalization." Nevertheless it can be said of "deconstruction," first, that the negative clichés that have been repeated over and over about it are false. "Deconstruction" is not nihilistic, nor anti-historical, nor mere play of language in the void, nor does it view literature or language generally as free play of language, nor is it committed to the notion that readers and critics are free to make texts mean anything they like. "Deconstruction," in all its diversity, is a certain kind of "critique of ideology," namely a kind that presupposes, as de Man put it in the interview with Rosso, that "one could approach the problems of ideology and by extension the problems of politics only on the basis of critical–linguistic analysis, which had to be done in its own terms, in the medium of language" (*The Resistance to Theory*, p. 121). This approach goes by way of identifying the linguistic constructions that are the basis of ideologies. Ideology is defined by de Man as "the confusion of linguistic with natural reality" (*The Resistance to Theory*, p. 11). Of special importance are those linguistic constructions that depend on thinking in terms of oppositions, literal versus metaphorical language, man against woman, inside against outside, and so on. An example would be the way the nationalism that is so important a part of "aesthetic ideology" leads to defining one group in opposition to another. This can lead, as in the case of Nazi Germany, to the horror of the slaughter of the Jews in the attempt to create an Aryan nation purified of all "polluting" elements.

Far from being without an interest in history or being without political import, "deconstruction," as de Man said in a crucial late essay, "The Resistance to Theory," is "more than any other mode of inquiry, including economics . . . a powerful and indispensable tool in the unmasking of ideological aberrations, as well as a determining factor in accounting for their occurrence. Those who reproach literary theory for being oblivious to social and historical (that is to say ideological) reality are merely stating their fear at having their own ideological mystifications exposed by the tool they are trying to discredit" (*The Resistance to Theory*, p. 11). It is fear of this power in "deconstruction" and in contemporary critical theory as a whole, in all its diversity, that accounts better than any other explanation for the unreasoning hostility, the abandoning of the canons of journalistic and academic responsibility, in the recent attacks on de Man, on "deconstruction" and on theory generally.

25

An open letter to Professor Jon Wiener

Department of English and Comparative Literature
University of California, Irvine, CA 92717
20 March 1988

Professor Jon Wiener
Department of History
University of California, Irvine

Professor Jon Wiener,
   I have been reluctant to write to you, since I think controversy among colleagues is likely to generate more heat than light, but both of us have responsibilities to the larger academic community and to wider communities as well. I wanted to wait, as I had recommended you should do too, until it was possible to see the full set of de Man's articles in *Les Cahiers du Libre Examen*, *Le Soir* and *Het Vlaamsche Land*, before writing. I also had waited to see if you would retract your article and try to correct its errors and unjustified insinuations. I know some at least of these have been pointed out to you by others.
   I think your de Man piece is one of the most misinformed, distorted, and irresponsible of all the journalistic essays I have seen on this subject, and that is saying quite a bit. You will say that you allowed both "sides" to speak in your essay and gave your readers the opportunity to judge for themselves, but the "evidence" you give leaves no doubt what conclusions you would draw and would expect your readers to draw both about de Man and about so-called "deconstruction." What you have allowed to be published has done great damage to the possibilities of rational and informed discussion of de Man's writings and of the issues they raise, damage both in this country and in Europe, where your errors have, as you must know, been reprinted, picked up and compounded. Thousands and thousands of readers both in this country and in Europe will have read your article and the ones that copied it as an accurate reporting of the facts. If de Man must be held responsible for what he wrote and for the effects of what he wrote, as I believe he must, I believe

also that you bear a great responsibility for the effects of what you have written. You will say that you wear two hats, one as a journalist and one as a historian, but surely your primary obligation is, or ought to be, the one common to both professions: the obligation to state the facts, responsibly and correctly. Your article has carried special weight and authority because it was written by a professor of history. Of course you are free, like everyone else, to pass judgment on de Man and his writings, and on "deconstruction" too, but surely this judgment should be based on an accurate identification of the facts to be judged and on a careful reading of the documents, particularly in a case of such gravity.

You quoted me correctly, as well as I can remember what I said. (It is amazing to me that you can think, as your recent letter to me suggests, that this is all I could find to quarrel with in your article.) You did not, however, heed my most important recommendation, namely that you should take the time to inform yourself about all de Man's wartime writings and about "deconstruction" before writing about it. You said when we talked on the phone, as I remember, that you had an urgent deadline and had to work fast. That may, sometimes, be an excuse for a journalist, who has time constraints, has no need to have expert knowledge about the subject on which he writes, and can work with opinions quickly gathered by phone, but it is not an excuse a historian can afford to make with anything he writes.

Your article is so full of errors, defamatory insinuations, and distortions that I hardly know where to begin in listing them. This includes what you say about "deconstruction," where almost everything you say is in error. It will be a tedious business to go through them all, but I shall try to do so. Since the errors of your essay have been so widely repeated and since the falsifications of so-called "deconstruction" in your article are exemplary of the characterizations that have appeared almost everywhere in the international media, it has a more than local importance to try to get things straight.

(1) De Man died in 1983, not 1984, at age 64, not 65.

(2) David Carroll has written you a letter about the "academic Waldheim" slur. It is an example of the ugly rhetoric of your essay throughout. What de Man wrote and published is so different from what Waldheim is said to have done that any analogy between them can only be said to be defamatory. In de Man's case it is a question of writing, publishing, and of the probable political effects of that.

(3) The two articles – "in one of the articles . . ., in another" – in *Le Soir* on the 'Jewish question' you refer to are in fact one article. How could you have made that mistake? Had you really read the article in question? Your paraphrase of it is woefully inadequate and misleading.

I am not saying that elements of fascist ideologies (primarily a dangerous belief in intrinsic national and racial characteristics and a view of history as developing "organically") and support for collaboration with the German occupant are not present in what de Man wrote for *Le Soir* and *Het Vlaamsche Land*. They are. Nor am I saying that de Man should not be held to account for what he wrote and its probable effects. He should. I am saying only that much more than that is present in those writings and that you present a distressingly inadequate report of what he actually said even in the group of writings available to you, I presume, even when you wrote your article – not to speak of the full set of writings. Did you really read them, or did you depend, as is clearly the case with de Man's later writings and with "deconstruction" generally, on what someone else told you they said?

(4) It is simply foolish to insinuate that, because Hans Robert Jauss taught as a visiting professor at Yale, he and de Man were a couple of old Nazis conspiring together. Since Jauss has been invited to lecture all over the place in the US, including UCI, I believe, the guilt you ascribe to de Man would be pretty widespread. A look at de Man's essay on Jauss in *The Resistance to Theory*, rather than the few paragraphs on him in *Blindness and Insight* which you mention, would have sufficed to clear up the "matter of [their] relationship." The essay is by no means a eulogy. In fact it is quite critical of Jauss.

(5) Kristeva's study of Céline is not anti-Semitic, but the reverse. Reading it – or even glancing at it in a hurry – might have saved you from making that mistake. De Man's praise of it has exactly the opposite meaning from the one you ascribe to it. He praises Kristeva's book for exposing the mechanisms of anti-Semitism.

(6) You say, "Nevertheless, one can assume that the young journalist who urged isolating Europe's Jews on an island did not find the deportations of 1942 objectionable." Let's be serious – journalistically and academically – and read what it says. He did not "urge," nor did he "propose," anything. The sentence in "Les Juifs dans la littérature actuelle" says, "En plus, on voit qu'une solution du problème juif qui viserait à la création d'une colonie juive isolée de l'Europe, n'entraînerait pas, pour la vie littéraire de l'Occident, de conséquences déplorables [In addition, one sees that a solution to the Jewish problem that would aim at creation of a Jewish colony isolated from Europe would not result, for the literary life of the West, in deplorable consequences]." That is a terrible thing to say, and it is terrifying to think of the way it may have given support to the deportations of Jews from Belgium that began over a year later. But you should explain what it says, not make things up. The article is restricted to what its title names, namely "contemporary literature," and

comments only on "literary life." Rather than "urging" the isolation of anyone, de Man unequivocally condemns what he calls "vulgar anti-Semitism" and vigorously criticizes the "myth" of a Jewish "pollution" of European literature. And he lists Franz Kafka among the four most important authors of modern literature. His article is in fact an implicit condemnation of the other articles adjacent to de Man's in this special page of *Le Soir* on "the Jewish question." These other articles, a hideous one on "Les deux faces du judaïsme," an attack on Freud, and a vilification of "la peinture juive," represent just that "vulgar anti-Semitism" which de Man vigorously rejects in his own article.

In addition, there *is* another article which raises, from a rather different angle, similar "questions." I gather you were not able to read this one, given your deadline, for had you read it you could not have failed to take notice of it. This one reviews a book on Charles Péguy, and begins with a fairly extensive recounting of Péguy's role in the Dreyfus Affair. De Man praises Péguy for his wholehearted defense of Dreyfus and his commitment to egalitarian socialism. He was a "Dreyfusard *jusqu'à bout*," writes de Man, with evident approval. Historians would surely understand the significance of the appellation "Dreyfusard" in that time and place. How about a little respect for history, and some attention to the documents?

(7) You quote Jeffrey Mehlman, whom you call "a practitioner of deconstruction" (!), as saying that de Man's articles in *Le Soir* "plugged the Nazi hit parade." The reality is far more complex. Did you give a journalistic glance, or cast a historian's gaze, at these articles, so as to verify the interpretation of your source? Did you look at de Man's articles on Montherlant's *Le Solstice de juin* (11 November 1941), on Brasillach's *Notre Avant-Guerre* (12 August 1941), or on Drieu's *Notes pour comprendre le siècle* (9 December 1941)? Even a brief inspection would have revealed, for example, that de Man is extremely critical of the political views expressed in Montherlant's book and insolently attacks his qualifications as a political and historical commentator. The other two are just as unkind. How did you miss them?

Your account of de Man's political position in those articles is a one-sided distortion of a complex matter. To say, as you do, that "out of a sense of malaise, of having been defeated by history," "the young de Man became a Fascist," lock, stock, and barrel, is simply wrong, not to mention unhistorical, and could not be based on a reading of the articles in question – which is, after all, what we are talking about. And it is your account that has been repeated all around the United States and in Europe by journalists who have taken your word for it. Perhaps because you are a professor of history as well as a journalist, and therefore speak with authority, these other journalists have made no attempt to read de Man's writings themselves or to verify the accuracy of your report.

(8) If you had been truly interested in exploring the question of whether "Paul de Man became a Fascist," or in actually reporting on his political convictions, there were other options open to you beyond the time-consuming reading of all those articles. Sometimes journalists interview witnesses. Surely relevant here is the testimony of two people who knew de Man during the war, Charles Dosogne, the first editor-in-chief of *Les Cahiers du Libre Examen*, of which de Man, as you know, was editor in 1940, before the Occupation, and Georges Lambrichs, a Belgian writer who was a close friend of Paul de Man in his early years and who after the war became an editor at Minuit and Gallimard in Paris. Two or three telephone calls and you could have quoted the former affirming that he never heard de Man, neither before nor during the war express a single anti-Semitic opinion or attitude. Or the second asserting that de Man was "anything but a collaborator," and that he had assisted French resistants in publishing and circulating a publication prohibited by the Germans in Paris (with texts by Eluard, Bataille, etc.), called *Exercice du silence*.

Sometimes journalists read other newspapers. A short walk to the library and you could have read in Belgium's biggest newspaper (the present-day *Le Soir*, 3 December 1987, 4) the words of an anonymous third person who knew de Man during the war (later identified as a certain Georges Goriély) and who, he said, had been at that time "*clandestin*, mêlé à la Résistance." "According to our source," wrote the newspaper, de Man was "idéologiquement, ni antisémite, ni même pro-nazi." Goriély told the Belgian reporter that he never (*jamais*) feared at all that de Man, who knew he was linked to the Resistance, would denounce him.

All of this information was not difficult to come by, surely not for the contributing editor of a journal with a reputation for breaking tough stories. Certainly not for a journalist with a sharp eye for "revelations" that would "shock and dismay." Not to mention for a historian. That is just the point I am making: in a matter of this gravity a historian has a responsibility to get as many of the facts as possible and to get them right, even to wait a little when it is known that important additional documents will soon be available, to make a few extra telephone calls, to be prepared to be patient, to take the time to read and to think before passing judgment. [Note added 11 August 1988: In the months since this letter was written a great deal more testimony has come in from those who knew Paul de Man in Belgium during the war. This new information confirms the fact that if de Man was not a member of the

Resistance he nevertheless cooperated in their work. It now appears, for example, that de Man probably lost his job with the publishing agency Dechenne in the spring of 1943 precisely because he had helped arrange the publication there of the Eluard, Bataille, *et al.* volume *Exercice du silence.*]

(9) Then there is the topic of the supposed "hero worship" of de Man by students and colleagues in the sentences you quote from Frank Lentricchia. You will say that you did not say this, that you were just quoting your sources accurately, but surely even a journalist has a responsibility not to pass on errors and defamatory insinuations. What you quote Lentricchia as saying is a condescending slur on all those students and colleagues who studied with de Man, read his work, and found it indispensable for their own work. You, with Lentricchia's help, imply that they were hypnotized by some kind of charismatic personality, as Mario was by the magician in Thomas Mann's allegory of the rise of Italian fascism, "Mario and the Magician." The facts are far otherwise. Charismatic teachers are abundant at the universities in which de Man taught. It takes more than that to attract the sustained attention of all those brilliant students and colleagues of such diverse orientation in literary study. The fact is that it was de Man's learning, rigor, and original insight into major works by Proust, Rousseau, Kant, Hegel, Wordsworth, Baudelaire, Yeats, and many others, into literary history, into the working of language generally, literary and otherwise, into the relation of literature and history, into literary history as such, and into literary theory that attracted students and colleagues to read his essays and attend his seminars. These features of his work will continue to draw serious students of literature to read his work.

Whatever de Man wrote in 1941–2, there is nothing whatever fascist, anti-Semite, or politically reactionary in what he wrote and published after 1953. Quite the reverse is the case. In fact I should say, now that I have had time to read those "early writings" and think about their relation to the later work of de Man, not that there is no connection between the two sets of writings, as it appeared to me when we talked by phone last January, but that the relation is one of reversal or putting in question. The special targets of his radical questioning of received opinions about particular authors, about literary history, and about the relation of literature to history in his later work were just those ideas about these topics that recur in the articles he wrote for *Le Soir*: notions about specific national and racial character and about the uniqueness of each national literature, notions about the independent and autonomous development of literature according to its own intrinsic laws and according to a model of organic development, that is, according to what he called in his latest essays "aesthetic ideology." Now having access to those early writings, I have a better understanding of the urgency with which de Man advised me, the first time we met, in 1966, not to read the later Heidegger but to go back to *Sein und Zeit* if I wanted to read Heidegger, or the equal urgency with which he vigorously put in question, at a conference that took place in Zürich about 1969, some ideas I proposed in a paper about the organic development of the novel toward greater and greater sophistication and complexity. I was prepared to believe that those ideas were in error, but reading these newly discovered "early writings" has given me a new understanding of what is potentially at stake politically in what might appear to be merely "academic" questions.

But already the articles in *Le Soir* present evidence of a transformation under way or of an intellectual battle within de Man's mind, for example in the difference between "Les Juifs dans la littérature actuelle" and the article on Charles Péguy published only two months later. One might in fact apply to his own case what he says of such changes in a review of a novel by one Herman de Man, *Maria et son charpentier*. Speaking of the implausibly rapid transformation from evil to good of the protagonist of this novel de Man says: "Presque toujours, le changement dans l'âme du personnage est présenté d'une manière trop brusque et trop rapide, alors qu'elle traînera en réalité sur longues périodes de transition durant lesquelles des forces contraires se disputent dans le coeur du héros [Almost always, the change in the soul of the personage is presented in too brusque and too rapid a manner, whereas in reality it will take place throughout long periods of transition during which contrary forces battle within the heart of the hero]" (4 March 1941). Nor is it the case that de Man's writings after 1953 are all of a piece, any more than the writings of 1941–2, though, as I have said, there is no trace remaining of the nationalist and organicist ideas of the "early writings" in the writings after 1953, except when they are identified as ever-present temptations in literary studies that must be vigorously contested. De Man's work was continually passing beyond positions previously held, and for a period of a decade or more after 1953 his work was within a region that might be called "phenomenological," in which the important categories were consciousness, intentionality, and temporality, though already with anticipations of the interest in figurative language that marked his work after the mid-sixties. The major essay, "The Rhetoric of Temporality," presented at Johns Hopkins in 1967, marks a turning point to a new phase. Thereafter the key terms in de Man's work tended to be linguistic ones: allegory, metaphor, prosopopoeia, rhetoric, irony, the distinction between constative and performative uses of language. Attention to history, politics, and to what he called "aesthetic ideology" becomes more explicit in his latest work, though it was present all along, especially in his constant concern to put in question the validity of period terms and the global generalizations they codify. "Romanticism" and "modernism" were his special concerns in this research.

Whatever de Man wrote in 1941–2, these later writings make him one of the most important literary critics and theorists of his time, indispensable reading for *our* time too, for reasons I shall try to specify later. Testimony to his importance is the fact that Mehlman, Lentricchia, and others of his hostile critics have been and remain fascinated by his work, obsessed with it, full of envy of it and resentment toward it. It is *their* fascination that is an inverse hero worship, not the sober reading, assessment, and practical use of his work by students and teachers all across the country, for example by the authors of the essays in *Reading de Man Reading* (edited by Lindsay Waters and Wlad Godzich, forthcoming from the University of Minnesota Press), or in the recent balanced essays by Geoffrey Hartman (in *The New Republic*), Jacques Derrida (in *Critical Inquiry*), and Jonathan Culler (forthcoming).

(10) Then there is what you say about "damage control" and the publication of the "early writings" in French. I was present at that meeting in Tuscaloosa. The collective decision was to acquire good copies of all of de Man's writings of 1941–2, to distribute them in photocopy to anyone interested, and to publish them with all possible speed so they would be widely available. You speak as if you think doing that was a way of hiding them – by publishing the original documents, in facsimile, in their original language. Think about that – it is an outrageous suggestion, and a strange thing for a historian to say. Surely you know that waiting to translate 400 pages of material would have taken a very long time. Now the articles – all the articles [including some discovered as recently as June (11 August 88)] – will be available this fall, providing a reliable basis for a reasonable discussion, and a translation, of all those pages. Our decision was for the utmost possible speed in making all the writings widely available. Does that sound like "damage control"? What sort of historian calls complete republication of original documents "damage control"? Is it "damage control" to try to correct and persuade you to retract the errors and defamatory insinuations of your article?

(11) The number of articles by de Man in *Le Soir* is of course not 92, as your incomplete information in January led you to say, but 170, as well as a careful search has been able to determine. These will all be included in the forthcoming University of Nebraska Press volume, along with the ten articles published in *Het Vlaamsche Land* and the three earlier texts from *Les Cahiers du Libre Examen* [as well as the even more recently

discovered articles in the *Bibliographie Dechenne* and in the prewar socialist student newspaper *Jeudi* (11 August 1988)].

(12) Moving on now to what is the real center of your article, and of all the others around the world that have repeated your falsehoods, namely an attempt to discredit and obliterate so-called "deconstruction" by making it continuous with de Man's supposed total commitment to fascism:

First, what you say about so-called "deconstruction" and Heidegger. You speak of Jacques Derrida, absurdly, as the "founder" of "deconstruction," as though it were a bank or a "school," in any case some kind of identifiable "it," and then go on to say two more utterly erroneous things. First, you say that "Heidegger's commitment to Nazism was much stronger than has previously been realized." In fact, as the serious European reviews and comments have shown, Farias' book has added little new to what has already been known for decades. Second, but much more heinous, especially in its context, is your false assertion that Heidegger is "the German philosopher acknowledged by Derrida as the intellectual progenitor of deconstruction." The facts are far otherwise. Both de Man and Derrida have been consistently, carefully, patiently critical of what Heidegger says. Heidegger has been one of the major targets of so-called "deconstruction," not its progenitor. De Man's "Tentation de la permanence," an essay of 1955 (well before he knew any work by Derrida, by the way) is a major essay exposing Heidegger's submission to a mystified aesthetic ideology. Another de Man essay rejecting Heidegger's belief that poetic language, as exemplified in Hölderlin, could speak "Being" directly, is "Heidegger's Exegeses of Hölderlin" (also 1955). Moreover, Derrida's *De l'esprit: Heidegger et la question* (1987) had been published when you wrote your article, not to speak of many earlier essays by Derrida on Heidegger, so you had had an opportunity to read them, if you had cared to learn something about the topic on which you were writing. *De l'esprit* is the best book I know that shows through careful reading of Heidegger how a certain fascist nationalism enters deeply into Heidegger's late philosophical works, not just into the *Rektoratsrede*. It is an instructive book. You should read it if you are interested in Heidegger and fascism.

(13) What is worst, most defamatory, about what you say about Heidegger and so-called "deconstruction" is that it is part of the assertions about "deconstruction" that are in fact the essential message of your article. The sequence of implied arguments or enthymemes goes like this, in a crescendo of errors: De Man was a fascist through and through in his "early writings." In his later writings he was a

"deconstructionist." His "deconstructionist" writings are all of a piece with his "early writings." Therefore all deconstructionists, including Derrida and me (I as "the leading deconstructionist in the United States and a friend of de Man," Derrida as the "founder" of "deconstruction"), are fascists. Moreover, Derrida has admitted that Heidegger, a fascist philosopher, is the "progenitor" of deconstruction. Therefore we come back again to the conclusion that all deconstructionists are fascists, including the two "leaders" mentioned. After you have published this, do you really expect me to sit down with you and have a friendly little chat about your article, as one of your notes to me suggests we should do. Let's be serious!

(14) The sequence of false argumentation that leads to that terrible implied accusation against me, Derrida, and all others who have worked in this mode of literary and philosophical study, goes by way of and depends absolutely on the account you give of so-called "deconstruction," with the help of Said, Mehlman, and Lentricchia. It is erroneous throughout. Everything you say about so-called "deconstruction" and about de Man's later writings is false, except your quotations from Esch, Hertz, and Graff. You will say that this is not your fault, that you informed yourself as best you could (mostly by way of phoning some self-proclaimed opponents of so-called "deconstruction"), but of course you had an obligation, particularly in view of the gravity of the charges you were bringing against "deconstruction," to get it right, to learn enough about the topic to know what you were talking about. And you do speak for yourself in your description of "deconstruction" at the bottom of third column, p. 22, and top of first column, p. 23, of your article. There you repeat the most erroneous clichés of previous journalistic accounts. Let me try to identify these.

(a) With all respect for my good friend Edward Said, I do not recognize the work of de Man, Derrida, or myself in what you quote from him. Are you sure you quoted him correctly? In any case, in de Man's work or Derrida's, "rhetoric" and "stated content" are not separated in the way you quote Said as saying, nor is it true that the "deconstructed meaning" (whatever *that* means) "locates itself" "in the range of decidable meanings." Said may have given a valiant try at a capsule definition, but, assuming you quoted him correctly, I would have to say he did not get very far toward a correct or coherent definition, though I do not suppose he intended to be other than helpful. To say of the so-called "deconstructionists," as you say Said said, that "their whole point is that their positions are not paraphrasable" is ridiculous. It would be as difficult to "paraphrase" in a sentence or two Said's argument in his admirable *Beginnings* as it would be to paraphrase in a sentence or two de Man's *Allegories of Reading* or Derrida's *Of Grammatology* or his recent *De l'esprit*. There is nothing whatsoever scandalous or unique to "deconstruction" in recognizing the difficulty and inherent dangers of oversimplication and outright falsification in attempting to paraphrase a complex intellectual position.

(b) The next paragraph, where you are more on your own, is much worse. You show no understanding of what is at stake in saying a war is a text. One of de Man's main points in his later work was that words have a terrible power to bring about what he called "the materiality of history." The effect of journalism, both of de Man's wartime writings and of what you and other journalists have written now about de Man, is a good example of that. As a good Marxist historian, as I am told you pretend to be, you surely do not believe that all those civilians in Nicaragua have been getting killed because the Contras and Sandinistas have been out having a little target practice? Or that we were in Vietnam for reasons that had nothing to do with words and the ideology expressed in "texts." Those wars, like all wars and revolutions, are "textual" through and through.

So-called "deconstruction" does not by any means "presuppose" that "literature is not part of knowable social and political reality," or that "one must be resigned to the impossibility of truth." Quite the reverse is the case. "Deconstruction" is in all its many forms a contribution to knowledge by being a contribution to good and accurate reading of "social and political reality" as well as of literary and philosophical texts and of the relation between the former and the latter. You must have picked up your ideas from an earlier article in *Newsweek* or some such source. You could never have learned them from a careful reading of even one work by de Man or Derrida.

Nor is "deconstruction" "nihilistic." Again, just the reverse is the case. I have written about the charge that "deconstruction" is "nihilistic" in my essay in *Deconstruction and Criticism*. "Nihilism," if it means anything precise, rather than being just a polemical name for something we do not like and want to call by a harsh word, is the name of a moment intrinsic to Western metaphysics when the highest values are devalued by the vanishing of what had seemed their necessary transcendent ground. Nothing could be further from that than the commitment of de Man, Derrida, or myself to a rigorous truth-telling about the nature of language, about the meaning of major texts in the Western tradition, about the relations of literature or philosophy to history.

Nor is "deconstruction" in any way "implicitly authoritarian," as you charge. Again the exact opposite is the case. Deconstruction works to free people from ideological mystifications and aberrancies, for example deeply ingrained notions about the organic development of literature as a separate "aesthetic" realm, or, on the other hand, the notion that a work of literature is entirely determined and can be entirely explained by its historical context. Far from being "authoritarian," "deconstruction" functions in manifold ways to free us from totalizing and totalitarian thinking, thinking, for example, that makes "deconstruction" one single, homogeneous, monolithic thing.

(c) Your next paragraph repeats two of the most common and most erroneous clichés about deconstruction, namely that it makes criticism "the creative activity of the period" and that it says "the critic [can] create meaning." This is your version of the false notion that deconstruction is an extreme form of "reader response" criticism and that it holds texts mean nothing in themselves, so the critic is free to make them mean anything he or she likes. Again, the exact opposite is the case. In his "Foreword" to Carol Jacobs' *The Dissimulating Harmony*, de Man, citing Hölderlin, gives full authority to the text to determine what happens in any act of reading that text:

> What makes a reading more or less true is simply the predicability, the necessity of its occurrence, regardless of the reader or of the author's wishes. "Es ereignet sich aber das Wahre" (not *die Wahrheit*) says Hölderlin, which can be freely translated, "What is true is what is bound to take place." And in the case of the reading of a text, what takes place is a necessary understanding. What marks the truth of such an understanding is not some abstract universal but the fact that it has to occur regardless of other considerations. . . . Reading . . . has to go against the grain of what one would want to happen in the name of what has to happen; this is the same as saying that understanding is an epistemological event prior to being an ethical or aesthetic value. (xi)

(d) Your account of "Excuses," de Man's essay on Rousseau's *Confessions*, is erroneous throughout, as is your account of what de Man means by "allegory." De Manian allegory has nothing to do with hidden autobiographical elements in a text. As for "Excuses," even if one were to read this essay as a disguised autobiographical confession, an extremely dubious, unauthorized, and unauthorizable procedure, however tempting it may be as a way to avoid reading what de Man really said, the meaning of the essay would still be the exact opposite of what you make it mean. The essay would give no comfort whatsoever to de Man himself or to anyone else who might hope to use a speech act to exonerate himself from some prior act. "Excuses" focuses on the disjunction between performative and cognitive dimensions of language. It says that, for Rousseau at least and perhaps in other cases too, an excuse is a performative use of language that never works. Far from functioning to free the excuser from a prior guilt, the excuse repeats the crime or even commits the crime from which it would free the excuser. "Excuses generate the very guilt they exonerate," says de Man, "though always in excess or by default," and "No excuse can hope to catch up with such a proliferation of guilt" (*Allegories of Reading*, 209).

(e) I turn, finally, to what you say, with the help of Frank Lentricchia, about the way de Man supposedly cuts off literature and literary study from history. Once more, what you say is the exact contrary of the truth. Far from being "antihistorical," de Man was in all his work, early and late, passionately concerned with the relation of literature to what he came to call "the materiality of history." De Man explored with great insight the ways in which literature makes history rather than just reflecting it, and he had a deep sense of the way apparently innocuous errors in conceptions about literary history and about the relation of literature to history as such (what he called "aesthetic ideology") can have disastrous political effects. One of his last and as yet unpublished essays, on Schiller, is extremely explicit about this, but the concern for history is manifest everywhere in what he wrote, for example in "The Resistance to Theory," when he says: "This does not mean that fictional narratives are not part of the world and of reality; their impact upon the world may be all too strong for comfort," or when, in an interview a few months before his death, he says, in response to Stefano Rosso's observation that the terms "ideology" and "politics" are now appearing frequently in his writing and lectures: "I don't think I ever was away from these problems, they were always uppermost in my mind. I have always maintained that one could approach the problems of ideology and by extension the problems of politics only on the basis of critical-linguistic analysis, which had to be done in its own terms, in the medium of language, and I felt I could approach those problems only after having achieved a certain control over those questions" (*The Resistance to Theory*, 11, 121). Those who affirm that de Man has no concern for history are really objecting to a vision of history that differs sharply from their own and that threatens their assumptions about the relations of literature and history.

This brings me to the concluding section of what I have to say. Why is it, exactly, that so-called "deconstruction" in particular and literary theory generally have been so violently attacked and so falsely described in your article and in the other journalistic ones? Why is it that the falsehoods have taken just the form they have taken, the claim, for example, that so-called "deconstruction" is anti-historical, nihilistic, and says works may be made to mean anything the interpreter wants them to mean, when in fact exactly the opposite is the case? Why is it that the discovery of these early writings by de Man has produced a violent outpouring of these clichés, a somnambulistic repetition of just these received opinions, as in the case of your article, written as if by a ventriloquist's dummy through whom a programmed procedure of thought control is speaking? Just why is it that so many supposedly responsible newspapers and weeklies leaped to condemn de Man without waiting to read what they were writing about – not to mention making a careful review of the evidence – and why is it that all made the move to condemn so-called "deconstruction" as something that would follow logically from the condemnation of de Man, again without waiting to read and reflect, to sift the evidence, as if one could say now, "Ah ha, we knew it all along, but now we have the proof: deconstruction is fascist"? Why is it that though *The Nation* is supposedly liberal or on the "left," so many newspapers and weeklies on the "right," even the extreme right, have leaped eagerly to repeat the falsehoods in your article? Why is it that the authors of so many of these attacks are, like you, professors as well as journalists, professor–journalists who use the prestige of their university positions to promulgate these falsehoods? Just what is at stake that would lead to the wholesale suspension of the ordinary rules of academic and journalistic responsibility?

No doubt this outpouring of falsehood is "overdetermined." It has many and perhaps contradictory "causes" and concomitant conditions, including, no doubt, plain stupidity and ignorance, though these would not account for just the form the errors have taken. But the essential reasons I think can be identified. As de Man himself put it one of the last times I saw him, a few days before his death, "the stakes are enormous." He was speaking, first and most immediately, of a deplorably ignorant and malicious essay by René Wellek in *The New Criterion* accusing de Man and others of "Destroying Literary Studies." A copy was on de Man's bedside table with a friendly inscription from Wellek. It attacks not only de Man, but also Derrida and me, and so-called "deconstruction" generally, more or less in the same terms as you do and repeats more or less the same falsehoods, gathered as far as I can see from the mass media and from academic gossip. It certainly could not be based on a careful reading of what we have written. You might want to reflect on what it means that a so-called Marxist historian like you finds himself allied with a conservative like Wellek who publishes in a place like *The New Criterion* against what seems to you both a common enemy. I shall have a bit more to say about that later.

But de Man's reference when he said "the stakes are enormous" was also to the wider context of the perpetual war on behalf of good reading (that is, rhetorical reading, or, to give it another of its more recent names, so-called "deconstructive" reading) as a major defense of literary studies and of other precious aspects of our culture against the ever-present danger of various sorts of totalizing or totalitarian thinking. Make no mistake about it. The real target of your article and of the other journalistic ones that preceded it and followed it, in the *New York Times*, in *La Quinzaine littéraire*, in the *Frankfurter Allgemeine Zeitung*, in various university newspapers, etc. is, whether consciously or "unconsciously," explicitly or implicitly, deliberately or by a somnambulistic happenstance, not de Man's early writings or his personality, but the kind of work with which his name is associated, that is, so-called "deconstruction," and, beyond that, literary theory generally – as the extension of the attack, in the *Newsweek* piece, from so-called "deconstruction" to the so-called "new historicists," what that piece, quoting Frederick Crews, calls "the new militant cultural materialism of the left," and as a recent attack, in *The Wall Street Journal*, on the Duke English Department for destroying canonical literary studies, unmistakably demonstrates.

In the name of what standards, implicit or explicit, does this league of the so-called left with the so-called right in American and European journalism take place? The clear aim of the writing on both political "sides" is to discredit and obliterate, as far as possible, de Man's work as a whole and that of his associates, to prevent it from being taught and students or anyone else from reading it. From that it is an easy step to a wholesale condemnation of literary theory generally. You will say that your article ends by saying no more than that "a revaluation of the politics of deconstruction and the writings of de Man is now at the top of the agenda of both the deconstructionists and their critics," but that, in its context, does not imply a rereading of de Man's work, only an acceptance of the juridical procedure of condemnation you have outlined in your article. Insofar as you are a Marxist theorist, as I am told you are, you were shooting yourself in the foot, as they say, by writing and publishing your article against de Man and "deconstruction," since you were participating, whether deliberately or inadvertently, in the current attempts to suppress theoretical reflection generally about literature and about the relation of literature to society. De Man's work is an invaluable part of that reflection, necessary reading, for example, for those young Marxists and Foucauldians, some of whom I named in my MLA Presidential address; necessary reading, for example, for those who want to understand what might be meant by the "material base" in its relation to ideology. Once again, it is a question of reading and of the taking of responsibility. And once again, it is de Man himself, in this case in one of his most powerful essays on the relations of literature, theory, history, and ideology, "The Resistance to Theory," who has in his later work said something essential on this topic, as on so many others in this region of thought and action:

> . . . what is it about literary theory that is so threatening that it provokes such strong resistances and attacks? It upsets rooted ideologies by

revealing the mechanics of their workings; it goes against a powerful philosophical tradition of which aesthetics is a prominent part; it upsets the established canon of literary works and blurs the borderlines between literary and non-literary discourse. By implication, it may also reveal the links between ideologies and philosophy. (*The Resistance to Theory*, 11).

De Man's formulations here help us to understand the violence of the outpouring of denunciations of de Man and of "deconstruction" based on errors of the sort I have identified in your essay. The violence is a reaction to the genuine threat posed by de Man's work and by that of the so-called deconstructionists generally to a powerful tradition of ideological assumptions about literature, about history, and about the relation of literature to human life. Fear of this power in "deconstruction" and in contemporary theory generally, in all its diversity, accounts better than any other explanation for the unreasoning hostility, the abandoning of the canons of journalistic and academic responsibility, in articles like yours and the many other subsequent attacks on de Man, on "deconstruction," and on critical theory as such. Insofar as the received opinions deconstruction challenges are "aberrations" and "mystifications," and they are that, they are exceedingly dangerous, politically and ethically, as all falsehood is. Insofar as literary study is politically, socially, and ethically useful, deconstruction as a form of such study performs a fundamental work of what might be called the "critique of ideology." It is not surprising that the resistance to it should be so strong, but it is also the case that the health of our culture depends on the presence of the lessons of deconstruction within what is most vital and productive in literary and cultural study today.

26

The function of literary theory at the present time

Not long ago Paul de Man could cheerfully say, with how much or how little of irony is impossible to know, that *the* task of criticism in the coming years would be a kind of imperialistic appropriation of all of literature by the method of rhetorical reading often called "deconstruction." "But there is absolutely no reason why analyses of the kind suggested here for Proust," said de Man, "would not be applicable, with proper modifications of technique, to Milton or to Dante or to Hölderlin. This will in fact be the test of literary criticism in the coming years."[1] It can hardly be said that this task has been carried out in the years since 1979 with much systematic rigor. This is true in spite of the widespread influence of "deconstruction," in spite of the many books and essays written about it, and in spite of the brilliant work of younger critics influenced by de Man. But there has been more talk about deconstruction, as a "theory" or as a "method," attempts to applaud it or to deplore it, than there has been an attempt to do it, to show that it is "applicable" to Milton or to Dante or to Hölderlin, or to Anthony Trollope and to Virginia Woolf.

In fact there has been a massive shift of focus in literary study since 1979 away from the "intrinsic," rhetorical study of literature toward study of the "extrinsic" relations of literature, its placement within psychological, historical, or sociological contexts.

All honor to the motivations which underlie this shift, the noble desire for social justice, for the improvement of the situation of women and minorities, for a clear understanding of the ideological presuppositions which invisibly manipulate us, of which the shift in commitment I am describing is surely a conspicuous example. And all honor to the impatience with the actual hard work of reading, the nagging sense that reading may be cut off from the real obligations of life, the desire to make the study of literature somehow count, have effects of power in society and in history. It is hard to imagine wholeheartedly admiring the man or woman who does not have some kind of passion for social justice and is willing to work for it.

385

The question is what this has to do with the study of literature. It is in defining that liaison that the difficulties and disagreements begin. My contention is that the study of literature has a great deal to do with history, society, the self, but that this relation is not a matter of thematic reflection within literature of these extra-linguistic forces and facts, but rather a matter of the way the study of literature offers perhaps the best opportunities to identify the nature of language as it may have effects on what de Man calls "the materiality of history." Here "reading," in the sense of a rhetorical analysis of the most vigilant and patient sort, is indispensable. How else are we going to know just what a given text is and says, what it can do? This can never be taken for granted beforehand, not even after that text has been overlaid by generations of commentary.

Since "reading" in this sense is indispensable to any responsible concern for the relations of literature to what is outside it, it would be a catastrophe for the study of literature if the insights of deconstruction, along with those of the New Criticism and of such critics as William Empson and Kenneth Burke, were to be forgotten or were to be relegated to an overpassed stage in some imagined historical "development," so that they no longer need to be taken seriously in the actual, present-day work of literary study. I should go so far as to say that, to paraphrase de Man, "the task of literary criticism in the coming years" will be mediation between the rhetorical study of literature, of which "deconstruction" is by far the most rigorous in recent times, and the now so irresistibly attractive study of the extrinsic relations of literature. Or rather, since, as Thomas Keenan reminds me, the word *mediation* is part of the vocabulary of dialectical thinking and suggests always the possibility of some synthesis or *Aufhebung*, usually at the expense of one or the other parties, it would be better to say "confrontation" or "encounter" or "negotiation of the non-negotiable," since, it may be, the rhetorical study of literature or of the "literariness" in any piece of language as soon as it is taken as a text is the encounter with that thing articulated within language which is altogether irreducible or explicable by historical, sociological, or psychological methods of interpretation. Even "encounter" or "confrontation" is misleading, since that thing of which I speak can never be seen face-to-face, only indirectly, as in those traces or tracks of the passage of a cosmic particle in a bubble chamber. In any case, without the rhetorical study of literature, focused on language, its laws, what it is, and what it can do, particularly on the role of figurative language in interfering with the straightforward working of grammar and logic, as the parasitical virus interferes with the working of the host cell, we can have no hope of understanding just what the role of literature might be in society, in history, and in individual human life.

In our anxiety to make the study of literature count we are always in danger of misplacing that role, of claiming too much for literature, for example, as a political or historical force, or of thinking of the teaching of literature as too explicitly political. No one can doubt that literature is performative, that it makes things happen, that it is a way of doing things with words, and no one can doubt that the teaching of literature always has a political component, perhaps most when I am most silent about its political implications, ignorant of them or indifferent to them. It is not so much that the performative effects of literature, for better or for worse, are overestimated, as that they are often located in the wrong place. Sociological theories of literature which reduce it to being a mere "reflection" of dominant ideologies in fact tend to limit its role to that of passive mirroring, a kind of unconscious anamorphosis of the real currents of power. Study of literature would then tell readers something they could probably learn better elsewhere, by direct study of historical documents, for example. De Man, on the other hand, goes so far as to say that "textual allegories on this level of rhetorical complexity [he is speaking of Jean-Jacques Rousseau's *Social Contract*] generate history" (*AR*, 277). In order to understand how it might be the case that a certain kind of language would make what we call history happen it is necessary first to understand what it means, in the case of a given text, to speak of it as a textual allegory with a high level of rhetorical complexity. It is necessary, that is, to *read* the *Social Contract* or whatever other text is our concern, no easy matter, nor one that happens as often as one would like, before going on to studying with confidence those extrinsic relations. To put this another way, those extrinsic relations themselves are intrinsic to the text. The distinction between intrinsic and extrinsic, like most such binary oppositions, turns out to be false and misleading. Those apparently "extrinsic" relations themselves require a rhetorical analysis, for example a clear understanding of the various figures of speech always necessary in one form or another to talk about the relation of a work of literature to its "context": reflection," which is metaphor; "context," which is metonymy; "ideology," which is anamorphosis, and so on.

It is in fact not the case that the work of de Man or Derrida is entirely "intrinsic," entirely concerned with language as such, limited to language in rarefied isolation from the extralinguistic. There is a fully elaborated theory of the historical, psychological, and ethical relations of literature already present, for example, in de Man's *Allegories of Reading*. Work he was doing in the last two or three years of his life was increasingly focused on such questions, no doubt as one more example of that almost universal shift to politics, history, and society which marks the specificity of the current moment in literary study. No doubt this present essay is yet another example of that. In an essay entitled "The Resistance to Theory," for example, de Man has this to say about the contribution of a rhetorical study of literature to social, political, and historical understanding:

> It would be unfortunate, for example, to confuse the materiality of the signifier with the materiality of what it signifies. This may seem obvious enough on the level of sight and sound, but is less so with regard to the more general phenomenality of space, time or especially of the self: no one in his right mind will try to grow grapes by the luminosity of the word "day," but it is very difficult not to conceive the pattern of one's past and future existence as in accordance with temporal and spatial schemes that belong to fictional narratives and not to the world. This does not mean that fictional narratives are not part of the world and of reality; their impact upon the world may well be all too strong for comfort. What we call ideology is precisely the confusion of linguistic with natural reality, of reference with phenomenalism. It follows that, more than any other mode of inquiry, including economics, the linguistics of literariness is a powerful and indispensable tool in the unmasking of ideological aberrations, as well as a determining factor in accounting for their occurrence. Those who reproach literary theory for being oblivious to social and historical (that is to say ideological) reality are merely stating their fear at having their own ideological mystifications exposed by the tool they are trying to discredit. They are, in short, very poor readers of Marx's *German Ideology*. (*RT*, 11)

One may wish to argue with this or to say that de Man has got the relation of the study of language and literature to politics all wrong, but only in bad faith could one say he does not explicitly account for the political and historical implications of his theory of language and his theory of what he calls "literariness." Or rather it would be better to speak of what he has written not as abstract theory but as praxis, since almost all of his work centers on the reading of some text or other, for example the series of essays on different works by Rousseau in *Allegories of Reading*. Or rather, to refine still further, what he has written, like all good literary study, is neither pure theory nor pure praxis, "practical criticism," nor yet a mixture of the two or something between the two, but a mode of interpretive language which is beyond this false and misleading opposition. One might call it "exemplification," but that would leave open the question, "exemplification of just what?" The answer must be that each good example of reading is an exemplification of other examples, according to a strange logic of synecdoche in a situation like literary study in which there exists no possibility of totalization or the establishment, once and for all, of an all-encompassing general theory. If, in any case, one of the simultaneously practical and theoretical dimensions of Paul de Man's work is a scrupulous accounting for the referential, historical, social, and political effects of literature, the same thing can just as decisively be demonstrated for Jacques Derrida, who has all along included consideration of the institutional, political, and social implications of his work, for example in *Positions*, or, more recently, in an interview entitled "Deconstruction in America."²

That the opponents of the rhetorical study of literature from both sides of the political spectrum continue to misrepresent it as ahistorical and apolitical may indicate the importance of what is in question here. The stakes, one can see, are enormous, both for literary study as such and for the function of literary study in society as it is now and as it is likely to be in the coming years. The stakes are enormous, that is, in continuing to think out the implications of a rhetorical study of literature for our political and ethical life.

The consensus on the function of the humanities in American life lasted until about the time I went to college in 1944. That consensus was largely the product of the humanism of Matthew Arnold as it was embodied in the curriculum of American colleges and universities. That curriculum was oriented primarily toward preparing white Anglo-Saxon middle-class males for professions: law, medicine, teaching, public service, business, the protestant ministry, and toward preparing white Anglo-Saxon middle-class women to be better wives, mothers, hostesses, and community servants. The idea was that you went off for four years to a protected and sequestered place, often protected and sequestered from the "opposite sex," and there assimilated the humanistic values by reading Plato, Shakespeare, Robert Browning, and so on, in preparation for entering society. The consensus about humanistic study saw it as primarily thematic and stylistic. Courses in the humanities were in aid of the assimilation of the best that has been thought and said in our Western tradition from the Bible and the Greeks on down. Such courses also provided models of style mostly taken from Victorian prose. In the required Freshman course I had at Oberlin College in 1944 we read Arnold, Newman, Mill, Huxley, and the Lang, Leaf, and Meyers translation of the Iliad. There was a general consensus on the canon a student of literature should read. It was primarily English: Chaucer, Shakespeare, Milton, Pope, Wordsworth, Tennyson, Arnold, T. S. Eliot, not a woman among them, and foreign works were usually read in translation, as is still the case in innumerable courses in "masterpieces of Western literature" across the United States today. This meant a general assumption of the translatability of works in that canon that happen to have been written in Latin, Greek, or Italian. In spite of lip service paid to "language requirements" and to the desirability of being able to read French, German, or Latin, the consensus I am describing depended fundamentally on the assumption that the great masterpieces in any language can and have been translated without significant loss into English. It is no wonder that those "language requirements" gradually eroded, since the necessity of reading Homer or Dante or Dostoevsky or Baudelaire or Nietzsche "in the original" was by no means generally recognized.

At that very moment, though I certainly did not know it, this consensus was breaking down. *Understanding Poetry* was already being tried out in a gingerly fashion in certain advanced classes in English at Oberlin, and the same thing was happening all across the country. The New Criticism was, as Walter Jackson Bate astutely recognizes,[3] a major blow at the consensus. As soon as you start assuming that anyone can read a poem, that no special knowledge or membership in a particular class with a particular education is necessary, and as soon as you shift, however benignly, from attention to *what* is said, the thematic content, to *how* it is said, to tone, style, figures of speech, devices of presentation, it is the beginning of the end for that consensus. Sooner or later some teachers or students will see that the how contaminates and undermines the what. The long-term effect of the New Criticism, that is, was far different from, perhaps exactly the opposite of, the conservative intentions of its founders. The birth of American deconstruction out of Paul de Man's participation in Reuben Brower's "Hum 6" course at Harvard might be taken as an allegory of that process.[4]

A second blow at the consensus was struck by the introduction of the discipline of comparative literature into the curriculum of American colleges and universities. However benignly intended and conservative in its intent, this move led ultimately to a recognition of an essential untranslatability from one language to another. This means, as Bate sees clearly, a breaking of the authority and domination of Departments of English, a gradual recognition of why it is one must study foreign languages: not to come back from them into English but to stay in them, to go native, one might say. From the point of view of that old Arnoldian consensus about the humanities both the New Criticism and the development of comparative literature were subversive. They were ultimately lethal invasions, destructive parasites within the host organism, generated by the organism itself.

To these two internal self-generated attacks on the old consensus about the humanities may be added social changes outside the university: the new assumption that all Americans ought to have a higher education; the rise of great public universities; the shift to a notion that women too should be educated for professional work (a change of incalculable importance); the gradual realization that the United States is a multilingual not a monolingual country; technological developments like television; jet planes that bring European scholars here in a few hours; extremely rapid translation of European "theoretical" works, so that they often appear in English first – in short, the general internationalization of humanistic study.

The result of all this crossing of borders has been a breakdown or dissolution of that old consensus. I do not think it can be reconstructed by fiat. At most, or at worst, a beguiling but ultimately repressive simulacrum can be reimposed in its place, as is in some quarters being attempted now. This is in fact perhaps the greatest danger to the humanities at the moment. By "repressive" I mean for example forcing a Latino or Thai in Los Angeles, a Puerto Rican in New York, an inner city African-American in either city to read only *King Lear*, *Great Expectations*, and other works from the old canon, and to read them for a "content" and according to theological assumptions that are prescribed beforehand. This is what Joseph Conrad called "The Suppression of Savage Customs," which, as you remember, turned into "Exterminate all the brutes." The Latino, Thai, African-American, or Puerto Rican is assumed to be a "brute" until she or he can be turned as much as possible into that white middle-class male for whom the canon was intended. The dissolution of the consensus about humanistic study, a dissolution in which both internal and external factors have, as I have said, cooperated, has meant an irrevocable breakdown of the canon, a breakdown of the assumption of translatability, and, finally, a breakdown of the assumption that humanistic education is primarily aesthetic (has to do with pleasure) and thematic (has to do with values).

What I mean by the shaking of the canon should not be misunderstood. I do not mean we should no longer read Sophocles, Dante, Shakespeare, Milton, Wordsworth, and the rest. Surely it is good that they still be read. But they are read differently now, partly as a result of new ways of reading which have shown that they are far more problematic than perhaps they once seemed, far less the secure and stable repositories of the values and ideas of our cultural tradition than some defenders of the canon still seem to think they are. Canonical works now can be seen as especially concentrated forms of universal features of language, the tendency of figurative language, for example, to subvert straightforward grammatical or logical meaning. In addition, canonical works are read differently now because they are read in a different context, by students brought up on television, cinema, and popular music, for example, or in courses in which they are set side by side with noncanonical works. The ideology of the traditional canon involves both the exclusion of noncanonical works and strong presuppositions about how the canonical works are to be read. The shaking of the canon is accomplished by the rejection of both these forms of delimitation.

What rationale for the study of the humanities should be put in the place of the old consensus? I think there can be only one answer.

Preservation, conservation, the keeping of the archives, the whole work of memory, remembering, and memorialization: yes, this remains an indispensable task of humanistic study. But our past is remembered differently now and some different things are now recalled into memory, for example, African-American literature and history or the history of women and writing by women. Memory and the storing and interpretation of what is remembered is not a passive but a vital and passionate act, an act each generation does anew and differently as it appropriates history for its own purposes. One of the important effects of the new modes of literary theory has been to redefine what it is that is worth remembering and what procedures of recovery and reinterpretation should be followed to make sure we remember what we want to remember.

Along with that perennial task of humanistic study, however, study of the humanities, in the present context of our multilingual, multiracial society, a society whose cultural traditions, for better or worse, are primarily shaped by the mass media, must become again focused on another traditional task, the teaching of *reading*. Courses in the literature departments should become primarily training in reading and writing, the reading of great works of literature, yes, but with a much broader notion of the canon, and along with that training in reading all the signs: paintings, movies, television, the newspaper, historical data, the data of material culture. An educated people these days, an informed electorate, is a people who can read, who can read all the signs, no easy thing to learn.[5]

Our fundamental task, the new rationale for the humanities, is to teach reading and the effective writing that can only come from or accompany a sophisticated ability to read. This transformation of the task of teachers in the humanities has come partly from radical changes in our society itself, and therefore from changes in the role of the universities and colleges that are a major institution within that society, and partly from accompanying internal changes in the disciplines themselves. The most conspicuous of the latter, especially in literary study, is the new centrality of theory. The future of literary theory is immense (to paraphrase Matthew Arnold) because it is the fundamental tool of both the tasks of humanistic study in the coming years as I have defined them: the work of archival remembering and the work of the teaching of critical reading as the primary means of combating that disastrous confusion of linguistic with material reality, one name for which is "ideology."

Notes

1. Paul de Man, *Allegories of Reading* (New Haven and London, 1979), pp. 16–17, henceforth *AR*. This essay was written before the discovery of the wartime

writings of Paul de Man, and the subsequent flood of essays in the mass media and elsewhere, about them. I have written elsewhere about de Man's early writings, but will say here that I remain as convinced as when I wrote this essay that de Man's later writings are indispensable to present-day study of literature.
2. Jacques Derrida, "Deconstruction in America," *Critical Exchange*, no. 17 (Winter, 1985), 1–33.
3. See Walter Jackson Bate, "The Crisis in English Studies," *Harvard Magazine*, **85**, 12 (1982), 46–53.
4. This is discussed in de Man's "The Return to Philology." *The Times Literary Supplement*, No. 4,158 (Friday, 10 December 1982), pp. 1355–6.
5. The final few pages of this essay are in part an elaboration of convictions briefly affirmed in the fourth of the Presidential Columns in Chapter 18, above. Though Jonathan Culler and I might conceivably disagree a bit about exactly what it means to teach good reading, I take heart from his substantial agreement with what I am saying here. Here are some sentences from a forthcoming essay by him entitled "The Future of Criticism," which I have just encountered as I have been typing up my own essay:

> But when one thinks about the future of our multi-lingual, multi-racial society, one finds it hard seriously to imagine the establishment of a common culture based on the Greeks or other classics. Such common culture as we have will inevitably be based on the mass media – especially films and television. Schools will not counter this culture effectively by requiring the study of particular historical artifacts, seeking to impose a canon. The struggle against the debilitating effects of mass culture must take place on a different front: by teaching critical thinking, perhaps by analyzing the ideological stakes and structures of mass media productions and exposing the interests at work in their functioning. Argument about what literary works and what historical knowledge to require will only distract attention from the pressing problem of how to insure that schools encourage intellectual activity, teach critical thinking, close reading, analysis of narrative structures and semiotic mechanisms.

(This essay is now in print in *Framing the Sign: Criticism and its Institutions* [Norman, Oklahoma, 1988]).

Index

A, in *Either/Or*, 281–2
À la recherche du temps perdu (Proust), 34–5, 45, 57, 84, 128, 307
Abrams, M. H., 79–94, 143, 150, 151, 185–192, 196
Adagia (Stevens), 267
Adam Bede (Eliot), 8
Adam, in *Paradise Lost*, 293–4
Adorno, T. W., 218
Aeschylus, 263
After Strange Gods (Eliot), 67
Agon (Bloom), 218
Alastor (Shelley), 156–7
Alastor, in *Alastor*, 159, 162
Alford, Henry, 283
Allegro, L' (Milton), 125
Allen, D. C., 72
Alter, Robert, 112
Althusser, Louis, 319
âme romantique et le rêve, L' (Béguin), 19, 20, 67, 80
Amiel, Henri-Frédéric, 14, 22, 39, 41, 46, 81
Ammons, A. R., 218, 222
Anatomy of Criticism (Frye), 10
Anaximander, 99
Anxiety of Influence, The (Bloom), 115
Aphrodite, 155, 158
Apollinaire, Guillaume, 17
Apollo, 122, 127
Aquinas, St Thomas, 79
Arac, Jonathan, 326
Arachne, 125
Ariadne, 122–3, 257, 280–1
Ariosto, Ludovico, 149
Aristotle, 49, 50, 87, 99–100, 175, 232–3, 234, 238, 240
"Arnold at the Present Time" (Goodheart), 267
Arnold, Matthew, 6, 64, 65, 171, 222, 263, 264, 265–8, 272, 278–9, 331, 332, 335, 338, 339, 389, 392
Ashbery, John, 218, 219
"Asphodel, That Greeny Flower"

(Williams), 11, 108
Ästhetik (Hegel), 270
Auden, W. H., 65
Auerbach, Eric, viii, 6, 72, 79, 81, 134, 174
"Aufgabe des Übersetzers, Die" (Benjamin), 340
Augustine, St, 49–50, 73, 75, 80, 82, 84, 85, 87, 90, 91
Austen, Jane, 31, 230

B, in *Either/Or*, 281, 284
Bachelard, Gaston, 3, 4, 6, 9, 11, 22–3, 26, 32, 112
Bakhtin, Mikhail, 112, 224, 319, 323
Bakhtin: Essays and Dialogues (Bakhtin), 323
Balzac, Honoré de, 15, 19, 25, 34, 37, 43, 45, 46, 81
Barthes, Roland, 52, 84, 95, 112, 113, 114, 121, 135, 296, 319
Bataille, Georges, 95, 373, 374
Bate, Walter Jackson, 192–3, 198, 264–5, 268, 269, 314, 336, 390
Baudelaire, Charles, 17, 27, 34, 37, 43, 45, 56, 65, 81, 340, 374, 390
Beckett, Samuel, 8, 66, 72, 139
Beginnings (Said), 113–14, 120, 122, 133–42, 378
Benjamin, Walter, 178, 319, 340
Bennet, Elizabeth, in *Pride and Prejudice*, 211, 212
Bentham, Jeremy, 267
Benveniste, Émile, 52
Beowulf, 72, 203
Bercovitch, Sacvan, 112
Bergson, Henri, 11, 47, 58
Bernanos, Georges, 19, 21, 46, 67
Beyond Formalism (Hartman), 115, 125
Beyond the Pleasure Principle (Freud), 249, 250
Béguin, Albert, viii, 4, 13, 14, 18–21, 22, 23, 27, 29, 32, 39, 47, 67–8, 80, 81
Bible, 80, 85, 90, 223, 278, 279, 330, 338
Bibliographie Dechenne, 377
Blackmur, R. P. 66

395

Blake, William, 8, 64, 79, 80, 82, 86, 92, 115
Blanchot, Maurice, 28, 32, 40, 66, 149, 277, 290, 300–1, 302
Bleak House (Dickens), 336
Blin, Georges, 8, 29
Bloom, Harold, 109, 112, 115, 120, 122, 124–5, 126, 127, 131, 149, 150, 151, 218–21, 319
Bloomfield, Morton, 72
Bloy, Léon, 19, 21, 67
Blumine, in *Sartor Resartus*, 280
Boehme, Jacob, 80
Booth, Wayne, 143, 173
Borges, J. L., 135, 139, 173, 194
boundary 2, 245
"Boy of Winander, The" (Wordsworth), 178, 195
Boyer, Ernest, 316
Bradley, F. H., 8–9
Brandi, Cesare, 121
Brasillach, Robert, 372
Breton, André, 17
"Bright Star" (Keats), 222
Brontë, Emily, ix
Brooke, Dorothea, in *Middlemarch*, 211, 212
Brooke, Mr, in *Middlemarch*, 207
Brooks, Cleanth, 193, 195, 263–4, 333
Brower, Reuben, 390
Browning, Robert, 35, 44, 115, 125, 166, 266, 389
Burke, Kenneth, 174, 193, 195, 215, 218, 235, 386
Butor, Michel, 139
Byron, George Gordon, 32

Cahiers du libre examen, Les, 359, 361, 363, 365, 369, 373, 376
Camus, Albert, 65, 66, 72
Capital (Marx), 271
Carlyle, Thomas, 79, 80, 264, 277, 278, 279, 280, 281, 284
Carroll, David, 327, 370
Carroll, Lewis (Charles Lutwidge Dodgson), 92
Casanova de Seingalt, Giacomo, 22, 46
Casaubon, Mr, in *Middlemarch*, 207
Celan, Paul, 322
Céline (Louis-Ferdinand Destouches), 371
Chamfort, Sébastien-Roch Nicolas, 45
Char, René, 25, 27, 46
Chase, Cynthia, ix, 326
Chateaubriand, François René, 32
Chaucer, Geoffrey, 64, 72, 109, 174, 203, 204, 389
Chollop, Mr, in *Martin Chuzzlewit*, 217
Chomsky, Noam, 245

Christian and the World of Unbelief, The (L. L. Miller), 65
Christianity and the Existentialists (ed. Michalson), 65
Christmas, Joe, in *Light in August*, 211
"Circles" (Emerson), 201, 224, 359
Classic, The (Kermode), 114
Claudel, Paul, 19, 20, 21, 25, 26, 39, 46, 49, 66
Clough Arthur Hugh, 266, 268, 331
Cohen, Ralph, 112
Coleridge, Samuel Taylor, 39, 43, 65, 80, 111, 149, 296
Collected Poems 1934 (Williams), 329
Colleoni, Bartolomeo, 69
"Comedian as the Letter C, The" (Stevens), 87
Condillac, Étienne Bonnot de, 39
Confessions (Augustine), 50, 82, 84, 90
Confessions (Rousseau), 380–1
Conrad, Joseph, 8, 134, 135, 136, 138, 333, 391
Constant, Benjamin, 14, 45
"Constructions in Analysis" (Freud), 245–6, 247–9
"Construing and Deconstructing" (Abrams), 185–92
Coomaraswamy, Ananda K., 66
Coquet, Jean-Claude, 121
Corneille, Pierre, 25, 45
"Corson's Inlet" (Ammons), 222
Cortez, Hernando, 309, 310
Crane, Hart, 218, 220
Cratylus, 311
Crews, Frederick, 238–9, 383
"crise de l'esprit, La" (Valéry), 69
Critical Inquiry, 113, 376
Critique of Judgement (Kant), 264–5, 267, 269–70, 271–2, 332
Critique of Pure Reason (Kant), 272
Culler, Jonathan, 113, 121, 134, 376
Curran, Edward, 295
Curtius, E. R., viii, 6, 7, 72, 79, 134
Cythna, in *Laon and Cythna*, 157, 162

Damien, in *The Pure and the Impure*, 207
Daniel Deronda (Eliot), 192
Dante Alighieri, 64, 70, 72, 73, 149, 155, 163, 176, 263, 338, 340, 385, 390, 391
De Mille, Cecil B., 333
de Man, Henri, 361–2
de Man, Herman, 375
de Man, Paul, ix, x, 10, 11, 47, 53, 84, 92, 95, 106, 113, 114, 115, 122, 123–4, 125, 127, 128, 131, 178, 196, 200, 206, 210, 219, 229, 231, 298, 313, 315, 317–8, 319, 322, 335, 341–84, 385, 387–8, 390

de Man, Paul, works:
"Allegorie (Julie)," 341–58
Allegories of Reading, 341–58, 364, 378, 387, 388
Blindness and Insight, 106, 114, 348, 364, 371
"Excuses (*Confessions*)," 380–1
"Foreword" to *The Dissimulating Harmony*, 380
"Heidegger's Exegeses of Hölderlin," 377
"Hypogram and Inscription," 322
"juifs dans la littérature actuelle, Les" ("The Jews in Contemporary Literature"), 364, 375
"Kant and Schiller," 365
"Proust et l'allégorie de la lecture," 128
"Resistance to Theory, The," 298, 317–18, 322, 363, 364–5, 381, 383–4, 387–8
Resistance to Theory, The, 365, 366–7, 371, 381
"Rhetoric of Blindness, The: Jacques Derrida's Reading of Rousseau," 106, 114
Rhetoric of Romanticism, 366
"Rhetoric of Temporality, The," 92, 345, 348–9, 364, 375
"Tentation de la permanence," 365, 377
Deconstruction and Criticism (Bloom et al.), 379
Dedlock, Sir Leicester, in *Bleak House*, 336
"Dejection: An Ode" (Coleridge), 296
Deleuze, Gilles, 52, 84, 91, 92, 93, 114
Demetz, Peter, 228
Democracy and Poetry (Warren), 112
Demogorgon (in *Prometheus Unbound*), 85
Demon of the World, The (Shelley), 156, 162, 166
Derrida, Jacques, viii, ix, x, xi, 52, 54–5, 84, 88, 90–1, 92, 93, 95, 96, 97–106, 113, 114, 115, 116, 120, 122, 125–7, 131, 135, 139, 142, 151, 174, 186, 187, 188, 189–90, 193, 194, 195, 197, 198, 200, 206, 218, 219, 223, 231, 236, 240, 246, 268–9, 282, 315, 319, 322, 334, 335, 348, 351–2, 364, 376, 377–9, 382, 387, 388–9

Derrida, Jacques, works:
De l'esprit: Heidegger et la question, 377, 378–9
De la grammatologie, 113, 187, 378
carte postale, La, 187
"Deconstruction in America," 389
"Des tours de Babel," 351
"différance, La," 92, 97, 104
dissémination, La, 90–1

"double séance, La," 126
Glas, 114, 120, 125, 187, 194
"Hors livre," 90–1
Marges, 104, 106
Mimesis, 114, 122
"Ousia et grammè," 99
"pharmacie de Platon, La," 120
Positions, 127, 389
"Principle of Reason, The: The University in the Eyes of its Pupils," 268–9
Schibboleth, 322
Signéponge, 187
"Structure, Sign, and Play," 95, 97, 100, 102, 197
Ulysse gramophone, 351–2
"White Mythology," 195, 223, 240, 322
Descartes, René, 7, 18, 23, 25, 39, 45, 46, 194, 340
"Destroying Literary Studies" (Wellek), 265, 382
"deux faces du judaïsme, Les," 372
Dewey, John, 218
Diacritics, 113, 133
dialectique de la durée, La (Bachelard), 11
Diary of a Seducer (Kierkegaard), 281–2
Dickens, Charles, 174, 212, 215, 217, 218, 308, 336
Dickinson, Emily, 218
Dickstein, Morris, 267
Diderot, Denis, 45, 215
Différence et répétition (Deleuze), 91, 92
Dilthey, Wilhelm, 13, 35, 43, 68, 69
Dionysus, 122, 127, 280–1, 286
Dissimulating Harmony, The (Jacobs), 196, 380
Divine Comedy, The (Dante), 64, 72, 281
Dobbin, William, in *Vanity Fair*, 144
Don Quixote (Cervantes), 211
Donne, John, 72
"Dora" ("Fragment of an Analysis of a Case of Hysteria") (Freud), 245, 246–7
Dosogne, Charles, 363, 373
Dostoevsky, Fyodor, 19, 67, 134, 390
Doubling and Incest, Repetition and Revenge (Irwin), 114
"Dover Beach" (Arnold), 222
Dreyfus, Alfred, 362, 372
Drieu la Rochelle, Pierre, 372
Du Bouchet, André, 28
du Bos, Charles, 13, 17
Dubois, Hubert, 363
Dupin (in "The Purloined Letter"), 139

écriture du désastre, L' (Blanchot), 300–1
Edith Wharton (Lewis), 112
Egoist, The (Meredith), 198–9

Einbildungskraft des Dichters, Die (Dilthey), 69
Either/Or (Kierkegaard), 140–1, 279, 281–2
Eliot, George, xii, 8, 9, 73, 109, 134, 192, 196, 233–7, 337
Eliot, T. S., 6, 7, 8–9, 10, 40, 43, 45, 66, 67, 72, 73, 80, 95, 97, 101, 109, 111, 389
Eluard, Paul, 17, 25, 46, 373, 374
Emblem and Expression (Paulson), 114
Emerson, Ralph Waldo, xii, 201, 218, 220, 221, 222, 223–5, 297, 359, 365
Emily, in *Epipsychidion*, 157, 159–60, 161, 166
Empedocles on Etna (Arnold), 338
Empson, William, 111, 174, 193, 195, 215, 235, 293, 330, 331, 386
"Encantadas, The" (Melville), 312
Enneads (Plotinus), 90
Epipsychidion (Shelley), 156, 157, 159–65
Eremita, Victor, in *Either/Or*, 281–2
Erlich, Victor, 112
Esau, 208
Esch, Deborah, 326, 378
Essays upon Epitaphs (Wordsworth), 222, 234
Europäische Literatur und lateinisches Mittelalter (Curtius), 6, 79
Eurydice, 32, 249
Eve, in *Paradise Lost*, 293–4
Excursion, The (Wordsworth), 87
Exercice du silence, 373, 374
Ezekiel, 149, 155, 156, 163

Faerie Queene, The (Spenser), 176, 286
Failing Distance, The: The Autobiographical Impulse in John Ruskin (Fellows), 112
"False Themes and Gentle Minds" (Hartman), 125
Farias, Victor, 377
Fate of Reading, The (Hartman), 114, 115, 125
Faulkner, William, 72, 218, 332
Fellows, Jay, 112
Felman, Shoshana, 113
Feuerbach, Ludwig, 73
Fénelon, François de Salignac de la Mothe-, 46
Fichte, Johann Gottlieb, 39, 80
Figures (Genette), 113, 128
Fish, Stanley, 173, 194, 219, 319
Fitzgerald, F. Scott, 111
Flaubert, Gustave, 25, 26, 27, 45, 46, 135
Flaubert: The Uses of Uncertainty (Culler), 113
Fleishman, Avrom, 114
folie du jour, La (Blanchot), 301
Fontenelle, Bernard Lo Bovier, Sieur de, 45

Forme et signification (Rousset), 26
Fors Clavigera (Ruskin), 122–3
Foucault, Michel, 52–3, 95, 114, 134, 135, 136, 139, 142, 319, 334, 383
Four Quartets (Eliot), 101, 109
Förster-Nietzsche, Elizabeth, 150
Frankfurter Allgemeine Zeitung, 359, 360, 383
Frank, Joseph, 10
Franklin, Benjamin, 310, 312
Franklin, Phyllis, 295
Freud, Sigmund, ix, 4, 51, 83, 111, 113, 120, 124, 129, 134, 135, 136, 137, 138–9, 149, 245–61, 271, 352–3, 372
From Baudelaire to Surrealism (Raymond), 17
Frost, Robert, 203
Frye, Northrop, 1, 6, 10, 111, 174, 197
Fuchs, K., 91
"Function of Criticism at the Present Time, The" (Arnold), 265
"Function of Rhetorical Study at the Present Time, The" (Miller), 194, 199
Fundamentals of Language (Jakobson and Hallé), 128

Gainsborough, Thomas, 114
Garland, Mary, in *Roderick Hudson*, 320
Gasché, Rodolphe, 197, 198
Gautier, Théophile, 45
Gawain, in *Sir Gawain and the Green Knight*, 149
Gearhart, Suzanne, 327
Genet, Jean, 194
Genette, Gérard, 84, 113, 121, 128
George, Stefan, 97
Georgia Review, The, 113
German Ideology (Marx), 388
Gide, André, 51
Gilby, Thomas, 65
Ginsberg, Allen, 80
Girard, René, 221
Glyph, 197
Goethe, Johann Wolfgang von, 32, 43, 45, 215, 309
Golden Bowl, The (James), 297, 301–2
Goldmann, Lucien, 5
Goodheart, Eugene, 267, 268, 269, 314
Gordon, Margaret (Lady Bannerman), 280
Gorgias (Plato), 232
Goriély, Georges, 363
Graff, Gerald, 198, 378
Graphesis: Perspectives in Literature and Philosophy (ed. Logan), 113
"Grasmere Journals" (Dorothy Wordsworth), 181
Great Chain of Being, The (Lovejoy), 79
Great Expectations (Dickens), 391
Green Knight, in "Sir Gawain and the Green Knight," 149

Green, Julien, 46
Green, Richard, 72
Gregory, St, 73
Greimas, A. J., 121
Groethuysen, Bernhard, 68
Grundrisse (Marx), 271
Guérin, Maurice de, 24, 46
Guillén, Jorge, 38, 40, 45
Gundolf, Friedrich, 13
Gwendolen, in *Daniel Deronda*, 192

H. D. (Hilda Doolittle), 95
Hamacher, Werner, 307
Hamann, Johann Georg, 19, 80
Hardy, Thomas, 6, 9, 67, 70, 134, 135, 144, 149, 155, 166, 185
Hartman, Geoffrey, 109, 114–15, 120, 122, 125, 126, 127, 131, 376
Hawthorne (James), 313
Hawthorne, Nathaniel, 313, 320, 321
Heart of Darkness (Conrad), 249
Hegel, G. W. F., ix, 80, 81, 90, 98, 113, 120, 194, 197, 219, 267, 270, 277, 321, 322, 323, 340, 374
Heidegger, Martin, 9, 11, 28, 53–54, 65, 95, 96, 97–106, 113, 149, 150–1, 178–9, 187, 194, 219, 246, 268, 277, 311, 352–3, 354, 365, 375, 377–8
Heidegger, Martin, works:
Frage nach dem Ding, Die, 179
Identität und Differenz, 99
Introduction to Metaphysics, An, 97
"Letter on Humanism," 98
Nietzsche, 268
On the Way to Language, 97
Poetry, Language, Thought, 97–8
Rektoratsrede, Die, 377
Sein und Zeit, 11, 53–4, 98, 375
"Spruch des Anaximander, Der," 104
"Ursprung des Kunstwerkes, Der," 101, 178–9
Zur Seinsfrage (The Question of Being), 150–1
Hemingway, Ernest, 111, 332, 362
Henchard, Michael, in *The Mayor of Casterbridge*, 211
Henri, in *The Demon of the World*, 159, 162
Henry Esmond (Thackeray), 143
Herbert, George, 72
Hertz, Neil, 378
Hesper, 155
Hirsch, E. D., 173
Hoffmann, E. T. A., 19
Hogarth, William, 114
Hollander, John, 114, 206
Holt, Mr (in *Henry Esmond*), 143
Homemade World, A (Kenner), 96–7, 111

Homer, 64, 67, 70, 97, 266, 308, 332, 338, 340, 390
Hopkins, Gerard Manley, 3, 66, 71, 125, 134, 135, 138, 281
Horner, Winifred, 231
Hölderlin, Friedrich, ix, 64, 65, 79, 80, 81, 97, 98, 196, 342, 365, 377, 380, 385
Hugo, Victor, 15, 46
Hume, David, 265
Husserl, Edmund, 9, 22–3, 28, 50, 140, 187, 364
Huxley, Thomas Henry, 389
Hyperion (Hölderlin), 81

Ianthe, in *The Demon of the World*, 159
"Idea of Order at Key West, The" (Stevens), 222, 223–5
Iliad (Homer), 67, 389
Imaginations (Williams), 101
Implied Reader, The (Iser), 112
In the American Grain (Williams), 309–13, 320
innomable, L' (Beckett), 211
Interpretation of Dreams, The (Freud), see *Traumdeutung, Die*
Inverted Bell, The (Riddel), 95–110, 113
Irigaray, Luce, 319
Irwin, John, 113, 114
Iser, Wolfgang, 112
"Ivy Wife, The" (Hardy), 144, 145

Jaccottet, Philippe, 28
Jacob, 208
Jacobs, Carol, ix, 196, 380
Jakobson, Roman, 95, 105, 121, 128–9
James, Henry, 45, 46, 138, 225–6, 297, 301–2, 313, 320, 321, 343
James, William, 218
Jameson, Fredric, 319, 334
Jauss, Hans Robert, 112, 371
Jay, Gregory, 326
Jean-Jacques Rousseau: la transparence et l'obstacle (Starobinski), 29
Jerusalem (Blake), 82, 89
Jesus Christ, 278, 279, 280, 281, 282, 283–4, 285, 348, 356
Jeudi, 377
Johnson, Samuel, 219
Jokes and the Unconscious (Freud), 167
Joseph Conrad and the Fiction of Autobiography (Said), 133
Joubert, Joseph, 22, 46, 66
Joyce, James, 8, 72, 208
Judgment, The (Kafka), 287
Julie (La nouvelle Héloïse) (Rousseau), 341, 345–6, 349, 350, 352, 355

Julie, in *Julie*, 345–6 349, 350
Jünger, Ernst, 150

Kabbalah and Criticism (Bloom), 115, 124
Kabbalah, 115, 124
Kafka, Franz, 8, 65, 66, 287, 308, 362, 372
Kant, Immanuel, ix, 111, 193, 194, 200, 263, 264–5, 266, 269–70, 271–2, 278, 332, 335, 374
Kaufmann, Walter, 113, 285
Keats, John, 2, 35, 63, 64, 80, 222, 266
Keenan, Thomas, 326, 386
Kenner, Hugh, 96–7, 106, 111
Kermode, Frank, 114
Khan, Kubla, 126
Kierkegaard, Søren, ix, 140–1, 277, 279–80, 281, 284, 349
Kincaid, James, 111
King Lear (Shakespeare), 391
Kleist, Heinrich von, ix, 215
Kofman, Sarah, 84, 122
Kojève, Alexandre, 98
Krieger, Murray, 1
Kristeva, Julia, 371
Kronik, John, 295
Kurtz, in *Heart of Darkness*, 249
La Fayette, Madame de, 45
Lacan, Jacques, viii, 4, 5, 10, 113, 120, 201, 218, 228, 245, 319
Laclos, Pierre (-Ambrose-François), Choderlos de, 46
Lacoue-Labarthe, Philippe, 122, 211, 327
Laius, 227
Lamartine, Alphonse de, 45, 46
Lambert, Richard, 317
Lambrichs, Georges, 363, 373
Languages of Criticism and the Sciences of Man, The (ed. Macksey and Donato), 100
Laon and Cythna (Shelley), 156, 157, 165
Laon, in *Laon and Cythna*, 157, 162
Lawrence, D. H., 6, 67, 80, 362
Lawrence, T. E., 134, 138
Leavis, F. R., 67
Leibniz, Gottfried Wilhelm, 42, 194, 268
Lentricchia, Frank, 315, 334, 374, 376, 378, 381
Letters on the Aesthetic Education of Man (Schiller), 332
Letters to Clough (Arnold), 263
Lettres édifiantes (Rasles), 310, 312
Levinas, Emmanuel, 53
Levine, George, 267
Lewis, C. S., 79
Lewis, R. W. B., 112
Levi-Strauss, Claude, 5, 6, 10, 74, 100, 160, 161, 197, 245
Linguistic Moment, The (Miller), 195

"Linguistics and Poetics" (Jakobson), 128
Littérature de l'âge baroque en France (Rousset), 26
Littérature et sensation (Richard), 27
Liu, Alan, x
Locke, John, 7, 215
Logan, Marie-Rose, 113
Logique du sens (Deleuze), 91
Lord Jim (Conrad), 240
Lord Jim, in *Lord Jim*, 212
Los Angeles Times, 359
Lovejoy, A. O., 9, 68, 69, 79, 112, 210
Loyola, St Ignatius, 71
Lucifer, 154, 155, 158, 165
Lucy poems (Wordsworth), 176–84, 190–1
Lucy, in "The Lucy Poems," 176–84
Lukacher, Ned, 327
Lukács, Georg, viii, 5, 6, 8
Luke, 282
Luther, Martin, 285
Lyotard, Jean–François, 113

Macpherson, James, 8
Madame Bovary (Flaubert), 25, 26
Magdalene, Mary, 281
Maisie, in *What Maisie Knew*, 343
maladie et la guérison, La (Raymond), 18
Mallarmé, Stephane, ix, 17, 19, 22, 27, 38, 46, 91, 126, 135, 196
Mallet, Rowland, in *Roderick Hudson*, 320
Manchester Guardian, 359
Mandela, Nelson, xi
Mann, Thomas, 8, 134, 135, 374
Map of Misreading, A (Bloom), 115
Marcel (in *À la recherche du temps perdu*), 128, 307
Maria et son charpentier (Herman de Man), 375
"Mario and the Magician" (Mann), 374
Mario, in "Mario and the Magician," 374
Maritain, Jacques, 65, 66
Marivaux, Pierre Carlet de Chamblain de, 46
Mark, 282
Marlow, in *Heart of Darkness*, 249
Marlowe, Christopher, 64
Marquez, García, 139
Martin Chuzzlewit (Dickens), 217, 220
Marx, Karl, 51, 80, 83, 113, 135, 140, 201, 218, 228, 245, 246, 271, 322, 323, 326, 334, 338, 379, 382, 383, 388
"massacre des innocents, Le" (Dubois), 363
Mather, Cotton, 312
Matthew poems (Wordsworth), 178
Matthew, 282, 283, 330
Maurus, Rhabanus, 72
Mayoux, Jean-Jacques, 112

McCarthy, Mary, 238
Mehlman, Jeffrey, 113, 314–15, 372, 376, 378
Melville, Herman, 65, 308, 312
Meredith, George, 9, 198–9, 234
Merleau-Ponty, Maurice, 9, 22–3, 26, 28, 135
Merrill, James, 218
"Meru" (Yeats), 69
"Métonymie chez Proust" (Genette), 128
Michelet, Jules, 46
Middlemarch (Eliot), 11, 196, 233–6, 337
Middleton, Clara, in *The Egoist*, 198–9, 212
Mill on the Floss, The (Eliot), 233
Mill, John Stuart, 325, 389
Miller, Perry, 112
Milne, A. A., 188
Milton, John, viii, xii, 67, 72, 80, 85, 96, 109, 125, 135, 149, 155, 194, 204, 230, 236, 263, 264, 266, 267, 293–4, 330, 331, 332, 333, 338, 340, 385, 389, 391
Mirror of Nature (Rorty), 218
MLN, 113
Modern Literature and the Religious Frontier (Scott), 65
Molière (Jean Baptiste Poquelin), 45
Monde nouveau, 365
"Monsieur Texte: On Jacques Derrida, his *Glas*" (Hartman), 114, 125
Montaigne, Michel Eyquem de, 25, 39, 43, 45, 46, 215
Montezuma, 309
Montherlant, Henry de, 363, 372
Moore, Marianne, 111
Moses and Monotheism (Freud), 137
Mosses from an Old Manse (Hawthorne), 313
Mounier, Emmanuel, 18
Mouvements premiers, 128
Murder in the Cathedral (Eliot), 64
Musil, Robert, 66
Musset, Alfred de, 46

Nancy, Jean-Luc, 122, 211, 327
Nation, The, 359, 360, 382
Natural Supernaturalism (Abrams), 79–94
Nature and Culture in the Iliad (Redfield), 114
Nerval, Gerard de, ix, 19, 24, 27, 41, 45, 81
Nestroy, Johann Nepomuk Eduard Ambrosius, 248
New Criterion, The, 382
New Directions in Literary History (ed. Cohen), 112
New Literary History, 113
New Republic, The, 376
New Science, The (Vico), 136
New Testament, 149, 279
New York Times, 359, 383

Newman, John Henry, 389
Newmark, Kevin, ix
Newsweek, 359, 360, 383
Nietzsche, Friedrich, ix, xii, 51, 52, 68, 79, 80, 83–4, 85–6, 88, 89, 91, 92–3, 95, 100, 113, 114, 121, 124, 128, 129–31, 133, 134, 136, 142, 149, 150, 152–3, 184, 198, 199, 215, 218, 231–2, 246, 263, 268, 273, 277–91, 322, 343, 353, 390
Nietzsche, Friedrich, works:
  Also Sprach Zarathustra, 277–91
  Birth of Tragedy, The, 84, 121, 127, 129–31
  Daybreak, 263, 277
  Dionysus-Dithyramben, 280–1
  Ecce Homo, 277, 278, 280, 284–7
  Genealogy of Morals, The, 88
  Human, All Too Human, 79
  "On Truth and Lie in an Extra-Moral Sense," 89
  Twilight of the Idols, The, 86
  Will to Power, The, 85, 89, 91, 133, 136, 142, 150, 152–3 184, 199
"Nineteen Hundred and Nineteen" (Yeats), 69, 195–6
"Noble Rider and the Sound of Words, The" (Stevens), 69
Norse sagas, 212
Norton *Anthology*, 215
Nostromo (Conrad), 136
"Notes" (Bakhtin), 323
Notes pour comprendre le siècle (Drieu la Rochelle), 372
"Notes Toward a Supreme Fiction" (Stevens), 117
Notre Avant-Guerre (Brasillach), 372
Nouvelle nouvelle revue français, 363
Novalis (Friedrich Leopold von Hardenberg), 19, 80, 81, 82
"Nutting" (Wordsworth), 180

Ocean King, in *Epipsychidion*, 160, 161, 162, 166
"Ode to Joy" (Schiller), 296
Odyssey, The (Homer), 212
Oedipus at Colonus (Sophocles), 330
Oedipus, 227
oeil vivant, L' (Starobinski), 29
Old Testament, 149
Olson, Regina, 280
Olson, Robert, 95
"On Edge" (Miller), 197, 199
Onze études sur la poésie moderne (Richard), 28
"Ordinary Evening in New Haven, An" (Stevens), 11

Orgoglio, in *The Faerie Queen*, 286
Orientalism (Said), 133
Orpheus, 32, 249
Ortega y Gasset, José, 68
Orwell, George, xi
"Out of the Cradle Endlessly Rocking" (Whitman), 222
Ovid (Publius Ovidius Naso), 16

Palliser, Plantagenet, in the Palliser novels, 211
Paracelsus (Philippus Aureolus Theophrastus Bombast von Hohenheim), 80
Paradise Lost (Milton), 264, 267, 293–4, 330, 333, 337
Parker, Andrew, 326
Parmenides, 40, 99, 100
Partial Magic (Alter), 112
pas au delà, Le (Blanchot), 290
Pascal, Blaise, 19, 22, 23, 24, 34, 43, 45, 46, 56, 67–8
Pater, Walter, 13, 32, 71
Paterson (Williams), 11, 95, 96, 98, 101, 102, 108
Paulson, Ronald, 114
Pautrat, Bernard, 84, 122
"peinture juive, La," 372
Peirce, Charles Sanders, 118, 218
Pensées (Joubert), 22
Penseroso, Il (Milton), 125
Perse, Saint-John, 28, 46
Péguy, Charles, 19, 21, 67, 363, 372, 375
Phaedo (Plato), 117, 129
Phaedrus (Plato), 232, 234
Phenomenology of Mind, The (Hegel), 81, 89, 90, 321
Philosophical Investigations (Wittgenstein), 9
Physics (Aristotle), 49
Picon, Gaëton, 25
Pip, in *Great Expectations*, 212
Plato, ix, 49, 50, 53, 69, 83, 87, 91, 93, 120, 145, 152, 175, 179, 187, 191, 194, 197, 220, 232, 234, 236, 237, 389
Plotinus, 80, 87
Poe, Edgar Allan, 39, 45, 46, 139
Poetry and Repression (Bloom), 115, 124
Poetry of George Herbert, The (Vendler), 111
Poésie et profondeur (Richard), 27
Poggioli, Renato, 363
Pogram, Elijah, in *Martin Chuzzlewit*, 217
Point of View for My Work as an Author (Kierkegaard), 279–80
Ponge, Francis, 28, 197, 296
Pooh, in *Winnie-the-Pooh*, 188
Poor Richard's Almanac (Franklin), 312
Pope, Alexander, 389

Poulet, Georges, viii, ix, 4, 7–8, 9, 10, 13, 14–15, 17, 21–5, 26, 29, 31–61, 112, 129, 198
Poulet, Georges, works:
Chemins actuels de la critique, Les, 56
distance intérieure, La, 40, 45, 46
espace proustien, L', 10, 45, 49, 56, 57
Études sur le temps humain, 40, 42, 44, 45, 56
Mesure de l'instant, 44, 45, 46, 49, 56, 57
métamorphoses du cercle, Les, 8, 10, 24, 40, 42–3, 45–6, 47
point de départ, Le, 22, 44, 45, 46, 49, 56, 57
Pound Era, The (Kenner), 111
Pound, Ezra, 95, 111
Pre-Socratics, 100, 277
"Preface" of 1853 (Arnold), 266
Prelude, The (Wordsworth), 80, 81, 82, 84, 89, 90, 92, 93, 138, 180, 222
Prévost, Abbé, 45
"Primitive Like an Orb, A" (Stevens), 11
Principles of Literary Criticism (Richards), 267
Problems of Dostoevsky's Poetics (Bakhtin), 112
Prometheus, 159
Prometheus Unbound (Shelley), 81, 85
Proust, Marcel, ix, 2, 7, 25, 39, 45, 46, 51, 56–7, 84, 85, 138, 307, 308, 353, 374, 385
Psychopathology of Everyday Life, The (Freud), 167
PTL, 174
Publications of the Modern Language Association, The, 174
Puritan Origins of the American Self, The (Bercovitch), 112
"Purloined Letter, The" (Poe), 139
Puttenham, Richard, 234
Pygmalion (Rousseau), 352–3

Queen Mab (Shelley), 156, 158
Quinzaine littéraire, La, 359, 383

Racine, Jean, 45, 46
Ramuz, Charles-Ferdinand, 14, 19
Rasles, Père Sebastien, 309–11, 312
"Rationality and Imagination in Cultural History" (Abrams), 143
Raymond, Marcel, viii, 4, 13, 14–15, 16–18, 19, 22, 23, 25, 27, 29, 32, 33, 37, 39, 47
Reading de Man Reading (Waters, Godzich, et al.), 376
Recluse, The (Wordsworth), 80, 85
"Red Wheelbarrow, The" (Williams), 96

Redfield, James M., 114
Renan, Ernest, 134, 135
Representations, 315
"Resolution and Independence" (Wordsworth), 108
Revelation, 80, 87, 149, 155
Reverdy, Pierre, 28, 46
Revolt of Islam, The (Shelley), 156, 157, 166
Rey, Jean-Michel, 84
Rêveries (Rousseau), 15
Rhetoric (Aristotle), 233
Richard, Jean-Pierre, viii, 4, 13, 22–3, 26–8, 29, 32, 36
Richards, I. A., 267
Ricoeur, Paul, 74, 352–3
Riddel, Joseph, 95–110, 113
Riffaterre, Michael, 229, 322
Rilke, Rainer Maria, 45, 66, 97, 308
Rimbaud, Arthur, 17, 27, 66, 81
Rivière, Jacques, 13, 17, 44
Robert, Marthe, 112
Robertson, D. W., Jr, 72
"Rock, The" (Stevens), 117, 130, 196
Roderick Hudson (James), 225, 320
roman de la rose, La (de Lorris and de Meung), 281
Room of One's Own, A (Woolf), 194
Rorty, Richard, 218
Rosso, Stefano, 365, 366, 381
Rotsel, R. W., 112
Rousseau, Jean-Jacques, ix, 14, 15, 25, 28, 34, 39, 41, 45, 46, 47, 56, 81, 100, 114, 142, 149, 155, 163, 189–90, 215, 341, 343, 344, 345–6 353, 364, 374, 380–1, 387, 388
Rousset, Jean, viii, 13, 15, 25–6, 29
Rowe, John, 326
Royle, Nicholas, x
"Ruined Cottage, The" (Wordsworth), 178
Ruskin, John, 13, 122–3, 293, 294
Ryan, Michael, 326–7

Sacred Discontent (Schneidau), 113
Said, Edward, 113–14 120, 122, 133–42, 315, 334, 378
Saint-Cyran, Abbé de (Jean Duvergier de Hauranne), 46
Saint-Martin, Louis-Claude de, 19
Saint-Preux, in *Julie*, 345, 349, 350
Sartor Resartus (Carlyle), 279, 280, 281, 282
Sartre, Jean-Paul, 4, 9, 29, 31, 46, 65, 187
Satan, in *Paradise Lost*, 293–4
Saussure, Ferdinand de, 52, 83, 113, 245, 319, 322
Scève, Maurice, 46
Schelling, Friedrich Wilhelm Joseph von, 80, 111

Schiller, Friedrich, 80, 265, 296, 332, 335, 381
Schlegel, Friedrich, 211
Schneidau, Herbert, 113
Scholes, Robert, 134
Schopenhauer, Arthur, 277
Scott, Nathan, Jr, 65, 314
Scotus, Duns, 71
Searle, John, 198, 314, 336
"Seashore" (Emerson), 222, 223–5
Second Discourse (Rousseau), 342, 345
Secret Agent, The (Conrad), 333
Sedley, Amelia, in *Vanity Fair*, 144
"Self-Reliance" (Emerson), 221
Sensitive Plant, The (Shelley), 156, 157
Serres, Michel, 113
Sénancour, Étienne Pivert de, 14, 222
Shakespeare, William, 63, 64, 65, 66, 109, 174, 194, 218, 236, 332, 338, 389, 391
Shaun, in *Finnegans Wake*, 208
Shaw, George Bernard, 8
Shelley, Percy Bysshe, ix, xii, 8, 64, 80, 85, 115, 125, 149–50, 151, 154–68, 194, 208, 209, 215, 221, 222, 263, 344
Shem, in *Finnegans Wake*, 208
Singleton, C. S., 72
Sir Gawain and the Green Knight, 281
"Slumber Did My Slumber Seal, A" (Wordsworth), 176–92, 196
Smart, Christopher, 8
Smelser, Neil, 316
Snow, C. P, 112
Social Contract (Rousseau), 354, 387
Socrates, 117, 121, 127, 129, 232, 234, 280
Soir, Le, 359, 361–5, 369, 371, 372, 373, 374, 376
solstice de juin, Le (Montherlant), 372
Sophist, The (Plato), 83, 152, 232
Sophists, 152
Sophocles, 222, 308, 330, 337, 391
"Spelt from Sibyl's Leaves" (Hopkins), 71
Spenser, Edmund, 72, 109, 149, 155, 194, 286
Spivak, Gayatri, 113, 327, 334
Spring and All (Williams), 108
Sprinker, Michael, 326
Sptizer, Leo, 134, 174
St John of the Cross, 64
Staël, Madame de, 46
Starobinski, Jean, viii, 13, 14, 28–9, 32–3, 35, 41
Stein, Gertrude, 321
Stein, in *Lord Jim*, 240
Stelling, Mr, in *The Mill on the Floss*, 233, 234
Stendhal (Henri Beyle), 8, 29, 46

Stevens, Wallace, xii, 2, 6, 9, 11, 64, 69, 79, 80, 87, 95, 96, 108, 109, 111, 115, 116, 117–18, 125, 127, 130, 149, 183, 193, 196, 203, 218, 219, 220, 222, 223–5, 230, 236, 247, 267, 308
"Strange Fits of Passion" (Wordsworth), 183
Strauss, Leo, 362–3
Structural Study of Autobiography, The (Mehlman), 113
Structuralist Poetics (Culler), 113, 121
Studies on Hysteria (Studien über Hysterie) (Freud), 245, 249–60
"Study of Poetry, The" (Arnold), 265–6
Style in Language (ed. Sebeok), 128
Suárez, Francisco, 71
Supervielle, Jules, 19, 46
Swedenborg, Emanuel, 220
Swift, Jonathan, 135

Taine, Hippolyte, 174
Tate, Allen, 65
Tave, Stuart M., 267
Tennyson's Major Poems (Kincaid), 111
Tennyson, Alfred, 115, 125, 208, 220, 266, 389
Tess of the d'Urbervilles (Hardy), 185
Teufelsdröck, Diogenes, in *Sartor Resartus*, 264, 280, 281, 282, 284
Thackeray, William Makepeace, 2, 144
Thaetetus (Plato), 179
Thales, 179, 183
Theory of Literature (Wellek and Warren), 174
Theseus, 122, 123, 280–1
Thoreau, Henry David, 222
Tieck, Ludwig, 19
Timaeus (Plato), 49
"To All Gentleness" (Williams), 11
To the Lighthouse (Woolf), 11
Todorov, Tzvetan, 121
Tolstoi, Leo, 340
"Tradition and the Individual Talent" (Eliot), 10, 67
Tragic Vision and the Christian Faith, The (ed. Scott), 65
Traumdeutung, Die (Freud), 120, 134, 136, 137, 245, 249–50, 259–60
Trilling, Lionel, 82, 335
"Triumph of Life, The" (Shelley), 149–50, 151, 154–6, 158, 159, 165, 166–7, 168, 208, 222, 344
Trollope (Snow), 112
Trollope, Anthony, 9, 31, 63, 385
Tulliver, Tom, in *The Mill on the Floss*, 233–6

Twentieth-Century Russian Literary Criticism (ed. Erlich), 112
"Two Aspects of Language and Two Types of Aphasic Disturbances" (Jakobson), 128

Ulysses (Joyce), 208, 211
"Ulysses" (Tennyson), 208
"Uncanny, The" (Freud), see "Unheimliche, Das"
Understanding Poetry (Brooks and Warren), 215, 390
Ungaretti, Giuseppe, 46
"Unheimliche, Das" (Freud), 129, 249
univers imaginaire de Mallarmé, L' (Richard), 27
Unmediated Vision, The (Hartman), 114, 115, 125
Über die Linie (Jünger), 150

Valéry, Paul, 17, 45, 69, 95, 115, 135, 140
Vanity Fair (Thackeray), 144
Vauvenargues, Luc de Clapiers, marquis de, 46
Vendler, Helen, 111
Venus, 154, 155, 165
Verloc, Winnie, in *The Secret Agent*, 333
Verrocchio, Andrea del, 69
Vesper, 154, 155
Vico, Giambattista, 133, 135, 136
Vigny, Alfred de, 45
Village Voice, 359
Virgil, 65, 66, 155, 308
Virginia Woolf (Fleishman), 114
Vision and Resonance: Two Senses of Poetic Form (Hollander), 114
Vlaamsche Land, Het, 359, 362, 364, 365, 369, 371, 376
Vorlesungen zur Phänomenologie des inneren Zeitbewusstseins (Husserl), 50

Wagner, Cosima, 280–1
Wagner, Richard, 67, 281
Waldheim, Kurt, 370
Wall Street Journal, 360, 383
Warminski, Andrzej, ix, 327
Warner, William Beaty, 332, 334
Warren, Austin, 174
Warren, Robert Penn, 112, 195
Waves, The (Woolf), 211
Webster, Noah, 356
Wellek, René, 174, 198, 265, 268, 314, 336, 382
What Maisie Knew (James), 343
Whitehead, Alfred North, 235
Whitman, Walt, 45, 46, 218, 219, 220, 222

Wiener, Jon, 369–84
Wilde, Oscar, 138
Wilder, Amos, 65
Williams, William Carlos, xii, 9, 1, 40, 95–110, 111, 125, 309–12, 320, 323, 329
Willoughby, in *The Egoist*, 212
"Windhover, The" (Hopkins), 71
Winstanley, Gerrard, 80
Wittgenstein, Ludwig, 9, 135
Wonders of the Invisible World (Mather), 312
Woolf, Virginia, 115, 194, 332, 385
Wordsworth, Dorothy, 176, 181
Wordsworth, William, ix, xii, 79, 80, 81, 82, 84, 85, 87, 96, 108, 109, 115, 149, 154, 155, 176–85, 204, 218, 220, 236, 266, 296, 308, 331, 338, 340, 374, 389, 391
"Wreck of the Deutschland, The" (Hopkins), 71

Yeats, William Butler, 6, 39, 66, 67, 69, 88, 115, 149, 155, 166, 195–6, 198, 218, 221, 297, 374
"Young Sycamore" (Williams), 329

Zarathustra, in *Also Sprach Zarathustra*, 278, 281, 282, 284, 287–90
Zerrissene, Der (Nestroy), 248
Zukofsky, Louis, 95